RANDOM HOUSE
ESSENTIAL
FRENCH
DICTIONARY

D0660368

RANDOM HOUSE ESSENTIAL FRENCH DICTIONARY

Originally published as *The Random House French Dictionary, Second Vest Pocket Edition.*

Edited by
Francesca L. V. Langbaum
University of Virginia

Revised by
Susan Husserl-Kapit, Ph.D.

BALLANTINE BOOKS • NEW YORK

Copyright © 1996 by Random House, Inc.

All rights reserved under International and Pan-American Copyright Conventions. No part of this book may be reproduced in any form or by any means, electronic or mechanical, including photocopying, without permission in writing from the publisher. All inquiries should be addressed to Reference & Information Publishing, Random House, Inc., 201 East 50th Street, New York, NY 10022-7703. Published in the United States by Ballantine Books, a division of Random House, Inc., New York, and simultaneously in Canada by Random House of Canada Limited, Toronto. The first edition of this work was published by Random House, Inc., in 1983. This second edition was originally published as *The Random House French Dictionary, Second Vest Pocket Edition,* by Reference & Information Publishing, Random House, Inc., in 1995.

Library of Congress Cataloging-in-Publication Data

Random House essential French dictionary / edited by Francesca L. V. Langbaum.
      p.   cm.
   ISBN 0-345-41079-3 (pbk.)
   1. French language—Dictionaries—English. 2. English language—Dictionaries—French. I. Langbaum, Francesca L. V. II. Random House (Firm)
PC2640.R27 1997
443'.21—dc20
                                                    96-43044
                                                        CIP

This edition published by arrangement with Random House, Inc.

Manufactured in the United States of America

First Ballantine Books Edition: February 1997

10 9 8 7 6 5 4 3 2 1

Concise Pronunciation Guide

The following concise guide describes the approximate pronunciation of the letters and frequent combinations of letters occurring in the French language. A study of it will enable the reader to pronounce French adequately most of the time. While the guide cannot list all the exceptions to the established pronunciations, or cover the manner in which adjacent words affect each other in speech, such exceptions and variations will readily be learned as one develops facility in the language.

French Letter	Description of Pronunciation
a, à	Between *a* in *calm* and *a* in *hat*.
â	Like *a* in *calm*.
ai	Like *e* in *bed*.
au	Like *oa* in *coat*.
b	As in English.
	At end of words, usually silent.
c	Before *e, i, y,* like *s*.
	Elsewhere, like *k*.
	When *c* occurs at the end of a word and is preceded by a consonant, it is usually silent.
ç	Like *s*.
cc	Before *e, i,* like *x*.
	Elsewhere, like *k*.
ch	Usually like *sh* in *short*.
	ch is pronounced like *k* in words of Greek origin before *a, o,* and *u* and before consonants.
d	At beginning and in middle of words, as in English.
	At end of words, usually silent.
e	At end of words, normally silent; indicates that preceding consonant letter is pronounced.
	Between two single consonant sounds, usually silent.
	Elsewhere, like English *a* in *sofa*.
é	Approximately like *a* in *hate*.
è, ê, ei	Like *e* in *bed*.
eau	Like *au*.
ent	Silent when it is the third person plural ending.
er (end of words)	At end of words of more than one syllable, usually like *a* in *hate,* the *r* being silent; otherwise like *air* in *chair*.
es	Silent at end of words.
eu	A vowel sound not found in English; like French *e,* but pronounced with the lips rounded as for *o*.
ez	At end of words, almost always like English *a* in hate, the *z* being silent.
f	As in English; silent at the end of a few words.
g	Before *e, i, y,* like *z* in *azure*.
	Elsewhere, like *g* in *get*.
	At end of words, usually silent.
gn	Like *ni* in *onion*.
gu	Before *e, i, y,* like *g* in *get*.
	Elsewhere, like g in get plus French *u* (see below).

French Letter	Description of Pronunciation
h	In some words, represents a slight tightening of the throat muscles (in French, called "aspiration")
	In most words, silent.
i, î	Like *i* in *machine*.
ill	(-il at end of words) like *y* in *yes*, in many but not all words.
j	Like *z* in *azure*.
k	As in English.
l	As in English, but always pronounced "bright," with tongue in front of mouth.
m, n	When double, and when single between two vowel letters or at beginning of word, like English m and n respectively. When single at end of syllable (at end of word or before another consonant), indicates nasalization of preceding vowel.
o	Usually like u in English *mud*, but rounder.
	When final sound in word, and often before *s* and *z*, like *ô*.
ô	Approximately like *oa* in *coat*.
oe, oeu	Like *eu*.
oi	Approximately like a combination of the consonant w and the *a* of *calm*.
ou, oû, où	Like *ou* in *tour*.
p	At end of words, usually silent.
	Between *m* and *t*, *m* and *s*, *r* and *s*, usually silent.
	Elsewhere, as in English.
pn, ps	Unlike English, when *pn* and *ps* occur at the beginning of words the *p* is usually sounded.
ph	Like *f*.
qu	Usually like *k*.
r	A vibration either of the uvula, or of the tip of the tongue against the upper front teeth.
	See above under *er*.
s	Generally, like *s* in *sea*.
	Single s between vowels, like *z* in *zone*.
	At end of words, normally silent.
sc	Before *e* or *i*, like *s*.
	Elsewhere, like *sk*.
t	Approximately like English t, but pronounced with tongue tip against teeth.
	At end of words, normally silent.
	When followed by *ie*, *ion*, *ium*, *ius*, and other diphthongs beginning with a vowel, *t* generally is like English *s* in *sea* (unless the *t* itself is preceded by an *s* or an *x*).
th	Like *t*.
u, û	A vowel sound not found in English; like the i in machine but with lips rounded as for *ou*.
ue	After *e* or *g* and before *il*, like *eu*.
v	As in English.
w	Usually like *v*; in some people's pronunciation, like English *w*.
x	Generally sounds like *ks;* but when the syllable *ex* begins a word and is followed by a vowel, *x* sounds like *gz*.
	At end of words, usually silent.
y	Generally like *i* in *machine;* but when between two vowels, like *y* in *yes*.
z	Like *z* in *zone*.
	At end of words, often silent (see above under *ez*).

Note on Pronunciation

A few minutes' study of the *Concise Pronunciation Guide* on pages v–vii will enable you to pronounce most French words without having to look each word up in the dictionary. For the relatively few cases in which the pronunciation does not follow the usual pattern, this dictionary provides a transcription in simple and familiar symbols.

ă   bat

ā   cape

â   dare

ä   calm

á   [a vowel intermediate in quality between the a of cat and the a of calm, but closer to the former]

ĕ   set

ē   bee

ĭ   big

ī   bite

N   [a symbol used to indicate nasalized vowels. There are four such vowels in French, found in *un bon vin blanc* (œN bōN văN bläN)]

ŏ   hot

ө   no

ô   order

œ   [a vowel made with the lips rounded in position for *o* as in *over*, while trying to say *a* as in *able*]

oi   oil

ŏŏ   book

ōө   ooze

ou   loud

ŭ   up

ū   cute

û   burn

Y   [a vowel made with the lips rounded in position for *oo* as in *ooze*, while trying to say *e* as in *easy*]

ə   [indicates the sound of *a* in *alone*, *e* in *system*, *i* in *easily*, *o* in *gallop*, *u* in *circus*]

Irregular Verbs

Infinitive	Pres. Part.	Past Part.	Pres. Indic.	Future
aller	allant	allé	vais	irai
asseoir	asseyant	assis	assieds	assiérai
atteindre	atteignant	atteint	atteins	atteindrai
avoir	ayant	eu	ai	aurai
battre	battant	battu	bats	battrai
boire	buvant	bu	bois	boirai
conduire	conduisant	conduit	conduis	conduirai
connaître	connaissant	connu	connais	connaîtrai
courir	courant	couru	cours	courrai
craindre	craignant	craint	crains	craindrai
croire	croyant	cru	crois	croirai
devoir	devant	dû	dois	devrai
dire	disant	dit	dis	dirai
dormir	dormant	dormi	dors	dormirai
écrire	écrivant	écrit	écris	écrirai
envoyer	envoyant	envoyé	envoie	enverrai
être	étant	été	suis	serai
faire	faisant	fait	fais	ferai
falloir	———	fallu	(il) faut	(il) faudra
joindre	joignant	joint	joins	joindrai
lire	lisant	lu	lis	lirai
mettre	mettant	mis	mets	mettrai
mourir	mourant	mort	meurs	mourrai
naître	naissant	né	nais	naîtrai
ouvrir	ouvrant	ouvert	ouvre	ouvrirai
plaire	plaisant	plu	plais	plairai
pleuvoir	pleuvant	plu	(il) pleut	(il) pleuvra
pouvoir	pouvant	pu	peux	pourrai
prendre	prenant	pris	prends	prendrai
recevoir	recevant	reçu	reçois	recevrai
rire	riant	ri	ris	rirai
savoir	sachant	su	sais	saurai
suffire	suffisant	suffi	suffis	suffirai
suivre	suivant	suivi	suis	suivrai
tenir	tenant	tenu	tiens	tiendrai
valoir	valant	valu	vaux	vaudrai
venir	venant	venu	viens	viendrai
vivre	vivant	vécu	vis	vivrai
voir	voyant	vu	vois	verrai
vouloir	voulant	voulu	veux	voudrai

Abbreviations

abbr.	abbreviation	*intr.*	intransitive
adj.	adjective	*lit.*	literal, literally
adv.	adverb	*m.*	masculine
arch.	architecture	*med.*	medical
arith.	arithmetic	*mil.*	military
art.	article	*n.*	noun
comm.	commercial	*naut.*	nautical
conj.	conjunction	*pl.*	plural
eccles.	ecclesiastical	*pred.*	predicate
f.	feminine	*prep.*	preposition
fig.	figurative	*pron.*	pronoun
geog.	geography	*sg.*	singular
geom.	geometry	*tr.*	transitive (used only with verbs which also have reflexive use to indicate intransitive meaning)
gramm.	grammar, grammatical		
interj.	interjection		
interr.	interrogative	*vb.*	verb

A

à, *prep.* at, in, to.

abaisser, *vb.* depress, lower.

abandon, *n.m.* desertion, abandonment.

abandonné, *adj.* forlorn.

abandonner, *vb.* forsake, leave (desert). **s'a.**, give up, resign oneself.

abasourdir, *vb.* astound.

abat-jour, *n.m.* lampshade.

abattage, *n.m.* slaughter.

abattement, *n.m.* depression, dejection.

abattoir, *n.m.* slaughterhouse.

abattre, *vb.* depress, reduce; slaughter. **s'a.**, alight.

abbaye, *n.f.* abbey.

abbé, *n.m.* abbot.

abbesse, *n.f.* abbess.

abcès, *n.m.* abscess.

abdiquer, *vb.* abdicate.

abdomen, *n.m.* abdomen.

abeille, *n.f.* bee.

aberrant, *adj.* absurd.

aberration, *n.f.* aberration.

abîme, *n.m.* abyss.

abîmer, *vb.* injure, spoil.

abject, *adj.* abject, low.

aboiement, *n.m.* barking.

abolir, *vb.* abolish.

abolition, *n.f.* abolition.

abominable, *adj.* vile, objectionable.

abondamment, *adv.* fully.

abondance, *n.f.* plenty.

abondant, *adj.* plentiful. **peu a.**, scanty.

abonder de, *vb.* abound in.

abonné, *n.m.* subscriber.

abonnement, *n.m.* subscription.

abonner, *vb.* **s'a.**, subscribe.

abord, 1. *n.m.* approach. 2. *adv.* **d'a.**, at first.

abordable, *adj.* approachable, affordable.

aborder, *vb.* accost.

aboutir, *vb.* end (in).

aboyer, *vb.* bark.

abrégé, *n.m.* summary.

abréger, *vb.* abridge, shorten, abbreviate.

abreuver, *vb.* water (animals).

abréviation, *n.f.* abbreviation.

abri, *n.m.* shelter. **à l'a. de**, safe from.

abricot, *n.m.* apricot.

abriter, *vb.* shelter.

abroger, *vb.* repeal.

abrupt (-pt), *adj.* steep.

abrutir, *vb.* exhaust. **s'a.**, become dazed.

absence, *n.f.* absence.

absent, *adj.* absent. **rester a.**, stay away.

absenter, *vb.* **s'a.**, go away.

abside, *n.f.* apse.

absinthe, *n.f.* absinthe.

absolu, *adj.* utter, absolute.

absolument, *adv.* absolutely.

absolution, *n.f.* absolution.

absorbant, *adj. and n.m.* absorbent.

absorbé dans, *adj.* intent on.

absorber, *vb.* engross, absorb. **s'a. dans**, pour over.

absorption, *n.f.* absorption.

absoudre, *vb.* absolve.

abstenir, *vb.* forbear. **s'a. de**, abstain from.

abstinence, *n.f.* abstinence.

abstraction, *n.f.* abstraction.

abstrait, *adj.* abstract.

absurde, *adj.* absurd, preposterous.

absurdité, *n.f.* nonsense, absurdity.

abus, *n.m.* abuse.

abuser de, *vb.* abuse.

académie, *n.f.* academy.

académique, *adj.* academic.

acajou, *n.m.* mahogany.

accablant, *adj.* oppressive.

accabler, *vb.* overwhelm, burden.

accalmie, *n.f.* lull.

accaparer, *vb.* get a corner on.

accéder, *vb.* reach.

accélérateur, *n.m.* accelerator.

accélération, *n.f.* acceleration.

accélérer, *vb.* quicken, hurry.

accent, *n.m.* stress, emphasis, accent.

accentuer, *vb.* accentuate, accent, emphasize.

acceptable, *adj.* acceptable.

acceptation, *n.f.* acceptance.

accepter, *vb.* accept, admit.

accepteur, *n.m.* accepter.

accès, *n.m.* access, approach; fit (of anger); bout (of fever).

accessible, *adj.* accessible.

accessoire, *n.m. and adj.* accessory, adjunct.

accident, *n.m.* crash, accident.

accidenté, *adj.* damaged; (terrain) hilly.

accidentel, *adj.* accidental.

acclamation, *n.f.* acclamation.

acclamer, *vb.* acclaim, cheer.

accommodant, *adj.* accommodating.

accommoder, *vb.* accommodate.

accompagnateur, *n.m.* accompanist, (travel) guide.

accompagnement, *n.m.* accompaniment.

accompagner, *vb.* accompany, go with.

accompli, *adj.* accomplished, complete, perfect.

accomplir, *vb.* accomplish, achieve, fulfill, carry out, perform.

accomplissement, *n.m.* performance, accomplishment, fulfillment, achievement.

accord, *n.m.* agreement, harmony; settlement; chord, tune. **être d'a.**, agree, concur.

accorder, *vb.* grant, bestow; allow; tune. **s'a.**, agree.

accouchement, *n.m.* delivery (baby).

accoucher, *vb.* deliver (baby).

accoucheur, *n.m.* **médecin-a.**, obstetrician.

accouder, *vb.* **s'a.,** lean.

accourir, *vb.* flock, run up.

accoutumer, *vb.* accustom, habituate.

accréditer, *vb.* accredit.

accro, *n.m.* (drug) addict.

accroc, *n.m.* tear, snag; hitch (fig.).

accrocher, *vb.* hook, hitch, hang (up).

accroissement, *n.m.* growth, addition.

accroître, *vb.* increase.

accroupir, *vb.* **s'a.,** squat, crouch.

accru, *adj.* greater, increased.

accueil, *n.m.* reception, greeting.

accueillir, *vb.* receive, greet.

acculer, *vb.* corner.

accumuler, *vb.* heap up.

accusateur, *n.m.* accuser.

accusatif, *n.m.* accusative.

accusation, *n.f.* accusation.

accusatrice, *n.f.* accuser.

accusé, *n.m.* defendant.

accuser, *vb.* arraign, accuse.

acerbe, *adj.* bitter.

acharné, *adj.* eager, relentless.

acharner, *vb.* **s'a.,** go at intensely.

achat, *n.m.* purchase.

acheminer, *vb.* start (toward).

acheter, *vb.* buy.

acheteur, *n.m.* buyer.

achèvement, *n.m.* completion.

achever, *vb.* complete, finish, achieve.

acide, *adj. and n.m.* acid.

acidité, *n.f.* acidity.

acier, *n.m.* steel.

acné, *n.f.* acne.

acolyte, *n.m.* associate.

acompte, *n.m.* deposit, installment.

à-côté, *n.m.* side-issue.

à-c.s, extras.

à-coup, *n.m.* jolt. **par à-c.s.,** by fits and starts.

acoustique, *n.f.* acoustics.

acquérir, *vb.* acquire, get, obtain.

acquiescement, *n.m.* acquiescence, compliance.

acquiescer à, *vb.* acquiesce, consent.

acquisition, *n.f.* acquisition, purchase.

acquittement, *n.m.* acquittal.

acquitter, *vb.* acquit.

âcre, *adj.* sharp.

acrobate, *n.m.f.* acrobat.

acrobatie, *n.f.* acrobatics.

acte, *n.m.* act. **a. notarié,** deed. **a. de naissance,** birth certificate.

acteur, *n.m.* actor.

actif, 1. *n.m.* assets (*comm.*). **2.** *adj.* active.

action, *n.f.* action, deed, act; (*comm.*) share.

action de contrôle en retour, *n.f.* feedback.

actionnaire, *n.m.* shareholder.

actionner, *vb.* operate.

activement, *adv.* busily.

activer, *vb.* activate, fan, hurry.

activité, *n.f.* activity.

actrice, *n.f.* actress.

actualiser, *vb.* update.

actualité, *n.f.* topicality.

actualités, *n.f.pl.* current events, TV news.

actuel, *adj.* present.

actuellement, *adv.* now, at present.

acuité, *n.f.* acuteness.

acuponcture, *n.f.* acupuncture.

adaptateur, *n.m.* adapter.

adaptation, *n.f.* adaptation.

adapter, *vb.* adapt, fit, adjust, suit.

additif, *n.m.* additive.

addition, *n.f.* addition, bill.

additionnel, *adj.* additional.

additionner, *vb.* add.

adepte, *n.m.f.* follower.

adéquat, *adj.* appropriate.

adhérent, *n.m.* member.

adhérer, *vb.* adhere, join.

adhésif, *adj.* adhesive.

adieu, *n.m. and interj.* goodbye, farewell. **faire ses adieux,** take one's leave.

adjacent, *adj.* adjacent.

adjectif, *n.m.* adjective.

adjoindre, *vb.* add, attach.

adjoint, *n.m.* fellow-worker, associate.

adjuger, *vb.* grant, award.

admettre, *vb.* allow, admit, grant.

administrateur, *n.m.* administrator, director, manager.

administratif, *adj.* administrative.

administration, *n.f.* administration, direction.

administrer, *vb.* administer, manage.

admirable, *adj.* admirable.

admirateur, *n.m.* admirer.

admiration, *n.f.* admiration.

admirer, *vb.* admire.

admissible, *adj.* eligible.

admission, *n.f.* confession, admission.

adolescence, *n.f.* adolescence.

adolescent, *adj. and n.m.* adolescent.

adonner, *vb.* **s'a. à,** indulge in, become addicted to.

adopter, *vb.* adopt.

adoptif, *adj.* adoptive.

adoption, *n.f.* adoption.

adoration, *n.f.* adoration.

adorer, *vb.* worship, adore.

adosser, *vb.* **s'a. à,** lean on.

adoucir, *vb.* soothe, soften, sweeten.

adresse, *n.f.* address; skill, ability.

adresser, *vb.* address (a letter); direct. **s'a. à,** apply to.

adroit, *adj.* skillful, clever, handy.

aduler, *vb.* adulate.

adulte, *adj. and n.m.f.* adult.

adultère, *n.m.* adultery.

adultérer, *vb.* adulterate.

advenir, *vb.* happen, occur.

adverbe, *n.m.* adverb.

adversaire, *n.m.f.* opponent.

adverse, *adj.* adverse.

adversité, *n.f.* adversity.

aéré, *adj.* airy.

aérer, *vb.* air (a room).

aérien, *adj.* aerial, overhead.

aérobic, *n.m.* aerobics.

aérodynamique, *adj.* streamlined, aerodynamic.

aérogare, *n.f.* airline (city) terminal.

aéroglisseur, *n.m.* hovercraft.

aérogramme, *n.m.* airmail letter, aerogram.

aéronautique, 1. *n.m.* aeronautics. **2.** *adj.* aeronautical.

aéroport, *n.m.* airport.

aérospatial, *adj.* aerospace.

affable, *adj.* affable.

affaiblir, *vb.* weaken.

affaire, *n.f.* affair, matter; deal; *(pl.)* business. **se tirer d'a.,** manage (somehow). **homme d'a,s,** businessman.

affairé, *adj.* busy.

affairer, *vb.* s'a., be busy.

affaissement, *n.m.* collapse.

affaisser, *vb.* s'a., collapse.

affaler, *vb.* s'a., collapse.

affamé, *adj.* hungry, famished.

affamer, *vb.* starve.

affectation, *n.f.* affectation.

affecter, *vb.* affect; assign.

affectif, *adj.* emotional.

affection, *n.f.* affection.

affectueux, *adj.* affectionate.

affermir, *vb.* strengthen.

affiche, *n.f.* poster.

afficher, *vb.* post, announce.

affilée (d'), *adv.* in a row.

affilier, *vb.* affiliate.

affiner, *vb.* refine.

affinité, *n.f.* affinity.

affirmatif, *adj.* affirmative.

affirmation, *n.f.* statement.

affirmer, *vb.* assert, state, maintain, testify, affirm.

affliction, *n.f.* affliction.

affligé, *adj.* sorrowful.

affliger, *vb.* distress, afflict, grieve.

affluence, *n.f.* crowd. **heures d'a.,** rush hour.

affluent, *n.m.* tributary.

affluer, *vb.* flow into.

affolement, *n.* panic.

affoler, *vb.* drive mad.

affranchir, *vb.* free.

affranchissement, *n.m.* postage.

affréter, *vb.* charter (boat).

affreusement, *adv.* terribly.

affreux, *adj.* dreadful, terrible, horrid, dire.

affront, *n.m.* affront, insult.

affronter, *vb.* confront, face.

afin, 1. a. de *prep.* in order to. **2.** *conj.* **a. que,** so that.

Africain, *n.m.* African.

africain, *adj.* African.

Afrique, *n.f.* Africa.

agacer, *vb.* vex, irritate.

âge, *n.m.* age. **d'un certain â.,** elderly. **le moyen â.,** the Middle Ages.

âgé, *adj.* aged.

agence, *n.f. (comm.)* agency.

agencer, *vb.* organize, arrange.

agenda, *n.m.* datebook.

agenouiller, *vb.* s'a., kneel.

agent, *n.m.* agent. **a. de police,** policeman. **a. de change,** stockbroker.

agglomération, *n.f.* built-up area, town.

aggloméré, *n.m.* chipboard.

agglomérer, *vb.* s'a., pile up.

agglutiner, *vb.* stick together.

aggraver, *vb.* aggravate.

agile, *adj.* nimble.

agir, *vb.* act. **s'a. de,** be a question of.

agitateur, *n.m.* agitator.

agitation, *n.f.* excitement, disturbance, commotion, flutter.

agité, *adj.* upset, excited.

agiter, *vb.* agitate, wave, wag, shake, stir. **s'a.,** toss; flutter.

agneau, *n.m.* lamb.

agonie, *n.f.* agony.

agoniser, *vb.* be dying.

agrafe, *n.f.* clasp, staple.

agrafer, *vb.* clasp, staple.

agrafeuse, *n.f.* stapler.

agrandir, *vb.* enlarge.

agréable, *adj.* likable, pleasant, enjoyable, agreeable.

agréer, *vb.* accept, consent.

agrégation, *n.f.* aggregation; fellowship.

agrément, *n.m.* pleasure, approval.

agresser, *vb.* attack.

agresseur, *n.m.* aggressor, attacker.

agressif, *adj.* aggressive, hostile.

agression, *n.f.* aggression.

agricole, *adj.* agricultural.

agriculture, *n.f.* agriculture.

agripper, *vb.* s'a. à, grab.

agroalimentaire, *n.m.* food industry.

agrumes, *n.m.pl.* citrus fruit(s).

aguerrir, *vb.* harden.

aguets, *n.m.pl.* être aux a., be on the look-out.

aguicher, *vb.* entice.

ahurir, *vb.* bewilder, fluster.

aide, *n.f.* help, aid.

aider, *vb.* help, aid.

aïe, *interj.* ouch!

aïeul, (ä yœl), *n.m.* grandfather.

aïeule, (ä yœl), *n.f.* grandmother.

aïeux, *n.m.pl.* ancestors.

aigle, *n.m.f.* eagle.

aiglefin, *n.m.* haddock.

aigre, *adj.* sour.

aigu, *m.* **aiguë** *f. adj.* shrill, sharp, pointed.

aiguille, *n.f.* needle.

aiguisé, *adj.* keen.

aiguiser, *vb.* sharpen.

ail, (ä ẽ) *n.m.* garlic.

aile, *n.f.* wing.

aileron, *n.m.* fin.

ailleurs, *adv.* elsewhere. **d'a.,** in addition, anyhow.

aimable, *adj.* kind, pleasant, amiable.

aimant, *n.m.* magnet.

aimer, *vb.* love, like.

aine, *n.f.* groin.

aîné (ẽ´ nä), **1.** *adj. and n.m.* elder. **2.** *adj.* eldest, senior.

ainsi, *adv.* thus, so, like this.

air, *n.m.* air, looks. **en plein a.,** in the open air.

aire, *n.f.* area.

aisance, *n.f.* ease, affluence.

aise, *n.f.* ease, comfort. **à l'a.,** comfortable.

aisé, *adj.* substantial, well-to-do; easy.

aisselle, *n.f.* armpit.

ajourner, *vb.* put off. **s'a.,** adjourn.

ajouter, *vb.* add.

ajustage, *n.m.* fitting.

ajuster, *vb.* fit, fix, adjust.

alarme, *n.f.* alarm.

alarmer, *vb.* alarm.

albâtre, *n.m.* alabaster.

albatros, *n.m.* albatross.

album, *n.m.* album.

albumine, *n.f.* albumin.

alcool, (-kôl), *n.m.* alcohol.

alcoolique , (-kôl-), *adj. and n.m.f.* alcoholic.

alcoolisé, *adj.* alcoholic (drink).

alcootest, *n.m.* Breathalyzer test.

alcôve, *n.f.* alcove.

aléas, *n.m.pl.* hazards.

aléatoire, *adj.* uncertain, random.

alentour, *adv.* around.

alentours, *n.m.pl.* neighborhood, surroundings.

alerte, *adj.* spry, active, alert.

algarade, *n.f.* altercation.

algèbre, *n.f.* algebra.

Alger, *n.f.* Algiers.

Algérie, *n.f.* Algeria.

Algérian, *n.m.* Algerian.

algérian, *adj.* Algerian.

algue, *n.f.* seaweed.

alias, *adv.* alias.

alibi, *n.m.* alibi.

aliéné, *n.m.* lunatic.

aliéner, *vb.* alienate.

aligner, *vb.* line up.

aliment, *n.m.* food.

alimentation, *n.f.* feeding.

alimenter, *vb.* feed.

alinéa, *n.m.* paragraph.

aliter, *vb.* **s'a.,** take to one's bed.

allaiter, *vb.* nurse, feed.

allécher, *vb.* tempt.

allée, *n.f.* path, avenue, aisle.

allégation, *n.f.* allegation.

alléger, *vb.* lighten, soothe.

allégresse, *n.f.* glee, delight, mirth.

alléguer, *vb.* plead, allege.

Allemagne, *n.f.* Germany.

Allemand, *n.m.* German (person).

allemand, 1. *n.m.* German (language). **2.** *adj.* German.

aller, *vb.* go. **s'en a.,** go away. **a. à,** fit. **se laisser a.,** drift. **a. bien,** be well. **a. mal,** be not well. **a. et retour,** round trip.

allergique, *adj.* allergic.

alliage, *n.m.* alloy.

alliance, *n.f.* alliance, union.

allié, 1. *n.m.* ally, relation. **2.** *adj.* allied.

allier, *vb.* ally. **s'a. à,** join with.

allô, *interj.* hello.

allocation, *n.f.* allowance. **a.s familiales,** family allowance.

allocution, *n.f.* short speech.

allonger, *vb.* lengthen, prolong.

allons, *interj.* well, come now.

allouer, *vb.* grant.

allume-cigare, *n.m.* cigar lighter.

allumer, *vb.* light.

allumette, *n.f.* match.

allure, *n.f.* pace, gait.

allusion, *n.f.* hint, allusion. **faire a. à,** allude to.

almanach, (-nä), *n.m.* almanac.

aloi, *n.m.* **de bon a.,** of genuine quality.

alors, 1. *adv.* then. **2.** *conj.* **a. que,** when.

alouette, *n.f.* lark.

aloudir, *vb.* weigh down.

Alpes, *n.f.pl.* Alps.

alphabet, *n.m.* alphabet.

alphabétiser, *vb.* teach to read and write.

alpinisme, *n.m.* mountaineering.

Alsace, *n.f.* Alsace.

altérer, *vb.* change.

alternatif, *adj.* alternate.

alternative, *n.f.* alternative.

alterner, *vb.* alternate.

Altesse, *n.f.* Highness (title).

altitude, *n.f.* altitude.

alto, *n.m.* viola.

altruisme, *n.m.* altruism.

aluminium, *n.m.* aluminum.

amabilité, *n.f.* kindness.

amadouer, *vb.* soothe, coax.

amaigrir, *vb.* to make thin(ner).

amalgame, *n.m.* combination.

amalgamer, *vb.* amalgamate.

amande, *n.f.* kernel; almond.

amant, *n.m.* lover.

amarrer, *vb.* moor.

amas, *n.m.* hoard, mass.

amasser, *vb.* hoard, gather, amass.

amateur, *n.m.* amateur. **a. de,** lover of.

ambassade, *n.f.* embassy.

ambassadeur, *n.m.* ambassador.

ambassadrice, *n.f.* ambassadress.

ambiance, *n.f.* atmosphere.

ambiant, *adj.* surrounding.

ambigu, *m.,* **ambiguë** *f. adj.* ambiguous.

ambiguïté, *n.f.* ambiguity.

ambitieux, *adj.* ambitious.

ambition, *n.f.* ambition.

ambre, *n.m.* amber.

ambulance, *n.f.* ambulance.

ambulant, *adj.* traveling.

âme, *n.f.* soul.

amélioration, *n.f.* improvement.

améliorer, *vb.* improve.

aménagement, *n.m.* development.

aménager, *vb.* fit up.

amende, *n.f.* fine. **mettre à l'a.,** fine.

amendement, *n.m.* amendment.

amender, *vb.* amend.

amener, *vb.* bring, lead.

amenuiser, *vb.* **s'a.,** dwindle, lessen.

amer, (-r), *adj.* bitter.

Américain, *n.m.* American.

américain, *adj.* American.

Amérique, *n.f.* America. **A. du Nord,** North America. **A. du Sud,** South America.

amertume, *n.f.* bitterness.

ameublement, *n.m.* furniture.

ami, *m.,* **amie** *f. n.* friend.

amiable, *adj.* conciliatory. **à l'a.,** out of court.

amiante, *n.m.* asbestos.

amical, *adj.* friendly, amicable.

amidon, *n.m.* starch.

amiral, *n.m.* admiral.

amitié, *n.f.* friendship.

ammoniaque, *n.f.* ammonia.

amniocentèse, *n.f.* amniocentesis.

amoindrir, *vb.* lessen, reduce.

amollir, *vb.* soften.

amonceler, *vb.* pile up. **s'a.,** pile up, *(fig.)* accumulate.

amont, *adv.* **en a.,** upstream, uphill.

amorce, *n.f.* bait, beginning.

amorcer, *vb.* bait, begin.

amorphe, *adj.* listless.

amortir, *vb.* deaden, soften.

amortisseur, *n.m.* shock absorber.

amour, *n.m.* love.

amoureux, 1. *n.m.* lover. 2. *adj.* in love, amorous.

amour-propre, *n.m.* vanity, pride, conceit.

ampère, *n.m.* amp(ere).

ample, *adj.* ample, spacious.

ampleur, *n.f.* plenty; compass.

amplificateur, *n.m.* amplifier.

amplifier, *vb.* increase, enlarge, develop.

ampoule, *n.f.* blister; (electric) bulb.

amputer, *vb.* amputate.

amusant, *adj.* funny, enjoyable.

amusement, *n.m.* fun, pastime, entertainment.

amuser, *vb.* entertain. s'a., have a good time.

amygdale, *n.f.* tonsil.

an, *n.m.* year.

analogie, *n.f.* analogy.

analogique, *adj.* analogue.

analogue, *adj.* similar, analogous.

analphabète, *n.m.f.* illiterate.

analyse, *n.f.* analysis.

analyser, *vb.* analyze.

ananas, *n.m.* pineapple.

anarchie, *n.f.* anarchy.

anathème, *n.m.* anathema.

anatomie, *n.f.* anatomy.

ancêtre, *n.m.* forefather, ancestor.

anche, *n.f.* reed.

anchois, *n.m.* anchovy.

ancien, *m.*, ancienne *f. adj.* ancient, old; former.

ancre, *n.f.* anchor.

ancrer, *vb.* anchor.

Andorre, *n.f.* Andorra.

andouille, *n.f.* sausage made of chitterlings; (colloqiuial) idiot.

âne, *m.*, ânesse *f. n.* ass, donkey.

anéantir, *vb.* annihilate, destroy.

anecdote, *n.f.* anecdote.

anémie, *n.f.* anemia.

ânerie, *n.f.* stupidity.

anesthésie, *n.f.* anesthesia.

anesthésique, *adj. and n.m.* anesthetic.

ange, *n.m.* angel.

angine, *n.f.* throat infection.

Anglais, *n.m.* Englishman.

anglais, *adj. and n.m.* English.

Anglaise, *n.f.* Englishwoman.

angle, *n.m.* angle, corner.

Angleterre, *n.f.* England.

angoissant, *adj.* in anguish.

angoisse, *n.f.* agony, pang, anguish.

anguille, *n.f.* eel.

anguleux, *adj.* angular.

anicroche, *n.f.* hitch.

animal, *adj. and n.m.* animal.

animateur, *n.m.* leader, organizer.

animation, *n.f.* animation.

animer, *vb.* enliven, animate.

anis, *n.m.* aniseed.

ankyloser, *vb.* s'a., become stiff.

animosité, *n.f.* animosity.

anneau, *n.m.* ring, circle.

année, *n.f.* year; vintage.

annexe, *n.m.* annex.

annexer, *vb.* annex.

annexion, *n.f.* annexation.

anniversaire, *n.m.* anniversary; birthday.

annonce, *n.f.* advertisement; announcement.

annoncer, *vb.* advertise; announce.

annotation, *n.f.* annotation.

annoter, *vb.* annotate.

annuaire, *n.m.* directory.

annuel, *adj.* yearly, annual.

annuité, *n.f.* annual payment.

annulaire, *n.m.* ring finger.

annulation, *n.f.* cancellation.

annuler, *vb.* cancel, void, annul.

anodin, *adj.* harmless, minor.

ânonner, *vb.* stammer.

anonyme, *adj.* anonymous.

anorak, *n.m.* anorak.

anorexie, *n.f.* anorexia.

anormal, *adj.* irregular, abnormal.

anse, *n.f.* handle; bay (water).

antagonisme, *n.m.* antagonism.

antarctique, *adj.* antarctic.

antécédent, *adj. and n.m.* antecedent.

antécédents, *n.m.pl.* record.

antenne, *n.f.* antenna.

antérieur, *adj.* previous; fore, front.

anthracite, *n.m.* anthracite.

antichambre, *n.f.* entrance hall.

anticipation, *n.f.* anticipation.

anticiper, *vb.* anticipate.

anticorps, *n.m.* antibody.

antidote, *n.m.* antidote.

antihistaminique, *n.m.* antihistamine.

Antilles, *n.f.pl.* West Indies.

antilope, *n.f.* antelope.

antinucléaire, *adj.* antinuclear.

antipathie, *n.f.* antipathy.

antiquaire, *n.m.* antique dealer.

antique, *adj.* ancient, antiquated, antique.

antiquité, *n.f.* antiquity.

antisémite, 1. *n.m.* anti-Semite. 2. *adj.* anti-Semitic.

antiseptique, *adj. and n.m.* antiseptic.

antre, *n.m.* den.

anxiété, *n.f.* anxiety, worry.

anxieux, *adj.* anxious.

août, (ōō), *n.m.* August.

apaiser, *vb.* allay, quiet, appease.

apanage, *n.m.* l'a. de, privilege of.

aparté, *n.m.* aside.

apathie, *n.f.* apathy.

apatride, *n.m.* stateless person.

apercevoir, *vb.* perceive. s'a. de, realize.

aperçu, *n.m.* outline.

apéritif, *n.m.* appetizer.

à-peu-près, *n.m.* approximation.

apeuré, *adj.* scared.

aphone, *adj.* voiceless.

apitoyer, *vb.* move (emotionally).

aplanir, *vb.* even off.

aplatir, *vb.* flatten.

aplomb, *n.m.* poise, boldness.

apogée, *n.m.* peak.

apologie, *n.f.* vindication.

apoplexie, *n.f.* apoplexy.

apostolique, *adj.* apostolic.

apostrophe, *n.f.* apostrophe.

apothéose, *n.f.* crowning glory.

apôtre, *n.m.* apostle.

apparaître, *vb.* appear.

appareil, *n.m.* gear, appliance, device. **a. photographique,** camera.

apparence, *n.f.* appearance, looks.

apparent, *adj.* noticeable, apparent.

apparenté, *adj.* related.

apparition, *n.f.* appearance, ghost.

appartement, *n.m.* apartment.

appartenir, *vb.* belong; pertain.

appât, *n.m.* bait.

appauvrir, *vb.* impoverish.

appel, *n.m.* call, appeal.

appeler, *vb.* call, summon, appeal. **s'a.,** be named.

appendice, *n.m.* appendix.

appesantir, *vb.* **s'a.,** grow heavier.

appétissant, *adj.* appetizing.

appétit, *n.m.* appetite.

applaudir, *vb.* applaud.

applaudissements, *n.m.pl.* applause.

applicable, *adj.* applicable.

application, *n.f.* application, industry.

appliqué, *adj.* industrious.

appliquer, *vb.* apply (put on), stick. **s'a.,** work hard.

appoint, *n.m.* contribution.

appointements, *n.m.pl.* salary.

apport, *n.m.* contribution.

apporter, *vb.* bring, fetch.

apposer, *vb.* affix.

appréciable, *adj.* appreciable.

appréciation, *n.f.* appreciation.

apprécier, *vb.* appreciate, value.

appréhension, *n.f.* apprehension.

apprendre, *vb.* learn. **a. à,** teach (to). **a. par cœur,** memorize.

apprenti, *n.m.* apprentice.

apprentissage, *n.m.* apprenticeship.

apprêt, *n.m.* preparation.

apprêter, *vb.* **s'a.,** prepare, get ready.

apprivoiser, *vb.* tame.

approbation, *n.f.* endorsement, approval, approbation.

approche, *n.f.* approach.

approcher, *vb.* **s'a. de,** approach, go toward.

approfondir, *vb.* deepen.

appropriation, *n.f.* appropriation.

approprier, *vb.* **s'a.,** take over, appropriate.

approuver, *vb.* approve.

approvisionnement, *n.m.* supply.

approvisioner, *vb.* supply.

approximatif, *adj.* approximate.

appui, (-pwē) *n.m.* support.

appuyer, (-pwē-) *vb.* support, endorse, advocate. **a. sur,** emphasize.

âpre, *adj.* bitter.

après, 1. *adv., prep.* after. **2.** *conj.* **a. que,** after. **d'a.,** according to.

après-demain, *n.m.* day after tomorrow.

après-midi, *n.m.f.* afternoon.

âpreté, *n.f.* harshness, bitterness.

à-propos, *n.m.* fitness.

apte à, *adj.* apt, suitable for.

aptitude, *n.f.* fitness, ability, aptitude.

aqualit, *n.m.* waterbed.

aquarelle, (-kwà-), *n.f.* watercolor.

aquarium, (-kwà-), *n.m.* aquarium.

aquatique, (-kwà-), *adj.* aquatic.

aqueux, *adj.* watery.

Arabe, *n.m.f.* Arab, Arabian.

arabe, 1. *n.m.* Arabic. **2.** *adj.* Arab, Arabian, Arabic.

arachide, *n.f.* peanut.

araignée, *n.f.* spider. **toile d'a.,** cobweb.

arbitrage, *n.m.* arbitration.

arbitraire, *adj.* arbitrary.

arbitre, *n.m.f.* umpire, arbitrator.

arbitrer, *vb.* arbitrate.

arbre, *n.m.* tree.

arbrisseau, *n.m.* shrub.

arc, (-k), *n.m.* arc, arch, bow.

arcade, *n.f.* arcade.

arc-boutant, *n.m.* flying buttress.

arc-en-ciel, *n.m.* rainbow.

archaïque, (àrk-), *adj.* archaic.

arche, *n.f.* arch (of bridge); ark. **a. de Noé,** Noah's Ark.

archéologie, *n.f.* archeology.

archet, *n.m.* bow.

archevêque, *n.m.* archbishop.

archi-, *prefix.* very.

archipel, *n.m.* archipelago.

architecte, *n.m.* architect.

architectural, *adj.* architectural.

architecture, *n.f.* architecture.

archives, *n.f.pl.* files, archives.

arctique, *adj.* arctic.

ardemment, *adv.* eagerly.

ardent, *adj.* eager, fiery, ardent.

ardeur, *n.f.* ardor.

ardoise, *n.f.* slate.

arène, *n.f.* arena, ring.

arête, *n.f.* fish bone.

argent, *n.m.* silver, money.

argenté, *adj.* silver(y).

argenterie, *n.f.* silverware.

Argentin, *n.m.* Argentine.

argentin, *adj.* Argentine.

argile, *n.f.* clay.

argot, *n.m.* slang.

argument, *n.m.* argument (reasoning).

argumenter, *vb.* argue (reason).

aride, *adj.* arid.

aristocrate, *n.m.f.* aristocrat.

aristocratie, *n.f.* aristocracy.

aristocratique, *adj.* aristocratic.

arithmétique, *n.f.* arithmetic.

arme, *n.f.* weapon; arm.

armée, *n.f.* army.

armement, *n.m.* armament.

arme nucléaire, *n.f.* nuclear weapon.

armer, *vb.* arm.

armistice, *n.m.* armistice.

armoire, *n.f.* cupboard, closet, wardrobe.

armure, *n.f.* armor.

arnaque, *n.f.* swindle.

aromatique, *adj.* aromatic.

arome, *n.m.* flavor, aroma.

arpenter, *vb.* pace.

arrache-pied, *adv.* d'a., relentlessly.

arracher, *vb.* snatch.

arrangement, *n.m.* arrangement, settlement.

arranger, *vb.* settle, trim, fix, arrange.

arrestation, *n.f.* arrest, apprehension. en état d'a., under arrest.

arrêt, *n.m.* stop.

arrêté, *n.m.* decree.

arrêter, *vb.* stop, check, halt, arrest.

arrhes, *n.f.pl.* deposit.

arrière, *adv.* behind, back. en a., backward. marche a., reverse (gear).

arriéré, 1. *n.m.* arrear. 2. *adj.* backward.

arrière-garde, *n.f.* rear guard.

arrivée, *n.f.* arrival.

arriver, *vb.* happen, reach, arrive.

arrogance, *n.f.* arrogance.

arrogant, *adj.* arrogant.

arroger, *vb.* arrogate, assume.

arrondir, *vb.* round off.

arrondissement, *n.m.* district.

arroser, *vb.* water, sprinkle; baste (meat).

arsenal, *n.m.* arsenal.

arsenic, *n.m.* arsenic.

art, *n.m.* art. beaux-a.s, fine arts.

artère, *n.f.* artery.

artériel, *adj.* arterial.

arthrite, *n.f.* arthritis.

arthrose, *n.f.* osteoarthritis.

artichaut, *n.m.* artichoke.

article, *n.m.* article, item; entry. a. de fond, editorial.

articulation, *n.f.* joint, articulation.

articuler, *vb.* articulate.

artifice, *n.m.* artifice.

artificiel, *adj.* artificial.

artificieux, *adj.* artful.

artillerie, *n.f.* artillery.

artisan, *n.m.* craftsman, artisan.

artiste, *n.m.f.* artist.

artistique, *adj.* artistic.

as, (äs), *n.m.* ace.

ascenseur, *n.m.* elevator.

ascension, *n.f.* ascent (of a mountain).

ascète, *n.m.f.* ascetic.

aseptique, *adj.* aseptic.

aseptiser, *vb.* disinfect.

Asiatique, *n.m.f.* Asian.

asiatique, *adj.* Asian.

Asie, *n.f.* Asia.

asile, *n.m.* haven, refuge, asylum.

aspect, (-pě), *n.m.* looks, appearance, aspect.

asperger, *vb.* sprinkle.

asperges, *n.f.pl.* asparagus.

aspérité, *n.f.* bump.

asphalte, *n.m.*, asphalt.

asphixier, *vb.* suffocate.

aspirateur, *n.m.* vacuum cleaner.

aspiration, *n.f.* aspiration, longing.

aspirer, *vb.* aspire, breathe.

aspirine, *n.f.* aspirin.

assaillant, *n.m.* assailant.

assaillir, *vb.* assail, attack.

assaisonner, *vb.* season.

assassin, *n.m.* assassin, murderer.

assassinat, *n.m.* assassination, murder.

assassiner, *vb.* assassinate, murder.

assaut, *n.m.* assault, attack.

assemblage, *n.m.* collection.

assemblée, *n.f.* congregation, assembly.

assembler, *vb.* convene, gather. s'a., assemble.

assener, *vb.* deal (a blow).

assentiment, *n.m.* assent.

asseoir, *vb.* seat. s'a., sit down.

assermenté, *adj.* sworn.

assertion, *n.f.* assertion.

asservir, *vb.* enslave.

assez (de), *adv.* enough (of); pretty much.

assidu, *adj.* assiduous, industrious.

assiduité, *n.f.* industry.

assiéger, *vb.* besiege.

assiette, *n.f.* plate.

assigner, *vb.* assign.

assimiler, *vb.* assimilate.

assis, *adj.* seated.

assistance, *n.f.* those present.

assister à, *vb.* attend, be present at.

association, *n.f.* soccer; association, company; connection.

associé, 1. *n.m.* partner, associate. 2. *adj.* associated.

associer, *vb.* associate.

assoiffé, *adj.* thirsty.

assombrir, *vb.* s'a., grow dark.

assommer, *vb.* murder, slaughter.

Assomption, *n.f.* (eccles.) Assumption.

assorti, *adj.* matching.

assortiment, *n.m.* assortment.

assortir, *vb.* match; tune.

assoupir, *vb.* s'a., get drowsy.

assouplir, *vb.* make supple.

assourdir, *vb.* deafen.

assouvir, *vb.* satisfy, appease.

assujetti, *adj.* subject.

assujettir, *vb.* subject.

assumer, *vb.* assume.

assurance, *n.f.* assurance, insurance.

assuré, *adj.* sure.

assurer, *vb.* insure; assure. s'a. de, make certain.

assureur, *n.m.* insurer.

astérisque, *n.m.* asterisk.

asthme, *n.m.* asthma.

astiquer, *vb.* polish.

astre, *n.m.* star.

astronaute, *n.m.* astronaut.

astronome, *n.m.* astronomer.

astronomie, *n.f.* astronomy.

astuce, *n.f.* shrewdness; trick.

astucieux, *adj.* tricky.

atelier, *n.m.* studio, (work)shop.

athée, *n.m.f.* atheist.

Athènes, *n.f.* Athens.

athlète, *n.m.f.* athlete.

athlétique, *adj.* athletic.

atlantique, *adj.* Atlantic.

atlas, (-s) *n.m.* atlas.

atmosphère, *n.f.* atmosphere.

atmosphérique, *adj.* atmospheric.

atome, *n.m.* atom.

atomique, *adj.* atomic.

atout, *n.m.* trump.

atroce, *adj.* atrocious, outrageous.

atrocité, *n.f.* atrocity.

attachement, *n.m.* attachment, affection.

attacher, *vb.* tie, fasten, join, attach.

attaque, *n.f.* attack.

attaquer, *vb.* attack.

attardé, *adj.* belated.

attarder, *vb.* **s'a.,** linger; delay.

atteindre, *vb.* reach, attain; strike.

atteint, *adj.* stricken.

atteinte, *n.f.* reach. **hors d'a.,** out of reach.

attelage, *n.m.* team.

atteler, *vb.* hitch up, harness.

attenant, *adj.* adjoining.

attendre, *vb.* wait (for), await. **s'a. à,** expect.

attendrir, *vb.* soften, move. **se laisser a.,** relent.

attendrissement, *n.m.* feeling, emotion.

attentat, *n.m.* criminal attack, outrage.

attente, *n.f.* expectation, wait.

attenter à, *vb.* make an attempt on.

attentif, *adj.* thoughtful, attentive.

attention, *n.f.* notice, heed, attention. **faire a.,** heed, pay attention.

atténuer, *vb.* extenuate.

atterrir, *vb.* land.

attester, *vb.* attest.

attirant, *adj.* attractive.

attirer, *vb.* attract, entice, lure.

attitude, *n.f.* attitude.

attouchement, *n.m.* touch.

attraction, *n.f.* attraction.

attrait, *n.m.* charm.

attraper, *vb.* catch.

attrayant, *adj.* attractive.

attribuer, *vb.* ascribe, attribute.

attribut, *n.m.* attribute, characteristic.

attrister, *vb.* grieve.

au, *m.,* **à la,** *f.,* **aux,** *pl. prep.* to the, in the.

aubaine, *n.f.* godsend.

aube, *n.f.* dawn.

auberge, *n.f.* inn.

aubergine, *n.f.* eggplant.

aubergiste, *n.m.* innkeeper.

aucun, *pron.* none.

aucunement, *adv.* not at all.

audace, *n.f.* audacity.

audacieux, *adj.* daring, bold.

au-delà, *adv.* beyond.

au-dessous, 1. *adv.* below. 2. *prep.* **au-d. de,** beneath, under.

au-dessus, 1. *adv.* above. 2. *prep.* **au-d. de,** over, above.

audience, *n.f.* audience.

Audimat, *n.m.* (trademark) TV ratings.

audiovisuel, *adj.* audiovisual.

auditeur, *n.m.* listener.

auditoire, *n.m.* audience, assembly.

auge, *n.f.* trough.

augmentation, *n.f.* increase, raise, rise.

augmenter, *vb.* increase.

augure, *n.m.* omen, augury. **de bon a.,** auspicious. **de mauvais a.,** ominous.

augurer, *vb.* augur.

aujourd'hui, *adv.* today.

aumône, *n.f.* alms.

aumônier, *n.m.* chaplain.

auparavant, *adv.* before (time).

auprès de, *prep.* next, near, beside.

auréole, *n.f.* halo.

aurore, *n.f.* dawn.

ausculter, *vb.* examine with a stethoscope.

auspice, *n.m.* auspice.

aussi, *adv.* too, also; so, as; therefore.

aussitôt, *adv.* immediately.

austère, *adj.* austere, severe.

austérité, *n.f.* austerity.

Australie, *n.f.* Australia.

Australien, *n.m.* Australian.

australien, *adj.* Australian.

autant, *adv.* so much, as much. **a. que,** as (so) much as. **d'a. que,** since. **a. plus,** so much the more.

autel, *n.m.* altar.

auteur, *n.m.* author, originator.

authentique, *adj.* true, genuine, authentic.

auto, *n.f.* auto.

auto-, *prefix.* self-, auto-.

autobus, (-s) *n.m.* bus.

automatique, *adj.* automatic.

automne, (-tôn) *n.m.* fall.

automobile, *n.f.* automobile.

autonomie, *n.f.* autonomy.

autopsie, *n.f.* autopsy.

autorail, *n.m.* train car.

autorisation, *n.f.* license, authorization.

autoriser, *vb.* authorize.

autoritaire, *adj.* authoritative.

autorité, *n.f.* authority.

autoroute, *n.f.* highway.

auto-stop, *n.m.* hitchhiking.

autour, 1. *adv.* around. 2. *prep.* **a. de,** around.

autre, 1. *adj.* other. 2. *pron.* other, else. **l'un l'a.,** one another. **quelqu'un d'a.,** someone else.

autrefois, *adv.* formerly.

autrement, *adv.* otherwise.

Autriche, *n.f.* Austria.

Autrichien, *n.m.* Austrian.

autrichien, *adj.* Austrian.

autruche, *n.f.* ostrich.

autrui, *pron.* someone else, others.

auxiliaire, *adj.* auxiliary.

avalanche, *n.f.* avalanche.

avaler, *vb.* swallow.

avance, *n.f.* advance. **d'a.,** beforehand. **en a.,** fast (clock).

avancé, *adj.* forward, advanced.

avancement, *n.m.* advance; advancement; promotion.

avancer, *vb.* proceed; come *or* go forward *or* onward.

avances, *n.f.pl.* advance. **faire des a. à,** make approaches to.

avant, 1. *n.m.* fore, bow. **2.** *adv., prep.* before. **3.** *conj.* **a. que,** before. **en a.,** forward, onward. **en a. de,** ahead of.

avantage, *n.m.* advantage.

avantageux, *adj.* advantageous; favorable; profitable.

avant-bras, *n.m.* forearm.

avant-garde, *n.f.* vanguard.

avant-hier, (-yâr), *n.m.* day before yesterday.

avant-toit, *n.m.* eaves.

avare, 1. *n.m.f.* miser. **2.** *adj.* miserly, stingy.

avarice, *n.f.* avarice.

avec, *prep.* with.

avenant, *adj.* comely. **à l'a.,** accordingly.

avenir, *n.m.* future.

Avent, *n.m.* *(eccles.)* Advent.

aventure, *n.f.* adventure.

aventurer, *vb.* **s'a.,** take a chance.

aventureux, *adj.* adventurous.

aventurier, *n.m.* adventurer.

avenue, *n.f.* avenue.

avérer, *vb.* **s'a.,** prove (to be).

averse, *n.f.* shower (rain).

aversion, *n.f.* aversion, dislike.

avertir, *vb.* notify, warn.

avertissement, *n.m.* warning.

avertisseur d'incendie, *n.m.* fire alarm.

aveu, *n.m.* admission, confession.

aveugle, *adj.* blind.

aveuglement, *n.m.* blindness.

aveuglément, *adv.* blindly.

aveugler, *vb.* blind.

aviateur, *n.m.* flier, aviator.

aviation, *n.f.* air force, aviation.

avide, *adj.* eager, greedy, avid.

avidité, *n.f.* greediness.

avilir, *vb.* debase, disgrace.

avion, *n.m.* airplane. **a. de bombardement,** bomber. **par a.,** via air mail.

avis, *n.m.* notice, opinion, advice *(comm.).*

aviser, *vb.* inform, notify. **s'a. (de),** decide.

avocat, *n.m.* lawyer; advocate.

avoine, *n.f.* oat.

avoir, *vb.* have. **il y a,** ago.

avortement, *n.m.* abortion.

avoué, *n.m.* attorney, lawyer.

avouer, *vb.* confess, admit, avow.

avril, (-l), *n.m.* April.

axe, *n.m.* axis.

axer, *vb.* center.

axiome, *n.m.* axiom.

ayatollah, *n.m.* ayatollah.

azote, *n.m.* nitrogen.

azur, *n.m.* azure, blue.

azuré, *adj.* azure.

B

babeurre *n.m.* buttermilk.

babil, *n.m.* babble.

babiller, *vb.* babble.

bâbord, *n.m.* *(naut.)* port.

babouin, *n.m.* baboon.

baby-foot, *n.m.* table football.

bac, *n.m.* ferryboat. **passage en b.,** ferry, high school diploma.

baccalauréat, *n.m.* high school diploma.

bachelier, *n.m.* graduate.

bachot, *n.m.* (colloquial) high school diploma.

bacille, (-l), *n.m.* bacillus.

bactérie, *n.f.* bacterium.

bactériologie, *n.f.* bacteriology.

badaud, *adj.* silly.

baffe, *n.f.* (colloquial) slap.

bagages, *n.m.pl.* luggage.

bagatelle, *n.f.* trifle.

bagnole, *n.f.* (colloquial) car.

bague, *n.f.* ring.

baguette, *n.f.* wand, stick; long, thin loaf of bread.

baie, *n.f.* bay; creek; berry.

baigner, *vb.* bathe.

baigneur, *n.m.* bather.

baignoire, (bĕn wär), *n.f.* bathtub.

bail, *n.m.* lease.

bâillement, *n.m.* yawn.

bâiller, *vb.* yawn.

bâillon, *n.m.* gag.

bain, *n.m.* bath.

baïonnette, *n.f.* bayonet.

baiser, *n.m. and vb.* kiss (hand, forehead, etc.).

baissé, *adj.* downcast.

baisser, *vb.* lower, sink.

bal, *n.m.* ball (dance).

balade, *n.f.* stroll.

baladeur, *n.m.* portable cassette player or radio; (trademark) Walkman.

balai, *n.m.* broom. **b. à laver,** mop.

balance, *n.f.* scales, balance.

balancement, *n.m.* rocking, swinging.

balancer, *vb.* rock, swing, sway. **se b.,** roll, hover.

balayer, *vb.* sweep.

balbutier, *vb.* stammer.

balcon, *n.m.* balcony.

baldaquin, *n.m.* canopy.

baleine, *n.f.* whale.

ballade, *n.f.* ballad.

balle, *n.f.* bullet, ball; bale.

ballet, *n.m.* ballet.

ballon, *n.m.* balloon.

ballot, *n.m.* bundle.

ballotter, *vb.* shake.

balnéaire, *adj.* seaside.

balsamique, *adj.* balmy.

bambin, *n.m.* small child.

bambou, *n.m.* bamboo.

ban, *n.m.* ban. **mettre au b.,** ban.

banal, *adj.* trite.

banane, *n.f.* banana.

banc, *n.m.* bench.

bancaire, *adj.* banking.

bandage, *n.m.* bandage.

bande, *n.f.* strip, stripe; pack, gang, band.

bande magnétique, *n.f.* tape.

bande vidéo, *n.f.* videotape.

bandit, *n.m.* bandit, robber, knave.

banlieue, *n.f.* suburbs.

bannière, *n.f.* banner.

bannir, *vb.* banish.

bannissement, *n.m.* banishment.

banque, *n.f.* bank. **billet de b.,** banknote.

banqueroute, *n.f.* bankruptcy.

banquet, *n.m.* banquet, feast.

banquier, *n.m.* banker.

baptême, (bä těm), *n.m.* christening, baptism.

baptiser, (bä tē-), *vb.* christen, baptize.

Baptiste, (bä tēst), *n.m.* Baptist.

baptistère, (bä tēs-), *n.m.* baptistery.

bar, *n.m.* bar; bass (fish).

baraque, *n.f.* booth, stall; (colloquial) house.

baratin, *n.m.* smooth talk.

barbare, 1. *n.m.f.* barbarian. 2. *adj.* barbarian, barbarous, wild.

barbarie, *n.f.* cruelty.

barbe, *n.f.* beard.

barbouiller, *vb.* daub, blur.

barbu, *adj.* bearded.

baril, *n.m.* barrel, keg.

baromètre, *n.m.* barometer.

baron, *n.m.* baron.

baroque, *adj.* baroque, weird.

barque, *n.f.* boat.

barrage, *n.m.* dam.

barre, *n.f.* bar, rail(ing). **b. du gouvernail,** helm.

barreau, *n.m.* bar.

barrer, *vb.* shut out.

barricade, *n.f.* barricade.

barrière, *n.f.* gate; bar, barrier; fence.

barrique, *n.f.* barrel, cask.

bas, *n.m.* stocking.

bas, *m.,* **basse** *f. adj.* base, low, soft. **en b.,** down(ward), downstairs. **b. côté,** aisle.

bascule, *n.f.* seesaw. **chaise à b.,** rocking-chair.

basculer, *vb.* fall over.

base, *n.f.* base, basis.

basilic, *n.m.* basil.

basket, *n.m.* basketball; sneaker.

Basque, *n.m.* Basque (person).

basque, 1. *n.m.* Basque (language). 2. *adj.* Basque.

basse, *n.f.* bass (voice).

basse-cour, *n.f.* barnyard.

bassesse, *n.f.* baseness.

bassin, *n.m.* basin, dock.

bataille, *n.f.* battle.

bataillon, *n.m.* battalion.

bâtard, *adj. and n.m.* bastard.

bateau, *n.m.* boat.

bâtiment, *n.m.* building.

bâtir, *vb.* build.

bâton, *n.m.* stick, staff.

battant, *n.m.* flap, door.

batte, *n.f.* bat.

battement, *n.m.* beat.

batterie, *n.f.* battery; drums.

battre, *vb.* beat, strike; flap, pulsate. **se b.,** fight.

baume, *n.m.* balm.

bavard, *adj.* talkative, gossipy.

bavardage, *n.m.* gossip, chatter.

bavarder, *vb.* gossip, chat(ter).

bavette, *n.f.* bib.

bavure, *n.f.* smudge, mistake.

bazar, *n.m.* bazaar.

BCBG, *adj.* preppy. (bon chic bon genre).

BD, *n.f.* comic strip. (bande dessinée).

béatitude, *n.f.* bliss.

beau, bel, *m.,* **belle** *f. adj.* beautiful, handsome, fair, lovely, fine. **avoir b.,** (to do something) in vain. **faire b.,** be fine (weather).

beaucoup (de), *adj.* a lot, a great deal; much, many. **de b.,** by far.

beau-frère, *n.m.* brother-in-law.

beau-père, *n.m.* father-in-law; stepfather.

beauté, *n.f.* beauty. **grain de b.,** mole.

bébé, *n.m.* baby.

bec, *n.m.* beak, bill; spot; burner; **b. sucré,** sweet tooth.

bécane, *n.f.* (colloquial) bike.

bêche, *n.f.* spade.

bêcher, *vb.* dig.

becqueter, *vb.* peck.

bée, *adj.* **rester bouche b.,** stand gaping.

bégayer, *vb.* stammer.

beignet, *n.m.* fritter.

bêler, *vb.* bleat.

Belge, *n.m.f.* Belgian.

belge, *adj.* Belgian.

Belgique, *n.f.* Belgium.

bélier, *n.m.* ram.

belle-fille, *n.f.* daughter-in-law.

belle-mère, *n.f.* mother-in-law; stepmother.

belligérant, *adj. and n.m.* belligerent.

bémol, *n.m.* flat (music).

bénédiction, *n.f.* blessing, benediction.

bénéfice, *n.m.* benefit, advantage, profit.

bénéficier, *vb.* benefit, profit.

bénin, *m.,* **bénigne** *f. adj.* benign.

bénir, *vb.* bless.

béquille, *n.f.* crutch.

berceau, *n.m.* cradle, bower.

bercer, *vb.* rock.

berge, *n.f.* bank (river, etc.).

berger, *n.m.* shepherd.

besogne, *n.f.* (piece of) work.

besoin, *n.m.* need, want. **avoir b.,** need.

bestiaux, *n.m.pl.* cattle.

bétail, *n.m.* cattle, animals.

bête, 1. *n.f.* beast, animal. 2. *adj.* stupid, dumb.

bêtise, *n.f.* nonsense.

béton, *n.m.* concrete.

betterave, *n.f.* beet.

Beur, *n.m.f.* North African in France of immigrant parents.

beurre, *n.m.* butter.

bévue, *n.f.* blunder, boner.

biais, *n.m.* slant; bias. **en b.,** at an angle.

bibelot, *n.m.* trinket.

biberon, *n.m.* baby's bottle.

Bible, *n.f.* Bible.

bibliothèque, *n.f.* library; bookcase.

biblique, *adj.* biblical.

bicyclette, *n.f.* bicycle. **faire de la b.**, cycle.

bidet, *n.m.* bidet.

bidon, *n.m.* can.

bidonville, *n.m.* shanty town.

bien, *n.m.* good; *(pl.)* goods, property, estate. **faire du b. à**, benefit.

bien, *adv.* well. **b. entendu**, of course. **aller b.**, be well. **vouloir b.**, be willing. **b. que**, although.

bien-aimé, *n.m. and adj.* darling.

bien-être, *n.m.* welfare.

bienfaisant, *adj.* beneficent, kind, humane.

bienfait, *n.m.* benefit.

bienfaiteur, *n.m.* benefactor.

bienheureux, *adj.* blessed.

bieséant, *adj.* proper.

bientôt, *adv.* soon.

bienveillance, *n.f.* benevolence, kindness.

bienveillant, *adj.* benevolent, kindly.

bienvenu, *adj.* welcome.

bière, *n.f.* beer, ale.

biffer, *vb.* cancel, erase.

bifteck, *n.m.* beefsteak.

bifuquer, *vb.* branch off, fork.

bigamie, *n.f.* bigamy.

bigot, *n.m.* bigot.

bigoterie, *n.f.* bigotry.

bijou, *n.m.* jewel.

bijouterie, *n.f.* jewelry.

bilan, *n.m.* balance sheet; outcome.

bile, *n.f.* bile. **se faire de la b.**, worry.

bilingue, *adj.* bilingual.

billard, *n.m.* billiards.

bille, *n.f.* marble (toy).

billet, *n.m.* ticket, note. **b. de banque**, banknote.

billetterie, *n.f.* ticket dispenser.

billion, (-l-), *n.m.* billion.

biochimie, *n.f.* biochemistry.

biographie, *n.f.* biography.

biologie, *n.f.* biology.

bis, **1.** *n.m.* encore. **2.** *adv.* A or a (in addresses).

biscuit, *n.m.* biscuit.

bise, *n.f.* (colloquial) kiss.

bisou, *n.m.* (colloquial) kiss.

bit, *n.m.* bit.

bizarre, *adj.* queer, odd, strange.

blâme, *n.m.* blame.

blâmer, *vb.* blame.

blanc, *m.*, **blanche** *f. adj.* white, blank. **en b.**, blank.

blancheur, *n.f.* whiteness.

blanchir, *vb.* whiten.

blanchisserie, *n.f.* laundry.

blasé, *adj.* sophisticated.

blasphème, *n.m.* blasphemy.

blasphémer, *vb.* curse, blaspheme.

blatte, *n.f.* cockroach.

blé, *n.m.* wheat.

bled, *n.m.* inland country.

blême, *adj.* pale.

blesser, *vb.* wound, hurt, injure.

blessure, *n.f.* wound, hurt, injury.

bleu, *adj.* blue; extremely rare (meat).

bloc, *n.m.* pad, block.

blocus, (-s), *n.m.* blockade.

blond, *adj.* fair, blond(e).

bloquer, *vb.* block.

blottir, *vb.* **se b.**, cower.

blouse, *n.f.* blouse.

blouson, *n.m.* windbreaker.

blue jeans, *n.m.pl.* blue jeans.

bluff, *n.m.* bluff.

bluffeur, *n.m.* bluffer.

bobine, *n.f.* spool, reel.

bœuf, (bœf), *n.m.* ox, beef. **jeune b.**, steer.

bogue, *n.m.* bug (computers).

Bohême, *n.f.* Bohemia.

bohème, **1.** *n.m.f.* bohemian, happy-go-lucky person. **2.** *n.f.* artistic underworld. **3.** *adj.* bohemian.

Bohémien, *n.m.* Bohemian; gypsy.

bohémien, *adj.* Bohemian.

boire, *vb.* drink. **b. à petits coups**, sip.

bois, *n.m.* wood, forest, lumber.

boiserie, *n.f.* woodwork.

boisseau, *n.m.* bushel.

boisson, *n.f.* beverage, drink.

boîte, *n.f.* box; can (food). **b. aux lettres**, mail-box.

boiter, *vb.* limp.

boiteux, *adj.* lame.

bol, *n.m.* bowl.

bombardement, *n.m.* bombardment.

bombarder, *vb.* bomb, bombard.

bombe, *n.f.* bomb, shell.

bombe à neutrons, *n.f.* neutron bomb.

bon, *m.*, **bonne** *f. adj.* good, kind. **de b. heure**, early. **b. marché**, cheap.

bon, *n.m.* bond.

bonbon, *n.m.* candy, bonbon.

bond, *n.m.* bound, leap.

bonder, *vb.* overcrowd, jam.

bondir, *vb.* bound, leap, spring.

bonheur, *n.m.* happiness.

bonhomme, *n.m.* fellow.

bonjour, *interj. and n.m.* good morning.

bonne, *n.f.* maid.

bonnement, *adv.* simply.

bonnet, *n.m.* cap, hood.

bonsoir, *interj. and n.m.* good evening.

bonté, *n.f.* kindness, goodness.

bord, *n.m.* edge, rim, brim. **b. du toit**, eaves.

bordeaux, *n.m.* Bordeaux (wine).

border, *vb.* bound, edge, border, hem.

borne, *n.f.* bound, limit.

borner, *vb.* bound, limit.

Bosnie-Herzégovine, *n.f.* Bosnia (and) Herzegovina.

bosquet, *n.m.* clump (trees).

bosse, *n.f.* bump.

bosselure, *n.f.* dent.

bosser, *vb.* (colloquial) work.

bossu, *adj.* hunchbacked.

botanique, *n.f.* botany.

botte, *n.f.* boot; bunch.

Bottin, *n.m.* (trademark) phone book.

bottine, *n.f.* ankle boot.

bouche, *n.f.* mouth.

boucher, *vb.* stop up.

boucher, *n.m.* butcher.
boucherie, *n.f.* butcher shop.
bouchon, *n.m.* cork.
boucle, *n.f.* curl, loop, buckle. **b. d'oreille**, earring.
boucler, *vb.* curl.
bouclier, *n.m.* shield.
bouder, *vb.* sulk.
boudin, *n.m.* black pudding.
boue, *n.f.* mud.
bouée, *n.f.* buoy.
boueur, *n.m.* scavenger.
boueux, *adj.* muddy.
bouffe, *n.f.* (colloquial) food, grub.
bouffée, *n.f.* puff.
bouffon, *n.m.* clown, fool.
bouffonerie, *n.f.* antic(s).
bouger, *vb.* stir, move, budge.
bougie, *n.f.* candle; spark plug.
bouillabaisse, *n.f.* bouillabaisse.
bouillir, *vb.* boil
bouilloire, *n.f.* kettle.
bouillon, *n.m.* broth.
bouillonner, *vb.* bubble.
bouillotte, *n.f.* kettle.
boulanger, *n.m.* baker.
boulangerie, *n.f.* bakery.
boule, *n.f.* ball.
bouleau, *n.m.* birch.
bouledogue, *n.m.* bulldog.
boulevard, *n.m.* boulevard.
bouleversement, *n.m.* upset.
bouleverser, *vb.* upset, overturn.
boulot, *n.m.* (colloquial) work.
boum, 1. *n.m.* bang. 2. *n.f.* party.
bouquet, *n.m.* cluster, bunch, bouquet.
bouquiniste, *n.m.* (secondhand) bookseller.
bourbeux, *adj.* sloppy.
bourdon, *n.m.* bumblebee.
bourdonnement, *n.m.* buzz.
bourdonner, *vb.* hum, buzz.
bourg, *n.m.* borough, village.
bourgeois, *adj.* middle-class, bourgeois.
bourgeoisie, *n.f.* middle class.
bourgeon, *n.m.* bud.

bourgeonner, *vb.* bud.
bourgogne, 1. *n.m.* Burgundy (wine). 2. *n.f.* **la B.**, Burgundy.
bourre, *n.f.* stuffing.
bourreau, *n.m.* executioner, hangman; brute.
bourrelet, *n.m.* pad.
bourrer, *vb.* stuff, pad.
bourru, *adj.* gruff.
bourse, *n.f.* purse, bag; stock exchange; scholarship, fellowship.
boursoufler, *vb.* bloat.
bousculer, *vb.* jostle.
bousiller, *vb.* bungle.
boussole, *n.f.* compass.
bout, *n.m.* end, tip, butt, stub.
bouteille, *n.f.* bottle.
boutique, *n.f.* shop.
bouton, *n.m.* button, bud; pimple.
boutonnière, *n.f.* buttonhole.
boxe, *n.f.* boxing.
boxeur, *n.m.* boxer.
boycotter, *vb.* boycott.
bracelet, *n.m.* bracelet.
braconnier, *n.m.* poacher.
brailler, *vb.* bawl.
braise, *n.f.* coals, embers.
brancard, *n.m.* stretcher.
branche, *n.f.* branch, bough, limb.
branché, *adj.* trendy.
brandir, *vb.* brandish.
branler, *vb.* waver.
braquer, *vb.* aim, point.
bras, *n.m.* arm.
brasse, *n.f.* fathom; breaststroke.
brasser, *vb.* brew.
brasserie, *n.f.* brewery; beer-joint.
bravade, *n.f.* bravado.
brave, *adj.* fine, good, brave.
braver, *vb.* brave, face, defy.
bravoure, *n.f.* courage.
break, *n.m.* station wagon.
brebis, *n.f.* lamb.
brèche, *n.f.* breach, gap.
bref, 1. *adj. m.*, **brève** *f.* brief, short. 2. *adv.* in short.
Brésil, *n.m.* Brazil.
Bretagne, *n.f.* Brittany.
brevet, *n.m.* commission. **b. d'invention**, patent.

bribe, *n.f.* scrap, bit.
bricoler, *vb.* do odd jobs.
bride, *n.f.* bridle.
brider, *vb.* curb.
bridge, *n.m.* bridge (game).
brièveté, *n.f.* brevity.
brigade, *n.f.* brigade.
brigadier, *n.m.* corporal.
brigant, *n.m.* robber, knave.
brillant, *adj.* brilliant, bright, glowing.
briller, *vb.* shine, glisten, glare.
brin, *n.m.* blade (grass).
brindille, *n.f.* twig.
brioche, *n.f.* bun.
brique, *n.f.* brick.
briquet, *n.m.* lighter. **pierre à b.**, flint.
brise, *n.f.* breeze.
briser, *vb.* break, shatter, smash.
britannique, *adj.* British.
brocart, *n.m.* brocade.
broche, *n.f.* spit, spindle; brooch.
brochette, *n.f.* skewer.
brochure, *n.f.* pamphlet.
broder, *vb.* embroider.
broderie, *n.f.* embroidery.
bronchite, *n.f.* bronchitis.
bronze, *n.m.* bronze.
broquette, *n.f.* tack.
brosse, *n.f.* brush.
brouhaha, *n.m.* uproar.
brouillard, *n.m.* fog, mist.
brouiller, *vb.* jumble, embroil; scramble (eggs). **se b.**, quarrel.
brouillon, *n.m.* (rough) draft.
broussailles, *n.f.pl.* brushwood.
brousse, *n.f.* **la b.**, the bush.
brouter, *vb.* browse.
broyer, *vb.* crush.
bruine, *n.f.* drizzle.
bruiner, *vb.* drizzle.
bruissement, *n.m.* rustle.
bruit, *n.m.* noise, clatter; report, rumor.
brûler, *vb.* burn.
brume, *n.f.* mist. **b. légère**, haze.
brumeux, *adj.* foggy, misty.
brun, *adj.* brown.
brune, *adj. and n.f.* brunette.

brusque, *adj.* abrupt, curt, blunt, gruff, brusque.
brut, *adj.* crude, gross.
Bruxelles, *n.f.* Brussels.
brutal, *adj.* brutal, savage.
brutalité, *n.f.* brutality.
brute, *n.f.* brute.
bruyant, *adj.* noisy, loud.
bruyère, *n.f.* heath, heather.
bûche, *n.f.* log.
bûcheron, *n.m.* wood-cutter.
budget, *n.m.* budget.

buffet, *n.m.* buffet.
buffle, *n.m.* buffalo.
buis, *n.m.* box (tree).
buisson, *n.m.* bush, shrub, thicket.
buissonneux, *adj.* bushy.
bulbe, *n.m.* bulb.
Bulgarie, *n.f.* Bulgaria.
bulle, *n.f.* bubble; (papal) bull.
bulletin, *n.m.* bulletin, ticket.

bureau, *n.m.* office, bureau; desk. **b. de location,** box office.
burin, *n.m.* chisel.
burlesque, *adj.* ludicrous.
bus, *n.m.* bus.
buste, *n.m.* bust.
but, *n.m.* aim, goal, purpose.
butin, *n.m.* spoils, booty.
butte, *n.f.* hill, knoll.
buvard, *n.m.* blotter.
buvette, *n.f.* bar.

C

ça *pron.* that.
cabane, *n.f.* cabin, hut.
cabaret, *n.m.* cabaret; tavern.
cabine, *n.f.* cabin, booth.
cabinet, *n.m.* closet; office. **c. de toilette,** lavatory. **c. de travail,** study.
câble, *n.m.* cable, rope.
câbler, *vb.* cable.
câblogramme, *n.m.* cablegram.
cacahuète, *n.f.* peanut.
cacao, *n.m.* cocoa.
cacher, *vb.* hide, conceal. **se c.,** lurk.
cacher, *m.,* **cachère** *f. adj.* kosher.
cachet, *n.m.* seal.
cadavre, *n.m.* corpse.
cadeau, *n.m.* gift, present.
cadence, *n.f.* cadence.
cadet, 1. *n.m.* cadet. **2.** *adj.* junior.
cadran, *n.m.* dial.
cadre, *n.m.* frame.
café, *n.m.* coffee; café.
cage, *n.f.* cage.
cahier, *n.m.* notebook.
caille, *n.f.* quail.
caillot, *n.m.* clot.
caillou, *n.m.* pebble.
caisse, *n.f.* crate, case, box.
caissier, *n.m.* cashier, teller.
cajoler, *vb.* coax.
calamité, *n.f.* calamity.
calcium, *n.m.* calcium.
calcul, *n.m.* calculation.
calculateur, *n.m.* calculator.
calculatrice, *n.f.* calculator.
calculer, *vb.* figure, reckon, calculate.

cale, *n.f.* hold (ship).
calembour, *n.m.* pun.
calendrier, *n.m.* calendar.
calibre, *n.m.* caliber.
calicot, *n.m.* calico.
callosité, *n.f.* callus.
calmant, *n.m.* sedative.
calme, *adj. and n.m.* quiet, calm.
calmer, *vb.* soothe, quiet, calm.
calomnie, *n.f.* slander.
calomnier, *vb.* slander.
calorie, *n.f.* calorie.
calotte, *n.f.* crown (of hat).
Calvaire, *n.m.* Calvary.
camarade, *n.m.f.* comrade; companion, mate.
camaraderie, *n.f.* companionship, fellowship.
cambrioleur, *n.m.* burglar.
camembert, *n.m.* Camembert cheese.
camera, *n.f.* camera.
caméscope, *n.m.* camcorder.
camion, *n.m.* truck.
camoufler, *vb.* camouflage.
camp, *n.m.* camp.
campagnard, 1. *n.m.* countryman, peasant. **2.** *adj.* peasant.
campagne, *n.f.* country; campaign.
camper, *vb.* camp.
camphre, *n.m.* camphor.
Canada, *n.m.* Canada.
Canadien, *n.m.* Canadian.
canadien, *adj.* Canadian.
canaille, *n.f.* rabble; scoundrel.
canal, *n.m.* channel, canal.

canapé, *n.m.* sofa, couch; canapé.
canard, *n.m.* duck.
canari, *n.m.* canary.
cancer, (-r), *n.m.* cancer.
cancérogène, *adj.* carcinogenic.
candeur, *n.f.* purity; candor.
candidat, *n.m.* candidate, applicant.
candidature, *n.f.* candidacy.
candide, *adj.* frank, open, candid.
canevas, *n.m.* canvas. **gros c.,** burlap.
canicule, *n.f.* heat wave.
canin, *adj.* canine.
canne, *n.f.* cane, stick.
canneberge, *n.f.* cranberry.
cannelle, *n.f.* cinnamon.
cannibale, *adj. and n.m.f.* cannibal.
canoë, (-ō ä), *n.m.* canoe.
canon, *n.m.* cannon.
canot, *n.m.* boat, canoe. **c. automobile,** motorboat.
cantaloup, *n.m.* cantaloupe.
cantine, *n.f.* canteen, dining hall.
cantique, *n.m.* hymn.
canton, *n.m.* district, canton.
caoutchouc, (-chōō), *n.m.* rubber.
cap, (-p), *n.m.* cape (headland).
capable, *adj.* efficient, fit, capable, competent.
capacité, *n.f.* capability; capacity.
cape, *n.f.* cape (clothing).
capitaine, *n.m.* captain.
capital, *adj. and n.m.* capital.

capitale, *n.f.* capital (city).
capitaliser, *vb.* capitalize.
capitalisme, *n.m.* capitalism.
capitaliste, *n.m.f.* capitalist.
caporal, *n.m.* corporal.
capot, *n.m.* hood.
capote, *n.f.* hood.
câpre, *n.f.* caper.
caprice, *n.m.* whim, fancy.
capricieux, *adj.* fickle, capricious.
capsule, *n.f.* capsule.
captif, *adj. and n.m.* captive.
captiver, *vb.* captivate, charm.
captivité, *n.f.* captivity.
capture, *n.f.* capture.
capturer, *vb.* capture.
capuchon, *n.m.* hood.
car, *conj.* for.
caractère, *n.m.* character, nature, disposition; type.
caractériser, *vb.* characterize; distinguish; mark.
caractéristique, *adj.* characteristic.
carafe, *n.f.* decanter, water-bottle.
caraïbe, *adj.* Caribbean.
Caraïbes, *n.f.pl.* **les C.,** the Caribbean.
caramel, *n.m.* caramel.
carat, *n.m.* carat.
caravane, *n.f.* caravan.
carbone, *n.m.* carbon.
carboniser, *vb.* char.
carburant, *n.m.* fuel.
carburateur, *n.m.* carburetor.
carcasse, *n.f.* shell; carcass.
cardinal, *n.m.* cardinal.
Carême, *n.m.* Lent.
caresse, *n.f.* caress.
caresser, *vb.* fondle, stroke, caress.
cargaison, *n.f.* cargo.
caricature, *n.f.* caricature.
carie, *n.f.* decay.
carillon, *n.m.* chime.
carilloner, *vb.* chime.
carnaval, *n.m.* carnival.
carnet, *n.m.* notebook.
carnivore, *adj.* carnivorous.
carotte, *n.f.* carrot.
carré, *n.m. and adj.* square.
carreau, *n.m.* diamond (cards); pane; tile.
carrefour, *n.m.* crossroads.

carrément, *adv.* bluntly, altogether.
carrière, *n.f.* career; scope; quarry.
carriole, *n.f.* (light) cart.
carrosse, *n.m.* coach.
cartable, *n.m.* school bag.
carte, *n.f.* chart, map, card.
   c. de crédit, credit card.
   c. du jour, bill of fare.
carton, *n.m.* cardboard; box, carton.
cartouche, *n.f.* cartridge.
cas, *n.m.* case; event.
cascade, *n.f.* waterfall.
cascadeur, *n.m.* stuntman.
case, *n.f.* pigeonhole; hut, shed.
caserne, *n.f.* barracks.
casier, *n.m.* filing cabinet, compartment.
casque, *n.m.* helmet.
casque a écouteurs, *n.m.pl.* headphones.
casquette, *n.f.* cap.
cassable, *adj.* breakable.
casse-croûte, *n.m.* snack.
casser, *vb.* break, crack.
casserole, *n.f.* pan.
cassette, *n.f.* **1.** casket. **2.** cassette.
cassis, *n.m.* black currant.
cassure, *n.f.* break.
caste, *n.f.* caste.
castor, *n.m.* beaver.
casuel, *adj.* casual.
catalogue, *n.m.* catalogue.
cataracte, *n.f.* cataract.
catarrhe, *n.m.* catarrh.
catastrophe, *n.f.* disaster, catastrophe.
catéchisme, *n.m.* catechism.
catégorie, *n.f.* category.
cathédrale, *n.f.* cathedral.
catholicisme, *n.m.* Catholicism.
catholique, *adj.* Catholic.
cauchemar, *n.m.* nightmare.
cause, *n.f.* case; cause.
causer, *vb.* chat; cause.
causerie, *n.f.* chat, talk.
causette, *n.f.* chat.
caution, *n.f.* bail, security.
cavalerie, *n.f.* cavalry.
cavalier, *n.m.* rider, horseman; escort.
cave, *n.f.* cellar, cavern.
cavité, *n.f.* cavity.

CD, *n.m.* compact disc.
ce, (sə) **cet** (sĕt) *m.,* **cette** (sĕt) *f.,* **ces** (sā) *pl. adj.* that, this.
ceci, *pron.* this.
cécité, *n.f.* blindness.
céder, *vb.* yield, give in, cede.
cédille, *n.f.* cedilla.
cèdre, *n.m.* cedar.
ceindre, *vb.* gird.
ceinture, *n.f.* belt, sash.
cela, *pron.* that.
célébration, *n.f.* celebration.
célèbre, *adj.* famous, noted.
célébrer, *vb.* celebrate.
célébrité, *n.f.* celebrity.
céleri, *n.m.* celery.
céleste, *adj.* heavenly, celestial.
célibataire, 1. *n.m.* bachelor. **2.** *adj.* single.
celle, *pron. f.* See **celui.**
cellule, *n.f.* cell.
celluloïd, (-lô ĕd) *n.m.* celluloid.
celtique, *adj.* Celtic.
celui, *m.,* **celle** *f.,* **ceux** *m.pl.,* **celles** *f.pl.* *pron.* the one; the other. **celui-ci,** this one; the latter. **celui-là,** that one; the former.
cendre, *n.f.* ashes, cinders.
cendrier, *n.m.* ashtray.
censé, *adj.* **être c. faire,** be supposed to do.
censeur, *n.m.* censor, vice-principal.
censure, *n.f.* censure.
censurer, *vb.* censor.
cent, *adj. and n.m.* hundred. **pour c.,** percent.
centaine, *n.f.* about a hundred.
centenaire, *adj. and n.m.* centenary, centennial.
centième, *adj.* hundredth.
centigrade, *adj.* centigrade.
centimètre, *n.m.* centimeter.
central, *adj.* central.
centraliser, *vb.* centralize.
centre, *n.m.* center.
cep, *n.m.* vine stock.
cependant, *adv.* however, still, yet.
cercle, *n.m.* circle, ring, hoop; club.
cercueil, *n.m.* coffin.

céréale, *adj. and n.f.* cereal.

cérémonial, *adj. and n.m.* ceremonial.

cérémonie, *n.f.* ceremony. **sans c.,** informal.

cérémonieux *adj.* formal, ceremonious.

cerf, (sĕr), *n.m.* deer.

cerf-volant, *n.m.* kite.

cerise, *n.f.* cherry.

certain, *adj.* certain, sure; *(pl.)* some.

certes, *adv.* indeed.

certificat, *n.m.* credentials; certificate.

certifier, *vb.* certify.

certitude, *n.f.* certainty, assurance.

cerveau, *n.m.* brain.

cervelle, *n.f.* brains.

cessation, *n.f.* stopping, cessation.

cesser, *vb.* stop, desist, cease.

cession, *n.f.* assignment (law).

cet, cette, *pron.* See **ce.**

chacun, *pron.* everybody, everyone; each.

chagrin, 1. *n.m.* grief, vexation. **2.** *adj.* fretful.

chagriner, *vb.* grieve.

chaîne, *n.f.* chain; range.

chaîne stéréo, *n.f.* stereo system.

chaînon, *n.m.* link.

chair, *n.f.* flesh.

chaire, *n.f.* pulpit, rostrum.

chaise, *n.f.* chair.

chaland, *n.m.* barge.

châle, *n.m.* shawl.

chaleur, *n.f.* warmth, heat, glow.

chaloupe, *n.f.* launch.

chambre, *n.f.* room, chamber; House (parliament). **c. à coucher,** bedroom.

chameau, *n.m.* camel.

chamois, *n.m.* chamois.

champ, *n.m.* field.

champagne, *n.m.* champagne.

champêtre, *adj.* rural.

champignon, *n.m.* mushroom.

champion, *n.m.* champion.

championnat, *n.m.* championship.

chance, *n.f.* luck; risk, chance.

chanceler, *vb.* stagger, reel.

chancelier, *n.m.* chancellor.

chandail, *n.m.* sweater.

chandelier, *n.m.* candlestick.

chandelle, *n.f.* candle.

change, *n.m.* exchange.

changeant, *adj.* changeable.

changement, *n.m.* change, shift.

changer, *vb.* alter, shift, change.

chanson, *n.f.* song.

chant, *n.m.* song, chant. **c. du coq,** cock-crow.

chantage, *n.m.* blackmail.

chanter, *vb.* sing, chant.

chanteur, *n.m.* singer.

chantier, *n.m.* (work)yard.

chaos, (k-), *n.m.* chaos.

chaotique, (k-), *adj.* chaotic.

chapeau, *n.m.* hat, bonnet.

chapelle, *n.f.* chapel.

chaperon, *n.m.* chaperon.

chapiteau, *n.m.* capital.

chapitre, *n.m.* chapter.

chapon, *n.m.* capon.

chaque, *adj.* every, each.

char, *n.m.* chariot. **c. d'assaut,** (military) tank.

charbon, *n.m.* coal. **c. de bois,** charcoal.

charcuterie, *n.f.* delicatessen.

charge, *n.f.* load, charge.

charger, *vb.* load, burden, charge.

chariot, *n.m.* wagon; baggage cart.

charisme, *n.m.* charisma.

charitable, *adj.* charitable.

charité, *n.f.* charity.

charlatan, *n.m.* charlatan.

charmant, *adj.* delightful, lovely, charming.

charme, *n.m.* spell, charm.

charmer, *vb.* charm.

charnel, *adj.* carnal.

charnu, *adj.* fleshy.

charpente, *n.f.* framework.

charpentier, *n.m.* carpenter.

charretier, *n.m.* carter.

charrette, *n.f.* cart.

charrue, *n.f.* plow.

charte, *n.f.* charter.

chasse, *n.f.* hunt(ing), chase.

châsse, *n.f.* shrine.

chasse-neige, *n.m.* snowplow.

chasser, *vb.* hunt, chase; drive away.

chasseur, *n.m.* hunter; bellboy.

châssis, *n.m.* (window) sash; chassis.

chaste, *adj.* chaste.

chasteté, *n.f.* chastity.

chat, *m.,* **chatte** *f. n.* cat.

châtaigne, *n.f.* chestnut.

château, *n.m.* mansion, castle.

châtier, *vb.* punish, chastise.

chaton, *n.m.* kitten.

chatouiller, *vb.* tickle.

chatouilleux, *adj.* ticklish.

chaud, *adj.* hot, warm.

chaudière, *n.f.* boiler.

chauffage, *n.m.* heating.

chauffer, *vb.* heat, warm.

chauffeur, *n.m.* driver, chauffeur.

chaumière, *n.f.* cottage.

chaussée, *n.f.* road.

chausser, *vb.* wear shoes. **se c.,** put on shoes.

chaussette, *n.f.* sock.

chaussure, *n.f.* footgear.

chauve, *adj.* bald.

chauve-souris, *n.f.* bat.

chaux, *n.f.* lime.

chavirer, *vb.* capsize.

chef, *n.m.* leader, chief.

chef-d'œuvre, (shĕ-), *n.m.* masterpiece.

chemin, *n.m.* road. **c. de fer,** railway. **à mi-c.,** halfway. **c. de table,** table runner.

chemineau, *n.m.* tramp.

cheminée, *n.f.* fireplace, chimney; funnel.

chemise, *n.f.* shirt. **c. de nuit,** nightgown.

chemisier, *n.m.* blouse.

chêne, *n.m.* oak.

chenille, *n.f.* caterpillar.

chèque, *n.m.* check.

chèque de voyage, *n.m.* traveler's check.

cher, (-r), *adj.* dear, expensive.

chercher, *vb.* seek, look for, search. **aller c.,** fetch.

chère, *n.f.* fare, food. **aimer la bonne c.,** be fond of good living. **faire bonne c.**, have a good meal.

chéri, *adj. and n.m.* beloved, darling.

chérir, *vb.* cherish.

chétif, *adj.* puny.

cheval, *n.m.* horse. **à c.**, on horseback. **monter à c.**, ride (horseback). **fer à c.**, horseshoe.

chevaleresque, *adj.* chivalrous.

chevalerie, *n.f.* chivalry.

chevalet, *n.m.* easel; knight.

chevalier, *n.m.* knight.

cheveu, *n.m., pl.* **cheveux**, hair.

cheville, *n.f.* ankle; peg.

chèvre, *n.f.* goat.

chevreau, *n.m.* kid.

chevreuil, *n.m.* roe.

chevron, *n.m.* rafter.

chevroter, *vb.* quaver.

chevrotine, *n.f.* buckshot.

chez, *prep.* at . . .'s (house, office, shop, etc.).

chic, *adj.* stylish.

chien, *n.m.* dog.

chienne, *n.f.* bitch.

chiffon, *n.m.* rag.

chiffonner, *vb.* crumple.

chiffre, *n.m.* figure.

chiffrer, *vb.* figure.

Chili, *n.m.* Chile.

Chilien, *n.m.* Chilean.

chilien, *adj.* Chilean.

chimie, *n.f.* chemistry.

chimiothérapie, *n.f.* chemotherapy.

chimique, *adj.* chemical.

chimiste, *n.m.f.* chemist.

Chine, *n.f.* China.

Chinois, *n.m.* Chinese (person).

chinois, 1. *n.m.* Chinese (language). 2. *adj.* Chinese.

chiper, *vb.* (colloquial) swipe.

chiquenaude, *n.f.* flip.

chirurgie, *n.f.* surgery.

chirurgien, *n.m.* surgeon.

chlore (k-), *n.m.* chlorine.

chloroforme, (k-), *n.m.* chloroform.

choc, *n.m.* shock, clash, brunt.

chocolat, *n.m.* chocolate.

chœur, (k-), *n.m.* choir, chorus.

choisir, *vb.* choose, select, pick.

choix, *n.m.* choice.

chômage, *n.m.* stoppage (of work).

chômer, *vb.* be unemployed.

choquer, *vb.* shock, clash.

choral, (k-), *adj.* choral.

chose, *n.f.* thing, matter. **quelque c.**, anything.

chou, *n.m.* cabbage.

choucroute, *n.f.* sauerkraut.

chouette, 1. *n.f.* owl. 2. *adj.* great, neat.

chou-fleur, *n.m.* cauliflower.

choyer, *vb.* pamper.

chrétien, (k-), *adj. and n.m.* Christian.

chrétienté, (k-), *n.f.* Christendom.

christianisme, (k-), *n.m.* Christianity.

chronique, (k-), 1. *n.f.* chronicle. 2. *adj.* chronic.

chronologique, (k-), *adj.* chronological.

chronomètre (k-), stopwatch.

chronométrer (k-), *vb.* time.

chrysanthème, (k-), *n.m.* chrysanthemum.

chuchoter, *vb.* whisper.

chut (shYt), *interj.* sh!

chute, *n.f.* fall, drop, downfall.

Chypre, *n.f.* Cyprus.

cible, *n.f.* target.

cicatrice, *n.f.* scar.

cidre, *n.m.* cider.

ciel, *n.m., sky. (pl.)* **cieux**, heaven.

cierge, *n.m.* (church) candle.

cigale, *n.m.* locust.

cigare, *n.m.* cigar.

cigarette, *n.f.* cigarette.

ci-gît, *adv. and vb.* here lies.

cigogne, *n.f.* stork.

ci-joint, *adj.* enclosed.

cil, (-l), *n.m.* eyelash.

cime, *n.f.* top, summit.

ciment, *n.m.* cement.

cimenter, *vb.* cement.

cimetière, *n.m.* churchyard, cemetery.

cinéaste, *n.m.f.* film-maker.

cinéma, *n.m.* cinema.

cinémathèque, *n.f.* film library.

cinglant, *adj.* scathing.

cinq, (-k), *adj. and n.m.* five.

cinquante, *adj. and n.m.* fifty.

cinquième, *adj. and n.m.f.* fifth.

cintre, *n.m.* semicircle; arch.

circonférence, *n.f.* circumference.

circonflexe, *adj.* circumflex.

circonscription, *n.f.* **c. électorale**, borough.

circonscrire, *vb.* circumscribe.

circonstance, *n.f.* event, circumstance. **c. critique**, emergency.

circonvenir, *vb.* circumvent.

circuit, *n.m.* circuit. **hors c.**, disconnected.

circulaire, *adj.* circular.

circulation, *n.f.* traffic; circulation.

circuler, *vb.* circulate, turn, revolve.

cire, *n.f.* wax.

cirer, *vb.* polish, shine.

cireur, *n.m.* bootblack.

cirque, *n.m.* circus.

cirrhose, *n.f.* cirrhosis.

cisailles, *n.f.pl.* shears.

ciseau, *n.m.* chisel; *(pl.)* scissors.

ciseler, *vb.* chisel.

citadelle, *n.f.* citadel.

citation, *n.f.* quotation, citation.

cité, *n.f.* city. **droit de c.**, citizenship.

citer, *vb.* quote, cite.

citoyen, *n.m.* citizen.

citron, *n.m.* lemon. **c. pressé**, lemonade.

citrouille, *n.f.* pumpkin.

civil, 1. *n.m.* civilian. 2. *adj.* civil.

civilisation, *n.f.* civilization.

civilisé, *adj.* civilized.

civiliser, *vb.* civilize.

civique, *adj.* civic.

clair, *adj.* clear, bright. **c. de lune**, moonlight.

clairière, *n.f.* glade, clearing.

clairon, *n.m.* bugle.

clameur, *n.f.* clamor, outcry.

clandestin, *adj.* clandestine.

clapoteux, *adj.* choppy (sea).

claque, *n.f.* slap.

claquement, *n.m.* smack.

claquer, *vb.* slap, smack; chatter (teeth); bang.

clarifier, *vb.* clarify.

clarinette, *n.f.* clarinet.

clarté, *n.f.* clarity; light.

classe, *n.f.* class.

classement, *n.m.* classification.

classer, *vb.* classify, order, file, grade.

classeur, *n.m.* file, filing cabinet.

classification, *n.f.* classification.

classifier, *vb.* classify.

classique, *adj.* classic, classical.

clause, *n.f.* clause.

clavecin, *n.m.* harpsicord.

clavicule, *n.f.* collarbone.

clavier, *n.m.* keyboard.

clef, (klā) **clé**, *n.f.* key.

clémence, *n.f.* clemency.

clément, *adj.* merciful.

clerc, *n.m.* clerk.

clergé, *n.m.* clergy.

clérical, *adj.* clerical.

cliché, *n.m.* cliché; snapshot; negative.

client, *n.m.* customer, patron, client.

clientèle, *n.f.* customers; practice.

cligner (de l'œil), *vb.* wink.

clignoter, *vb.* blink, wink.

clignotant, *n.m.* turn signal.

climat, *n.m.* climate.

climatisation, *n.f.* air conditioning.

climatiser, *vb.* air-condition.

clin, *n.m.* **c. d'œil**, wink.

clinique, **1.** *n.f.* clinic. **2.** *adj.* clinical.

cloche, *n.f.* bell.

clocher, *n.m.* belfry. **de c.**, parochial.

cloison, *n.f.* partition.

cloître, *n.m.* cloister, convent.

clôture, *n.f.* fence.

clou, *n.m.* nail.

clouer, *vb.* nail, tack.

club, (-b), *n.m.* club.

coaguler, *vb.* coagulate.

coalition, *n.f.* coalition.

coasser, *vb.* croak (frogs).

cobaye, *n.m.* guinea pig.

coca, *n.m.* Coke (trade-marked name of soft drink).

cocaïne, *n.f.* cocaine.

cochon, *n.m.* pig.

coco, *n.m.* **noix de c.**, coconut.

cocon, *n.m.* cocoon.

cocotte, *n.f.* casserole.

cocu, *n.m.* cuckold.

code, *n.m.* code; laws.

code postal, *n.m.* zip code.

cœur, *n.m.* heart.

coffre, *n.m.* bin; coffer.

cognac, *n.m.* brandy, cognac.

cogner, *vb.* bump, strike, run into, knock (down).

cohérent, *adj.* coherent.

cohésion, *n.f.* cohesion.

coiffer, *vb.* dress (hair).

coiffeur, *n.m.* hairdresser, barber.

coiffure, *n.f.* hairdo.

coin, *n.m.* corner, wedge.

coincé, *adj.* stuck; inhibited.

coincer, *vb.* get stuck, jam.

coïncidence, (kō ăn-), *n.f.* coincidence.

coïncider, (kō ăn-), *vb.* coincide.

col, *n.m.* collar; pass.

colère, *n.f.* anger, temper. **en c.**, angry.

colimaçon, *n.m.* snail.

colique, *n.f.* diarrhea.

colis, *n.m.* parcel.

collaborateur, *n.m.* fellow-worker.

collaboration, *n.f.* assistance, collaboration.

collaborer, *vb.* work together, collaborate.

collant, *n.m.* pantyhose.

collatéral, *adj. and n.m.* collateral.

colle, *n.f.* glue, paste.

collecte, *n.f.* collection.

collectif, *adj.* collective.

collection, *n.f.* collection.

collectionneur, *n.m.* collector.

collège, *n.m.* secondary school.

collègue, *n.m.f.* colleague.

coller, *vb.* glue, paste, stick.

collier, *n.m.* necklace; collar (dog).

colline, *n.f.* hill.

collision, *n.f.* collision.

colombe, *n.f.* dove.

Colombie, *n.f.* Colombia.

colon, *n.m.* settler, colonist.

colonel, *n.m.* colonel.

colonial, *adj.* colonial.

colonie, *n.f.* settlement, colony.

coloniser, *vb.* colonize.

colonne, *n.f.* column.

coloré, *adj.* colorful.

colorer, *vb.* color.

colossal, *adj.* huge, colossal.

colosse, *n.m.* giant, colossus.

colporter, *n.m.* peddle.

colporteur, *n.m.* peddler.

combat, *n.m.* fight, battle. **hors de c.**, disabled.

combattant, *adj. and n.m.* combatant.

combattre, *vb.* fight.

combien (de), *adv.* how much, how many.

combinaison, *n.f.* combination; slip, B.V.D.'s.

combine, *n.f.* trick, scheme.

combiné, *n.m.* (phone) receiver.

combiner, *vb.* devise, combine.

comble, *n.m.* climax, top.

combler, *vb.* heap up, fill.

combustible, **1.** *n.m.* fuel. **2.** *adj.* combustible.

combustion, *n.f.* combustion.

comédie, *n.f.* comedy.

comédien, *n.m.* actor, comedian.

comestible, *adj.* edible.

comète, *n.f.* comet.

comique, *adj.* funny, comic(al).

comité, *n.m.* committee.

commandant, *n.m.* major, commander.

commande, *n.f.* order; commission.

commandement, *n.m.* command, commandment.

commander, *vb.* order, command.

commanditer, *vb.* finance.

comme, 1. *adv.* as, how. **2.** *prep.* as, like. **c. il faut,** proper, decent.

commémoratif, *adj.* memorial.

commémorer, *vb.* commemorate.

commencement, *n.m.* beginning, start.

commencer, *vb.* begin, start.

comment, *adv.* how.

commentaire, *n.m.* comment, commentary.

commentateur, *n.m.* commentator.

commenter, *vb.* comment on.

commerçant, *n.m.* trader.

commerce, *n.m.* trade, commerce.

commercer, *vb.* trade.

commercial, *adj.* commercial.

commettre, *vb.* commit.

commis, *n.m.* clerk.

commissaire, *n.m.* commissary, commissioner.

commissariat, *n.m.* police station.

commission, *n.f.* errand; commission.

commode, 1. *n.f.* dresser, bureau. **2.** *adj.* handy, convenient; comfortable.

commodité, *n.f.* convenience.

commun, *adj.* joint, common.

communauté, *n.f.* community.

commune, *n.f.* commune, town(ship).

communicatif, *adj.* communicative.

communication, *n.f.* communication.

communion, *n.f.* communion.

communiquer, *vb.* communicate.

communisme, *n.m.* communism.

communiste, *adj. and n.m.f.* communist.

commutateur, *n.m.* switch.

compacité, *n.f.* compactness.

compact, (-kt), *adj.* compact.

compact disc, *n.m.* compact disc.

compagne, *n.f.* mate, companion.

compagnie, *n.f.* company.

compagnon, *n.m.* mate, fellow, companion.

comparable, *adj.* comparable.

comparaison, *n.f.* comparison.

comparaître, *vb.* appear.

comparatif, *adj. and n.m.* comparative.

comparer, *vb.* compare.

compartiment, *n.m.* compartment.

compas, *n.m.* compass.

compassion, *n.f.* sympathy, compassion.

compatible, *adj.* compatible.

compatissant, *adj.* sympathetic, compassionate.

compatriote, *n.m.f.* compatriot.

compensation, *n.f.* amends; compensation.

compenser, *vb.* compensate.

compétence, *n.f.* qualification, efficiency, competence.

compétition, *n.f.* competition.

compiler, *vb.* compile.

complaire, *vb.* please.

complaisance, *n.f.* kindness, compliance.

complaisant, *adj.* obliging, kind.

complément, *n.m.* object; complement.

complet, 1. *n.m.* suit. **2.** *adj.* full, thorough, complete.

compléter, *vb.* complete.

complexe, *adj. and n.m.* complex.

complexité, *n.f.* complexity.

complication, *n.f.* complication.

complice, *n.m.f.* party to, accomplice.

compliment, *n.m.* compliment.

compliqué, *adj.* intricate, involved, complicated.

compliquer, *vb.* complicate.

complot, *n.m.* plot.

comporter, *vb.* **se c.,** act, behave.

composant, *adj. and n.m.* component.

composé, *adj. and n.m.* compound.

composer, *vb.* compound, compose.

compositeur, *n.m.* composer.

composition, *n.f.* essay, theme, composition.

composter, *vb.* date-stamp, punch.

compote, *n.f.* stewed fruit.

compréhensible, *adj.* understandable.

compréhensif, *adj.* comprehensive.

compréhension, *n.f.* comprehension.

comprendre, *vb.* understand, realize; comprise, include. **c. mal,** misunderstand.

compresse, *n.f.* compress.

compression, *n.f.* compression.

comprimé, *n.m.* tablet *(med.).*

comprimer, *vb.* compress.

compromettre, *vb.* compromise.

compromis, *n.m.* compromise.

comptabilité, *n.f.* accounting, bookkeeping.

comptable, *n.m.* accountant.

comptant, *adv.* **payer c.,** pay cash.

compte, *n.m.* account, count. **rendre c. de,** account for. **tenir c. de,** allow for.

compte-gouttes, *n.m.* dropper.

compter, *vb.* count, reckon. **c. sur,** rely on.

compteur, *n.m.* meter.

comptoir, *n.m.* counter.

comte, *n.m.* count.

comté, *n.m.* county.

comtesse, *n.f.* countess.

concave, *adj.* concave.

concéder, *vb.* grant, concede.

concentration, *n.f.* concentration.

concentrer, *vb.* condense; concentrate.

concept, (-pt), *n.m.* concept.

conception, *n.f.* conception.

concernant, *prep.* concerning.

concerner, *vb.* concern.

concert, *n.m.* concert.

concerter, *vb.* organize, prepare.

concession, *n.f.* grant, license, admission, concession.

concessionnaire, *n.m.* dealer.

concevable, *adj.* conceivable.

concevoir, *vb.* conceive, imagine.

concierge, *n.m.f.* janitor, doorkeeper, porter.

concile, *n.m.* council.

conciliation, *n.f.* conciliation.

concilier, *vb.* reconcile, conciliate.

concis, *adj.* concise.

concision, *n.f.* conciseness.

concitoyen, *n.m.* fellow citizen.

concluant, *adj.* conclusive.

conclure, *vb.* complete, conclude, infer.

conclusion, *n.f.* conclusion.

concombre, *n.m.* cucumber.

concourir, *vb.* concur, contribute, compete.

concours, *n.m.* contest.

concret, *adj.* concrete.

concrétiser, *vb.* put in concrete form.

concurrence, *n.f.* competition.

concurrent, *n.m.* rival, competitor.

condamnation, (-dà nä-), *n.f.* conviction, condemnation, sentence.

condamner, (-dä nä), *vb.* convict, doom, condemn, sentence.

condensation, *n.f.* condensation.

condenser, *vb.* condense.

condescendance, *n.f.* condescension.

condescendre, *vb.* condescend.

condiment, *n.m.* condiment.

condisciplé, *n.m.* classmates.

condition, *n.f.* condition.

conditionnel, *adj. and n.m.* conditional.

conditionnement, *n.m.* conditioning.

conditionner, *vb.* condition.

condoléance, *n.f.* condolence. **faire ses c.s à,** condole with.

condominium, *n.m.* condominium.

conducteur, *n.m.* conductor.

conduire, *vb.* lead, take, drive, conduct. **se c.,** behave, act.

conduite, *n.f.* behavior, conduct.

cône, *n.m.* cone.

cône de charge, *n.m.* warhead.

confection, *n.f.* making (e.g. clothes); ready-made garment.

confédération, *n.f.* confederacy, confederation.

confédéré, *adj. and n.m.* confederate.

conférence, *n.f.* lecture, talk, conference.

conférer, *vb.* confer, grant.

confesser, *vb.* confess, admit.

confesseur, *n.m.* confessor.

confession, *n.f.* denomination; confession.

confiance, *n.f.* trust, belief, confidence. **digne de c.,** dependable.

confiant, *adj.* confident.

confidence, *n.f.* confidence.

confident, *n.m.* confidant.

confidentiel, *adj.* confidential.

confier, *vb.* confide, entrust. **se c. à,** trust.

configuration, *n.f.* configuration.

confiner, *vb.* confine, limit.

confirmation, *n.f.* confirmation.

confirmer, *vb.* confirm.

confiserie, *n.f.* confectionery.

confisquer, *vb.* confiscate.

confit, *adj.* candied.

confiture, *n.f.* jam, jelly.

conflit, *n.m.* conflict.

confondre, *vb.* confuse, confound.

confondu, *adj.* overwhelmed.

conforme à, *adv.* in accordance with.

conformément, *adv.* in accordance.

conformer, *vb.* conform. **se c. à,** comply with.

conformité, *n.f.* accordance.

confort, *n.m.* comfort.

confortable, *adj.* cozy, snug, comfortable.

confrère, *n.m.* colleague.

confronter, *vb.* confront.

confus, *adj.* confused.

confusion, *n.f.* confusion.

congé, *n.m.* discharge; leave of absence.

congédier, *vb.* discharge, dismiss.

congélateur, *n.m.* freezer.

congeler, *vb.* congeal.

congénère, *n.m.f.* fellow human.

congénital, *adj.* congenital.

congestion, *n.f.* congestion.

conglomération, *n.f.* conglomeration.

congrès, *n.m.* congress, assembly, conference.

conjecture, *n.f.* guess, conjecture.

conjoint, 1. *n.m.* spouse, **2.** *adj.* joint.

conjonction, *n.f.* conjunction.

conjugaison, *n.f.* conjugation.

conjugal, *adj.* conjugal.

conjuguer, *vb.* conjugate.

conjuration, *n.f.* conspiracy.

conjurer, *vb.* conspire, plot.

connaissance, *n.f.* knowledge, acquaintance. **sans c.,** unconscious. **faire la c. de,** meet.

connaisseur, *n.m.* connoisseur.

connaître, *vb.* be acquainted with, know.

connecté, *adj.* on line.

connecter, *vb.* connect.

connexion, *n.f.* connection.

conquérir, *vb.* conquer.

conquête, *n.f.* conquest.

consacrer, *vb.* consecrate, devote, dedicate, hallow.

conscience, *n.f.* conscience, consciousness.

consciencieux, *adj.* conscientious.

conscient, *adj.* conscious.

conscription, *n.f.* draft.

conscrit, *adj. and n.m.* conscript.

consécration, *n.f.* consecration.

consécutif, *adj.* consecutive.

conseil, *n.m.* advice, counsel; council, board; staff.

conseiller, 1. *vb.* advise, counsel, **2.** *n.m.* advisor.

consentement, *n.m.* consent.

consentir, *vb.* consent, assent, accede.

conséquence, *n.f.* outgrowth, result, consequence.

conséquent, *adj.* consequent; consistent. **par c.,** consequently.

conservateur, *adj. and n.m.* conservative.

conservation, *n.f.* conservation.

conservatoire, *n.m.* academy; conservation area.

conserve, *n.f.* canned food, pickle.

conserver, *vb.* keep; preserve, can.

considérable, *adj.* considerable.

considération, *n.f.* consideration.

considérer, *vb.* consider.

consigne, *n.f.* checkroom; (*mil.*) orders.

consigne automatique, *n.f.* (luggage) locker.

consigner, *vb.* consign.

consistance, *n.f.* consistency.

consistant, *adj.* consistent.

consister, *vb.* consist.

consœur, *n.f.* (female) colleague.

consolateur, *n.m.* comforter.

consolation, *n.f.* comfort, solace.

console, *n.f.* bracket.

consoler, *vb.* comfort, console.

consolider, *vb.* consolidate, strengthen.

consommateur, *n.m.* consumer.

consommation, *n.f.* consumption; end, consummation.

consommé, *adj.* consummate.

consommer, *vb.* consummate, complete; consume.

consomption, *n.f.* consumption.

consonne, *n.f.* consonant.

conspirateur, *n.m.* conspirator.

conspiration, *n.f.* conspiration.

conspirer, *vb.* conspire.

conspuer, *vb.* boo.

constamment, *adv.* continually, constantly.

constance, *n.f.* constancy, firmness.

constant, *adj.* constant, firm.

constat, *n.m.* certified report, statement.

constater, *vb.* observe, state as a fact.

constellation, *n.f.* constellation.

consternation, *n.f.* dismay.

consterné, *adj.* aghast.

consterner, *vb.* dismay.

constipation, *n.f.* constipation.

constipé, *adj.* constipated; tense.

constituant, *adj.* constituent.

constituer, *vb.* constitute.

constitution, *n.f.* constitution.

constitutionnel, *adj.* constitutional.

constructeur, *n.m.* builder.

constructif, *adj.* constructive.

construction, *n.f.* construction.

construire, *vb.* construct, build.

consul, *n.m.* consul.

consulat, *n.m.* consulate.

consultation, *n.f.* consultation.

consulter, *vb.* consult.

consumer, *vb.* consume.

contact, (-kt), *n.m.* touch, contact.

contagieux, *adj.* contagious.

contagion, *n.f.* contagion.

contaminer, *vb.* contaminate.

conte, *n.m.* tale, story.

contemplation, *n.f.* contemplation.

contempler, *vb.* survey, observe, contemplate.

contemporain, *adj.* contemporary.

contenance, *n.f.* compass, capacity.

contenir, *vb.* hold, restrain, contain.

content de, *adj.* glad of, contented with. **c. de soi-même,** complacent.

contentement, *n.m.* content(ment), satisfaction. **c. de soi-même,** complacency.

contenter, *vb.* please, satisfy.

contentieux, *n.m.* litigation.

contenu, *n.m.* contents.

conter, *vb.* tell.

contestable, *adj.* questionable.

contestataire, *n.m.* protester.

contester, *vb.* challenge (dispute), object to, contest.

conteur, *n.m.* story-teller.

contexte, *n.m.* context.

contigu, *m.,* **contiguë** *f. adj.* adjoining.

continent, *n.m.* continent.

continental, *adj.* continental.

contingences, *n.f.pl.* contingencies.

contingent, *n.m.* quota.

continu, *adj.* continuous.

continuation, *n.f.* continuation, continuance.

continuel, *adj.* continual.

continuer, *vb.* carry on, keep on, go on, continue.

continuité, *n.f.* continuity.

contorsion, *n.f.* contortion.

contour, *n.m.* outline.

contourner, *vb.* go round.

contraceptif, *n.m.* contraceptive.

contracter, *vb.* contract.

contraction, *n.f.* contraction.

contractuel, *n.m.* traffic warden.

contradiction, *n.f.* discrepancy, contradiction.

contradictoire, *adj.* contradictory.

contraindre, *vb.* coerce, force.
contrainte, *n.f.* compulsion.
contraire, 1. *n.m.* reverse. **2.** *adj.* contrary. **au c.,** on the contrary.
contrarier, *vb.* thwart, vex, annoy, oppose, keep (from).
contrariété, *n.f.* annoyance.
contraste, *n.m.* contrast.
contraster, *vb.* contrast.
contrat, *n.m.* contract.
contravention, *n.f.* traffic ticket.
contre, *prep.* against.
contre-balancer, *vb.* counterbalance.
contrebande, *n.f.* smuggling; contraband.
contrecarrer, *vb.* thwart.
contre-cœur, *adv.* **à c.,** unwillingly.
contrecoup, *n.m.* consequence.
contredire, *vb.* contradict.
contrée, *n.f.* district, province.
contrefaire, *vb.* forge, counterfeit.
contrefort, *n.m.* buttress.
contremaître, *n.m.* foreman.
contre-partie, *n.f.* counterpart.
contrepoids, (-pwä), *n.m.* counterbalance.
contresens, *n.m.* misinterpretation.
contretemps, *n.m.* mishap.
contribuer, *vb.* contribute.
contribution, *n.f.* share, contribution; tax.
contrôle, *n.m.* check.
contrôle des naissances, *n.m.* birth control, contraception.
contrôler, *vb.* control, check.
contrôleur, *n.m.* checker, collector.
controverse, *n.f.* controversy.
contusion, *n.f.* bruise, contusion.
convaincre, *vb.* convince.
convaincu, *adj.* positive.
convalescence, *n.f.* convalescence.

convalescent, *n.m.* convalescent.
convenable, *adj.* becoming, appropriate, suitable, congenial.
convenance, *n.f.* convenience.
convenir à, *vb.* suit, fit, befit, agree.
convention, *n.f.* convention; contract.
conventionnel, *adj.* conventional.
convenu, *adj.* agreed.
converger, *vb.* converge.
conversation, *n.f.* talk, conversation.
converser, *vb.* talk, converse.
conversion, *n.f.* conversion, change.
convertir, *vb.* convert, transform.
convexe, *adj.* convex.
conviction, *n.f.* conviction.
convive, *n.m.* guest, companion.
convivial, *adj.* convivial, user-friendly.
convocation, *n.f.* summons.
convoi, *n.m.* convoy, funeral procession.
convoiter, *vb.* covet.
convoitise, *n.f.* covetousness.
convoquer, *vb.* summon, call.
convulsion, *n.f.* convulsion.
coopératif, (kō ô-), *adj.* cooperative.
coopération, (kō ô-), *n.f.* cooperation.
coopérative, (kō ô-), *n.f.* cooperative.
coopérer, (kō ô-), *vb.* cooperate.
coordonner, (kō ôr-), *vb.* coordinate.
copain, *n.m.* pal, chum.
copie, *n.f.* copy; exercise.
copier, *vb.* copy.
copieux, *adj.* copious.
copine, *n.f.* (female) pal, chum.
coq, (-k), *n.m.* rooster.
coque, *n.f.* **œuf à la c.,** boiled egg.
coquet, *adj.* flirtatious, pretty.
coquille, *n.f.* shell.

coquin, *adj. and n.m.* rogue, rascal.
cor, *n.m.* horn; corn.
corail, *n.m., pl.* **coraux,** coral.
corbeau, *n.m.* raven, crow.
corbeille, *n.f.* basket.
corde, *n.f.* rope, string, cord.
cordial, *adj.* hearty, cordial.
cordon, *n.m.* rope.
cordonnier, *n.m.* shoemaker.
Corée, *n.f.* Korea.
coreligionnaire, *n.m.* member of the same religion.
corne, *n.f.* horn.
corneille, *n.f.* crow.
cornemuse, *n.f.* bagpipe.
cornet, *n.m.* cone.
cornichon, *n.m.* gherkin.
corporation, *n.f.* corporation.
corporel, *adj.* bodily.
corps, *n.m.* body.
corpulent, *adj.* burly.
corpuscule, (-sk-), *n.m.* corpuscle.
correct, (-kt), *adj.* right, correct.
correcteur, *n.m.* proofreader, examiner.
correction, *n.f.* correction, correctness; beating.
corrélation, *n.f.* correlation.
correspondance, *n.f.* (train) connection: similarity; correspondence.
correspondant, 1. *n.m.* correspondent. **2.** *adj.* similar, corresponding.
correspondre, *vb.* correspond.
corriger, *vb.* mend, reclaim, correct.
corroborer, *vb.* corroborate.
corroder, *vb.* corrode.
corrompre, *vb.* bribe, corrupt.
corrompu, *adj.* corrupt.
corruption, *n.f.* bribery, graft, corruption.
corsage, *n.m.* bodice, blouse.
Corse, *n.f.* Corsica. *n.m.f.* Corsican.
corse, *adj.* Corsican.
corset, *n.m.* corset.
cortège, *n.m.* procession.
corvée, *n.f.* chore.

cosmétique, *adj. and n.m.* cosmetic.

cosmonaute, *n.m.* cosmonaut.

cosmopolite, *adj. and n.m.f.* cosmopolitan.

costaud, *adj.* strong, sturdy.

costume, *n.m.* attire, dress.

cote, *n.f.* quotation, rating.

côte, *n.f.* rib; coast.

côté, *n.f.* side, way. **mettre de c.,** put to one side (save; discard). **à c. de,** beside.

coteau, *n.m.* hill.

côtelette, *n.f.* chop, cutlet.

coton, *n.m.* cotton.

cou, *n.m.* neck.

couche, *n.f.* layer; bed; stratum; diaper.

coucher, *vb.* put to bed. **se c.,** lie down; set.

couchette, *n.f.* bunk, berth.

coucou, *n.m.* cuckoo.

coude, *n.m.* elbow.

coudoyer, *vb.* jostle.

coudre, *vb.* sew, stitch.

couette, *n.f.* duvet.

couler, *vb.* flow, sink, run; cast (metal).

couleur, *n.f.* hue, color; suit (cards).

couloir, *n.m.* corridor.

coup, *n.m.* blow, stroke, hit, bump, knock, cast. **c. de feu,** discharge (gun). **c. d'œil,** glance, look. **c. de pied,** kick. **c. de poing,** punch.

coupable, *adj.* guilty, to blame.

coupe, *n.f.* cut; goblet. **c. de cheveux,** haircut.

couper, *vb.* cut.

couple, *n.f.* couple, pair.

coupler, *vb.* couple.

coupole, *n.f.* dome.

coupon, *n.m.* remnant; coupon.

coupure, *n.f.* cut, clipping.

cour, *n.f.* court(yard).

courage, *n.m.* bravery, pluck, courage.

courageux, *adj.* brave.

couramment, *adv.* fluently.

courant, 1. *adj.* current. **peu c.,** unusual. **au c.,** well informed. **2.** *n.m.* stream, current. **c. d'air,** draft.

courbe, *n.f.* curve, sweep.

courber, *vb.* bend, curve.

courbure, *n.f.* curvature.

coureur, *n.m.* runner; womanizer.

courgette, *n.f.* zucchini.

courir, *vb.* run.

couronne, *n.f.* crown, wreath.

couronnement, *n.m.* coronation.

couronner, *vb.* crown.

courrier, *n.m.* mail.

courroie, *n.f.* strap.

courroux, *n.m.* wrath.

cours, *n.m.* course.

course, *n.f.* race, errand.

coursier, *n.m.* messenger.

court, 1. *adj.* short. **2.** *n.m.* (tennis) court.

courtepointe, *n.f.* quilt.

courtier, *n.m.* broker.

courtisan, *n.m.* courtier.

courtois, *adj.* courteous.

courtoisie, *n.f.* courtesy.

couscous, *n.m.* couscous.

cousin, *n.m.* cousin.

coussin, *n.m.* cushion.

coussinet, *n.m.* bearing.

coût, *n.m.* cost.

couteau, *n.m.* knife.

coutellerie, *n.f.* cutlery.

coûter, *vb.* cost.

coûteux, *adj.* expensive, costly.

coutume, *n.f.* custom.

couture, *n.f.* seam. **haute couture,** high fashion.

couturière, *n.f.* dressmaker.

couvée, *n.f.* brood.

couvent, *n.m.* convent.

couver, *vb.* brood, hatch; smolder.

couvercle, *n.m.* lid, cover.

couvert, 1. *n.m.* cover. **2.** *adj.* covered, cloudy.

couverture, *n.f.* blanket, cover; (*pl.*) bedclothes.

couvre-feu, *n.m.* curfew.

couvrir, *vb.* cover.

crabe, *n.m.* crab.

crachat, *n.m.* spit.

cracher, *vb.* spit.

craie, *n.f.* chalk.

craindre, *vb.* fear.

crainte, *n.f.* fear, dread, awe.

craintif, *adj.* fearful.

cramoisi, *adj. and n.m.* crimson.

crampe, *n.f.* cramp.

crampon, *n.m.* clamp, cramp iron.

cramponner, *vb.* **se c.,** cling.

crâne, *n.m.* skull.

crapaud, *n.m.* toad.

craquement, *n.m.* crack.

craquer, *vb.* crack, break down.

crasse, *n.f.* grime.

cratère, *n.m.* crater.

cravate, *n.f.* necktie.

crayon, *n.m.* pencil.

créance, *n.f.* belief. **lettres de c.,** credentials.

créancier, *n.m.* creditor.

créateur, *m.,* **créatrice** *f.* **1.** *adj.* creative. **2.** *n.* creator.

création, *n.f.* creation.

créature, *n.f.* creature.

crèche, *n.f.* day-care center.

crédit, *n.m.* credit.

credo, *n.m.* creed.

crédule, *adj.* credulous.

créer, *vb.* create.

crème, *n.f.* cream, custard.

crémerie, *n.f.* dairy store.

créneau, *n.m.* slot.

Créole, *n.m.* Creole.

crêpe, *n.f.* pancake; crepe.

crépuscule, (-sk-), *n.m.* dusk.

crête, *n.f.* ridge, crest.

crétin, *n.m.* dunce.

cretonne, *n.f.* cretonne.

creuser, *vb.* dig.

creuset, *n.m.* crucible.

creux, *adj. and n.m.* hollow.

crevasse, *n.f.* crevice.

crevé, *adj.* exhausted.

crever, *vb.* burst; die.

crevette, *n.f.* shrimp.

cri, *n.m.* cry, call.

criard, *adj.* garish.

crible, *n.m.* sieve.

crier, *vb.* yell, shout.

crime, *n.m.* crime.

criminel, *adj.* criminal.

crinière, *n.f.* mane.

crise, *n.f.* crisis.

crisper, *vb.* tense, clench.

cristal, *n.m.* crystal.

cristallin, *adj.* crystalline.

cristalliser, *vb.* crystallize.

critère, *n.m.* criterion.

critérium, *n.m.* criterion.

critique, 1. *n.m.f.* critic. 2. *n.f.* criticism. 3. *adj.* critical.

critiquer, *vb.* criticize.

croasser, *vb.* croak.

Croatie, *n.f.* Croatia.

croc, (-ō), *n.m.* hook.

croche, *n.f.* quaver (music).

crochet, *n.m.* bracket, hook.

crochu, *adj.* hooked.

crocodile, *n.m.* crocodile.

croire, *vb.* believe.

croisade, *n.f.* crusade.

croisé, *n.m.* crusader.

croiser, *vb.* cross.

croiseur, *n.m.* cruiser.

croisière, *n.f.* cruise.

croissance, *n.f.* growth.

croissant, *n.m.* crescent; croissant (pastry).

croître, *vb.* grow.

croix, *n.f.* cross.

croquant, *adj.* crisp.

croque-monsieur, *n.m.* grilled ham and cheese sandwich.

croquer, *vb.* crunch; sketch.

croquet, *n.m.* croquet.

croquis, *n.m.* sketch.

crosse, *n.f.* (golf) club; butt (gun).

crotale, *n.m.* rattlesnake.

crouler, *vb.* fall apart.

croup, *n.m.* croup.

croupir, *vb.* wallow.

croustiller, *vb.* be crispy.

croûte, *n.f.* crust.

croûton, *n.m.* crouton.

croyable, *adj.* believable.

croyance, *n.f.* belief.

croyant, *n.m.* believer.

cru, *adj.* raw.

cruauté, *n.f.* cruelty.

cruche, *n.f.* pitcher.

crucifier, *vb.* crucify.

crucifix, *n.m.* crucifix.

crudités, *n.f.pl.* raw vegetables.

cruel, *adj.* cruel.

cryochirurgie, *n.f.* cryosurgery.

Cuba, *n.m.* Cuba.

Cubain, *n.m.* Cuban.

cubain, *adj.* Cuban.

cube, *n.m.* cube.

cubique, *adj.* cubic.

cueillir, *vb.* pick.

cuiller, *n.f.* spoon. c. à thé, teaspoon. c. à bouche, tablespoon.

cuillerée, *n.f.* spoonful.

cuir, *n.m.* leather.

cuirassé, *n.m.* battleship.

cuire, *vb.* cook; sting, smart.

cuisine, *n.f.* kitchen, cooking.

cuisinier, *n.m.* cook.

cuisse, *n.f.* thigh.

cuisson, *n.m.* cooking.

cuivre, *n.m.* copper. c. jaune, brass.

cul-de-sac, *n.m.* blind alley.

culinaire, *adj.* culinary, cooking.

culotte, *n.f.* breeches, panties.

culpabilité, *n.f.* guilt.

culte, *n.m.* worship; cult.

cultivé, *adj.* cultured.

cultiver, *vb.* cultivate; grow, raise.

culture, *n.f.* culture, cultivation; farming.

culturel, *adj.* cultural.

cure, *n.f.* cure, treatment.

curé, *n.m.* (parish) priest.

curieux, *adj.* curious.

curiosité, *n.f.* curiosity, curio.

curseur, *n.m.* cursor.

cursif, *adj.* cursive.

cuticule, *n.f.* cuticle.

cuve, *n.f.* vat.

cuver, *vb.* ferment.

cuvette, *n.f.* (wash) basin.

cuvier, *n.m.* washtub.

cycle, *n.m.* cycle.

cycliste, *n.m.f.* cyclist.

cyclomoteur, *n.m.* moped.

cyclone, *n.m.* cyclone.

cygne, *n.m.* swan.

cylindre, *n.m.* cylinder.

cylindrique, *adj.* cylindrical.

cymbale, *n.f.* cymbal.

cynique, 1. *n.m.* cynic. 2. *adj.* cynical.

cynisme, *n.m.* cynicism.

cyprès, *n.m.* cypress.

czar, *n.m.* czar.

D

d'abord *adv.* first, at first.

dactylo, *n.m.f.* typist.

dada, *n.m.* hobby-horse.

daigner, *vb.* deign.

daim, *n.m.* buck.

daine, *n.f.* doe.

dais, *n.m.* canopy.

dalle, *n.f.* slab, flag(stone).

daltonien, *adj.* color-blind.

dame, *n.f.* lady.

damner, (dä nā), *vb.* damn.

dancing, *n.m.* dance hall.

Danemark, *n.m.* Denmark.

danger, *n.m.* danger.

dangereux, *adj.* dangerous.

Danois, *n.m.* Dane.

danois, *adj. and n.m.* Danish (language).

dans, *prep.* in, into.

danse, *n.f.* dance.

danser, *vb.* dance.

danseur, *n.m.* dancer.

dard, *n.m.* dart.

date, *n.f.* date (calendar).

dater, *vb.* date.

datte, *n.f.* date (fruit).

dauphin, *n.m.* dolphin.

davantage, *adv.* more, further.

de, *prep.* of, from, by, about; some.

dé, *n.m.* die; thimble.

débacle, *n.m.* downfall.

débarcadère, *n.m.* wharf.

débardeur, *n.m.* tank top.

débarquer, *vb.* land.

débarrasser, *vb.* rid.

débat, *n.m.* debate.

débattre, *vb.* canvass; debate.

débile, *adj.* weak, stupid.

débit, *n.m.* delivery (speech); sale; debit.

débiter, *vb.* sell (retail).

débiteur, *n.m.* debtor.

déblayer, *vb.* clear.

déborder, *vb.* overflow.

déboucher, *vb.* flow (into); uncork.

débourser, *vb.* disburse.

debout, *adv.* up. **être d., stand.**

débrancher, *vb.* unplug.

débris, *n.m.pl.* wreck, debris.

débrouiller, *vb.* disentangle. **se d., manage.**

début, *n.m.* beginning, first appearance, debut.

débuter, *vb.* make one's first appearance; begin.

décadence, *n.f.* decay; decadence.

decafféiné, *adj.* decaffeinated.

décalage, *n.m.* gap.

décaler, *vb.* shift.

décapiter, *vb.* behead.

décéder, *vb.* die.

décembre, *n.m.* December.

décence, *n.f.* decency.

décennie, *n.f.* decade.

décent, *adj.* decent.

décentraliser, *vb.* decentralize.

déception, *n.f.* disappointment.

décerner, *vb.* award.

décès, *n.m.* death.

décevoir, *vb.* disappoint.

décharge, *n.f.* discharge.

décharger, *vb.* unload, discharge.

décharné, *adj.* gaunt.

déchausser, *vb.* take off shoes.

déchets, (-à) *n.m.pl.* waste.

déchets nucléaires, *n.m.pl.* nuclear waste.

déchiffrer, *vb.* decipher.

déchirer, *vb.* tear; rend.

déchirure, *n.f.* tear; rent.

décibel, *n.m.* decibel.

décider, *vb.* prevail upon, decide.

décimal, *adj.* decimal.

décisif, *adj.* decisive.

décision, *n.f.* decision.

déclamer, *vb.* recite.

déclaration, *n.f.* statement, declaration.

déclarer, *vb.* state, declare.

déclencher, *vb.* release, set off.

déclic, *n.m.* trigger.

déclin, *n.m.* ebb.

décliner, *vb.* decline.

décoller, *vb.* take off.

décolorer, *vb.* bleach, fade.

décomposer, *vb.* spoil, decompose.

déconcerter, *vb.* baffle, disconcert; embarrass.

décongestionnant, *adj.* decongestant.

déconseiller, *vb.* advise against.

décontracté, *adj.* relaxed.

décor, *n.m.* scenery.

décoratif, *adj.* decorative.

décoration, *n.f.* decoration, trimming.

décorer, *vb.* decorate.

découper, *vb.* carve (meat).

découragé, *adj.* despondent.

découragement, *n.m.* discouragement.

décourager, *vb.* dishearten, discourage.

découverte, *n.f.* discovery.

découvreur, *n.m.* discoverer.

découvrir, *vb.* uncover, detect, discover.

décrépit, *adj.* decrepit.

décret, *n.m.* decree.

décréter, *vb.* enact.

décrire, *vb.* describe.

décrocher, *vb.* unhook.

dédaigneux, *adj.* scornful.

dédain, *n.m.* scorn, disdain.

dedans, *n.m.* inside, within.

dédicace, *n.f.* dedication.

dédier, *vb.* dedicate.

déduction, *n.f.* deduction.

déduire, *vb.* infer, deduce, deduct.

déesse, *n.f.* goddess.

défaillance, *n.f.* weakness.

défaire, *vb.* undo.

défaite, *n.f.* defeat.

défaut, *n.m.* flaw, fault, failure, lack. **à d. de,** for want of.

défavorable, *adj.* unfavorable.

défavoriser, *vb.* put at a disadvantage.

défectueux, *adj.* faulty, defective.

défendeur, *n.m.* defendant.

défendre, *vb.* forbid, defend.

défense, *n.f.* prohibition, plea, defense.

défenseur, *n.m.* advocate, defender.

défensif, *adj.* defensive.

déférer, *vb.* defer.

défi, *n.m.* challenge, defiance.

défiance, *n.f.* mistrust.

déficit, (-t), *n.m.* deficit.

défier, *vb.* challenge, defy. **se d. de,** mistrust.

défigurer, *vb.* deface.

défiler, *vb.* march off.

défini, *adj.* definite.

définir, *vb.* define.

définitif, *adj.* final, definitive.

définition, *n.f.* definition.

déformer, *vb.* distort, deform.

défouler, *vb.* let off steam.

défraîchi, *adj.* dingy.

défricher, *vb.* reclaim; clear.

défunt, *adj. and n.m.* deceased.

dégagé, *adj.* breezy.

dégât, *n.m.* damage.

dégénérer, *vb.* degenerate.

dégoût, *n.m.* distaste, disgust.

dégoûtant, *adj.* foul, disgusting.

dégoûter, *vb.* disgust.

dégoutter, *vb.* drip.

dégradation, *n.f.* degradation.

dégrader, *vb.* degrade.

degré, *n.m.* degree, step.

déguisement, *n.m.* disguise.

déguiser, *vb.* disguise.

dehors, *adv.* outdoors, outside. **en d. de,** apart from.

déifier, *vb.* deify.

déité, *n.f.* deity.

déjà, *adv.* already.

déjeter, *vb.* make unsymmetrical.

déjeuner, *n.m. and vb.* lunch, breakfast. **petit d.,** breakfast.

déjouer, *vb.* foil, thwart.

delà, *adv.* beyond. **au d. de,** over, past, beyond.

délabrement, *n.m.* decay.

délabrer, *vb.* ruin, wreck.

délacer, *vb.* unlace.

délai, *n.m.* delay.

délaissement, *n.m.* desertion.

délaisser, *vb.* desert.

délassement, *n.m.* relaxation.

délasser, *vb.* refresh.

délateur, *n.m.* informer.

délavé, *adj.* faded, pallid.

délayer, *vb.* dilute with water.

délectable, *adj.* delicious.

délectation, *n.f.* enjoyment.

délecter, *vb.* delight.

délégation, *n.f.* delegation.

délégué, *n.m.* delegate.

déléguer, *vb.* delegate.

délester, *vb.* relieve of ballast.

délétère, *adj.* harmful; offensive.

délibératif, *adj.* deliberative.

délibération, *n.f.* deliberation.

délibéré, *adj.* deliberate.

délibérer, *vb.* deliberate.

délicat, *adj.* delicate, tactful.

délicatesse, *n.f.* delicacy.

délices, *n.f.pl.* delight.

délicieux, *adj.* delicious.

délié, *adj.* slender; keen.

délier, *vb.* untie.

délimiter, *vb.* mark the limits of.

délinéer, *vb.* delineate.

délinquant, 1. *n.m.* delinquent, offender. 2. *adj.* delinquent.

délirant, *adj.* delirious.

délire, *n.m.* frenzy.

délirer, *vb.* rave.

délit, *n.m.* offense, crime.

délivrance, *n.f.* rescue, deliverance.

délivrer, *vb.* rescue, set free, deliver.

déloger, *vb.* dislodge.

déloyal, *adj.* disloyal.

déloyauté, *n.f.* disloyalty.

deltaplane, *n.m.* hang glider.

déluge, *n.m.* deluge.

déluré, *adj.* clever, cute.

démagogue, *n.m.* demagogue.

demain, *adv.* tomorrow.

demande, *n.f.* application, request, inquiry, claim. **d. en mariage,** proposal.

demander, *vb.* ask, request. **se d.,** wonder.

demandeur, *n.m.* plaintiff.

démangeaison, *n.f.* itch.

démanger, *vb.* itch.

démanteler, *vb.* dismantle.

démaquiller, *vb.* remove makeup.

démarcation, *n.f.* demarcation.

démarche, *n.f.* walk; bearing; step.

démarrage, *n.m.* start.

démarrer, *vb.* unmoor; start off.

démarreur, *n.m.* (self-)starter.

démasquer, *vb.* unmask; expose, reveal.

démêlant, *n.m.* conditioner.

démêler, *vb.* disentangle.

démembrement, *n.m.* dismemberment.

démembrer, *vb.* dismember.

déménagement, *n.m.* moving.

déménager, *vb.* move.

déménageur, *n.m.* furniture mover.

démence, *n.f.* insanity.

démener, *vb.* struggle.

dément, *adj.* insane.

démenti, *n.m.* denial.

démentir, *vb.* deny, refute.

démesuré, *adj.* measureless, immense.

démettre, *vb.* se d. (de), resign.

demeure, *n.f.* abode.

demeurer, *vb.* dwell.

demi, *n.m. and adj.* half.

demi-cercle, *n.m.* semicircle.

demi-dieu, *n.m.* demigod.

demi-frère, *n.m.* stepbrother.

demi-heure, *n.f.* half an hour.

démilitariser, *vb.* demilitarize.

demi-place, *n.f.* half price; half fare.

demi-saison, *adj.* between-season.

demi-sœur, *n.f.* stepsister.

demi-solde, *n.f.* half-pay.

démission, *n.f.* resignation.

démobilisation, *n.f.* demobilization.

démobiliser, *vb.* demobilize.

démocrate, *n.m.f.* democrat.

démocratie, *n.f.* democracy.

démocratique, *adj.* democratic.

démodé, *adj.* old-fashioned.

demoiselle, *n.f.* young lady. **d. d'honneur,** bridesmaid.

démolir, *vb.* demolish.

démolition, *n.f.* demolition.

démon, *n.m.* demon.

démonétiser, *vb.* demonetize.

démoniaque, *adj.* demonic.

démonstratif, *adj.* effusive; demonstrative.

démonstration, *n.f.* demonstration.

démonter, *vb.* take down; dismantle.

démontrable, *adj.* demonstrable.

démontrer, *vb.* demonstrate.

démoralisation, *n.f.* demoralization.

démoraliser, *vb.* demoralize.

démouler, *vb.* remove from a mold.

démuni, *adj.* lacking, impoverished.

dénationaliser, *vb.* denationalize.

dénaturer, *vb.* denature.

dénégation, *n.f.* denial.

dénigrer, *vb.* disparage.

dénivelé, *adj.* not level.

dénombrement, *n.m.* enumeration; census.

dénombrer, *vb.* count.

dénomination, *n.f.* denomination, designation.

dénommer, *vb.* name.

dénoncer, *vb.* report, denounce.

dénonciation, *n.f.* denunciation.

dénoter, *vb.* denote.

dénouement, *n.m.* result, outcome.

dénouer, *vb.* untie.

denrée, *n.f.* foodstuff, produce.

dense, *adj.* dense.

densité, *n.f.* density.

dent, *n.f.* tooth. **mal de d.s,** toothache. **brosse à d.s,** toothbrush.

dentaire, *adj.* dental.

denté, *adj.* cogged.

dentelle, *n.f.* lace.

dentifrice, *n.m.* tooth paste or powder.

dentiste, *n.m.* dentist.

dentition, *n.f.* dentition.

denture, *n.f.* set of natural teeth.

dénuder, *vb.* denude.

dénué, *adj.* destitute, bare.

dénuement, *n.m.* destitution.

dénuer, *vb.* divest.

déodorant, *n.m.* deodorant.

dépannage, *n.m.* emergency repairs.

dépanner, *vb.* repair; help out.

dépareillé, *adj.* odd (unmatched).

départ, *n.m.* departure.

département, *n.m.* department.

départir, *vb.* divide in shares.

dépassé, *adj.* outdated.

dépasser, *vb.* outrun, pass.

dépayser, *vb.* disorient, confuse.

dépêche, *n.f.* dispatch.

dépêcher, *vb.* se d., hurry.

dépeindre, *vb.* portray.

dépendance, *n.f.* annex (to a building).

dépendant, *adj.* dependent.

dépendre, *vb.* depend.

dépens, *n.m.pl.* expenses.

dépense, *n.f.* expenditure, expense.

dépenser, *vb.* spend, expend.

dépérir, *vb.* waste away; decline.

dépeupler, *vb.* depopulate.

déphasé, *adj.* disoriented.

dépiécer, *vb.* dismember.

dépit, *n.m.* spite. **en d. de,** despite.

déplacement, *n.m.* displacement.

déplacé, *adj.* out of place.

déplacer, *vb.* displace, move, shift.

déplaire à, *vb.* displease.

déplaisant, *adj.* displeasing.

déplanter, *vb.* transplant.

déplantoir, *n.m.* trowel.

dépliant, *n.m.* leaflet.

déplier, *vb.* unfold.

déploiement, *n.m.* deployment.

déplorable, *adj.* wretched, deplorable.

déplorer, *vb.* deplore.

déployer, *vb.* deploy.

déplumer, *vb.* pluck.

déportation, *n.f.* deportation.

déportements, *n.m.pl.* misconduct.

déporter, *vb.* deport.

déposant, *n.m.* depositor.

déposer, *vb.* deposit, set down, depose.

dépositaire, *n.m.f.* trustee.

déposséder, *vb.* oust; dispossess.

dépôt, *n.m.* deposit, depot. **d. de vivres,** commissary.

dépotoir, *n.m.* rubbish dump.

dépouille, *n.f.* hide, skin, pelt.

dépouiller, *vb.* strip. **se d. de,** shed.

dépourvu, *adj.* devoid; needy.

dépoussiéreur, *n.m.* vacuum cleaner.

dépravation, *n.f.* depravity.

dépraver, *vb.* deprave.

dépréciation, *n.f.* depreciation.

déprécier, *vb.* depreciate, cheapen.

déprédation, *n.f.* depredation.

dépression, *n.f.* depression.

déprimer, *vb.* depress.

depuis, *adv. and prep.* since. **d. que,** *conj.* since.

députation, *n.f.* delegation.

député, *n.m.* representative, deputy.

déraciné, *adj.* rootless.

déraciner, *vb.* uproot, eradicate.

dérailler, *vb.* derail; talk nonsense.

déraison, *n.f.* unreason.

déraisonnable, *adj.* unreasonable.

dérangement, *n.m.* disturbance.

déranger, *vb.* disturb, trouble.

déraper, *vb.* skid.

derechef, *adv.* once again.

dérégler, *vb.* upset, disorder.

dérider, *vb.* smooth; cheer up.

dérision, *n.f.* derision. **tourner en d.,** deride.

dérisoire, *adj.* ridiculous, derisory.

dérivation, *n.f.* derivation, etymology.

dérive, *n.f.* drift. **à la d.,** adrift.

dériver, *vb.* derive; drift.

dernier, *adj.* last, latter.

dernièrement, *adv.* lately.

dérober, *vb.* rob. **se d.,** steal away.

dérouiller, *vb.* remove the rust from.

dérouler, *vb.* unroll, unfold.

déroute, *n.f.* rout.

dérouter, *vb.* mislead; confuse.

derrière, *n.m., adv. and prep.* behind.

derviche, *n.m.* dervish.

dès, *prep.* since. **d. que,** *conj.* as soon as.

désabuser, *vb.* disillusion.

désaccord, *n.m.* disagreement.

désaccoutumer, *vb.* break of a habit.

désaffecté, *adj.* disused.

désaffecter, *vb.* close down.

désaffection, *n.f.* alienation.

désagréable, *adj.* nasty, distasteful.

désagrégation, *n.f.* disintegration.

désaligné, *adj.* out of alignment.

désaltérer, *vb.* quench (one's) thirst.

désapprobation, *n.f.* disapproval.

désapprouver, *vb.* disapprove.

désarçonner, *vb.* disconcert.

désarmement, *n.m.* disarmament.

désarmer, *vb.* disarm.

désarroi, *n.m.* disorder.

désastre, *n.m.* disaster.

désastreux, *adj.* disastrous.

désavantage, *n.m.* disadvantage.

désaveu, *n.m.* denial.

désavouer, *vb.* disown.

désaxé, *adj. and n.m.* unbalanced (person).

descendance, *n.f.* descent.

descendant, 1. *n.m.* offspring, descendant. **2.** *adj.* downward, descending.

descendre, *vb.* go down, come down, alight, descend.

descente, *n.f.* raid; descent.

descriptif, *adj.* descriptive.

description, *n.f.* description.

désembarquer, *vb.* disembark, unload.

désemparé, *adj.* distraught.

désenchanter, *vb.* disenchant.

désenivrer, *vb.* sober up.

déséquilibre, *n.m.* imbalance.

déséquilibrer, *vb.* throw off balance.

désert, *n.m.* wilderness, desert.

déserter, *vb.* desert.

déserteur, *n.m.* deserter.

désertion, *n.f.* desertion.

désespéré, *adj.* hopeless, forlorn, desperate.

désespérer, *vb.* despair.

désespoir, *n.m.* desperation, despair.

déshabiller, *vb.* undress.

déshériter, *vb.* disinherit.

déshonnête, *adj.* improper, indecent.

déshonneur, *n.m.* disgrace, dishonor.

déshonorant, *adj.* dishonorable.

déshonorer, *vb.* disgrace, dishonor.

déshydrater, *vb.* dehydrate.

désignation, *n.f.* nomination.

désigner, *vb.* appoint, nominate; point out; designate.

désillusion, *n.f.* disillusion.

désinfectant, *n.m.* disinfectant.

désinfecter, *vb.* disinfect, fumigate.

désinfection, *n.f.* disinfection.

désintégration, *n.f.* disintegration.

désintégrer, *vb.* disintegrate.

désintéressé, *adj.* unselfish.

désintéressement, *n.m.* unselfishness.

désintoxication, *n.f.* detoxification.

désinvolte, *adj.* casual.

désir, *n.m.* desire, wish.

désirable, *adj.* desirable.

désirer, *vb.* desire, wish.

désireux, *adj.* desirous.

désistement, *n.m.* withdrawal.

désobéir à, *vb.* disobey.

désobéissance, *n.f.* disobedience.

désobéissant, *adj.* disobedient.

désobligeant, *adj.* disagreeable.

désodorisant, *n.m.* air freshener, deodorant.

désœuvré, *adj.* idle.

désolation, *n.f.* desolation.

désolé, *adj.* disconsolate; desolate.

désoler, *vb.* desolate.

désopilant, *adj.* hilarious.

désordonné, *adj.* disorderly.

désordonner, *vb.* upset, confuse.

désordre, *n.m.* disorder.

désorganisation, *n.f.* disorganization.

désorganiser, *vb.* disorganize.

désorienté, *adj.* disoriented.

désormais, *adv.* henceforth.

despote, *n.m.* despot.

despotique, *adj.* despotic.

despotisme, *n.m.* despotism.

dessécher, *vb.* dry out, parch; drain.

dessein, *n.m.* plan, intent.

desserrer, *vb.* loosen.

dessert, *n.m.* dessert.

desservir, *vb.* serve; clear away.

dessin, *n.m.* drawing, design, sketch.

dessinateur, *n.m.* designer.

dessiner, *vb.* draw, design. se d., loom.

dessous, *n.m.* underside. **en d., au-d. de,** beneath, underneath.

dessus, *n.m.* top. **en d., au-d. de,** above. **d. de lit,** bedspread.

déstabiliser, *vb.* destabilize.

destin, *n.m.* fate, destiny.

destinataire, *n.m.f.* addressee.

destination, *n.f.* destination. **à d. de,** bound for.

destinée, *n.f.* destiny.

destiner, *vb.* destine, intend.

destituer, *vb.* dismiss.

destructeur, *adj.* destructive.

destructif, *adj.* destructive.

destruction, *n.f.* destruction.

désuet, *adj.* obsolete.

désuétude, *n.f.* disuse.

désunion, *n.f.* disunion.

désunir, *vb.* disconnect.

détaché, *adj.* loose.

détachement, *n.m.* detachment.

détacher, *vb.* detach. **se d.,** stand out.

détail, *n.m.* item; particular, detail. **au d.,** at retail.

détaillant, *n.m.* retailer.

détailler, *vb.* retail, itemize; detail.

détaxe, *n.f.* tax refund.

détaxer, *vb.* reduce the tax on.

détective, *n.m.* detective.

déteindre, *vb.* run (of colors).

détendre, *vb.* release; relax. **se d.,** relax.

détenir, *vb.* detain.

détente, *n.f.* **1.** trigger. **2.** (politics) détente.

détention, *n.f.* custody, detention.

détenu, *n.m.* prisoner.

détergent, *n.m.* detergent.

détérioration, *n.f.* deterioration.

détériorer, *vb.* deteriorate.

détermination, *n.f.* determination.

déterminer, *vb.* determine, fix.

détestable, *adj.* detestable, hateful.

détester, *vb.* abhor, loathe, detest.

détonation, *n.f.* detonation.

détoner, *vb.* detonate.

détour, *n.m.* turn; detour.

détourné, *adj.* devious.

détourner, *vb.* turn away; divert; avert; embezzle.

détracteur, *n.m.* critic.

détresse, *n.f.* trouble, distress.

détriment, *n.m.* detriment.

détritus, *n.m.pl.* rubbish.

détroit, *n.m.* strait.

détruire, *vb.* destroy.

dette, *n.f.* debt.

D.E.U.G., *n.m.* advanced (university) degree.

deuil, *n.m.* mourning.

deux, *adj. and n.m.* two. **tous les d.,** both.

deuxième, *adj.* second.

deux-points, *n.m.* colon.

dévaler, *vb.* hurtle down.

dévaliser, *vb.* rob.

dévaliseur, *n.m.* robber.

dévaloriser, *vb.* devalue.

dévaluation, *n.f.* devaluation.

devancer, *vb.* be ahead of.

devant, 1. *n.m.* front. **2.** *prep.* before, in front of.

devanture, *n.f.* window, (shop) front.

dévastation, *n.f.* devastation.

dévaster, *vb.* devastate.

déveine, *n.f.* bad luck.

développement, *n.m.* development.

développer, *vb.* develop.

devenir, *vb.* become.

déverser, *vb.* divert.

dévêtir, *vb.* undress, disrobe.

déviation, *n.f.* deviation.

dévider, *vb.* unwind.

dévier, *vb.* turn away.

deviner, *vb.* guess.

devinette, *n.f.* puzzle, riddle.

devis, *n.m.* estimate.

dévisager, *vb.* stare at.

devise, *n.f.* motto; currency (finance).

dévisser, *vb.* unscrew.

dévoiler, *vb.* unveil, disclose, reveal.

devoir, *n.m.* duty.

devoir, *vb.* owe; be supposed to; have to; (conditional) ought.

dévorer, *vb.* devour.

dévot, *adj.* devout.

dévotion, *n.f.* devotion.

dévoué, *adj.* devoted.

dévouement, *n.m.* devotion.

dévouer, *vb.* dedicate, devote.

dextérité, *n.f.* dexterity.

diabète, *n.m.* diabetes.

diabétique, *adj. and n.m.f.* diabetic.

diable, *n.m.* devil.

diablerie, *n.f.* mischief.

diabolique, *adj.* diabolic.

diacre, *n.m.* deacon.

diacritique, *adj.* diacritic.

diadème, *n.m.* diadem.

diagnostic, *n.m.* diagnosis.

diagnostiquer, *vb.* diagnose.

diagonal, *adj.* diagonal.

diagramme, *n.m.* diagram.

dialectal, *adj.* dialect.

dialecte, *n.m.* dialect.

dialogue, *n.m.* dialogue.

dialoguer, *vb.* converse, talk together.

diamant, *n.m.* diamond.

diamétral, *adj.* diametric.

diamètre, *n.m.* diameter.

diaphane, *adj.* diaphanous.

diaphragme, *n.m.* diaphragm.

diapositive, *n.f.* slide (photography).

diarrhée, *n.f.* diarrhea.

diathermie, *n.f.* diathermy.

diatribe, *n.f.* diatribe.

dictateur, *n.m.* dictator.

dictature, *n.f.* dictatorship.

dictée, *n.f.* dictation.

dicter, *vb.* dictate.

diction, *n.f.* diction.

dictionnaire, *n.m.* dictionary.

dicton, *n.m.* maxim, proverb.

didactique, *adj.* didactic.

dièse, *adj. and n.m.* sharp (music).

diesel, *adj and n.m.* diesel.

diète, *n.f.* diet.

diététique, *adj.* dietetic.

Dieu, *n.m.* God.

diffamant, *adj.* libelous.

diffamateur, *n.m.* libeler.

diffamation, *n.f.* libel.

diffamer, *vb.* defame.

différence, *n.f.* difference.

différenciation, *n.f.* differentiation.

différencier, *vb.* differentiate.

différend, *n.m.* difference, dispute.

différent, *adj.* different.

différer, *vb.* defer; differ.

difficile, *adj.* arduous, hard; difficult; fastidious.

difficilement, *adv.* with difficulty.

difficulté, *n.f.* trouble; difficulty.

difficulté psychologique, *n.f.* hangup.

difforme, *adj.* deformed.

difformité, *n.f.* deformity.

diffus, *adj.* diffuse.

diffuser, *vb.* diffuse, broadcast.

diffusion, *n.f.* spread, diffusion; broadcasting.

digérer, *vb.* digest.

digestible, *adj.* digestible.

digestif, 1. *adj.* digestive. **2.** *n.m.* after-dinner liqueur.

digestion, *n.f.* digestion.

digital, *adj.* digital.

digitaline, *n.f.* digitalis.

digne, *adj.* worthy.

dignitaire, *n.m.* dignitary.

dignité, *n.f.* dignity.

digression, *n.f.* digression.

digue, *n.f.* dike, dam.

dilapidation, *n.f.* waste.

dilater, *vb.* expand, dilate.

dilemme, *n.m.* dilemma.

dilettante, *n.m.* amateur.

diligence, *n.f.* diligence.

diligent, *adj.* diligent.

diluer, *vb.* dilute.

dilution, *n.f.* dilution.

dimanche, *n.m.* Sunday.

dimension, *n.f.* dimension.

diminuer, *vb.* lessen, decrease, diminish.

diminutif, *adj. and n.m.* diminutive.

diminution, *n.f.* decrease.

dinde, *n.f.* turkey.

dindon, *n.m.* turkey.

dîner, 1. *n.m.* dinner. **2.** *vb.* dine.

dîneur, *n.m.* diner.

dingue, *adj.* (colloquial) crazy.

diphtérie, *n.f.* diphtheria.

diphtongue, *n.f.* diphthong.

diplomate, *n.m.* diplomat.

diplomatie, *n.f.* diplomacy.

diplomatique, *adj.* diplomatic.

diplôme, *n.m.* diploma.

dipsomane, *n.m.f.* dipsomaniac.

dipsomanie, *n.f.* dipsomania.

dire, *vb.* say, tell. **vouloir d.,** mean. **c'est-à-d.,** namely; that is.

direct, *adj.* direct.

directement, *adv.* directly.

directeur, *n.m.* manager, director.

directif, *adj.* guiding.

direction, *n.f.* management, leadership, direction.

directive, *n.f.* instruction.

directorat, *n.m.* directorate.

dirigeable, *adj. and n.m.* dirigible.

dirigeant, *adj.* ruling.

diriger, *vb.* manage, boss; steer, direct.

dirigisme, *n.m.* interventionism.

discernable, *adj.* barely visible.

discernement, *n.m.* discernment, judgment.

discerner, *vb.* discern.

disciple, *n.m.* follower, disciple.

disciplinaire, *adj.* disciplinary.

discipline, *n.f.* discipline.

discipliner, *vb.* discipline.

disco, *adj.* disco.

discontinu, *adj.* intermittent.

discontinuer, *vb.* discontinue.

disconvenance, *n.f.* unsuitability.

discordance, *n.f.* discord.

discorde, *n.f.* discord.

discothèque, *n.f.* discotheque.

discourir, *vb.* speak one's views.

discours, *n.m.* speech, oration, talk, discourse.

discourtois, *adj.* discourteous.

discrédit, *n.m.* disrepute.

discréditer, *vb.* disparage.

discret, *adj.* discreet.

discrétion, *n.f.* discretion.

discrimination, *n.f.* discrimination.

disculper, *vb.* exonerate.

discursif, *adj.* discursive.

discussion, *n.f.* argument, discussion.

discutable, *adj.* debatable.

discuter, *vb.* argue, debate, discuss.

disette, *n.f.* famine.

diseur, *n.m.* talker.

disgrâce, *n.f.* disgrace.

disgracier, *vb.* put out of favor.

disjoindre, *vb.* sever, disjoint.

dislocation, *n.f.* dislocation.

disloquer, *vb.* dislocate.

disparaître, *vb.* disappear.

disparate, *adj.* unlike; badly matched.

disparition, *n.f.* disappearance.

disparu, *n.m.* missing person; dead person.

dispendieux, *adj.* expensive.

dispensaire, *n.m.* dispensary.

dispensation, *n.f.* dispensation.

dispense, *n.f.* military exemption.

dispenser, *vb.* dispense.

disperser, *vb.* scatter, disperse.

dispersion, *n.f.* dispersal.

disponible, *adj.* available.

disposé, *adj.* disposed. **d. d'avance,** predisposed. **peu d.,** reluctant.

disposer, *vb.* arrange.

dispositif, *n.m.* device.

disposition, *n.f.* arrangement, disposal, disposition.

disproportionné, *adj.* disproportionate.

dispute, *n.f.* row, fight, quarrel, dispute.

disputer, *vb.* dispute. **se d.,** quarrel.

disquaire, *n.m.* record dealer.

disqualifier, *vb.* disqualify.

disque, *n.m.* disk, record.

disquette, *n.f.* floppy disk, diskette.

dissemblable, *adj.* unlike.

dissemblance, *n.f.* dissimilarity.

disséminer, *vb.* scatter.

dissension, *n.f.* dissension.

dissentiment, *n.m.* dissent.

disséquer, *vb.* dissect.

dissertation, *n.f.* essay.

dissimulation, *n.f.* pretense.

dissimuler, *vb.* dissemble, pretend.

dissipation, *n.f.* dissipation.

dissiper, *vb.* dispel, waste, dissipate.

dissolu, *adj.* dissolute.

dissolution, *n.f.* dissolution.

dissonant, *adj.* discordant.

dissoudre, *vb.* dissolve.

dissuader, *vb.* dissuade.

distance, *n.f.* distance.

distancer, *vb.* outdistance.

distant, *adj.* distant.

distillation, (-l-), *n.f.* distillation.

distiller, (-l-), *vb.* distill.

distillerie, (-l-), *n.f.* distillery.

distinct, (-kt), *adj.* distinct.

distinctif, *adj.* distinctive.

distinction, *n.f.* distinction.

distingué, *adj.* distinguished.

distinguer, *vb.* discriminate; make out; distinguish.

distraction, *n.f.* distraction; pastime.

distraire, *vb.* distract, amuse. **se d.,** have fun.

distrait, *adj.* absentminded.

distribuer, *vb.* give out, deal out, distribute.

distributeur, *n.m.* distributor.

distribution, *n.f.* distribution; delivery; cast.

district, (-trèk), *n.m.* district.

dit, *adj.* called.

diurétique, *adj. and n.m.* diuretic.

diurne, *adj.* diurnal.

divaguer, *vb.* ramble.

divan, *n.m.* davenport, couch.

divergence, *n.f.* divergence.

diverger, *vb.* diverge.

divers, *adj.* various.

diversifier, *vb.* diversify.

diversion, *n.f.* diversion.

diversité, *n.f.* diversity.

divertir, *vb.* divert, entertain. **se d.,** enjoy oneself.

divertissement, *n.m.* diversion.

dividende, *n.m.* dividend.

divin, *adj.* divine.

divinateur, *n.m.* soothsayer.

divinité, *n.f.* divinity.

diviser, *vb.* part, divide.

divisible, *adj.* divisible.

division, *n.f.* division.

divorce, *n.m.* divorce.

divorcer, *vb.* divorce.

divulguer, *vb.* divulge.

dix, (-s), *adj. and n.m.* ten.

dix-huit, (-z-), *adj. and n.m.* eighteen.

dix-huitième, (-z-), *adj. and n.m.f.* eighteenth.

dixième, (-z-), *adj. and n.m.f.* tenth.

dix-neuf, (-z-), *adj. and n.m.* nineteen.

dix-sept, (-s-), *adj. and n.m.* seventeen.

dizaine, *n.f.* (group of) ten.

docile, *adj.* docile.

docilité, *n.f.* docility.

docte, *adj.* learned, wise.

docteur, *n.m.* doctor.

doctorat, *n.m.* doctorate.

doctrine, *n.f.* doctrine.

document, *n.m.* document.

documentaliste, *n.m.f.* researcher.

documenter, *vb.* document.

dodo, *n.m.* (colloquial) **faire d.,** go to sleep.

dodu, *adj.* plump.

dogmatique, *adj.* dogmatic.

dogma, *n.m.* dogma.

dogue, *n.m.* watchdog.

doigt, (dwä), *n.m.* finger. **d. de pied,** toe.

doit, *n.m.* debit.

doléances, *n.f.pl.* grievances.

dollar, *n.m.* dollar.

domaine, *n.m.* domain, property.

dôme, *n.m.* dome.

domestique, 1. *n.m.f.* servant. 2. *adj.* domestic.

domicile, *n.m.* residence.

dominant, *adj.* dominant.

domination, *n.f.* sway, domination, dominion.

dominer, *vb.* rule, dominate.

domino, *n.m.* domino.

dommage, *n.m.* injury; damage. **c'est d.,** that's too bad. **quel d.!,** what a pity!

dompter, *vb.* tame, subdue.

don, *n.m.* gift.

donateur, *n.m.* donor.

donation, *n.f.* donation.

donc, (-k), *adv.* therefore.

donjon, *n.m.* dungeon.

donne, *n.f.* deal (cards).

donner, *vb.* give.

donneur, *n.m.* giver.

dont, *pron.* whose, of which.

dopage, *n.m.* doping.

doper, *vb.* dope.

dorénavant, *adv.* hereafter.

dorer, *vb.* gild.

dorloter, *vb.* coddle.

dormant, *adj.* dormant; asleep.

dormir, *vb.* sleep.

dortoir, *n.m.* dormitory.

dos, *n.m.* back.

dosage, *n.m.* mixture.

dose, *n.f.* dose.

doser, *vb.* decide the amount.

dossier, *n.m.* record.

dot, (-t), *n.f.* dowry.

doter, *vb.* endow.

douaire, *n.m.* dowry.

douane, *n.f.* customs, customs house.

douanier, *n.m.* customs officer.

double, *adj. and n.m.* double. **faire le d. de,** duplicate.

doubler, *vb.* double.

doublure, *n.f.* lining.

doucement, *adv.* gently.

doucereux, *adj.* sugary; oversweet.

douceur, *n.f.* sweetness; gentleness, meekness.

douche, *n.f.* shower bath; douche.

doucher, *vb.* **se d.,** take a shower.

doudoune, *n.m.* anorak.

douer, *vb.* endow.

douille, *n.f.* socket.

douleur, *n.f.* pain, ache; sorrow, grief.

douloureux, *adj.* painful.

doute, *n.m.* doubt.

douter, *vb.* doubt. **se d. de,** suspect.

douteux, *adj.* dubious, doubtful, questionable.

douve, *n.f.* ditch.

doux, *m.,* **douce** *f. adj.* soft, sweet, gentle, mild, meek.

douzaine, *n.f.* dozen.

douze, *adj. and n.m.* twelve.

douzième, *adj. and n.m.f.* twelfth.

doyen, *n.m.* dean.

dragée, *n.f.* sugar-coated pill.

dragon, *n.m.* dragon; dragoon.

draguer, *vb.* dredge; try to pick up.

drainage, *n.m.* drainage.

drainer, *vb.* drain.

dramatique, *adj.* dramatic.

dramatiser, *vb.* dramatize.

dramaturge, *n.m.* playwright.

drame, *n.m.* drama.

drap, *n.m.* sheet.

drapeau, *n.m.* flag.

draper, *vb.* drape.

draperie, *n.f.* drapery.

drapier, *n.m.* clothier.

dresser, *vb.* draw up.

dressoir, *n.m.* dresser.

drive, *n.m.* drive (tennis).

drogue, *n.f.* drug.

droguer, *vb.* drug.

droguerie, *n.f.* hardware store.

droguiste, *n.m.* owner or keeper of a hardware store.

droit, 1. *n.m.* right; law; claim. 2. *adj. and adv.* (up)right, straight, fair. **d. d'auteur,** copyright.

droite, *n.f.* right. **à d.,** (to the) right.

droitier, *n.m.* right-handed person.

droiture, *n.f.* uprightness.

drôle, *adj.* funny.

du, *m.,* **de la,** *f.,* **des,** *pl. prep.* some, any.

dû, *m.,* **due** *f. adj.* due.

duc, *n.m.* duke.

duché, *n.m.* dukedom.

duchesse, *n.f.* duchess.

ductile, *adj.* ductile.

duel, *n.m.* duel.

duelliste, *n.m.* duelist.

dûment, *adv.* duly.

dune, *n.f.* dune.

duo, *n.m.* duet.

dupe, *n.f.* dupe.

duper, *vb.* trick.

duperie, *n.f.* trickery.

duplicité, *n.f.* duplicity.

dur, *adj.* hard, tough.

durabilité, *n.f.* durability.

durable, *adj.* lasting, durable.

durant, *prep.* during.

durcir, *vb.* harden.

durcissement, *n.m.* hardening.

durée, *n.f.* duration.

durement, *adv.* hard, harshly, strongly.

durer, *vb.* last.
dureté, *n.f.* hardness.
duvet, *n.m.* down.
duveté, *adj.* downy.

dynamique, *adj.* dynamic.
dynamite, *n.f.* dynamite.
dynamo, *n.f.* dynamo.
dynastie, *n.f.* dynasty.

dynastique, *adj.* dynastic.
dysenterie, *n.f.* dysentery.
dyslexie, *n.f.* dyslexia.
dyspepsie, *n.f.* dyspepsia.

E

eau *n.f.* water. **faire e.**, leak.
eau-de-vie, *n.f.* brandy.
eau-forte, *n.f.* nitric acid.
ébahir, *vb.* amaze.
ébahissement, *n.m.* amazement.
ébarber, *vb.* trim, clip.
ébattre, *vb.* **s'é.**, frolic.
ébauche, *n.f.* outline.
ébaucher, *vb.* outline.
ébène, *n.m.* ebony.
ébéniste, *n.m.* cabinetmaker.
ébénisterie, *n.f.* cabinet work.
éblouir, *vb.* dazzle.
éblouissement, *n.m.* dazzle, amazement.
éboulement, *n.m.* cave-in.
ébouriffer, *vb.* ruffle.
ébranler, *vb.* shake.
ébriété, *n.f.* drunkenness.
ébullition, *n.f.* boiling point.
écaille, *n.f.* scale.
écarlate, *adj. and n.f.* scarlet.
écart, *n.m.* separation. **à l'é.**, aloof.
écarté, *adj.* isolated; lonely.
écartement, *n.m.* gap, separation.
écarter, *vb.* set aside.
ecclésiastique, *adj. and n.m.* ecclesiastic.
écervelé, *adj.* scatterbrained.
échafaud, *n.m.* scaffold.
échafaudage, *n.m.* scaffolding.
échalote, *n.f.* shallot.
échancrer, *vb.* scallop, notch.
échange, *n.m.* exchange.
échangeable, *adj.* exchangeable.
échanger, *vb.* exchange.
échantillon, *n.m.* sample.
échappatoire, *n.f.* loophole.
échappement, *n.m.* exhaust.
échapper, *vb.* escape.
écharde, *n.f.* splinter.

écharpe, *n.f.* scarf; sling.
échasse, *n.f.* stilt.
échauder, *vb.* scald.
échauffer, *vb.* heat up.
échéance, *n.f.* maturity (finance).
échec, *n.m.* failure.
échecs, (-shĕ), *n.m.pl.* chess.
échelle, *n.f.* ladder; scale.
échelon, *n.m.* step; echelon.
échevelé, *adj.* dishevelled.
échine, *n.f.* spine.
échiner, *vb.* work like a slave.
écho, (-kō), *n.m.* echo.
échoir, *vb.* fall due.
échoppe, *n.f.* booth, stall.
échouer, *vb.* fail. **faire é.**, frustrate.
éclabousser, *vb.* splash.
éclair, *n.m.* flash.
éclairage, *n.m.* lighting.
éclaircie, *n.f.* clearing.
éclaircir, *vb.* clear up.
éclairer, *vb.* (en)lighten, light, clear up, clarify.
éclaireur, *n.m.* scout.
éclat, *n.m.* chip, splinter; burst; brilliance, radiance, glamour.
éclatant, *adj.* bursting; loud; brilliant.
éclatement (de pneu), *n.m.* blowout.
éclater, *vb.* burst out.
éclectique, *adj.* eclectic.
éclipse, *n.f.* eclipse.
éclipser, *vb.* eclipse.
éclore, *vb.* hatch; open, blossom.
écluse, *n.f.* lock.
écœurant, *adj.* sickly, disgusting.
écœurer, *vb.* disgust.
école, *n.f.* school.
écolier, *n.m.* schoolboy.
écologie, *n.f.* ecology.
écologique, *adj.* ecological.

écologiste, *n.m.f.* ecologist; environmentalist.
économe, *adj.* economical.
économie, *n.f.* economy. **é. politique**, economics.
économique, *adj.* economic(al).
économiser, *vb.* economize.
économiste, *n.m.f.* economist.
écope, *n.f.* ladle.
écoper, *vb.* ladle or bail out.
écorce, *n.f.* bark.
écorcher, *vb.* skin.
écorchure, *n.f.* gall.
Écossais, *n.m.* Scotchman, Scotsman.
écossais, *adj.* Scotch, Scottish.
Écosse, *n.f.* Scotland.
écosystème, *n.m.* ecosystem.
écot, *n.m.* share.
écouler, *vb.* drain. **s'é.**, flow, elapse.
écoute, *n.f.* listening.
écouter, *vb.* listen (to).
écouteur, *n.m.* listener.
écran, *n.m.* screen.
écraser, *vb.* crush.
écrémer, *vb.* skim.
écrevisse, *n.f.* crayfish.
écrier, *vb.* **s'é.**, exclaim.
écrin, *n.m.* case, box.
écrire, *vb.* write. **machine à é.**, typewriter.
écrit, *adj.* written.
écriteau, *n.m.* notice.
écritoire, *n.f.* inkstand.
écriture, *n.f.* writing, scripture.
écrivain, *n.m.* writer.
écrou, *n.m.* nut.
écrouler, *vb.* **s'é.**, fall to pieces.
écru, *adj.* natural, off-white.
écu, *n.m.* shield.
écueil, *n.m.* reef; pitfall.
écuelle, *n.f.* bowl, dish.
écume, *n.f.* lather, foam.

écuménique, *adj.* ecumenical.

écureuil, *n.m.* squirrel.

écurie, *n.f.* stable.

écusson, *n.m.* escutcheon.

écuyer, (-kwē-), *n.m.* squire.

édenté, *adj.* toothless.

édifice, *n.m.* building.

édifier, *vb.* build; edify.

édit, *n.m.* edict.

éditer, *vb.* publish.

éditeur, *n.m.* publisher.

édition, *n.f.* edition, publishing.

éditorial, *adj.* editorial.

éducateur, *n.m.* educator.

éducation, *n.f.* breeding, education.

éduquer, *vb.* educate, train.

effacer, *vb.* erase, efface.

effarant, *adj.* alarming.

effarer, *vb.* alarm.

effectif, *adj.* effective, actual.

effectivement, *adv.* effectively.

effectuer, *vb.* effect.

efféminé, *adj.* effeminate.

effet, *n.m.* effect; (*pl.*) belongings. **en e.,** as a matter of fact, indeed.

efficace, *adj.* effective.

efficacité, *n.f.* efficacy.

effigie, *n.f.* effigy.

effleurer, *vb.* skim, graze.

effluves, *n.m.pl.* exhalations.

effondrement, *n.m.* collapse.

effondrer, *vb.* **s'e.,** collapse, sink.

efforcer, *vb.* **s'e.,** endeavor, try hard.

effort, *n.m.* endeavor, strain, exertion, effort.

effrayant, *adj.* fearful.

effrayer, *vb.* frighten, scare, startle.

effréné, *adj.* unrestrained; frantic.

effriter, *vb.* **s'e.,** crumble.

effroi, *n.m.* fright.

effronté, *adj.* brazen.

effronterie, *n.f.* effrontery.

effroyable, *adj.* appalling.

effusion, *n.f.* shedding.

égal, *adj.* even, equal, same.

également, *adv.* equally.

égaler, *vb.* equal.

égaliser, *vb.* equalize.

égalité, *n.f.* equality, evenness.

égard, *n.m.* regard, consideration, esteem. **à l'é. de,** as for. **plein d'é.s,** considerate.

égaré, *adj.* astray.

égarement, *n.m.* aberration.

égarer, *vb.* mislay, bewilder. **s'é.,** go astray, get lost.

égayer, *vb.* cheer up.

église, *n.f.* church.

égoïsme, *n.m.* selfishness, egoism.

égoïste, *adj.* selfish.

égorger, *vb.* kill.

égotisme, *n.m.* egotism.

égout, *n.m.* sewer.

égoutter, *vb.* drain; drip.

égratigner, *vb.* scratch.

égratignure, *n.f.* scratch.

Égypte, *n.m.* Egypt.

Égyptien, *n.m.* Egyptian.

égyptien, *adj.* Egyptian.

éhonté, *adj.* brazen, shameless.

éjecter, *vb.* eject.

élaboration, *n.f.* working out, elaboration; data processing.

élaborer, *vb.* draft, elaborate.

élan, *n.m.* elk; zest.

élancé, *adj.* slim.

élancer, *vb.* **s'é.,** dash.

élargir, *vb.* widen, increase, enlarge.

élasticité, *n.f.* elasticity.

élastique, *adj. and n.m.* elastic.

électeur, *n.m.* voter.

électif, *adj.* elective.

élection, *n.f.* election.

électoral, *adj.* electoral.

électricien, *n.m.* electrician.

électricité, *n.f.* electricity.

électrique, *adj.* electric, electrical.

électrocardiogramme, *n.m.* electrocardiogram.

électrochoc, *n.m.* electric shock treatment.

électrocuter, *vb.* electrocute.

électroménager, *adj.* **appareils é.s,** household appliances.

électron, *n.m.* electron.

électronique, *adj.* electronic.

électrophone, *n.m.* record-player.

élégance, *n.f.* elegance.

élégant, *adj.* elegant, smart, stylish.

élégie, *n.f.* elegy.

élément, *n.m.* element.

élémentaire, *adj.* elementary.

éléphant, *n.m.* elephant.

élevage, *n.m.* breeding.

élévation, *n.f.* elevation.

élève, *n.m.f.* pupil.

élevé, *adj.* lofty.

élever, *vb.* raise. **s'é.,** arise; soar.

éleveur, *n.m.* breeder.

élider, *vb.* elide.

éligibilité, *n.f.* eligibility.

éligible, *adj.* eligible.

élimination, *n.f.* elimination.

éliminer, *vb.* eliminate.

élire, *vb.* elect.

élite, *n.f.* elite.

elle, *pron.f.* she, her; (*pl.*) they, them (*f.*).

elle-même, *pron.* herself.

ellipse, *n.m.* ellipse.

élocution, *n.f.* elocution.

éloge, *n.m.* praise.

éloigné, *adj.* remote.

éloignement, *n.m.* distance.

éloigner, *vb.* take away. **s'é.,** go away, recede.

élongation, *n.f.* pulled muscle.

éloquence, *n.f.* eloquence.

éloquent, *adj.* eloquent.

élu, *adj.* chosen.

éluder, *vb.* evade, elude.

émacié, *adj.* emaciated.

émail, *n.m.* enamel.

émancipation, *n.f.* emancipation.

émanciper, *vb.* emancipate.

émaner, *vb.* emanate.

emballage, *n.m.* wrapping.

emballer, *vb.* pack.

embarcadère, *n.m.* wharf.

embarcation, *n.f.* craft.

embargo, *n.m.* embargo.

embarquement, *n.m.* loading, boarding.

embarquer, *vb.* embark.

embarras, *n.m.* embarrassment; trouble, fix.

embarrassant, *adj.* embarrassing, awkward.

embarrasser, *vb.* embarrass.

embaucher, *vb.* hire.
embaumé, *adj.* balmy.
embaumer, *vb.* perfume; embalm.
embellir, *vb.* beautify.
embêter, *vb.* bore, irritate.
emblème, *n.m.* emblem.
embolie, *n.f.* embolism.
embouchure, *n.f.* mouth.
embourber, *vb.* bog.
embouteillage, *n.m.* traffic jam.
embranchement, *n.m.* junction.
embrasser, *vb.* embrace, kiss.
embrayage, *n.m.* clutch.
embrayer, *vb.* let in the clutch.
embrouillement, *n.m.* tangle, mix-up.
embrouiller, *vb.* perplex; entangle.
embrun, *n.m.* spray.
embuscade, *n.f.* ambush.
émeraude, *n.f.* emerald.
émerger, *vb.* emerge.
émerveiller, *vb.* astonish.
émetteur, *n.m.* transmitter.
émettre, *vb.* emit, send forth, issue.
émeute, *n.f.* riot.
émietter, *vb.* crumble.
émigrant, *n.m.* emigrant.
émigration, *n.f.* emigration.
émigré, *n.m.* political exile.
émigrer, *vb.* (e)migrate.
émincer, *vb.* cut into thin slices.
éminemment, *adv.* eminently.
éminence, *n.f.* eminence.
éminent, *adj.* eminent.
émission, *n.f.* issue.
emmagasinage, *n.m.* storage.
emmagasiner, *vb.* store.
emmener, *vb.* take away.
émoi, *n.m.* commotion.
émotif, *adj.* emotional.
émotion, *n.f.* emotion, feeling.
émoussé, *adj.* blunt.
émouvant, *adj.* moving.
émouvoir, *vb.* move.
empailler, *vb.* stuff.
empaler, *vb.* impale.
empan, *n.m.* span.

emparer, *vb.* **s'e. de,** take possession of.
empêchement, *n.m.* prevention.
empêcher, *vb.* prevent, stop, hinder, inhibit.
empereur, *n.m.* emperor.
empester, *vb.* stink.
empêtrer, *vb.* entangle.
emphase, *n.f.* emphasis.
emphatique, *adj.* emphatic.
empiéter, *vb.* encroach, trespass.
empire, *n.m.* empire.
empirer, *vb.* worsen.
empirique, *adj.* empirical.
emplette, *n.f.* purchase. **faire des e.s,** shop.
emplir, *vb.* fill.
emploi, *n.m.* employment, use; job.
employé, *n.m.* employee, clerk, (public) servant.
employer, *vb.* employ, use.
employeur, *n.m.* employer.
empoigner, *vb.* grab.
empois, *n.m.* starch.
empoisonné, *adj.* poisonous.
empoisonner, *vb.* poison.
emporter, *vb.* take away. **s'e.,** get angry.
empreinte, *n.f.* print, impression.
empressé, *adj.* solicitous.
empressement, *n.m.* eagerness.
empresser, *vb.* **s'e.,** be eager.
emprise, *n.f.* expropriation; influence.
emprisonnement, *n.m.* imprisonment.
emprisonner, *vb.* imprison.
emprunt, *n.m.* loan.
emprunter, *vb.* borrow from.
emprunteur, *n.m.* borrower.
ému, *adj.* touched, stirred.
émule, *n.* rival, competitor.
émulsion, *n.f.* lotion.
en, 1. *prep.* in, into. **2.** *adv.* thence; of it; some, any.
encadrer, *vb.* frame.
encaisser, *vb.* cash; tolerate.
en-cas, *n.m.* reserve.
enceinte, *adj.f.* pregnant.
encens, *n.m.* incense.
enchaîner, *vb.* chain.
enchantement, *n.m.* enchantment.

enchanter, *vb.* delight, charm, enchant.
enchère, *n.f.* bid. **vente aux e.s,** auction.
enclore, *vb.* fence in, enclose.
enclos, 1. *n.m.* enclosure, **2.** *adj.* shut in.
enclume, *n.f.* anvil.
encoche, *n.f.* notch.
encoignure, *n.f.* corner.
encoller, *vb.* paste.
encombrant, *adj.* cumbersome.
encombré, *adj.* crowded.
encombrement, *n.m.* congestion.
encombrer, *vb.* crowd, clutter, block up.
encontre, *adv.* **à l'e.,** toward, counter (to).
encore, *adv.* still, yet, again.
encourageant, *adj.* encouraging.
encouragement, *n.m.* encouragement.
encourager, *vb.* encourage, urge, promote.
encourir, *vb.* incur.
encre, *n.f.* ink.
encrier, *n.m.* inkwell.
encyclopédie, *n.f.* encyclopedia.
endetté, *adj.* indebted.
endiguer, *vb.* dam up.
endimanché, *adj.* in one's Sunday best.
endive, *n.f.* endive, chicory.
endocrinologie, *n.f.* endocrinology.
endolori, *adj.* painful.
endommager, *vb.* damage.
endormi, *adj.* asleep.
endormir, *vb.* put to sleep. **s'e.,** go to sleep.
endossement, *n.m.* endorsement.
endosser, *vb.* endorse; shoulder.
endroit, *n.m.* place.
enduire, *vb.* smear, daub.
endurance, *n.f.* endurance.
endurant, *adj.* patient.
endurcir, *vb.* harden.
endurcissement, *n.m.* hardening.
énergie, *n.f.* energy.
énergique, *adj.* energetic.

énervant, *adj.* enervating.

énervé, *adj.* nervous.

énerver, *vb.* irritate.

enfance, *n.f.* childhood.
première e., infancy.

enfant, *n.m.f.* child.

enfantement, *n.m.* childbirth.

enfanter, *vb.* bear (children).

enfantillage, *n.m.* childishness.

enfantin, *adj.* childish.

enfariner, *vb.* coat with flour.

enfer, (-r), *n.m.* hell.

enfermer, *vb.* shut in.

enfiévrer, *vb.* excite, inspire.

enfin, *adv.* finally, at last.

enflammer, *vb.* inflame.

enfler, *vb.* swell.

enflure, *n.f.* swelling.

enfoncer, *vb.* sink.

enfouir, *vb.* bury.

enfourchure, *n.f.* bifurcation; crotch of a tree.

enfreindre, *vb.* violate.

enfuir, *vb.* **s'e.,** run away, flee, elope.

enfumer, *vb.* fill or cover with smoke.

engagé, *adj.* committed.

engageant, *adj.* personable, charming.

engagement, *n.m.* pledge, agreement, engagement.

engager, *vb.* hire, engage. **s'e.,** volunteer.

engelure, *n.f.* chilblain.

engendrer, *vb.* beget.

engin, *n.m.* machine; engine, motor.

englober, *vb.* include.

engloutir, *vb.* devour.

engorgement, *n.m.* choking.

engouement, *n.m.* infatuation.

engouffrer, *vb.* engulf.

engourdir, *vb.* dull.

engrais, *n.m.* fertilizer.

engraisser, *vb.* fatten.

engraver, *vb.* strand or ground (a ship).

engrenage, *n.m.* gear.

engrener, *vb.* engage (gears).

engueuler, *vb.* (colloquial) bawl out.

enhardir, *vb.* make bolder.

enième, *adj.* (colloquial) umpteenth.

énigmatique, *adj.* enigmatic.

énigme, *n.f.* riddle, puzzle, enigma.

enivrant, *adj.* intoxicating.

enivrement, *n.m.* intoxication.

enivrer, *vb.* intoxicate. **s'e.,** get drunk.

enjambée, *n.f.* stride.

enjamber, *vb.* stride.

enjeu, *n.m.* stake.

enjoindre, *vb.* enjoin; call upon.

enjôlement, *n.m.* cajolery.

enjôler, *vb.* cajole.

enjoliver, *vb.* beautify.

enjoué, *adj.* playful.

enjouement, *n.m.* playfulness.

enlacer, *vb.* entwine; interlace; embrace.

enlaidir, *vb.* make or become ugly.

enlevable, *adj.* detachable.

enlèvement, *n.m.* removal, abduction.

enlever, *vb.* take away, remove, abduct.

enliser, *vb.* **s'e.,** sink.

enneigé, *adj.* snow-covered.

ennemi, *adj. and n.m.* enemy.

ennoblir, *vb.* exalt; ennoble.

ennui, (-nwē), *n.m.* nuisance, bore, bother; boredom.

ennuyer, *vb.* bore, annoy, vex, bother, irk.

ennuyeux, *adj.* boring, tedious, dull.

énoncer, *vb.* enunciate.

énonciation, *n.f.* enunciation.

énorme, *adj.* enormous.

énormité, *n.f.* enormity.

enquérir, *vb.* inquire.

enquête, *n.f.* inquiry.

enquiquiner, *vb.* irritate.

enraciner, *vb.* root. **s'e.,** take root.

enragé, *adj.* rabid.

enrageant, *adj.* infuriating.

enrager, *vb.* be, go mad. **s'e.,** get angry.

enregistrement, *n.m.* registration, recording; checking.

enregistrer, *vb.* record, register, list; check (luggage).

enrhumer, *vb.* **s'e.,** catch a cold.

enrichir, *vb.* enrich.

enrober, *vb.* coat, envelop.

enrôlement, *n.m.* enlistment, enrollment.

enrôler, *vb.* enlist, enroll.

enroué, *adj.* hoarse.

enrouement, *n.m.* hoarseness.

enrouler, *vb.* **s'e.,** roll up, twist, wind.

enseignant, *n.m.* teacher.

enseigne, *n.f.* sign, ensign.

enseignement, *n.m.* teaching, instruction.

enseigner, *vb.* teach.

ensemble, **1.** *n.m.* set. **2.** *adv.* together.

ensevelir, *vb.* bury.

ensoleillé, *adj.* sunny.

ensommeillé, *adj.* sleepy.

ensorceler, *vb.* bewitch.

ensuite, *adv.* then, next, afterwards.

ensuivre, *vb.* **s'e.,** ensue.

entablement, *n.m.* entablature.

entacher, *vb.* taint, besmirch.

entailler, *vb.* hack (notch).

entamer, *vb.* begin.

entassement, *n.m.* accumulation.

entasser, *vb.* heap up.

ente, *n.f.* scion (horticulture).

entendement, *n.m.* understanding, sense.

entendre, *vb.* hear; understand. **s'e.,** get on together.

entendu, *adj.* understood, agreed. **bien e.,** of course.

enténébré, *adj.* gloomy.

entente, *n.f.* understanding, agreement.

entériner, *vb.* ratify.

enterrement, *n.m.* burial.

enterrer, *vb.* bury.

entêté, *adj.* perverse.

entêtement, *n.m.* stubbornness.

entêter, *vb.* **s'e.,** be stubborn, insist.

enthousiasme, *n.m.* enthusiasm.

enthousiaste, 1. *n.m.f.* enthusiast. 2. *adj.* enthusiastic. e. de, keen on.

entichement, *n.m.* infatuation.

entier, *adj.* whole, complete, entire.

entité, *n.f.* entity.

entonner, *vb.* start to sing.

entonnoir, *n.m.* funnel.

entorse, *n.f.* sprain.

entourage, *n.m.* circle of friends; surroundings.

entourer, *vb.* surround, encircle.

entournure, *n.f.* armhole.

entr'acte, *n.m.* intermission.

entr'aide, *n.f.* mutual assistance.

entrailles, *n.f.pl.* bowels.

entrain, *n.m.* zest.

entraînant, *adj.* rousing.

entraîner, *vb.* draw along; involve, entail; coach, train.

entraîneur, *n.m.* coach.

entrant, *adj.* incoming.

entrave, *n.f.* obstacle.

entraver, *vb.* clog.

entre, *prep.* among, between.

entre-clos, *adj.* ajar.

entre-deux, *n.m.* interval.

entrée, *n.f.* admission, entry; main course.

entreface, *n.f.* interface.

entregent, *n.m.* tact; spirit.

entrelacer, *vb.* interlace.

entremets, (-mě), *n.m.* (side) dish; dessert.

entremetteur, *n.m.* intermediary.

entreposer, *vb.* store.

entreposeur, *n.m.* warehouseman.

entrepôt, *n.m.* warehouse.

entreprenant, *adj.* enterprising.

entreprendre, *vb.* undertake.

entrepreneur, *n.m.* contractor. e. de pompes funèbres, undertaker.

entreprise, *n.f.* concern, undertaking.

entrer (dans), *vb.* enter, come in, go in. laisser e., admit.

entretenir, *vb.* entertain. s'e., converse.

entretien, *n.m.* maintenance; conference; talk, conversation.

entrevoir, *vb.* glimpse.

entrevue, *n.f.* interview.

entr'ouvert, *adj.* ajar.

entr'ouvrir, *vb.* open halfway.

énumération, *n.f.* enumeration.

énumérer, *vb.* enumerate.

envahir, *vb.* invade.

envahissement, *n.m.* invasion.

enveloppe, *n.f.* envelope; wrapping.

envelopper, *vb.* envelop, wrap, enfold.

envergure, *n.f.* scope.

envers, 1. *n.m.* wrong side. 2. *prep.* toward.

enviable, *adj.* enviable.

envie, *n.f.* envy, desire. avoir e. de, want to, feel like.

envier, *vb.* envy.

envieux, *adj.* envious.

environ, *prep. and adv.* around, about; approximately.

environnement, *n.m.* surroundings.

environnementaliste, *n.m.f.* environmentalist.

environner, *vb.* surround.

environs, *n.m.pl.* surroundings.

envisager, *vb.* consider.

envoi, *n.m.* shipment, sending.

envoler, *vb.* s'e., fly away.

envoûter, *vb.* bewitch.

envoyé, *n.m.* envoy.

envoyer, *vb.* send.

enzyme, *n.f.* enzyme.

éon, *n.m.* eon.

épais, *adj.* thick.

épaisseur, *n.f.* thickness.

épaissir, *vb.* thicken.

épancher, *vb.* shed (blood).

épanouir, *vb.* s'é., bloom.

épargne, *n.f.* savings.

épargner, *vb.* save, spare.

éparpiller, *vb.* scatter.

épars, *adj.* scattered, sparse.

éparvin, *n.m.* spavin.

épatant, *adj.* (*colloq.*) grand.

épate, *n.f.* swagger.

épatement, *n.m.* amazement.

épater, *vb.* amaze.

épaule, *n.f.* shoulder.

épaulette, *n.f.* epaulette.

épave, *n.f.* wreck.

épée, *n.f.* sword.

épeler, *vb.* spell.

épellation, *n.f.* spelling.

éperdu, *adj.* distracted.

éperlan, *n.m.* smelt.

éperon, *n.m.* spur.

éperonner, *vb.* spur.

épervier, *n.m.* hawk.

épeuré, *adj.* frightened.

éphémère, *adj.* ephemeral, fleeting.

épice, *n.f.* spice.

épicé, *adj.* spicy.

épicerie, *n.f.* grocery.

épicier, *n.m.* grocer.

épidémie, *n.f.* epidemic.

épiderme, *n.m.* epidermis.

épidermique, *adj.* epidermal.

épier, *vb.* spy.

épigramme, *n.f.* epigram.

épilatoire, *adj. and n.m.* depilatory.

épilepsie, *n.f.* epilepsy.

épileptique, *adj. and n.m.f.* epileptic.

épilogue, *n.m.* epilogue.

épinards, (-når), *n.m.pl.* spinach.

épine, *n.f.* spine, thorn. é. dorsale, spinal column.

épinet, *n.f.* spinet.

épineux, *adj.* thorny.

épingle, *n.f.* pin. é. à cheveux, hairpin. é. anglaise, safety pin.

épingler, *vb.* pin.

épique, *adj.* epic.

épiscopal, *adj.* Episcopal.

épisode, *n.m.* episode.

épisodique, *adj.* episodic.

épistolaire, *adj.* epistolary.

épitaphe, *n.f.* epitaph.

épithète, *n.f.* epithet.

épitomé, *n.m.* epitome.

épître, *n.f.* epistle.

éploré, *adj.* tearful.

épluche-légumes, *n.m.* (potato) peeler.

éplucher, *vb.* peel.

épointé, *adj.* dull, blunted.

éponge, *n.f.* sponge.

éponger, *vb.* sponge up.

épopée, *n.f.* epic.

époque, *n.f.* epoch.

épouffé, *adj.* breathless, panting.

épouiller, *vb.* delouse.

épouse, *n.f.* wife.

épouser, *vb.* marry.

épouseur, *n.m.* suitor.

épousseter, *vb.* dust.

époussette, *n.f.* duster.

époustouflant, *adj.* staggering.

épouvantable, *adj.* terrible.

épouvante, *n.f.* fright.

épouvanter, *vb.* frighten.

époux, *n.m.* husband.

épreindre, *vb.* squeeze.

éprendre, *vb.* s'é., fall in love.

épreuve, *n.f.* trial, test; ordeal; proof.

éprouver, *vb.* experience.

éprouvette, *n.f.* test tube.

épuisant, *adj.* exhausting.

épuisement, *n.m.* exhaustion.

épuiser, *vb.* exhaust.

épuration, *n.f.* purification.

épurer, *vb.* purify.

équanimité, (-kwā-), *n.f.* equanimity.

équateur, (-kwā-), *n.m.* equator.

équation, (-kwā-), *n.f.* equation.

équatorial, (-kwā-), *adj.* equatorial.

équestre, *adj.* equestrian.

équidistant, *adj.* equidistant.

équilibre, *n.m.* poise.

équilibrer, *vb.* balance.

équilibriste, *n.* tightrope walker.

équinoxe, *n.m.* equinox.

équinoxial, *adj.* equinoctial.

équipage, *n.m.* crew.

équipe, *n.f.* team, crew, gang; shift.

équipement, *n.m.* equipment.

équiper, *vb.* equip.

équipier, *n.m.* team member.

équitable, *adj.* fair.

équitation, *n.f.* (horse) riding.

équité, *n.f.* equity.

équivalent, *adj.* and *n.m.* equivalent.

équivaloir, *vb.* equal in value.

équivoque, *adj.* equivocal.

érable, *n.m.* maple.

éradication, *n.f.* eradication.

éraflure, *n.m.* scratch; graze.

érailler, *vb.* unravel.

ère, *n.f.* era.

érection, *n.f.* erection; construction.

éreintant, *adj.* exhausting.

éreinter, *vb.* exhaust.

erg, *n.m.* erg.

ergoter, *vb.* quibble.

ériger, *vb.* erect.

ermitage, *n.m.* hermitage.

ermite, *n.m.* hermit.

éroder, *vb.* erode.

érosif, *adj.* erosive.

érosion, *n.f.* erosion.

érotique, *adj.* erotic.

errant, *adj.* wandering.

erratique, *adj.* erratic.

errer, *vb.* wander; err.

erreur, *n.f.* mistake, error.

erroné, *adj.* erroneous.

éructation, *n.f.* belch.

éructer, *vb.* belch.

érudit, *adj.* learned, scholarly.

érudition, *n.f.* learning.

éruption, *n.f.* rash, eruption.

érysipèle, *n.m.* erysipelas.

escabeau, *n.m.* stool.

escadrille, *n.f.* (ships) flotilla; (airplanes) squadron.

escadron, *n.m.* squadron.

escalade, *n.f.* climbing; escalation.

escalader, *vb.* scale; escalate.

escalator, *n.m.* escalator.

escale, *n.f.* stopover.

escalier, *n.m.* stairs.

escalope, *n.f.* cutlet.

escamotage, *n.m.* legerdemain.

escamoter, *vb.* evade, get around.

escamoteur, *n.m.* conjurer, magician.

escapade, *n.f.* escapade.

escarcelle, *n.f.* wallet.

escargot, *n.m.* snail.

escarmouche, *n.f.* skirmish.

escarole, *n.f.* chicory, endive.

escarpé, *adj.* abrupt.

escarpement, *n.m.* steepness.

eschare, *n.f.* scab; bedsore.

esclandre, *n.m.* slander.

esclavage, *n.m.* slavery.

esclave, *n.m.f.* slave.

escompte, *n.m.* discount.

escorte, *n.f.* escort.

escorter, *vb.* escort.

escouade, *n.f.* squad.

escrime, *n.f.* fencing.

escrimer, *vb.* fight.

escrimeur, *n.m.* swordsman.

escroc, (-ō), *n.m.* swindler.

escroquer, *vb.* swindle.

escroquerie, *n.f.* swindle.

esculent, *adj.* esculent.

espace, *n.m.* space.

espacé, *adj.* at great intervals.

espacer, *vb.* space out.

espadon, *n.m.* swordfish.

espadrille, *n.f.* rope sandal.

Espagne, *n.f.* Spain.

Espagnol, *n.m.* Spaniard.

espagnol, *adj.* and *n.m.* Spanish.

espalier, *n.m.* espalier.

espèce, *n.f.* species, kind; (*pl.*) cash.

espérance, *n.f.* hope.

espéranto, *n.m.* Esperanto.

espérer, *vb.* hope.

espiègle, *adj.* mischievous.

espièglerie, *n.f.* mischief.

espion, *n.m.* spy.

espionnage, *n.m.* espionage.

espionner, *vb.* spy on.

esplanade, *n.f.* esplanade.

espoir, *n.m.* hope.

esprit, *n.m.* spirit, mind, wit. Saint-E., Holy Ghost.

esquif, *n.m.* skiff.

Esquimau, *m.,* Esquimaude, *f. n.* Eskimo.

esquimau, *adj.* Eskimo.

esquinancie, *n.m.* quinsy.

esquinter, *vb.* exhaust, tire out.

esquisse, *n.f.* sketch.

esquisser, *vb.* sketch.

esquiver, *vb.* dodge.

essai, *n.m.* essay; attempt; experiment; assay.

essaim, *n.m.* swarm.

essaimer, *vb.* swarm.

essayer, *vb.* try; assay.

essence, *n.f.* gasoline; essence.

essentiel, *adj.* essential.

esseulement, *n.m.* solitude.

essieu, *n.m.* axle.

essor, *n.m.* flight; rapid expansion.

essorer, *vb.* dry.

essoufflé, *adj.* breathless.

essoufflement, *n.m.* breathlessness.

essuie-glace, *n.m.* windshield wiper.

essuyer, *vb.* wipe.

est, (-t), *n.m.* east.

estacade, *n.f.* stockade.

estafette, *n.f.* courier.

estafier, *n.m.* bodyguard.

estagnon, *n.m.* oil drum.

estaminet, *n.m.* bar, taproom.

estampe, *n.f.* engraving.

estampille, *n.f.* trademark.

esthète, *n.m.* esthete.

esthéticienne, *n.f.* beautician.

esthétique, *adj.* aesthetic.

estimable, *adj.* estimable.

estimateur, *n.m.* estimator; appraiser.

estimatif, *adj.* estimated.

estimation, *n.f.* estimate.

estime, *n.f.* esteem; estimation.

estimer, *vb.* esteem; estimate, value, rate.

estival, *adj.* of summer.

estivant, *n.m.* summer tourist.

estiver, *vb.* spend the summer.

estoc, *n.m.* tree trunk.

estomac, (mä), *n.m.* stomach.

estomper, *vb.* blur. s'e., soften, become blurred.

estourbir, *vb.* kill.

estrade, *n.f.* platform; stage.

estragon, *n.m.* tarragon.

estropié, 1. *n.m.* cripple. 2. *adj.* crippled.

estropier, *vb.* cripple.

estuaire, *n.m.* estuary.

estudiantin, *adj.* student.

esturgeon, *n.m.* sturgeon.

et, *conj.* and.

étable, *n.f.* barn.

établi, *n.m.* worktable.

établir, *vb.* settle; establish.

établissement, *n.m.* establishment.

étage, *n.m.* floor, story.

étagère, *n.f.* whatnot shelf.

étain, *n.m.* tin.

étal, *n.m.* stall.

étalage, *n.m.* display.

étalager, *vb.* display.

étaler, *vb.* display; spread.

étalon, *n.m.* standard.

étameur, *n.m.* tinsmith.

étamine, *n.f.* coarse muslin; stamen.

étampe, *n.f.* stamp.

étamper, *vb.* stamp.

étanche, *adj.* impervious.

étancher, *vb.* quench; stanch.

étang, *n.m.* pond.

étape, *n.f.* stage.

état, *n.m.* state.

étatisé, *adj.* state-controlled.

état-major, *n.m.* staff.

États-Unis, *n.m.pl.* United States.

été, *n.m.* summer.

éteindre, *vb.* extinguish, put out.

éteint, *adj.* extinct.

étendage, *n.m.* clotheslines.

étendard, *n.m.* standard.

étendre, *vb.* extend, spread, reach.

étendu, *adj.* extensive.

étendue, *n.f.* extent.

éternel, *adj.* everlasting.

éterniser, *vb.* perpetuate.

éternité, *n.f.* eternity.

éternuement, *n.m.* sneeze.

éternuer, *vb.* sneeze.

éther, (-r), *n.m.* ether.

éthéré, *adj.* ethereal.

Éthiopie, *n.f.* Ethiopia.

éthique, *n.f.* ethics.

ethnie, *n.f.* ethnic group.

ethnique, *adj.* ethnic.

étinceler, *vb.* sparkle.

étincelle, *n.f.* spark, sparkle.

étincellement, *n.m.* sparkle, glitter.

étiolement, *n.m.* atrophy.

étioler, *vb.* blanch.

étiqueter, *vb.* label.

étiquette, *n.f.* label, tag; etiquette.

étirer, *vb.* stretch out.

étoffe, *n.f.* stuff, material, cloth.

étoffer, *vb.* stuff.

étoile, *n.f.* star.

étoiler, *vb.* bespangle.

étonnement, *n.m.* astonishment.

étonner, *vb.* astonish.

étouffé, *adj.* braised.

étouffer, *vb.* smother.

étourderie, *n.f.* thoughtlessness.

étourdi, *adj.* thoughtless.

étourdir, *vb.* daze.

étourdissant, *adj.* dazing.

étourdissement, *n.m.* dizziness.

étrange, *adj.* strange.

étranger, *n.m. and adj.* alien.

étranglement, *n.m.* strangulation.

étrangler, *vb.* strangle.

étrave, *n.f.* stem, bow.

être, 1. *n.m.* being. 2. *vb.* be.

étrécir, *vb.* shrink.

étreindre, *vb.* clasp.

étreinte, *n.f.* clasp; hug, embrace.

étrier, *n.m.* stirrup.

étrille, *n.f.* currycomb.

étroit, *adj.* narrow.

Étrusque, *n.m.f.* Etruscan.

étrusque, *adj.* Etruscan.

étude, *n.f.* study.

étudiant, *n.m.* student.

étudier, *vb.* study.

étui, *n.m.* 1. case. 2. needle case.

étuve, *n.f.* steam room.

étymologie, *n.f.* etymology.

étymologique, *adj.* etymological.

eucalyptus, *n.m.* eucalyptus.

eucharistie, *n.f.* eucharist.

eunuque, *n.m.* eunuch.

euphémique, *adj.* euphemistic.

euphémisme, *n.m.* euphemism.

euphonie, *n.f.* euphony.

euphonique, *adj.* euphonic.

euphorie, *n.f.* euphoria.

Europe, *n.f.* Europe.

Européen, *n.m.* European.

européen, *adj.* European.

euthanasie, *n.f.* euthanasia.

eux, *pron. m.pl.* them.

évacuable, *adj.* able to be evacuated.

évacuation, *n.f.* evacuation.

évacuer, *vb.* evacuate.

évader, *vb.* **s'é.,** escape.
évaluateur, *n.m.* appraiser.
évaluation, *n.f.* appraisal.
évaluer, *vb.* evaluate, rate, assess.
évangélique, *adj.* evangelic.
évangéliste, *n.m.* evangelist.
évangile, *n.m.* gospel.
évanouir, *vb.* **s'é.,** fade away; faint.
évanouissement, *n.m.* fainting fit.
évaporation, *n.f.* evaporation.
évaporer, *vb.* evaporate.
évasif, *adj.* evasive.
évasion, *n.f.* escape.
évêché, *n.m.* bishopric.
éveil, *n.m.* alertness.
éveillé, *adj.* sprightly.
éveiller, *vb.* wake.
événement, *n.m.* event.
éventail, *n.m.* fan.
éventrer, *vb.* disembowel.
éventualité, *n.f.* possibility.
éventuel, *adj.* possible.
éventuellement, *adv.* possibly.
évêque, *n.m.* bishop.
éviction, *n.f.* eviction.
évidemment, *adv.* evidently.
évidence, *n.f.* evidence. **en é.,** conspicuous.
évident, *adj.* obvious, evident.
évider, *vb.* scoop out.
évier, *n.m.* sink.
évincer, *vb.* oust.
éviscérer, *vb.* eviscerate, disembowel.
évitable, *adj.* avoidable.
éviter, *vb.* avoid.
évocateur, *adj.* evocative.
évocation, *n.f.* evocation.
évolué, *adj.* mature.
évolution, *n.f.* evolution.
évoquer, *vb.* evoke.
exact, **(-kt),** *adj.* exact, precise.
exactement, *adv.* exactly.
exactitude, *n.f.* precision.
exagération, *n.f.* exaggeration.
exagéré, *adj.* excessive.
exagérer, *vb.* exaggerate.
exaltant, *adj.* exciting.
exaltation, *n.f.* exaltation.
exalté, *adj.* impassioned.

exalter, *vb.* exalt, elate.
examen, *n.m.* examination.
examiner, *vb.* examine.
exaspération, *n.f.* exasperation.
exaspérer, *vb.* exasperate, aggravate.
exaucer, *vb.* grant.
excavateur, *n.m.* steam shovel.
excavation, *n.f.* excavation.
excaver, *vb.* excavate.
excédent, *n.m.* excess; overweight.
excéder, *vb.* exceed.
excellence, *n.f.* excellence; excellency, highness.
excellent, *adj.* excellent.
exceller, *vb.* excel.
excentrique, *adj.* eccentric.
excepté, *prep.* except.
excepter, *vb.* except.
exception, *n.f.* exception.
exceptionnel, *adj.* exceptional.
excès, *n.m.* excess.
excessif, *adj.* excessive, extreme.
exciser, *vb.* excise; cut out.
excitabilité, *n.f.* excitability.
excitable, *adj.* excitable.
excitant, **1.** *n.m.* stimulant. **2.** *adj.* stimulating.
exciter, *vb.* excite.
exclamatif, *adj.* exclamatory.
exclamation, *n.f.* exclamation.
exclamer, *vb.* exclaim.
exclure, *vb.* exclude.
exclusif, *adj.* exclusive.
exclusion, *n.f.* exclusion.
excommunication, *n.f.* excommunication.
excommunier, *vb.* excommunicate.
excorier, *vb.* excoriate.
excrément, *n.m.* excrement.
excréter, *vb.* excrete.
excrétion, *n.f.* excretion.
excroissance, *n.f.* (out)growth.
excursion, *n.f.* excursion.
excursionniste, *n.m.f.* excursionist.
excusable, *adj.* excusable.
excuse, *n.f.* plea; excuse.
excuser, *vb.* excuse. **s'e. de,** apologize for.

exécrable, *adj.* atrocious.
exécrer, *vb.* loathe.
exécuter, *vb.* perform; enforce.
exécuteur, *n.m.* executor.
exécutif, *adj. and n.m.* executive.
exécution, *n.f.* performance; enforcement; execution.
exemplaire, 1. *n.m.* copy. **2.** *adj.* exemplary.
exemple, *n.m.* instance, example.
exempt, *adj.* exempt.
exempt de droits, *adj.* duty-free.
exempter, *vb.* exempt.
exemption, *n.f.* exemption.
exerçant, *adj.* practicing.
exercer, *vb.* exercise; drill, train. **s'e.,** practice.
exercice, *n.m.* exercise; drill, practice.
exhalation, *n.f.* exhalation.
exhaler, *vb.* exhale.
exhaustion, *n.f.* exhaust.
exhiber, *vb.* show, present; exhibit.
exhibition, *n.f.* exhibition.
exhortation, *n.f.* exhortation.
exhorter, *vb.* exhort.
exhumer, *vb.* exhume.
exigeant, *adj.* demanding.
exigence, *n.f.* requirement.
exiger, *vb.* require, exact, demand.
exigu, *m.* **exiguë** *f.* *adj.* tiny.
exil, **(-l),** *n.m.* exile.
exilé, *n.m.* exile.
exiler, *vb.* banish.
existant, *adj.* existent.
existence, *n.f.* existence.
exister, *vb.* exist.
exode, *n.m.* exodus.
exonération, *n.f.* exoneration.
exonérer, *vb.* exonerate.
exorbitant, *adj.* exorbitant.
exorciser, *vb.* exorcise.
exotique, *adj.* exotic.
expansible, *adj.* expansible.
expansif, *adj.* expansive.
expansion, *n.f.* expansion.
expatriation, *n.f.* expatriation.
expatrié, *n.* exile, expatriate.
expectorant, *adj. and n.m.* expectorant.

expectorer, *vb.* expectorate.

expédient, *n.m.* makeshift.

expédier, *vb.* dispatch.

expéditif, *adj.* expeditious.

expédition, *n.f.* dispatch; expedition, shipment.

expérience, *n.f.* experience; experiment.

expérimental, *adj.* experimental.

expérimentation, *n.f.* experimentation.

expérimenté, *adj.* experienced.

expert, *adj. and n.m.* expert.

expiable, *adj.* expiable.

expiation, *n.f.* atonement.

expier, *vb.* atone for.

expiration, *n.f.* expiration.

expirer, *vb.* expire.

explétif, *n.m. and adj.* expletive.

explicatif, *adj.* explanatory.

explication, *n.f.* explanation.

explicite, *adj.* explicit, clear.

expliquer, *vb.* explain.

exploit, *n.m.* feat, exploit.

exploitation, *n.f.* exploitation; working.

exploiter, *vb.* exploit.

explorateur, *n.m.* explorer.

exploratif, *adj.* exploratory.

exploration, *n.f.* exploration.

explorer, *vb.* explore.

exploser, *vb.* explode.

explosible, *adj.* explosive.

explosif, *adj. and n.m.* explosive.

explosion, *n.f.* blast, explosion.

exportation, *n.f.* export, exportation.

exporter, *vb.* export.

exposé, *n.m.* account, statement.

exposer, *vb.* expound; expose; exhibit.

exposition, *n.f.* exposition; exposure; show, display.

exprès, 1. *n.m.* special delivery. 2. *adj.* express. 3. *adv.* on purpose.

express, *n.m.* espresso.

expressif, *adj.* expressive.

expression, *n.f.* expression.

exprimable, *adj.* expressible.

exprimer, *vb.* express.

exproprier, *vb.* expropriate.

expulser, *vb.* expel.

expulsion, *n.f.* expulsion.

expurgation, *n.f.* expurgation.

expurger, *vb.* expurgate.

exquis, *adj.* exquisite.

exsangue, *adj.* bloodless.

exsuder, *vb.* exude.

extase, *n.f.* ecstasy.

extasier, *vb.* s'e. sur, rave about.

extatique, *adj.* ecstatic.

extensif, *adj.* extensive.

extension, *n.f.* extension.

exténuation, *n.f.* extenuation.

exténuer, *vb.* extenuate, exhaust.

extérieur, 1. *n.m.* exterior. 2. *adj.* exterior, outer.

extérieurement, *adv.* externally.

extermination, *n.f.* extermination.

exterminer, *vb.* exterminate.

externat, *n.m.* day school.

externe, *adj.* external.

exterritorialité, *n.f.* extraterritoriality.

extincteur, *n.m.* fire extinguisher.

extinction, *n.f.* extinction.

extirper, *vb.* extirpate, root out.

extorquer, *vb.* extort.

extorsion, *n.f.* extortion.

extra, *adj.* first-rate.

extra-, *prefix* extra.

extraction, *n.f.* extraction; descent.

extrader, *vb.* extradite.

extradition, *n.f.* extradition.

extra-fin, *adj.* extremely fine.

extraire, *vb.* extract.

extrait, *n.m.* extract; abstract.

extraordinaire, *adj.* extraordinary, unusual.

extraordinairement, *adv.* extraordinarily.

extravagance, *n.f.* extravagance.

extravagant, *adj.* extravagant.

extraverti, *n.m.* extrovert.

extrême, *adj. and n.m.* extreme.

extrémiste, *n.m.f.* extremist.

extrémité, *n.f.* extremity.

extrinsèque, *adj.* extrinsic.

extroverti, *n.m.* extrovert.

extrusion, *n.f.* extrusion.

exubérance, *n.f.* exuberance.

exubérant, *adj.* exuberant.

exultation, *n.f.* exultation.

exulter, *vb.* exult.

F

fable *n.f.* fable.

fabliau, *n.m.* fabliau.

fabricant, *n.m.* maker, manufacturer.

fabricateur, *n.m.* forger.

fabrication, *n.f.* make.

fabrique, *n.f.* factory.

fabriquer, *vb.* manufacture.

fabuleux, *adj.* fabulous.

fabuliste, *n.m.* fabulist.

fac, *n.f.* (colloquial) university.

façade, *n.f.* front.

face, *n.f.* face. en f. de, opposite. faire f. à, confront.

facétie, *n.f.* joke, prank.

facétieux, *adj.* facetious.

facette, *n.f.* facet.

fâché, *j.* angry; sorry.

fâcher, *vb.* anger, offend; grieve. se f., get angry.

fâcherie, *n.f.* quarrel, argument.

fâcheux, *adj.* upleasant.

facial, *adj.* facial.

facile, *adj.* easy.

facilité, *n.f.* fluency; ease.

faciliter, *vb.* facilitate, make easy.

façon, *n.f.* way, manner, fashion. **de f. à,** so as to.

faconde, *n.f.* glibness; fluency.

façonner, *vb.* shape, fashion.

facsimilé, *n.m.* facsimile.

facteur, *n.m.* factor, element; mail carrier.

factice, *adj.* artificial.

factieux, *adj.* factious; quarrelsome.

faction, *n.f.* faction, party.

factionnaire, *n.m.* sentry.

facture, *n.f.* invoice, bill.

facturer, *vb.* bill; send an invoice to.

facultatif, *adj.* optional.

faculté, *n.f.* faculty.

fadaise, *n.f.* nonsense.

fade, *adj.* insipid.

fadeur, *n.f.* insipidity.

fagot, *n.m.* bundle.

faible, *adj.* weak, faint, dim, feeble.

faiblement, *adv.* feebly, weakly.

faiblesse, *n.f.* weakness, frailty; dimness.

faiblir, *vb.* weaken.

faïence, *n.f.* earthenware.

faille, *n.f.* fault.

failli, *adj. and n.m.* bankrupt.

faillibilité, *n.f.* fallibility.

faillible, *adj.* fallible.

faillir, *vb.* fail.

faillite, *n.f.* bankruptcy.

faim, *n.f.* hunger.

fainéant, *n.m.* loafer.

faire, *vb.* make, do. **f. part,** inform. **f. mal à,** hurt. **f. voir,** show.

faire-part, *n.m.* announcement.

faisable, *adj.* feasible.

faisan, *n.m.* pheasant.

faisceau, *n.m.* bundle; beam.

fait, *n.m.* fact. **tout à f.,** wholly.

falaise, *n.f.* cliff.

fallacieux, *adj.* fallacious.

falloir, *vb.* be necessary. **comme il faut,** decent.

falot, *n.m.* lamp.

falsificateur, *n.* forger; falsifier.

falsification, *n.f.* falsification.

falsifier, *vb.* falsify.

famélique, *adj.* starving.

fameux, *adj.* famous.

familial, *adj.* family.

familiariser, *vb.* familiarize.

familiarité, *n.f.* familiarity.

familier, *adj.* familiar.

familièrement, *adv.* familiarly.

famille, *n.f.* family, household.

famine, *n.f.* famine.

fanatique, *adj. and n.m.f.* fanatic.

fanatisme, *n.m.* fanaticism.

faner, *vb.* fade.

fanfare, *n.f.* fanfare.

fanfaronnade, *n.f.* boast.

fange, *n.f.* filth; vice.

fantaisie, *n.f.* fancy, fantasy.

fantaisiste, *adj.* eccentric.

fantasme, *n.m.* fantasy.

fantastique, *adj.* fantastic.

fantoche, *n.m.* puppet.

fantôme, *n.m.* phantom, ghost; joke.

faon, *n.m.* fawn.

faramineux, *adj.* phenomenal.

farce, *n.f.* stuffing; farce.

farceur, *n.m.* jokester.

farcir, *vb.* stuff.

fard, *n.m.* facial makeup.

fardeau, *n.m.* burden.

farfelu, *adj.* weird.

farinacé, *adj.* farinaceous.

farine, *n.f.* meal, flour.

farniente, *n.m.* idleness.

farouche, *adj.* fierce; sullen, shy.

fascinant, *adj.* fascinating.

fascination, *n.f.* fascination.

fascine, *n.f.* faggot (of wood).

fasciner, *vb.* fascinate.

fascisme, *n.m.* fascism.

fasciste, *n.m.f.* fascist.

faste, *n.m.* ostentation.

fast-food, *n.m.* fast-food establishment.

fastidieux, *adj.* dull.

fat, *adj.* foppish.

fatal, *adj.* mortal, fatal.

fatalisme, *n.m.* fatalism.

fataliste, *n.m.f.* fatalist.

fatalité, *n.f.* fatality; misfortune.

fatidique, *adj.* fateful.

fatigant, *adj.* tiring.

fatigue, *n.f.* weariness.

fatiguer, *vb.* tire.

fatuité, *n.f.* smugness.

faubourg, *n.m.* suburb.

faubourien, *adj.* suburban.

fauché, *adj.* broke.

faucher, *vb.* mow.

faucheur, *n.m.* reaper, mower.

faucille, *n.f.* sickle.

faucon, *n.m.* hawk.

fauconneau, *n.m.* young falcon.

fauconnerie, *n.f.* falconry.

faufil, *n.m.* basting thread.

faufiler, *vb.* baste.

faune, *n.f.* fauna, wildlife.

faussaire, *n.m.f.* forger; liar.

faussement, *adv.* falsely.

fausser, *vb.* pervert, warp, distort.

fausset, *n.m.* falsetto; spigot, faucet.

fausseté, *n.f.* falseness.

faute, *n.f.* fault, mistake. **f. de,** for want of.

fauteuil, *n.m.* armchair.

fauteur, *n.m.* trouble-maker.

fautif, *adj.* faulty, wrong.

fauve, *adj.* wild.

faux, 1. *n.m.* forgery. **2.** *n. f.* scythe.

faux, *m.,* **fausse** *f. adj.* false, wrong; spurious; counterfeit.

faux-filet, *n.m.* sirloin.

faveur, *n.f.* favor. **en f. de,** on behalf of.

favorable, *adj.* conducive, favorable.

favorablement, *adv.* favorably.

favori, *n.m.* whisker.

favori, *m.,* **favorite** *f. adj. and n.* favorite.

favoriser, *vb.* favor.

favoritisme, *n.m.* favoritism.

fax, *n.m.* fax (machine).

faxer, *vb.* fax.

fayot, *n.m.* kidney bean.

féal, *adj.* faithful.

fébrile, *adj.* feverish.

fécal, *adj.* fecal.

fécond, *adj.* fertile.

féconder, *vb.* fertilize.

fécondité, *n.f.* fertility.

féculent, *adj.* starchy.

fédéral, *adj.* federal.

fédéraliser, *vb.* federalize.

fédéraliste, *n.m.f. and adj.* federalist.

fédération, *n.f.* confederacy, federation.

fédérer, *vb.* federate.

fée, *n.f.* fairy.

féerie, *n.f.* fairyland.

féerique, *adj.* fairylike.

feindre, *vb.* feign, pretend.

feinte, *n.f.* feint.

fêler, *vb.* crack.

félicitation, *n.f.* congratulation.

félicité, *n.f.* bliss.

féliciter, *vb.* congratulate.

félin, *adj.* feline.

félon, *adj.* disloyal.

fêlure, *n.f.* crack.

femelle, *adj. and n.f.* female.

féminin, *adj.* female, feminine.

féministe, *n.m.f.* feminist.

femme, *n.f.* woman, wife. **f. de chambre,** chambermaid.

fémoral, *adj.* femoral.

fémure, *n.m.* thighbone.

fendille, *n.f.* crack.

fendiller, *vb.* se f., crack.

fendoir, *n.m.* cleaver.

fendre, *vb.* split, rip.

fenêtre, *n.f.* window.

fenil, *n.m.* hayloft.

fenouil, *n.m.* fennel.

fente, *n.f.* crack; rip, split.

féodal, *adj.* feudal.

féodalité, *n.f.* feudalism.

fer (-r), *n.m.* iron., **chemin de f.,** railway. **fil de f.,** wire. **f. à cheval,** horseshoe.

fermail, *n.m.* brooch; clasp.

ferme, *n.f.* farm. **maison de f.,** farmhouse.

ferme, *adj.* firm, steady, fast.

fermement, *adv.* firmly.

ferment, *n.m.* ferment.

fermentation, *n.f.* fermentation.

fermenter, *vb.* ferment.

fermer, *vb.* close. **f. à clef,** lock.

fermeté, *n.f.* firmness.

fermeture, *n.f.* closing.

fermier, *n.m.* farmer.

féroce, *adj.* fierce.

férocité, *n.f.* ferocity.

ferraille, *n.f.* old iron.

ferreux, *adj.* ferrous.

ferrique, *adj.* ferric.

ferroviaire, *adj.* rail(way).

fertile, *adj.* fertile.

fertilisant, *n.m.* fertilizer.

fertilisation, *n.f.* fertilization.

fertiliser, *vb.* fertilize.

fertilité, *n.f.* fertility.

férule, *n.f.* cane, rod.

fervemment, *adv.* fervently.

fervent, *adj.* fervent.

ferveur, *n.f.* fervor.

fesse, *n.f.* buttock.

fessée, *n.f.* spanking.

fesser, *vb.* spank.

festin, *n.m.* feast.

festiner, *vb.* feast.

festival, *n.m.* festival.

feston, *n.m.* festoon.

fête, *n.f.* feast, party. **jour de f.,** holiday.

fêter, *vb.* fete.

fétiche, *n.m.* fetish.

fétide, *adj.* fetid.

feu, *n.m.* fire. **f. de joie,** bonfire. **f. d'artifice,** fireworks. **prendre f.,** catch fire. **coup de f.,** shot.

feu, *adj.* late (deceased).

feuillage, *n.m.* foliage.

feuille, *n.f.* leaf; sheet; foil.

feuillet, *n.m.* leaf.

feuilleter, *vb.* skim (book); roll and turn (pastry).

feuilleton, *n.m.* serial, TV series.

feutre, *n.m.* felt.

fève, *n.f.* bean.

février, *n.m.* February.

fez, *n.m.* fez.

fi, *interj.* fie!

fiable, *adj.* reliable.

fiacre, *n.m.* cab.

fiançailles, *n.f.pl.* engagement, betrothal.

fiancé, *n.m.* fiancé.

fiancer, *vb.* betroth.

fiasco, *n.m.* fiasco.

fibre, *n.f.* fiber.

fibreux, *adj.* fibrous.

ficeler, *vb.* tie up.

ficelle, *n.f.* string, twine.

fiche, *n.f.* slip (of paper).

ficher, *vb.* se f. de, care nothing about.

fichier, *n.m.* card index, file.

fichu, *adj.* ruined.

fictif, *adj.* fictitious.

fiction, *n.f.* fiction.

fidèle, *adj.* faithful.

fidélité, *n.f.* fidelity, loyalty, allegiance.

fief, *n.m.* fief.

fiel, *n.m.* gall.

fiente, *n.f.* dung.

fier, **(-r),** *adj.* proud.

fier, *vb.* se f., trust.

fierté, *n.f.* trust.

fièvre, *n.f.* fever.

fiévreux, *adj.* feverish.

fifre, *n.m.* fife(r).

figer, *vb.* coagulate.

figue, *n.f.* fig.

figurant, *n.m.* extra (film).

figuratif, *adj.* figurative.

figure, *n.f.* face; figure.

figurer, *vb.* figure, imagine. se f., fancy.

fil, **(-l),** *n.m.* thread, string. **f. de fer,** wire.

filament, *n.m.* filament.

filature, *n.f.* spinning mill.

file, *n.f.* file.

filer, *vb.* spin.

filet, *n.m.* net.

filial, *adj.* filial.

filière, *n.f.* network.

filin, *n.m.* rope.

fille, *n.f.* daughter. **jeune f.,** girl. **vieille f.,** old maid.

fillette, *n.f.* little girl.

filleul, *n.m.* godson.

film, *n.m.* film.

filmer, *vb.* film.

filou, *n.m.* thief.

fils, **(fēs),** *n.m.* son.

filtrant, *adj.* filtering.

filtration, *n.f.* filtration.

filtre, *n.m.* filter.

filtrer, *vb.* filter.

fin, **1.** *n.f.* end. **2.** *adj.* fine; sharp; clever.

final, *adj.* final.

finaliste, *n.m.f.* finalist.

finalité, *n.f.* finality.

finance, *n.f.* finance.

financer, *vb.* finance.

financier, **1.** *n.m.* financier. **2.** *adj.* financial.

finasser, *vb.* finesse.

finesse, *n.f.* fineness; slimness.

finir, *vb.* finish.

Finlande, *n.f.* Finland.

Finnois, *n.m.* Finn.

finnois, *adj. and n.m.* Finnish.

firmament, *n.m.* firmament.

firme, *n.f.* company.

fisc, *n.m.* tax authorities.

fiscal, *adj.* fiscal.

fissure, *n.f.* fissure.

fiston, *n.m.* (colloquial) son.

fixation, *n.f.* fixation.

fixe, *adj.* set, fixed.

fixer, *vb.* fix, settle; stare at.

fixité, *n.f.* fixity.

flaccidité, *n.f.* flabbiness.

flacon, *n.m.* bottle.

flagellation, *n.f.* flagellation.

flageller, *vb.* flog.

flageolet, *n.m.* kidney bean.

flagrant, *adj.* flagrant.

flair, *n.m.* flair.

flairer, *vb.* smell.

flamand, *adj.* Flemish.

flambant, *adj.* flaming.

flambeau, *n.m.* torch.

flambée, *n.f.* blaze.

flamber, *vb.* blaze.

flamboyant, *adj.* flaming; flamboyant.

flamboyer, *vb.* flame, flare.

flamme, *n.f.* flame.

flan, *n.m.* custard pie.

flanc, *n.m.* side, flank.

flanchet, *n.m.* flank (of beef).

flanelle, *n.f.* flannel.

flâner, *vb.* saunter, stroll; loiter, loaf.

flâneur, *n.m.* idler.

flanquer, *vb.* flank.

flaque, *n.f.* puddle.

flash, *n.m.* flash, news flash.

flasque, *adj.* flabby.

flatter, *vb.* flatter.

flatterie, *n.f.* flattery.

flatteur, *n.m.* flatterer.

fléau, *n.m.* scourge, plague.

flèche, *n.f.* arrow.

fléchir, *vb.* bend.

flegmatique, *adj.* phlegmatic.

flegme, *n.m.* phlegm.

flemmard, *n.m.* lazybones.

flemme, *n.f.* laziness.

flet, *n.m.* flounder.

flétan, *n.m.* halibut.

flétrir, *vb.* wilt, wither.

fleur, *n.f.* flower, blossom, bloom.

fleuret, *n.m.* foil.

fleuri, *adj.* flowery.

fleurir, *vb.* flower, bloom, blossom.

fleuriste, *n.m.f.* florist.

fleuve, *n.m.* river.

flexibilité, *n.f.* flexibility.

flexible, *adj.* flexible.

flic, *n.m.* (colloquial) cop.

flipper, *n.m.* pinball.

flirt, (-t), *n.m.* flirtation.

flirter, *vb.* flirt.

flocon, *n.m.* flake.

flore, *n.f.* flora.

florissant, *adj.* prosperous, flourishing.

flot, *n.m.* wave. **à f.**, afloat.

flottant, *adj.* floating; irresolute.

flotte, *n.f.* fleet.

flottement, *n.m.* fluctuation; wavering.

flotter, *vb.* float.

flou, *adj.* hazy, indistinct.

fluctuation, *n.f.* fluctuation.

fluctuer, *vb.* fluctuate.

fluet, *m.*, **fluette** *f. adj.* thin, delicate.

fluide, *adj. and n.m.* fluid, liquid.

fluidité, *n.f.* fluidity.

fluor, *n.m.* fluoride.

fluorescent, *adj.* fluorescent.

flûte, *n.f.* flute.

flûté, *adj.* soft; flutelike.

fluvial, *adj.* river.

flux, *n.m.* flow, flux.

fluxion, *n.f.* inflammation.

foi, *n.f.* faith; trust.

foie, *n.m.* liver.

foin, *n.m.* hay.

foire, *n.f.* fair.

fois, *n.f.* time. **à la f.**, at once.

foison, *n.f.* abundance.

foisonner, *vb.* abound.

folâtre, *adj.* frisky.

folâtrer, *vb.* frolic.

folichon, *adj.* playful.

folie, *n.f.* mania, madness, folly.

folklore, *n.m.* folklore.

follement, *adv.* foolishly.

follet, *adj.* merry, playful.

fomenter, *vb.* foment.

foncé, *adj.* dark.

foncer, *vb.* deepen.

fonction, *n.f.* function.

fonctionnaire, *n.m.* official, civil servant.

fonctionnement, *n.m.* operation, working.

fonctionner, *vb.* function, work.

fonctions, *n.f.pl.* office.

fond, *n.m.* bottom, (back)ground. **à f.**, thorough(ly). **au f.**, fundamentally.

fondamental, *adj.* basic, fundamental.

fondateur, *n.m.* founder.

fondation, *n.f.* foundation, establishment.

fondé, *adj.* authentic; (comm.) funded.

fondement, *n.m.* foundation.

fonder, *vb.* found.

fonderie, *n.f.* foundry.

fondre, *vb.* melt; fuse.

fondrière, *n.f.* bog.

fonds, *n.m.* fund.

fondu, *adj.* melted, molten.

fongus, (-s), *n.m.* fungus.

fontaine, *n.f.* fountain.

fonte, *n.f.* melting.

fonts, *n.m.pl.* font.

foot, *n.m.* (colloquial) football.

football, *n.m.* football.

footing, *n.m.* walking; jogging.

forain, *n.m.* peddler.

forçat, *n.m.* convict.

force, *n.f.* strength, force; emphasis.

forcé, *adj.* forced; far-fetched.

forcément, *adv.* of necessity.

forcené, *adj.* frantic.

forceps, *n.m.* forceps.

forcer, *vb.* force, compel.

forcir, *vb.* thrive.

forer, *vb.* bore, drill.

forestier, *n.m.* forest ranger.

foret, *n.m.* drill.

forêt, *n.f.* forest.

foreuse, *n.f.* drill.

forfait, *n.m.* crime; forfeit; contract.

forfaiture, *n.f.* mishandling.

forfanterie, *n.f.* bragging.

forge, *n.f.* forge.

forger, *vb.* forge.

forgeron, *n.m.* blacksmith.

forgeur, *n.m.* forger; inventor.

formaliser, *vb.* formalize.

formaliste, *adj.* formal; precise.

formalité, *n.f.* formality, ceremony.

formater, *vb.* format.

formation, *n.f.* formation, training.

forme, *n.f.* shape, form.

formel, *adj.* formal.

former, *vb.* form, shape.

formidable, *adj.* tremendous; formidable.

formulaire, *n.m.* form.

formule, *n.f.* formula; form.

formuler, *vb.* formulate, draw up.

fort, 1. *n.m.* fort. **2.** *adj.* strong, loud. **3.** *adv.* hard.

forteresse, *n.f.* fort(ress).

fortifiant, *adj.* strengthening.

fortification, *n.f.* fortification.

fortifier, *vb.* strengthen.

fortuit, *adj.* accidental.

fortuité, *n.f.* fortuitousness.

fortune, *n.f.* fortune.

fortuné, *adj.* lucky, fortunate.

fosse, *n.f.* pit.

fossé, *n.m.* ditch; dike.

fossette, *n.f.* dimple.

fossile, *n.m.* fossil.

fossoyer, *vb.* dig a trench.

fou, *m.,* **folle** *f. adj.* mad, crazy, demented.

foudre, *n.m.* thunderbolt.

foudroyant, *adj.* terrifying, crushing.

foudroyer, *vb.* crush, blast.

fouet, *n.m.* whip, lash.

fouetter, *vb.* flog, whip.

fougère, *n.f.* fern.

fougue, *n.f.* ardor.

fougueux, *adj.* fiery, impetuous.

fouille, *n.f.* excavation.

fouiller, *vb.* ransack.

fouillis, *n.m.* litter, mess.

fouir, *vb.* dig, burrow.

foulard, *n.m.* scarf.

foule, *n.f.* crowd, mob.

fouler, *vb.* trample.

foulure, *n.f.* sprain; wrench.

four, *n.m.* oven.

fourbe, 1. *n.m.* knave. **2.** *adj.* scheming.

fourberie, *n.f.* knavery.

fourbir, *vb.* polish.

fourche, *n.f.* fork.

fourchette, *n.f.* fork.

fourgon, *n.m.* wagon.

fourmi, *n.f.* ant.

fourmillement, *n.m.* swarming; tingling.

fourmiller, *vb.* mill; swarm.

fourneau, *n.m.* stove, furnace.

fournée, *n.f.* batch.

fourniment, *n.m.* equipment.

fournir de, *vb.* supply, furnish.

fournisseur, *n.m.* tradesman.

fournitures, *n.f.pl.* supplies.

fourrage, *n.m.* fodder, forage.

fourrager, *vb.* forage.

fourré, *adj.* lined (of clothing); thick; wooded.

fourreau, *n.m.* sheath.

fourrer, *vb.* thrust in. **se f.,** interfere, meddle.

fourreur, *n.m.* furrier.

fourrure, *n.f.* fur.

fourvoyer, *vb.* mislead.

foutaise, *n.f.* (colloquial) rubbish.

foyer, *n.m.* focus; hearth. **f. domestique,** home.

frac, *n.m.* dress coat.

fracas, *n.m.* crash; rattle; noise; ado.

fracasser, *vb.* **se f.,** shatter.

fraction, *n.f.* fraction.

fracture, *n.f.* fracture.

fracturer, *vb.* break, fracture.

fragile, *adj.* brittle, delicate, frail, fragile.

fragilité, *n.f.* fragility.

fragment, *n.m.* fragment.

fragmenter, *vb.* divide up.

fraîcheur, *n.f.* freshness, coolness.

fraîchir, *vb.* freshen.

frais, *n.m.pl.* expense(s), cost, fee.

frais, *m.,* **fraîche** *f. adj.* fresh, cool.

fraise, *n.f.* strawberry; ruffle.

framboise, *n.f.* raspberry.

franc, 1. *n.m.* franc. **2.** *adj.m.,* **franche** *f.* frank, open.

Français, *n.m.* Frenchman.

français, *adj. and n.m.* French.

Française, *n.f.* Frenchwoman.

France, *n.f.* France.

franchement, *adv.* frankly.

franchir, *vb.* clear, cross.

franchise, *n.f.* frankness.

franciser, *vb.* make French.

franc-maçon, *n.m.* Freemason.

franco, *adv.* postage paid.

francophone, *adj.* French-speaking.

francophonie, *n.f.* French-speaking communities.

franc-parler, *n.m.* frankness.

franc-tireur, *n.m.* sniper; freelancer.

frange, *n.f.* fringe.

frangible, *adj.* breakable.

frapper, *vb.* strike, hit, rap, knock. **f. du pied,** stamp.

frasque, *n.f.* prank.

fraternel, *adj.* brotherly.

fraterniser, *vb.* fraternize.

fraternité, *n.f.* brotherhood.

fraude, *n.f.* fraud.

frauder, *vb.* defraud.

fraudeur, *n.m.* smuggler.

frauduleux, *adj.* fraudulent.

frayer, *vb.* open up; rub.

frayeur, *n.f.* fright.

fredaine, *n.f.* prank.

fredonner, *vb.* hum.

frégate, *n.f.* frigate.

frein, *n.m.* brake; check.

freiner, *vb.* brake; restrain.

frelater, *vb.* adulterate.

frêle, *adj.* frail.

frelon, *n.m.* hornet.

frémir, *vb.* tremble. **faire f.,** thrill.

frémissement, *n.m.* shiver; thrill.

frêne, *n.m.* ash (tree).

frénésie, *n.f.* frenzy.

frénétique, *adj.* frantic.

fréquemment, *adv.* often.

fréquence, *n.f.* frequency.

fréquent, *adj.* frequent.

fréquenter, *vb.* frequent, associate with.

frère, *n.m.* brother.

fresque, *n.f.* fresco.

fret, *n.m.* freight.

fréter, *vb.* charter (ship); freight.

frétillant, *adj.* lively.

frétiller, *vb.* wag; quiver.

fretin, *n.m.* young fish.
frette, *n.f.* hoop.
friand, *adj.* dainty; fond (of).
friandise, *n.f.* love of delicacies; candy.
fric, *n.m.* (colloquial) money, dough, bread.
fricoter, *vb.* cook, stew.
friction, *n.f.* friction.
frictionner, *vb.* chafe.
frigidaire, *n.m.* (trademark) refrigerator.
frigide, *adj.* frigid.
frigo, *n.m.* frozen meat; fridge.
frigorifier, *vb.* freeze; refrigerate.
frileux, *adj.* chilly; susceptible to cold.
frime, *n.f.* pretense, sham.
frimer, *vb.* put on an act.
fringant, *adj.* lively, frisky.
friper, *vb.* crush, rumple.
fripier, *n.m.* secondhand clothing dealer.
fripon, 1. *adj.* knavish. **2.** *n.m.* rascal.
friponnerie, *n.f.* roguery.
fripouille, *n.f.* rascal.
frire, *vb.* fry.
frisé, *adj.* curly.
friser, *vb.* curl.
frisoir, *n.m.* (hair) curler.
frisson, *n.m.* shudder, shiver.
frissonnement, *n.m.* shudder, shivering.
frissonner, *vb.* shudder, shiver.
frites, *n.f.pl.* French fries.

friture, *n.f.* frying.
frivole, *adj.* frivolous.
frivolité, *n.f.* frivolity.
froc, *n.m.* (monk's) frock.
froid, *adj. and n.m.* cold. **un peu f.,** chilly. **avoir f.,** be cold.
froideur, *n.f.* coldness.
froissé, *adj.* bruised. **être f. de,** resent.
froissement, *n.m.* crumpling; rustling, jostling.
froisser, *vb.* crease, wrinkle; bruise, hurt.
frôler, *vb.* graze.
fromage, *n.m.* cheese.
froment, *n.m.* wheat.
froncement, *n.m.* puckering, contraction.
froncer, *vb.* pucker. **f. les sourcils,** frown.
frondaison, *n.f.* foliage.
fronde, *n.f.* sling.
fronder, *vb.* sling; censure.
front, *n.m.* forehead.
frontière, *n.f.* boundary, border; frontier.
frottement, *n.m.* rubbing.
frotter, *vb.* rub.
frou-frou, *n.m.* rustle.
fructueux, *adj.* fruitful.
frugal, *adj.* frugal.
frugalité, *n.f.* frugality.
fruit, *n.m.* fruit.
fruiterie, *n.f.* fruit store.
fruitier, *n.m.* fruit seller.
fruste, *adj.* uncultivated.
frustrer, *vb.* frustrate.
fugace, *adj.* fleeting.

fugitif, *adj.* fugitive.
fugue, *n.f.* flight, escape.
fuir, *vb.* flee; shun; leak.
fuite, *n.f.* escape, flight; leak.
fume-cigarette, *n.m.* cigarette holder.
fumée, *n.f.* smoke.
fumer, *vb.* smoke.
fumeur, *n.m.* one who smokes.
fumeux, *adj.* smoky.
fumier, *n.m.* dung.
fumiste, *n.m.* shirker.
fumisterie, *n.f.* con.
funèbre, *adj.* funereal.
funérailles, *n.f.pl.* funeral.
funeste, *adj.* disastrous.
fureter, *vb.* pry.
fureur, *n.f.* fury.
furibond, *adj.* furious.
furie, *n.f.* fury.
furieux, *adj.* furious.
furtif, *adj.* sly.
fuseau, *n.m.* spindle.
fusée, *n.f.* rocket.
fuser, *vb.* melt; spread.
fusible, *n.m.* fuse wire.
fusil, *n.m.* rifle.
fusiller, (-zēl yā), *vb.* shoot.
fusion, *n.f.* merger; meltdown.
fusionner, *vb.* merge.
futé, *adj.* cunning, crafty.
futile, *adj.* futile.
futur, *adj. and n.m.* future.
futurologie, *n.f.* futurology.
fuyant, *adj.* passing, transitory; fugitive.
fuyard, *n.* fugitive.

G

gâcher *vb.* mess.
gâchette, *n.f.* trigger.
gâchis, *n.m.* waste.
gadoue, *n.f.* sludge.
gaffe, *n.f.* blunder.
gage, *n.m.* pledge, wage.
gageure, *n.f.* bet.
gagnant, *n.m.* winner.
gagner, *vb.* earn, gain, win, beat (in a game).
gai, *adj.* cheerful, cheery, merry, gay.
gaieté, *n.f.* mirth, cheer, merriment, gaiety.
gaillard, *adj.* hearty, sound.

gain, *n.m.* gain, profit.
gaine, *n.f.* girdle.
galant, 1. *n.m.* beau. **2.** *adj.* gallant, civil, courteous. **g. homme,** gentleman.
galanterie, *n.f.* courtesy, compliment.
galaxie, *n.f.* galaxy.
galbe, *n.m.* outline, contour.
galère, *n.f.* galley, ship.
galerie, *n.f.* gallery; balcony (theater).
galet, *n.m.* boulder.
galette, *n.f.* flat cake.

Galles, *n.f.pl.* **le pays de G.,** Wales.
Gallois, *n.m.* Welshman.
gallois, *adj. and n.m.* Welsh.
gallon, *n.m.* gallon.
galon, *n.m.* stripe, braid.
galop, *n.m.* gallop.
galoper, *vb.* gallop.
galvaudé, *adj.* worthless.
gambader, *vb.* frolic.
gamin, *n.m.* boy; urchin.
gamme, *n.f.* scale.
gangster, (-r), *n.m.* gangster.
gant, *n.m.* glove.
ganterie, *n.f.* glove shop.

garage, *n.m.* garage.

garagiste, *n.m.f.* garage keeper, car mechanic.

garant, *n.m.* sponsor.

garantie, *n.f.* guarantee, pledge.

garantir, *vb.* guarantee, pledge; warrant.

garçon, *n.m.* boy; waiter; bachelor; flight attendant.

garçonnière, *n.f.* bachelor's apartment.

garde, *n.f.* watch, guard; custody. **prendre g. à,** beware of. **avant-g.,** vanguard. **g. du corps,** bodyguard.

garde-boue, *n.m.* fender.

garde-feu, *n.m.* fender (fireplace).

garde-manger, *n.m.* pantry.

garder, *vb.* guard, keep, mind.

garderie, *n.f.* nursery, daycare center.

garde-robe, *n.f.* wardrobe.

gardeur, *n.m.* keeper.

gardien, *n.m.* keeper, guard, watchman, guardian.

gare, 1. *n.f.* station. **2.** *interj.* look out!

garer, *vb.* garage, park.

gargariser, *vb.* **se g.,** gargle.

gargarisme, *n.m.* gargle.

gargouille, *n.f.* gargoyle.

garnement, *n.m.* rascal.

garni, *adj.* furnished; garnished.

garnir, *vb.* trim, garnish.

garnison, *n.f.* garrison.

garniture, *n.f.* fittings.

gars, *n.m.* chap, guy.

gas-oil, *n.m.* diesel (oil).

gaspillage, *n.m.* waste.

gaspiller, *vb.* waste, squander.

gastronomique, *adj.* gastronomic.

gâteau, *n.m.* cake. **g. de miel,** honeycomb. **g. sec,** cookie.

gâter, *vb.* spoil.

gâterie, *n.f.* excessive indulgence.

gâteux, *adj.* senile.

gauche, *adj. and n.f.* left. **à g.,** on *or* to the left. *adj.* awkward, clumsy.

gaucher, *n.m.* left-handed person.

gaucherie, *n.f.* clumsiness.

gaufre, *n.f.* waffle.

gaule, *n.f.* pole.

gaulois, *adj.* Gallic; bawdy.

gausser, *vb.* **se g. de,** mock, banter.

gaver, *vb.* force-feed.

gaz, (-z), *n.m.* gas.

gaze, *n.f.* gauze.

gazette, *n.f.* newspaper.

gazeux, *adj.* gassy, gaseous. **boisson gazeuse,** carbonated drink.

gazoduc, *n.m.* gas pipeline.

gazon, *n.m.* turf, lawn.

gazouillement, *n.m.* warble, twitter.

géant, *n.m.* giant.

geindre, *vb.* moan, whine.

gel, *n.m.* frost; gel.

gelé, *adj.* frozen.

gelée, *n.f.* jelly; frost.

geler, *vb.* freeze.

gélule, *n.f.* capsule.

gelures, *n.f.pl.* frostbite.

gémir, *vb.* groan, wail, moan.

gémissement, *n.m.* groan, moan.

gênant, *adj.* troublesome, bothersome.

gencive, *n.f.* gum.

gendarme, *n.m.* policeman.

gendarmerie, *n.f.* police force.

gendre, *n.m.* son-in-law.

gêne, *n.f.* trouble, uneasiness. **être à la g.,** be uneasy.

gêné, *adj.* uneasy.

généalogie, *n.f.* pedigree.

gêner, *vb.* hinder, be in the way; embarrass; bother.

général, *adj. and n.m.* general, overhead *(comm.).* **quartier g.,** headquarters.

généraliser, *vb.* generalize.

généralissime, *n.m.* commander-in-chief.

généraliste, *n.m.f.* general practitioner.

généralité, *n.f.* generality.

génération, *n.f.* generation.

généreusement, *adv.* generously.

généreux, *adj.* generous, liberal.

générosité, *n.f.* generosity.

génial, *adj.* of genius, highly original; (colloquial) fantastic.

génie, *n.m.* genius; engineer corps. **soldat du g.,** engineer.

genièvre, *n.m.* gin.

génisse, *n.f.* heifer.

genou, *n.m.* knee; (*pl.*) lap.

genre, *n.m.* kind, gender.

gens, *n.m.f.pl.* people, persons, folk.

gentiane, *n.f.* gentian.

gentil, *m.,* **gentille** *f. adj.* pleasant, nice.

gentilhomme, *n.m.* nobleman; peer.

gentillesse, *n.f.* prettiness, gracefulness.

géographie, *n.f.* geography.

géographique, *adj.* geographical.

géologie, *n.f.* geology.

géométrie, *n.f.* geometry.

géométrique, *adj.* geometric.

gérance, *n.f.* managership.

géranium, *n.m.* geranium.

gérant, *n.m.* manager, director, superintendent.

gerbe, *n.f.* sheaf.

gerçure, *n.f.* chap.

gérer, *vb.* manage.

germain, *adj.* first (of cousins).

germe, *n.f.* germ.

germer, *vb.* sprout.

gésir, *vb.* lie.

geste, *n.m.* gesture.

gesticuler, *vb.* gesticulate.

gestion, *n.f.* management.

ghetto, *n.m.* ghetto.

gibier, *n.m.* game.

giboulée, *n.f.* sudden storm.

gicler, *vb.* spurt.

gifler, *vb.* slap.

gigantesque, *adj.* great, huge.

gigot, *n.m.* leg (of meat).

gigue, *n.f.* leg; jig.

gilet, *n.m.* vest. **g. de dessous,** undershirt.

gingembre, *n.m.* ginger.

girafe, *n.f.* giraffe.

girofle, *n.m.* **clou de g.,** clove.

giron, *n.m.* lap.

gisement, *n.m.* deposit.

gitan, *n.m.* gypsy.

gîte, *n.m.* lodging, bed.

givre, *n.m.* frost.

glabre, *adj.* smooth-shaven.

glaçage, *n.m.* frosting.

glace, *n.f.* ice; ice cream; mirror.

glacé, *adj.* icy, frozen.

glacer, *vb.* freeze.

glacial, *adj.* icy.

glacier, *n.m.* glacier.

glacière, *n.f.* icebox.

glacis, *n.m.* slope.

glaçon, *n.m.* block of ice; ice cube.

glaise, *n.f.* clay.

gland, *n.m.* acorn.

glande, *n.f.* gland.

glaner, *vb.* glean.

glapir, *vb.* yelp; screech.

glas, *n.m.* knell.

glissade, *n.f.* slide, slip.

glissant, *adj.* slippery.

glisser, *vb.* slide, slip. **se g.,** creep, sneak.

global, *adj.* entire.

globe, *n.m.* globe. **g. de l'œil,** eyeball.

globule, *n.m.* corpuscle.

gloire, *n.f.* glory.

glorieux, *adj.* glorious.

glorifier, *vb.* glorify.

glose, *n.f.* criticism; gloss.

glossaire, *n.m.* glossary.

glousser, *vb.* cluck.

glouton, *adj.* gluttonous.

gluant, *adj.* sticky.

goal, *n.m.* goalkeeper.

gobelet, *n.m.* goblet.

gober, *vb.* swallow.

godasse, *n.f.* (colloquial) shoe.

goéland, *n.m.* seagull.

goinfre, *n.m.* glutton.

golfe, *n.m.* gulf.

gomme, *n.f.* gum; eraser.

gommeux, *adj.* gummy.

gond, *n.m.* hinge.

gonflé, *adj.* swollen; full of nerve.

gonfler, *vb.* inflate; swell.

gonfleur, *n.m.* tire pump.

gorge, *n.f.* throat; gorge.

gorger, *vb.* cram.

gosier, *n.m.* throat.

gosse, *n.m.f.* kid (child).

gothique, *adj.* Gothic.

goudron, *n.m.* tar.

gouffre, *n.m.* gulf, abyss.

goujat, *n.m.* boor, cad.

goulu, *adj.* gluttonous.

gourde, *n.f.* flask.

gourer, *vb.* (colloquial) **se g.,** make a mistake.

gourmand, 1. *n.m.* glutton. **2.** *adj.* greedy.

gourmander, *vb.* scold.

gourmandise, *n.f.* greediness.

gourmer, *vb.* curb.

gourmet, *n.m.* epicure.

gourmette, *n.f.* curb (horse).

gourou, *n.m.* guru.

gousse, *n.f.* shell, pod.

goût, *n.m.* taste, relish.

goûter, 1. *n.m.* snack. **2.** *vb.* taste, relish.

goutte, *n.f.* drop; gout.

goutteux, *adj.* gouty.

gouttière, *n.f.* gutter.

gouvernail, *n.m.* rudder, helm.

gouvernante, *n.f.* governess.

gouvernement, *n.m.* government.

gouverner, *vb.* govern, rule, steer.

gouverneur, *n.m.* governor.

grabuge, *n.m.* squabble.

grâce, *n.f.* grace. **faire g. de,** spare.

gracier, *vb.* pardon.

gracieux, *adj.* graceful, gracious.

grade, *n.m.* grade, rank.

gradé, *n.m.* non-commissioned officer.

gradin, *n.m.* step, tier.

graduel, *adj.* gradual.

graduer, *vb.* graduate.

graffiti, *n.m.pl.* graffiti.

grain, *n.m.* grain, seed, berry, kernel. **g. de beauté,** mole.

graine, *n.f.* seed, berry.

graissage, *n.m.* greasing.

graisse, *n.f.* grease, fat.

graisser, *vb.* grease.

grammaire, *n.f.* grammar.

gramme, *n.m.* gram.

grand, *adj.* big, great, tall. **grand'chose,** much.

grandement, *adv.* grandly, greatly.

grandeur, *n.f.* size, height, greatness.

grandiose, *adj.* grand.

grandir, *vb.* grow.

grand-mère, *n.f.* grandmother.

grand-père, *n.m.* grandfather.

grange, *n.f.* barn.

granit, (-t), *n.m.* granite.

graphique, *n.m.* chart.

grappe, *n.f.* bunch, cluster.

gras, *m.,* **grasse** *f.* *adj.* fat, stout.

grassement, *adj.* plentifully.

grasset, *adj.* plump.

grassouillet, *adj.* plump.

gratification, *n.f.* bonus.

gratifier, *vb.* bestow.

gratin, *n.m.* cheese topping.

gratis, (-s), *adv.* free.

gratitude, *n.f.* gratitude.

gratte-ciel, *n.m.* skyscraper.

gratter, *vb.* scrape, scratch.

gratuit, *adj.* free.

grave, *adj.* grave.

graveleux, *adj.* gritty.

graver, *vb.* engrave.

graveur, *n.m.* engraver.

gravier, *n.m.* gravel.

gravir, *vb.* climb.

gravité, *n.f.* gravity.

graviter, *vb.* gravitate.

gravure, *n.f.* engraving. **g. à l'eau-forte,** etching.

gré, *n.m.* pleasure.

Grec, *m.,* **Grecque** *f. n.* Greek (person).

grec, *n.m.* Greek (language).

grec, *m.,* **grecque** *f. adj.* Greek.

Grèce, *n.f.* Greece.

gréement, *n.m.* rig.

gréer, *vb.* rig.

greffer, *vb.* graft, transplant.

greffier, *n.m.* clerk.

grêle, 1. *n.f.* hail. **2.** *adj.* thin, slight.

grêler, *vb.* hail.

grêlon, *n.m.* hailstone.

grelotter, *vb.* shiver.

grenade, *n.f.* grenade; pomegranate.

grenier, *n.m.* attic.

grenouille, *n.f.* frog.

grève, *n.f.* strike. **se mettre en g.,** strike.

gréviste, *n.m.f.* striker.

gribouiller, *vb.* scribble.
grief, *n.m.* grievance.
grièvement, *adv.* seriously.
griffe, *n.f.* claw, clutch.
griffer, *vb.* seize; scratch.
griffonner, *vb.* scribble.
grignoter, *vb.* nibble.
gril, *n.m.* grill.
grillade, *n.f.* broiling.
grille, *n.f.* grate, gate.
grille-pain, *n.m.* toaster.
griller, *vb.* broil, roast, toast.
grillon, *n.m.* cricket.
grimace, *n.f.* grimace.
grimacer, *vb.* make faces.
grimer, *vb.* make up.
grimper, *vb.* climb.
grincer, *vb.* creak, grate, grind.
grippe, *n.f.* flu.
gris, *adj.* gray; drab; drunk.
griser, *vb.* get drunk.
grive, *n.f.* thrush.
grogner, *vb.* growl, snarl, grumble.
grommeler, *vb.* mutter.
gronder, *vb.* scold, nag; roar, rumble.

gros, *m.,* **grosse** *f. adj.* overly large; gross, stout, rough. **en g.,** wholesale.
groseille, *n.f.* currant.
grossesse, *n.f.* pregnancy.
grosseur, *n.f.* size, thickness.
grossier, *adj.* coarse, crude, gross.
grossièreté, *n.f.* coarseness.
grossir, *vb.* magnify, grow.
grossiste, *n.m.* wholesaler.
grosso modo, *adv.* roughly.
grotesque, *adj.* grotesque.
grotte, *n.f.* cave, grotto.
grouiller, *vb.* stir, swarm.
groupe, *n.m.* group, party; cluster.
groupement, *n.m.* grouping.
grouper, *vb.* group.
grue, *n.f.* crane.
gruyère, *n.m.* Gruyère (cheese).
gué, *n.m.* ford. **traverser à g.,** wade.
guêpe, *n.f.* wasp.
guère, *adv.* hardly.
guérilla, *n.f.* guerrilla warfare.

guérir, *vb.* cure, heal.
guérison, *n.f.* cure.
guerre, *n.f.* war.
guerrier, *adj.* warlike.
guetter, *vb.* watch (for).
gueule, *n.f.* mouth, (colloquial) mouth, face.
gueuler, *vb.* bawl (out).
gueux, *n.m.* beggar, tramp.
guichet, *n.m.* ticket window.
guide, *n.m.* guide(book).
guider, *vb.* guide.
guidon, *n.m.* handlebars.
guignol, *n.m.* Punch and Judy show; puppet; clown.
guillemets, *n.m.pl.* quotation marks, inverted commas.
guillotine, *n.f.* guillotine.
guingan, *n.m.* gingham.
guirlande, *n.f.* garland.
guise, *n.f.* way, manner.
guitare, *n.f.* guitar.
gymnase, *n.m.* gymnasium.
gymnastique, *n.f.* gymnastics.
gynecologie, *n.f.* gynecology.
gynécologiste, *n.m.f.* gynecologist.

H

habile *adj.* clever, skillful, smart, able.
habileté, *n.f.* craft, ability.
habillement, *n.m.* apparel.
habillements masculins, *n.m.pl.* menswear.
habiller, *vb.* dress.
habilleur, *n.m.,* **habilleuse** *f.* dresser.
habit, *n.m.* coat; attire; (*pl.*) clothes.
habitant, *n.m.* inhabitant, resident.
habitation, *n.f.* dwelling.
habiter, *vb.* inhabit, live.
habitude, *n.f.* habit, practice. **d'h.,** customarily. **avoir l'h. de,** be accustomed to.
habitué, *n.m.* regular visitor, regular (client).
habituel, *adj.* customary, usual.
habituer, *vb.* get used to.
hâbleur, *n.m.* boaster.
hache, *n.f.* ax.

hacher, *vb.* mince, chop, hack up.
hachette, *n.f.* hatchet.
hachis, *n.m.* hash.
hagard, *adj.* haggard.
haie, *n.f.* hedge.
haillon, *n.m.* rag.
haine, *n.f.* hatred.
haineux, *adj.* hating.
haïr, *vb.* hate.
haïssable, *adj.* hateful.
halage, *n.m.* towage.
hâle, *n.m.* tan; sunburn.
haleine, *n.f.* breath.
haler, *vb.* haul, tow.
hâler, *vb.* tan. **se h.,** become sunburned.
haleter, *vb.* pant, gasp.
hall, *n.m.* hall.
halle, *n.f.* market.
hallucination, *n.f.* hallucination.
halte, *n.f.* halt.
haltère, *n.m.* dumbbell.
hamac, *n.m.* hammock.

hamburger, *n.m.* hamburger.
hameau, *n.m.* hamlet.
hameçon, *n.m.* hook.
hampe, *n.f.* handle.
hanche, *n.f.* hip.
handicap, *n.m.* handicap.
handicapé, *n.m.* handicapped (person).
hangar, *n.m.* shed.
hanter, *vb.* haunt.
hantise, *n.f.* obsession.
happer, *vb.* snap.
harcèlement, *n.m.* hassle, harassment.
harceler, *vb.* worry, bother; hassle; harass.
hardes, *n.f.pl.* togs.
hardi, *adj.,* bold.
hardiesse, *n.f.* boldness.
hareng, *n.m.* herring.
hargneux, *adj.* cross, snarling.
haricot, *n.m.* bean.
harmonie, *n.f.* harmony.

harmonieux, *adj.* harmonious.

harmoniser, *vb.* put in tune, harmonize.

harnacher, *vb.* harness.

harnais, *n.m.* harness.

harpe, *n.f.* harp.

harpin, *n.m.* boat hook.

hasard, *n.m.* chance. **au h.** or **par h.,** at random.

hasarder, *vb.* venture.

hasardeux, *adj.* hazardous, unsafe.

hâte, *n.f.* haste, hurry. **à la h.,** hastily.

hâter, *vb.* hasten, hurry.

hâtif, *adj.* early, hasty.

hausse, *n.f.* rise, increase.

haussement, *n.m.* raising; shrug.

hausser, *vb.* raise; shrug.

haussier, *n.m.* bull (stock exchange).

haut, 1. *n.m.* top. **2.** *adj.* high, loud. **à haute voix,** aloud. **en h.,** up, above.

hautain, *adj.* haughty, lofty, proud.

hautbois, *n.m.* oboe.

haute fidélité, *n.f.* high fidelity.

hautement, *adv.* highly.

hauteur, *n.f.* height; haughtiness. **être à la h. de,** be up to.

hauturier, *adj.* seagoing.

hâve, *adj.* wan, gaunt.

havre, *n.m.* haven.

havresac, *n.m.* knapsack.

hebdo, *n.m.* (colloquial) weekly.

hebdomadaire, *adj.* weekly.

héberger, *vb.* shelter.

hébété, *adj.* dull.

hébreu, 1. *n.m.* Hebrew (language). **2.** *adj.* Hebrew.

hécatombe, *n.f.* slaughter.

hectare, *n.m.* hectare.

hégémonie, *n.f.* hegemony.

hein, *interj.* huh?

hélas, (-s), *interj.* alas!

héler, *vb.* call, hail.

hélice, *n.f.* propeller.

hélicoptère, *n.m.* helicopter.

helvétique, *adj.* Swiss.

hématome, *n.m.* bruise.

hémisphère, *n.m.* hemisphere.

hémorragie, *n.f.* hemorrhage.

hennir, *vb.* neigh.

hépatite, *n.f.* hepatitis.

héraut, *n.m.* herald.

herbage, *n.m.* grass, pasture.

herbe, *n.f.* grass, herb; marijuana. **mauvaise h.,** weed.

herbeux, *adj.* grassy.

héréditaire, *adj.* hereditary.

hérésie, *n.f.* heresy.

hérétique, 1. *n.m.f.* heretic. **2.** *adj.* heretic, heretical.

hérisser, *vb.* bristle.

hérisson, *n.m.* hedgehog.

héritage, *n.m.* inheritance.

hériter, *vb.* inherit.

héritier, *n.m.* heir.

hermétique, *adj.* (sealed) tight.

hermine, *n.f.* ermine.

hernie, *n.f.* hernia.

héroïne, *n.f.* heroine; heroin (drug).

héroïque, *adj.* heroic.

héroïsme, *n.m.* heroism.

héros, *n.m.* hero.

hertz, *n.m.* hertz.

hésitation, *n.f.* hesitation.

hésiter, *vb.* hesitate, waver, falter.

hétéroclite, *adj* heterogeneous.

hétérogène, *adj.* heterogeneous.

hétérosexuel, *adj.* heterosexual.

hêtre, *n.m.* beech.

heure, *n.f.* hour; time. **de bonne h.,** early.

heureusement, *adv.* happily, luckily.

heureux, *adj.* glad, happy; lucky, fortunate; successful.

heurt, *n.m.* blow, shock.

heurter, *vb.* collide (with).

heurtoir, *n.m.* (door) knocker.

hexagone, *n.m.* hexagon. **L'h.,** France.

hibou, *n.m.* owl.

hideux, *adj.* hideous.

hier, (-r), *adv.* yesterday.

hiérarchie, *n.f.* hierarchy.

hi-fi, *adj. and n.m.* hi-fi.

hilare, *adj.* hilarious.

hilarité, *n.f.* hilarity.

Hindou, *n.m.* Hindu.

hindou, *adj.* Hindu.

hippodrome, *n.m.* race course.

hippopotame, *n.m.* hippopotamus.

hirondelle, *n.f.* swallow.

hispanique, *adj.* Hispanic.

hisser, *vb.* hoist.

histoire, *n.f.* history; story; to-do, fuss.

historien, *n.m.* historian.

historique, *adj.* historic.

hiver, (-r), *n.m.* winter.

hiverner, *vb.* **s'h.,** hibernate.

hocher, *vb.* shake, nod.

hochet, *n.m.* rattle.

hockey, *n.m.* hockey.

hoirie, *n.f.* inheritance.

hold-up, *n.m.* hold-up.

Hollandais, *n.m.* Hollander, Dutchman.

hollandais, *adj. and n.m.* Dutch.

Hollande, *n.f.* Holland; the Netherlands.

hologramme, *n.m.* hologram.

holographie, *n.f.* holography.

homard, *n.m.* lobster.

homicide, *n.m.* homicide.

hommage, *n.m.* homage.

hommasse, *adj.* mannish.

homme, *n.m.* man. **h. d'affaires,** businessman.

homogène, *adj.* of the same kind, homogeneous.

homologue, *n.m.* counterpart.

homonyme, *n.m.* namesake.

homosexuel, *adj.* homosexual.

Hongrie, *n.f.* Hungary.

Hongrois, *n.m.* Hungarian (person).

hongrois, 1. *n.m.* Hungarian (language). **2.** *adj.* Hungarian.

honnête, *adj.* honest.

honnêteté, *n.f.* honesty, fairness.

honneur, *n.m.* honor, credit.

honorable, *adj.* honorable.

honoraires, *n.m.pl.* fee.

honorer, *vb.* honor.

honorifique, *adj.* honorary.

honte, *n.f.* shame. **avoir h. de,** be ashamed of. **faire h. à.,** shame.

honteux, *adj.* ashamed; shameful.

hôpital, *n.m.* hospital.

hoquet, *n.m.* hiccup.

horaire, *n.m.* timetable.

horde, *n.f.* horde.

horizon, *n.m.* horizon.

horizontal, *adj.* horizontal.

horloge, *n.f.* clock.

horloger, *n.m.* watchmaker.

hormis, *prep.* except.

horreur, *n.f.* horror.

horrible, *adj.* horrible, ghastly.

horrifier, *vb.* horrify.

horrifique, *adj.* hair-raising.

horripiler, *vb.* annoy.

hors, *prep.* except (for).

hors-bord, *n.m.* outboard boat.

hors de, *prep.* out of, outside.

hors-taxe, *adj.* duty-free.

horticole, *adj.* horticultural.

hospice, *n.m.* refuge.

hospitalier, *adj.* hospitable.

hospitaliser, *vb.* hospitalize; shelter.

hospitalité, *n.f.* hospitality.

hostie, *n.f.* (*eccles.*) host.

hostile, *adj.* hostile.

hostilité, *n.f.* hostility.

hôte, *n.m.* host; guest.

hôtel, *n.m.* hotel; mansion. **h. de ville,** city hall.

hôtelier, *n.m.* innkeeper.

hôtesse, *n.f.* hostess.

hôtesse de l'air, *n.f.* stewardess, flight attendant.

hotte, *n.f.* basket carried on back.

houblon, *n.m.* hop (plant).

houe, *n.f.* hoe.

houer, *vb.* hoe.

houille, *n.f.* coal.

houillère, *n.f.* coal mine.

houle, *n.f.* surge.

houleux, *adj.* stormy, rough.

houppe, *n.f.* tuft; powder puff.

hourra, *n.m.* cheer.

housse, *n.f.* covering.

houx, *n.m.* holly.

hublot, *n.m.* porthole.

huer, *vb.* shout, hoot.

huile, *n.f.* oil.

huiler, *vb.* oil.

huileux, *adj.* oily.

huissier, *n.m.* usher.

huit, *adj.* and *n.m.* eight.

huitième, *adj.* and *n.m.f.* eighth.

huître, *n.f.* oyster.

humain, *adj.* human; humane.

humanitaire, *adj.* humanitarian.

humanité, *n.f.* humanity.

humble, *adj.* lowly, humble.

humecter, *vb.* moisten.

humer, *vb.* suck up, sniff up.

humeur, *n.f.* humor; mood, temper.

humide, *adj.* damp, humid.

humidité, *n.f.* moisture.

humiliation, *n.f.* humiliation.

humilier, *vb.* humiliate, humble.

humilité, *n.f.* humility.

humoristique, *adj.* humorous.

humour, *n.m.* humor.

hune, *n.f.* (*naut.*) top.

huppe, *n.f.* tuft, crest.

hurlement, *n.m.* noise, howling.

hurler, *vb.* howl, roar, yell.

hutte, *n.f.* hut, shed.

hybride, *adj.* and *n.m.* hybrid.

hydratant, *adj.* moisturizing.

hydravion, *n.m.* seaplane.

hydroélectrique, *adj.* hydroelectric.

hydrogène, *n.m.* hydrogen.

hyène, *n.f.* hyena.

hygiène, *n.f.* sanitation; hygiene.

hygiénique, *adj.* hygienic.

hymne, *n.m.* hymn; *n.f.* church hymn.

hypermarché, *n.m.* very large supermarket; hypermarket.

hypnotiser, *vb.* hypnotize.

hypocondriaque, *adj.* and *n.m.f.* hypochondriac.

hypocrisie, *n.f.* hypocrisy.

hypocrite, 1. *n.m.f.* hypocrite. **2.** *adj.* hypocritical.

hypothèque, *n.f.* mortgage.

hypothéquer, *vb.* mortgage.

hypothèse, *n.f.* hypothesis.

hystérectomie, *n.f.* hysterectomy.

hystérie, *n.f.* hysteria.

hystérique, *adj.* hysterical.

I

ici *adv.* here. **d'i.,** hence.

ictère, *n.m.* jaundice.

idéal, *adj.* and *n.m.* ideal.

idéaliser, *vb.* idealize.

idéalisme, *n.m.* idealism.

idéaliste, *n.m.f.* idealist.

idée, *n.f.* idea, notion.

identification, *n.f.* identification.

identifier, *vb.* identify.

identique, *adj.* identical.

identité, *n.f.* identity.

idéologie, *n.f.* ideology.

idiome, *n.m.* idiom.

idiot, *adj.* and *n.m.* idiot(ic).

idiotie, *n.f.* idiocy.

idiotisme, *n.m.* idiom.

idolâtrer, *vb.* idolize.

idole, *n.f.* idol.

idyllique, *adj.* idyllic.

if, *n.m.* yew.

ignare, *adj.* ignorant.

ignoble, *adj.* ignoble.

ignorance, *n.f.* ignorance.

ignorant, *adj.* ignorant.

ignorer, *vb.* not know.

il, (ēl), *pron.* he, it; (*pl.*) they.

île, *n.f.* island.

illégal, (-l-), *adj.* illegal.

illégitime, (-l-), *adj.* illegitimate.

illettré, (-l-), *adj.* illiterate.

illicite, (-l-), *adj.* illicit.

illimité, (-l-), *adj.* boundless.

illogique, (-l-), *adj.* illogical.

illuminer, (-l-), *vb.* light, illuminate.

illusion, (-l-), *n.f.* illusion; delusion.

illustration 50 FRENCH-ENGLISH

illustration, (-l-), *n.f.* illustration.

illustre, (-l-), *adj.* illustrious, famous.

illustrer, (-l-), *vb.* illustrate.

îlot, *n.m.* small island.

image, *n.f.* picture.

imaginaire, *adj.* fancied, imaginary.

imaginatif, *adj.* imaginative.

imagination, *n.f.* imagination.

imaginer, *vb.* imagine.

imam, *n.m.* imam.

imbattable, *adj.* unbeatable.

imbécile, 1. *n.m.f.* idiot. **2.** *adj.* idiotic.

imbécillité, *n.f.* imbecility; stupidity.

imberbe, *adj.* beardless.

imbiber, *vb.* soak; steep.

imbu, *adj.* imbued; steeped.

imitation, *n.f.* imitation, copy.

imiter, *vb.* imitate, copy; mimic.

immaculé, *adj.* immaculate.

immangeable, *adj.* uneatable.

immatériel, *adj.* incorporeal.

immatriculer, *vb.* matriculate.

immédiat, *adj.* immediate.

immense, *adj.* immense, great, huge.

immensité, *n.f.* immensity.

immerger, *vb.* immerse.

immeuble, *n.m.* real estate.

immigrer, *v.b.* immigrate.

imminent, *adj.* imminent.

immiscer, *vb.* **s'i.,** meddle, interfere.

immixtion, *n.f.* mixing; interference.

immobile, *adj.* motionless.

immobilier, *adj.* property.

immodéré, *adj.* immoderate.

immoler, *vb.* sacrifice. **s'i.,** sacrifice oneself.

immonde, *adj.* filthy.

immoral, *adj.* immoral.

immortaliser, *vb.* immortalize.

immortalité, *n.f.* immortality.

immortel, *adj. and n.m.* immortal.

immuable, *adj.* unchangeable.

immuniser, *vb.* immunize.

immunité, *n.f.* immunity.

impact, *n.m.* impact.

impair, *adj.* odd (number).

impalpable, *adj.* intangible.

impardonnable, *adj.* unforgivable.

imparfait, *adj. and n.m.* imperfect.

impartial, *adj.* impartial.

impasse, *n.f.* dead end.

impassible, *adj.* impassive.

impatience, *n.f.* impatience.

impatient, *adj.* impatient.

impatienter, *vb.* provoke.

impayable, *adj.* invaluable; very funny.

impeccable, *adj.* faultless.

impécunieux, *adj.* impecunious.

impénétrable, *adj.* impenetrable.

impératif, *adj. and n.m.* imperative.

impératrice, *n.f.* empress.

imperceptible, *adj.* imperceptible.

imperfection, *n.f.* imperfection.

impérial, *adj.* imperial.

impérialisme, *n.m.* imperialism.

impérieux, *adj.* domineering.

impérissable, *adj.* imperishable.

imperméabiliser, *vb.* waterproof.

imperméable, 1. *n.m.* raincoat. **2.** *adj.* waterproof.

impersonnel, *adj.* impersonal.

impertinence, *n.f.* impertinence.

impertinent, *adj.* saucy.

impétueux, *adj.* headlong, impetuous.

impie, *adj.* impious.

impitoyable, *adj.* merciless, pitiless, ruthless.

implanter, *vb.* establish; implant.

impliquer, *vb.* involve; imply.

implorer, *vb.* implore, beg.

impoli, *adj.* rude, impolite, discourteous.

impolitesse, *n.f.* discourtesy.

impopulaire, *adj.* unpopular.

importance, *n.f.* significance, importance.

important, *adj.* momentous, important.

importateur, *n.m.* importer.

importation, *n.f.* import.

importer, *vb.* matter; import.

importun, *adj.* tiresome, bothersome; importunate.

importuner, *vb.* pester, keep bothering.

importunité, *n.f.* importunity.

imposable, *adj.* taxable.

imposer, *vb.* impose; tax; enforce.

imposition, *n.f.* imposition.

impossibilité, *n.f.* impossibility. **dans l'i. de,** unable to.

impossible, *adj.* impossible.

imposteur, *n.m.* fraud (person), faker, impostor.

imposture, *n.f.* imposture, deception.

impôt, *n.m.* tax, tariff.

impotent, *adj.* weak, infirm.

impôt sur les ventes, *n.m.* sales tax.

imprécis, *adj.* imprecise.

imprégner, *vb.* impregnate, imbue.

imprenable, *adj.* impregnable.

impression, *n.f.* print, impression.

impressionnable, *adj.* sensitive, impressionable.

impressionnant, *adj.* impressive.

impressionner, *vb.* affect.

imprévisible, *adj.* unforeseeable.

imprévoyance, *n.f.* improvidence.

imprévoyant, *adj.* not foresighted.

imprévu, *adj.* unexpected, unforeseen.

imprimante, *n.f.* printer.

imprimé, *n.m.* printed matter.

imprimer, *vb.* impress; print.

imprimerie, *n.f.* printery, printing.
imprimeur, *n.m.* printer.
improbable, *adj.* improbable.
improbité, *n.f.* dishonesty.
improductif, *adj.* unproductive.
impromptu, *adv., adj. and n.m.* impromptu.
impropre, *adv.* improper, unfit.
improviste, *adv.* à l'i., all of a sudden.
imprudence, *n.f.* indiscretion.
impudence, *n.f.* impudence.
impudicité, *n.f.* lewdness.
impuissance, *n.f.* impotence.
impuissant, *adj.* impotent; powerless, helpless.
impulsif, *adj.* impulsive.
impulsion, *n.f.* impulse, spur.
impunément, *adv.* with impunity.
impunité, *n.f.* impunity.
impur, *adj.* impure.
impureté, *n.f.* impurity.
imputer, *vb.* impute.
inabordable, *adj.* inaccessible.
inaccessible, *adj.* inaccessible.
inaccoutumé, *adj.* unusual.
inachevé, *adj.* unfinished.
inactif, *adj.* inactive, indolent.
inadapté, *adj.* maladjusted.
inadmissible, *adj.* unacceptable.
inadvertance, *n.f.* oversight.
inanimé, *adj.* lifeless.
inanité, *n.f.* uselessness.
inaperçu, *adj.* unperceived.
inattaquable, *adj.* unassailable.
inattendu, *adj.* unexpected.
inaugurer, *vb.* inaugurate.
inavouable, *adj.* unavowable, shameful.
incalculable, *adj.* countless, incalculable.
incapable, *adj.* unable.
incapacité, *n.f.* incapacity.
incarcérer, *vb.* imprison.
incarnat, *adj.* flesh-colored, rosy.
incarner, *vb.* embody.

incartade, *n.f.* insult, prank.
incendie, *n.m.* fire.
incendier, *vb.* set fire to.
incertain, *adj.* uncertain.
incertitude, *n.f.* suspense.
incessamment, *adv.* incessantly; immediately.
incessant, *adj.* incessant.
inceste, *n.m.* incest.
incident, *n.m.* incident.
incinérer, *vb.* cremate; incinerate.
incisif, *adj.* incisive.
incision, *n.f.* incision.
inciter, *vb.* incite.
inclinaison, *n.f.* slope.
inclination, *n.f.* bow, nod; propensity.
incliner, *vb.* slant; nod, bow. s'i., lean.
inclure, *vb.* include, enclose.
inclus, *adj.* included. ci-inclus, enclosed, herewith.
inclusif, *adj.* inclusive.
incohérent, *adj.* incoherent.
incolore, *adj.* colorless.
incomber, *vb.* devolve upon.
incombustible, *adj.* incombustible.
incommode, *adj.* uncomfortable, inconvenient.
incommoder, *vb.* inconvenience.
incomparable, *adj.* incomparable.
incompatible, *adj.* incompatible.
incompétence, *n.f.* incompetence.
incomplet, *adj.* imperfect, unfinished.
incompréhension, *n.m.* lack of understanding.
incompris, *adj.* unappreciated, not understood.
inconditionnel, *adj.* unquestioning.
inconduite, *n.f.* misconduct.
incongru, *adj.* unseemly.
inconnu, *adj.* unknown.
inconscient, *adj. and n.m.* unconscious.
inconséquent, *adj.* inconsistent.
inconsidéré, *adj.* thoughtless.
inconsistant, *adj.* weak, inconsistent.

inconstant, *adj.* fickle.
incontestable, *adj.* unquestionable.
incontesté, *adj.* unquestioned.
incontinent, 1. *adj.* incontinent. 2. *adv.* immediately.
incontrôlable, *adj.* not verifiable.
inconvenance, *n.f.* impropriety.
inconvénient, *n.m.* inconvenience.
incorporer, *vb.* embody.
incorrect, *adj.* incorrect.
incrédule, *adj.* incredulous.
incriminer, *vb.* accuse.
incroyable, *adj.* incredible.
incroyant, *n.m.* unbeliever.
inculper, *vb.* charge, accuse.
inculquer, *vb.* instill.
inculte, *adj.* uncultivated; unkempt.
incurable, *adj.* incurable.
incurie, *n.f.* carelessness, neglect.
incursion, *n.f.* incursion.
Inde, *n.f.* India.
indécent, *adj.* indecent.
indécis, *adj.* doubtful, vague, dim.
indéfini, *adj.* indefinite.
indéfinissable, *adj.* nondescript.
indéfrisable, *n.f.* permanent wave.
indélicat, *adj.* indelicate.
indélicatesse, *n.f.* indelicacy; blunder.
indemne, *adj.* unharmed.
indemniser, *vb.* compensate for.
indemnité, *n.f.* indemnity.
indépendance, *n.f.* independence.
indépendant, *adj.* independent.
index, (-ks) *n.m.* index; forefinger.
indicateur, *n.m.* timetable; informer.
indicatif, *adj. and n.m.* indicative.
indicatif interurbain, *n.m.* area code.
indication, *n.f.* indication.
indice, *n.m.* sign, proof.

indicible, *adj.* unspeakable, inexpressible.

Indien, *n.m.* Indian.

indien, *adj.* Indian.

indifférence, *n.f.* indifference.

indifférent, *adj.* indifferent.

indigène, *n.m.f.* native.

indigent, *adj.* destitute.

indigeste, *adj.* indigestible.

indignation, *n.f.* indignation, anger.

indigne, *adj.* worthless, unworthy.

indigné, *adj.* indignant.

indigner, *vb.* anger.

indiquer, *vb.* indicate, point out.

indirect, *adj.* indirect.

indiscret, *adj.* indiscreet.

indiscutable, *adj.* indisputable.

indispensable, *adj.* indispensable, essential.

indisposer, *vb.* indispose; set against.

indisposition, *n.f.* ailment.

indistinct, *adj.* indistinct.

individu, *n.m.* individual, person.

individuel, *adj.* individual.

indomptable, *adj.* adamant; unconquerable.

indu, *adj.* undue; not ordinary.

induire, *vb.* induce; infer.

indulgence, *n.f.* indulgence.

indulgent, *adj.* lenient; indulgent.

indûment, *adv.* unduly.

industrie, *n.f.* industry.

industriel, *adj.* industrial.

inébranlable, *adj.* immovable, firm.

inédit, *adj.* unpublished.

inefficace, *adj.* ineffectual.

inégal, *adj.* uneven, unequal.

inégalité, *n.f.* inequality; irregularity.

inepte, *adj.* inept; stupid.

ineptie, *n.f.* inept action.

inépuisable, *n.f.* inexhaustible.

inertie, *n.f.* inertia.

inestimable, *adj.* priceless.

inévitable, *adj.* inevitable.

inexact, *adj.* inexact.

inexécutable, *adj.* impracticable.

inexplicable, *adj.* inexplicable.

inexprimable, *adj.* inexpressible.

infaillible, *adj.* infallible.

infâme, *adj.* infamous.

infamie, *n.f.* infamy.

infanterie, *n.f.* infantry.

infarctus, *n.f.* coronary (thrombosis).

infatigable, *adj.* untiring.

infécond, *adj.* barren, sterile.

infect, *adj.* infected; rotten.

infecter, *vb.* infect.

infection, *n.f.* infection.

inférieur, *adj. and n.m.* inferior, low(er).

infériorité, *n.f.* inferiority.

infernal, *adj.* infernal.

infester, *vb.* infest.

infidèle, *adj.* disloyal, unfaithful, false.

infidélité, *n.f.* infidelity.

infime, *adj.* lowest; tiny.

infini, *adj. and n.m.* infinite.

infinité, *n.f.* infinity.

infinitif, *n.m.* infinitive.

infirme, *adj. and n.m.f.* invalid.

infirmer, *vb.* invalidate; weaken.

infirmière, *n.f.* nurse.

infirmité, *n.f.* infirmity.

inflammation, *n.f.* inflammation.

inflation, *n.f.* inflation.

infliger, *vb.* inflict.

influence, *n.f.* influence.

influent, *adj.* influential.

information, *n.f.* inquiry; (*pl.*) news.

informatique, *n.f.* computer science.

informatiser, *vb.* computerize.

informe, *adj.* shapeless.

informer, *vb.* inform. **i. de,** acquaint with.

infraction, *n.f.* breach.

infructueux, *adj.* fruitless.

infuser, *vb.* infuse. **faire i.,** brew.

ingambe, *adj.* nimble.

ingénieur, *n.m.* engineer.

ingénieux, *adj.* ingenious.

ingéniosité, *n.f.* ingenuity.

ingénu, *adj.* naive; ingenuous.

ingrat, *adj.* ungrateful.

ingrédient, *n.m.* ingredient.

inguérissable, *adj.* incurable.

inhabile, *adj.* awkward; incapable.

inhabituel, *adj.* unusual.

inhalation, *n.f.* inhalation.

inhiber, *vb.* inhibit.

inhospitalier, *adj.* inhospitable.

inhumain, *adj.* cruel, inhuman.

inimitié, *n.f.* enmity.

inique, *adj.* unfair.

initial, *adj.* initial.

initiale, *n.f.* initial.

initialiser, *vb.* format.

initiative, *n.f.* initiative.

initier, *vb.* initiate.

injecté, *adj.* **i. de sang,** bloodshot.

injecter, *vb.* inject.

injection, *n.f.* injection.

injonction, *n.f.* injunction.

injures, *n.f.pl.* abuse.

injurier, *vb.* abuse; insult.

injurieux, *adj.* abusive; insulting, offensive.

injuste, *adj.* unfair.

injustice, *n.f.* injustice.

inlassable, *adj.* untiring.

inné, *adj.* innate.

innocence, *n.f.* innocence.

innocent, *adj.* innocent.

innocenter, *vb.* declare innocent.

innombrable, *adj.* countless.

innovation, *n.f.* innovation.

inoccupé, *adj.* idle; unoccupied.

inoculer, *vb.* inoculate.

inodore, *adj.* odorless.

inoffensif, *adj.* innocuous, harmless.

inondation, *n.f.* flood.

inonder, *vb.* flood.

inopiné, *adj.* unexpected.

inoubliable, *adj.* unforgettable.

inouï, *adj.* unheard-of.

inox(ydable), *adj.* stainless.

inquiet, *adj.* restless, anxious, uneasy.

inquiéter, *vb.* trouble. **s'i.,** worry.

inquiétude, *n.f.* misgiving, worry.

insaisissable, *adj.* imperceptible.

insalubre, *adj.* unhealthy.

inscription, *n.f.* incription, entry.

inscrire, *vb.* inscribe; enter.

insecte, *n.m.* bug, insect.

insensé, *adj.* mad.

insensible, *adj.* insensible, unfeeling.

inséparable, *adj.* inseparable.

insérer, *vb.* insert.

insigne, *n.m.* badge, sign.

insignifiant, *adj.* petty, insignificant.

insinuer, *vb.* hint.

insipide, *adj.* tasteless; dull.

insistance, *n.f.* insistence.

insister, *vb.* insist.

insolation, *n.f.* sunstroke.

insolence, *n.f.* insolence.

insolite, *adj.* unusual.

insomnie, *n.f.* insomnia.

insondable, *adj.* bottomless.

insouciant, *adj.* casual, careless.

insoumis, *adj.* rebellious.

inspecter, *vb.* examine, survey.

inspecteur, *n.m.* inspector.

inspection, *n.f.* inspection.

inspiration, *n.f.* inspiration.

inspirer, *vb.* inspire.

instable, *adj.* temperamental; unsteady, unstable.

installer, *vb.* install.

instamment, *adv.* urgently.

instance, *n.f.* entreaty; instance; authority.

instant, *n.m.* instant. **à l'i.,** at once.

instantané, 1. *n.m.* snapshot. **2.** *adj.* instantaneous.

instinct, *n.m.* instinct.

instinctif, *adj.* instinctive.

instituer, *vb.* institute.

institut, *n.m.* institute.

instituteur, *n.m.* teacher.

institution, *n.f.* institution, institute.

institutrice, *n.f.* teacher.

instructeur, *n.m.* teacher.

instructif, *adj.* instructive.

instruction, *n.f.* education, instruction; (*pl.*) directions.

instruire, *vb.* educate, teach, intruct.

instrument, *n.m.* instrument.

instrumentation, *n.f.* orchestration.

insu, *n.m.* **à l'i. de,** unknown to.

insuccès, *n.m.* failure.

insuffisance, *n.f.* deficiency.

insuffisant, *adj.* deficient.

insulaire, 1. *n.m.* islander. **2.** *adj.* insular.

insuline, *n.f.* insulin.

insulte, *n.f.* affront, insult.

insulter, *vb.* affront, insult.

insurgé, *adj. and n.m.* insurgent.

insurger, *vb.* **s'i.,** revolt.

insurmontable, *adj.* insuperable.

intact, (-kt), *adj.* intact.

intarissable, *adj.* inexhaustible.

intègre, *adj.* upright.

intégrisme, *n.m.* fundamentalism.

intégrité, *n.f.* integrity.

intellect, *n.m.* intellect.

intellectuel, *adj. and n.m.* intellectual.

intelligence, *n.f.* intelligence.

intelligent, *adj.* intelligent.

intelligible, *adj.* intelligible; audible.

intempérie, *n.f.* inclemency (of weather).

intempestif, *adj.* untimely.

intenable, *adj.* unbearable.

intendance, *n.f.* administration.

intendant, *n.m.* director.

intendante, *n.f.* matron.

intense, *adj.* intense.

intensif, *adj.* intensive.

intensité, *n.f.* intensity.

intention, *n.f.* intention.

intentionné, *adj.* intentioned.

intentionnel, *adj.* intentional.

interactif, *adj.* interactive.

intercéder, *vb.* intercede.

intercepter, *vb.* intercept.

interdiction, *n.f.* ban.

interdire, *vb.* forbid.

intéressant, *adj.* interesting.

intéresser, *vb.* interest, concern, affect.

intérêt, *n.m.* interest.

intérieur, *adj. and n.m.* interior.

interjection, *n.f.* interjection.

interlocuteur, *n.m.* speaker; person one is speaking to.

interloquer, *vb.* embarrass.

intermède, *n.m.* interlude.

intermédiaire, 1. *adj.* intermediate. **2.** *n.m.f.* intermediary.

interminable, *adj.* interminable.

internat, *n.m.* boarding school.

international, *adj.* international.

interne, 1. *adj.* internal. **2.** *n.m.f.* resident student.

interner, *vb.* intern.

interpellation, *n.f.* questioning.

interpeller, *vb.* ask.

interphone, *n.m.* intercom.

interposer, *vb.* interpose.

interprétation, *n.f.* interpretation.

interprète, *n.m.f.* interpreter.

interpréter, *vb.* interpret.

interrogateur, 1. *n.m.* examiner. **2.** *adj.* questioning.

interrogation, *n.f.* interrogation.

interrogatoire, *n.m.* cross-examination.

interroger, *vb.* question.

interrompre, *vb.* interrupt.

interrupteur, *n.m.* switch.

interruption, *n.f.* break, intermission, interruption.

interurbain, *n.m.* long-distance telephone service.

intervalle, *n.m.* interval.

intervenir, *vb.* interfere.

intervention, *n.f.* interference.

intervertir, *vb.* transpose.

interview, *n.m. or f.* interview.

interviewer, *vb.* interview.

intestin, *n.m.* bowels.

intimation, *n.f.* notification.

intime, *adj.* intimate.

intimer, *vb.* notify.

intimider, *vb.* daunt, intimidate.

intimité, *n.f.* intimacy.
intituler, *vb.* entitle.
intolérance, *n.f.* intolerance.
intonation, *n.f.* intonation.
intoxication, *n.f.* poisoning.
intoxiquer, *vb.* poison; brainwash.
intraitable, *adj.* intractable, difficult to deal with.
intrépide, *adj.* fearless.
intrigant, 1. *adj.* intriguing. 2. *n.m.* schemer.
intrigue, *n.f.* plot, intrigue.
intriguer, *vb.* intrigue; puzzle.
intrinsèque, *adj.* intrinsic.
introduction, *n.f.* introduction.
introduire, *vb.* introduce, insert.
introuvable, *adj.* unfindable.
intrus, *n.m.* intruder.
introverti, *n.m.* introvert.
intrusion, *n.f.* intrusion; trespass.
intuitif, *adj.* intuitive.
intuition, *n.f.* intuition.
inusité, *adj.* unusual.
inutile, *adj.* useless, needless.
invalide, 1. *n.m.f.* invalid. 2. *adj.* disabled, invalid.
invalider, *vb.* invalidate.
invasion, *n.f.* invasion.
invectiver, *vb.* abuse, revile.
inventaire, *n.m.* inventory.
inventer, *vb.* invent.
inventeur, *n.m.* inventor.
invention, *n.f.* invention.

inventorier, *vb.* inventory, catalogue.
inverse, *adj.* inverted, inverse.
investigateur, 1. *adj.* searching. 2. *n.m.* investigator.
investigation, *n.f.* investigation, inquiry.
investir, *vb.* invest.
invétéré, *adj.* inveterate.
invincible, *adj.* invincible.
invisible, *adj.* invisible.
invitation, *n.f.* invitation.
invité, *n.m.* guest.
inviter, *vb.* invite, ask.
involontaire, *adj.* involuntary.
invoquer, *vb.* call upon.
invraisemblable, *adj.* improbable.
iode, *n.m.* iodine.
Irak, *n.m.* Iraq.
Iran, *n.m.* Iran.
iris, (-s), *n.m.* iris.
irisé, *adj.* iridescent.
Irlandais, *n.m.* Irishman.
irlandais, *adj.* Irish.
Irlande, *n.f.* Ireland.
ironie, *n.f.* irony.
ironique, *adj.* ironical.
irradier, *vb.* radiate.
irraisonnable, *adj.* irrational.
irrationnel, *adj.* irrational.
irréel, *adj.* unreal.
irréfléchi, *adj.* thoughtless, rash.
irrégulier, *adj.* irregular.
irréligieux, *adj.* irreligious.
irrésistible, *adj.* irresistible.

irrésolu, *adj.* irresolute.
irrespectueux, *adj.* disrespectful.
irrévérence, *n.f.* disrespect.
irrigation, *n.f.* irrigation.
irriguer, *vb.* irrigate.
irritation, *n.f.* irritation.
irriter, *vb.* irritate, anger; provoke.
Islam, *n.m.* Islam.
islamique, *adj.* Islamic.
Islande, *n.f.* Iceland.
isolateur, *adj.* insulating.
isolement, *n.m.* isolation.
isoler, *vb.* isolate.
isoloire, *n.m.* polling booth.
Israël, *n.m.* Israel.
Israélien, *n.m.* Israeli.
israélien, *adj.* Israeli.
Israélite, *n.m.* Jew.
israélite, *adj.* Jewish.
issue, *n.f.* issue, outlet; outcome.
isthme, *n.m.* isthmus.
Italie, *n.f.* Italy.
Italien, *n.m.* Italian (person).
italien, 1. *n.m.* Italian (language). 2. *adj.* Italian.
italique, 1. *n.m.* italics. 2. *adj.* italic.
itinéraire, *n.m.* route, itinerary.
ivoire, *n.m.* ivory.
ivre, *adj.* drunk, intoxicated.
ivresse, *n.f.* drunkenness, intoxication.
ivrogne, *n.m.f.* drunkard.
ivrognerie, *n.f.* drunkenness.

J ⚥

jaboter *vb.* prattle.
jacasser, *vb.* chatter.
jachère, *n.f.* fallow.
jacinthe, *n.f.* hyacinth.
jadis, (-s), *adv.* formerly.
jaillir, *vb.* gush, spurt.
jaillissement, *n.m.* gush, spurt.
jais, *n.m.* jet (mineral).
jalon, *n.m.* staff; landmark.
jalonner, *vb.* mark out.
jalouser, *vb.* envy.
jalousie, *n.f.* jealousy.
jaloux, *adj.* jealous.
jamais, *adv.* ever; never.

jambe, *n.f.* leg.
jambière, *n.f.* legging.
jambon, *n.m.* ham.
jante, *n.f.* rim.
janvier, *n.m.* January.
Japon, *n.m.* Japan.
Japonais, *n.m.* Japanese (person).
japonais, 1. *n.m.* Japanese (language). 2. *adj.* Japanese.
japper, *vb.* yelp.
jaquette, *n.f.* jacket.
jardin, *n.m.* garden.
jardinage, *n.m.* gardening.

jardinier, *n.m.* gardener.
jargon, *n.m.* jargon.
jarre, *n.f.* jar.
jarretière, *n.f.* garter.
jaser, *vb.* jabber.
jasmin, *n.m.* jasmine.
jatte, *n.f.* bowl.
jaunâtre, *adj.* yellowish.
jaune, 1. *adj.* yellow. 2. *n.m.* yolk (of egg).
jaunir, *vb.* turn yellow.
jaunisse, *n.f.* jaundice.
jazz, *n.m.* jazz.
je, (jə), *pron.* I.
jeans, *n.m.pl.* jeans.

jésuite, *n.m.* Jesuit.
jet, *n.m.* jet (water, gas).
jetable, *adj.* disposable.
jetée, *n.f.* pier.
jeter, *vb.* throw.
jeton, *n.m.* token.
jeu, *n.m.* play, game. **mettre en j.,** stake.
jeudi, *n.m.* Thursday.
jeune, *adj.* young, youthful.
jeûne, *n.m.* fast.
jeûner, *vb.* fast.
jeunesse, *n.f.* youth.
joaillerie, *n.f.* jewelry.
joaillier, *n.m.* jeweler.
job, *n.m.* (colloquial) job.
jobard, *n.m.* fool.
joie, *n.f.* joy.
joindre, *vb.* join.
joint, *n.m.* joint.
jointure, *n.f.* joint (esp. of the body).
joli, *adj.* pretty.
joliment, *adv.* prettily; awfully.
jonc, *n.m.* rush (plant).
joncher, *vb.* scatter.
jonction, *n.f.* junction.
jongler, *vb.* juggle.
jongleur, *n.m.* juggler.
jonquille, *n.f.* jonquil.
Jordanie, *n.f.* Jordan.
joue, *n.f.* cheek.
jouer, *vb.* play.
jouet, *n.m.* toy.
joueur, *n.m.* player.
joufflu, *adj.* chubby-cheeked, chubby.

joug, (-g), *n.m.* yoke.
jouir, *vb.* enjoy.
jouissance, *n.f.* enjoyment.
jouisseur, *n.m.* pleasure-seeker.
jour, *n.m.* day, daylight. **j. de fête,** holiday. **point du j.,** dawn.
journal, *n.m.* newspaper, journal; diary.
journalier, *adj.* daily.
journalisme, *n.m.* journalism.
journaliste, *n.m.f.* journalist.
journée, *n.f.* day.
journellement, *adv.* daily.
joute, *n.f.* joust.
jovialité, *n.f.* jollity.
joyau, *n.m.* jewel.
joyeux, *adj.* joyful.
jubilé, *n.m.* jubilee.
jubiler, *vb.* exult.
judaïsme, *n.m.* Judaism.
judas, *n.m.* peephole.
judiciare, *adj.* judicial; legal.
judicieux, *adj.* wise; judicious.
juge, *n.m.* judge.
jugement, *n.m.* judgment, reason. **mettre en j.,** try.
juger, *vb.* judge.
jugulaire, *adj.* jugular.
Juif, *m.,* Juive *f. n.* Jew.
juif, *m.,* juive *f. adj.* Jewish.
juillet, *n.m.* July.
juin, *n.m.* June.

jules, *n.m.* (colloquial) guy.
jumeau, *m.,* jumelle *f. adj. and n.* twin.
jumeler, *vb.* couple, join.
jumelles, *n.f.pl.* opera glasses.
jument, *n.f.* mare.
jungle, *n.f.* jungle.
jupe, *n.f.* skirt.
jupon, *n.m.* petticoat.
jurer, *vb.* swear.
juridiction, *n.f.* jurisdiction.
juridique, *adj.* judicial, legal.
jurisconsulte, *n.m.f.* jurist; lawyer.
jurisprudence, *n.f.* jurisprudence.
juriste, *n.m.f.* jurist.
juron, *n.m.* oath.
jury, *n.m.* jury.
jus, *n.m.* juice; gravy.
jusque, *prep.* up to. **jusqu'à,** as far as; until. **jusqu'ici,** hitherto.
juste, **1.** *adj.* just, fair, right. **2.** *adv.* just.
justement, *adv.* precisely, exactly.
justesse, *n.f.* accuracy, precision.
justice, *n.f.* justice, fairness.
justifiant, *adj.* justifying.
justification, *n.f.* justification.
justifier, *vb.* justify.
juteux, *adj.* juicy.
juvénile, *adj.* juvenile.

K

kaki *adj.* khaki.
kangourou, *n.m.* kangaroo.
karaté, *n.m.* karate.
kasher, *adj.* kosher.
képi, *n.m.* cap.
kermesse, *n.f.* fair.
kidnapper, *vb.* kidnap.

kif, *n.m.* marijuana.
kilogramme, *n.m.* kilogram.
kilohertz, *n.m.* kilohertz.
kilométrage, *n.m.* mileage.
kilomètre, *n.m.* kilometer.
kilométrique, *adj.* kilometric.

kinésithérapeute, *n.m.f.* physiotherapist.
kiosque, *n.m.* kiosk; newsstand; bandstand.
klaxon, *n.m.* car horn.
kyrielle, *n.f.* litany.
kyste, *n.m.* cyst.

L

la *pron.* her; it *(f.)*.

là, *adv.* there.

là-bas, *adv.* yonder, out there.

labeur, *n.m.* labor.

labo, *n.m.* (colloquial) lab.

laboratoire, *n.m.* laboratory.

laborieux, *adj.* industrious, laborious.

labour, *n.m.* plowing.

labourer, *vb.* plow.

labyrinthe, *n.m.* maze.

lac, *n.m.* lake.

lacérer, *vb.* lacerate; tear up.

lacet, *n.m.* shoelace; winding.

lâche, 1. *n.m.f.* coward. **2.** *adj.* cowardly; loose.

lâchement, *adv.* loosely; shamefully.

lâcher, *vb.* loosen; let go. **l. pied,** give ground, flee.

lâcheté, *n.f.* cowardice.

lacis, *n.m.* network.

laconique, *adj.* laconic.

lacrymogène, *adj.* **gaz l.,** tear gas.

lacté, *adj.* milky.

lacune, *n.f.* gap, blank.

ladre, *adj.* stingy, mean.

lagune, *n.f.* lagoon.

laid, *adj.* ugly.

laideron, *n.m.* ugly person.

laideur, *n.f.* ugliness.

lainage, *n.m.* woolen goods.

laine, *n.f.* wool.

laineux, *adj.* woolly; downy.

laïque, (lä ēk,) *n.m.* layman.

laisse, *n.f.* leash.

laisser, *vb.* let; leave.

laisser-aller, *n.m.* freedom; negligence.

laissez-passer, *n.m.* pass.

lait, *n.m.* milk.

laitage, *n.m.* dairy foods.

laiterie, *n.f.* dairy.

laiteux, *adj.* milky.

laitier, *n.m.* milkman.

laiton, *n.m.* brass.

laitue, *n.f.* lettuce.

lambeau, *n.m.* rag.

lambin, *adj.* slow, dawdling.

lame, *n.f.* blade.

lamé, *adj.* gold- or silver-trimmed.

lamelle, *n.f.* (microscope) slide.

lamentable, *adj.* sad, grievous.

lamentation, *n.f.* lamentation.

lamenter, *vb.* mourn, lament.

laminer, *vb.* laminate.

lampadaire, *n.m.* lamp; street lamp.

lampe, *n.f.* lamp. **l. de poche,** flashlight.

lamper, *vb.* drink, gulp.

lampion, *n.m.* Chinese lantern.

lampiste, *n.m.* lamplighter.

lance, *n.f.* lance.

lancer, *vb.* hurl; launch.

lanceur, *n.m.* pitcher.

lancinant, *adj.* throbbing (of pain).

lande, *n.f.* wasteland; moor.

landeau, *n.m.* baby carriage.

langage, *n.m.* language.

langoureux, *adj.* languishing.

langouste, *n.f.* crayfish, crawfish.

langue, *n.f.* tongue; language.

languette, *n.f.* tonguelike strip.

langueur, *n.f.* languor.

languir, *vb.* pine, languish.

languissant, *adj.* languid.

lanière, *n.f.* strap, thong.

lanterne, *n.f.* lantern.

lapider, *vb.* stone; abuse.

lapin, *n.m.* rabbit.

laps, *n.m.* lapse of time.

lapsus, (-SYS), *n.m.* slip.

laquais, *n.m.* footman, lackey.

laque, *n.f.* shellac; hairspray.

larcin, *n.m.* larceny, theft.

lard, *n.m.* bacon, fat.

larder, *vb.* lard; pierce.

large, *adj.* wide.

largesse, *n.f.* generosity.

largeur, *n.f.* width.

larguer, *vb.* drop, let go.

larme, *n.f.* tear.

larmoyer, *vb.* weep, whimper.

larron, *n.m.* thief.

laryngite, *n.f.* laryngitis.

las, *adj.* weary.

lascif, *adj.* lewd, wanton.

laser, *n.m.* laser.

lasser, *vb.* weary.

lassitude, *n.f.* weariness.

latéral, *adj.* lateral.

Latin, *n.m.* Latin (person).

latin, 1. *n.m.* Latin (language). **2.** *adj.* Latin.

latitude, *n.f.* latitude.

latte, *n.f.* lath.

laurier, *n.m.* bay, laurel.

lavabo, *n.m.* lavatory.

lavage, *n.m.* washing.

lavande, *n.f.* lavender.

lavandière, *n.f.* laundress.

lavement, *n.m.* enema.

laver, *vb.* wash.

lavette, *n.f.* dishrag.

laxatif, *n.m.* laxative.

le, (lǝ) *m.,* **la** *f.,* **les** *pl.* **1.** *art.* the. **2.** *pron.* him, her, it.

lécher, *vb.* lick.

lèche-vitrines, *n.m.* window shopping.

leçon, *n.f.* lesson.

lecteur, *n.m.* reader.

lecture, *n.f.* reading.

légal, *adj.* lawful, legal.

légaliser, *vb.* legalize.

légalité, *n.f.* legality.

légataire, *n.m.* legatee.

légation, *n.f.* legation.

légendaire, *adj.* legendary.

légende, *n.f.* legend; inscription.

léger, *adj.* light.

légèreté, *n.f.* lightness.

légion, *n.f.* legion.

législateur, *n.m.* legislator.

législatif, *adj.* legislative.

législation, *n.f.* legislation.

législature, *n.f.* legislature.

légitime, *adj.* legitimate, lawful.

legs, *n.m.* bequest.

léguer, *vb.* bequeath.

légume, *n.m.* vegetable.

lendemain, *n.m.* the next day.

lent, *adj.* slow.

lenteur, *n.f.* slowness.

lentille, *n.f.* lentil; lens.

léopard, *n.m.* leopard.

lèpre, *n.f.* leprosy.

lépreux, 1. *adj.* leprous. 2. *n.m.* leper.

lequel, *pron.* which, who.

les, *pron.* them.

lesbien, *adj.* lesbian.

lesbienne, *n.f.* lesbian.

léser, *vb.* wrong, hurt.

lésine, *n.f.* stinginess.

lésion, *n.f.* wrong; lesion.

lessive, *n.f.* laundry.

lessiveuse, *n.f.* washing machine.

lest, (-t), *n.m.* ballast.

leste, *adj.* nimble, clever.

lettre, *n.f.* letter.

lettré, *adj.* lettered, literate.

leucémie, *n.f.* leukemia.

leur, 1. *pron.* to them; le leur, la leur, theirs. 2. leur *m.f.*, leurs *pl. adj.* their.

leurre, *n.m.* lure, trap.

leurrer, *vb.* lure.

levain, *n.m.* yeast; leaven.

levée, *n.f.* embankment, levee.

lever, *vb.* raise. se l., get up.

levier, *n.m.* lever.

lèvre, *n.f.* lip.

lévrier, *n.m.* greyhound.

lexique, *n.m.* lexicon.

lézard, *n.m.* lizard.

lézarde, *n.f.* crevice.

liaison, *n.f.* connection, linkage.

liant, *adj.* supple; affable.

liasse, *n.f.* file; wad.

Liban, *n.m.* Lebanon.

libelle, *n.m.* libel.

libeller, *vb.* draw up, word.

libéral, *adj.* liberal.

libérateur, *n.m.* rescuer.

libérer, *vb.* free.

liberté, *n.f.* freedom, liberty.

libertin, 1. *adj.* wanton. 2. *n.* libertine.

libraire, *n.m.* bookseller.

librairie, *n.f.* bookstore.

libre, *adj.* free.

libre-échange, *n.m.* free trade.

Libye, *n.f.* Libya.

licence, *n.f.* license.

licencié, *n.m.* licensee; holder of university degree.

licencier, *v.b.* dismiss, lay off.

licencieux, *adj.* licentious.

licite, *adj.* lawful.

licorne, *n.f.* unicorn.

licou, *n.m.* halter.

lie, *n.f.* dreg.

liège, *n.m.* cork.

lien, *n.m.* bond, link, tie.

lier, *vb.* bind, tie, link.

lierre, *n.m.* ivy.

lieu, *n.m.* place. au l. de, instead of.

lieu-commun, *n.m.* commonplace.

lieue, *n.f.* league (distance).

lieutenant, *n.m.* lieutenant.

lièvre, *n.m.* hare.

ligne, *n.f.* line.

lignée, *n.f.* offspring.

ligoter, *vb.* bind up.

ligue, *n.f.* league.

liguer, *vb.* league.

lilas, *n.m.* lilac.

limaçon, *n.m.* snail.

lime, *n.f.* file; lime (fruit).

limer, *vb.* file.

limier, *n.m.* bloodhound.

limitation, *n.f.* limitation.

limitation des naissances, *n.f.* birth control, contraception.

limite, *n.f.* limit, border.

limiter, *vb.* limit, confine.

limoger, *vb.* dismiss.

limon, *n.m.* mud, slime.

limonade, *n.f.* lemon soda.

limoneux, *adj.* muddy.

limpide, *adj.* clear, limpid.

lin, *n.m.* flax.

linceul, *n.m.* shroud.

linéaire, *adj.* lineal.

linge, *n.m.* linen; wash.

lingerie, *n.f.* linen goods; underwear.

linguistique, *adj.* linguistic.

linon, *n.m.* lawn (sheer linen).

linteau, *n.m.* lintel.

lion, *n.m.* lion.

lippu, *adj.* thick-lipped.

liqueur, *n.m.* liquid; liqueur.

liquidation, *n.f.* liquidation; settling.

liquide, *adj. and n.m.* liquid, fluid.

liquider, *vb.* liquidate.

liquoreux, *adj.* sweet.

lire, *vb.* read.

lis, (-s), *n.m.* lily.

liséré, *n.m.* piping, border.

liseur, *n.m.* reader.

liseuse, *n.f.* bookmark.

lisible, *adj.* legible.

lisière, *n.f.* edge.

lisse, *adj.* smooth.

lisser, *vb.* smooth.

liste, *n.f.* list, roll.

lit, *n.m.* bed.

litanie, *n.f.* litany.

lit-cage, *n.m.* (folding) cot.

lit de la mer, *n.m.* seabed.

literie, *n.f.* bedding.

litière, *n.f.* litter.

litige, *n.m.* litigation.

litigieux, *adj.* litigious.

litre, *n.m.* liter.

littéraire, *adj.* literary.

littéral, *adj.* literal.

littérature, *n.f.* literature.

littoral, *n.m.* coast.

liturgie, *n.f.* liturgy.

livide, *adj.* livid.

livraison, *n.f.* delivery. l. contre remboursement, C.O.D.

livre, *n.f.* pound.

livre, *n.m.* book.

livre de poche, *n.m.* paperback.

livrée, *n.f.* livery.

livrer, *vb.* deliver.

livresque, *adj.* bookish, from books.

livreur, *n.m.* delivery man.

local, *adj.* local.

localiser, *vb.* locate.

localité, *n.f.* locality.

locataire, *n.m.f.* tenant.

location, *n.f.* renting.

loch, (-k), *n.m.* log.

locomotive, *n.f.* locomotive.

locuste, *n.f.* locust.

locution, *n.f.* locution, phrase.

loge, *n.f.* box.

logement, *n.m.* lodging.

loger, *vb.* lodge.

logiciel, *n.m.* software.

logique, 1. *n.f.* logic. 2. *adj.* logical.

logis, *n.m.* dwelling.

loi, *n.f.* law.

loin, *adv.* far, away.

lointain, *adj.* distant.

loir, *n.m.* dormouse.

loisible, *adj.* optional, allowable.

loisir, *n.m.* leisure.
Londres, *n.m.* London.
long, *m.,* **longue** *f. adj.* long.
longe, *n.f.* leash; loin (of veal).
longer, *vb.* go along.
longeron, *n.m.* beam, girder.
longitude, *n.f.* longitude.
longtemps, *adv.* long.
longueur, *n.f.* length.
look, *n.m.* (colloquial) look, image.
lopin, *n.m.* small piece, plot.
loquace, *adj.* talkative.
loque, *n.f.* morsel, rag.
loquet, *n.m.* latch.
loqueteux, *adj.* tattered.
lorgner, *vb.* glance at; ogle.
lorgnon, *n.m.* glasses.
loriot, *n.m.* oriole.
lors, *adv.* then. **l. de,** at the time of.
lorsque, *conj.* when.
losange, *n.m.* diamond, lozenge.
lot, *n.m.* lot, prize.
loterie, *n.f.* raffle, lottery.
lotion, *n.f.* lotion.
lotir, *vb.* divide, apportion.
loto, *n.m.* lotto, lottery.
louable, *adj.* praiseworthy.
louage, *n.m.* hire.
louange, *n.f.* praise.

louche, *adj.* shady.
loucher, *vb.* squint.
louer, *vb.* praise; hire, rent.
loueur, *n.m.* one who rents.
loup, *n.m.* wolf.
loupe, *n.f.* magnifying glass.
louper, *vb.* (colloquial) spoil, botch.
loup-garou, *n.m.* werewolf.
lourd, *adj.* heavy.
lourdaud, *n.m.* clod.
lourdeur, *n.f.* heaviness; dullness.
lorve, *n.f.* she-wolf.
loyal, *adj.* loyal.
loyauté, *n.f.* loyalty.
loyer, *n.m.* rent.
lubricité, *n.f.* lewdness.
lubrifier, *vb.* lubricate.
lucarne, *n.f.* attic window.
lucide, *adj.* lucid.
lucidité, *n.f.* clearness.
luciole, *n.f.* firefly.
lueur, *n.f.* gleam.
luge, *n.f.* sled.
lugubre, *adj.* doleful, dismal, lugubrious.
lui, *pron.* he; to him, to her.
lui-même, *pron.* himself, itself.
luire, *vb.* gleam.
luisant, *adj.* shiny.
lumière, *n.f.* light.
lumineux, *adj.* luminous.

lunaire, *adj.* lunar.
lunatique, *adj.* whimsical.
lunch, *n.m.* buffet lunch.
lundi, *n.m.* Monday.
lune, *n.f.* moon. **l. de miel,** honeymoon. **clair de l.,** moonlight.
lunetier, *n.m.* optician.
lunettes, *n.f.pl.* glasses.
lustre, *n.m.* chandelier; luster; five-year period.
lustrer, *vb.* polish, gloss.
luth, *n.m.* lute.
lutiner, *vb.* tease.
lutte, *n.f.* strife, struggle, contest.
lutter, *vb.* struggle, contend.
luxe, *n.m.* luxury.
Luxembourg, *n.m.* Luxembourg.
luxer, *vb.* dislocate.
luxueux, *adj.* luxurious.
luxure, *n.f.* lust.
luzerne, *n.f.* alfalfa.
lycée, *n.m.* high school.
lycéen, *n.m.* high-school student.
lymphatique, *adj.* lymphatic.
lynchage, *n.m.* lynching.
lyncher, *vb.* lynch.
lyre, *n.f.* lyre.
lyrique, *adj.* lyric.
lys, *n.m.* lily.

M

M. (abbr. for **Monsieur**), *n.m.* Mr.
macabre, *adj.* macabre, ghastly.
macadam, *n.m.* macadam.
macédoine, *n.f.* salad; mixture.
macérer, *vb.* macerate, soak.
mâcher, *vb.* chew.
machin, *n.m.* thing, gadget.
machinal, *adj.* mechanical.
machination, *n.f.* plot, scheme.
machine, *n.f.* machine. **m. à copier,** copier. **m. à écrire,** typewriter.
machiner, *vb.* plot.
machiniste, *n.m.f.* machinist.
macho, *n.m.* (colloquial) macho.

mâchoire, *n.f.* jaw.
mâchonner, *vb.* mumble; munch.
maçon, *n.m.* mason.
maculer, *vb.* spot, blot.
Madame, *n.f.* Madam, Mrs.
madeleine, *n.f.* light cake.
Mademoiselle, *n.f.* Miss.
Madone, *n.f.* Madonna.
mafia, *n.f.* mafia.
magasin, *n.m.* store.
magazine, *n.m.* magazine.
mages, *n.m.pl.* Magi, Wise Men.
Maghreb, *n.m.* North Africa.
magicien, *n.m.* magician.
magie, *n.f.* magic.
magique, *adj.* magic.
magistral, *adj.* masterly, authoritative.

magistrat, *n.m.* magistrate.
magistrature, *n.f.* judiciary.
magnanime, *adj.* magnanimous.
magnat, *n.m.* magnate.
magnétique, *adj.* magnetic.
magnétophone, *n.m.* tape recorder.
magnétoscope, *n.m.* videorecorder.
magnificence, *n.f.* magnificence.
magnifique, *adj.* magnificent.
magouille, *n.f.* scheming.
mahométan, *adj.* Mohammedan.
mai, *n.m.* May.
maigre, *adj.* lean, thin, meager.

maigrir, *vb.* lose weight.

maille, *n.f.* stitch; mesh.

maillot, *n.m.* shorts; T-shirt. **m. de bain,** bathing suit.

main, *n.f.* hand. **sous la m.,** handy.

main-d'œuvre, *n.f.* manpower.

maintenant, *adv.* now. **dès m.,** henceforth.

maintenir, *vb.* maintain.

maintien, *n.m.* upkeep; behavior.

maire, *n.m.* mayor.

mairie, *n.f.* city hall.

mais, *conj.* but.

maïs, (mä ēs), *n.m.* corn.

maison, *n.f.* house.

maisonnée, *n.f.* household.

maître, *n.m.* master, teacher.

maîtresse, *n.f.* mistress, teacher.

maîtrise, *n.f.* mastery.

maîtriser, *vb.* master, overcome.

majesté, *n.f.* majesty.

majestueux, *adj.* majestic.

majeur, *adj.* major.

majordome, *n.m.* majordomo.

majorer, *vb.* increase price, over-price.

majoritaire, *adj.* majority.

majorité, *n.f.* majority.

majuscule, *n.f.* capital.

mal, 1. *n.m.* harm, ill, evil. **2.** *adv.* badly. **faire m. à,** hurt. **avoir m. à,** have a pain in.

malade, 1. *n.m.f.* sick person, patient. **2.** *adj.* sick.

maladie, *n.f.* disease, illness, sickness.

maladif, *adj.* sickly.

maladresse, *n.f.* awkwardness.

maladroit, *adj.* awkward.

malaise, *n.m.* discomfort.

malappris, *adj.* ill-bred.

malaria, *n.f.* malaria.

malavisé, *adj.* indiscreet, ill-advised.

Malaisie, *n.f.* Malaysia.

malchance, *n.f.* bad luck, mishap.

maldonne, *n.f.* misdeal.

mâle, *adj. and n.m.* male.

malédiction, *n.f.* curse.

maléfice, *n.m.* witchery, evil spell.

malencontre, *n.f.* unlucky incident.

malencontreux, *adj.* unlucky.

malentendu, *n.m.* misunderstanding.

malfaiteur, *n.m.* malefactor.

malfamé, *adj.* ill-famed.

malgré, *prep.* despite.

malhabile, *adj.* awkward, dull.

malheur, *n.m.* misfortune, accident.

malheureux, *adj.* unfortunate; unhappy, miserable.

malhonnête, *adj.* dishonest.

malhonnêteté, *n.f.* dishonesty.

malice, *n.f.* mischief, malice.

malicieux, *adj.* malicious, roguish.

malin, m., maligne f. adj. sharp, sly; malignant.

malingre, *adj.* sickly, puny.

malintentionné, *adj.* ill-disposed.

malle, *n.f.* trunk.

mallette, *n.f.* small suitcase.

malnutrition, *n.f.* malnutrition.

malotru, *n.m.* boor, lout.

malpropre, *adj.* messy.

malpropreté, *n.f.* messiness.

malsain, *adj.* unhealthy.

malséant, *adj.* improper.

Malte, *n.f.* Malta.

maltraiter, *vb.* misuse.

malveillant, *adj.* malevolent.

malvenu, *adj.* without any right.

malversation, *n.f.* embezzlement.

maman, *n.f.* mamma.

mamelle, *n.f.* udder.

mamelon, *n.m.* nipple; hillock.

mamie, *n.f.* (colloquial) granny.

mammifère, *n.m.* mammal.

manche, *n.m.* handle. *f.* sleeve. **La M.,** the English Channel.

manchette, *n.f.* cuff.

manchon, *n.m.* muff.

manchot, *n.m.* one-armed person.

mandarine, *n.f.* tangerine.

mandat, *n.m.* warrant, writ, mandate. **m.-poste,** money order.

mandataire, *n.m.* agent, proxy.

mander, *vb.* send for, inform.

manège, *n.m.* horsemanship.

manette, *n.f.* handle, lever; joystick.

mangeable, *adj.* eatable.

mangeoire, *n.f.* manger.

manger, *vb.* eat.

maniable, *adj.* manageable; easygoing.

maniaque, 1. *n.m.f.* maniac. **2.** *adj.* maniac, maniacal.

manie, *n.f.* mania.

manier, *vb.* handle; wield.

manière, *n.f.* manner.

maniéré, *adj.* affected.

manière de vivre, *n.f.* life style.

manif (-f), *n.f.* (colloquial) demo.

manifestation, *n.f.* demonstration.

manifeste, 1. *n.m.* manifesto, petition. **2.** *adj.* manifest, evident, overt.

manifester, *vb.* manifest, show.

manigance, *n.f.* trick, intrigue.

manipuler, *adj.* manipulate.

manivelle, *n.f.* crank; winch.

mannequin, *n.m.* dummy; model.

manœuvre, *n.f.* maneuver.

manoir, *n.m.* country house, estate.

manquant, 1. *adj.* missing. **2.** *n.m.* absentee.

manque, *n.m.* lack.

manquer, *vb.* miss, lack; fail.

mansarde, *n.f.* attic.

mansuétude, *n.f.* mildness, kindness.

manteau, *n.m.* cloak, coat.

manucure, *n.m.f.* manicurist.

manuel, *adj. and n.m.* manual.

manufacture, *n.f.* manufacture.

manuscrit, *adj. and n.m.* manuscript.

manutention, *n.f.* management.

maquereau, *n.m.* mackerel; (colloquial) pimp.

maquette, *n.f.* preliminary sketch or model.

maquillage, *n.m.* makeup.

maquis, *n.m.* scrub land; Resistance fighters.

maquisard, *n.m.* Resistance fighter.

marais, *n.m.* marsh.

marasme, *n.m.* slump.

marâtre, *n.f.* stepmother.

maraude, *n.f.* marauding.

marbre, *n.m.* marble.

marchand, *n.m.* merchant.

marchander, *vb.* bargain, haggle.

marchandises, *n.f.pl.* goods.

marche, *n.f.* march, step.

marché, *n.m.* market, bargain. **bon m.,** cheap.

marchepied, *n.m.* running-board.

marcher, *vb.* walk, step, march; run (machine).

marcheur, *n.m.* pedestrian.

mardi, *n.m.* Tuesday.

mare, *n.f.* pool.

marécage, *n.m.* bog.

marécageux, *adj.* marshy.

maréchal, *n.m.* marshal.

marée, *n.f.* tide.

mareyeur, *n.m.* fish seller.

margarine, *n.f.* margarine.

marge, *n.f.* margin.

margelle, *n.f.* edge, brink.

marguerite, *n.f.* daisy.

mari, *n.m.* husband.

mariage, *n.m.* marriage.

marié, 1. *n.m.* bridegroom. **2.** *adj.* married.

mariée, *n.f.* bride.

marie-jeanne, *n.f.* marijuana.

marier, *vb.* marry.

marijuana, *n.f.* marijuana.

marin, 1. *n.m.* sailor. **2.** *adj.* marine. **fusilier m.,** marine.

marinade, *n.f.* mixture for pickling.

marine, *n.f.* navy.

mariner, *vb.* pickle.

marionnette, *n.f.* puppet.

maritime, *adj.* marine.

marmite, *n.f.* pot.

marmiter, *vb.* blast (with gunfire).

marmonner, *vb.* mumble.

marmot, *n.m.* kid, brat.

marmotter, *vb.* mumble.

Maroc (-k), *n.m.* Morocco.

marocain, *adj. and n.m.* Moroccan.

maroquinerie, *n.f.* leather goods.

marotte, *n.f.* fad.

marque, *n.f.* brand, mark.

marquer, *vb.* mark.

marqueur, *n.m.* marker, scorekeeper.

marquis, *n.m.* marquis.

marraine, *n.f.* godmother; sponsor.

marrant, *adj.* funny.

marron, *n.m.* chestnut; brown.

marronier, *n.m.* chestnut tree.

mars, (-s), *n.m.* March.

marteau, *n.m.* hammer.

marteler, *vb.* hammer.

martial, *adj.* warlike.

martre, *n.m.* marten.

martyr, *n.m.* martyr.

martyre, *n.m.* martyrdom.

marxisme, *n.m.* Marxism.

mascarade, *n.f.* masquerade.

mascotte, *n.f.* mascot.

masculin, *adj.* masculine.

maso, *n.m.* (colloquial) masochist.

masochiste, *n.m.f.* masochist.

masque, *n.m.* mask.

masquer, *vb.* mask.

massacre, *n.m.* slaughter.

massage, *n.m.* massage.

masse, *n.f.* mass.

masser, *vb.* mass; massage.

massif, *adj.* massive, solid.

massue, *n.f.* club.

mastiquer, *vb.* chew.

mat, (-t) *adj.* dull.

mât, (mä) *n.m.* mast.

matelas, *n.m.* mattress.

matelot, *n.m.* sailor.

matérialiser, *vb.* materialize.

matérialisme, *n.m.* materialism.

matérialiste, *n.m.f.* materialist. *adj.* materialistic.

matériaux, *n.m.pl.* stuff, materials.

matériel, *adj.* material, real.

maternel, *adj.* native; maternal.

maternité, *n.f.* maternity.

mathématique, *adj.* mathematical.

mathématiques, *n.f.pl.* mathematics.

maths, *n.f.pl.* (colloquial) math.

matière, *n.f.* matter. **table des m.s,** index.

matin, *n.m.* morning.

mâtin, *n.m.* big dog.

matinal, *adj.* early.

matinée, *n.f.* morning.

matineux, *adj.* rising early.

matois, *adj.* cunning, sly.

matou, *n.m.* tomcat.

matraque, *n.f.* heavy club.

matrice, *n.f.* womb.

matricule, *n.f.* roster, registration.

matriculer, *vb.* enroll, register.

matrimonial, *adj.* marital.

mâture, *n.f.* masts (of boats).

maturité, *n.f.* maturity.

maudire, *vb.* curse.

maudit, *adj.* cursed, miserable.

maugréer, *vb.* curse, grumble.

maussade, *adj.* glum, sullen, cross.

mauvais, *adj.* bad.

maxime, *n.f.* maxim.

maximum, *n.m.* maximum.

mayonnaise, *n.f.* mayonnaise.

mazout, *n.m.* (fuel) oil.

me, (mə), *pron.* me; myself.

méandre, *n.m.* winding.

mec, *n.m.* (colloquial) guy.

mécanicien, *n.m.* mechanic, engineer.

mécanique, *adj.* mechanical.

mécaniser, *vb.* mechanize.

mécanisme, *n.m.* mechanism, machinery.

mécano, *n.m.* mechanic.

méchamment, *adv.* maliciously.

méchanceté, *n.f.* wickedness, malice.

méchant, *adj.* wicked, malicious.

mèche, *n.f.* lock (hair); wick, fuse.

mécompte, *n.m.* error; disappointment.

méconnaissable, *adj.* unrecognizable.

méconnaître, *vb.* fail to recognize.

mécontent, *adj.* discontented.

mécontentement, *n.m.* discontent.

mécontenter, *vb.* dissatisfy.

mécréant, *n.m.* unbeliever.

médaille, *n.f.* medal.

médaillon, *n.m.* locket.

médecin, *n.m.* physician.

médecine, *n.f.* medicine.

médiateur, *n.m.* mediator; ombudsman (in France).

médiation, *n.f.* mediation.

médiatique, *adj.* media.

médical, *adj.* medical.

médicament, *n.m.* medicine.

médicinal, *adj.* medicinal.

médiéval, *adj.* medieval.

médiocre, *adj.* mediocre.

médiocrité, *n.f.* mediocrity.

médire, *vb.* slander, defame.

médisance, *n.f.* slander.

méditation, *n.f.* meditation.

méditer, *vb.* meditate; muse, brood.

Méditerranée, *n.f.* the Mediterranean.

méditerranéen, *adj.* Mediterranean.

médium, *n.m.* medium.

méduse, *n.f.* jellyfish.

méduser, *vb.* stupefy.

méfait, *n.m.* crime, misdeed.

méfiance, *n.f.* distrust.

méfiant, *adj.* distrustful.

méfier, *vb.* **se m. de,** distrust.

mégarde, *n.f.* heedlessness.

mégère, *n.f.* vixen, shrew.

mégot, *n.m.* cigarette butt.

meilleur, *adj.* better, best.

mélancolie, *n.f.* melancholy.

mélancolique, *adj.* melancholy.

mélange, *n.m.* mixture.

mélasse, *n.f.* molasses.

mêlée, *n.f.* struggle.

mêler, *vb.* mix. **se m. de,** meddle in.

mélèze, *n.m.* larch.

melliflu, *adj.* sweet, honeyed.

mélo, 1. *n.m.* melodrama. **2.** *adj.* melodramatic.

mélodie, *n.f.* melody.

mélodieux, *adj.* melodious.

mélodique, *adj.* melodic.

mélodrame, *n.m.* melodrama.

mélomane, *n.m.* lover of music.

melon, *n.m.* melon.

membrane, *n.f.* membrane.

membre, *n.m.* member, limb.

membrure, *n.f.* frame, limbs.

même, 1. *adj.* same, very; self. **moi-m.,** myself; **lui-m.,** himself, etc. **2.** *adv.* even. **de m.,** likewise. **tout de m.,** notwithstanding. **mettre à m. de,** enable to.

mémé, *n.f.* (colloquial) granny.

mémento, *n.m.* memento, notebook.

mémoire, *n.f.* memory; memoir.

mémorable, *adj.* memorable.

mémorandum, *n.m.* memorandum.

mémorial, *n.m.* memorial; memoirs.

menaçant, *adj.* threatening.

menace, *n.f.* threat.

menacer, *vb.* threaten.

ménage, *n.m.* household.

ménagement, *n.m.* discretion.

ménager, 1. *n.m.* manager. **2.** *vb.* manage.

ménagère, *n.f.* housewife; housekeeper.

ménagerie, *n.f.* menagerie.

mendiant, *n.m.* beggar.

mendicité, *n.f.* begging.

mendier, *vb.* beg.

menées, *n.f.pl.* schemes.

mener, *vb.* lead.

ménestrel, *n.m.* minstrel.

ménétrier, *n.m.* country fiddler.

meneur, *n.m.* leader, ringleader.

méningite, *n.f.* meningitis.

ménopause, *n.f.* menopause.

menottes, *n.f.pl.* handcuffs.

mensonge, *n.m.* falsehood, lie.

mensonger, *adj.* false, deceptive.

mensualité, *n.f.* remittance paid monthly.

mensuel, *adj.* monthly.

mensurable, *adj.* measurable.

mental, *adj.* mental.

mentalité, *n.f.* mentality.

menterie, *n.f.* lie.

menteur, *n.m.* liar.

menthe, *n.f.* mint.

mention, *n.f.* mention.

mentionner, *vb.* mention.

mentir, *vb.* lie.

menton, *n.m.* chin.

menu, 1. *n.m.* menu. **2.** *adj.* little, minute.

menuet, *n.m.* minuet.

menuiserie, *n.f.* woodwork.

menuisier, *n.m.* carpenter.

méprendre, *vb.* **se m.,** be mistaken.

mépris, *n.m.* contempt, scorn.

méprisable, *adj.* mean, contemptible.

méprisant, *adj.* contemptuous.

méprise, *n.f.* mistake, misunderstanding.

mépriser, *vb.* scorn, despise.

mer, (-r), *n.f.* sea. **mal de m.,** seasickness.

mercantile, *adj.* mercantile.

mercenaire, *adj. and n.m.* mercenary.

mercerie, *n.f.* haberdashery.

merci, *n.f.* thanks; mercy.

mercredi, *n.m.* Wednesday.

mercure, *n.m.* mercury.

mère, *n.f.* mother.

méridien, *n.m.* meridian.

méridional, *adj.* southern.

meringue, *n.f.* meringue.

méritant, *adj.* meritorious.

mérite, *n.m.* merit, desert.

mériter, *vb.* merit, deserve.

méritoire, *adj.* meritorious.

merle, *n.m.* blackbird.

merveille, *n.f.* marvel.

merveilleux, *adj.* wonderful, marvelous.

mésalliance, *n.f.* misalliance.

mésallier, *vb.* marry badly.

mésaventure, *n.f.* accident, mishap.

Mesdames, *pl.* of **Madame.**

Mesdemoiselles, *pl.* of **Mademoiselle.**

mésestime, *n.f.* low opinion or repute.

mésintelligence, *n.f.* difficulty, discord.

mesquin, *adj.* shabby, mean, stingy.

mesquinerie, *n.f.* meanness.

message, *n.m.* message.

messager, *n.m.* messenger.

messe, *n.f.* Mass.

Messie, *n.m.* Messiah.

Messieurs, *pl.* of **Monsieur.**

mesurage, *n.m.* measurement.

mesure, *n.f.* measure. **à m. que,** as.

mesuré, *adj.* measured, cautious.

mesurer, *vb.* measure.

métairie, *n.f.* small farm.

métal, *n.m.* metal.

métallique, *adj.* metallic.

métallurgie, *n.f.* metallurgy.

métamorphose, *n.f.* transformation.

métaphore, *n.f.* metaphor.

métaphysique, 1. *n.f.* metaphysics. **2.** *adj.* metaphysical.

métayer, *n.m.* small farmer.

météo, *n.f.* weather report.

météore, *n.m.* meteor.

météorologie, *n.f.* meteorology.

métèque, *n.m.f.* alien.

méthode, *n.f.* method.

méthodique, *adj.* methodical, systematic.

méticuleux, *adj.* meticulous.

métier, *n.m.* loom; craft, trade.

métis, *adj.* hybrid, crossbred.

métrage, *n.m.* measurement.

mètre, *n.m.* meter.

métrique, *adj.* metric.

métro, *n.m.* subway.

métropole, *n.f.* metropolis; native land.

métropolitain, *adj.* metropolitan.

mets, *n.m.* food, dish.

mettable, *adj.* wearable.

metteur, *n.m.* **m. en scène,** play director.

mettre, *vb.* put, place, set. **se m. à,** begin.

meuble, *n.m.* piece of furniture; (*pl.*) furniture.

meubler, *vb.* furnish, outfit.

meule, *n.f.* stack.

meunier, *n.m.* miller.

meurtre, *n.m.* murder.

meurtrier, *n.m.* murderer.

meurtrière, *n.f.* murderess.

meurtrir, *vb.* bruise.

meurtrissure, *n.f.* bruise.

meute, *n.f.* dog pack; mob.

Mexicain, *n.m.* Mexican.

mexicain, *adj.* Mexican.

Mexique, *n.m.* Mexico.

mezzanine, *n.f.* mezzanine.

mi, *adj.* mid, half.

miaou, *n.m.* mew.

miauler, *vb.* mew.

mica, *n.m.* mica.

miche, *n.f.* loaf of bread.

micro, *n.m.* microphone, mike; micro.

microbe, *n.m.* microbe.

microfiche, *n.f.* microfiche.

microforme, *n.f.* microform.

micro-ondes, *n.m.* microwave oven.

microphone, *n.m.* microphone.

microplaquette, *n.f.* (micro)chip.

microprocesseur, *n.m.* microprocessor.

microscope, *n.m.* microscope.

microscopique, *adj.* microscopic.

midi, *n.m.* noon; south.

midinette, *n.f.* young saleswoman.

mie, *n.f.* crumb.

miel, *n.m.* honey.

mielleux, *adj.* honeyed, sweet.

mien, *pron.* **le mien, la mienne,** mine.

miette, *n.f.* crumb.

mieux, *adv.* better, best.

mièvre, *adj.* affected.

mignard, *adj.* dainty, mincing.

mignon, 1. *adj.* delicate, dainty. **2.** *n.m.* darling.

migraine, *n.f.* headache.

migration, *n.f.* migration.

mijoter, *vb.* cook slowly, simmer.

mil, (mēl), *n.m.* thousand.

milice, *n.f.* militia.

milieu, *n.m.* middle, center; environment.

militaire, *adj.* military.

militant, *adj.* militant.

militarisme, *n.m.* militarism.

militer, *vb.* militate.

mille, (-l), **1.** *n.m.* mile. **2.** *adj. and n.m.f.* thousand.

millénaire, *n.m.* millenium.

millet, *n.m.* millet.

milliard, *n.m.* billion.

millier, (-l-), *n.m.* thousand.

milligramme, (-l-), *n.m.* milligram.

millimètre, *n.m.* millimeter.

million, (-l-), *n.m.* million.

millionnaire, (-l-), *adj. and n.m.f.* millionaire.

mime, *n.m.* mime, mimic.

mimique, *adj.* mimic.

minable, *adj.* shabby, poor.

minauder, *vb.* simper.

mince, *adj.* slender, slight, thin.

minceur, *n.f.* slimness.

mine, *n.f.* mine; mien; lead.

miner, *vb.* mine; wear away; weaken.

minerai, *n.m.* ore.

minéral, *adj. and n.m.* mineral.

minet, *n.m.* (colloquial) kitty.

mineur, 1. *n.m.* miner. **2.** *adj. and n.m.* minor.

miniature, *n.f.* miniature.

miniaturiser, *vb.* miniaturize.

minibus, *n.m.* minibus.

minier, *adj.* of mines.

minime, *adj.* very small.

minimum, *n.m.* minimum.

mini-ordinateur, *n.m.* minicomputer.

ministère, *n.m.* ministry, department, board.

ministériel, *adj.* ministerial.

ministre, *n.m.* minister. **premier m.,** prime minister, premier.

Minitel, *n.m.* (trademark) Minitel (videotext terminal and service).

minorité, *n.f.* minority.

minotier, *n.m.* miller.

minuit, *n.m.* midnight.

minuscule, *adj.* minute.

minute, *n.f.* minute.

minuterie, *n.f.* time switch.

minutie, *n.f.* trifle; care with details.

minutieux, *adj.* minute.

mioche, *n.m.f.* urchin.

miracle, *n.m.* miracle.

miraculeux, *adj.* miraculous.

mirage, *n.m.* mirage.

mirer, *vb.* aim at, look at.

mirifique, *adj.* wonderful.

miroir, *n.m.* mirror.

miroiter, *vb.* glisten.

misanthrope, 1. *n.m.f.* misanthrope. **2.** *adj.* misanthropic.

mise, *n.f.* putting; mode. **m. en scène,** setting.

miser, *vb.* bid.

misérable, *adj.* miserable, wretched, squalid.

misère, *n.f.* misery.

miséreux, *adj.* poor, miserable.

miséricorde, *n.f.* mercy.

miséricordieux, *adj.* merciful.

misogyne, 1. *n.m.f.* misogynist. **2.** *adj.* woman-hating; misogynist.

missel, *n.m.* missal.

missile, *n.m.* missile.

mission, *n.f.* mission.

missionnaire, *adj. and n.m.f.* missionary.

missive, *n.f.* missive.

mistral, *n.m.* mistral wind.

mitaine, *n.f.* mitten.

mite, *n.f.* moth.

mi-temps, *n.f.* half-time, part-time.

miteux, *adj.* shabby.

mitiger, *vb.* moderate.

mitoyen, *adj.* midway; jointly owned.

mitrailleuse, *n.f.* machine gun.

mixage, *n.m.* (sound) mixing.

mixte, *adj.* mixed, joint.

Mlle., (abbr. for **Mademoiselle**), *n.f.* Miss.

Mme., (abbr. for **Madame**), *n.f.* Mrs.

mobile, *adj.* movable.

mobilier, *adj.* movable.

mobilisation, *n.f.* mobilization.

mobiliser, *vb.* mobilize.

mobilité, *n.f.* mobility; instability.

moche, *adj.* ugly.

modalité, *n.f.* mode.

mode, *n.f.* fashion, mode; mood; *pl.* millinery. **à la m.,** fashionable.

modèle, *n.m.* model, pattern.

modeler, *vb.* model, shape.

modelliste, *n.m.f.* dress designer.

modem, *n.m.* modem.

modérateur, *n.m.* moderator.

modération, *n.f.* moderation.

modéré, *adj.* moderate.

modérer, *vb.* check, moderate.

moderne, *adj.* modern.

moderniser, *vb.* modernize.

modernité, *n.f.* modernity.

modeste, *adj.* modest.

modestie, *n.f.* modesty.

modicité, *n.f.* small quantity.

modification, *n.f.* alteration.

modifier, *vb.* modify, qualify.

modique, *adj.* moderate, unimportant.

modiste, *n.f.* milliner.

modulation, *n.f.* modulation.

module, *n.m.* module.

moduler, *vb.* modulate.

moelle, *n.f.* marrow.

moelleux, (mwä ly), *adj.* mellow, soft.

mœurs, (-s), *n.f.pl.* manner(s), custom.

moi, 1. *n.m.* ego. **2.** *pron.* me.

moignon, *n.m.* stump.

moi-même, *pron.* myself; I myself.

moindre, *adj.* less, lesser, least.

moine, *n.m.* monk.

moineau, *n.m.* sparrow.

moins, *adv.* less, least. **au m.,** at least. **à m. que,** unless.

moire, *n.f.* watered silk.

mois, *n.m.* month.

moisi, *adj.* moldy.

moisir, *vb.* mold.

moisissure, *n.f.* mold.

moisson, *n.f.* harvest, crop.

moissonner, *vb.* reap, harvest.

moissonneur, *n.m.* harvester.

moissonneuse, *n.f.* reaping machine.

moite, *adj.* moist.

moiteur, *n.f.* dampness.

moitié, *n.f.* half. **à m.,** half.

molaire, *adj. and n.f.* molar.

môle, *n.m.* pier.

molécule, *n.f.* molecule.

molester, *vb.* molest.

mollah, *n.m.* mullah.

mollasse, *adj.* flabby, soft.

mollesse, *n.f.* softness; weakness.

mollet, 1. *adj.* soft. **œufs m.s,** soft-boiled eggs. **2.** *n.m.* calf of leg.

molletière, *n.f.* legging.

molleton, *n.m.* heavy flannel.

mollir, *vb.* soften, slacken.

mollusque, *n.m.* mollusk.

môme, *n.m.f.* (colloquial) kid.

moment, *n.m.* moment.

momentané, *adj.* momentary.

mon, *m.,* **ma** *f.,* **mes** *pl. adj.* my.

monacal, *adj.* pertaining to monks.

Monaco, *n.m.* Monaco.

monarchie, *n.f.* monarchy.

monarchiste, *n.m.f.* monarchist.

monarque, *n.m.* monarch.

monastère, *n.m.* monastery.

monastique, *adj.* monastic.

monceau, *n.m.* pile.

mondain, *adj.* worldly.

monde, *n.m.* world; people. **tout le m.,** everybody, everyone. **mettre au m.,** bear.

mondial, *adj.* worldwide.

monétaire, *adj.* monetary.

moniteur, *n.m.* monitor.

monnaie, *n.f.* change; money, currency. **Hôtel de la M.,** mint.

monnayer, *vb.* mint.

monocle, *n.m.* monocle.

monogramme, *n.m.* monogram.

monologue, *n.m.* monologue.

monologuer, *vb.* soliloquize.

monoplan, *n.m.* monoplane.

monopole, *n.m.* monopoly.

monopoliser, *vb.* monopolize.

monosyllabe, *n.m.* monosyllable.

monosyllabique, *adj.* monosyllabic.

monotone, *adj.* monotonous.

monotonie, *n.f.* monotony, dullness.

monseigneur, *n.m.* title of honor; My Lord.

Monsieur, *n.m.,* gentleman, sir; Mr.

monstre, *n.m.* monster.

monstrueux, *adj.* monstrous.

monstruosité, *n.f.* monstrosity.

mont, *n.m.* mountain, hill.

montage, *n.m.* carrying up; setting; (film) editing.

montagnard, *n.m.* mountaineer.

montagne, *n.f.* mountain.

montagneux, *adj.* mountainous.

montant, *n.m.* amount.

mont-de-piété, *n.m.* pawnshop.

monté, *adj.* mounted; supplied.

montée, *n.f.* ascent, rise, climb.

monter, *vb.* go up, mount, climb, rise.

montre, *n.f.* watch; display. **m.-bracelet,** wristwatch.

montrer, *vb.* show.

montreur, *n.m.* showman.

montueux, *adj.* hilly.

monture, *n.f.* mount; setting.

monument, *n.m.* monument.

monumental, *adj.* monumental.

moquer, *vb.* **se m. de,** make fun of, mock, laugh at.

moquerie, *n.f.* mockery, ridicule.

moquette, *n.f.* wall-to-wall carpeting.

moqueur, *adj.* mocking.

moral, *adj.* ethical, moral.

morale, *n.f.* morals, morality. *m.* morale.

moraliser, *vb.* moralize.

moraliste, *n.m.f.* moralist.

moralité, *n.f.* morals, morality.

morbide, *adj.* morbid.

morceau, *n.m.* piece, bit, morsel. **gros m.,** lump, chunk.

morceler, *vb.* cut up.

mordant, *adj.* pointed.

mordiller, *vb.* nibble.

mordre, *vb.* bite.

morfondre, *vb.* chill.

morgue, *n.f.* morgue.

moribond, *adj.* dying.

morne, *adj.* bleak, dismal, dreary.

morose, *adj.* morose.

morosité, *n.f.* moroseness.

morphine, *n.f.* morphine.

morphinomane, *n.* drug addict.

morphologie, *n.f.* morphology.

mors, *n.m.* horse's bit.

morse, *n.m.* walrus.

morsure, *n.f.* bite.

mort, 1. *n.m.* dummy; dead man. **2.** *n.f.* death. **3.** *adj.* dead.

mortaise, *n.f.* mortise.

mortalité, *n.f.* mortality.

mortel, *adj.* deadly, mortal.

morte-saison, *n.f.* off season.

mortier, *n.m.* mortar.

mortifier, *vb.* mortify.

mort-né, *adj.* stillborn.

mortuaire, *adj.* mortuary.

morue, *n.f.* cod.

mosaïque, (-ä ĕk), *n.f.* mosaic.

Moscou, *n.m.* Moscow.

mosquée, *n.f.* mosque.

mot, *n.m.* word; cue.

motard, *n.m.* biker; motorcycle cop.

motel, *n.m.* motel.

moteur, *n.m.* motor.

motif, *n.m.* motive.

motion, *n.f.* motion.

motiver, *vb.* motivate, justify.

motocyclette, *n.f.* motorcycle.

motocycliste, *n.m.* motorcyclist.

motorisé, *adj.* having transportation.

motte, *n.f.* clod.

mou, *m.,* **molle** *f.* *adj.* soft.

mouchard, *n.m.* spy.

moucharder, *vb.* spy.

mouche, *n.f.* fly.

moucher, *vb.* blow the nose.

moucheron, *n.m.* gnat.

moucheté, *adj.* spotted.

moucheture, *n.f.* spot.

mouchoir, *n.m.* handkerchief.

moudre, *vb.* grind.

moue, *n.f.* pout, wry face.

mouette, *n.f.* gull.

moufette, *n.f.* skunk.

moufle, *n.f.* mitten.

mouillage, *n.m.* wetting.

mouillé, *adj.* wet.

mouiller, *vb.* soak.

moulage, *n.m.* cast (from mold).

moule, 1. *n.m.* mold. **2.** *n.f.* mussel.

mouler, *vb.* mold.

mouleur, *n.m.* molder.

moulin, *n.m.* mill.

moulinette, *n.f.* vegetable shredder.

moulure, *n.f.* molding.

mourant, *adj.* dying.

mourir, *vb.* die.

mouron, *n.m.* pimpernel.

mousquetaire, *n.m.* musketeer.

mousse, *n.f.* moss; foam, lather.

mousseline, *n.f.* muslin.

mousser, *vb.* foam, froth.

mousseux, *adj.* foaming.

mousson, *n.m.* monsoon.

moustache, *n.f.* mustache, whisker.

moustiquaire, *n.f.* mosquito net.

moustique, *n.m.* mosquito.

moutarde, *n.f.* mustard.

mouton, *n.m.* sheep; mutton.

moutonner, *vb.* curl; make woolly.

mouture, *n.f.* grinding.

mouvant, *adj.* moving, shifting.

mouvement, *n.m.* movement, stir.

mouvoir, *vb.* move.

moyen, 1. *n.m.* means; medium. **2.** *adj.* middle, average.

moyennant, *prep.* by means of.

moyenne, *n.f.* average.

Moyen Orient, *n.m.* Middle East.

muabilité, *n.f.* changeability.
mucilage, *n.m.* mucilage.
mue, *n.f.* molting; changing (esp. of voice).
muer, *vb.* molt (animals); break, change (voice).
muet, *m.*, **muette** *f. adj.* dumb, mute.
mufle, *n.m.* cad.
mugir, *vb.* roar, bellow.
mugissement, *n.m.* roaring, bellowing.
muguet, *n.m.* lily of the valley.
mulâtre, *adj. and n.m.f.* mulatto.
mulet, *n.m.* mule.
muletier, *n.m.* muleteer.
mulot, *n.m.* field mouse.
multinational, *adj.* multinational.
multiple, *adj.* multiple, manifold.
multiplicande, *n.m.* multiplicand.
multiplication, *n.f.* multiplication.
multiplicité, *n.f.* multiplicity.
multiplier, *vb.* multiply.
multitude, *n.f.* multitude.
municipal, *adj.* municipal.
municipalité, *n.f.* municipality.
munificence, *n.f.* munificence, liberality.

munificent, *adj.* very generous.
munir, *vb.* provide, supply.
munitionner, *vb.* provision, supply.
munitions, *n.f.pl.* ammunition.
muqueux, *adj.* mucous.
mur, *n.m.* wall.
mûr, *adj.* ripe, mature.
muraille, *n.f.* wall.
mural, *adj.* mural.
mûre, *n.f.* blackberry.
mûrier, *n.m.* mulberry tree.
mûrir, *vb.* ripen, mature.
murmure, *n.m.* murmur.
murmurer, *vb.* murmur.
musarder, *vb.* waste time, dawdle.
muscade, *n.f.* nutmeg.
muscle, *n.m.* muscle.
musculaire, *adj.* muscular.
musculeux, *adj.* muscular.
muse, *n.f.* muse.
museau, *n.m.* muzzle.
musée, *n.m.* museum.
museler, *vb.* muzzle; gag.
muselière, *n.f.* muzzle.
muser, *vb.* trifle, dawdle.
musette, *n.f.* lunchbag; accordion.
musical, *adj.* musical.
musicien, 1. *adj.* musical. 2. *n.m.* musician.
musique, *n.f.* music.

musulman, *adj. and n.m.* Mohammedan.
mutabilité, *n.f.* mutability.
mutation, *n.f.* change, replacement.
mutilation, *n.f.* mutilation.
mutiler, *vb.* mutilate, mangle, mar.
mutin, *adj.* refractory, mutinous.
mutiner, *vb.* **se m.**, mutiny, revolt.
mutinerie, *n.f.* mutiny.
mutisme, *n.m.* muteness, lack of speech.
mutuel, *adj.* mutual.
myope, *adj.* nearsighted.
myopie, *n.f.* nearsightedness.
myosotis, *n.m.* forget-me-not.
myriade, *n.f.* myriad.
myrrhe, *n.f.* myrrh.
myrte, *n.m.* myrtle.
mystère, *n.m.* mystery.
mystérieux, *adj.* mysterious, weird.
mysticisme, *n.m.* mysticism.
mystification, *n.f.* hoax.
mystifier, *vb.* mystify.
mystique, *adj.* mystic.
mythe, *n.m.* myth.
mythique, *adj.* mythical.
mythologie, *n.f.* mythology.

N

nabot *n.m.* dwarf.
nacre, *n.f.* mother-of-pearl.
nacré, *adj.* pearly.
nage, *n.f.* act of swimming.
nageoire, *n.f.* fin.
nager, *vb.* swim.
nageur, *n.m.* swimmer.
naguère, *adv.* a short time ago.
naïf, (nä ēf) *m.*, **naïve** *f. adj.* naive.
nain, *adj. and n.m.* dwarf.
naissance, *n.f.* birth.
naissant, *adj.* beginning; new-born.
naître, *vb.* be born.

naïveté, (nä ēv-), *n.f.* simplicity.
nantir, *vb.* give as security; furnish.
nantis, *n.m.pl.* the well-to-do.
nantissement, *n.m.* pledge, guarantee.
naphte, *n.m.* naphtha.
nappe, *n.f.* tablecloth.
narcisse, *n.m.* daffodil.
narcotique, *n.m.* narcotic.
narguer, *vb.* defy, flout.
narine, *n.f.* nostril.
narrateur, *n.m.* narrator, storyteller.

narration, *n.f.* narrative, recital.
narrer, *vb.* narrate, relate.
nasal, *adj.* nasal.
naseau, *n.m.* nostril.
nasiller, *vb.* talk with a nasal voice.
nasse, *n.f.* fish trap.
natal, *adj.* native.
natalité, *n.f.* birthrate.
natation, *n.f.* swimming.
natif, *adj. and n.m.* native.
nation, *n.f.* nation.
national, *adj.* national.
nationalisation, *n.f.* nationalization.
nationaliser, *vb.* nationalize.

nationalisme, *n.m.* nationalism.

nationalité, *n.f.* nationality.

nativité, *n.f.* nativity.

naturaliser, *vb.* naturalize; (of animals) stuff.

naturalisme, *n.m.* naturalism, naturalness.

naturaliste, *n.m.f.* naturalist.

nature, *n.f.* nature.

naturel, 1. *n.m.* nature. 2. *adj.* natural.

naufrage, *n.m.* shipwreck.

naufragé, *adj.* shipwrecked.

nauséabond, *adj.* nauseous, offensive.

nausée, *n.f.* nausea.

nautique, *adj.* nautical.

nautisme, *n.m.* water sports.

naval, *adj.* naval.

navet, *n.m.* turnip.

navette spatiale, *n.f.* space shuttle.

navigable, *adj.* navigable.

navigateur, *n.m.* navigator, seaman.

navigation, *n.f.* seafaring, navigation.

naviguer, *vb.* sail, navigate.

navire, *n.m.* ship.

navrant, *adj.* distressing, causing grief.

navrer, *vb.* wound; grieve.

né, *adj.* born.

néanmoins, *adv.* yet, nevertheless, however.

néant, *n.m.* nothing(ness).

nébuleux, *adj.* cloudy; worried.

nécessaire, *adj.* requisite, necessary.

nécessité, *n.f.* necessity. **n. préalable**, prerequisite.

nécessiter, *vb.* make necessary or imperative.

nécessiteux, *adj.* needy.

nécrologe, *n.m.* obituary.

néerlandais, *adj.* Dutch (language).

nef, *n.f.* nave.

néfaste, *adj.* ill-omened, unlucky.

négatif, *adj.* negative.

négation, *n.f.* negation; negative word.

négative, *n.f.* negative argument or opinion.

négligé, 1. *adj.* neglected, sloppy. 2. *n.m.* state of undress.

négligeable, *adj.* negligible.

négligence, *n.f.* neglect.

négligent, *adj.* negligent.

négliger, *vb.* overlook, neglect.

négoce, *n.m.* commerce, trade.

négociable, *adj.* negotiable.

négociant, *n.m.* merchant.

négociation, *n.f.* negotiation.

négocier, *vb.* negotiate.

nègre, *adj.* and *n.m.* black, Negro.

négresse, *n.f.* a black woman.

neige, *n.f.* snow.

neiger, *vb.* snow.

neigeux, *adj.* snowy.

néon, *n.m.* neon.

néophyte, *n.m.* neophyte, convert.

Néo-Zélandais, *n.* New Zealander.

néphrite, *n.f.* nephritis.

nerf, (něr), *n.m.* nerve.

nerveux, *adj.* nervous.

nervosité, *n.f.* nervousness.

net, (-t) *m.*, **nette** *f.* *adj.* net, clear; clean, neat.

netteté, *n.f.* clearness, neatness.

nettoyer, *vb.* clean, scour.

nettoyeur, *n.m.* one who or that which cleans.

neuf, *adj.* and *n.m.* nine.

neuf, *m.*, **neuve** *f.* *adj.* brand-new.

neutraliser, *vb.* counteract.

neutralité, *n.f.* neutrality.

neutre, *adj.* and *n.m.* neutral.

neutron, *n.m.* neutron.

neuvième, *adj.* and *n.m.f.* ninth.

neveu, *n.m.* nephew.

névralgie, *n.f.* neuralgia.

névrite, *n.f.* neuritis.

névrose, *n.f.* neurosis.

névrosé, *adj.* and *n.m.* neurotic.

nez, *n.m.* nose.

ni, *conj.* nor. **ni ... ni ...**, neither ... nor ....

niais, *adj.* foolish.

niaiserie, *n.f.* silliness, trifle.

niche, *n.f.* alcove.

nichée, *n.f.* brood.

nicher, *vb.* **se n.**, nestle.

nickel, *n.m.* nickel.

nicotine, *n.f.* nicotine.

nid, *n.m.* nest.

nièce, *n.f.* niece.

nielle, *n.f.* wheat blight.

nier, *vb.* deny.

nigaud, *n.m.* fool, simpleton.

nihilisme, *n.m.* nihilism.

nimbe, *n.m.* halo.

n'importe, *interj.* never mind.

nippes, *n.f.pl.* old clothes.

nitrate, *n.m.* nitrate.

niveau, *n.m.* level. **au n. de**, level with.

niveler, *vb.* make level; survey.

nivellement, *n.m.* leveling; surveying.

noble, 1. *n.m.* nobleman, peer. 2. *adj.* noble.

noblesse, *n.f.* nobility.

noce, *n.f.* wedding. **faire la n.**, revel.

noceur, *n.m.* gay blade.

nocif, *adj.* harmful.

noctambule, *n.m.f.* sleepwalker; noctambulist.

nocturne, *adj.* nocturnal.

Noël, (nöël), *n.m.* Christmas; carol.

nœud, (nœ), *n.m.* knot.

noir, *adj.* and *n.m.* black.

noircir, *vb.* blacken.

noisetier, *n.m.* hazel (tree).

noisette, 1. *n.f.* hazelnut. 2. *adj.* light reddish brown.

noix, *n.f.* nut, walnut.

nolis, *n.m.* freight.

nom, *n.m.* name; noun.

nomade, *adj.* wandering, roaming.

nombre, *n.m.* number.

nombrer, *vb.* number.

nombreux, *adj.* numerous, manifold.

nombril, *n.m.* navel.

nominal, *adj.* nominal.

nominatif, *adj.* and *n.m.* nominative.

nomination, *n.f.* nomination, appointment.

nommément, *adv.* particularly, namely.

nommer, *vb.* name; nominate, appoint.

non, *adv.* no. **n. plus,** neither.
non-aligné, *adj.,* non-aligned.
nonchalamment, *adv.* carelessly, nonchalantly.
nonchalant, *adj.* nonchalant.
non-combattant, *adj. and n.m.* non-combatant.
nonne, *n.f.* nun.
nonobstant, *prep.* in spite of, notwithstanding.
nonpareil, *adj.* unequaled.
non-sens, *n.m.* nonsense.
nord, *n.m.* north.
normal, *adj.* normal.
normand, *adj.* Norman; equivocal.
Normandie, *n.f.* Normandy.
norme, *n.f.* norm.
Norvège, *n.f.* Norway.
Norvégien, *n.m.* Norwegian (person).
norvégien, 1. *n.m.* Norwegian (language). **2.** *adj.* Norwegian.
nostalgie, *n.f.* nostalgia.
notabilité, *n.f.* notability.
notable, 1. *n.m.* notable. **2.** *adj.* remarkable, notable.
notaire, *n.m.* lawyer, notary.
notamment, *adv.* particularly.
notation, *n.f.* notation.
note, *n.f.* note, bill; grade.

noter, *vb.* note.
notice, *n.f.* notice, review.
notification, *n.f.* notification.
notifier, *vb.* notify.
notion, *n.f.* notion.
notoire, *adj.* notorious.
notoriété, *n.f.* notoriety.
notre, *sg.,* **nos** *pl. adj.* our.
nôtre, *pron.* **le n.,** ours.
nouer, *vb.* tie.
noueux, *adj.* knotty.
nouilles, *n.f.pl.* noodles.
nounours, *n.m.* teddy bear.
nourrice, *n.f.* (wet) nurse.
nourricier, *adj.* nourishing; of nursing.
nourrir, *vb.* feed, nourish, foster.
nourrisson, *n.m.* infant.
nourriture, *n.f.* food, nourishment.
nous, *pron.* we, us, ourselves.
nouveau, *m.,* **nouvelle** *f. adj.* new, fresh. **de n.,** anew.
nouveauté, *n.f.* novelty.
nouvel an, *n.m.* new year.
nouvelle, *n.f.* news.
nouvellement, *adv.* recently, newly.
Nouvelle-Zélande, *n.f.* New Zealand.
novembre, *n.m.* November.
novice, *n.m.f.* novice.

noviciat, *n.m.* novitiate.
noyade, *n.f.* drowning.
noyau, *n.m.* kernel, nucleus.
noyauter, *vb.* infiltrate.
noyer, *vb.* drown.
noyer, *n.m.* walnut (tree).
nu, *adj.* naked, bare.
nuage, *n.m.* cloud; gloom.
nuageux, *adj.* cloudy.
nuance, *n.m.* shade, degree.
nucléaire, *adj.* nuclear.
nudité, *n.f.* bareness.
nuée, *n.f.* cloud; swarm.
nuire, *vb.* injure, harm.
nuisible, *adj.* injurious, hurtful.
nuit, *n.f.* night.
nul, *adj.* no, none; void. **nulle part,** nowhere.
nullement, *adv.* not at all.
nullité, *n.f.* nonentity.
numéraire, *n.m.* cash.
numéral, *adj. and n.m.* numeral.
numérique, *adj.* numerical.
numéro, *n.m.* number.
nu-pieds, *adj.* barefoot.
nuptial, *adj.* bridal.
nuque, *n.f.* nape.
nu-tête, *adj.* bareheaded.
nutritif, *adj.* nutritious.
nutrition, *n.f.* nutrition.
nylon, *n.m.* nylon.
nymphe, *n.f.* nymph.

O

oasis (-s), *n.f.* oasis.
obéir, *vb.* obey.
obéissance, *n.f.* obedience.
obéissant, *adj.* obedient.
obélisque, *n.m.* obelisk.
obérer, *vb.* burden with debt.
obèse, *adj.* obese.
obésité, *n.f.* obesity.
objecter, *vb.* object.
objecteur, *n.m.* **o. de conscience,** conscientious objector.
objectif, *adj. and n.m.* objective.
objection, *n.f.* objection.
objet, *n.m.* object.
obligation, *n.f.* obligation.
obligatoire, *adj.* compulsory, mandatory, binding.
obligeance, *n.f.* obligingness.

obliger, *vb.* oblige, accommodate.
oblique, *adj.* slanting; devious.
oblitération, *n.f.* obliteration.
oblitérer, *vb.* obliterate.
oblong, *adj.* oblong.
obnubilé, *adj.* obsessed.
obscène, *adj.* filthy, obscene.
obscénité, *n.f.* obscenity.
obscur, *adj.* obscure, dark, dim.
obscurcir, *vb.* darken, obscure.
obscurcissement, *n.m.* darkening; state of being obscure.
obscurément, *adv.* obscurely.
obscurité, *n.f.* darkness, dimness, obscurity.

obséder, *vb.* harass, haunt.
obsèques, *n.f.pl.* funeral.
obséquieusement, *adv.* obsequiously.
obséquieux, *adj.* obsequious.
observance, *n.f.* observance.
observateur, *n.m.* observer.
observation, *n.f.* observation, remark.
observer, *vb.* observe, watch.
obsession, *n.f.* obsession.
obstacle, *n.m.* obstacle, bar.
obstétrical, *adj.* obstetrical.
obstétrique, *n.f.* obstetrics.
obstination, *n.f.* stubbornness.
obstiné, *adj.* obstinate, stubborn.
obstiner, *vb.* **s'o.,** persist.
obstruction, *n.f.* obstruction.

obstruer, *vb.* obstruct, stop up.

obtempérer, *vb.* obey.

obtenir, *vb.* obtain, get.

obtention, *n.f.* obtaining.

obtus, *adj.* obtuse, dull, stupid.

obus, (-s), *n.m.* shell.

obusier, *n.m.* howitzer.

occasion, *n.f.* opportunity, chance; bargain.

occasionnel, *adj.* occasional.

occasionner, *vb.* cause, bring about.

occident, *n.m.* west.

occidental, *adj.* western.

occulte, *adj.* occult.

occupant, *n.m.* occupant, tenant.

occupation, *n.f.* pursuit; occupation.

occupé, *adj.* busy.

occuper, *vb.* occupy, busy. **s'o. de**, attend to.

occurrence, *n.f.* occurrence.

océan, *n.m.* ocean.

océanique, *adj.* oceanic.

ocre, *n.f.* ochre.

octane, *n.m.* octane.

octave, *n.f.* octave.

octobre, *n.m.* October.

octroyer, *vb.* grant.

oculaire, *adj.* ocular.

oculiste, *n.m.f.* oculist.

ode, *n.f.* ode.

odeur, *n.f.* odor, scent, perfume.

odieux, *adj.* hateful, obnoxious, odious.

odorant, *adj.* having a fragrant odor.

odorat, *n.m.* (sense of) smell.

œil, *n.m.*, *pl.* **yeux**, eye. **coup d'o.**, glance.

œillade, *n.f.* wink, quick look.

œillère, *n.f.* eyetooth.

œillet, *n.m.* carnation.

œuf, *n.m.* egg.

œuvre, *n.f.* work.

offensant, *adj.* offensive.

offense, *n.f.* offense.

offenser, *vb.* offend.

offenseur, *n.m* offender.

offensif, *adj.* offensive.

offensive, *n.f.* offensive.

offensivement, *adv.* offensively.

office, *n.m.* office, pantry; (church) service.

officiant, *n.m.* one who officiates.

officiel, *adj.* official.

officier, **1.** *n.m.* officer; mate. **2.** *vb.* officiate.

officieux, *adj.* officious.

offrande, *n.f.* offering.

offre, *n.f.* offer.

offrir, *vb.* offer, present.

offusquer, *vb.* obscure, shadow; irritate.

ogive, *n.f.* warhead.

ogre, *n.m.* ogre.

oie, *n.f.* goose.

oignon, (ô nyôN), *n.m.* onion; bulb.

oindre, *vb.* anoint.

oiseau, *n.m.* bird.

oiselet, *n.m.* small bird.

oiseux, *adj.* idle, empty, useless.

oisif, *adj.* idle.

oisillon, *n.m.* young bird.

oisiveté, *n.f.* idleness.

oléagineux, *adj.* oily.

oléoduc, *n.m.* oil pipeline.

olivâtre, *adj.* olive-colored.

olive, *n.f.* olive.

olivier, *n.m.* olive tree.

olympique, *adj.* Olympic.

ombilical, *adj.* umbilical.

ombrage, *n.m.* shade.

ombragé, *adj.* shady.

ombrager, *vb.* shade.

ombrageux, *adj.* suspicious, doubtful.

ombre, *n.f.* shade, shadow.

ombrelle, *n.f.* parasol.

ombreux, *adj.* shady.

omelette, *n.f.* omelet.

omettre, *vb.* omit.

omission, *n.f.* omission.

omnibus, (-s), *n.m.* bus.

omnipotent, *adj.* omnipotent.

omoplate, *n.f.* shoulder blade.

on, *pron.* one (indef. subj.).

once, *n.f.* ounce.

oncle, *n.m.* uncle.

onction, *n.f.* unction.

onctueux, *adj.* unctuous.

onde, *n.f.* wave.

ondé, *adj.* wavy.

on-dit, *n.m.* rumor.

ondoyer, *vb.* wave.

ondulation, *n.f.* wave. **o. permanente**, permanent wave.

onduler, *vb.* wave.

onéreux, *adj.* burdensome.

ongle, *n.m.* (finger)nail.

onglée, *n.f.* numb feeling.

onguent, *n.m.* salve, ointment.

onomatopée, *n.f.* onomatopœia.

onze, *adj.* and *n.m.* eleven.

onzième, *adj.* and *n.m.f.* eleventh.

opacité, *n.f.* opacity.

opale, *n.f.* opal.

opaque, *adj.* opaque.

opéra, *n.m.* opera.

opérateur, *n.m.* operator; cameraman.

opération, *n.f.* operation; transaction.

opératoire, *adj.* operative.

opéré, *n.m.* patient undergoing surgery.

opérer, *vb.* operate.

opérette, *n.f.* operetta.

opiner, *vb.* hold or express an opinion.

opiniâtre, *adj.* stubborn.

opiniâtreté, *n.f.* stubbornness.

opinion, *n.f.* opinion.

opium, *n.m.* opium.

opportun, *adj.* timely.

opportunité, *n.f.* timeliness.

opposant, *n.m.* opponent.

opposé, *adj.* opposite, averse.

opposer, *vb.* oppose. **s'o. à**, oppose, resist.

opposition, *n.f.* opposition.

oppresser, *vb.* weigh heavily on.

oppresseur, *n.m.* oppressor.

oppressif, *adj.* oppressive.

oppression, *n.f.* oppression.

opprimer, *vb.* oppress.

opprobre, *n.m.* disgrace, infamy.

opter, *vb.* select, decide.

opticien, *n.m.* optician.

optimisme, *n.m.* optimism.

optimiste, **1.** *adj.* optimistic. **2.** *n.m.f.* optimist.

option, *n.f.* option.

optique, *adj.* optic.
opulence, *n.f.* opulence, riches.
opuscule, *n.m.* small work.
or, 1. *n.m.* gold. **2.** *conj.* now.
oracle, *n.m.* oracle.
orage, *n.m.* storm.
orageusement, *adv.* turbulently, stormily.
orageux, *adj.* stormy.
oraison, *n.f.* prayer, oration.
oral, *adj.* oral.
orange, *n.f.* orange.
oranger, *n.m.* orange tree.
orateur, *n.m.* speaker, orator.
oratoire, *adj.* oratorical. **art o.,** oratory.
orbe, *n.m.* orb, sphere.
orbite, *n.m.* orbit; socket (as of eye).
orchestre, (-k-), *n.m.* orchestra, band.
orchestrer, (-k-), *vb.* orchestrate.
orchidée, *n.f.* orchid.
ordinaire, *adj. and n.m.* ordinary.
ordinal, *adj. and n.m.* ordinal.
ordinateur, *n.m.* computer.
ordonnance, *n.f.* prescription; ordinance, decree.
ordonné, *adj.* orderly, tidy.
ordonner, *vb.* order, ordain, bid, command.
ordre, *n.m.* order. **de premier o.,** first-rate.
ordure, *n.f.* filth, garbage, refuse.
ordurier, *adj.* foul.
oreille, *n.f.* ear.
oreiller, *n.m.* pillow.
oreillons, *n.m.pl.* mumps.
orfèvrerie, *n.f.* gold or silver jewelry.
organdi, *n.m.* organdy.
organe, *n.m.* organ (body).
organigramme, *n.m.* flow chart, organization chart.
organique, *adj.* organic.
organisateur, 1. *n.m.* organizer. **2.** *adj.* organizing.
organisation, *n.f.* organization, arrangement.
organiser, *vb.* organize.
organisme, *n.m.* organism.
organiste, *n.m.f.* organist.

orgasme, *n.m.* orgasm, climax.
orge, *n.f.* barley.
orgelet, *n.m.* sty (of eye).
orgie, *n.f.* orgy.
orgue, *n.m.* organ (instrument).
orgueil, *n.m.* pride.
orgueilleux, *adj.* proud, haughty.
Orient, *n.m.* Orient, East.
Oriental, *n.m.* Oriental.
oriental, *adj.* Oriental, eastern.
orientation, *n.f.* positioning.
orienté, *adj.* slanted.
orienter, *vb.* orient.
orifice, *n.m.* orifice, hole.
originaire, *adj.* original, native.
originairement, *adv.* originally.
original, 1. *n.m.* eccentric person. **2.** *adj.* original.
originalement, *adv.* originally; unusually.
originalité, *n.f.* originality.
origine, *n.f.* origin, source.
originel, *adj.* original.
oripeau, *n.m.* tinsel.
orme, *n.m.* elm.
orné, *adj.* ornate.
ornement, *n.m.* ornament, adornment, trimming.
ornemental, *adj.* ornamental.
ornementation, *n.f.* ornamentation.
orner, *vb.* adorn, trim.
ornière, *n.f.* rut, track.
ornithologie, *n.f.* ornithology.
orphelin, *n.m.* orphan.
orphelinat, *n.m.* orphanage.
orphéon, *n.m.* choral group.
orteil, *n.m.* toe.
orthodoxe, *adj.* orthodox.
orthodoxie, *n.f.* orthodoxy.
orthographe, *n.f.* spelling, orthography.
orthographier, *vb.* spell.
ortie, *n.f.* nettle.
os, *n.m.* bone.
oscillant, *adj.* oscillating.
oscillation, *n.f.* sway.
osciller, *vb.* fluctuate, oscillate.
osé, *adj.* attempted, bold.

oser, *vb.* dare.
osier, *n.m.* willow.
ossature, *n.f.* bony structure, skeleton.
ossements, *n.m.pl.* human remains.
osseux, *adj.* bony.
ossifier, *vb.* ossify.
ostensible, *adj.* ostensible.
ostentation, *n.f.* ostentation.
ostraciser, *vb.* ostracize.
otage, *n.m.* hostage.
ôter, *vb.* take off; take away.
otite, *n.f.* ear infection.
ou, *conj.* or. **ou . . . ou . . .,** either . . . or . . . .
où, *adv.* where.
ouailles, *n.f.pl.* religious congregation.
ouate, *n.f.* cotton; padding.
ouater, (wä-), *vb.* pad.
oubli, *n.m.* forgetfulness; oblivion.
oublier, *vb.* forget.
oubliettes, *n.f.pl.* dungeon.
oublieux, *adj.* forgetful.
ouest, (wĕst), *n.m.* west.
oui, (wē), *adv.* yes.
ouï-dire, *n.m.* gossip, hearsay.
ouïe, *n.f.* hearing; gill.
ouïr, *vb.* hear.
ouragan, *n.m.* hurricane.
ourler, *vb.* hem.
ourlet, *n.m.* hem.
ours, (-s), *n.m.* bear. **o. blanc,** polar bear.
ourson, *n.m.* bear cub.
outil, *n.m.* tool, implement.
outillage, *n.m.* quantity of tools, equipment.
outiller, *vb.* supply with tools.
outrage, *n.m.* outrage.
outrageant, *adj.* outrageous.
outrager, *vb.* outrage, affront.
outrance, *n.f.* extreme degree. **à o.,** to the very end.
outre, *adv. and prep.* beyond. **en o.,** besides, furthermore.
outré, *adj.* excessive, extreme.
outrecuidant, *adj.* excessively bold and forward.
outre-mer, *adv.* across the seas.

outrer, *vb.* overdo, irritate.
ouvert, *adj.* open.
ouverture, *n.f.* opening, gap; overture.
ouvrable, *adj.* work, workable.
ouvrage, *n.m.* work.
ouvrer, *vb.* work.

ouvreuse, *n.f.* usher or usherette.
ouvrier, *n.m.* workman; *pl.* labor.
ouvrir, *vb.* open.
ouvroir, *n.m.* workroom or workshop.
ovaire, *n.m.* ovary.

ovale, *adj. and n.m.* oval.
ovation, *n.f.* ovation.
overdose, *n.f.* overdose.
ovni, *n.m.* UFO.
ovule, *n.f.* egg.
oxyder, *vb.* oxidize.
oxygène, *n.m.* oxygen.
ozone, *n.f.* ozone.

P

pacage *n.m.* land used for pasture.
pacemaker, *n.m.* pacemaker.
pacificateur, 1. *adj.* pacifying. **2.** *n.m.* peacemaker.
pacification, *n.f.* peacemaking.
pacifier, *vb.* pacify, appease, soothe.
pacifique, *adj.* pacific, peaceful, peaceable.
pacifisme, *n.m.* pacifism.
pacotille, *n.f.* small wares.
pacte, *n.m.* covenant, pact.
pactiser, *vb.* make a pact, compromise.
pagaie, *n.f.* paddle.
pagaille, *n.f.* mess.
pagale, *n.f.* disorder, rush.
paganisme, *n.m.* paganism.
pagayer, *vb.* paddle.
pagayeur, *n.m.* paddler.
page, 1. *n.m.* page (boy). **2.** *n.f.* page (in book).
pages centrales, *n.f.pl.* centerfold.
pagination, *n.f.* pagination.
paginer, *vb.* number pages.
pagode, *n.f.* pagoda.
paie, *n.f.* pay.
paiement, payement, *n.m.* payment.
païen, *adj. and n.m.* pagan, heathen.
paillard, *adj.* lewd, indecent.
paillasse, *n.f.* mattress of straw; ticking.
paillasson, *n.m.* (door)mat.
paille, *n.f.* straw; defect (in gems).
paillette, *n.f.* spangle; defect.
pain, *n.m.* bread, loaf. **petit p.,** roll.
pair, 1. *n.m.* peer. **2.** *adj.* even (number), equal.
paire, *n.f.* pair.

pairesse, *n.f.* peeress.
pairie, *n.f.* peerage.
paisible, *adj.* peaceful.
paître, *vb.* graze.
paix, *n.f.* peace.
Pakistan, *n.m.* Pakistan.
palabre, *n.m.* palaver.
palais, *n.m.* palace; palate.
palan, *n.m.* gear for hoisting.
palatal, *adj.* palatal.
pale, *n.f.* blade; paddle.
pâle, *adj.* pale.
palefrenier, *n.m.* groom.
Palestine, *n.f.* Palestine.
palet, *n.m.* quoit.
paletot, *n.m.* overcoat.
palette, *n.f.* palette.
pâleur, *n.f.* paleness.
palier, *n.m.* stair landing.
pâlir, *vb.* grow pale or dim.
palissade, *n.f.* paling, fence.
pâlissant, *adj.* becoming pale.
palliatif, *n.m.* palliative; stopgap measure.
palmarès, *n.m.* list of winners.
palme, *n.f.* palm.
palmier, *n.m.* palm (tree).
palpable, *adj.* palpable.
palper, *vb.* touch, feel.
palpitant, *adj.* fluttering, palpitating.
palpiter, *vb.* flutter, beat, palpitate.
paludéen, *adj.* marshy.
paludisme, *n.m.* malaria.
pâmer, *vb.* se p., faint.
pamphlet, *n.m.* pamphlet; satire.
pamphlétaire, *n.m.* pamphleteer.
pamplemousse, *n.m.* grapefruit.
pan, *n.m.* side, piece, flap.
panacée, *n.f.* panacea.

panache, *n.m.* plume; spirit.
panais, *n.m.* parsnip.
pancarte, *n.f.* sign, placard.
pandit, *n.m.* pundit.
pané, *adj.* dotted with bread crumbs.
panier, *n.m.* basket.
panique, *adj. and n.f.* panic.
panne, *n.f.* fat; accident, breakdown.
panneau, *n.m.* panel.
panoplie, *n.f.* outfit; display.
panorama, *n.m.* panorama.
panse, *n.f.* paunch, cud.
pansement, *n.m.* dressing.
panser, *vb.* groom; dress.
pantalon, *n.m.* trousers.
panteler, *vb.* pant, gasp.
panthère, *n.f.* panther.
pantomime, *n.f.* pantomime.
pantoufle, *n.f.* slipper.
pantoufler, *vb.* act silly.
paon, (pän), *n.m.* peacock.
papa, *n.m.* daddy.
papal, *adj.* papal.
papauté, *n.f.* papacy.
pape, *n.m.* pope.
paperasse, *n.f.* waste paper; official documents.
paperassier, *adj.* scribbling, petty.
papeterie, *n.f.* stationery.
papetier, *n.m.* stationer.
papier, *n.m.* paper.
papier à notes, *n.m.* notepaper.
papier à tapisser, *n.m.* wallpaper.
papier peint, *n.m.* wallpaper.
papillon, *n.m.* butterfly.
papillonner, *vb.* flutter, trifle.
papoter, *vb.* prate, prattle.
pâque, *n.f.* Passover.
paquebot, *n.m.* small liner, packet.
pâquerette, *n.f.* daisy.

Pâques, *n.m.* Easter.

paquet, *n.m.* package, parcel, bundle; deck (cards).

par, *prep.* by; through.

parabole, *n.f.* parabola; parable.

parachever, *vb.* perfect.

parachute, *n.m.* parachute.

parade, *n.f.* parade, procession.

parader, *vb.* parade, show off.

paradis, *n.m.* paradise.

paradoxal, *adj.* paradoxical.

paradoxe, *n.m.* paradox.

paraffine, *n.f.* paraffin.

parage, *n.m.* ancestry, descent; locality.

parages, *n.m.pl.* vicinity.

paragraphe, *n.m.* paragraph.

paraître, *vb.* appear, seem.

parallèle, *adj. and n.m.f.* parallel.

paralyser, *vb.* paralyze.

paralysie, *n.f.* paralysis.

paralytique, *adj. and n.m.f.* paralytic.

paramètre, *n.m.* parameter.

parangon, *n.m.* model, paragon.

paranoïa, *n.f.* paranoia.

paraphraser, *vb.* paraphrase.

parapluie, *n.m.* umbrella.

parasite, *n.m.* parasite.

parasol, *n.m.* parasol.

paratonnerre, *n.m.* lightning rod.

paravent, *n.m.* screen.

parc, (-k), *n.m.* park.

parcelle, *n.f.* part, instalment.

parce que, *conj.* because.

parchemin, *n.m.* parchment.

parcimonie, *n.f.* parsimony.

parcomètre, *n.m.* parking meter.

parcourir, *vb.* run through.

parcours, *n.m.* course, journey.

par-dessous, *adv. and prep.* under(neath).

pardessus, *n.m.* overcoat.

par-dessus, *adv. and prep.* above, over.

pardon, 1. *n.m.* pardon, forgiveness. **2.** *interj.* sorry!

pardonner, *vb.* forgive, pardon.

pardonneur, *n.m.* pardoner.

pare-balles, *adj.* bulletproof.

pare-boue, *n.m.* mudguard.

pare-brise, *n.m.* windshield.

pare-chocs, *n.m.* bumper.

pareil, *adj.* like.

parent, *n.m.* relative; (*pl.*) parents.

parenté, *n.f.* relationship.

parenthèse, *n.f.* parenthesis.

parer, *vb.* attire, deck out; parry.

paresse, *n.f.* sloth.

paresser, *vb.* laze, waste time.

paresseux, *adj.* lazy.

parfaire, *vb.* complete, finish up.

parfait, *adj.* perfect.

parfois, *adv.* sometimes.

parfum, *n.m.* perfume.

parfumé, *adj.* fragrant.

parfumer, *vb.* perfume.

parfumerie, *n.f.* perfumery.

pari, *n.m.* bet.

paria, *n.m.* outcast.

parier, *vb.* bet.

parieur, *n.m.* one who bets.

Parisien, *n.m.* Parisian.

parisien, *adj.* Parisian.

parité, *n.f.* equality, parity.

parjure, *n.m.* perjury.

parjurer, *vb.* se p., commit perjury.

parking, *n.m.* parking lot.

parlant, *adj.* speaking, chatty.

parlement, *n.m.* parliament.

parlementaire, *adj.* parliamentary.

parlementer, *vb.* parley.

parler, *vb.* talk, speak.

parleur, *n.m.* one who speaks or talks.

parloir, *n.m.* parlor.

parmi, *prep.* among.

parodie, *n.f.* parody.

parodier, *vb.* parody, imitate.

paroi, *n.f.* wall lining.

paroisse, *n.f.* parish.

paroissial, *adj.* parochial.

parole, *n.f.* speech, word. **prendre la p.,** take the floor.

paroxysme, *n.m.* peak.

parquer, *vb.* park, enclose.

parquet, *n.m.* floor.

parqueterie, *n.f.* parquetry.

parrain, *n.m.* godfather.

parsemer, *vb.* spread, strew.

part, *n.f.* share, part. **de la p. de,** on behalf of. **quelque p.,** somewhere. **nulle p.,** nowhere. **faire p. à,** share; inform.

partage, *n.m.* partition, sharing, share.

partager, *vb.* share, divide.

partance, *n.f.* going, sailing.

partant, *n.m.* one who leaves.

partenaire, *n.m.f.* partner.

parti, *n.m.* party.

partial, *adj.* partial.

partialité, *n.f.* bias, partiality.

participant, *adj. and n.m.* participant.

participation, *n.f.* participation, share.

participe, *n.m.* participle.

participer, *vb.* partake, take part.

particularité, *n.f.* peculiarity.

particule, *n.f.* particle.

particulier, *adj.* particular; private; peculiar, special.

partie, *n.f.* part, party.

partiel, *adj.* partial.

partir, *vb.* depart, leave, go (come) away, sail.

partisan, *n.m.* partisan, follower.

partitif, *adj.* partitive.

partition, *n.f.* score (music).

partout, *adv.* everywhere, throughout. **p. où,** wherever.

parure, *n.f.* ornament.

parution, *n.f.* publication, appearance.

parvenir, *vb.* reach.

parvenu, *n.m.* upstart.

pas, 1. *n.m.* step, pace. **faux p.,** slip. **2.** *adv.* not. **p. du tout,** not at all.

passable, *adj.* fair.

passage, *n.m.* aisle, passage, alley.

passager, 1. *n.m.* passenger. **2.** *adj.* passing, fugitive.

passant, *n.m.* passer-by.

passavant, *n.m.* permit.

passe, *n.f.* passing, permit.

passé, *adj. and n.m.* past.

passe-partout, *n.m.* skeleton key; passport.

passeport, *n.m.* passport.

passer, *vb.* pass; go by; spend; strain. **se p. de,** go without.

passereau, *n.m.* sparrow.

passerelle, *n.f.* bridge.

passe-temps, *n.m.* pastime.

passible, *adj.* capable of feeling.

passif, *adj. and n.m.* passive.

passion, *n.f.* passion.

passionné, *adj.* passionate.

passionnel, *adj.* concerning or due to passion.

passionner, *vb.* interest, excite. **se p.,** be eager or excited over.

passoire, *n.f.* device for straining.

pastel, *n.m.* crayon.

pastèque, *n.f.* watermelon.

pasteur, *n.m.* pastor.

pasteuriser, *vb.* pasteurize.

pastille, *n.f.* lozenge, cough drop.

pastis, *n.m.* aniseed liquor.

pastoral, *adj.* pastoral.

pataud, *adj.* awkward.

patauger, *vb.* flounder.

pâte, *n.f.* paste, dough, batter.

pâté, *n.m.* block; pie.

patelin, *n.m.* (colloquial) village.

patenôtre, *n.f.* (Lord's) prayer.

patent, *adj.* patent, evident.

patente, *n.f.* license.

patenter, *vb.* license.

paterne, *adj.* paternal.

paternel, *adj.* paternal.

paternité, *n.f.* fatherhood.

pâteux, *adj.* pasty, thick, muddy.

pathétique, *adj.* pathetic.

pathologie, *n.f.* pathology.

patience, *n.f.* patience.

patient, *adj. and n.m.* patient.

patienter, *vb.* wait.

patin, *n.m.* skate.

patiner, *vb.* skate.

patineur, *n.m.* skater.

patinoire, *n.f.* skating rink.

pâtir, *vb.* suffer.

pâtisserie, *n.f.* pastry.

patois, *n.m.* dialect; gibberish.

pâtre, *n.m.* shepherd.

patriarche, *n.m.* patriarch.

patricien, *adj. and n.m.* patrician.

patrie, *n.f.* native country, homeland.

patrimoine, *n.m.* patrimony.

patriote, *n.m.f.* patriot.

patriotique, *adj.* patriotic.

patriotisme, *n.m.* patriotism.

patron, *n.m.* employer, boss; model, pattern; patron.

patronat, *n.m.* management, employers.

patronner, *vb.* patronize, support.

patrouille, *n.f.* patrol

patrouiller, *vb.* patrol

patte, *n.f.* paw, leg; flap.

pâturage, *n.m.* pasture.

pâture, *n.f.* fodder; pasture.

paume, *n.f.* palm.

paumé, 1. *n.m.* loser. **2.** *adj.* lost.

paupière, *n.f.* eyelid.

pause, *n.f.* pause.

pauvre, *adj.* poor.

pauvreté, *n.f.* poverty.

pavaner, *vb.* **se p.,** swagger, strut.

pavé, *n.m.* pavement.

paver, *vb.* pave.

pavillon, *n.m.* pavilion.

pavot, *n.m.* poppy.

payant, *adj.* paying, profitable.

paye, *n.f.* payment, salary.

payement, *n.m.* payment.

payer, *vb.* pay, settle.

payeur, *n.m.* payer.

pays, *n.m.* country.

paysage, *n.m.* landscape, scenery.

paysager, *adj.* of the country, rural.

paysan, *n.m.* peasant.

Pays-Bas, les, *n.m.pl.* Holland; the Netherlands.

péage, *n.m.* toll, tollgate.

peau, *n.f.* skin, hide.

pêche, *n.f.* peach; fishing.

péché, *n.m.* sin.

pécher, *vb.* sin.

pêcher, 1. *vb.* fish. **2.** *n.m.* peach tree.

pêcherie, *n.f.* fishing place.

pécheur, *m.,* **pécheresse** *f.* **1.** *n.* sinner. **2.** *adj.* sinful.

pêcheur, *n.m.* fisherman.

pécule, *n.f.* savings.

pécuniare, *adj.* pecuniary.

pédagogie, *n.f.* pedagogy.

pédale, *n.f.* pedal.

pédalo, *n.m.* pedal boat.

pédant, *adj. and n.m.* pedant, pedantic.

pédanterie, *n.f.* pedantry.

pédé(raste), *n.m.* homosexual.

pédestre, *adj.* pedestrian.

pédiatre, *n.m.* pediatrician.

pédicure, *n.m.* podiatrist.

pègre, *n.f.* underworld.

peigne, *n.m.* comb.

peigner, *vb.* comb.

peignoir, *n.m.* dressing-gown.

peindre, *vb.* paint, portray, depict.

peine, *n.f.* pain; penalty. **à p.,** hardly, barely; **faire de la p. à,** pain, *vb.;* **valoir la p. de,** be worth while to; **se donner la p.,** take the trouble.

peiner, *vb.* labor; grieve.

peintre, *n.m.* painter.

peinture, *n.f.* paint, painting.

péjoratif, *adj.* pejorative.

pelage, *n.m.* coat.

pelé, *adj.* bald, uncovered.

pêle-mêle, *adv.* pell-mell.

peler, *vb.* peel, pare.

pèlerin, *n.m.* pilgrim.

pèlerinage, *n.m.* pilgrimage.

pèlerine, *n.f.* cape.

pélican, *n.m.* pelican.

pelle, *n.f.* shovel.

pelletier, *n.m.* furrier.

pellicule, *n.f.* film.

pelote, *n.f.* ball, pellet.

peloton, *n.m.* ball; group of soldiers.

pelouse, *n.f.* lawn.

peluche, *n.f.* **animal en p.,** stuffed animal.

pelure, *n.f.* peel.

pénal, *adj.* penal.

pénalité, *n.f.* penalty.

penaud, *adj.* sheepish.

penchant, *n.m.* bent, liking, tendency.

pencher, *vb.* tilt, lean, droop. **se p.,** bend.

pendaison, *n.f.* hanging (execution).

pendant, *prep.* during; pending. **p. que,** as, while.

pendentatif, *n.m.* pendant.

penderie, *n.f.* wardrobe.

pendiller, *vb.* dangle.

pendre, *vb.* hang.

pendule, *n.m.* pendulum. *n.f.* clock.

pénétrable, *adj.* penetrable.

pénétrant, *adj.* keen.

pénétration, *n.f.* penetration.

pénétrer, *vb.* penetrate, pervade.

pénible, *adj.* painful.

pénicilline, *n.f.* penicillin.

péninsule, *n.f.* peninsula.

pénis, *n.m.* penis.

pénitence, *n.f.* penance.

pénitencier, *n.m.* penitentiary.

pénitent, *adj. and n.m.* penitent.

penne, *n.f.* feather.

pénombre, *n.f.* gloom, shadow.

pensée, *n.f.* thought; pansy.

penser, *vb.* think.

penseur, *n.m.* thinker.

pensif, *adj.* thoughtful, pensive.

pension, *n.f.* board; pension.

pensionnaire, *n.m.f.* boarder.

pensionnat, *n.m.* boarding school.

pente, *n.f.* slope, slant.

Pentecôte, *n.f.* Whitsun, Pentecost.

pénurie, *n.f.* penury, scarcity.

pépé, *n.m.* (colloquial) grandpa.

pépier, *vb.* chirp.

pépin, *n.m.* pip, kernel; (colloquial) problem.

pépinière, *n.f.* nursery (plants).

pépite, *n.f.* nugget.

perçant, *adj.* sharp.

perce, *n.f.* boring tool.

percée, *n.f.* opening; breakthrough.

perce-neige, *n.f.* snowdrop.

percepteur, *n.m.* tax collector.

perception, *n.f.* perception; collecting.

percer, *vb.* pierce, bore.

percevoir, *vb.* collect, amass; perceive.

perche, *n.f.* pole, perch.

percher, *vb.* se p., perch.

perchoir, *n.m.* perch.

perclus, *adj.* lame, crippled.

percolateur, *n.m.* percolator.

percussion, *n.f.* percussion.

percuter, *vb.* hit, strike.

perdition, *n.f.* perdition.

perdre, *vb.* lose; waste.

perdrix, *n.f.* partridge.

père, *n.m.* father.

péremptoire, *adj.* peremptory.

perfection, *n.f.* perfection.

perfectionnement, *n.m.* improvement, finishing.

perfectionner, *vb.* perfect, finish.

perfectionniste, *adj. and n.m.f.* perfectionist.

perfide, *adj.* treacherous.

perfidie, *n.f.* treachery.

perforation, *n.f.* perforation.

perforer, *vb.* perforate, drill.

péricliter, *vb.* collapse.

péridural, *adj.* **anesthésie p.,** epidural.

péril, (-l) *n.m.* peril, danger.

périlleux, *adj.* perilous, dangerous.

périmé, *adj.* outdated, expired.

périmètre, *n.m.* perimeter.

période, *n.f.* period, term, stage.

périodique, *adj.* periodic.

péripétie, *n.f.* shift of luck.

périphérique, *adj.* outlying, peripheral.

périr, *vb.* perish.

périscope, *n.m.* periscope.

périssable, *adj.* perishable.

perle, *n.f.* pearl, bead.

perlé, *adj.* pearly, perfect.

permanence, *n.f.* permanence.

permanent, *adj.* permanent.

perméable, *adj.* permeable.

permettre, *vb.* permit, allow.

permis, *n.m.* permit, license.

permission, *n.f.* permission; leave (of absence), furlough.

permissionnaire, *n.m.f.* one having a permit; one on leave.

permuter, *vb.* change, exchange.

pernicieux, *adj.* pernicious.

pérorer, *vb.* harangue, argue.

Pérou, *n.m.* Peru.

perpendiculaire, *adj.* perpendicular.

perpétrer, *vb.* commit.

perpétuel, *adj.* perpetual.

perpétuer, *vb.* perpetuate.

perplexe, *adj.* perplexed, undecided.

perplexité, *n.f.* perplexity.

perquisition, *n.f.* exploration, search.

perron, *n.m.* flight of steps.

perroquet, *n.m.* parrot.

perruque, *n.f.* wig.

persan, *adj. and n.m.* Persian.

perse, *adj.* Persian.

persécuter, *vb.* persecute.

persécution, *n.f.* persecution.

persévérance, *n.f.* perseverance.

persévérant, *adj.* persevering, resolute.

persévérer, *vb.* persevere.

persienne, *n.f.* blind, shutter.

persifler, *vb.* banter, ridicule.

persil, *n.m.* parsley.

Persique, *adj.* **le golfe P.,** the Persian Gulf.

persistance, *n.f.* persistence.

persistant, *adj.* persistent.

persister, *vb.* persist.

personnage, *n.m.* personage; character.

personnalité, *n.f.* personality.

personne, 1. *n.f.* person. **2.** *pron.* nobody.

personnel, 1. *n.m.* personnel, staff. **2.** *adj.* personal.

personnifier, *vb.* personify.

perspective, *n.f.* perspective, prospect.

perspicace, *adj.* discerning.

perspicacité, *n.f.* insight.

persuader, *vb.* persuade, convince; induce.

persuasif, *adj.* persuasive.

perte, *n.f.* loss, waste; (*pl.*) casualties.

pertinence, *n.f.* pertinence.

pertinent, *adj.* relevant, pertinent.

perturbateur, *n.m.* agitator, disturber.

perturbation, *n.f.* disruption.
perturber, *vb.* disrupt.
pervenche, *n.f.* periwinkle.
pervers, *adj.* perverse, contrary.
pervertir, *vb.* pervert.
pesant, *adj.* heavy, ponderous.
pesanteur, *n.f.* weight, dullness.
peser, *vb.* weigh.
pessimisme, *n.m.* pessimism.
pessimiste, *n.m.f.* pessimist.
peste, *n.f.* pestilence; nuisance.
pester, *vb.* **p. contre,** curse against.
pestilence, *n.f.* pestilence, plague, nuisance.
pétale, *n.m.* petal.
pétanque, *n.f.* bowling.
pétiller, *vb.* twinkle, crackle.
petit, 1. *adj.* little, small, petty. **2.** *n.m.* cub.
petite-fille, *n.f.* granddaughter.
petitesse, *n.f.* smallness, pettiness.
petit-fils, (-fēs), *n.m.* grandson.
petit-gris, *n.m.* fur of the squirrel.
pétition, *n.f.* petition.
pétitionner, *vb.* request, ask.
petits-enfants, *n.m.pl.* grandchildren.
petits-pois, *n.m.pl.* peas.
pétrifiant, *adj.* petrifying.
pétrifier, *vb.* petrify or (se p.) become petrified.
pétrin, *n.m.* (colloquial) jam, fix.
pétrir, *vb.* knead, mold.
pétrole, *n.m.* petroleum, kerosene.
pétulance, *n.f.* petulance.
peu, 1. *n.m.* little; few. **2.** *adv.* not. **p. à p.,** gradually.
peuplade, *n.f.* tribe, clan.
peuple, *n.m.* people.
peupler, *vb.* people.
peuplier, *n.m.* poplar.
peur, *n.f.* fear. **avoir p.,** be afraid. **de p. que . . . ne,** lest.
peureux, *adj.* shy, timid.

peut-être, *adv.* perhaps, maybe.
phallocrate, *adj.* macho.
phallocratie, *n.f.* machismo.
phantasme, *n.m.* fantasy.
phare, *n.m.* beacon, lighthouse; headlight.
pharmacie, *n.f.* drugstore, pharmacy.
pharmacien, *n.m.* druggist.
phase, *n.f.* phase.
phénix, *n.m.* phoenix; superior person.
phénoménal, *adj.* phenomenal.
phénomène, *n.m.* phenomenon; freak.
philanthrope, *n.m.* philanthropist.
philanthropie, *n.f.* philanthropy.
philatélie, *n.f.* stamp collecting.
Philippines, *n.f.pl.* the Philippines.
philosophe, *n.m.f.* philosopher.
philosophie, *n.f.* philosophy.
philosophique, *adj.* philosophical.
phobie, *n.f.* phobia.
phonéticien, *n.m.* phonetician.
phonétique, *adj. and n.f.* phonetic, phonetics.
phonographe, *n.m.* phonograph.
phoque, *n.m.* seal.
phosphorescent, *adj.* luminous.
photo, *n.f.* photograph.
photocopie, *n.f.* photocopy.
photocopieur, *n.m.* photocopier.
photographe, *n.m.f.* photographer.
photographie, *n.f.* photograph; photography.
phrase, *n.f.* sentence.
phtisie, *n.f.* consumption.
phtisique, *adj. and n.m.* consumptive.
physicien, *n.m.* physical scientist.
physionomie, *n.f.* looks, expression.
physique, 1. *n.f.* physics. **2.** *adj.* physical.

piailler, *vb.* peep, squeal.
pianiste, *n.m.f.* pianist.
piano, *n.m.* piano.
pic, *n.m.* peak.
pichet, *n.m.* jug.
pick-up, *n.m.* phonograph.
picoter, *vb.* prick, peck.
pièce, *n.f.* piece; coin; patch; room. **p. de théâtre,** play.
pied, *n.m.* foot. **aller à p.,** walk. **coup de p.,** kick.
pied-à-terre, *n.m.* temporary quarters.
piédestal, *n.m.* pedestal.
pied-noir, *n.m.* Algerianborn French person.
piège, *n.m.* snare, trap.
pierre, *n.f.* stone.
pierreries, *n.f.pl.* jewelry, gems.
pierreux, *adj.* full of stone or grit.
pierrot, *n.m.* clown in pantomime.
piété, *n.f.* piety.
piétiner, *vb.* trample; mark time.
piéton, *n.m.* pedestrian.
piètre, *adj.* pitiful, mean, wretched.
pieu, *n.m.* stake, pile.
pieuvre, *n.f.* octopus.
pieux, *adj.* pious.
pigeon, *n.m.* pigeon, dove.
piger, *vb.* (colloquial) understand.
pigiste, *n.m.f.* freelance(r).
pile, *n.f.* stack; battery.
piler, *vb.* crush; beat someone.
pilier, *n.m.* pillar, column.
pillage, *n.m.* plundering.
piller, *vb.* plunder.
pilotage, *n.m.* piloting; driving piles.
pilote, *n.m.f.* pilot.
piloter, *vb.* pilot, lead.
pilule, *n.f.* pill.
piment, *n.m.* chili.
pimenter, *vb.* flavor, season.
pimpant, *adj.* stylish, smart.
pin, *n.m.* pine.
pinacle, *n.m.* pinnacle.
pinard, *n.m.* (colloquial) (cheap) wine.
pince, *n.f.* clip; (*pl.*) pliers.
pinceau, *n.m.* paintbrush.
pince-nez, *n.m.* eyeglasses.

pincer, *vb.* pinch, nip.
pinte, *n.f.* pint.
pioche, *n.f.* pickax.
piocher, *vb.* dig.
piocheur, *n.m.* digger.
pion, *n.m.* pawn, peon.
pioncer, *vb.* nap, sleep.
pionnier, *n.m.* pioneer.
pipe, *n.f.* pipe.
pipeline, *n.m.* pipeline.
piper, *vb.* catch, decoy, trick.
piquant, *adj.* sharp. **mot p.,** quip.
pique, *n.m.* spade.
pique-nique, *n.m.* picnic.
piquer, *vb.* prick, sting.
piquet, *n.m.* picket, peg, stake.
piqûre, *n.f.* prick, sting, puncture.
pirate, *n.m.f.* pirate.
pirate de l'air, *n.m.f.* hijacker.
piraterie, *n.f.* piracy.
pire, *adj.* worse, worst.
pirouette, *n.f.* pirouette.
pis, *adv.* worse, worst.
piscine, *n.f.* pool.
pissenlit, *n.m.* dandelion.
pistache, *n.f.* pistachio.
piste, *n.f.* track.
pistolet, *n.m.* pistol.
piston, *n.m.* piston; strings (influence).
pistonner, *vb.* help, push; pull strings for.
pitance, *n.f.* meager amount, as of food.
piteux, *adj.* pitiful.
pitié, *n.f.* pity, mercy.
pitoyable, *adj.* pitiful, miserable.
pitre, *n.m.* clown.
pittoresque, *adj.* picturesque, colorful.
pivoine, *n.f.* peony.
pivot, *n.m.* pivot.
pivoter, *vb.* turn, pivot, revolve.
pizza, *n.f.* pizza.
placard, *n.m.* closet; poster.
placarder, *vb.* post, display.
place, *n.f.* place, room.
placement, *n.m.* investment; placing.
placer, *vb.* invest; place.
placet, *n.m.* petition, demand.

placide, *adj.* placid.
placidité, *n.f.* placidness.
plafond, *n.m.* ceiling.
plafonner, *vb.* reach one's ceiling.
plage, *n.f.* beach.
plagiaire, *n.m.f.* one who plagiarizes.
plagiat, *n.m.* plagiarism.
plagier, *vb.* plagiarize.
plaid, *n.m.* plaid.
plaider, *vb.* plead.
plaideur, *n.m.* pleader.
plaidoirie, *n.f.* lawyer's speech.
plaie, *n.f.* wound, sore.
plaignant, *n.m.* plaintiff.
plaindre, *vb.* pity. **se p.,** complain.
plaine, *n.f.* plain.
plainte, *n.f.* complaint.
plaintif, *adj.* mournful.
plaire, *vb.* please. **s'il vous plaît,** if you please.
plaisance, *n.f.* pleasure, ease.
plaisant, *adj.* joking.
plaisanter, *vb.* joke.
plaisanterie, *n.f.* joke.
plaisir, *n.m.* pleasure.
plan, *n.m.* plan; plane; schedule, scheme. **premier p.,** foreground.
planche, *n.f.* board, shelf, plank.
planche à roulettes, *n.f.* skateboard.
plancher, *n.m.* floor.
planer, *vb.* glide; hover.
planétaire, 1. *adj.* planetary. **2.** *n.m.* planetarium.
planète, *n.f.* planet.
planeur, *n.m.* glider (plane).
planifier, *vb.* plan.
plantation, *n.f.* plantation.
plante, *n.f.* plant; sole.
planter, *vb.* plant.
planteur, *n.m.* planter.
planton, *n.m.* military orderly.
plantureux, *adj.* fertile, rich.
plaque, *n.f.* plate, slab. **p. de projection,** lantern-slide.
plaquer, *vb.* plate; abandon.
plaquette, *n.f.* booklet; plaque.
plastic, *n.m.* plastic explosive.
plastique, *adj.* plastic.

plastiquer, *adj.* blow up.
plastronner, *vb.* pose, strut jauntily.
plat, 1. *n.m.* dish, platter. **2.** *adj.* flat. **œuf sur le p.,** fried egg.
platane, *n.m.* plane-tree.
plat-bord, *n.m.* gunwale.
plateau, *n.m.* plateau; tray.
plate-bande, *n.f.* flower bed.
plate-forme, *n.f.* platform.
platine, 1. *n.f.* platen, plate; turntable. **2.** *n.m.* platinum.
platitude, *n.f.* flatness.
plâtras, *n.m.* rubbish, rubble.
plâtre, *n.m.* plaster; cast (*med.*).
plausible, *adj.* plausible.
plébéien, *adj.* ignoble.
plébiscite, *n.m.* plebiscite.
plein, *adj.* full; crowded.
pleinement, *adv.* fully.
plénier, *adj.* complete, plenary.
plénitude, *n.f.* fullness.
pléthore, *n.f.* overabundance, plethora.
pleurer, *vb.* cry, weep, lament, mourn.
pleurésie, *n.f.* pleurisy.
pleurnicher, *vb.* complain, whine.
pleurs, *n.m.pl.* tears, weeping.
pleutre, *n.m.* cad, coward.
pleuvoir, *vb.* rain.
pli, *n.m.* envelope; fold, pleat, crease.
pliable, *adj.* pliable.
pliant, *n.m.* folding chair.
plier, *vb.* fold, bend.
plissement, *n.m.* fold, folding.
plisser, *vb.* pleat.
plomb, *n.m.* lead.
plomberie, *n.f.* plumbing.
plombier, *n.m.* plumber.
plongeoir, *n.m.* diving board.
plongeon, *n.m.* plunge, dive.
plonger, *vb.* plunge, dive, dip.
plongeur, *n.m.* diver; dishwasher.
plouf, *interj. and n.m.* splash, plop.
ploutocrate, *n.m.* plutocrat.
ployer, *vb.* incline, bend.

pluie, *n.f.* rain.
pluie radioactive, *n.f.* fallout.
plumage, *n.m.* feathers.
plume, *n.f.* pen; feather.
plumeau, *n.m.* feather duster.
plumer, *vb.* pluck.
plumet, *n.m.* plume.
plumeux, *adj.* feathery.
plumier, *n.m.* pen or pencil case.
plupart, *n.f.* greater part, majority. **pour la p.,** mostly.
pluralité, *n.f.* plurality.
pluriel, *adj. and n.m.* plural.
plus, *adv.* more, most. **ne . . . p.,** no more. **non p.,** neither. **en p.,** extra.
plusieurs, *adj. and pron.* several.
plus-que-parfait, *n.m.* pluperfect.
plus-value, *n.f.* profit.
plutôt, *adv.* rather.
pluvieux, *adj.* rainy, wet.
pneu, *n.m.* tire.
pneumatique, *abbr.* **pneu,** *n.m.* tire.
pneumonie, *n.f.* pneumonia.
pochade, *n.f.* hasty sketch.
poche, *n.f.* pocket.
pocher, *vb.* poach.
pocheter, *vb.* pocket.
pochette, *n.f.* little pocket; handkerchief.
pochoir, *n.m.* stencil.
poêle, *n.m.* stove.
poème, *n.m.* poem.
poésie, *n.f.* poem, poetry.
poète, *n.m.* poet.
poétique, *adj.* poetic.
poids, (pwä) *n.m.* weight.
poignant, *adj.* poignant, keen.
poignard, *n.m.* dagger.
poignarder, *vb.* stab.
poigne, *n.f.* grip, power.
poignée, *n.f.* handful; handle.
poignet, *n.m.* wrist; cuff.
poil, (pwäl) *n.m.* hair.
poilu, 1. *adj.* hairy. **2.** *n.m.* French soldier.
poinçon, *n.m.* punch.
poing, *n.m.* fist.
point, *n.m.* point, dot, period; stitch. **p. de vue,** point of view. **p. du jour,** dawn. **ne . . . p.,**

none. **être sur le p. de,** be about to. **au p.,** in focus. **deux p.s,** colon. **p. d'interrogation,** question mark.
pointage, *n.m.* pointing; *(mil.)* sighting.
pointe, *n.f.* point, tip, touch (small amount).
pointer, *vb.* point, aim; check in.
pointeur, *n.m.* pointer, checker.
pointillage, *n.m.* dotting.
pointiller, *vb.* dot; tease.
pointilleux, *adj.* fussy, precise.
pointu, *adj.* pointed.
pointure, *n.f.* size (shoe).
point-virgule, *n.m.* semicolon.
poire, *n.f.* pear.
poireau, *n.m.* leek.
poireauter, *vb.* hang around.
poirier, *n.m.* pear tree.
pois, *n.m.* pea; dot.
poison, *n.m.* poison.
poisser, *vb.* make gluey or sticky.
poisson, *n.m.* fish.
poissonnerie, *n.f.* fish store.
poissonneux, *adj.* filled with fish.
poissonnier, *n.m.* fish dealer.
poitrinaire, *adj. and n.m.f.* consumptive.
poitrine, *n.f.* chest.
poivre, *n.m.* pepper.
poivrer, *vb.* spice with pepper.
poivrier, *n.m.* pepper plant.
poivron, *n.m.* pepper.
poix, *n.f.* pitch.
polaire, *adj.* polar.
pôle, *n.m.* pole.
polémique, *n.f.* argument.
poli, 1. *adj.* civil, polite. **2.** *n.m.* polish.
police, *n.f.* police; (insurance) policy.
policer, *vb.* refine.
polichinelle, *n.m.* Punch (puppet).
policier, *n.m.* policeman. **roman p.,** detective story.
polir, *vb.* polish.
polisseur, *n.m.* polisher.

polisson, 1. *n.m.* gamin, scamp. **2.** *adj.* running wild.
polissonnerie, *n.f.* naughty action or remark.
politesse, *n.f.* good manners.
politicien, *n.m.f.* politician, political schemer.
politique, 1. *n.f.* policy, politics. **2.** *adj.* politic, political.
polka, *n.f.* polka.
pollen, *n.m.* pollen.
polluer, *vb.* pollute.
pollution, *n.f.* pollution.
Pologne, *n.f.* Poland.
Polonais, *n.m.* Pole.
polonais, *adj. and n.m.* Polish.
poltron, 1. *adj.* craven, cowardly. **2.** *n.m.* coward.
poltronnerie, *n.f.* cowardly behavior.
polycopier, *vb.* duplicate.
polygame, 1. *n.m.f.* polygamist. **2.** *adj.* polygamous.
polygamie, *n.f.* polygamy.
polygone, *n.m.* polygon.
polyvalent, *adj.* varied, versatile.
pommade, *n.f.* pomade, salve.
pomme, *n.f.* apple. **p. de terre,** potato.
pommeau, *n.m.* pommel.
pommette, *n.f.* cheekbone.
pommier, *n.m.* apple tree.
pompe, *n.f.* pump; pomp.
pomper, *vb.* pump.
pompeux, *adj.* pompous.
pompier, *n.m.* fireman.
pompiste, *n.m.f.* gas station attendant.
pompon, *n.m.* pompom, tuft.
ponce, *n.f.* pumice.
ponctualité, *n.f.* punctuality.
ponctuation, *n.f.* punctuation.
ponctuel, *adj.* punctual.
ponctuer, *vb.* punctuate.
pondre, *vb.* lay (eggs).
poney, *n.m.* pony.
pont, *n.m.* bridge; deck.
pontife, *n.m.* pontiff.
pont-levis, *n.m.* drawbridge.
ponton, *n.m.* pontoon.
pop, *adj. and n.m.* pop (music).

popeline, *n.f.* poplin.

popote, *n.f.* mess (military).

populace, *n.f.* mob.

populaire, *adj.* popular.

populariser, *vb.* popularize.

popularité, *n.f.* popularity.

population, *n.f.* population.

populeux, *adj.* populous.

porc, *n.m.* pig, pork.

porcelaine, *n.f.* china.

porc-épic, *n.m.* porcupine.

porche, *n.m.* porch.

porcherie, *n.f.* pigpen.

pore, *n.m.* pore.

poreux, *adj.* porous.

porno, *adj.* porn.

pornographie, *n.f.* pornography.

port, *n.m.* port, harbor; carrying; postage.

portable, *adj.* wearable.

portail, *n.m.* portal.

portant, *adj.* bien/mal p., in good/ill health.

portatif, *adj.* portable.

porte, *n.f.* door, gate.

porte-affiches, *n.m.* billboard.

porte-avions, *n.m.* aircraft carrier.

portée, *n.f.* range, import, scope, reach; litter. hors de p., out of reach.

portefaix, *n.m.* porter.

portefeuille, *n.m.* wallet, case, portfolio.

portemanteau, *n.m.* cloak rack.

portement, *n.m.* carrying.

porte-monnaie, *n.m.* purse.

porte-parole, *n.m.* spokesman.

porter, *vb.* carry, bear; wear. se p., be (in health).

porte-rame, *n.m.* oarlock.

porteur, *n.m.* porter, bearer.

portier, *n.m.* doorman, porter.

portière, *n.f.* door-curtain.

portion, *n.f.* portion, share.

portique, *n.m.* portico, porch.

porto, *n.m.* port wine.

portrait, *n.m.* portrait.

portraitiste, *n.m.f.* painter of portraits.

Portugais, *n.m.* Portuguese (person).

portugais, 1. *n.m.* Portuguese (language). 2. *adj.* Portuguese.

Portugal, *n.m.* Portugal.

pose, *n.f.* pose, attitude.

posé, *n.f.* poised, set.

poser, *vb.* place, stand, set, lay. se p., settle, alight.

poseur, *n.m.* person or thing that places or applies; affected person.

positif, *adj. and n.m.* positive.

position, *n.f.* stand, place, position.

positiviste, *n.m.f.* positivist.

posologie, *n.f.* dosage.

posséder, *vb.* own, possess.

possesseur, *n.m.* possessor.

possessif, *adj. and n.m.* possessive.

possession, *n.f.* possession.

possibilité, *n.f.* possibility.

possible, *adj.* possible. tout son p., one's utmost.

postal, *adj.* postal.

poste, *n.f.* mail. mettre à la p., mail. p. restante, general delivery.

poste, *n.m.* post. p. d'essence, gas station. p. de secours, first-aid station.

poster, *vb.* post (letter); place.

postérieur, *adj.* rear, posterior.

postérité, *n.f.* posterity.

posthume, *adj.* posthumous.

postiche, *adj.* false, unnecessary.

postier, *n.m.* postal worker.

post-scriptum, *n.m.* postscript.

postulant, *n.m.* applicant.

postuler, *vb.* apply for.

posture, *n.f.* posture.

pot, *n.m.* pot, pitcher, jar.

potable, *adj.* drinkable.

potage, *n.m.* soup.

potager, *adj.* vegetable.

potasse, *n.f.* potash.

pot-au-feu, *n.m.* stew.

pot-de-vin, *n.m.* tip, bribe.

pote, *n.m.* (colloquial) buddy.

poteau, *n.m.* post.

potée, *n.f.* potful.

potelé, *adj.* chubby.

potence, *n.f.* gallows.

potentat, *n.m.* potentate.

potentiel, *adj. and n.m.* potential.

poterie, *n.f.* pottery.

poterne, *n.f.* postern.

potier, *n.m.* potter.

potins, *n.m.pl.* gossip.

potion, *n.f.* potion.

potiron, *n.m.* pumpkin.

pou, *n.m.* louse.

poubelle, *n.f.* garbage can.

pouce, *n.m.* thumb; inch.

pouding, *n.m.* pudding.

poudre, *n.f.* powder.

poudrer, *vb.* powder.

poudreux, *adj.* full of powder or dust.

poudrier, *n.m.* compact (cosmetic).

poudroyer, *vb.* be dusty.

pouilleux, *adj.* infested with lice.

poulailler, *n.m.* henhouse.

poulain, *n.m.* colt.

poule, *n.f.* hen, chicken.

poulet, *n.m.* chicken.

poulette, *n.f.* pullet.

poulie, *n.f.* pulley.

poulpe, *n.m.* octopus.

pouls, *n.m.* pulse.

poumon, *n.m.* lung.

poupe, *n.f.* poop (of ship).

poupée, *n.f.* doll.

poupin, *adj.* smart, chic.

pour, *prep.* for; in order to. p. que, so that.

pourboire, *n.m.* tip, gratuity.

pourceau, *n.m.* hog.

pour-cent, *n.m.* percent.

pourcentage, *n.m.* percentage.

pourchasser, *vb.* pursue.

pourfendeur, *n.m.* killer, bully.

pourparlers, *n.m.pl.* discussion, parley.

pourpoint, *n.m.* doublet.

pourpre, *adj.* purple.

pourquoi, *adv.* why.

pourri, *adj.* rotten.

pourrir, *vb.* rot, spoil.

pourriture, *n.f.* pursuit.

poursuite, *n.f.* pursuit.

poursuivant, *n.m.* one who sues or prosecutes.

poursuivre, *vb.* pursue; sue, prosecute.

pourtant, *adv.* however.

pourvoi, *n.m.* appeal (at court).

pourvoir, *vb.* provide, supply. **p. à,** cater to.

pourvoyeur, *n.m.* caterer, purveyor.

pourvu que, *conj.* provided that.

pousse, *n.f.* shoot, sprouting.

poussée, *n.f.* push.

pousser, *vb.* push, urge, drive; grow.

poussette, *n.f.* stroller.

poussier, *n.m.* coal dust.

poussière, *n.f.* dust.

poussiéreux, *adj.* dusty.

poussin, *n.m.* newly hatched chick.

poussoir, *n.m.* push-button.

poutre, *n.f.* beam.

pouvoir, 1. *vb.* be able, can, may. **2.** *n.m.* power.

prairie, *n.f.* meadow.

praline, *n.f.* burnt almond.

praticable, *adj.* practicable.

praticien, *n.m.* practitioner.

pratique, 1. *n.f.* practice, exercise. **2.** *adj.* practical.

pratiquement, *adv.* practically, virtually.

pratiquer, *vb.* practice, exercise.

pré, *n.m.* meadow.

préalable, *adj.* preliminary.

préambule, *n.m.* preamble.

préau, *n.m.* yard, as of a prison.

préavis, *n.m.* advance notice.

précaire, *adj.* precarious.

précaution, *n.f.* precaution, discretion.

précédent, *n.m.* precedent.

précéder, *vb.* precede; come (go) before.

précepte, *n.m.* precept.

précepteur, *n.m.* tutor.

prêche, *n.m.* sermon.

prêcher, *vb.* preach.

précieux, *adj.* precious, valuable.

préciosité, *n.f.* preciosity.

précipice, *n.m.* precipice.

précipitamment, *adv.* headlong.

précipitation, *n.f.* hurry.

précipité, *adj.* hasty.

précipiter, *vb.* precipitate. **se p.,** rush, hasten.

précis, *adj.* precise, exact, accurate.

précisément, *adv.* precisely, definitely, just so.

préciser, *vb.* specify.

précision, *n.f.* accuracy, precision.

précité, *adj.* previously cited.

précoce, *adj.* precocious.

précocité, *n.f.* precociousness.

précompter, *vb.* deduct in advance.

préconçu, *adj.* preconceived.

préconiser, *vb.* extol, praise.

préconnaissance, *n.f.* foreknowledge.

précurseur, *n.m.* precursor.

prédécesseur, *n.m.* predecessor.

prédestination, *n.f.* predestination.

prédicateur, *n.m.* preacher.

prédiction, *n.f.* prediction.

prédilection, *n.f.* preference, predilection.

prédire, *vb.* foretell, predict.

prédisposer, *vb.* predispose.

prédisposition, *n.f.* predisposition.

prédominant, *adj.* predominant.

prééminence, *n.f.* preeminence.

préfabriquer, *adj.* prefabricated.

préface, *n.f.* preface.

préfecture, *n.f.* prefecture, district.

préférable, *adj.* preferable.

préférence, *n.f.* preference.

préférer, *vb.* prefer.

préfet, *n.m.* prefect.

préfixe, *n.m.* prefix.

préfixer, *vb.* fix in advance.

prégnant, *adj.* pregnant.

préhistorique, *adj.* prehistoric.

préjudice, *n.m.* injury.

préjudiciel, *adj.* interlocutory (as in law).

préjugé, *n.m.* prejudice.

préjuger, *vb.* prejudge.

prélasser, *vb.* **se p.,** bask, lounge.

prélat, *n.m.* prelate.

prélèvement, *n.m.* deduction in advance.

prélever, *vb.* deduct previously.

préliminaire, *adj.* preliminary.

prélude, *n.m.* prelude.

prématuré, *adj.* premature.

préméditation, *n.f.* premeditation.

préméditer, *vb.* premeditate.

prémices, *n.f.pl.* first fruits, first works.

premier, *adj.* first, foremost; early; former.

prémisse, *n.f.* premise.

prémonition, *n.f.* premonition.

prémunir, *vb.* warn, take precautions.

prendre, *vb.* take.

preneur, *n.m.* buyer.

prénom, *n.m.* given name.

prénommé, *adj.* previously named.

préoccupation, *n.f.* care, worry.

préoccuper, *vb.* worry.

prépaiement, *n.m.* prepayment.

préparatifs, *n.m.pl.* preparation.

préparation, *n.f.* preparation.

préparatoire, *adj.* preparatory.

préparer, *vb.* prepare.

prépondérance, *n.f.* preponderance.

prépondérant, *adj.* preponderant.

préposé, *n.m.* one in charge.

préposition, *n.f.* preposition.

préretraite, *n.f.* early retirement.

prérogative, *n.f.* prerogative.

près, 1. *adv.* near. **2.** *prep.* **p. de,** near. **de p.,** nearby.

présage, *n.m.* omen.

présager, *vb.* (fore)bode.

presbyte, *adj.* far-sighted.

presbytère, *n.m.* parsonage, presbytery.

prescription, *n.f.* prescription.

prescrire, *vb.* prescribe.
préséance, *n.f.* precedence.
présélection, *n.f.* triage.
présence, *n.f.* presence; attendance.
présent, *adj. and n.m.* present.
présentable, *adj.* presentable.
présentation, *n.f.* presentation, introduction.
présentement, *adv.* now, at present.
présenter, *vb.* present; introduce. **se p. à l'esprit,** come to mind.
préservatif, *n.m.* condom.
préservation, *n.f.* preservation.
préserver, *vb.* preserve.
présidence, *n.f.* presidency.
président, *n.m.* president, chairman.
présidente, *n.f.* chairwoman.
présidentiel, *adj.* presidential.
présider, *vb.* preside.
présomptif, *adj.* apparent, presumed.
présomptueux, *adj.* presumptuous.
presque, *adv.* almost, nearly.
presqu'île, *n.f.* peninsula.
pressage, *n.m.* pressing.
pressant, *adj.* urgent.
presse, *n.f.* press; crowd.
pressé, *adj.* hurried.
pressentiment, *n.m.* foreboding, misgiving.
pressentir, *vb.* foresee.
presse-papiers, *n.m.* paperweight.
presser, *vb.* press; urge; hurry.
pressing, *n.m.* dry cleaner.
pression, *n.f.* pressure.
pressoir, *n.m.* machine or device for squeezing.
pressurer, *vb.* squeeze, put pressure on.
prestance, *n.f.* imposing appearance.
prestation, *n.f.* allowance; performance.
preste, *adj.* dexterous, nimble.
prestesse, *n.f.* vivacity, nimbleness.

prestige, *n.m.* prestige; illusion.
prestigieux, *adj.* enchanting.
présumer, *vb.* presume.
présupposer, *vb.* presuppose.
prêt, 1. *n.m.* loan. **2.** *adj.* ready.
prêtable, *adj.* lendable.
prétendant, *n.m.* claimant.
prétendre, *vb.* claim.
prétendu, *adj.* supposed, so-called.
prétentieux, *adj.* pretentious.
prétention, *n.f.* claim.
prêter, *vb.* lend.
prêteur, *n.m.* lender.
prétexte, *n.m.* pretext.
prétexter, *vb.* pretend, feign.
prêtre, *n.m.* priest.
prêtresse, *n.f.* priestess.
preuve, *n.f.* proof.
preux, *adj. and n.m.* gallant, brave.
prévaloir, *vb.* prevail.
prévenance, *n.f.* attentiveness, obligingness.
prévenant, *adj.* considerate.
prévenir, *vb.* prevent; warn.
préventif, 1. *adj.* preventive. **2.** *n.m.* deterrent.
prévention, *n.f.* bias; prevention.
prévenu, *adj.* partial, biased.
prévision, *n.f.* forecast, expectation, prediction.
prévoir, *vb.* foresee.
prévôt, *n.m.* provost.
prévoyance, *n.f.* foresight.
prévoyant, *adj.* farseeing, prudent.
prier, *vb.* beg; pray.
prière, *n.f.* prayer.
prieur, *n.m.* prior.
prieuré, *n.m.* priory.
primaire, *adj.* primary.
primauté, *n.f.* preeminence, primacy.
prime, 1. *n.f.* premium; subsidy. **2.** *adj.* first; accented.
primé, *adj.* prize-winning.
primer, *vb.* outdo, excel.
primeur, *n.f.* freshness, earliness.
primitif, *adj.* primitive; original.
primordial, *adj.* primordial.
prince, *n.m.* prince.

princesse, *n.f.* princess.
princier, *adj.* princely.
principal, *adj.* chief, main, principal.
principauté, *n.f.* principality.
principe, *n.m.* principle.
printanier, *adj.* of spring.
printemps, *n.m.* spring.
priorité, *n.f.* priority.
prisable, *adj.* estimable.
prise, *n.f.* grasp, hold, grip. **p. de courant,** (electric) plug.
prisée, *n.f.* appraisal.
priser, *vb.* appraise; prize; take (drugs).
priseur, *n.m.* auctioneer, appraiser.
prisme, *n.m.* prism.
prison, *n.f.* jail, prison.
prisonnier, *n.m.* prisoner.
privation, *n.f.* privation, want, hardship.
privé, *adj.* private.
priver, *vb.* deprive.
privilège, *n.m.* privilege, license.
privilégier, *vb.* license.
prix, *n.m.* price, charge, fare; prize, award.
prix-courant, *n.m.* list of prices.
probabilité, *n.f.* probability, chances.
probable, *adj.* likely, probable.
probant, *adj.* convincing.
probité, *n.f.* probity.
problématique, *adj.* problematical.
problème, *n.m.* problem.
procédé, *n.m.* procedure, process.
procéder, *vb.* proceed.
procédure, *n.f.* proceeding.
procès, *n.m.* trial; (law)suit.
procession, *n.f.* procession.
processionnel, *adj.* processional.
processus, *n.m.* process.
procès-verbal, *n.m.* minutes (of meeting).
prochain, 1. *n.m.* neighbor. **2.** *adj.* next.
prochainement, *adv.* soon.
proche, *adj.* near, close.
Proche-Orient, *n.m.* Near East.

proclamation, *n.f.* proclamation.

proclamer, *vb.* proclaim.

procréation, *n.f.* procreation.

procurer, *vb.* procure, get.

procureur, *n.m.* prosecuting attorney.

prodigalement, *adv.* prodigally.

prodigalité, *n.f.* extravagance.

prodige, *n.m.* prodigy.

prodigieux, *adj.* wondrous.

prodigue, *adj.* extravagant, lavish, profuse.

prodiguer, *vb.* lavish.

producteur, *n.m.* producer.

productif, *adj.* productive.

production, *n.f.* production.

productivité, *n.f.* productivity.

produire, *vb.* produce, yield, breed.

produit, *n.m.* product, commodity.

proéminence, *n.f.* prominence.

proéminent, *adj.* prominent, standing out,

prof, *n.m.* teacher.

profane, *adj.* profane.

profaner, *vb.* misuse, debase, profane.

proférer, *vb.* say, utter.

professer, *vb.* profess.

professeur, *n.m.* professor, teacher.

profession, *n.f.* profession.

professionnel, *adj.* professional.

professoral, *adj.* professorial.

professorat, *n.m.* professorship; teaching.

profil, (-1), *n.m.* profile.

profiler, *vb.* show a profile of.

profit, *n.m.* profit.

profitable, *adj.* profitable.

profiter, *vb.* profit.

profiteur, *n.m.* profiteer.

profond, *adj.* deep, profound; in-depth.

profondeur, *n.f.* depth.

profus, *adj.* profuse.

profusion, *n.f.* profusion, excess.

progéniture, *n.f.* offspring.

programmation, *n.f.* programming.

programme, *n.m.* program.

progrès, *n.m.* progress, advance.

progresser, *vb.* progress.

progressif, *adj.* progressive.

progressiste, *n.m.* progressive.

prohiber, *vb.* prohibit.

prohibitif, *adj.* prohibitive.

prohibition, *n.f.* prohibition.

proie, *n.f.* prey.

projecteur, *n.m.* projector.

projectile, *n.m.* missile.

projection, *n.f.* projection.

projet, *n.m.* project, plan. **p. de loi**, bill.

projeter, *vb.* project, plan.

prolétaire, *adj. and n.m.* proletarian.

prolétariat, *n.m.* proletariat.

prolifération, *n.f.* proliferation.

prolifique, *adj.* prolific.

prolixe, *adj.* verbose.

prologue, *n.m.* prologue.

prolongation, *n.f.* extension, prolongation.

prolonger, *vb.* extend, prolong.

promenade, *n.f.* excursion; walk; ride.

promener, *vb.* take out. **se p.**, take a walk (ride).

promeneur, *n.m.* walker.

promesse, *n.f.* promise.

promettre, *vb.* promise.

promiscuité, *n.f.* promiscuity; crowding.

promontoire, *n.m.* promontory.

promoteur, *n.m.* promoter.

promotion, *n.f.* promotion.

promouvoir, *vb.* promote.

prompt, *adj.* prompt.

promptitude, *n.f.* quickness.

promulguer, *vb.* promulgate.

prôner, *vb.* lecture to, praise.

pronom, *n.m.* pronoun.

prononcer, *vb.* pronounce, utter; deliver.

prononciation, *n.f.* pronunciation.

pronostic, *n.m.* prognosis; prediction.

propagande, *n.f.* propaganda.

propagandiste, *n.m.f.* propagandist.

propagateur, *n.m.* propagator.

propagation, *n.f.* propagation.

propager, *vb.* propagate.

propension, *n.f.* inclination, propensity.

prophète, *n.m.* prophet.

prophétie, *n.f.* prophecy.

prophétique, *adj.* prophetic.

prophétiser, *vb.* prophesy.

propice, *adj.* favorable. **peu p.**, unfavorable.

propitiation, *n.f.* propitiation, conciliation.

proportion, *n.f.* proportion.

proportionné, *adj.* proportionate.

proportionnel, *adj.* proportional.

proportionner, *vb.* keep in proportion.

propos, *n.m.* subject; discourse. **à p.**, relevant. **à p. de**, with regard to.

proposable, *adj.* suitable, appropriate.

proposer, *vb.* propose; move. **se p. de**, intend, mean.

proposition, *n.f.* proposal, proposition.

propre, *adj.* proper; clean; neat; own. **peu p.**, unfit.

propreté, *n.f.* cleanliness, neatness.

propriétaire, *n.m.f.* proprietor.

propriété, *n.f.* property (landed), estate.

propulser, *vb.* push, propel.

propulseur, *n.m.* propeller.

propulsion, *n.f.* propulsion.

proroger, *vb.* postpone, extend time limit.

prosaïque, (-zä ĕk), *adj.* prosaic.

prosaïsme, *n.m.* prosaicness, dullness.

prosateur, *n.m.* writer of prose.

proscription, *n.f.* proscription.

proscrire, *vb.* outlaw, proscribe.

proscrit, *adj. and n.m.* exile(d); forbidden.

prose, *n.f.* prose.
prosodie, *n.f.* prosody.
prospecter, *vb.* search, as for gold.
prospecteur, *n.m.* prospector.
prospectus (-s), *n.m.* leaflet, pamphlet.
prospère, *adj.* prosperous.
prospérer, *vb.* flourish, thrive, prosper.
prospérité, *n.f.* prosperity.
prosterner, *vb.* prostrate.
prostituée, *n.f.* prostitute.
prostitution, *n.f.* prostitution.
protagoniste, *n.m.f.* main character.
protecteur, 1. *n.m.* protector; patron. **2.** *adj.* protective.
protecteur du citoyen, *n.m.* ombudsman (in Quebec).
protection, *n.f.* protection.
protectorat, *n.m.* protectorate.
protéger, *vb.* protect; patronize, foster.
protéine, *n.f.* protein.
protestant, *adj. and n.m.* Protestant.
protestantisme, *n.m.* Protestantism.
protestation, *n.f.* protest.
protester, *vb.* protest.
protêt, *n.m.* protest.
prothèse, *n.f.* artificial aid, as a denture.
protocole, *n.m.* protocol.
prototype, *n.m.* prototype.
protubérance, *n.f.* protuberance.
proue, *n.f.* prow, front.
prouesse, *n.f.* prowess.
prouver, *vb.* prove.
provenance, *n.f.* place of origin; product.
provençal, 1. *adj.* of Provence. **2.** *n.m.* language of Provence.
provende, *n.f.* provender, foodstuffs.
provenir, *vb.* come from.
proverbe, *n.m.* proverb, saying.
proverbial, *adj.* proverbial.
providence, *n.f.* providence.
providentiel, *adj.* providential.
province, *n.f.* province.

provincial, *adj. and n.m.* provincial.
provincialisme, *n.m.* provincialism.
proviseur, *n.m.* principal, headmaster.
provision, *n.f.* supply, store, provision.
provisoire, *adj.* temporary.
provocateur, *n.m.* one who provokes action.
provocation, *n.f.* provocation.
provoquer, *vb.* provoke.
proximité, *n.f.* closeness, proximity.
prude, 1. *n.f.* prude. **2.** *adj.* prudish.
prudence, *n.f.* caution, prudence.
prudent, *adj.* cautious, prudent.
pruderie, *n.f.* prudishness.
prune, *n.f.* plum.
pruneau, *n.m.* prune.
prunelle, *n.f.* pupil (of eye).
prunier, *n.m.* plum tree.
Prusse, *n.f.* Prussia.
Prussien, *n.m.* Prussian (person).
prussien, *adj.* Prussian.
psalmiste, *n.m.* psalmist.
psaume, *n.m.* psalm.
psautier, *n.m.* psalm book.
pseudonyme, *n.m.* pseudonym.
psychanalyse, (-k-), *n.f.* psychoanalysis.
psychédélique, (-k-), *adj.* psychedelic.
psychiatre, (-k-), *n.m.* psychiatrist.
psychiatrie, (-k-), *n.f.* psychiatry.
psychique, (-k-), *adj.* psychic.
psychologie, (-k-), *n.f.* psychology.
psychologique, (-k-), *adj.* psychological.
psychologue, (-k-), *n.m.f.* psychologist.
psychose, (-k-), *n.f.* psychosis.
psychothérapie, (-k-), *n.f.* psychotherapy.
puant, *adj.* foul; shameful.

pub, *n.f.* advertising; advertisement.
puberté, *n.f.* puberty.
public, 1. *adj. m.,* **publique** *f.* public. **2.** *n.m.* public; audience (theater).
publication, *n.f.* publication.
publiciste, *n.m.f.* publicist.
publicité, *n.f.* publicity, advertisement(s).
publier, *vb.* publish, issue.
puce, *n.f.* flea.
pucelle, *n.f.* young girl, virgin.
pudeur, *n.f.* modesty.
pudibond, *adj.* prudish.
pudique, *adj.* modest.
puer, *vb.* smell, have an offensive odor.
puéril, (-l), *adj.* childish.
pugiliste, *m.* boxer.
puîné, *adj.* younger (of a brother or sister).
puis, *adv.* then.
puisard, *n.m.* cesspool.
puisatier, *n.m.* well-digger.
puiser, *vb.* draw up, derive.
puisque, *conj.* since, as.
puissamment, *adv.* very, powerfully.
puissance, *n.f.* power.
puissant, *adj.* potent, powerful, mighty.
puits, (pwē), *n.m.* well; shaft.
pull(-over), *n.m.* sweater.
pulluler, *vb.* breed abundantly, multiply.
pulmonaire, *adj.* pulmonary.
pulpe, *n.f.* pulp.
pulpeux, *adj.* pulpy.
pulsar, *n.m.* pulsar.
pulsation, *n.f.* pulsation, beating.
pulvérisateur, *n.m.* vaporizer, spray.
pulvériser, *vb.* spray; pulverize.
punaise, *n.f.* bedbug; thumbtack.
punir, *vb.* punish.
punitif, *adj.* punitive.
punition, *n.f.* punishment.
pupille, (-l), *n.m.f.* ward; pupil (of the eye).
pupitre, *n.m.* desk.
pur, *adj.* pure.
purée, *n.f.* mash.

purement, *adv.* purely, solely.

pureté, *n.f.* purity.

purgatoire, *n.m.* purgatory.

purge, *n.f.* purge.

purger, *vb.* purge.

purification, *n.f.* purification.

purifier, *vb.* purify, cleanse.

puritain, *adj. and n.m.* Puritan.

pur-sang, *n.m.* thoroughbred.

purulent, *adj.* purulent.

pusillanime, *adj.* fainthearted.

pustule, *n.f.* pimple.

putain, *n.f.* (colloquial) whore.

putois, *n.m.* skunk; polecat.

putréfier, *vb.* corrupt, rot, spoil.

putride, *adj.* putrid.

putsch, *n.m.* putsch.

puzzle, *n.m.* jigsaw (puzzle).

pygmée, *n.m.* Pygmy.

pyjama, *n.m.* pajamas.

pyramidal, *adj.* pyramidal, overwhelming.

pyramide, *n.f.* pyramid.

Pyrénées, *n.f.pl.* the Pyrenees.

Q Ⅹ

quadragénaire (kw-), *n.m.* person in his forties.

quadrangle, (kw-), *n.m.* quadrangle.

quadrillé, *adj.* checked, ruled off.

quadriphonique, (kw-), *adj.* quadraphonic.

quadrupède, (kw-), *n.m. and adj.* quadruped.

quadruple, (kw-), *adj.* quadruple.

quai, *n.m.* pier, dock; (station) platform.

qualification, *n.f.* qualification.

qualifier, *vb.* qualify.

qualité, *n.f.* quality, nature, grade.

quand, *adv.* when.

quant à, *prep.* as to, as for.

quantité, *n.f.* amount, quantity.

quarantaine, *n.f.* quarantine.

quarante, *adj. and n.m.* forty.

quart, *n.m.* fourth, quarter.

quartier, *n.m.* district, quarter. **q. général,** headquarters.

quartz, (kw-), *n.m.* quartz.

quasar, (kw-), *n.m.* quasar.

quasi, *adv.* nearly, quasi.

quasiment, *adv.* almost.

quatorze, *adj. and n.m.* fourteen.

quatrain, *n.m.* quatrain.

quatre, *adj. and n.m.* four.

quatre-vingt-dix, *adj. and n.m.* ninety.

quatre-vingts, *adj. and n.m.* eighty.

quatrième, *adj. and n.m.f.* fourth.

quatuor, (kw-), *n.m.* quartet.

que, 1. *pron.* whom, which, that. **2.** *conj.* that, than.

quel, *adj.* which, what; of what kind.

quelconque, *adj.* of any kind, ordinary.

quelque, *adj.* some, any. **q. chose,** something. **q. part,** somewhere.

quelquefois, *adv.* sometimes.

quelques, *adj.* a few.

quelques-uns, *pron.* a few.

quelqu'un, *pron.* somebody.

querelle, *n.f.* quarrel.

quereller, *vb.* quarrel (with); scold.

querelleur, 1. *n.m.* quarreler. **2.** *adj.* inclined to quarrel.

question, *n.f.* question; issue, matter.

questionner, *vb.* question.

quête, *n.f.* quest, seeking.

quêter, *vb.* seek, look for.

queue, (kœ,) *n.f.* tail; line. **faire la q.,** stand in line.

qui, 1. *interr. pron.* who, whom. **2.** *rel. pron.* who, which. **q. que,** whoever.

quiconque, *pron.* whoever.

quiétude, *n.f.* quiet, tranquility.

quignon, *n.m.* large piece of bread.

quincaillerie, *n.f.* hardware.

quinine, *n.f.* quinine.

quinquagénaire, *n.m.* person in his fifties.

quintal, *n.m.* unit of weight (100 kilograms).

quinte, *n.f.* **q. de toux,** coughing fit.

quintuple, *n.m.* five times.

quinze, *adj. and n.m.* fifteen.

quinzième, *adj. and n.m.f.* fifteenth.

quiproquo, *n.m.* misunderstanding.

quittance, *n.f.* receipt.

quitte, *adj.* free, quit, released.

quitter, *vb.* quit, leave.

quoi, *pron. and interj.* what.

quoique, *conj.* though.

quote-part, *n.f.* quota.

quotidien, *adj.* daily.

R

rabâcher *vb.* keep repeating.

rabais, *n.m.* reduction.

rabaisser, *vb.* diminish, lower.

rabattre, *vb.* put down, suppress, quell.

rabbin, *n.m.* rabbi.

rabbinique, *adj.* rabbinical.

rabot, *n.m.* plane.

raboter, *vb.* plane, perfect.

raboteux, *adj.* rugged.

rabougri, *adj.* puny, stunted.

raccommodage, *n.m.* fixing, mending.

raccommoder, *vb.* mend.

raccompagner, *vb.* take back.

raccorder, *vb.* join, bring together.

raccourci, *n.m.* shortcut.

raccourcir, *vb.* shorten, curtail.

raccourcissement, *n.m.* shortening, curtailing.

raccrocher, *vb.* hook up, hang up; recover.

race, *n.f.* race.

rachat, *n.m.* redemption.

racheter, *vb.* redeem.

rachitique, *adj.* rickety, affected with rickets.

rachitisme, *n.m.* rickets.

racine, *n.f.* root.

raciste, *n.m.f.* racist.

racket, *n.m.* racketeering.

raclage, *n.m.* action of scraping.

racler, *vb.* scrape.

racoler, *vb.* recruit, esp. by fraud.

racontars, *n.m.pl.* gossip.

raconter, *vb.* tell, narrate, recount.

raconteur, *n.m.* story-teller.

radar, *n.m.* radar.

radeau, *n.m.* raft.

radiant, *adj.* radiant.

radiateur, *n.m.* radiator.

radiation, *n.f.* radiation.

radical, *adj. and n.m.* radical.

radier, *vb.* radiate; erase.

radieux, *adj.* radiant, beaming, glorious.

radio, *n.f.* radio; wireless; x-ray.

radio-actif, *adj.* radioactive.

radiocassette, *n.f.* radio and cassette player.

radiodiffuser, *vb.* broadcast.

radio-émission, *n.f.* broadcast.

radiogramme, *n.m.* radiogram.

radiographie, *n.f.* radiography.

radiophonique, *adj.* radio.

radis, *n.m.* radish.

radium, *n.m.* radium.

radoter, *vb.* babble, drivel.

radoub, *n.m.* refitting (of ship).

radoucir, *vb.* quiet, soften, appease.

rafale, *n.f.* blast, gust, squall.

raffermir, *vb.* make stronger or more secure.

raffinement, *n.m.* refinement.

raffiner, *vb.* refine.

raffinerie, *n.f.* refinery.

raffoler, *vb.* dote on, be mad about.

rafistoler, *vb.* mend, patch.

rafle, *n.f.* (police) raid.

rafler, *vb.* carry off.

rafraîchir, *vb.* refresh.

rafraîchissement, *n.m.* refreshment.

rage, *n.f.* rage, fury; rabies.

rager, *vb.* be angry, rage.

rageur, *n.m.* irritable person.

ragôt, *n.m.* nasty gossip.

ragoût, *n.m.* stew.

ragoûtant, *adj.* tasty, pleasing.

ragréer, *vb.* refinish, renovate.

raid, *n.m.* raid.

raide, *adj.* stiff; taut; steep.

raideur, *n.f.* stiffness.

raidir, *vb.* stiffen.

raie, *n.f.* streak; part (in hair).

raifort, *n.m.* horseradish.

rail, *n.m.* rail.

railler, *vb.* make fun of.

raillerie, *n.f.* jesting.

railleur, *n.m.* scoffer, jester.

rainure, *n.f.* groove.

rais, *n.m.* ray, spoke.

raisin, *n.m.* grape(s). **r. sec,** raisin.

raison, *n.f.* reason, judgment. **avoir r.,** be right.

raisonnable, *adj.* reasonable, rational.

raisonnement, *n.m.* reason; argument.

raisonner, *vb.* reason.

rajeunir, *vb.* rejuvenate.

rajuster, *vb.* readjust.

râle, *n.m.* rail (bird); rattle in throat.

ralentir, *vb.* slacken, slow down.

râler, *vb.* rattle (in dying); groan.

rallier, *vb.* rally.

rallonger, *vb.* make an addition to, lengthen.

rallye, *n.m.* rally.

ramadam, *n.m.* Ramadan.

ramage, *n.m.* flower pattern; chirping; babble.

ramassé, *adj.* thick-set, dumpy.

ramasser, *vb.* pick up.

ramasseur, *n.m.* collector.

rame, *n.f.* oar.

rameau, *n.m.* branch.

ramener, *vb.* bring (take) back.

rameneur, *vb.* restorer.

ramer, *vb.* row.

rameur, *n.m.* rower.

ramifier, *vb.* divide into branches, ramify.

ramille, *n.f.* twig.

ramollir, *vb.* soften; weaken.

rampe, *n.f.* banister; ramp.

ramper, *vb.* crawl, creep.

rance, 1. *adj.* rancid. **2.** *n.m.* rancidness.

rancœur, *n.f.* rancor.

rançon, *n.f.* ransom.

rancune, *n.f.* grudge, spite, rancor. **garder de la r.,** bear a grudge.

rancunier, *adj.* rancorous, bitter.

randonnée, *n.f.* walk, hike, ride.

rang, *n.m.* row; rank.

rangée, *n.f.* file, row.

ranger, *vb.* rank, array, (ar)range.

ranimer, *vb.* revive.

rapace, *adj.* predatory; greedy.

rapatrier, *vb.* repatriate.

râpe, *n.f.* file, rasp.

râper, *vb.* grate.

rapide, 1. *n.m.* rapid. **2.** *adj.* rapid, fast, quick.

rapidité, *n.f.* rapidity.

rapiécer, *vb.* patch.

rapière, *n.f.* rapier.

rapin, *n.m.* art student, pupil.

rapiner, *vb.* plunder, rob.

rappel, *n.m.* recall, repeal; reminder.

rappeler, *vb.* recall, remind. **se r.,** remember.

rapport, *n.m.* report; relation.

rapporter, *vb.* bring back; report. **se r. à,** relate to, refer to.

rapporteur, *n.m.* (court) reporter; tattle-tale.

rapprochement, *n.m.* bringing close, junction.

rapprocher, *vb.* bring together. **se r. de,** approximate.

rapt, *n.m.* rape, kidnapping.

raquette, *n.f.* racket; snowshoe.

rare, *adj.* scarce, rare.

raréfier, *vb.* rarefy.

rarement, *adv.* seldom.

rareté, *n.f.* rarity, uniqueness, scarcity.

ras, *adj.* smooth-shaven; open.

raser, *vb.* shave.

rasoir, *n.m.* razor.

rassasier, *vb.* cloy, sate.

rassemblement, *n.m.* rally.

rassembler, *vb.* gather, congregate; muster.

rasseoir, *vb.* reseat. **se r.,** be seated again.

rasséréner, *vb.* clear up (weather).

rassis, *adj.* stale.

rassurer, *vb.* reassure, comfort.

rat, *n.m.* rat.

ratatiner, *vb.* shrivel, shrink.

rate, *n.f.* spleen.

raté, *adj.* failed.

râteau, *n.m.* rake.

râteler, *vb.* rake.

râtelier, *n.m.* rack.

rater, *vb.* miss.

ratière, *n.f.* rat trap.

ratifier, *vb.* ratify.

ration, *n.f.* ration.

rationnel, *adj.* rational.

rationnement, *n.m.* rationing.

rationner, *vb.* ration.

ratissoire, *n.f.* scraper, rake.

rattacher, *vb.* fasten.

rattraper, *vb.* overtake, catch up with.

rature, *n.f.* erasure.

raturer, *vb.* erase, blot out.

rauque, *adj.* hoarse; raucous.

ravage, *n.m.* havoc.

ravager, *vb.* lay waste.

ravaler, *vb.* restore.

ravauder, *vb.* mend, patch.

ravi, *adj.* delighted.

ravigoter, *vb.* enliven, refresh.

ravin, *n.m.* ravine.

ravir, *vb.* ravish; delight.

ravissant, *adj.* ravishing, charming; ravenous.

ravissement, *n.m.* rapture.

ravisseur, *n.m.* ravisher, robber.

ravitailler, *vb.* resupply, refuel.

raviver, *vb.* revive.

rayé, *adj.* striped.

rayer, *vb.* streak; cross out.

rayon, *n.m.* ray, beam; shelf. **r. x,** x-ray.

rayonnant, *adj.* beaming.

rayonne, *n.f.* rayon.

rayonnement, *n.m.* radiation; radiance.

rayonner, *vb.* radiate, beam.

rayure, *n.f.* streak, blemish.

raz-de-marée, *n.m.* tidal wave.

re-, ré-, *prefix.* re-, again.

réabonnement, *n.m.* renewal of subscription.

réabonner, *vb.* renew, resubscribe.

réacteur, *n.m.* jet engine.

réaction, *n.f.* reaction. **avion à r.,** jet-plane.

reactionnaire, *adj. and n.m.f.* reactionary.

réadapter, *vb.* readjust.

réagir, *vb.* react.

réalisable, *adj.* realizable.

réalisateur, *n.m.* director; producer.

réalisation, *n.f.* attainment, carrying out.

réaliser, *vb.* realize; produce; direct. **se r.,** materialize.

réaliste, 1. *n.m.f.* realist. **2.** *adj.* realist, realistic.

réalité, *n.f.* reality.

réassurer, *vb.* reinsure.

rébarbatif, *adj.* forbidding.

rebattre, *vb.* repeat, beat again.

rebattu, *adj.* trite.

rebelle, 1. *n.m.f.* rebel. **2.** *adj.* rebel, rebellious.

rebeller, *vb.* se r., rebel.

rébellion, *n.f.* rebellion.

rebondi, *adj.* plump.

rebondir, *vb.* bounce.

rebondissement, *n.m.* new development.

rebord, *n.m.* border, edge.

rebuffade, *n.f.* rebuff, rebuke.

rebut, *n.m.* trash, refuse, junk, rubbish.

rebuter, *vb.* rebuke, discard.

récalcitrant, *adj.* stubborn.

receler, *vb.* accept stolen goods; hide.

récemment, *adv.* recently.

recensement, *n.m.* census.

recenser, *vb.* make a census.

récent, *adj.* recent.

réceptacle, *n.m.* receptacle.

récepteur, *n.m.* receiver.

réceptif, *adj.* receptive.

réception, *n.f.* reception; receipt.

récession, *n.f.* recession.

recette, *n.f.* recipe; receipt; (*pl.*) returns.

receveur, *n.m.* conductor; receiver.

recevoir, *vb.* receive, get; entertain.

réchapper, *vb.* escape, get out.

recharge, *n.f.* refill.

réchaud, *n.m.* food warmer, chafing dish.

réchauffer, *vb.* warm again; excite.

recherche, *n.f.* inquiry, (re)search; quest.

rechercher, *vb.* seek again, investigate.

rechigner, *vb.* balk.

rechute, *n.f.* relapse.

récif, *n.m.* reef.

récipient, *n.m.* container.

réciproque, *adj.* mutual.

récit, *n.m.* account.

réciter, *vb.* recite, tell.

réclamation, *n.f.* complaint.

réclame, *n.f.* advertisement.

réclamer, *vb.* claim, demand.

reclus, 1. *adj.* withdrawn, secluded. **2.** *n.m.* recluse.

réclusion, *n.f.* (solitary) confinement.

recoin, *n.m.* recess, corner.

récolte, *n.f.* crop, harvest.

récolter, *vb.* harvest, gather.

recommandable, *adj.* advisable.

recommandation, *n.f.* recommendation.

recommander, *vb.* recommend; register (letter).

recommencer, *vb.* start again.

récompense, *n.f.* reward.

récompenser, *vb.* reward.

réconcilier, *vb.* reconcile.

reconduire, *vb.* accompany, show out, dismiss.

réconfort, *n.m.* comfort.

reconnaissance, *n.f.* recognition; gratitude.

reconnaissant, *adj.* grateful.

reconnaître, *vb.* recognize; admit, acknowledge.

reconstituer, *vb.* rebuild, restore.

recourir, *vb.* resort.

recours, *n.m.* resort, recourse. avoir r. à, resort to; appeal to.

recouvrement, *n.m.* recovery.

recouvrer, *vb.* recover, retrieve.

recouvrir, *vb.* re-cover, cover completely.

récréation, *n.f.* amusement.

récréer, *vb.* entertain. se r., amuse oneself.

recroqueviller, *vb.* se r., curl up, huddle up.

recrudescence, *n.f.* fresh outbreak.

recrue, *n.f.* recruit.

recruter, *vb.* recruit.

rectangle, *n.m.* rectangle.

recteur, *n.m.* rector.

rectificatif, *n.m.* correction.

rectifier, *vb.* rectify, correct.

reçu, *n.m.* receipt.

recueil, *n.m.* collection, compilation.

recueillir, *vb.* gather, collect, glean.

recul, *n.m.* kick, recoil.

reculade, *n.f.* backing, retreat.

reculer, *vb.* recoil, draw back, go back.

récupérer, *vb.* recover, get back; rehabilitate.

récuser, *vb.* challenge; reject.

recycler, *vb.* recycle.

rédacteur, *n.m.* editor.

rédaction, *n.f.* editorial staff.

reddition, *n.f.* surrendering.

rédemption., *n.f.* redemption.

redevance, *n.f.* rental charge, license fee.

rédiger, *vb.* draw up.

redingote, *n.f.* frock-coat.

redire, *vb.* repeat, echo, reveal.

redoubler, *vb.* intesify, increase; repeat (class).

redoutable, *adj.* redoubtable, alarming.

redouter, *vb.* dread.

redresser, *vb.* straighten.

réduction, *n.f.* reduction, decrease, cut.

réduire, *vb.* reduce. se r. à, amount to.

réduit, *n.m.* retreat, hovel.

réel, *adj.* real, actual.

réfection, *n.f.* reconstruction; refreshments.

réfectoire, *n.m.* dining-room.

référence, *n.f.* reference.

référer, *vb.* refer.

refermer, *vb.* close up or again.

réfléchir, *vb.* reflect, consider, ponder.

reflet, *n.m.* reflection.

refléter, *vb.* reflect.

réflexe, *adj. and n.m.* reflex.

réflexion, *n.f.* reflection, consideration, thought.

refluer, *vb.* return to source, ebb.

reflux, *n.m.* ebb.

refondre, *vb.* cast again; remodel, improve.

réformateur, **1.** *adj.* reforming. **2.** *n.m.* reformer, crusader.

réforme, *n.f.* reform, reformation.

réformer, *vb.* reform.

refoulement, *n.m.* forcing back, retreat.

refouler, *vb.* drive back, repel.

réfractaire, *adj.* refractory.

réfrigérant, *n.m.* refrigerator.

réfrigérer, *vb.* put under refrigeration.

refroidir, *vb.* chill, cool.

refroidissement, *n.m.* cooling, refrigeration, chill.

refuge, *n.m.* refuge.

réfugié, *n.m.* refugee.

réfugier, *vb.* se r., take refuge.

refus, *n.m.* refusal, denial.

refuser, *vb.* refuse, withhold, deny.

réfutation, *n.f.* rebuttal.

réfuter, *vb.* disprove, refute.

regagner, *vb.* regain, recover.

regain, *n.m.* regrowth, renewal.

régal, *n.m.* feast, repast.

régaler, *vb.* entertain, treat.

regard, *n.m.* look.

regarder, *vb.* look (at); concern.

régence, *n.f.* regency.

régénérer, *vb.* regenerate.

régent, *adj. and n.m.* regent.

régenter, *vb.* direct, dominate.

régie, *n.f.* management, control; control room.

régime, *n.m.* diet; government; direction.

régiment, *n.m.* regiment.

région, *n.f.* area, region.

régional, *adj.* regional.

régir, *vb.* rule.

régisseur, *n.m.* (stage) manager.

registre, *n.m.* register, record.

réglage, *n.m.* adjusting, tuning.

règle, *n.f.* rule; ruler.

règlement, *n.m.* regulation; settlement.

réglementaire, *adj.* according to regulations.

régler, *vb.* regulate; rule; settle.

règne, *n.m.* reign.

régner, *vb.* reign.

régression, *n.f.* regression.

regret, *n.m.* regret.

regrettable, *adj.* regrettable.

regretter, *vb.* regret, be sorry for.

régulariser, *vb.* regularize.

régularité, *n.f.* regularity.

régulateur, *n.m.* regulator.

régulier, *adj.* regular.

réhabiliter, *vb.* rehabilitate.

rehausser, *vb.* enhance.

rein, *n.m.* kidney; (*pl.*) loins; back.

reine, *n.f.* queen.

réinsertion, *n.f.* reintegration, rehabilitation.

réintégrer, *vb.* return to, reinstate.

réitérer, *vb.* reiterate.

rejet, *n.m.* rejection.

rejeter, *vb.* reject.

rejeton, *n.m.* plant shoot; offspring.

rejoindre, *vb.* rejoin; catch up with, overtake.

réjouir, *vb.* rejoice, delight, cheer up.

réjouissance, *n.f.* festivity.

relâche, *n.m.* respite; (theater) closing.

relâché, *adj.* loose.

relâcher, *vb.* relax, slacken.

relais, *n.m.* relay.

relance, *n.f.* boost.

relater, *vb.* relate.

relatif, *adj.* relative.

relation, *n.f.* relation, connection.

relaxation, *n.f.* relaxation, release.

relayer, *vb.* relay.

reléguer, *vb.* relegate, banish.

relève, *n.f.* (*mil.*) relief, replacement.

relèvement, *n.m.* bearing.

relever, *vb.* lift; relieve; point out.

relief, *n.m.* relief. **mettre en r.,** emphasize.

relier, *vb.* bind; link.

relieur, *n.m.* binder, esp. of books.

religieuse, *n.f.* nun.

religieux, *adj.* religious.

religion, *n.f.* religion.

reliquaire, *n.m.* receptacle for relic.

relique, *n.f.* relic.

relire, *vb.* reread.

reliure, *n.f.* binding.

reluire, *vb.* shine, glisten.

remanier, *vb.* redo, modify.

remarquable, *adj.* remarkable; noticeable.

remarque, *n.f.* remark.

remarquer, *vb.* remark; notice.

rembarrer, *vb.* drive back; put in one's place.

remblai, *n.m.* embankment.

rembourrer, *vb.* stuff.

remboursement, *n.m.* refund.

rembourser, *vb.* repay, refund.

remède, *n.m.* remedy, cure.

remédiable, *adj.* remediable.

remédier, *vb.* remedy.

remerciement, *n.m.* thanks.

remercier, *vb.* thank.

remettre, *vb.* put back; restore; remit; pardon; deliver. **se r.,** recover.

réminiscence, *n.f.* reminiscence.

remise, *n.f.* discount; delivery.

rémission, *n.f.* remmission.

remontant, *n.m.* tonic.

remonte-pente, *n.m.* ski lift.

remontrance, *n.f.* remonstrance.

remontrer, *vb.* show anew, point out error.

remords, (-môr), *n.m.* remorse.

remorquer, *vb.* tow.

remorqueur, *n.m.* tug(boat).

rémouleur, *n.m.* sharpener, grinder.

remous, *n.m.* eddy.

rempart, *n.m.* bulwark, rampart.

remplaçant, *n.m.* substitute.

remplacer, *vb.* replace, substitute.

rempli, *n.m.* tuck, hitch.

remplier, *vb.* take a tuck in.

remplir, *vb.* fill; carry out; crowd.

remporter, *vb.* take away, bring back; win.

remuer, *vb.* stir. **se r.,** bustle.

rémunérer, *vb.* pay.

renaissance, *n.f.* rebirth, revival.

renaître, *vb.* be reborn, get new life.

renard, *n.m.* fox; sly person.

rencontre, *n.f.* meeting. **aller à la r. de,** go to meet.

rencontrer, *vb.* meet; come across.

rendement, *n.m.* output.

rendez-vous, *n.m.* date, appointment.

rendre, *vb.* give back; repay; surrender. **se r. compte de,** realize.

rendu, *adj.* tired out, all in.

rêne, *n.f.* rein.

rené, *adj.* born-again.

renégat, *adj. and n.m.* renegade.

renfermé, *adj.* withdrawn.

renfermer, *vb.* enclose.

renfler, *vb.* swell, inflate.

renforcer, *vb.* reinforce.

renfort, *n.m.* reinforcement, aid.

renfrogner, *vb.* **se r.,** scowl, frown.

rengaine, *n.f.* often-told story.

renifler, *vb.* sniff.

renne, *n.m.* reindeer.

renom, *n.m.* renown, repute.

renommée, *n.f.* fame, renown.

renoncer, *vb.* renounce, give up, forego.

renonciation, *n.f.* renunciation.

renouement, *n.m.* renewing, retying.

renouer, *vb.* tie up (again).

renouveau, *n.m.* springtime.

renouveler, *vb.* renew, renovate.

renouvellement, *n.m.* renewal.

rénover, *vb.* renovate.

renseignements, *n.m.pl.* information.

renseigner, *vb.* inform. **se r.,** inquire.

rentable, *adj.* profitable.

rente, *n.f.* income; interest; annuity.

rentier, *n.m.* one who lives off interest on investments.

rentrée, *n.f.* return.

rentrer, *vb.* go back, go home.

renversant, *adj.* amazing, overwhelming.

renverser, *vb.* overthrow, overturn; reverse.

renvoi, *n.m.* dismissal; return.

renvoyer, *vb.* send back, return; dismiss.

repaire, *n.m.* den, animal's lair.

repaître, *vb.* feed, feast.

répandre, *vb.* diffuse, scatter, spill.

répandu, *adj.* prevalent, widespread.

reparaître, *vb.* reappear.

réparateur, *n.m.* restorer, repairer.

réparation, *n.f.* repair; amends.

réparer, *vb.* repair; make up for, make amends for.

repartie, *n.f.* reply, quick retort.

repartir, *vb.* leave again; retort.

répartir, *vb.* apportion, allot, distribute.

repas, *n.m.* meal.

repasser, *vb.* press; pass; look over.

repentir, 1. *n.m.* repentance. **2.** *vb.* **se r.,** repent.

répercussion, *n.f.* repercussion.

répercuter, *vb.* reverberate, echo.

repère, *n.m.* guiding mark.

repérer, *vb.* spot, locate.

répertoire, *n.m.* list, repertory.

répéter, *vb.* repeat; rehearse.

répétition, *n.f.* repetition; rehearsal.

répit, *n.m.* respite.

replacer, *vb.* replace.

replier, *vb.* fold again or up.

réplique, *n.f.* rejoinder; cue.

répliquer, *vb.* rejoin.

répondant, *n.m.* respondent, bail.

répondeur, *n.m.* answering machine.

répondre, *vb.* answer, reply. **r. de,** vouch for.

réponse, *n.f.* answer, reply.

report, *n.m.* (in bookkeeping) amount brought forward.

reportage, *n.m.* reporting.

reporter, 1. *n.m.* reporter. **2.** *vb.* carry or take back.

repos, *n.m.* rest.

reposer, *vb.* rest, repose.

repousser, *vb.* push back, repel; spurn.

repoussoir, *n.m.* foil.

répréhensible, *adj.* objectionable.

répréhension, *n.f.* reprehension, censure.

reprendre, *vb.* take back; resume.

représailles, *n.f.pl.* retaliation.

représentant, *n.m.* representative.

représentatif, *adj.* representative.

représentation, *n.f.* representation, performance.

représenter, *vb.* represent.

répressif, *adj.* repressive.

répression, *n.f.* repression.

réprimande, *n.f.* reproof, rebuke, reprimand.

réprimander, *vb.* chide, reprove, reprimand.

réprimer, *vb.* quell.

reprise, *n.f.* recovery; turn; darn. **à plusieurs r.s,** repeatedly.

repriser, *vb.* darn.

réprobation, *n.f.* reprobation.

reproche, *n.m.* reproach.

reprocher, *vb.* reproach.

reproduction, *n.f.* reproduction.

reproduction exacte, *n.f.* clone.

reproduire, *vb.* reproduce.

réprouver, *vb.* censure.

reptile, *n.m.* reptile.

républicain, *adj. and n.m.* republican.

république, *n.f.* republic.

répudier, *vb.* repudiate.

répugnance, *n.f.* repugnance.

répulsion, *n.f.* repulsion.

réputation, *n.f.* reputation.

réputer, *vb.* consider, esteem.

requête, *n.f.* request, plea.

requin, *n.m.* shark.

requis, *adj.* required, necessary.

réquisition, *n.f.* requisition.

rescousse, *n.f.* rescue.

réseau, *n.m.* network.

réserve, *n.f.* reserve, reservation; qualification. **de r.,** spare, extra.

réservé, *adj.* aloof, reticent.

réserver, *vb.* reserve.

réserviste, *n.m.f.* reservist *(mil.).*

réservoir, *n.m.* tank, reservoir.

résidant, *adj.* resident.

résidence, *n.f.* residence, dwelling.

résider, *vb.* reside.

résidu, *n.m.* residue.

résignation, *n.f.* resignation.

résigner, *vb.* resign.

résiliation, *n.f.* cancelling.

résine, *n.f.* resin.

résistance, *n.f.* endurance, resistance.

résister, *vb.* resist.

résolu, *adj.* resolute.

résolument, *adv.* resolutely.

résolution, *n.f.* resolution.

résonnance, *n.f.* resonance.

résonnant, *adj.* resonant.

résonner, *vb.* resound.

résorber, *vb.* **se r.,** be reduced, be absorbed.

résoudre, *vb.* resolve, solve.

respect, (-spè). *n.m.* respect.

respectable, *adj.* decent, respectable.

respecter, *vb.* respect.

respectif, *adj.* respective.

respectueux, *adj.* respectful.

respiration, *n.f.* respiration, breathing.

respirer, *vb.* breathe.

resplendir, *vb.* gleam resplendently.

responsabilité, *n.f.* responsibility.

responsable, *adj.* responsible; accountable, liable.

ressaisir, *vb.* regain possession.

ressasser, *vb.* keep going over.

ressemblance, *n.f.* likeness.

ressembler, *vb.* resemble. **se r.,** look alike.

ressentiment, *n.m.* resentment.

ressentir, *vb.* feel, resent, show.

resserrer, *vb.* tighten, compress.

ressort, *n.m.* spring; elasticity.

ressortir, *vb.* stand out.

ressortissant, *n.m.* national, citizen.

ressource, *n.f.* resort, resource.

ressusciter, *vb.* revive, resuscitate.

restant, *n.m.* remainder.

restaurant, *n.m.* restaurant.

restaurateur, *n.m.* restorer; restaurant owner.

restauration, *n.f.* restoration; catering.

restaurer, *vb.* restore.

reste, *n.m.* remainder, rest, remnant.

rester, *vb.* remain, stay.

restituer, *vb.* give back, restore.

restoroute, *n.m.* restaurant along highway.

restreindre, *vb.* restrict.

restrictif, *adj.* restrictive.

restriction, *n.f.* restriction.

résultat, *n.m.* outcome, upshot, result.

résulter, *vb.* result.

résumé, *n.m.* summing up.

résumer, *vb.* sum up.

résurrection, *n.f.* resurrection; revival.

rétablir, *vb.* restore, reestablish. **se r.,** recover.

rétablissement, *n.m.* recovery.

retard, *n.m.* delay. **en r.,** late; slow.

retarder, *vb.* delay, retard; be slow.

retenir, *vb.* retain; keep; hold (back); detain. **se r. de,** refrain from.

rétentif, *adj.* retentive.

retentir, *vb.* resound.

retentissant, *adj.* reechoing.

retenue, *n.f.* deduction; detention; reticence.

réticence, *n.f.* silence, reticence.

retirer, *vb.* withdraw. **se r.,** retire, retreat.

retombées, *n.f.pl.* fallout.

rétorquer, *vb.* retort.

retoucher, *vb.* retouch, alter.

retour, *n.m.* return. **de r.,** back.

retourner, *vb.* go back, return; invert. **se r.,** turn around.

retrait, *n.m.* contraction, retraction.

retraite, *n.f.* retreat; privacy.

retrancher, *vb.* cut off, curtail.

retransmettre, *vb.* broadcast.

rétrécir, *vb.* shrink, contract.

rétribution, *n.f.* salary, recompense.

rétroactif, *adj.* retroactive; retrospective.

rétrograde, *adj.* reactionary; backward-looking.

retrousser, *vb.* turn up.

retrouver, *vb.* find; recover.

rétroviseur, *n.m.* rear-view mirror.

réunion, *n.f.* meeting, convention, reunion.

réunir, *vb.* unite. **se r.,** assemble.

réussi, *adj.* successful.

réussir, *vb.* succeed.

réussite, *n.f.* successful outcome.

revanche, *n.f.* revenge. **en r.,** in return.

rêve, *n.m.* dream.

réveil, *n.m.* awaking; revival.

réveille-matin, *n.m.* alarm clock.

réveiller, *vb.* wake (up), rouse, arouse.

réveillon, *n.m.* Christmas Eve; New Year's Eve.

révélateur, 1. *adj.* revealing. **2.** *n.m.* revealer.

révélation, *n.f.* revelation.

révéler, *vb.* disclose, reveal.

revenant, *n.m.* ghost, specter.

revendeur, *n.m.* retailer, old-clothes dealer.

revendication, *n.f.* claim, demand.

revendiquer, *vb.* claim.

revenir, *vb.* come back, return, recur; amount to.

revenu, *n.m.* income, revenue.

rêver, *vb.* dream.

réverbère, *n.m.* street lamp.

réverbérer, *vb.* reverberate.

révéremment, *adv.* reverently.

révérence, *n.f.* reverence; bow, curtsy.

révérend, *adj.* reverend.

révérer, *vb.* revere.

rêverie, *n.f.* dreaming, reverie.

revers, *n.m.* reverse, wrong side; lapel.

revêtir, *vb.* clothe; assume.

rêveur, 1. *n.m.* dreamer. **2.** *adj.* pensive.

revirement, *n.m.* change of mind, reversal.

réviser, *vb.* revise.

réviseur, *n.m.* reviser, inspector.

révision, *n.f.* revision, review.

revivre, *vb.* revive.

révocation, *n.f.* revocation, annulment.

revoir, *vb.* see again. **au r.,** good-bye.

révolte, *n.f.* revolt.

révolter, *vb.* **se r.,** revolt.

révolu, *adj.* past.

révolution, *n.f.* revolution, turn.

révolutionnaire, *adj. and n.m.f.* revolutionary.

revolver, *n.m.* revolver.

révoquer, *vb.* revoke.

revue, *n.f.* review, magazine.

rez-de-chaussée, *n.m.* ground floor.

rhétorique, *n.f.* rhetoric.

rhinocéros, *n.m.* rhinoceros.

Rhône, *n.m.* Rhone.

rhubarbe, *n.f.* rhubarb.

rhum, *n.m.* rum.

rhumatisme, *n.m.* rheumatism.

rhume, *n.m.* cold.

ricaner, *vb.* laugh objectionably.

riche, *adj.* rich, wealthy.

richesse, *n.f.* wealth.

ricocher, *vb.* ricochet, spring back.

rictus, *n.m.* grin; grimace.

ride, *n.f.* wrinkle, ripple.

rideau, *n.m.* curtain.

rider, *vb.* ripple, wrinkle.

ridicule, 1. *n.m.* ridicule. **2.** *adj.* ridiculous.

ridiculiser, *vb.* ridicule.

rien, *pron.* nothing.

rieur, *n.m.* laugher.

rigide, *adj.* rigid.

rigidité, *n.f.* rigidity.

rigole, *n.f.* ditch, gutter.

rigoler, *vb.* laugh.

rigolo, *m.,* rigolote *f. adj.* funny.

rigoureux, *adj.* rigorous.

rigueur, *n.f.* rigor.

rime, *n.f.* rhyme.

rimer, *vb.* rhyme.

rince-doigts, *n.m.* finger bowl.

rincer, *vb.* rinse.

ringard, *adj.* old-fashioned.

ripaille, *n.f.* feasting, revelry.

riposte, *n.f.* retort.

rire, 1. *n.m.* laugh, laughter. 2. *vb.* laugh.

ris, *n.m.* laugh; reef in a sail; sweetbread.

risée, *n.f.* laugh, mocking.

risible, *adj.* laughable.

risque, *n.m.* risk.

risquer, *vb.* risk.

risque-tout, *n.m.* daredevil.

rissoler, *vb.* brown, as in cooking.

rite, *n.m.* rite.

rituel, *adj.* ritual.

rivage, *n.m.* shore, bank.

rival, *adj. and n.m.* rival.

rivaliser, *vb.* compete, rival.

rivalité, *n.f.* rivalry.

rive, *n.f.* bank.

river, *vb.* clinch.

riverain, *n.m.* local resident.

rivet, *n.m.* rivet.

rivière, *n.f.* river.

rixe, *n.f.* brawl.

riz, *n.m.* rice.

rizière, *n.f.* rice field.

robe, *n.f.* dress, gown, frock, robe.

robinet, *n.m.* faucet, tap.

robot, *n.m.* robot.

robuste, *adj.* hardy, strong, robust.

roc, *n.m.* rock.

rocailleux, *adj.* rocky, rough.

roche, *n.f.* rock.

rocher, *n.m.* rock.

rocheux, *adj.* rocky.

rock, *adj.* rock (music).

rôder, *vb.* prowl.

rôdeur, *n.m.* prowler.

rogner, *vb.* pare, trim down.

rognon, *n.m.* kidney.

rogue, *adj.* proud, arrogant.

roi, *n.m.* king.

rôle, *n.m.* role, part.

Romain, *n.m.* Roman (person).

romain, *adj.* Roman.

roman, *n.m.* novel.

romance, *n.f.* ballad.

romancier, *n.m.* novelist.

romanesque, *adj.* romantic.

roman-feuilleton, *n.m.* serial.

romanichel, *n.m.* gypsy.

romantique, *adj.* romantic.

romarin, *n.m.* rosemary.

rompre, *vb.* break.

ronce, *n.f.* bramble.

rond, 1. *n.m.* round; circle. 2. *adj.* round.

ronde, *n.f.* round, patrol.

rondelle, *n.f.* washer; slice.

rondeur, *n.f.* roundness.

rond-point, *n.m.* traffic circle.

ronflement, *n.m.* snoring, roar.

ronfler, *vb.* snore.

ronger, *vb.* gnaw; fret.

rongeur, *adj. and n.m.* rodent.

ronronner, *vb.* purr, murmur.

rosace, *n.f.* rose window.

rosaire, *n.m.* rosary.

rosbif, *n.m.* roast beef.

rose, 1. *n.f.* rose. 2. *adj.* pink.

rosé, *adj.* pinkish.

roseau, *n.m.* reed.

rosée, *n.f.* dew.

rosier, *n.m.* rosebush.

rossignol, *n.m.* nightingale.

rôt, *n.m.* roast (meat).

rotation, *n.f.* rotation.

rotatoire, *adj.* rotary.

roter, *vb.* belch.

rôti, *n.m.* roast.

rôtir, *vb.* roast.

rôtisserie, *n.f.* grillroom.

rotondité, *n.f.* rotundity.

rotule, *n.f.* kneecap.

roturier, *adj.* commonplace, vulgar.

rouage, *n.m.* gearwheel, part, cog.

roublardise, *n.f.* cunningness.

roucouler, *vb.* coo.

roue, *n.f.* wheel.

roué, 1. *n.m.* rake, debauchee. 2. *adj.* crafty.

rouge, 1. *n.m.* rouge. 2. *adj.* red. r. foncé, maroon.

rouge-gorge, *n.m.* robin.

rougeole, *n.f.* measles.

rougeur, *n.f.* flush, blush.

rougir, *vb.* blush.

rouille, *n.f.* rust.

rouiller, *vb.* rust.

rouir, *vb.* soak.

rouleau, *n.m.* roll, roller, scroll, coil.

roulement, *n.m.* rolling, winding; rotation.

rouler, *vb.* roll, wind.

roulette, *n.f.* little wheel, caster.

roulis, *n.m.* roll.

Roumain, *n.m.* Romanian (person).

roumain, 1. *n.m.* Romanian (language). 2. *adj.* Romanian.

Roumanie, *n.f.* Romania.

rouquin, *n.m.* redhead.

rousseur, *n.f.* redness. tache de r., freckle.

roussir, *vb.* scorch.

route, *n.f.* road, way, course, route. en r., under way. en r. pour, on the way to.

routine, *n.f.* routine.

routinier, *adj.* routine.

roux, *adj. and n.m.* red, reddish-brown.

royal, *adj.* royal, regal.

royaliste, *adj. and n.m.f.* royalist.

royaume, *n.m.* kingdom.

royauté, *n.f.* royalty.

ruban, *n.m.* ribbon, tape.

rubéole, *n.f.* German measles.

rubis, *n.m.* ruby.

rubrique, *n.f.* red ocher; heading.

ruche, *n.f.* hive.

rude, *adj.* rough, gruff, harsh; rugged.

rudement, *adv.* terribly (hard).

rudesse, *n.f.* harshness.

rudiment, *n.m.* rudiment, element.

rudimentaire, *adj.* rudimentary.

rudoyer, *vb.* bully.

rue, *n.f.* street, road.
ruée, *n.f.* rush.
ruelle, *n.f.* lane, alley.
ruer, *vb.* se r., rush.
rugby, *n.m.* Rugby.
rugbyman, *n.m.* Rugby player.
rugir, *vb.* roar.
rugissement, *n.m.* roar.
rugueux, *adj.* rugged, harsh.
ruine, *n.f.* ruin.
ruiner, *vb.* ruin.

ruineux, *adj.* ruinous.
ruisseau, *n.m.* brook, creek; gutter.
ruisseler, *vb.* stream, flow.
rumeur, *n.f.* rumor; noise.
ruminant, *adj. and n.m.* ruminant.
ruminer, *vb.* chew the cud.
rupture, *n.f.* break, rupture.
rural, *adj.* rural.
ruse, *n.f.* trick; cunning.
rusé, *adj.* sly, cunning.

Russe, *n.m.f.* Russian (person).
russe, 1. *n.m.* Russian (language). **2.** *adj.* Russian.
Russie, *n.f.* Russia.
rusticité, *n.f.* rusticity, uncouthness.
rustique, *adj.* rustic.
rustre, *adj. and n.m.* boor, boorish.
rythme, *n.m.* rhythm.
rythmique, *adj.* rhythmical.

S

sabbat *n.m.* Sabbath.
sable, *n.m.* sand.
sablé, *n.m.* shortbread biscuit.
sabler, *vb.* sand; quaff.
sablier, *n.m.* sandbox; sandman; hourglass.
sablonneux, *adj.* sandy.
sablonnière, *n.f.* sand pit.
sabord, *n.m.* porthole.
sabot, *n.m.* hoof; wooden shoe.
sabotage, *n.m.* sabotage.
saboter, *vb.* sabotage.
saboteur, *n.m.* saboteur; awkward bungler.
sabre, *n.m.* saber.
sac, *n.m.* sack, bag. **s. à main,** pocketbook. **s. à air,** airbag.
saccade, *n.f.* jerk.
saccager, *vb.* ransack, sack, plunder.
saccharine, *n.f.* saccharin.
sacerdoce, *n.m.* priesthood.
sachet, *n.m.* sachet; packet.
sacre, *n.m.* consecration, coronation.
sacré, *adj.* sacred.
sacrement, *n.m.* sacrament.
sacrer, *vb.* crown, consecrate; curse.
sacrifice, *n.m.* sacrifice.
sacrifier, *vb.* sacrifice.
sacrilège, *n.m.* sacrilege.
sacristain, *n.m.* sexton.
sac tyrolien, *n.m.* backpack.
sadique, *adj.* sadistic.
sadisme, *n.m.* sadism.
sagace, *adj.* shrewd.
sagacité, *n.f.* sagacity.

sage, 1. *n.m.* sage. **2.** *adj.* wise, good.
sage-femme, *n.f.* midwife.
sagesse, *n.f.* wisdom.
Sahara, *n.m.* Sahara (desert).
saignant, *adj.* rare (meat).
saignée, *n.f.* bleeding.
saigner, *vb.* bleed.
saillant, *adj.* prominent, projecting.
saillie, *n.f.* projection.
saillir, *vb.* protrude.
sain, *adj.* healthy, sound, wholesome. **s. d'esprit,** sane.
saindoux, *n.m.* lard.
saint, 1. *n.m.* saint. **2.** *adj.* holy.
Saint-Esprit, *n.m.* Holy Ghost.
sainteté, *n.f.* holiness.
saisie, *n.f.* seizure.
saisir, *vb.* seize, grasp, snatch, grab.
saisissement, *n.m.* chill; seizure.
saison, *n.f.* season.
salade, *n.f.* salad.
saladier, *n.m.* salad bowl or dish.
salaire, *n.m.* wages, earnings, pay.
salarié, 1. *adj.* salaried. **2.** *n.m.* person earning a salary.
sale, *adj.* dirty.
salé, *adj.* salty.
saler, *vb.* salt.
saleté, *n.f.* dirt.
salière, *n.f.* saltcellar.
salin, *adj.* salt, salty.
salir, *vb.* get dirty.

salive, *n.f.* saliva.
salle, *n.f.* (large) room, hall, auditorium, (hospital) ward. **s. de classe,** classroom. **s. de bain,** bathroom.
salon, *n.m.* parlor.
salopette, *n.f.* overalls.
saltimbanque, *n.m.f.* charlatan; buffoon, acrobat.
salubre, *adj.* healthful.
salubrité, *n.f.* healthfulness.
saluer, *vb.* bow, greet, salute.
salut, *n.m.* bow, salute; salvation.
salutaire, *adj.* wholesome, beneficial.
salutation, *n.f.* greeting.
salve, *n.f.* salvo, salute.
samedi, *n.m.* Saturday.
SAMU, *n.m.* paramedics.
sanctifier, *vb.* hallow.
sanction, *n.f.* sanction.
sanctionner, *vb.* sanction, countenance.
sanctuaire, *n.m.* sanctuary.
sandale, *n.f.* sandal.
sang, *n.m.* blood.
sang-froid, *n.m.* calmness, composure.
sanglant, *adj.* bloody.
sangler, *vb.* strap, fasten.
sanglier, *n.m.* (wild) boar.
sanglot, *n.m.* sob.
sangloter, *vb.* sob.
sangsue, *n.f.* leech.
sanguin, *adj.* pertaining to blood.
sanguinaire, *adj.* bloodthirsty.
sanitaire, *adj.* sanitary.

sans, *prep.* without, out of. **s. doute,** without doubt. **s. plomb,** unleaded. **s. repos,** restless. **s. valeur,** worthless. **s. nom,** nameless.

sans-souci, *adj.* carefree, careless.

santé, *n.f.* health.

Saoudien, *n.m.* Saudi (person).

Saoudien, *adj.* Saudi Arabian.

saoul (sōō), *adj.* drunk.

saper, *vb.* sap, weaken.

saphir, *n.m.* sapphire.

sapin, *n.m.* fir.

sarcasme, *n.m.* sarcasm.

sarcastique, *adj.* sarcastic.

sarcler, *vb.* weed, root out.

Sardaigne, *n.f.* Sardinia.

sardine, *n.f.* sardine.

sardonique, *adj.* sardonic.

satanique, *adj.* satanic.

satellite, *n.m.* satellite.

satin, *n.m.* satin.

satire, *n.f.* satire.

satiriser, *vb.* satirize.

satisfaction, *n.f.* satisfaction.

satisfaire, *vb.* satisfy.

satisfaisant, *adj.* satisfactory.

saturer, *vb.* saturate.

satyre, *n.m.* satyr.

sauce, *n.f.* sauce. **s. piquante,** hot sauce.

saucisse, *n.f.* sausage.

saucisson, *n.m.* (slicing) sausage.

sauf, **1.** *prep.* but. **2.** *adj.* safe. **sain et s.,** safe and sound.

sauf-conduit, *n.m.* safe-conduct.

sauge, *n.f.* sage.

saugrenu, *adj.* absurd, preposterous.

saule, *n.f.* willow.

saumon, *n.m.* salmon.

saumure, *n.f.* brine.

saut, *n.m.* spring, jump.

saute, *n.f.* wind shift.

sauter, *vb.* spring, jump, leap, skip. **faire s.,** blow up.

sauterelle, *n.f.* grasshopper.

sautiller, *vb.* hop.

sauvage, **1.** *n.m.f.* savage. **2.** *adj.* wild, savage.

sauvegarde, *n.f.* safeguard.

sauvegarder, *vb.* safeguard; (computers) save, back up.

sauve-qui-peut, *n.m.* stampede, panic.

sauver, *vb.* save. **se s.,** run away.

sauvetage, *n.m.* salvage.

sauveteur, *n.m.* rescuer, saver.

sauveur, *n.m.* savior; Savior.

savane, *n.f.* prairie.

savant, **1.** *n.m.* scholar. **2.** *adj.* learned.

saveur, *n.f.* flavor, savor, zest.

savoir, **1.** *vb.* know, be aware, have knowledge. **vouloir s.,** wonder. **2.** *n.m.* knowledge.

savoir-faire, *n.m.* poise, ability.

savoir-vivre, *n.m.* breeding, manners.

savon, *n.m.* soap.

savonner, *vb.* soap, lather.

savourer, *vb.* relish.

savoureux, *adj.* tasty.

saxo(phone), *n.m.* sax(ophone).

scabreux, *adj.* improper; risky.

scalper, *vb.* scalp.

scandale, *n.m.* scandal.

scandaleux, *adj.* scandalous.

scandaliser, *vb.* shock.

scander, *vb.* scan.

Scandinave, *n.m.f.* Scandinavian (person).

scandinave, *adj.* Scandinavian.

Scandinavie, *n.f.* Scandinavia.

scaphandre, *n.m.* diving suit; space suit.

scarabée, *n.m.* beetle.

scarlatine, *n.f.* scarlet fever.

sceau, *n.m.* seal.

scélérat, *n.m.* villain, criminal, knave, ruffian.

sceller, *vb.* seal.

scénario, *n.m.* scenario.

scène, *n.f.* scene; stage.

scénique, *adj.* scenic.

scepticisme, *n.m.* skepticism.

sceptique, **1.** *n.m.f.* skeptic. **2.** *adj.* skeptical.

sceptre, *n.m.* scepter.

schéma, *n.m.* diagram.

schématique, *adj.* digrammatic; oversimplified.

schisme, *n.m.* schism.

schizophrène, (sk-), *adj.* schizophrenia.

sciatique, *n.f.* sciatica.

scie, *n.f.* saw.

science, *n.f.* science.

science-fiction, *n.f.* science fiction.

scientifique, **1.** *adj.* scientific. **2.** *n.m.f.* scientist.

scier, *vb.* saw.

scinder, *vb.* divide.

scintiller, *vb.* twinkle.

scission, *n.f.* cutting, division.

sclérose, *n.f.* sclerosis.

scolaire, *adj.* scholastic. **système s.,** school system.

scolastique, *adj.* scholastic.

scooter, *n.m.* (motor) scooter.

score, *n.m.* score.

Scotch, *n.m.* Scotish whisky; (trademark) Scotch tape.

scout, (-t), *n.m.* scout.

scrofule, *n.f.* scrofula.

scrupule, *n.m.* scruple.

scrupuleux, *adj.* scrupulous.

scruter, *vb.* scan, scrutinize.

scrutin, *n.m.* ballot, poll.

sculpter, (-lt-), *vb.* carve.

sculpteur, (-lt-), *n.m.* sculptor.

sculpture, (-lt-), *n.f.* sculpture.

se, (sə), *pron.* himself, herself, itself, oneself, themselves, each other.

séance, *n.f.* sitting; session; meeting.

séant, *adj.* sitting, proper.

seau, *n.m.* pail, bucket.

sec, *m.,* sèche *f.* *adj.* dry.

sécession, *n.f.* secession.

sèche-cheveux, *n.m.* hair dryer.

sécher, *vb.* dry.

sécheresse, *n.f.* dryness, drought.

séchoir, *n.m.* dryer.

second, (-g-), *adj.* second.

secondaire, (-g-), *adj.* secondary.

seconde, (-g-), *n.f.* second.

seconder, (-g-), *vb.* second, help.

secouer, *vb.* shake, rouse.

secourir, *vb.* relieve, succor, help.

secours, *n.m.* help, relief. **premiers s.,** first aid. **poste de s.,** first-aid station. **au s.!,** help!

secousse, *n.f.* jar, shock.

secret, *adj. and n.m.* secret.

secrétaire, *n.m.f.* secretary.

sécréter, *vb.* secrete.

sécrétion, *n.f.* secretion.

sectaire, *adj.* sectarian.

secte, *n.f.* sect.

secteur, *n.m.* district, sector.

section, *n.f.* section.

sectionner, *vb.* cut into sections.

Sécu, *n.f.* Social Security.

séculaire, *adj.* secular.

séculier, *adj.* secular, lay.

sécuriser, *vb.* make (someone) feel secure.

sécurité, *n.f.* safety.

sédatif, *adj. and n.m.* sedative.

sédentaire, *adj.* sedentary, stationary.

séditieux, *adj.* seditious.

sédition, *n.f.* sedition.

séduction, *n.f.* seduction.

séduire, *vb.* seduce, attract, allure.

séduisant, *adj.* attractive.

segment, *n.m.* segment.

ségrégation, *n.f.* segregation.

seigle, *n.m.* rye.

seigneur, *n.m.* lord, peer.

seigneurie, *n.f.* lordship.

sein, *n.m.* bosom, breast.

séisme, *n.m.* earthquake.

seize, *adj. and n.m.* sixteen.

seizième, *adj. and n.m.f.* sixteenth.

séjour, *n.m.* stay. **lieu de s.,** resort.

séjourner, *vb.* sojourn.

sel, *n.m.* salt.

sélection, *n.f.* selection.

self(-service), *n.m.* self-service.

selle, *n.f.* saddle.

seller, *vb.* saddle.

sellette, *n.f.* little stool or saddle.

selon, *prep.* according to.

seltz, *n.m.* **eau de s.,** soda water.

semailles, *n.f.pl.* sowing.

semaine, *n.f.* week; weekly pay.

semblable, *adj.* similar, alike.

semblant, *n.m.* show; appearance. **faire s.,** make believe.

sembler, *vb.* seem, appear.

semelle, *n.f.* sole (shoe).

semence, *n.f.* seed.

semer, *vb.* sow.

semestre, *n.m.* semester.

semeur, *n.m.* sower.

sémillance, *n.f.* briskness, liveliness.

séminaire, *n.m.* seminar; seminary.

semi-remorque, *n.f.* semi-trailer.

sémitique, *adj.* Semitic.

semoncer, *vb.* lecture, scold.

semoule, *n.f.* semolina.

sénat, *n.m.* senate.

sénateur, *n.m.* senator.

sénile, *adj.* senile.

sénilité, *n.f.* senility.

sens, (-s) *n.m.* meaning, sense; direction.

sensation, *n.f.* sensation, feeling.

sensationnel, *adj.* sensational.

sensé, *adj.* sensible.

sensibiliser, *vb.* make sensitive.

sensibilité, *n.f.* sensitivity.

sensible, *adj.* sensitive; conscious (of).

sensitif, *adj.* oversensitive.

sensualisme, *n.m.* sensualism.

sensualité, *n.f.* sensuality.

sensuel, *adj.* sensual.

sentence, *n.f.* sentence.

sentencieux, *adj.* sententious.

senteur, *n.f.* smell.

sentier, *n.m.* path.

sentiment, *n.m.* feeling.

sentimental, *adj.* sentimental.

sentimentalité, *n.f.* sentimentality.

sentinelle, *n.f.* sentry.

sentir, *vb.* feel; smell.

séparable, *adj.* separable.

séparation, *n.f.* separation, parting.

séparatiste, *adj.* separatist.

séparé, *adj.* separate.

séparer, *vb.* separate, segregate. **se s.,** part.

sept, (sĕt), *adj. and n.m.* seven.

septembre, *n.m.* September.

septième, (sĕt-), *adj. and n.m.f.* seventh.

septique, *adj.* septic.

sépulcre, *n.m.* sepulcher.

sépulture, *n.f.* burial (place).

sequelles, *n.f.pl.* after-effects, aftermath.

séquence, *n.f.* sequence.

séquestrer, *vb.* withdraw.

serein, *adj.* serene, placid.

sérénade, *n.f.* serenade.

sérénité, *n.f.* serenity.

serf, 1. *n.m.* serf. **2.** *adj.* in serfdom or the like.

sergent, *n.m.* sergeant.

série, *n.f.* series.

sérieux, 1. *adj.* serious, sober, grave. **2.** *n.m.* gravity.

serin, *n.m.* canary.

seringue, *n.f.* syringe.

serment, *n.m.* oath.

sermon, *n.m.* sermon.

sermonner, *vb.* lecture, preach.

séropostif, *adj.* HIV-positive.

serpent, *n.m.* snake, serpent.

serpenter, *vb.* wind, wander.

serpillière, *n.f.* floor-cloth.

serre, *n.f.* greenhouse; claw.

serré, *adj.* tight.

serre-joint, *n.m.* clamp.

serrer, *vb.* tighten, squeeze, press; crowd; shake (hands). **s. dans ses bras,** hug.

serrure, *n.f.* lock.

sérum, *n.m.* serum.

servage, *n.m.* servitude.

servant, 1. *adj.* serving. **2.** *n.m.* server; gunner.

servante, *n.f.* maid.

serveuse, *n.f.* waitress.

serviable, *adj.* helpful.

service, *n.m.* service, favor. **être de s.,** be on duty.

serviette, *n.f.* napkin; towel; briefcase.

servile, *adj.* menial.

servilité, *n.f.* servility.

servir, *vb.* serve. se s. de, use. ne s. à rien, be of no use.

serviteur, *n.m.* attendant, servant.

servitude, *n.f.* slavery.

session, *n.f.* session.

seuil, *n.m.* threshold.

seul, *adj.* alone, only, single.

seulement, *adv.* only, solely.

sève, *n.f.* sap.

sévère, *adj.* severe, stern.

sévérité, *n.f.* severity, rigor.

sévir, *vb.* punish, rage.

sevrer, *vb.* wean, withhold.

sexe, *n.m.* sex; sex organ(s).

sexisme, *n.m.* sexism.

sexiste, *adj.* sexist.

sexuel, *adj.* sexual.

seyant, *adj.* becoming, suitable.

shampooing, *n.m.* shampoo.

short, *n.m.* (pair of) shorts.

shrapnel, *n.m.* shrapnel.

si, 1. *adv.* so, so much; yes. si ... que, however (+*adj.*). 2. *conj.* if, whether.

Sicile, *n.f.* Sicily.

sida, SIDA, *n.m.* AIDS.

sidérurgie, *n.f.* iron and steel industry.

siècle, *n.m.* century.

siège, *n.m.* seat; siege.

siéger, *vb.* sit, convene, reside.

sien, *pron.* le sien, la sienne, his, hers, its.

sieste, *n.f.* siesta.

siffler, *vb.* whistle, hiss.

sifflerie, *n.f.* hissing, whistling.

sifflet, *n.m.* whistle.

sigle, *n.m.* abbreviation, acronym.

signal, *n.m.* signal.

signalement, *n.m.* description, details.

signaler, *vb.* point out.

signataire, *n.m.f.* signatory.

signature, *n.f.* signature.

signe, *n.m.* sign. s. de la tête, nod. faire s. à, beckon.

signer, *vb.* sign. se s., cross oneself.

significatif, *adj.* significant, meaningful.

signification, *n.f.* significance, meaning.

signifier, *vb.* signify, mean.

silence, *n.m.* silence.

silencieux, *adj.* noiseless, silent.

silex, *n.m.* flint.

silhouette, *n.f.* outline, silhouette.

silicium, *n.m.* silicon.

sillage, *n.m.* wake, course.

sillon, *n.m.* furrow.

sillonner, *vb.* plow.

similaire, *adj.* similar.

simple, *adj.* plain, simple, mere; no-frills.

simplicité, *n.f.* simplicity.

simplifier, *vb.* simplify.

simpliste, *adj.* simplistic.

simulacre, *n.m.* pretense, sham.

simulation, *n.f.* simulation.

simuler, *vb.* pretend.

simultané, *adj.* simultaneous.

sincère, *adj.* candid, sincere.

sincérité, *n.f.* candor, sincerity.

singe, *n.m.* monkey; imitator.

singer, *vb.* imitate, ape.

singularité, *n.f.* singularity; peculiar trait.

singulier, *adj. and n.m.* singular; peculiar, strange.

sinistre, 1. *n.m.* disaster, damage. 2. *adj.* sinister.

sinistré, 1. *n.m.* disaster victim. 2. *adj.* disaster-stricken.

sinon, *conj.* otherwise.

sinueux, *adj.* winding, sinuous.

sirène, *n.f.* siren; mermaid.

sirop, *n.m.* syrup.

siroter, *vb.* sip.

site, *n.m.* site.

sitôt, *adv.* as soon (as).

situation, *n.f.* situation; position, location, office.

situer, *vb.* situate, locate.

six, (sēs), *adj. and n.m.* six.

sixième, (-z-), *adj. and n.m.f.* sixth.

ski, *n.m.* ski. faire du s., ski.

skieur, *n.m.* skier.

Slave, 1. *adj.* Slavonic. 2. *n.m.f.* Slav.

slip, *n.m.* underpants, panties.

SMIC, *n.m.* minimum wage.

smoking, *n.m.* dinner jacket, tuxedo.

snak(-bar), *n.m.* snackbar.

snob, *n.m.* snob.

sobre, *adj.* temperate, sober.

sobriété, *n.f.* moderation, temperance.

sobriquet, *n.m.* nickname.

soc, *n.m.* plowshare.

sociable, *adj.* sociable.

social, *adj.* social.

socialisme, *n.m.* socialism.

socialiste, *adj. and n.m.f.* socialist.

société, *n.f.* society; company.

sociologie, *n.f.* sociology.

sociologue, *n.m.f.* sociologist.

sœur, *n.f.* sister.

sofa, *n.m.* sofa.

soi-disant, *adj.* so-called.

soie, *n.f.* silk; bristle.

soierie, *n.f.* silk goods.

soif, *n.f.* thirst. avoir s., be thirsty.

soigné, *adj.* trim. mal s., sloppy.

soigner, *vb.* tend, look after, take care of.

soigneux, *adj.* careful.

soi-même, *pron.* oneself.

soin, *n.m.* care. prendre s. de, take care of.

soir, *n.m.* evening. hier s., last night. ce s., tonight. le s., at night.

soirée, *n.f.* evening.

soit, *vb.* so be it. s. ... s., whether ... or. s. que, whether.

soixantaine, *n.f.* about sixty.

soixante, (-s-), *adj. and n.m.* sixty.

soixante-dix, *adj. and n.m.* seventy.

sol, *n.m.* earth, soil, ground.

solaire, *adj.* solar.

soldat, *n.m.* soldier.

solde, *n.m.* balance.

sole, *n.f.* sole (fish).

solécisme, *n.m.* solecism.

soleil, *n.m.* sun, sunshine. **coucher du s.,** sunset. **lever du s.,** sunrise.

solennel, *adj.* solemn.

solenniser, *vb.* solemnize.

solennité, *n.f.* solemnity.

solex, *n.m.* (trademark) moped.

solidaire, *adj.* jointly binding.

solidariser, *vb.* **se s.,** unite, join together.

solidarité, *n.f.* joint responsibility.

solide, *adj. and n.m.* solid.

solidifier, *vb.* solidify.

solidité, *n.f.* solidity.

soliloque, *n.m.* soliloquy.

soliste, *n.m.f.* soloist.

solitaire, *adj.* lonely, lonesome.

solitude, *n.f.* solitude.

solliciter, *vb.* solicit, ask, apply.

sollicitude, *n.f.* solicitude.

soluble, *adj.* soluble.

solution, *n.f.* solution.

solvable, *adj.* solvent.

sombre, *adj.* dark, dim, gloomy, somber.

sombrer, *vb.* sink.

sommaire, *n.m.* summary.

sommation, *n.f.* appeal, summons.

somme, 1. *n.f.* amount, sum. **2.** *n.m.* nap.

sommeil, *n.m.* sleep. **avoir s.,** be sleepy.

sommeiller, *vb.* doze, slumber.

sommer, *vb.* summon.

sommet, *n.m.* top, peak, summit.

somnifère, *n.m.* sleeping pill.

somnolence, *n.f.* drowsiness.

somnolent, *adj.* drowsy, sleepy.

somptueux, *adj.* lavish, sumptuous.

son, *m.,* **sa** *f.,* **ses** *pl. adj.* his, her, its.

son, *n.m.* sound, ring; bran.

sonate, *n.f.* sonata.

sondage, *n.m.* (opinion) poll.

sonde, *n.f.* sounding line; probe; catheter; feeding tube.

sonder, *vb.* fathom; probe.

songe, *n.m.* dream.

songer, *vb.* think of, dream.

songeur, 1. *adj.* dreamy, thoughtful. **2.** *n.m.* dreamer.

sonner, *vb.* sound, ring, strike.

sonnerie, *n.f.* ringing.

sonnette, *n.f.* bell.

sonore, *adj.* sonorous.

sonorisation, *n.f.* public address system.

sophiste, *n.m.f.* sophist.

sophistiqué, *adj.* sophisticated.

soprano, *n.m.* soprano.

sorbet, *n.m.* sorbet.

sorcellerie, *n.f.* sorcery.

sorcier, *n.m.* wizard.

sorcière, *n.f.* witch.

sordide, *adj.* sordid.

sort, *n.m.* lot.

sorte, *n.f.* sort, kind. **de s. que,** so that.

sortie, *n.f.* exit, way out.

sortilège, *n.m.* sorcery.

sortir, *vb.* go (come, get) out.

sot, *m.,* **sotte** *f. adj.* silly, stupid, foolish, dumb.

sottise, *n.f.* foolishness.

sou, *n.m.* cent. **sans le s.,** penniless.

soubassement, *n.m.* basement.

soubresaut, *n.m.* bound, jerk.

souche, *n.f.* stub, stump.

souci, *n.m.* care, worry, concern.

soucier, *vb.* **se s. (de),** care, worry (about).

soucieux, *adj.* anxious.

soucoupe, *n.f.* saucer. **s. volante,** flying saucer.

soudain, *adj.* sudden.

soudaineté, *n.f.* suddenness.

soude, *n.f.* soda.

souder, *vb.* solder, fuse.

souffle, *n.m.* breath.

souffler, *vb.* blow.

soufflet, *n.m.* bellows; blow, slap.

souffleter, *vb.* slap one's face.

souffrance(s), *n.f. (pl.)* misery, pain, suffering.

souffrir, *vb.* suffer, bear.

soufre, *n.m.* sulphur.

souhait, *n.m.* wish.

souhaiter, *vb.* wish for.

souiller, *vb.* soil, defile.

souillure, *n.f.* stain, dirt.

soûl, (sōō), *adj.* drunk.

soulager, *vb.* relieve, alleviate.

soûler, *vb.* fill with food and drink, inebriate.

soulèvement, *n.m.* uprising.

soulever, *vb.* lift, raise, arouse.

soulier, *n.m.* shoe.

souligner, *vb.* underline.

soumettre, *vb.* submit, subdue.

soumis, *adj.* obedient, submissive.

soumission, *n.f.* submission.

soupape, *n.f.* valve.

soupçon, *n.m.* suspicion.

soupçonner, *vb.* suspect.

soupçonneux, *adj.* suspicious.

soupe, *n.f.* soup.

souper, *n.m.* supper.

soupir, *n.m.* sigh.

soupirant, *n.m.* suitor.

soupirer, *vb.* sigh. **s. après,** yearn for.

souple, *adj.* flexible.

souplesse, *n.f.* suppleness, pliability.

source, *n.f.* source; spring.

sourcil, *n.m.* eyebrow.

sourciller, *vb.* frown.

sourcilleux, *adj.* haughty, disdainful.

sourd, *adj.* deaf.

sourd-muet, *n.m.* deaf mute.

souriant, *adj.* cheerful.

souricière, *n.f.* (mouse)trap.

sourire, *n.m. and vb.* smile.

souris, *n.f.* mouse.

sournois, *adj.* sly.

sous, *prep.* under.

souscription, *n.f.* subscription.

souscrire, *vb.* subscribe.

sous-entendre, *vb.* imply.

sous-estimer, *vb.* underestimate.

sous-louer, *vb.* sublet.

sous-marin, *n.m.* submarine.

sous-produit, *n.m.* by-product.

soussigné, *adj.* undersigned.

sous-sol, *n.m.* basement.
sous-titre, *n.m.* subtitle.
soustraction, *n.f.* subtraction.
soustraire, *vb.* subtract.
sous-traitant, *n.m.* subcontractor.
sous-vêtements, *n.m.pl.* underwear.
soutane, *n.f.* cassock.
soute, *n.f.* storeroom.
soutenir, *vb.* support, uphold, maintain; claim; back up.
soutenu, *adj.* steady.
souterrain, *adj.* underground.
soutien, *n.m.* support.
soutien-gorge, *n.m.* brassiere.
souvenance, *n.f.* recall, recollection.
souvenir, 1. *n.m.* remembrance, memory. **2.** *vb.* se s. de, remember.
souvent, *adv.* often.
souverain, *n.m.* ruler, sovereign.
souveraineté, *n.f.* sovereignty.
Soviétique, *n.m.f.* Soviet citizen.
soviétique, *adj.* Soviet.
soyeux, *adj.* silky.
spacieux, *adj.* spacious.
spasme, *n.m.* spasm.
spatial, *adj.* space.
spatule, *n.f.* spatula.
spécial, *adj.* special.
spécialiser, *vb.* specialize.
spécialiste, *n.m.f.* specialist.
spécialité, *n.f.* specialty.
spécifier, *vb.* specify.
spécifique, *adj.* specific.
spécimen, *n.m.* specimen.
spectacle, *n.m.* sight, show.
spectaculaire, *adj.* spectacular.
spectateur, *n.m.* spectator.
spectre, *n.m.* ghost; spectrum.
spéculation, *n.f.* speculation.
spéculer, *vb.* speculate.
sphère, *n.f.* sphere.
spinal, *adj.* spinal.
spiral, *adj.* spiral.
spirale, *n.f.* spiral.
spirite, *n.m.f.* spiritualist.

spiritisme, *n.m.* spiritualism.
spirituel, *adj.* spiritual; witty.
spiritueux, *adj.* pertaining to alcohol.
splendeur, *n.f.* splendor.
splendide, *adj.* splendid.
spolier, *vb.* plunder, pillage.
spontané, *adj.* spontaneous.
spontanéité, *n.f.* spontaneity.
sporadique, *adj.* sporadic.
sport, *n.m.* sport.
sportif, *adj.* sporting, athletic, sports.
spot, *n.m.* spot(light).
squatter, 1. *n.m.* squatter. **2.** *vb.* squat in.
squelette, *n.m.* skeleton.
stabiliser, *vb.* stabilize.
stabilité, *n.f.* stability.
stable, *adj.* stable, steady.
stage, *n.m.* training or instruction period.
stagflation, *n.f.* stagflation.
stagiaire, *n.m.f.* trainee.
stagnant, *adj.* stagnant.
stalle, *n.f.* stall.
stance, *n.f.* stanza.
standard, *n.m.* switchboard.
standardiste, *n.m.f.* phone operator.
starter, *n.m.* (car) choke.
station, *n.f.* stand, stop, station (subway).
stationnaire, *adj.* stationary.
stationnement, *n.m.* parking.
stationner, *vb.* park.
station-service, *n.f.* gas/service station.
statique, *adj.* static.
statistique, *n.f.* statistics.
statue, *n.f.* statue.
statuer, *vb.* decree, decide.
stature, *n.f.* stature.
statut, *n.m.* statute.
steak, *n.m.* steak.
sténographe, *n.m.f.* stenographer.
sténographie, *n.f.* stenography.
stéréo, *n.f. and adj.* stereo.
stéréophonique, *adj.* stereophonic.
stérile, *adj.* barren.
stérilet, *n.m.* coil, IUD.
stériliser, *vb.* sterilize.
stéthoscope, *n.m.* stethoscope.

stigmatiser, *vb.* mark, stigmatize.
stimulant, *n.m.* stimulus.
stimuler, *vb.* stimulate.
stipuler, *vb.* stipulate.
stoïque, *adj. and n.m.f.* stoic.
stop, *n.m.* stop sign; hitchhiking.
store, *n.m.* (window) shade, blind.
strapontin, *n.m.* folding seat.
stratagème, *n.m.* stratagem.
stratégie, *n.f.* strategy.
stratégique, *adj.* strategic.
stressant, *adj.* stressful.
strict, (-kt), *adj.* severe, strict.
strier, *vb.* mark, streak, groove.
structure, *n.f.* structure.
stuc, *n.m.* stucco.
studieux, *adj.* studious.
stupéfait, *adj.* astounded.
stupéfiant, *n.m.* narcotic, dope.
stupéfier, *vb.* astound.
stupeur, *n.f.* amazement.
stupide, *adj.* stupid.
stupidité, *n.f.* stupidity.
style, *n.m.* style.
styler, *vb.* train, teach.
stylet, *n.m.* stiletto.
stylographe, stylo, *n.m.* fountain pen.
suavité, *n.f.* suavity.
subalterne, *adj. and n.m.f.* junior (rank).
subdiviser, *vb.* subdivide.
subir, *vb.* undergo, bear.
subit, *adj.* sudden.
subjectif, *adj.* subjective.
subjonctif, *adj. and n.m.* subjunctive.
subjuguer, *vb.* subdue, overcome.
sublime, *adj.* sublime, exalted.
submerger, *vb.* submerge, flood.
subordonné, *adj. and n.m.* subordinate.
subordonner, *vb.* subordinate.
subornation, *n.f.* bribing.
subreptice, *adj.* surreptitious.
subséquent, *adj.* subsequent.
subside, *n.m.* subsidy.

subsister, *vb.* subsist, live.

substance, *n.f.* substance.

substantiel, *adj.* substantial.

substantif, *n.m.* noun.

substituer, *vb.* substitute.

substitution, *n.f.* substitution.

subtil, (-l), *adj.* subtle.

subtilité, *n.f.* subtlety.

subvenir, *vb.* provide.

subvention, *n.f.* grant, subsidy.

subventionner, *vb.* subsidize.

subversif, *adj.* subversive.

suc, *n.m.* juice.

succéder à, *vb.* succeed, follow.

succès, *n.m.* success, hit.

successeur, *n.m.* successor.

successif, *adj.* successive.

succession, *n.f.* succession.

succion, *n.f.* suction.

succomber, *vb.* succumb.

succursale, *n.f.* branch office.

sucer, *vb.* suck.

sucre, *n.m.* sugar.

sucrer, *vb.* add sugar.

sucreries, *n.f.pl.* sweets.

sud, (-d), *n.m.* south.

sudation, *n.f.* sweating.

sud-est, *n.m.* southeast.

sud-ouest, *n.m.* southwest.

Suède, *n.f.* Sweden.

Suédois, *n.m.* Swede (person).

suédois, *adj. and n.m.* Swedish.

suer, *vb.* sweat.

sueur, *n.m.* sweat.

suffire, *vb.* suffice.

suffisance, *n.f.* adequacy; conceit.

suffisant, *adj.* sufficient, adequate; conceited.

suffixe, *n.m.* suffix.

suffoquer, *vb.* suffocate.

suffrage, *n.m.* suffrage.

suggérer, *vb.* suggest.

suggestion, *n.f.* suggestion.

suicide, *n.m.* suicide.

suicider, *vb.* **se s.,** kill oneself.

suie, *n.f.* soot.

suif, *n.m.* tallow.

suinter, *vb.* seep.

Suisse, **1.** *n.m.* Swiss (person). **2.** *n.f.* Switzerland.

suisse, *adj.* Swiss.

suite, *n.f.* sequence; retinue; *(pl.)* results, aftermath. **et ainsi de s.,** and so on. **tout de s.,** at once.

suivant, **1.** *n.m.* follower. **2.** *adj.* next, following, subsequent. **3.** *prep.* by, according to.

suivi, *adj.* followed, coherent.

suivre, *vb.* follow; attend. **faire s.,** forward.

sujet, **1.** *n.m.* subject; topic. **2.** *adj.* subject. **s. à,** liable to.

sujétion, *n.f.* subjection, slavery.

superbe, *adj.* superb, magnificent.

super(carburant), *n.m.* high-octane gasoline.

superette, *n.f.* small supermarket.

superficie, *n.f.* surface.

superficiel, *adj.* superficial, shallow.

superflu, *adj.* superfluous.

supérieur, *adj. and n.m.* superior, higher, upper; senior.

supériorité, *n.f.* superiority.

superlatif, *adj. and n.m.* superlative.

supermarché, *n.m.* supermarket.

superpuissance, *n.f.* superpower.

superstar, *n.f.* superstar.

superstitieux, *adj.* superstitious.

superstition, *n.f.* superstition.

suppléant, *adj. and n.m.* assistant, substitute.

suppléer, *vb.* substitute.

supplément, *n.m.* supplement.

supplémentaire, *adj.* extra. **heures s.s,** overtime.

supplice, *n.m.* punishment, torture.

supplier, *vb.* beseech, entreat, beg, supplicate.

support, *n.m.* support, stand.

supportable, *adj.* tolerable.

supporter, *vb.* support; bear, stand, endure.

supposer, *vb.* suppose, assume.

supposition, *n.f.* assumption, conjecture, supposition.

suppôt, *n.m.* implement, tool, agent.

suppression, *n.f.* suppression.

supprimer, *vb.* suppress, put down; take out.

supputation, *n.f.* computation.

supputer, *vb.* compute.

suprématie, *n.f.* supremacy.

suprême, *adj.* supreme.

sur, *prep.* on, upon, over.

sûr, *adj.* safe, sure, secure.

surabonder, *vb.* be very abundant.

suranné, *adj.* out-of-date.

surcharge, *n.f.* excess load.

surcharger, *vb.* overload.

surcroît, *n.m.* addition.

surdité, *n.f.* deafness.

suret, *adj.* sour.

sûreté, *n.f.* safety, security, reliability.

surf, *n.m.* surf.

surface, *n.f.* surface, area.

surgélateur, *n.m.* deep freeze.

surgir, *vb.* spring up, arise.

surhumain, *adj.* superhuman.

surintendant, *n.m.* superintendent.

sur-le-champ, *adv.* at once, immediately.

surlendemain, *n.m.* two days later.

surmener, *vb.* overwork.

surmonter, *vb.* overcome, surmount.

surnager, *vb.* float.

surnaturel, *adj. and n.m.* supernatural.

surnom, *n.m.* nickname.

surpasser, *vb.* surpass.

surpeuplé, *adj.* overpopulated.

surplis, *n.m.* surplice.

surplomber, *vb.* overhang.

surplus, *n.m.* surplus, excess.

surprendre, *vb.* surprise.

surprise, *n.f.* surprise.

sursaut, *n.m.* start.

sursauter, *vb.* give a start.

sursis, *n.m.* delay, putting off.
surtaxe, *n.f.* surtax.
surtout, 1. *n.m.* overcoat. **2.** *adv.* above all.
surveillance, *n.f.* supervision, watch.
surveillant, *n.m.* superintendent.
surveiller, *vb.* supervise, watch over.
survenir, *vb.* happen.
survêtement, *n.m.* track suit.
survie, *n.f.* survival.
survivance, *n.f.* survival.
survivre, *vb.* survive.
susceptible, *adj.* susceptible; liable.
susciter, *vb.* arouse, provoke.
suspect, (-kt), *adj.* suspicious.
suspecter, *vb.* suspect.
suspendre, *vb.* suspend, hang, sling.

suspens, *adv.* **en s.,** in suspense.
suspense, *n.m.* suspense.
suspension, *n.f.* suspension.
suspicion, *n.f.* suspicion.
sustenter, *vb.* sustain, bulwark.
svelte, *adj.* slender, slim.
sweat-shirt, (swĕt shœrt), *n.m.* sweatshirt.
syllabe, *n.f.* syllable.
sylphide, *n.f.* sylph.
sylvestre, *adj.* sylvan, woody.
sylviculture, *n.f.* forestry.
symbole, *n.m.* symbol.
symboliser, *vb.* symbolize.
symétrie, *n.f.* symmetry.
sympa, *adj.* nice.
sympathie, *n.f.* sympathy. **avoir de la s. pour,** like.
sympathique, *adj.* congenial, likeable.
sympathiser, *vb.* sympathize.
symphonie, *n.f.* symphony.

symptôme, *n.m.* symptom.
synchroniser, *vb.* synchronize.
syncape, *n.f.* blackout.
syndic, *n.m.f.* association/union representative.
syndical, *adj.* of a trade union.
syndicat, *n.m.* syndicate. **s. ouvrier,** trade union.
syndiqué, *n.m.* (trade) union member.
syndrome, *n.m.* syndrome.
synonyme, *n.m.* synonym.
syntaxe, *n.f.* syntax.
synthèse, *n.f.* synthesis.
synthétique, *adj.* synthetic.
Syrie, *n.f.* Syria.
Syrien, *adj.* Syrian (person).
syrien, *adj.* Syrian.
systématique, *adj.* systematic.
système, *n.m.* system.

T

tabac (-bǎ), *n.m.* tobacco.
tabagie, *n.f.* smoking.
tabernacle, *n.m.* tabernacle.
table, *n.f.* table. **t. des matières,** index.
tableau, *n.m.* picture. **t. noir,** blackboard.
tabler, *vb.* count on, depend.
tablette, *n.f.* tablet.
tableur, *n.m.* spreadsheet.
tablier, *n.m.* apron.
tabou, *n.m.* taboo.
tabouret, *n.m.* stool.
tache, *n.f.* spot, stain, blot, smear.
tâche, *n.f.* task; assignment.
tacher, *vb.* spot, stain, blot.
tâcher, *vb.* try.
tacite, *adj.* tacit, silent.
taciturne, *adj.* unspeaking.
tact, (-kt), *n.m.* tact.
tacticien, *n.m.* tactician.
tactique, 1. *adj.* of tactics, tactical. **2.** *n.f.* tactics.
taffetas, *n.m.* taffeta.
taie, *n.f.* **t. d'oreiller,** pillowcase.
taillade, *n.f.* slash.
taille, *n.f.* waist, figure; size.
tailler, *vb.* trim, cut.

tailleur, *n.m.* tailor.
taire, *vb.* keep quiet. **se t.,** be silent.
talent, *n.m.* ability, talent.
talon, *n.m.* heel; (check) stub.
talus, *n.m.* slope.
tambour, *n.m.* drum.
tambourin, *n.m.* tambourine.
tamis, *n.m.* sieve.
tampon, *n.m.* plug, pad. **t. hygiénique,** tampon.
tamponner, *vb.* plug; run together.
tan, *n.m.* tan (leather).
tandis que, *conj.* while, whereas.
tangible, *adj.* tangible.
tanguer, *vb.* cover with pitch.
tant, *adv.* so much, so many. **t. que,** as long as.
tante, *n.f.* aunt.
tantième, *n.m.* part, percentage.
tantôt, *adv.* presently, soon.
tapage, *n.m.* din.
tapageur, *adj.* rowdy.
taper, *vb.* pat, knock, tap; type.

tapir, *vb.* **se t.,** squat, cower, lurk.
tapis, *n.m.* carpet, rug.
tapisserie, *n.f.* tapestry.
tapissier, *n.m.* upholsterer.
taquiner, *vb.* tease.
taquinerie, *n.f.* teasing.
tard, *adv.* late.
tarder, *vb.* delay.
tardif, *adj.* slow, tardy, late.
tare, *n.f.* defect.
tarière, *n.f.* auger.
tarif, *n.m.* scale of charges; rate; fare. **t. douanier,** tariff.
tartan, *n.m.* plaid.
tarte, *n.f.* pie.
tartine, *n.f.* slice of bread.
tartre, *n.m.* tartar.
tas, *n.m.* heap, pile.
tasse, *n.f.* cup.
tasser, *vb.* pack, fill up.
tâter, *vb.* feel.
tâtonner, *vb.* grope.
taudis, *n.m.* hovel, slum.
taupe, *n.f.* mole.
taureau, *n.m.* bull.
taux, *n.m.* rate.
taverne, *n.f.* tavern.

taxe, *n.f.* tax. **t. (à la) valeur ajoutée,** value-added tax.

taxer, *vb.* tax, assess.

taxi, *n.m.* cab, taxi.

Tchécoslovaquie, *n.f.* Czechoslovakia.

te, (tə**),** *pron.* you, yourself.

technicien, *n.m.* technician.

technique, 1. *n.f.* technique. **2.** *adj.* technical.

technologie, *n.f.* technology.

teindre, *vb.* dye.

teint, *n.m.* complexion.

teinte, *n.f.* tint, shade.

teinter, *vb.* tint, stain.

teinture, *n.f.* dye.

teinturier, *n.m.* dry-cleaner; dyer.

tel, *adj.* such.

télé, *n.f.* TV.

télécommande, *n.f.* remote control.

télécommunitions, *n.f.pl.* telecommunications.

télécopie, *n.f.* fax.

télécopieur, *n.m.* fax machine.

télédistribution, *n.f.* cable TV.

télégramme, *n.m.* telegram.

télégraphe, *n.m.* telegraph.

télégraphie, *n.f.* telegraphy. **t. sans fil,** *abbr.* **T.S.F.,** radio, wireless.

télégraphier, *vb.* telegraph.

téléguider, *vb.* operate by remote control, radio-control.

télématique, *n.f.* computer communications.

téléphone, *n.m.* telephone. **coup de t.,** telephone call.

téléphoner, *vb.* telephone.

télescope, *n.m.* telescope.

télescoper, *vb.* crash, run together.

téléspectateur, *n.m.* TV viewer.

téléviseur, *n.m.* TV set.

télévision, *n.f.* television.

télex, *n.m.* telex.

tellement, *adv.* so much.

téméraire, *adj.* rash.

témoignage, *n.m.* testimony; token.

témoigner, *vb.* testify.

témoin, *n.m.* witness.

tempe, *n.f.* temple (anatomy).

tempérament, *n.m.* temper, temperament.

tempérance, *n.f.* temperance.

tempérant, *adj.* temperate.

température, *n.f.* temperature.

tempéré, *adj.* temperate.

tempérer, *vb.* moderate, calm, lessen.

tempête, *n.f.* storm, tempest.

tempétueux, *adj.* tempestuous.

temple, *n.m.* temple.

temporaire, *adj.* temporary.

temporiser, *vb.* temporize, evade.

temps, (tä**n),** *n.m.* time; weather.

tenace, *adj.* tenacious.

ténacité, *n.f.* tenacity.

tenailles, *n.f.pl.* tongs.

tendance, *n.f.* tendency, trend, leaning.

tendre, 1. *adj.* tender, fond, loving. **2.** *vb.* tend, extend.

tendresse, *n.f.* tenderness, fondness.

tendu, *adj.* tense; uptight.

ténèbres, *n.f.pl.* gloom, darkness.

ténébreux, *adj.* dismal.

teneur, *n.m.* **t. de livres,** bookkeeper.

tenir, *vb.* hold.

tennis, (-s), *n.m.* tennis.

ténor, *n.m.* tenor.

tension, *n.f.* strain; stress.

tentacule, *n.m.* tentacle.

tentatif, *adj.* tentative.

tentation, *n.f.* temptation.

tentative, *n.f.* attempt.

tente, *n.f.* tent; awning.

tenter, *vb.* tempt, try, attract.

tenture, *n.f.* wallcovering.

tenue, *n.f.* rig; conduct, manners.

ténuité, *n.f.* tenuity, unimportance.

térébenthine, *n.f.* turpentine.

terme, *n.m.* term, period; end.

terminaison, *n.f.* ending.

terminal, *adj. and n.m.* terminal.

terminer, *vb.* end.

terminologie, *n.f.* terminology.

terminus, *n.m.* terminus.

terne, *adj.* drab, dull, dim, dingy.

ternir, *vb.* tarnish, dull.

terrain, *n.m.* ground(s).

terrasse, *n.f.* terrace.

terrasser, *vb.* heap up, embank; knock down, conquer.

terre, *n.f.* earth, ground, land. **pomme de t.,** potato. **à t.,** ashore.

terrestre, *adj.* earthly.

terreur, *n.f.* terror, fright, fear.

terrible, *adj.* terrible, awful; (colloquial) terrific.

terrifier, *vb.* terrify.

terrine, *n.f.* terrine, pâté.

territoire, *n.m.* territory.

terroir, *n.m.* soil.

terroriser, *vb.* terrorize.

terrorisme, *n.m.* terrorism.

tertre, *n.m.* mound.

tesson, *n.m.* broken piece, fragment.

testament, *n.m.* testament, will.

testateur, *n.m.* testator.

tester, *vb.* test.

testicule, *n.m.* testicle.

tête, *n.f.* head. **tenir t. à,** cope with.

téter, *vb.* suck.

téton, *n.m.* breast.

têtu, *adj.* stubborn.

texte, *n.m.* text.

textile, *adj.* textile.

textuel, *adj.* textual.

texture, *n.f.* texture.

Thaïlande, *n.f.* Thailand.

thé, *n.m.* tea.

théâtral, *adj.* theatrical.

théâtre, *n.m.* theater.

théière, *n.f.* teapot.

thème, *n.m.* theme.

théologie, *n.f.* theology.

théorie, *n.f.* theory.

théorique, *adj.* theoretical.

thérapie, *n.f.* therapy.

thermomètre, *n.m.* thermometer.

thermostat, *n.m.* thermostat.

thésauriser, *vb.* hoard.

thèse, *n.f.* thesis.

thon, *n.m.* tuna.

thym, *n.m.* thyme.

ticket, *n.m.* check, ticket, coupon.

tiède, *adj.* lukewarm.

tiédir, *vb.* make or become cool.

tien, *pron.* le tien, la tienne, yours.

tiers, *n.m.* third.

Tiers Monde, *n.m.* Third World.

tige, *n.f.* stem, stalk.

tigre, *n.m.* tiger.

tilleul, *n.m.* linden, lime tree.

timbre, *n.m.* stamp. t.-poste, postage stamp.

timbrer, *vb.* stamp.

timide, *adj.* timid, shy, coy, bashful.

timidité, *n.f.* timidity.

timoré, *adj.* timorous.

tintamarre, *n.m.* racket.

tinter, *vb.* ring, knell, tinkle.

tir, *n.m.* shooting, firing.

tirage, *n.m.* printing, print; circulation, edition.

tirailleur, *n.m.* sharpshooter.

tire, *n.f.* pull, yank.

tire-bouchon, *n.m.* corkscrew.

tirer, *vb.* draw, pull; shoot.

tiret, *n.m.* blank; dash.

tiroir, *n.m.* drawer.

tisane, *n.f.* drink, herbal tea.

tisser, *vb.* weave.

tisserand, *n.m.* weaver.

tissu, *n.m.* web; cloth, fabric.

titre, *n.m.* title, right.

titrer, *vb.* invest with a title.

titulaire, *n.m.* incumbent.

toast, (-t), *n.m.* toast.

toaster, *vb.* toast.

toi, *pron.* you.

toile, *n.f.* web; canvas; linen.

toilette, *n.f.* toilet; dressing, dress.

toison, *n.f.* fleece.

toit, *n.m.* roof.

toiture, *n.f.* roofing.

tolérance, *n.f.* tolerance.

tolérer, *vb.* tolerate, bear.

tomate, *n.f.* tomato.

tombe, *n.f.* grave.

tombeau, *n.m.* tomb.

tombée, *n.f.* fall, decline.

tomber, *vb.* fall. laisser t., drop.

tome, *n.m.* volume.

ton, *n.m.* tone, pitch.

ton, *m.*, ta *f.*, tes *pl. adj.* your.

tonalité, *n.f.* dial tone, tone, key.

tondeuse, *n.f.* (lawn) mower.

tondre, *vb.* shear; mow.

tonique, *adj. and n.m.* tonic.

tonne, *n.f.* ton; barrel.

tonneau, *n.m.* cask, barrel.

tonner, *vb.* thunder.

tonnerre, *n.m.* thunder.

topaze, *n.f.* topaz.

topographie, *n.f.* topography.

torche, *n.f.* torch.

tordre, *vb.* twist, wrench, wring. se t., writhe.

torpeur, *n.f.* torpor.

torpille, *n.f.* torpedo.

torrent, *n.m.* torrent.

torride, *adj.* torrid.

torse, *n.m.* torso.

tort, *n.m.* wrong. avoir t., be wrong.

tortiller, *vb.* twist, wiggle.

tortionnaire, *n.m.f.* torturer.

tortu, *adj.* crooked.

tortue, *n.f.* turtle, tortoise.

torture, *n.f.* torture.

torturer, *vb.* torture.

tôt, *adv.* soon, early.

total, *adj. and n.m.* total.

totalisateur, *n.m.* adding machine.

totaliser, *vb.* total, add up.

totalitaire, *adj.* totalitarian.

totalité, *n.f.* entirety.

toubib (-b) *n.m.* (colloquial) doctor.

touchant, *prep.* concerning.

touche, *n.f.* key.

toucher, 1. *n.m.* touch. 2. *vb.* touch; collect; affect; border on.

touffe, *n.f.* tuft, bunch.

touffu, *adj.* bushy.

toujours, *adv.* always, still, ever, yet.

toupie, *n.f.* top (child's toy).

tour, 1. *n.m.* turn; trick; stroll. faire le t. de, go around. 2. *n.f.* tower.

tourbe, *n.f.* rabble.

tourbillon, *n.m.* whirl. t. d'eau, whirlpool. t. de vent, whirlwind.

tourbilloner, *vb.* whirl.

tourelle, *n.f.* turret.

touriste, *n.m.f.* tourist.

tourment, *n.m.* torment.

tourmenter, *vb.* torment.

tournage, *n.m.* (film) shooting.

tourne-disques, *n.m.* record player.

tournedos, *n.f.* beefsteak.

tournée, *n.f.* round.

tourner, *vb.* turn, revolve, spin.

tournesol, *n.m.* sunflower.

tournevis, *n.m.* screwdriver.

tournoi, *n.m.* tournament.

tournure, *n.f.* figure; turn of phrase.

tousser, *vb.* cough.

tout, 1. *adj.m.*, toute *f.*, tous *m.pl.*, toutes *f.pl.* all, each, every. 2. *pron.* everything. tous les deux, both. t. d'un coup, all at once. t. de même, all the same. pas du t., not at all.

toutefois, *adv.* however.

tout-puissant, *adj.* almighty.

toux, *n.f.* cough.

toxicomane, *n.m.f.* drug addict.

toxique, *adj.* toxic.

tracasser, *vb.* worry.

trace, *n.f.* trace, step, track, footprint.

tracer, *vb.* outline, trace.

tracteur, *n.m.* tractor.

traction, *n.f.* traction.

tradition, *n.f.* tradition.

traditionnel, *adj.* traditional.

traducteur, *n.m.* translator.

traduction, *n.f.* translation.

traduire, *vb.* translate.

trafic, *n.m.* traffic.

trafiquer, *vb.* traffic; carry on dealings.

tragédie, *n.f.* tragedy.

tragique, *adj.* tragic.

trahir, *vb.* betray.

trahison, *n.f.* treason.

train, *n.m.* train.

traînard, *n.m.* loiterer, dawdler.

traîne, *n.f.* train of dress.

traîneau, *n.m.* sled, sleigh.

traîner, *vb.* drag, haul.

traire, *vb.* milk.

trait, *n.m.* feature; draft; shot. **t. d'union,** hyphen.

traité, *n.m.* treaty.

traitement, *n.m.* treatment. **t. de données,** data processing. **t. de texte,** word processing.

traiter, *vb.* treat, deal; process.

traiteur, *n.m.* caterer.

traître, *n.m.* traitor.

traîtrise, *n.f.* treachery.

trajet, *n.m.* crossing.

trame, *n.f.* web (woof); plan, plot.

tramer, *vb.* devise.

tramway, *n.m.* streetcar.

tranchant, *adj.* sharp, crisp.

tranche, *n.f.* slice.

tranchée, *n.f.* trench.

trancher, *vb.* cut.

tranquille, (-l), *adj.* quiet. **laisser t.,** leave alone.

tranquilliser, (-l-), *vb.* soothe, make tranquil.

tranquillité, (-l-), *n.f.* quiet, stillness.

transaction, *n.f.* transaction.

transe, *n.f.* fright, fear.

transférer, *vb.* transfer.

transformer, *vb.* transform.

transfuser, *vb.* transfuse.

transfusion, *n.f.* transfusion.

transitif, *adj.* transitive.

transition, (-z-), *n.f.* transition.

transitoire, (-z-), *adj.* transitory.

transmettre, *vb.* transmit, convey, send.

transmetteur, *n.m.* transmitter.

transmission, *n.f.* transmission.

transparent, *adj.* transparent.

transpiration, *n.f.* perspiration.

transpirer, *vb.* perspire.

transplanter, *vb.* transplant.

transport, *n.m.* transfer, transport, transportation; bliss, ecstasy. **t.s en commun,** mass transport.

transporter, *vb.* transport, transfer, convey.

transposer, *vb.* transpose.

transsexuel, *adj.* transsexual.

traumatiser, *vb.* traumatize.

travail, *n.m.* work, job, labor.

travailler, *vb.* work.

travailleur, 1. *n.m.* worker, laborer. 2. *adj.* industrious.

travée, *n.f.* span.

travers, *n.m.* breadth. **à t.,** across, through. **de t.,** askance, awry.

traversée, *n.f.* crossing.

traverser, *vb.* cross.

traversin, *n.m.* bolster.

travesti, *adj.* transvestite.

travestir, *vb.* disguise.

trébucher, *vb.* stumble, trip.

trèfle, *n.m.* clover; club (cards).

treillis, *n.m.* denim.

treize, *adj. and n.m.* thirteen.

tréma, *n.m.* dieresis.

tremblement, *n.m.* trembling. **t. de terre,** earthquake.

trembler, *vb.* tremble, shake, quake.

trembloter, *vb.* quiver.

trémousser, *vb.* flutter.

trempe, *n.f.* temper, cast.

tremper, *vb.* soak, drench, temper.

trentaine, *n.f.* about thirty.

trente, *adj. and n.m.* thirty.

trépasser, *vb.* die.

trépied, *n.m.* tripod, trivet.

très, *adv.* very.

trésor, *n.m.* treasure, treasury; darling.

trésorier, *n.m.* treasurer.

tressaillement, *n.m.* thrill; start.

tressaillir, *vb.* thrill; start.

tresse, *n.f.* braid.

tresser, *vb.* braid.

tréteau, *n.m.* trestle.

trêve, *n.f.* truce.

tri, *n.m.* sorting, selection.

triangle, *n.m.* triangle.

tribade, *n.f.* lesbian.

tribu, *n.f.* tribe.

tribulation, *n.f.* tribulation.

tribut, *n.m.* tribute.

tributaire, *adj.* tributary.

tricher, *vb.* cheat.

tricherie, *n.f.* cheating.

tricolore, *adj.* three-colored; (French) blue, white, red; (*fig.*) France.

tricot, *n.m.* knitting; undershirt; sweater.

tricoter, *vb.* knit.

trier, *vb.* sort.

trimestre, *n.m.* term.

trimestriel, *adj.* quarterly.

trinquer, *vb.* touch glasses in making a toast.

triomphant, *adj.* triumphant.

triomphe, *n.m.* triumph.

triompher, *vb.* triumph.

triple, *adj. and n.m.* triple.

tripoter, *vb.* fiddle with, dabble in; bother.

triste, *adj.* sad.

tristesse, *n.f.* sadness.

trivial, *adj.* trivial.

trivialité, *n.f.* triviality.

troc, *n.m.* barter.

trois, *adj. and n.m.* three.

troisième, *adj.and n.m.f.* third.

trompe, *n.f.* horn, trumpet; elephant's trunk.

trompe l'œil, *n.m.* trompe l'œil style of painting.

tromper, *vb.* deceive, cheat. **se t.,** be wrong, make a mistake.

tromperie, *n.f.* deceit.

trompette, *n.f.* trumpet.

trompeur, *adj.* deceitful.

tronc, *n.m.* trunk.

trône, *n.m.* throne.

trop, *adv.* too; too much, too many.

trophée, *n.m.* trophy.

tropical, *adj.* tropical.

tropique, *n.m.* tropic.

troquer, *vb.* barter, dicker, trade.

trot, *n.m.* trot.

trotter, *vb.* trot.

trottiner, *vb.* trot, jog.

trottoir, *n.m.* sidewalk.

trou, *n.m.* hole.

trouble, *n.m.* disturbance, riot.

troublé, *adj.* anxious, worried.

troubler, *vb.* perturb.

trouer, *vb.* pierce, bore.

trouille, *n.f.* (colloquial) **avoir la t.,** be scared to death.

troupe, *n.f.* troop.
troupeau, *n.m.* herd, flock, drove.
troupier, *n.m.* soldier, trooper.
trousseau, *n.m.* bunch; outfit.
trousser, *vb.* truss up, turn up.
trouvaille, *n.f.* discovery; find.
trouver, *vb.* find. **se t.,** be located.
truc, *n.m.* trick; thing.
truelle, *n.f.* trowel.
truite, *n.f.* trout.
truquer, *vb.* fake.
trust, *n.m.* trust.
T.S.F., *n.f.* radio.
tu, *pron.* you.

tube, *n.m.* tube, pipe.
tuberculeux, *adj.* tuberculous.
tuberculose, *n.f.* tuberculosis.
tuer, *vb.* kill.
tuerie, *n.f.* slaughter, massacre.
tueur, *n.m.* killer.
tuile, *n.f.* tile.
tulipe, *n.f.* tulip.
tuméfier, *vb.* make swollen.
tumulte, *n.m.* tumult, turmoil, uproar.
tunique, *n.f.* tunic.
Tunisie, *n.f.* Tunisia.
Tunisien, *n.m.* Tunisian (person).
tunisien, *adj.* Tunisian.
tunnel, *n.f.* tunnel.

Turc, *m.,* **Turque** *f. n.* Turk.
turc, *n.m.* Turkish (language).
turc, *m.,* **turque** *f. adj.* Turkish.
Turquie, *n.f.* Turkey.
tutelle, *n.f.* tutelage, protection.
tuteur, *n.m.* guardian.
tutoyer, *vb.* address familiarly as "tu."
tuyau, *n.f.* pipe; hose.
tympan, *n.m.* eardrum.
type, *n.m.* type; fellow, guy.
typique, *adj.* typical.
tyran, *n.m.* tyrant.
tyrannie, *n.f.* tyranny.
tyranniser, *vb.* tyrannize.
tzigane, *n.m.f.* gypsy.

U

ubiquité *n.f.* ubiquity.
ulcère, *n.m.* ulcer.
ultérieur, *adj.* ulterior, further.
ultime, *adj.* ultimate, last.
un, *m.,* **une** *f.* **1.** *art.* a. **2.** *adj. and n.* one.
unanime, *adj.* unanimous.
unanimité, *n.f.* unanimity.
uni, *adj.* united; plain; even.
unifier, *vb.* unify.
uniforme, *adj. and n.m.* uniform.
union, *n.f.* union.
unique, *adj.* unique; only.
unir, *vb.* unite.

unisexuel, *adj.* unisex.
unisson, *n.m.* unison.
unité, *n.f.* unit, unity.
univers, *n.m.* universe.
universel, *adj.* universal.
université, *n.f.* university, college.
urbain, *adj.* urban.
urbanisme, *n.m.* city planning.
urgence, *n.f.* urgency, emergency.
urgent, *adj.* urgent, pressing.
urine, *n.f.* urine.
urne, *n.f.* urn; ballot box.
urticaire, *n.f.* hives.

usage, *n.m.* use; custom.
usager, *adj.* for daily use.
usé, *adj.* shabby, worn-out.
user, *vb.* wear out.
usine, *n.f.* factory.
ustensile, *n.f.* utensil.
usuel, *adj.* usual.
usure, *n.f.* wear and tear; usury; interest.
usurper, *vb.* usurp.
utile, *adj.* helpful, useful.
utilisation, *n.f.* use.
utiliser, *vb.* use.
utilité, *n.f.* utility.
utopie, *n.f.* utopia.

V

vacance *n.f.* vacancy; *(pl.)* vacation.
vacarme, *n.m.* uproar.
vaccin, *n.m.* vaccine.
vacciner, *vb.* vaccinate.
vache, *n.f.* cow.
vaciller, (-l-), *vb.* waver.
vacuité, *n.f.* emptiness, vacuity.
vagabond, *adj.* vagrant.
vagabonder, *vb.* roam, tramp.
vagin, *n.m.* vagina.

vague, 1. *n.f.* wave. **2.** *adj.* vague.
vaguer, *vb.* wander.
vaillant, *adj.* valiant, brave, gallant.
vain, *adj.* idle; vain, futile.
vaincre, *vb.* defeat.
vainqueur, *n.m.* victor.
vaisseau, *n.m.* ship.
vaisselle, *n.f.* dishes.
valable, *adj.* valid; worthwhile.

valeur, *n.f.* valor; value, worth; *(pl.)* securities.
valeureux, *adj.* brave, valorous.
valide, *adj.* valid.
valise, *n.f.* suitcase.
vallée, *n.f.* valley.
vallon, *n.m.* valley, vale.
valoir, *vb.* be worth. **v. mieux,** be better.
valorisé, *adj.* valued.
valoriser, *vb.* add value to.
valse, *n.f.* waltz.

vandale, *n.m.f.* vandal.

vanille, *n.f.* vanilla.

vanité, *n.f.* conceit, vanity.

vaniteux, *adj.* vain.

vantard, *adj.* boastful.

vanter, *vb.* extol. **se v.,** boast, brag.

vapeur, 1. *n.m.* steamship. **2.** *n.f.* vapor, steam.

vaporisateur, *n.f.* vaporizer, spray.

variation, *n.f.* variation, change.

varicelle, *n.f.* chicken pox.

varier, *vb.* vary.

variété, *n.f.* variety.

variole, *n.f.* smallpox.

vase, *n.m.* vase, jar, pot.

vasectomie, *n.f.* vasectomy.

vaseux, *adj.* slimy; hazy.

vassal, *n.m.* vassal.

vaste, *adj.* vast, spacious.

vaurien, *n.m.* worthless person, idler.

veau, *n.m.* calf.

vedette, *n.f.* (movie) star.

végéter, *vb.* vegetate.

véhicule, *n.m.* vehicle.

veille, *n.f.* eve, day before.

veiller, *vb.* watch over, sit up.

veine, *n.f.* vein; luck.

véliplanchiste, *n.m.f.* windsurfer.

vélo, *n.m.* bike.

vélomoteur, *n.m.* moped.

velours, *n.m.* velvet. **v. côtelé,** corduroy.

velouté, *adj.* like velvet.

velu, *adj.* hairy.

vendange, *n.f.* vintage.

vendeur, *n.m.* seller; clerk, salesman.

vendre, *vb.* sell.

vendredi, *n.m.* Friday.

vénéneux, *adj.* poisonous.

vénérer, *vb.* venerate.

vengeance, *n.f.* revenge.

venger, *vb.* avenge. **se v.,** get revenge.

venimeux, *adj.* poisonous.

venin, *n.m.* poison.

venir, *vb.* come. **v. de,** have just. . . . **à v.,** forthcoming.

vent, *n.m.* wind.

vente, *n.f.* sale.

venteux, *adj.* windy.

ventilateur, *n.m.* fan.

ventiler, *vb.* ventilate.

ventre, *n.m.* belly.

venue, *n.f.* advent, arrival.

vêpres, *n.f.pl.* vespers.

ver, (-r), *n.m.* worm.

veracité, *n.f.* veracity.

véranda, *n.f.* porch.

verbe, *n.m.* verb.

verbeux, *adj.* wordy, verbose.

verdeur, *n.f.* greenness, sharpness; vigor.

verdict, (-kt), *n.m.* verdict.

verdir, *vb.* make or become green.

verdure, *n.f.* greenery.

verge, *n.f.* rod.

verger, *n.m.* orchard.

verglas, *n.m.* sleet.

vérification, *n.f.* check.

vérifier, *vb.* check, confirm.

véritable, *adj.* genuine, real.

verité, *n.f.* truth.

vermine, *n.f.* vermin.

vermouth, *n.m.* vermouth.

vernir, *vb.* varnish.

vernis, *n.m.* varnish.

vérole, *n.f.* **petite v.,** smallpox.

verre, *n.m.* glass.

verrou, *n.m.* bolt.

verrouiller, *vb.* bolt.

vers, 1. *n.m.* verse. **2.** *prep.* toward.

verse, *adj.* **tomber à v.,** pour.

verser, *vb.* pour; shed.

versifier, *vb.* versify.

version, *n.f.* version, translation.

vert, *adj.* green.

vertèbre, *n.f.* vertebra.

vertical, *adj.* upright, vertical.

vertige, *n.m.* dizziness.

vertigineux, *adj.* dizzy.

vertu, *n.f.* virtue.

vertueux, *adj.* virtuous.

verveux, *adj.* lively, animated.

vessie, *n.f.* bladder.

veste, *n.f.* jacket.

vestiaire, *n.m.* cloak-room.

vestibule, *n.m.* hall, lobby.

vestige, *n.m.* vestige, remains.

veston, *n.m.* jacket, coat.

vêtement, *n.m.* garment; *(pl.)* clothes.

vétéran, *n.m.* veteran.

vétérinaire, *n.m.f.* veterinary.

vêtir, *vb.* clothe.

véto, *n.m.* veto.

veuf, *n.m.* widower.

veuve, *n.f.* widow.

vexation, *n.f.* vexation.

vexer, *vb.* vex.

viaduc, *n.m.* viaduct.

viande, *n.f.* meat.

vibrant, *adj.* vibrant, vibrating.

vibration, *n.f.* vibration.

vibrer, *vb.* vibrate.

vicaire, *n.m.* vicar.

vice, *n.m.* vice.

vice-roi, *n.m.* viceroy.

vicieux, *adj.* depraved, wrong.

vicomte, *n.m.* viscount.

victime, *n.f.* victim.

victoire, *n.f.* victory.

victorieux, *adj.* victorious.

victuailles (věk tyĭ), *n.f.pl.* provisions.

vidange, *n.f.* emptying, cleaning.

vide, 1. *n.m.* emptiness, vacuum, blank, gap. **2.** *adj.* empty, void, vacant, blank.

videocassette, *n.f.* videocassette.

vidéodisque, *n.m.* videodisc.

vider, *vb.* empty, drain.

vie, *n.f.* life.

vieil, *adj.* old.

vieillard, *n.m.* old man.

vieille, 1. *n.f.* old woman. **2.** *adj.f.* old.

vieillesse, *n.f.* old age.

vieillir, *vb.* age.

Vienne, *n.f.* Vienna.

vierge, *n.f.* virgin.

Viêt-nam, Vietnam, *n.m.* Vietnam.

Vietnamien, *(m.),* **Vietnamienne** *(f)* *n.* Vietnamese (person).

vietnamien, *n.m. and adj.* Vietnamese.

vieux, *adj.m.* old.

vif, *m.,* **vive** *f.* *adj.* lively, quick, brisk, bright, vivacious.

vif-argent, *n.m.* quicksilver.

vigie, *n.f.* lookout man or station.

vigilance, *n.f.* vigilance.

vigilant, *adj.* watchful.

vigne, *n.f.* vine; vineyard.

vigneron, *n.m.* wine grower.

vignoble, *n.m.* vineyard.

vigoureux, *adj.* lusty, hardy, vigorous.

vigueur, *n.f.* vigor, force.

vil, (-l), *adj.* vile.

vilain, *adj.* ugly, mean, wicked.

village, (-l-), *n.m.* village.

ville, (-l), *n.f.* city, town.

villégiature, (-l-), *n.f.* country holiday.

vin, *n.m.* wine.

vinaigre, *n.m.* vinegar.

vindicatif, *adj.* vindictive.

vingt, (văɴ), *adj. and n.m.* twenty.

vingtaine, (văɴ-), *n.f.* score; about twenty.

vingtième (văɴ-), *adj. and n.m.f.* twentieth.

viol, *n.m.* rape, violation.

violateur, *n.m.* violator.

violation, *n.f.* violation.

violemment, *adj.* violently.

violence, *n.f.* violence.

violent, *adj.* violent.

violer, *vb.* violate.

violet, *adj.* purple, violet.

violette, *n.f.* violet.

violon, *n.m.* violin.

violoncelle, *n.m.* cello.

vipère, *n.f.* viper.

virement, *n.m.* transfer.

virgule, *n.f.* comma.

viril, (-l), *adj.* manly.

virilité, *n.f.* manhood.

virtuel, *adj.* virtual.

virtuose, *n.m.f.* virtuoso.

virus, (-s), *n.m.* virus.

vis, (-s), *n.f.* screw.

visa, *n.m.* visa.

visage, *n.m.* face.

vis-à-vis, *adv.* opposite, across from.

viser, *vb.* aim.

visibilité, *n.f.* visibility.

visible, *adj.* visible.

visière, *n.f.* visor; keenness.

vision, *n.f.* vision.

visionnaire, *adj. and n.m.f.* visionary.

visite, *n.f.* call, visit.

visiter, *vb.* visit.

visiteur, *n.m.* visitor.

visqueux, *adj.* viscous, sticky.

visser, *vb.* screw.

visuel, *adj.* visual.

vital, *adj.* vital.

vitalité, *n.f.* vitality.

vitamine, *n.f.* vitamin.

vite, *adv.* quick, fast.

vitesse, *n.f.* speed, rate; gear. **changer de v.,** shift gears.

viticole, *adj.* wine.

viticulteur, *n.m.* wine grower.

vitrail, *n.m.* (church) window.

vitre, *n.f.* pane.

vitrine, *n.f.* display case, shop window.

vitupération, *n.f.* vituperation.

vivace, *adj.* long-lived; perennial (of plant).

vivacité, *n.f.* vivacity.

vivant, *adj.* alive.

vivement, *adv.* quickly, smartly, vividly.

vivre, *vb.* live.

vocabulaire, *n.m.* vocabulary.

vocal, *adj.* vocal.

vocation, *n.f.* vocation.

vodka, *n.f.* vodka.

vœu, (vœ), *n.m.* vow.

vogue, *n.f.* vogue.

voguer, *vb.* sail.

voici, *vb.* here is, behold.

voie, *n.f.* track, road. **v. d'eau,** leak.

voilà, *vb.* there is; behold.

voile, *n.m.* veil; sail.

voiler, *vb.* veil, hide.

voilure, *n.f.* sails.

voir, *vb.* see. **faire v.,** show.

voirie, *n.m.* dump; highway maintenance.

voisin, 1. *n.m.* neighbor. **2.** *adj.* nearby, adjoining.

voisinage, *n.m.* neighborhood.

voisiner, *vb.* act like a neighbor.

voiture, *n.f.* car; carriage. **en v.!,** all aboard!

voix, *n.f.* voice.

vol, *n.m.* flight; theft, robbery; ripoff.

volage, *adj.* fickle.

volaille, *n.f.* fowl, poultry.

volant, *n.m.* steering wheel.

volatil, *adj.* volatile.

volcan, *n.m.* volcano.

volcanique, *adj.* volcanic.

volée, *n.f.* flight, covey; herd.

voler, *vb.* fly; steal, rob; rip off.

volet, *n.m.* shutter, blind.

voleur, *n.m.* thief, robber.

vol frété, *n.m.* charter flight.

volontaire, 1. *n.m.f.* volunteer. **2.** *adj.* voluntary, volunteer.

volonté, *n.f.* will.

volontiers, *adv.* gladly, willingly.

voltigement, *n.m.* flutter.

voltiger, *vb.* flutter; hover.

volubilité, *n.f.* volubility, glibness.

volume, *n.m.* volume.

volumineux, *adj.* bulky.

volupté, *n.f.* pleasure, voluptuousness.

vomir, *vb.* vomit.

vorace, *adj.* voracious.

votant, *n.m.* voter.

vote, *n.m.* vote.

voter, *vb.* vote.

votre, *sg.,* **vos** *pl. adj.* your.

vôtre, *pron.* **le v.,** yours.

vouer, *vb.* vow.

vouloir, *vb.* want, wish, will. **v. dire,** mean. **v. savoir,** wonder. **v. bien,** be willing. **en v. à,** bear a grudge against.

vous, *pron.* you, yourself.

voûte, *n.f.* vault.

voûter, *vb.* arch.

vouvoyer, *vb.* address politely as "vous."

voyage, *n.m.* journey, trip.

voyager, *vb.* travel.

voyageur, *n.m.* traveler, passenger.

voyageur de banlieue, *n.m.* commuter.

voyant, 1. *n.m.* clairvoyant. **2.** *adj.* gaudy, flashy.

voyelle, *n.f.* vowel.

vrai, *adj.* true, real.

vraisemblable, *adj.* probable, likely.

vraisemblance, *n.f.* probability.

vue, *n.f.* view, sight.

vue d'ensemble, *n.f.* overview.

vulcaniser, *vb.* vulcanize.

vulgaire, *adj.* vulgar, rude.

vulgariser, *vb.* popularize.

vulgarité, *n.f.* vulgarity.

vulnérable, *adj.* vulnerable.

W, X, Y, Z ❧

wagon, *n.m.* coach, car.
wagon-lits, *n.m.* sleeping car.
wagon-restaurant, *n.m.* diner, dining-car.
walkman, *n.m.* (trademark) Walkman.
Wallon, *n.m. and adj.* Walloon.
watt, *n.m.* watt.
week-end, *n.m.* weekend.
whisky, *n.m.* whiskey.
xénophobe (ks-), *n.m.f. and adj.* xenophobic (person).
xérès, (ks-), *n.m.* sherry.

xylophone, (ks-), *n.m.* xylophone.
y, *adv.* there, in it, to it.
yacht, *n.m.* yacht.
yaourt, *n.m.* yogurt.
yoga, *n.m.* yoga.
Yougoslave, *n.m.f.* Yugoslav (person).
yougoslave, *adj.* Yugoslav.
Yougoslavie, *n.f.* Yugoslavia.
yuppie, *n.m.f.* yuppie.
zèbre, *n.m.* zebra.
zèle, *n.m.* zeal.
zélé, *adj.* zealous.

zénith, *n.m.* zenith.
zéro, *n.m.* zero.
zeste, *n.m.* peel, zest.
zézayer, *vb.* lisp.
zibeline, *n.f.* sable.
zigzaguer, *vb.* zigzag.
zinc, *n.m.* zinc; (bar) counter.
zodiaque, *n.m.* zodiac.
zone, *n.f.* zone, district; slum.
zoologie, *n.f.* zoology.
zoologique, *adj.* zoological. jardin z., zoo.

A

a, *art.* un *m.,* une *f.*

aardvark, *n.* aardvark *m.*

aback, *adv.* déconcerté.

abacus, *n.* abaque *m.*

abandon, *vb.* abandonner.

abandon, *n.* abandon *m.*

abandoned, *adj.* abandonné.

abandonment, *n.* abandon *m.*

abase, *vb.* abaisser, avilir.

abasement, *n.* abaissement *m.,* avilissement *m.*

abash, *vb.* déconcerter.

abate, *vb.* diminuer.

abatement, *n.* diminution *f.*

abbess, *n.* abbesse *f.*

abbey, *n.* abbaye *f.*

abbot, *n.* abbé *m.*

abbreviate, *vb.* abréger.

abbreviation, *n.* abréviation *f.*

abdicate, *vb.* abdiquer.

abdication, *n.* abdication *f.*

abdomen, *n.* abdomen *m.*

abdominal, *adj.* abdominal.

abduct, *vb.* enlever.

abduction, *n.* enlèvement *m.*

abductor, *n.* ravisseur *m.*

aberrant, *adj.* aberrant, égaré.

aberration, *n.* égarement *m.*

abet, *vb.* aider, encourager, appuyer.

abetment, *n.* encouragement *m.,* appui *m.*

abettor, *n.* aide *m.,* complice *m.*

abeyance, *n.* suspension *f.*

abhor, *vb.* détester.

abhorrence, *n.* aversion extrême *f.,* horreur *f.*

abhorrent, *adj.* odieux, répugnant (à).

abide, *vb.* (tolerate) supporter; (remain) demeurer; **(a. by the law)** respecter la loi.

abiding, *adj.* constant, durable.

ability, *n.* talent *m.*

abject, *adj.* abject.

abjuration, *n.* abjuration *f.*

abjure, *vb.* abjurer, renoncer à.

abjurer, *n.* personne (*f.*) qui abjure.

ablative, *adj. and n.* ablatif *m.*

ablaze, *adj.* en feu, en flammes.

able, *adj.* capable; **(to be a.)** pouvoir.

able-bodied, *adj.* fort, robuste.

able-bodied seaman, *n.* marin (*m.*) de première classe.

ablution, *n.* ablution *f.*

ably, *adv.* capablement.

abnegate, *vb.* nier.

abnegation, *n.* abnégation *f.*

abnormal, *adj.* anormal.

abnormality, *n.* irrégularité *f.*

abnormally, *adv.* anormalement.

aboard, 1. *adv.* (*naut.*) à bord; **(all a.)** en voiture. **2.** *prep.* à bord de.

abode, *n.* demeure *f.*

abolish, *vb.* abolir.

abolishment, *n.* abolissement *m.*

abolition, *n.* abolition *f.*

abominable, *adj.* abominable.

abominate, *vb.* abominer.

abomination, *n.* abomination *f.*

aboriginal, *adj.* aborigène, primitif.

aborigines, *n.* aborigènes *m.pl.*

abort, *vb.* faire avorter.

abortion, *n.* avortement *m.*

abortive, *adj.* abortif, manqué.

abound, *vb.* abonder (en).

about, 1. *adv.* (approximately) à peu près; (around) autour; **(to be a. to)** être sur le point de. **2.** *prep.* (concerning) au sujet de; (near) auprès de; (around) autour de.

about-face, *n.* volte-face *f.*

above, 1. *adv.* au-dessus. **2.** *prep.* (higher than) au-dessus de; (more than) plus de.

aboveboard, 1. *adj.* ouvert, franc. **2.** *adv.* ouvertement, franchement.

abrasion, *n.* abrasion *f.*

abrasive, *adj.* abrasif.

abreast, *adv.* de front.

abridge, *vb.* abréger.

abridgment, *n.* abrégé *m.,* réduction *f.*

abroad, *adv.* à l'étranger.

abrogate, *vb.* abroger.

abrogation, *n.* abrogation *f.*

abrupt, *adj.* brusque; (steep) escarpé.

abruptly, *adv.* brusquement, subitement.

abruptness, *n.* brusquerie *f.,* précipitation *f.*

abscess, *n.* abcès *m.*

abscond, *vb.* disparaître, se dérober.

absence, *n.* absence *f.*

absent, *adj.* absent.

absentee, *n.* absent *m.,* manquant *m.*

absinthe, *n.* absinthe *f.*

absolute, *adj.* absolu.

absolutely, *adv.* absolument.

absoluteness, *n.* pouvoir absolu *m.;* arbitraire *m.*

absolution, *n.* absolution *f.*

absolutism, *n.* absolutisme *m.*

absolve, *vb.* absoudre.

absorb, *vb.* absorber.

absorbed, *adj.* absorbé, préoccupé.

absorbent, *n. and adj.* absorbant *m.*

absorbing, *adj.* absorbant, préoccupant.

absorption, *n.* absorption *f.*

abstain from, *vb.* s'abstenir de.

abstemious, *adj.* abstème.

abstinence, *n.* abstinence *f.*

abstract, 1. *n.* (book) extrait *m.* **2.** *adj.* abstrait.

abstracted, *adj.* détaché, pensif.

abstraction, *n.* abstraction *f.*

abstruse, *adj.* caché, abstrus.

absurd, *adj.* absurde.
absurdity, *n.* absurdité *f.*
absurdly, *adv.* absurdement.
abundance, *n.* abondance *f.*
abundant, *adj.* abondant.
abundantly, *adv.* abondamment.
abuse, 1. *n.* (misuse) abus *m.;* (insult) injures *f.pl.* **2.** *vb.* abuser de, injurier.
abusive, *adj.* (insulting) injurieux.
abusively, *adv.* abusivement, injurieusement.
abut, *vb.* s'embrancher (sur), aboutir (à).
abutment, *n.* contrefort *m.;* (of a bridge) culée *f.*
abysmal, *adj.* exécrable.
abyss, *n.* abîme *m.*
academic, *adj.* académique.
academic freedom, *n.* liberté (*f.*) de l'enseignement.
academy, *n.* académie *f.*
acanthus, *n.* acanthe *f.*
accede, *vb.* consentir.
accelerate, *vb.* accélérer.
acceleration, *n.* accélération *f.*
accelerator, *n.* accélérateur *m.*
accent, *n.* accent *m.*
accentuate, *vb.* accentuer.
accept, *vb.* accepter.
acceptability, *n.* acceptabilité *f.*
acceptable, *adj.* acceptable.
acceptably, *adv.* agréablement.
acceptance, *n.* acceptation *f.*
access, *n.* accès *m.*
accessible, *adj.* accessible.
accession, *n.* accession *f.*
accessory, *n. and adj.* accessoire *m.*
accident, *n.* accident *m.*
accidental, *adj.* accidentel.
accidentally, *adv.* accidentellement, par hasard.
acclaim, *vb.* acclamer.
acclamation, *n.* acclamation *f.*
acclimate, *vb.* acclimater.
acclivity, *n.* montée *f.,* rampe *f.*
accolade, *n.* accolade *f.*
accommodate, *vb.* (lodge) loger; (oblige) obliger.

accommodating, *adj.* accommodant, obligeant.
accommodation, *n.* (lodging) logement *m.*
accompaniment, *n.* accompagnement *m.*
accompanist, *n.* accompagnateur *m.,* accompagnatrice *f.*
accompany, *vb.* accompagner.
accomplice, *n.* complice *m.f.*
accomplish, *vb.* accomplir.
accomplished, *adj.* accompli, achevé.
accord, *n.* accord *m.*
accordance, *n.* conformité *f.*
accordingly, *adv.* (correspondingly) à l'avenant; (therefore) donc.
according to, *prep.* selon.
accordion, *n.* accordéon *m.*
accost, *vb.* aborder.
account, *n.* (comm.) compte *m.;* (narrative) récit *m.*
accountable for, *adj.* responsable de.
accountant, *n.* comptable *m.*
account for, *vb.* rendre compte de.
accounting, *n.* comptabilité *f.*
accouter, *vb.* habiller, équiper.
accouterments, *n.* équipements *m.pl.,* accoutrements *m.pl.*
accredit, *vb.* accréditer.
accretion, *n.* accroissement *m.*
accrual, *n.* accroissement *m.*
accrue, *vb.* provenir.
accrued interest, *n.* intérêt (*m.*) cumulé.
accumulate, *vb.* entasser.
accumulation, *n.* entassement *m.*
accumulative, *adj.* (thing) qui s'accumule, (person) qui accumule.
accumulator, *n.* accumulateur *m.,* accumulatrice *f.*
accuracy, *n.* précision *f.*
accurate, *adj.* précis.
accursed, *adj.* maudit, exécrable.
accusation, *n.* accusation *f.*

accusative, *n. and adj.* accusatif *m.*
accuse, *vb.* accuser.
accused, *n. and adj.* accusé *m.,* accusée *f.*
accuser, *n.* accusateur *m.,* accusatrice *f.*
accustom, *vb.* accoutumer.
accustomed, *adj.* accoutumé, habituel.
ace, *n.* as *m.*
acerbity, *n.* acerbité *f.,* âpreté *f.*
acetate, *n.* acétate *m.*
acetic acid, *n.* acide (*m.*) acétique.
acetylene, *n.* acétylène *m.*
ache, 1. *n.* douleur *f.* **2.** *vb.* faire mal à.
achieve, *vb.* accomplir.
achievement, *n.* accomplissement *m.*
acid, *adj. and n.* acide *m.*
acidify, *vb.* acidifier.
acidity, *n.* acidité *f.*
acidosis, *n.* acidose *f.*
acid test, *n.* épreuve (*f.*) concluante.
acidulous, *adj.* acidulé.
acknowledge, *vb.* reconnaître; (**a. receipt of**) accuser réception de.
acme, *n.* comble *m.,* apogée *m.*
acne, *n.* acné *f.*
acolyte, *n.* acolyte *m.*
acorn, *n.* gland *m.*
acoustics, *n.* acoustique *f.*
acquaint, *vb.* informer (de); (**be a.ed with**) connaître.
acquaintance, *n.* connaissance *f.*
acquainted, *adj.* connu, familier (avec).
acquiesce in, *vb.* acquiescer à.
acquiescence, *n.* acquiescement *m.*
acquire, *vb.* acquérir.
acquirement, *n.* acquis *m.,* acquisition *f.*
acquisition, *n.* acquisition *f.*
acquisitive, *adj.* porté à acquérir.
acquit, *vb.* acquitter.
acquittal, *n.* acquittement *m.*
acre, *n.* arpent *m.,* acre *f.*
acreage, *n.* superficie *f.*

acrid, *adj.* âcre.

acrimonious, *adj.* acrimonieux.

acrimony, *n.* acrimonie *f.*, aigreur *f.*

acrobat, *n.* acrobate *m.f.*

across, 1. *prep.* à travers; (on the other side of) de l'autre côté de. 2. *adv.* en travers.

acrostic, *n.* acrostiche *m.*

acrylic, *n.* acrylique *m.*

act, 1. *n.* acte *m.* 2. *vb.* (do) agir; (play) jouer; (behave) se conduire.

acting, 1. *n.* (theater) jeu *m.*; feinte *f.* 2. *adj.* (taking the place of) suppléant; *(comm.)* gérant.

actinism, *n.* actinisme *m.*

actinium, *n.* actinium *m.*

action, *n.* action *f.*

activate, *vb.* activer.

activation, *n.* activation *f.*

activator, *n.* activateur *m.*

active, *adj.* actif.

activity, *n.* activité *f.*

actor, *n.* acteur *m.*

actress, *n.* actrice *f.*

actual, *adj.* réel.

actuality, *n.* réalité *f.*, actualité *f.*

actually, *adv.* réellement, véritablement, en effet.

actuary, *n.* actuaire *m.*

actuate, *vb.* mettre en action, animer.

acumen, *n.* finesse *f.*, pénétration *f.*

acupuncture, *n.* acuponcture *f.*

acute, *adj.* *(geom.)* aigu *m.*, aiguë *f.*; (mind) fin.

acutely, *adv.* vivement, d'une manière poignante.

acuteness, *n.* finesse *f.*, vivacité *f.*

ad, *n.* annonce *f.*

adage, *n.* adage *m.*, proverbe *m.*

adamant, *adj.* indomptable.

Adam's apple, *n.* pomme *(f.)* d'Adam.

adapt, *vb.* adapter.

adaptability, *n.* faculté *(f.)* d'adaptation.

adaptable, *adj.* adaptable.

adaptation, *n.* adaptation *f.*

adapter, *n.* qui adapte.

adaptive, *adj.* adaptable.

add, *vb.* (join) ajouter; *(arith.)* additionner.

adder, *n.* vipère *f.*

addict, *n.* toxicomane, *m.f.*

addicted, *adj.* adonné (à).

addition, *n.* addition *f.*

additional, *adj.* additionel.

additive, *n.* additif *m.*

addle, 1. *vb.* corrompre, rendre couvi (of eggs). 2. *adj.* couvi, pourri.

address, 1. *n.* (on letters, etc.) adresse *f.*; (speech) discours *m.* 2. *vb.* (a letter) adresser; (a person) adresser la parole à.

addressee, *n.* destinataire *m.f.*

adduce, *vb.* alléguer, avancer.

adenoid, *adj. and n.* adénoïde *f.*

adeptly, *adv.* habilement, adeptement.

adeptness, *n.* habileté *f.*

adequacy, *n.* suffisance *f.*

adequate, *adj.* suffisant.

adequately, *adv.* suffisamment, convenablement.

adhere, *vb.* adhérer.

adherence, *n.* adhérence *f.*, attachement *m.*

adherent, *n.* adhérent *m.*

adhesion, *n.* adhésion *f.*

adhesive, *adj.* adhésif.

adhesiveness, *n.* propriété d'adhérer *f.*

ad hoc, *adj.* improvisé.

adieu, *n. and adv.* adieu *m.*

adjacent, *adj.* adjacent.

adjective, *n.* adjectif *m.*

adjoin, *vb.* adjoindre, être contigu (à).

adjourn, *vb.* ajourner, *tr.*; s'ajourner, *intr.*

adjournment, *n.* ajournement *m.*

adjudicate, *vb.* juger.

adjunct, *n. and adj.* adjoint *m.*, accessoire *m.*

adjust, *vb.* ajuster, arranger, régler.

adjuster, *n.* ajusteur *m.*

adjustment, *n.* ajustement *m.*, accommodement *m.*

adjutant, *n.* capitaine (*m.*) adjudant major.

ad-lib, *vb.* improviser.

administer, *vb.* administrer.

administration, *n.* administration *f.*

administrative, *adj.* administratif.

administrator, *n.* administrateur *m.*

admirable, *adj.* admirable.

admirably, *adv.* admirablement.

admiral, *n.* amiral *m.*

admiralty, *n.* amirauté *f.*

admiration, *n.* admiration *f.*

admire, *vb.* admirer.

admirer, *n.* admirateur *m.*

admiringly, *adv.* avec admiration.

admissible, *adj.* admissible.

admission, *n.* (entrance) entrée *f.*; (confession) aveu *m.*

admit, *vb.* (let in) laisser entrer; (confess) avouer.

admittance, *n.* entrée *f.*

admittedly, *adv.* de l'aveu de tout le monde.

admixture, *n.* mélange *m.*

admonish, *vb.* réprimander.

admonition, *n.* admonition *f.*, avertissement *m.*

ad nauseam, *adv.* à n'en plus finir.

ado, *n.* fracas *m.*

adolescence, *n.* adolescence *f.*

adolescent, *adj. and n.* adolescent *m.f.*

adopt, *vb.* adopter.

adoption, *n.* adoption *f.*

adorable, *adj.* adorable.

adoration, *n.* adoration *f.*

adore, *vb.* adorer.

adorn, *vb.* orner.

adornment, *n.* ornement *m.*

adrenal glands, *n.pl.* capsules *(f.pl.)* surrénales.

adrenalin, *n.* adrénaline *f.*

Adriatic (Sea), *n.* Adriatique *f.*

adrift, *adv.* *(naut.)* à la dérive.

adroit, *adj.* adroit.

adulate, *vb.* aduler.

adulation, *n.* adulation *f.*

adult, *adj. and n.* adulte *m.f.*

adulterant, *n.* adultérant *m.*

adulterate, *vb.* adultérer; (of wines, milk, etc.) frelater.

adulterer, *n.* adultère *m.*

adulteress, *n.* femme adultère *f.*

adultery, *n.* adultère *m.*

advance, 1. *n.* (motion forward) avancement *m.;* (progress) progrès *m.;* (pay) avances *f.pl.;* **(in a.)** d'avance. **2.** *vb.* avancer.

advanced, *adj.* avancé.

advancement, *n.* avancement *m.,* progrès *m.*

advantage, *n.* avantage *m.*

advantageous, *adj.* avantageux.

advantageously, *adv.* avantageusement.

advent, *n.* venue *f.; (eccles.)* Avent *m.*

adventitious, *adj.* adventice, fortuit.

adventure, *n.* aventure *f.*

adventurer, *n.* aventurier *m.*

adventurous, *adj.* aventureux.

adventurously, *adv.* aventureusement.

adverb, *n.* adverbe *m.*

adverbial, *adj.* adverbial.

adversary, *n.* adversaire *m.*

adverse, *adj.* adverse.

adversely, *adv.* défavorablement, d'une manière hostile.

adversity, *n.* adversité *f.*

advert, *vb.* faire allusion (à).

advertise, *vb.* annoncer; **(a. a product)** faire de la réclame pour un produit.

advertisement, *n.* publicité *f.,* réclame *f.;* (in a paper) annonce *f.;* (on a wall) affiche *f.*

advertiser, *n.* annonceur *m.*

advertising, *n.* publicité *f.,* annonce (newspaper) *f.*

advice, *n.* conseil *m.; (comm.)* avis *m.*

advisability, *n.* convenance *f.,* utilité *f.*

advisable, *adj.* recommandable.

advisably, *adv.* convenablement.

advise, *vb.* conseiller.

advisedly, *adv.* de propos délibéré.

advisement, *n.* délibération.

advocacy, *n.* défense *f.,* plaidoyer *m.*

advocate, 1. *n.* (law) avocat *m.;* (supporter) défenseur *m.* **2.** *vb.* appuyer.

aegis, *n.* égide *f.*

aerate, *vb.* aérer.

aeration, *n.* aération *f.*

aerial, *adj.* aérien.

aerially, *adv.* d'une manière aérienne.

aerie, *n.* aire *f.*

aerobics, *n.* aérobic *m.*

aerodynamic, *adj.* aérodynamique.

aerogram, *n.* aérogramme *m.*

aeronautics, *n.* aéronautique *f.*

aerosol, *n.* atomiseur *m.*

aerospace, *adj.* aérospatial.

aesthetic, *adj.* esthétique.

afar, *adv.* loin, de loin.

affability, *n.* affabilité *f.*

affable, *adj.* affable.

affably, *adv.* affablement.

affair, *n.* affaire *f.*

affect, *vb.* (move) toucher; (concern) intéresser; (pretend) affecter.

affectation, *n.* affectation *f.*

affected, *adj.* maniéré.

affecting, *adj.* touchant, émouvant.

affection, *n.* affection *f.*

affectionate, *adj.* affectueux.

affectionately, *adv.* affectueusement.

afferent, *adj.* afférent.

affiance, *vb.* fiancer.

affidavit, *n.* attestation (sous serment) *f.*

affiliate, *vb.* affilier.

affiliation, *n.* affiliation *f.*

affinity, *n.* affinité *f.*

affirm, *vb.* affirmer.

affirmation, *n.* affirmation *f.*

affirmative, *adj.* affirmatif.

affirmatively, *adv.* affirmativement.

affix, *vb.* apposer.

afflict, *vb.* affliger (de).

affliction, *n.* affliction *f.*

affluence, *n.* affluence *f.,* opulence *f.*

affluent, *adj.* affluent, opulent.

afford, *vb.* (have the means to) avoir les moyens de.

affray, *n.* bagarre *f.,* tumulte *m.*

affront, 1. *n.* affront *m.* **2.** *vb.* insulter.

afield, *adv.* aux champs, en campagne; **(go far a.)** aller très loin.

afire, *adv.* en feu.

afloat, *adv.* à flot, en train.

aforementioned, *adj.* mentionné plus haut, susdit.

aforesaid, *adj.* susdit, ledit.

afraid, *pred. adj.* (be afraid) avoir peur.

afresh, *adv.* de nouveau.

Africa, *n.* Afrique *f.*

African, 1. *n.* Africain *m.* **2.** *adj.* africain.

aft, *adv.* à l'arrière.

after, 1. *adv. and prep.* après. **2.** *conj.* après que.

aftereffect, *n.* effet *m.*

aftermath, *n.* suites *f. pl.*

afternoon, *n.* après-midi *m. or f.*

aftershave, *n.* lotion après-rasage *f.*

afterthought, *n.* réflexion (*f.*) tardive.

afterward, *adv.* ensuite.

again, *adv.* de nouveau, encore; **(a. and a.)** maintes et maintes fois.

against, *prep.* contre.

agape, *adv.* bouche bée.

agate, *n.* agate *f.*

age, 1. *n.* âge *m.* **2.** *vb.* vieillir.

aged, *adj.* vieux, âgé.

ageism, *n.* attitude (*f.*) discriminative basée sur l'âge.

ageless, *adj.* qui ne vieillit jamais.

agency, *n.* (*comm.*) agence *f.*

agenda, *n.* ordre du jour *m.;* agenda *m.*

agent, *n.* agent *m.*

agglutinate, *vb.* agglutiner.

agglutination, *n.* agglutination *f.*

aggrandize, *vb.* agrandir.

aggrandizement, *n.* agrandissement *m.*

aggravate, *vb.* (intensify) aggraver; (exasperate) exaspérer.

aggravation, *n.* aggravation *f.,* agacement *m.*

aggregate, *n.* masse *f.*

aggregation, *n.* agrégation *f.,* assemblage *m.*

aggression, *n.* agression *f.*

aggressive, *adj.* agressif.

aggressively, *adv.* agressivement.

aggressiveness, *n.* caractère (*m.*) agressif.

aggressor, *n.* agresseur *m.*

aggrieved, *adj.* affligé.

aghast, *adj.* consterné.

agile, *adj.* agile.

agility, *n.* agilité *f.*

agitate, *vb.* agiter.

agitation, *n.* agitation *f.*

agitator, *n.* agitateur *m.*

agnostic, *n. and adj.* agnostique *m.*

ago, *adv.* il y a (*always precedes*).

agonized, *adj.* torturé, déchirant.

agony, *n.* (anguish) angoisse *f.;* (death agony) agonie *f.*

agrarian, *adj.* agraire, agrarien.

agree, *vb.* être d'accord.

agreeable, *adj.* agréable.

agreeably, *adv.* agréablement.

agreement, *n.* accord *m.*

agriculture, *n.* agriculture *f.*

ahead, 1. *adv. and interj.* en avant. **2.** *prep.* (a. of) en avant de.

aid, 1. *n.* aide *f.;* (first a.) premiers secours; (first-a.station) poste de secours. **2.** *vb.* aider.

aide, *n.* aide *m.,* assistant *m.*

AIDS, *n.* SIDA *m.*

ail, *vb. intr.* être souffrant.

ailing, *adj.* malade.

ailment, *n.* indisposition *f.*

aim, 1. *n.* (fig.) but *m.* **2.** *vb.* viser.

aimless, *adj.* sans but.

aimlessly, *adv.* sans but, à la dérive.

air, 1. *n.* air *m.;* (a. force) aviation *f.;* (by a. mail) par avion; **(in the open a.)** en plein air. **2.** *vb.* aérer.

airbag, *n.* (in automobiles) sac à air *m.*

air base, *n.* champ (*m.*) d'aviation.

airborne, *adj.* par voie de l'air.

air-condition, *vb.* climatiser.

air conditioner, *n.* climatiseur *m.*

air conditioning, *n.* climatisation *f.*

aircraft, *n.* avions *m.pl.;* (a. carrier) porte-avions *m.*

air gun, *n.* fusil à vent.

airing, *n.* aérage *m.,* tour *m.*

airline, *n.* ligne (*f.*) aérienne.

airliner, *n.* avion *m.*

air mail, *n.* poste (*f.*) aérienne.

airplane, *n.* avion *m.*

air pollution, *n.* pollution (*f.*) de l'air.

airport, *n.* aéroport *m.*

air pressure, *n.* pression (*f.*) d'air.

air raid, *n.* raid (*m.*) aérien.

airsick, *adj.* (to be a.) avoir le mal d'air.

airtight, *adj.* imperméable à l'air, étanche.

air-traffic controller, *n.* aiguilleur (*m.*) du ciel.

airy, *adj.* (well-aired) aéré; (light) léger.

aisle, *n.* (passageway) passage *m.; (arch.)* bas côté *m.*

ajar, *adv.* entr'ouvert.

akin, *adj.* allié (à), parent (de).

alacrity, *n.* empressement *m.*

alarm, *n.* alarme *f.*

alarmist, *n.* alarmiste *m.*

alas, *interj.* hélas.

albeit, *conj.* bien que.

albino, *n.* albinos *m.*

album, *n.* album *m.*

alcohol, *n.* alcool *m.*

alcoholic, *adj.* alcoolique, alcoolisé.

alcove, *n.* (recess) niche *f.;* (sleeping alcove) alcôve *f.*

ale, *n.* bière *f.*

alert, *adj.* alerte.

alfalfa, *n.* luzerne *f.*

algebra, *n.* algèbre *f.*

Algeria, *n.* Algérie *f.*

algorithm, *n.* algorithme *m.*

alias, 1. *n.* nom d'emprunt *m.* **2.** *adv.* autrement nommé, dit.

alibi, *n.* alibi *m.*

alien, *adj.* étranger.

alienate, *vb.* aliéner.

alight, *vb.* (descend) descendre; (stop after descent) s'abattre.

align, *vb.* aligner.

alike, 1. *adj.* semblable; (be a.) se ressembler. **2.** *adv.* également.

alimentary canal, *n.* canal (*m.*) alimentaire.

alimony, *n.* pension (*f.*) alimentaire.

alive, *adj.* vivant.

alkali, *n.* alcali *m.*

alkaline, *adj.* alcalin.

all, 1. *adj.* tout *m.sg.,* toute *f.sg.,* tous *m.pl.,* toutes *f.pl.* **2.** *adv. and pron.* (everything) tout; (above a.) surtout; (a. at once) tout d'un coup; (a. the same) tout de même; (that's a.) c'est tout; (not at a.) pas du tout; (everybody) tous; (a. of you) vous tous.

allay, *vb.* apaiser.

allegation, *n.* allégation *f.*

allege, *vb.* alléguer.

allegiance, *n.* fidélité *f.*

allegory, *n.* allégorie *f.*

allergy, *n.* allergie *f.*

alleviate, *vb.* soulager.

alley, *n.* (in town) ruelle *f.;* (blind a.) cul-de-sac *m.*

alliance, *n.* alliance *f.*

allied, *adj.* allié.

alligator, *n.* alligator *m.*

all-night, *adj.* qui dure toute la nuit.

allocate, *vb.* assigner.

allot, *vb.* (grant) accorder; (distribute) répartir.

allotment, *n.* partage *m.,* lot *m.*

all-out, 1. *adj.* total. **2.** *adv.* à fond.

allow, *vb.* (permit) permettre; (admit) admettre; (grant) accorder; (a. for) tenir compte de.

allowance, *n.* (money granted) allocation *f.;* (food) ration *f.;* (tolerance) tolérance *f.;* (pension) rente *f.;* **(weekly a.)** semaine *f.*

alloy, *n.* alliage *m.*

all right, *adv.* très bien.

allude to, *vb.* faire allusion à.

allure, *vb.* séduire.

allusion, *n.* allusion *f.*

ally, 1. *n.* allié *m.* **2.** *vb.* allier.

almanac, *n.* almanach *m.*

almighty, *adj.* tout-puissant.

almond, *n.* amande *f.*

almost, *adv.* presque.

alms, *n.* aumône *f.*

aloft, *adv.* en haut.

alone, *adj.* seul; **(let a.)** laisser tranquille.

along, 1. *prep.* le long de. **2.** *adv.* **(come a.!)** venez donc!

alongside, *prep.* le long de.

aloof, 1. *adv.* à l'écart. **2.** *adj.* réservé.

aloud, *adv.* à haute voix.

alpaca, *n.* alpaga (fabric) *m.;* alpaca (animal) *m.*

alphabet, *n.* alphabet *m.*

alphabetical, *adj.* alphabétique.

alphabetize, *vb.* alphabétiser.

Alps, *n.pl.* Alpes *f.pl.*

already, *adv.* déjà.

also, *adv.* aussi.

altar, *n.* autel *m.*

alter, *vb.* changer.

alteration, *n.* modification *f.*

altercation, *n.* altercation *f.,* dispute *f.*

alternate, 1. *n.* remplaçant *m.* **2.** *adj.* alternatif. **3.** *vb.* alterner.

alternative, *n.* alternative *f.*

alternator, *n.* alternateur *m.*

although, *conj.* bien que.

altitude, *n.* altitude *f.*

altogether, *adv.* tout à fait.

altruism, *n.* altruisme *m.*

alum, *n.* alun *m.*

aluminum, *n.* aluminium *m.*

Alzheimer's (disease), *n.* maladie (*f.*) d'Alzheimer.

always, *adv.* toujours.

amalgam, *n.* amalgame *n.*

amalgamate, *vb.* amalgamer; (computer) fusionner.

amass, *vb.* amasser.

amateur, *n.* amateur *m.*

amaze, *vb.* étonner.

amazement, *n.* stupeur *f.*

amazing, *adj.* étonnant.

ambassador, *n.* ambassadeur *m.,* ambassadrice *f.*

amber, *n.* ambre *m.*

ambidextrous, *adj.* ambidextre.

ambiguity, *n.* ambiguïté *f.*

ambiguous, *adj.* ambigu *m.,* ambiguë *f.*

ambition, *n.* ambition *f.*

ambitious, *adj.* ambitieux.

ambivalent, *adj.* ambigu, ambivalent.

amble, *vb.* errer.

ambulance, *n.* ambulance *f.*

ambulatory, *adj.* ambulatoire.

ambush, *n.* embuscade *f.*

ameliorate, *vb.* améliorer.

amenable, *adj.* responsable, soumis (à), sujet (à).

amend, *vb.* amender.

amendment, *n.* amendement *m.*

amenity, *n.* aménité *f.,* agrément *m.*

America, *n.* Amérique *f.;* **(North A.)** A. du Nord; **(South A.)** A. du Sud.

American, 1. *n.* Américain *m.* **2.** *adj.* américain.

amethyst, *n.* améthyste *f.*

amiable, *adj.* aimable.

amicable, *adj.* amical.

amid, *prep.* au milieu de.

amidships, *adv.* par le travers.

amiss, *adv.* de travers.

amity, *n.* amitié *f.*

ammonia, *n.* ammoniaque *f.*

ammunition, *n.* munitions (*f.pl.*) de guerre.

amnesia, *n.* amnésie *f.*

amnesty, *n.* amnistie *f.*

amniocentesis, *n.* amniocentèse *f.*

amoeba, *n.* amibe *f.*

among, *prep.* parmi, entre.

amoral, *adj.* amoral.

amorous, *adj.* amoureux.

amorphous, *adj.* amorphe.

amortize, *vb.* amortir.

amount, 1. *n.* (sum) somme *f.;* (quantity) quantité *f.* **2.** *vb.* **(a. to)** (sum) se monter à; (summary) se réduire à.

amp, *n.* (colloquial) amp(ère) *m.*

ampere, *n.* ampère *m.*

amphibian, *n.* amphibie *m.*

amphibious, *adj.* amphibie.

amphitheater, *n.* amphithéâtre *m.*

ample, *adj.* ample.

amplify, *vb.* amplifier.

amplifier, *n.* amplifacateur *m.*

amputate, *vb.* amputer.

amputee, *n.* amputé *m.*

amuse, *vb.* amuser.

amusement, *n.* amusement *m.*

an, *art.* un *m.,* une *f.*

anachronism, *n.* anachronisme *m.*

analog, *adj.* analogique.

analogous, *adj.* analogue.

analogy, *n.* analogie *f.*

analysis, *n.* analyse *f.*

analyst, *n.* analyste *m.f.*

analytic, *adj.* analytique.

analyze, *vb.* analyser.

anarchy, *n.* anarchie *f.*

anathema, *n.* anathème *m.*

anatomy, *n.* anatomie *f.*

ancestor, *n.* ancêtre *m.*

ancestral, *adj.* d'ancêtres, héréditaire.

ancestry, *n.* aïeux, *m.pl.*

anchor, 1. *vb.* ancrer. **2.** *n.* ancre *f.*

anchorperson, *n.* présentateur *m.,* présentatrice *f.*

anchorage, *n.* mouillage *m.,* ancrage *m.*

anchovy, *n.* anchois *m.*

ancient, *adj.* ancien *m.,* ancienne *f.*

ancillary, *adj.* auxiliaire.

and, *conj.* et.

anecdote, *n.* anecdote *f.*

anemia, *n.* anémie *f.*

anesthetic, *adj. and n.* anesthésique *m.*

anesthetist, *n.* anesthésiste *m.f.*

anew, *adv.* de nouveau.

angel, *n.* ange *m.*

anger, *n.* colère *f.*

angle, 1. *n.* angle *m.;* (at an a.) en biais. 2. *vb.* (fish) pêcher à la ligne.

Anglican, *adj. and n.* anglican.

angry, *adj.* fâché; (to get a.) se fâcher.

anguish, *n.* angoisse *f.*

angular, *adj.* anguleux.

aniline, *n.* aniline *f.*

animal, *n. and adj.* animal *m.*

animate, *vb.* animer.

animated, *adj.* animé.

animated cartoon, *n.* dessin animé *m.*

animation, *n.* animation *f.*

animosity, *n.* animosité *f.*

anise, *n.* anis *m.*

ankle, *n.* cheville *f.*

annals, *n.pl.* annales *f.pl.*

annex, *n.* (to a building) dépendance *f.*

annexation, *n.* annexion *f.*

annihilate, *vb.* anéantir.

anniversary, *n.* anniversaire *m.*

annotate, *vb.* annoter.

annotation, *n.* annotation *f.*

announce, *vb.* annoncer.

announcement, *n.* annonce *f.*

announcer, *n.* speaker *m.*

annoy, *vb.* (vex) contrarier; (bore) ennuyer.

annoyance, *n.* contrariété *f.*

annual, *adj.* annuel.

annuity, *n.* annuité *f.*, rente annuelle *f.*

annul, *vb.* annuler.

anode, *n.* anode *f.*

anoint, *vb.* oindre.

anomalous, *adj.* anomal, irrégulier.

anonymous, *adj.* anonyme.

another, *adj. and pron.* un autre *m.*, une autre *f.;* (one a.) l'un l'autre.

answer, 1. *vb.* répondre. 2. *n.* réponse *f.*

answerable, *adj.* responsable (de), susceptible de réponse.

ant, *n.* fourmi *f.*

antacid, *adj.* antiacide.

antagonism, *n.* antagonisme *m.*

antagonist, *n.* antagoniste *m.*

antagonistic, *adj.* en opposition (à), hostile (à), opposé (à).

antagonize, *vb.* s'opposer à.

antarctic, *adj.* antarctique.

antecedent, *adj. and n.* antécédent *m.*

antedate, *vb.* antidater.

antelope, *n.* antilope *f.*

antenna, *n.* antenne *f.*

anterior, *adj.* antérieur.

anteroom, *n.* antichambre *m. or f.*

anthem, *n.* (national) hymne national *m.*

anthology, *n.* anthologie *f.*

anthracite, *n.* anthracite *m.*

anthrax, *n.* anthrax *m.*

anthropology, *n.* anthropologie *f.*

antiaircraft, *adj.* contreavion, antiaérien.

antibiotic, *n.* antibiotique *m.*

antibody, *n.* anticorps *m.*

antic, *n.* bouffonerie *f.*

anticipate, *vb.* (advance) anticiper; (expect) s'attendre à; (foresee) prévoir.

anticipation, *n.* anticipation *f.*

anticlerical, *adj.* anticlérical.

anticlimax, *n.* anticlimax *m.*

antidote, *n.* antidote *m.*

antifreeze, *n.* antigel *m.*

antihistamine, *n.* antihistaminique *m.*

antimony, *n.* antimoine *m.*

antinuclear, *adj.* antinucléaire.

antipathy, *n.* antipathie *f.*

antiquated, *adj.* desuet, vieilli.

antique, *n.* antique *m.;* (a. dealer) antiquaire *m.*

antiquity, *n.* antiquité *f.*

anti-Semite, *n.* antisémite *m.*

anti-Semitic, *adj.* antisémite.

antiseptic, *adj. and n.* antiseptique *m.*

antisocial, *adj.* antisocial.

antithesis, *n.* antithèse *f.*

antitoxin, *n.* antitoxine *f.*

antler, *n.* andouiller *m.*

anus, *n.* anus *m.*

anvil, *n.* enclume *f.*

anxiety, *n.* anxiété *f.*

anxious, *adj.* inquiet *m.*, inquiète *f.*

any, 1. *adj.* (in questions, for "some") du *m.sg.*, de la *f.sg.*, des *pl.;* (not ... a.) ne ... pas de; (no matter which) n'importe quel; (every) tout. 2. *pron.* (a. of it or them, with verb) en.

anybody, *pron.* (somebody) quelqu'un; (somebody, implying negation) personne; (not ... a.) ne ... personne; (no matter who) n'importe qui.

anyhow, *adv.* en tout cas; d'une manière quelconque.

anyone, *pron. see* anybody.

anything, *pron.* (something) quelque chose; (something, implying negation) rien; (not ... a.) ne ... rien; (no matter what) n'importe quoi.

anyway, *adv. see* anyhow.

anywhere, *adv.* n'importe où.

apart, 1. *adv.* à part. 2. *prep.* (a. from) en dehors de.

apartheid, *n.* apartheid *m.*

apartment, *n.* appartement *m.*

apathetic, *adj.* apathique.

apathy, *n.* apathie *f.*

ape, 1. *n.* singe *m.* 2. *vb.* singer.

aperture, *n.* ouverture *f.*

apex, *n.* sommet *m.*

aphorism, *n.* aphorisme *m.*

aphrodisiac, *n. and adj.* aphrodisiaque.

apiary, *n.* rucher *m.*

apiece, *adv.* chacun.

apocalypse, *n.* apocalypse *f.*

apogee, *n.* apogée *m.*

apologetic, *adj.* use verb s'excuser.

apologist, *n.* apologiste *m.*

apologize for, *vb.* s'excuser de.

apology, *n.* excuses *f.pl.*

apoplectic, *adj.* apoplectique.

apoplexy, *n.* apoplexie *f.*

apostate, *n.* apostat *m.*

apostle, *n.* apôtre *m.*

apostolic, *adj.* apostolique.

apostrophe, *n.* apostrophe *f.*

appall, *vb.* épouvanter.

apparatus, *n.* appareil *m.*

apparel, *n.* habillement *m.*

apparent, *adj.* apparent.

apparition, *n.* apparition *f.*

appeal, 1. *n.* appel *m.* **2.** *vb.* **(a. to)** en appeler à.

appear, *vb.* (become visible) apparaître; (seem) sembler.

appearance, *n.* (apparition) apparition *f.;* (semblance) apparence *f.;* (aspect) aspect *m.*

appease, *vb.* apaiser.

appeaser, *n.* personne qui apaise.

appellant, *n.* appelant *m.*

appellate, *adj.* d'appel.

append, *vb.* attacher; apposer, ajouter.

appendage, *n.* accessoire *m.,* apanage *m.*

appendectomy, *n.* appendéctomie *f.*

appendicitis, *n.* appendicite *f.*

appendix, *n.* appendice *m.*

appetite, *n.* appétit *m.*

appetizer, *n.* (drink) apéritif *m.*

appetizing, *adj.* appétissant.

applaud, *vb.* applaudir.

applause, *n.* applaudissements *m.pl.*

apple, *n.* pomme *f.*

applesauce, *n.* compote (*f.*) de pommes.

appliance, *n.* appareil *m.*

applicable, *adj.* applicable.

applicant, *n.* postulant *m.*

application, *n.* (request) demande *f.*

applied, *adj.* appliqué.

apply, *vb.* **(a. to somebody)** s'adresser à; **(a. for a job)** solliciter; (put on) appliquer; **(a. oneself)** s'appliquer.

appoint, *vb.* (a person) nommer; (time, place) désigner.

appointment, *n.* (meeting) rendez-vous *m.;* **(make an a. with)** donner un rendezvous à; (nomination) nomination *f.*

apportion, *vb.* répartir.

apposition, *n.* apposition *f.*

appraisal, *n.* évaluation *f.*

appraise, *vb.* priser.

appreciable, *adj.* appréciable.

appreciate, *vb.* apprécier.

appreciation, *n.* appréciation *f.*

apprehend, *vb.* saisir.

apprehension, *n.* (seizure) arrestation *f.;* (understanding) compréhension *f.;* (fear) appréhension *f.*

apprehensive, *adj.* craintif.

apprentice, *n.* apprenti *m.*

apprenticeship, *n.* stage *m.*

apprise, *vb.* prévenir, informer.

approach, 1. *n.* approche *f.;* **(make a.s to)** faire des avances à. **2.** *vb.* s'approcher de.

approachable, *adj.* abordable, accessible.

approbation, *n.* approbation *f.*

appropriate, 1. *adj.* convenable. **2.** *vb.* s'approprier.

appropriation, *n.* appropriation *f.*

approval, *n.* approbation *f.*

approve, *vb.* approuver.

approximate, 1. *adj.* approximatif. **2.** *vb.* se rapprocher (de).

approximately, *adv.* approximativement, à peu près.

approximation, *n.* approximation *f.*

appurtenance, *n.* appartenance *f.,* dépendance *f.*

apricot, *n.* abricot *m.*

April, *n.* avril *m.*

apron, *n.* tablier *m.*

apropos, *adj.* à propos.

apse, *n.* abside *f.*

apt, *adj.* (likely to) sujet à; (suitable for) apte à; (appropriate) à propos; (clever) habile.

aptitude, *n.* aptitude *f.*

aqualung, *n.* scaphandre autonome *m.*

aquarium, *n.* aquarium *m.*

Aquarius, *n.* le Verseau.

aquatic, *adj.* aquatique.

aqueduct, *n.* aqueduc *m.*

aqueous, *adj.* aqueux.

aquiline, *adj.* aquilin.

Arab, 1. *n.* Arabe *m.f.* **2.** *adj.* arabe.

Arabic, *adj. and n.* arabe *m.*

arable, *adj.* arable, labourable.

arbiter, *n.* arbitre *m.*

arbitrary, *adj.* arbitraire.

arbitrate, *vb.* arbitrer.

arbitration, *n.* arbitrage *m.*

arbitrator, *n.* arbitre *m.*

arbor, *n.* (bower) berceau *m.*

arboreal, *adj.* arboricole.

arc, *n.* arc *m.*

arcade, *n.* arcade *f.*

arch, 1. *n.* arc *m.;* (of bridge) arche *f.* **2.** *adj.* espiègle.

archaeology, *n.* archéologie *f.*

archaic, *adj.* archaïque.

archbishop, *n.* archevêque *m.*

archdiocese, *n.* archidiocèse *m.*

archduke, *n.* archiduc *m.*

archenemy, *n.* ennemi (*m.*) de toujours.

archer, *n.* archer *m.*

archery, *n.* tir à l'arc *m.*

archetype, *n.* achétype *m.,* modèle *m.*

archipelago, *n.* archipel *m.*

architect, *n.* architecte *m.*

architectural, *adj.* architectural.

architecture, *n.* architecture *f.*

archives, *n.* archives *f.pl.*

archway, *n.* voûte *f.,* passage (sous une voûte) *m.*

arctic, *adj.* arctique.

ardent, *adj.* ardent.

ardor, *n.* ardeur *f.*

arduous, *adj.* difficile.

area, *n.* (geom.) aire *f.;* (locality) région *f.;* (surface) surface *f.*

area code, *n.* indicatif (*m.*) interurbain.

arena, *n.* arène *f.*

Argentina, *n.* Argentine *f.*

argentine, *adj.* argentin.

argue, *vb.* (reason) argumenter; (indicate) prouver; (discuss) discuter.

argument, *n.* (reasoning) argument *m.;* (dispute) discussion *f.*

argumentative, *adj.* disposé à argumenter, raisonneur.

aria, *n.* air *m.,* chanson *f.*

arid, *adj.* aride.

arise, *vb.* (move upward) s'élever; (originate from) provenir de.

aristocracy, *n.* aristocratie *f.*

aristocrat, *n.* aristocrate *m.f.*

aristocratic, *adj.* aristocratique.

arithmetic, *n.* arithmétique *f.*

ark, *n.* arche *f.*

arm, 1. *n.* (limb) bras *m.;* (weapon) arme *f.* **2.** *vb.* armer.

armament, *n.* armement *m.*

armchair, *n.* fauteuil *m.*

armed forces, *n.* forces armées *f.pl.*

armed robbery, *n.* vol (*m.*) à main armée.

armful, *n.* brassée *f.*

armhole, *n.* emmanchure *f.,* entournure *f.*

armistice, *n.* armistice *m.*

armor, *n.* armure *f.*

armory, *n.* (drill hall) salle (*f.*) d'exercice.

armpit, *n.* aisselle *f.*

armrest, *n.* accoudoir *m.*

arms, *n.* armes *f.pl.*

army, *n.* armée *f.*

arnica, *n.* arnica *f.*

aroma, *n.* arome *m.*

aromatic, *adj.* aromatique.

around, 1. *adv.* autour. **2.** *prep.* autour de.

arouse, *vb.* (stir) soulever; (awake) réveiller; (anger, passion) exciter.

arraign, *vb.* accuser, poursuivre en justice.

arrange, *vb.* arranger.

arrangement, *n.* arrangement *m.*

array, 1. *n.* (military) rangs *m.pl.;* (display) étalage *m.* **2.** *vb.* ranger.

arrear, *n.* arriéré *m.*

arrest, 1. *n.* (capture) arrestation *f.;* (military) arrêts *m.pl.;* (halt) arrêt *m.* **2.** *vb.* arrêter.

arrival, *n.* arrivée *f.*

arrive, *vb.* arriver.

arrogance, *n.* arrogance *f.*

arrogant, *adj.* arrogant.

arrogate, *vb.* usurper; (a. to oneself) s'arroger.

arrow, *n.* flèche *f.*

arrowhead, *n.* pointe (*f.*) de flèche; (plant) sagittaire *f.*

arsenal, *n.* arsenal *m.*

arsenic, *n.* arsenic *m.*

arson, *n.* crime d'incendie *m.*

art, *n.* art *m.;* (fine a.s) beaux-arts.

artefact, *n.* objet fabriqué *m.*

arterial, *adj.* artériel.

arteriosclerosis, *n.* artériosclérose *f.*

artery, *n.* artère *f.*

artesian well, *n.* puits artésien *m.*

artful, *adj.* (crafty) artificieux; (skillful) adroit.

arthritis, *n.* arthrite *f.*

artichoke, *n.* artichaut *m.*

article, *n.* article *m.*

articulate, *vb.* articuler.

articulation, *n.* articulation *f.*

artifice, *n.* artifice *m.*

artificial, *adj.* artificiel.

artificiality, *n.* nature artificielle *f.*

artillery, *n.* artillerie *f.*

artisan, *n.* artisan *m.*

artist, *n.* artiste *m.*

artistic, *adj.* artistique.

artistry, *n.* habileté *f.*

artless, *adj.* ingénu, naïf.

as, 1. *adv.* comme; (as . . . as) aussi . . . que; (as much as) autant que; (such as) tel que. **2.** *conj.* (so . . . as) de façon à; (while) pendant que; (since) puisque; (progress) à mesure que. **3.** *prep.* (as to) quant à.

asbestos, *n.* asbeste *m.*

ascend, *vb.* monter.

ascendancy, *n.* ascendant *m.*

ascendant, *adj.* ascendant, supérieur.

ascent, *n.* montée *f.;* (of a mountain) ascension *f.*

ascertain, *vb.* s'assurer (de).

ascetic, *n.* ascétique *m.*

ascribe, *vb.* attribuer.

ash, *n.* cendre *f.;* (tree) frêne *m.*

ashamed, *adj.* honteux; (be a. of) avoir honte de.

ashen, *adj.* cendré, gris pâle.

ashore, *adv.* à terre; (go a.) débarquer.

ashtray, *n.* cendrier *m.*

Ash Wednesday, *n.* mercredi (*m.*) des cendres.

Asia, *n.* Asie *f.*

Asian, 1. *n.* Asiatique *m.f.* **2.** *adj.* asiatique.

aside, *adv.* de côté.

ask, *vb.* demander à; (invite) inviter.

askance, *adv.* de travers, obliquement.

askew, *adv. and adj.* de travers.

asleep, *adj.* endormi.

asp, *n.* aspic *m.*

asparagus, *n.* asperges *f.pl.*

aspect, *n.* aspect *m.*

asperity, *n.* aspérité *f.,* rudesse *f.*

aspersion, *n.* aspersion *f.*

asphalt, *n.* asphalte *m.*

asphyxia, *n.* asphyxie *f.*

asphyxiate, *vb.* asphyxier.

aspirant, *n.* aspirant *m.*

aspirate, *vb.* aspirer.

aspiration, *n.* aspiration *f.*

aspirator, *n.* aspirateur *m.*

aspire, *vb.* aspirer.

aspirin, *n.* aspirine *f.*

ass, *n.* âne *m.,* ânesse *f.*

assail, *vb.* assaillir.

assailable, *adj.* attaquable.

assailant, *n.* assaillant *m.*

assassin, *n.* assassin *m.*

assassinate, *vb.* assassiner.

assassination, *n.* assassinat *m.*

assault, *n.* assaut *m.*

assay, 1. *n.* essai *m.,* vérification *f.,* épreuve *f.* **2.** *vb.* essayer.

assemblage, *n.* assemblage *m.*

assemble, *vb.* assembler, *tr.;* s'assembler, *intr.*

assembly, *n.* assemblée *f.*

assent, 1. *n.* assentiment *m.* **2.** *vb.* consentir.

assert, *vb.* affirmer.

assertion, *n.* assertion *f.*

assertive, *adj.* assertif.

assertiveness, *n.* qualité d'être assertif.

assess, *vb.* (tax) taxer; (evaluate) évaluer.

assessor, *n.* assesseur *m.*

assets, *n.pl. (comm.)* actif *m.;* (property) biens *m.pl.*

asseverate, *vb.* affirmer solennellement.

asseveration, *n.* affirmation *f.*

assiduous, *adj.* assidu.

assiduously, *adv.* assidûment.

assign, *vb.* assigner.

assignable, *adj.* assignable, transférable.

assignation, *n.* assignation *f.*, rendez-vous *m.*

assignment, *n.* (law) cession *f.;* (school) tâche *f.*, devoir *m.*

assimilate, *vb.* assimiler, *tr.;* s'assimiler, *intr.*

assimilation, *n.* assimilation *f.*

assimilative, *adj.* assimilatif, assimilateur.

assistance, *n.* aide *f.*

assistant, *n.* aide *m.f.*

assist in, *vb.* aider à.

associate, *vb.* associer, *tr.;* s'associer, *intr.*

association, *n.* association *f.*

assonance, *n.* assonance *f.*

assort, *vb.* assortir.

assorted, *adj.* assorti.

assortment, *n.* assortiment *m.*

assuage, *vb.* adoucir, apaiser.

assume, *vb.* (take) prendre; (appropriate) s'arroger; (feign) simuler; (suppose) supposer.

assuming, *adj.* prétentieux, arrogant.

assumption, *n.* supposition *f.;* (eccles.) Assomption *f.*

assurance, *n.* assurance *f.*

assure, *vb.* assurer.

assured, *adj.* assuré.

assuredly, *adv.* assurément.

aster, *n.* aster *m.*

asterisk, *n.* astérisque *m.*

astern, *adv.* à l'arrière, de l'arrière.

asteroid, *n.* astéroïde *m.*

asthma, *n.* asthme *m.*

astigmatism, *n.* astigmatisme *m.*

astir, *adj.* agité, debout.

astonish, *vb.* étonner.

astonishment, *n.* étonnement *m.*

astound, *vb.* stupéfier.

astral, *adj.* astral.

astray, *adj.* égaré; (go a.) s'égarer.

astride, *adv.* à califourchon.

astringent, *n. and adj.* astringent *m.*

astrology, *n.* astrologie *f.*

astronaut, *n.* astronaute *m.*

astronomy, *n.* astronomie *f.*

astute, *adj.* fin.

asunder, *adv.* (apart) écartés; (to pieces) en morceaux;

asylum, *n.* asile *m.*

asymmetry, *n.* asymétrie *f.*

at, *prep.* (time, place, price) à; (someone's house, shop, etc.) chez.

ataxia, *n.* ataxie *f.*

atheist, *n.* athée *m.f.*

athlete, *n.* athlète *m.f.*

athletic, *adj.* athlétique.

athletics, *n.* sports *m.pl.*

athwart, *adv.* de travers.

Atlantic, *adj.* atlantique.

Atlantic Ocean, *n.* océan Atlantique *m.*

atlas, *n.* atlas *m.*

atmosphere, *n.* atmosphère *f.*

atmospheric, *adj.* atmosphérique.

atoll, *n.* atoll *m.*

atom, *n.* atome *m.*

atomic, *adj.* atomique.

atomic bomb, *n.* bombe atomique *f.*

atomic energy, *n.* énergie atomique *f.*

atomic theory, *n.* théorie atomique *f.*

atomic warfare, *n.* guerre atomique *f.*

atomic weight, *n.* poids atomique *m.*

atonal, *adj.* atonal.

atone for, *vb.* expier.

atonement, *n.* expiation *f.*

atrocious, *adj.* atroce.

atrocity, *n.* atrocité *f.*

atrophy, *n.* atrophie *f.*

atropine, *n.* atropine *f.*

attach, *vb.* attacher.

attaché, *n.* attaché *m.*

attaché case, *n.* mallette *f.*, attaché-case *m.*

attachment, *n.* attachement *m.;* (device) accessoire *m.*

attack, 1. *n.* attaque *f.* **2.** *vb.* attaquer.

attacker, *n.* agresseur *m.*

attain, *vb.* atteindre.

attainable, *adj.* qu'on peut atteindre.

attainment, *n.* (realization) réalisation *f.;* (knowledge) connaissance *f.*

attempt, *n.* tentative *f.*

attend, *vb.* (give heed to) faire attention à; (medical) soigner; (serve) servir; (meeting) assister à; (lectures) suivre; (see to) s'occuper de.

attendance, *n.* service *m.;* présence *f.*

attendant, *n.* serviteur *m.;* (retinue) suite *f.*

attention, *n.* attention *f.;* (pay a. to) faire attention à.

attentive, *adj.* attentif.

attentively, *adv.* attentivement.

attenuate, *vb.* atténuer.

attest, *vb.* attester.

attic, *n.* grenier *m.*

attire, 1. *n.* costume *m.* **2.** *vb.* parer, *tr.;* se parer, *intr.*

attitude, *n.* attitude *f.*

attorney, *n.* avoué *m.*

attract, *vb.* attirer.

attraction, *n.* attraction *f.*

attractive, *adj.* attrayant.

attributable, *adj.* attribuable, imputable.

attribute, 1. *n.* attribut *m.* **2.** *vb.* attribuer, imputer (à).

attrition, *n.* attrition *f.;* (war of a.) guerre (*f.*) d'usure.

attune, *vb.* accorder, mettre à l'unisson.

auburn, *adj.* châtain roux.

auction, *n.* vente (*f.*) aux enchères.

auctioneer, *n.* commissaire-priseur *m.*

audacious, *adj.* audacieux.

audacity, *n.* audace *f.*

audible, *adj.* intelligible.

audience, *n.* (listeners) auditoire *m.;* (interview) audience *f.*

audiovisual, *adj.* audiovisuel.

audiovisual aids, *n.* supports audiovisuels *m.pl.*

audit, 1. *vb.* vérifier (des comptes). **2.** *n.* vérification (des comptes) *f.*

audition, *n.* audition *f.*

auditor, *n.* vérificateur *m.,* censeur *m.*

auditorium, *n.* salle *f.*

auditory, *adj.* auditif.

auger, *n.* tarière *f.*

augment, *vb.* augmenter.

augur, *vb.* augurer.

August, *n.* août *m.*

aunt, *n.* tante *f.*

au pair, *n.* jeune fille (*f.*) au pair.

aura, *n.* atmosphère *f.*

auspice, *n.* auspice *m.*

auspicious, *adj.* de bon augure.

austere, *adj.* austère.

austerity, *n.* austérité *f.*

Australia, *n.* Australie *f.*

Australian, 1. *n.* Australien *m.* **2.** *adj.* australien.

Austria, *n.* Autriche *f.*

Austrian, 1. *n.* Autrichien *m.* **2.** *adj.* autrichien.

authentic, *adj.* authentique.

authenticate, *vb.* authentiquer, valider.

authenticity, *n.* authenticité *f.*

author, *n.* auteur *m.*

authoritarian, *adj.* autoritaire.

authoritative, *adj.* autoritaire.

authoritatively, *adv.* avec autorité, en maître.

authority, *n.* autorité *f.*

authorization, *n.* autorisation *f.*

authorize, *vb.* autoriser.

austistic, *adj.* autistique.

auto, *n.* auto *f.*

autobiography, *n.* autobiographie *f.*

autocracy, *n.* autocratie *f.*

autocrat, *n.* autocrate *m.*

autograph, 1. *n.* autographe *m.* **2.** *vb.* autographier.

autoimmune, *adj.* auto-immune.

automatic, *adj.* automatique.

automatically, *adv.* automatiquement.

automation, *n.* automatisation *f.*

automobile, *n.* automobile *f.*

automotive, *adj.* automoteur.

autonomously, *adv.* d'une manière autonome.

autonomy, *n.* autonomie *f.*

autopsy, *n.* autopsie *f.*

autumn, *n.* automne *m.*

auxiliary, *adj.* auxiliaire.

avail, *vb.* servir; (**be of no a.**) ne servir à rien.

available, *adj.* disponible.

avalanche, *n.* avalanche *f.*

avarice, *n.* avarice *f.*

avariciously, *adv.* avec avarice.

avenge, *vb.* venger.

avenger, *n.* vengeur *m.,* vengeresse *f.*

avenue, *n.* avenue *f.*

average, 1. *n.* moyenne *f.* **2.** *adj.* moyen.

averse, *adj.* opposé.

aversion, *n.* aversion *f.*

avert, *vb.* détourner.

aviary, *n.* volière *f.*

aviation, *n.* aviation *f.*

aviator, *n.* aviateur *m.*

aviatrix, *n.* aviatrice *f.*

avid, *adj.* avide.

avocado, *n.* avocat *m.*

avocation, *n.* distraction *f.,* profession *f.,* métier *m.*

avoid, *vb.* éviter.

avoidable, *adj.* évitable.

avoidance, *n.* action d'éviter *f.*

avow, *vb.* avouer.

avowal, *n.* aveu *m.*

avowed, *adj.* avoué, confessé.

avowedly, *adj.* de son propre aveu, ouvertement.

await, *vb.* attendre.

awake, *vb.* éveiller, *tr.;* s'éveiller, *intr.*

awaken, *vb. see* **awake.**

award, 1. *n.* (prize) prix *m.;* (law) sentence *f.* **2.** *vb.* décerner.

aware, *adj.* (**be a.**) savoir; (**not to be a.**) ignorer.

awash, *adv.* dans l'eau.

away, *adv.* loin; (**go a.**) s'en aller; (**a. from**) absent de.

awe, *n.* crainte *f.*

awesome, *adj.* inspirant du respect.

awful, *adj.* affreux.

awhile, *adv.* pendant quelque temps.

awkward, *adj.* (clumsy) gauche; (embarrassing) embarrassant.

awning, *n.* tente *f.*

awry, *adv.* de travers.

ax, *n.* hache *f.*

axiom, *n.* axiome *m.*

axis, *n.* axe *m.*

axle, *n.* essieu *m.*

ayatollah, *n.* ayatollah *m.*

azure, 1. *n.* azur *m.* **2. adj.** azuré.

B

babble *vb.* babiller.

babbler, *n.* babillard *m.*

babe, *n.* enfant *m.f.*

baboon, *n.* babouin *m.*

baby, *n.* bébé *m.*

babyish, *adj.* enfantin.

baby-sit, *vb.* garder les enfants.

baby-sitter, *n.* baby-sitter *m.f.*

bachelor, *n.* célibataire *m.;* (**B. of Arts/Science**) licencié(e) ès lettres/sciences.

bacillus, *n.* bacille *m.*

back, 1. *n.* dos *m.* **2.** *vb.* (**b. up, go b.**) reculer; (**uphold**) soutenir. **3.** *adv.* en arrière.

backache, *n.* mal de/aux reins *m.*

backbone, *n.* épine dorsale *f.*

backer, *n.* partisan *m.*

backfire, *vb.* (car) pétarader; (plans) mal tourner.

background, *n.* fond *m.,* arrière-plan *m.*

backhand, *adj.* donné avec le revers de la main.

backing, *n.* soutien *m.*

backlash, *n.* contrecoup *m.*, répercussion *f.*

backlog, *n.* réserve *f.*

back out, *vb.* se retirer.

backpack, *n.* sac à dos *m.*

backside, *n.* derrière *m.*

backstage, *adv.* dans les coulisses.

backup, (computer) **1.** *n.* sauvegarde *f.* **2.** *adj.* de sauvegarde.

backward, *adj.* en arrière.

backwardness, *n.* retard *m.*

backwards, *adv.* en arrière.

backwater, **1.** *n.* eau stagnante *f.* **2.** *vb.* aller en arrière (dans l'eau.)

backwoods, *n.* forêts vierges *f.pl.*

backyard, *n.* arrière-cour *f.*

bacon, *n.* porc (*m.*) salé et fumé, lard *m.*

bacteria, *n.* bactéries *f.pl.*

bacteriologist, *n.* bactériologue *m.f.*

bacteriology, *n.* bactériologie *f.*

bacterium, *n.* bactérie *f.*

bad, *adj.* mauvais; (wicked) méchant.

badge, *n.* insigne *m.*

badger, *vb.* ennuyer.

badly, *adv.* mal.

badness, *n.* mauvaise qualité *f.*; (wickedness) méchanceté *f.*

baffle, *vb.* déconcerter.

bafflement, *n.* confusion *f.*

bag, *n.* sac *m.*; (suitcase) valise *f.*

baggage, *n.* bagage *m.*

baggage cart, *n.* (airport) chariot *m.*

baggage claim, *n.* bulletin (*m.*) de bagage.

baggy, *adj.* bouffant.

bagpipe, *n.* cornemuse *f.*

Bahamas, *n.* les Bahamas *f.pl.*

bail, **1.** *n.* (law) caution *f.* **2.** *vb.* (b. out water) vider (l'eau.)

bailiff, *n.* huissier *m.*

bait, *n.* appât *m.*

bake, *vb.* faire cuire au four, *tr.*

baker, *n.* boulanger *m.*

bakery, *n.* boulangerie *f.*

baking, *n.* boulangerie *f.*

baking powder, *n.* levure *f.*

baking soda, *n.* bicarbonate (*m.*) de sodium.

balance, **1.** *n.* (equilibrium) équilibre *m.*; (bank) solde *m.* (account, scales) balance *f.* **2.** *vb.* balancer, *tr.*

balance sheet, *n.* bilan *m.*

balcony, *n.* balcon *m.*; (theater) galerie *f.*

bald, *adj.* chauve.

baldness, *n.* calvitie *f.*; (fig.) sécheresse *f.*

bale, *n.* balle *f.*

balk, *vb.* frustrer.

balky, *adj.* regimbé.

ball, *n.* (games, bullet) balle *f.*; (round object) boule *f.*; (dance) bal *m.*

ballad, *n.* (song) romance *f.*; (poem) ballade *f.*

ballast, *n.* lest *m.*

ball bearing, *n.* roulement (*m.*) à billes.

ballerina, *n.* ballerine *f.*

ballet, *n.* ballet *m.*

ballistic, *adj.* balistique; (b. missile) engin (*m.*) balistique.

balloon, *n.* ballon *m.*

ballot, *n.* scrutin *m.*; (b. box) urne *f.*

ballpoint pen, *n.* stylo (*m.*) à bille.

ballroom, *n.* salon de bal *m.*

balm, *n.* baume *m.*

balmy, *adj.* embaumé; doux.

balsa, *n.* balsa *f.*

balsam, *n.* baume *m.*

balustrade, *n.* balustrade *f.*

bamboo, *n.* bambou *m.*

ban, **1.** *n.* ban *m.* **2.** *vb.* mettre au ban, *tr.*

banal, *adj.* banal.

banana, *n.* banane *f.*

band, *n.* bande *f.*; (music) orchestre *m.*

bandage, *n.* bandage *m.*

Band-Aid, *n.* pansement adhésif *m.*

bandanna, *n.* foulard *m.*

bandbox, *n.* carton (de modiste) *m.*

bandit, *n.* bandit *m.*

bandmaster, *n.* chef de musique *m.*

bandsman, *n.* musicien *m.*

bandstand, *n.* kiosque *m.*

bandwagon, *n.* (jump on the b.) (fig.) monter dans le train en marche.

baneful, *adj.* pernicieux.

bang, **1.** *n.* coup *m.*; (b.s) frange *f.* **2.** *vb.* frapper.

banish, *vb.* bannir.

banishment, *n.* bannissement *m.*

banister, *n.* rampe *f.*

banjo, *n.* banjo *m.*

bank, *n.* banque *f.*; (river) rive *f.*

bank account, *n.* compte (*m.*) en banque.

bankbook, *n.* livret de banque *m.*

banker, *n.* banquier *m.*

banking, *n.* banque *f.*, affaires de banque *f.pl.*

bank note, *n.* billet de banque *m.*

bankrupt, *adj. and n.* failli *m.*

bankruptcy, *n.* faillite *f.*

bank statement, *n.* relevé (*m.*) de compte.

banner, *n.* bannière *f.*

banquet, *n.* banquet *m.*

banter, **1.** *n.* badinage *m.* **2.** *vb.* badiner, railler.

baptism, *n.* baptême *m.*

baptismal, *adj.* baptismal.

Baptist, *n.* Baptiste *m.*

baptistery, *n.* baptistère *m.*

baptize, *vb.* baptiser.

bar, *n.* (drinks) bar *m.*; (metal) barre *f.*; (law) barreau *m.*

barb, *n.* barbillon *m.*

barbarian, barbarous, *adj. and n.* barbare *m.f.*

barbarism, *n.* barbarie *f.*; (gramm.) barbarisme *m.*

barbecue, *n.* barbecue *m.*

barbed wire, *n.* fil (*m.*) de fer barbelé.

barbell, *n.* haltère *m.*

barber, *n.* coiffeur *m.*

barbiturte, *n.* barbiturique *m.*

bar code, *n.* code (*m.*) à barres.

bare, **1.** *adj.* nu. **2.** *vb.* découvrir.

bareback, *adv.* à dos nu.

barefoot, *adv.* nu-pieds.

barely, *adv.* à peine.

bareness, *n.* nudité *f.*

bargain, 1 *n.* marché *m.* **2.** *vb.* marchander.

barge, *n.* chaland *m.*

barium, *n.* barium *m.*

bark, 1. *n.* (tree) écorce *f.;* (dog) aboiement *m.* **2.** *vb.* (dog) aboyer.

barley, *n.* orge *f.*

barmaid, *n.* serveuse *f.*

barman, *n.* barman *m.*

barn, *n.* (grain) grange *f.;* (livestock) étable *f.*

barnacle, *n.* (shellfish) anatife *m.;* (goose) barnache *f.*

barnyard, *n.* basse-cour *f.*

barometer, *n.* baromètre *m.*

barometric, *adj.* barométrique.

baron, *n.* baron *m.*

baroness, *n.* baronne *f.*

baronial, *adj.* baronnial, seigneurial.

baroque, *adj.* baroque.

barracks, *n.* caserne *f.*

barrage, *n.* barrage *m.*

barred, *adj.* barré, empêché, exclus, défendu.

barrel, *n.* tonneau *m.*

barren, *adj.* stérile.

barrenness, *n.* stérilité *f.*

barricade, *n.* barricade *f.*

barrier, *n.* barrière *f.*

barring, *prep.* sauf.

barroom, *n.* buvette *f.*, comptoir *m.*, bar *m.*

bartender, *n.* barman *m.*

barter, 1. *n.* troc *m.* **2.** *vb.* échanger, troquer.

base, 1. *n.* base *f.* **2.** *adj.* bas *m.*, basse *f.* **3.** *vb.* baser, fonder.

baseball, *n.* baseball *m.*

baseboard, *n.* moulure de base *f.*

basement, *n.* sous-sol *m.*

baseness, *n.* bassesse *f.*

bash, *vb.* frapper.

bashful, *adj.* timide.

bashfully, *adv.* timidement, modestement.

bashfulness, *n.* timidité *f.*, modestie *f.*

basic, *adj.* fondamental.

basil, *n.* basilic *m.*

basin, *n.* (wash) cuvette *f.;* (river) bassin *m.*

basis, *n.* base *f.*

bask, se chauffer, *intr.*

basket, *n.* (with handle) panier *m.;* (without handle) corbeille *f.*

basketball, *n.* basket(ball) *m.*

Basque, 1. *n.* Basque *m.f.* **2.** *adj.* basque.

bass, *n.* (music) basse *f.;* (fish) bar *m.*

bassinet, *n.* bercelonnette *f.*

bassoon, *n.* basson *m.*

bastard, *n.* bâtard *m.*, (law) enfant naturel *m.;* (vulgar) salaud *m.*

baste, *vb.* (cooking) arroser; (sewing) faufiler.

bat, *n.* (animal) chauve-souris *f.;* (baseball) batte *f.*

batch, *n.* fournée *f.*

bate, *vb.* rabattre, diminuer.

bath, *n.* bain *m.*

bathe, *vb.* se baigner.

bather, *n.* baigneur *m.*

bathing, *n.* baignade *f.*

bathing cap, *n.* bonnet (*m.*) de bain.

bathing suit, *n.* maillot (*m.*) de bain.

bathrobe, *n.* peignoir (*m.*) de bain.

bathroom, *n.* salle (*f.*) de bain.

bathtub, *n.* baignoire *f.*

baton, *n.* bâton *m.*

battalion, *n.* bataillon *m.*

batter, *n.* (cooking) pâte *f.*

battery, *n.* (military) batterie *f.;* (electric) pile *f.*

battle, 1. *n.* bataille *f.* **2.** *vb.* lutter.

battlefield, *n.* champ (*m.*) de bataille.

battleship, *n.* cuirassé *m.*

bauxite, *n.* bauxite *f.*

bawdy, *adj.* paillard.

bawl, *vb.* brailler.

bay, *n.* (geography) baie *f.;* (plant) laurier *m.*

bayonet, *n.* baïonnette *f.*

bazaar, *n.* bazar *m.*

be, *vb.* être.

beach, *n.* plage *f.*

beachhead, *n.* (haut de) plage *f.*

beacon, *n.* phare *m.*

bead, *n.* perle *f.*

beading, *n.* ornement de grains *m.*

beady, *adj.* comme un grain, couvert de grains.

beak, *n.* bec *m.*

beaker, *n.* gobelet *m.*, coupe *f.*

beam, 1. *n.* (construction) poutre *f.;* (light) rayon *m.* **2.** *vb.* rayonner.

beaming, *adj.* rayonnant.

bean, *n.* haricot *m.*

bear, 1. *n.* ours *m.;* (teddy b.) ourson *m.* **2.** *vb.* (carry) porter; (endure) supporter; (birth) enfanter.

bearable, *adj.* supportable.

beard, *n.* barbe *f.*

bearded, *adj.* barbu.

beardless, *adj.* imberbe.

bearer, *n.* porteur *m.*

bearing, *n.* (person) maintien *m.;* (machinery) coussinet *m.;* (naut.) relèvement *m.*

bearskin, *n.* peau (*f.*) d'ours.

beast, *n.* bête *f.*

beat, 1. *vb.* battre. **2.** *n.* battement *m.*

beaten, *adj.* battu.

beatify, *vb.* béatifier.

beating, *n.* battement *m.*, rossée *f.*

beau, *n.* galant *m.*

beautician, *n.* esthéticien(ne) *m.(f.).*

beautiful, *adj.* beau (bel) *m.*, belle *f.*

beautifully, *adv.* admirablement.

beautify, *vb.* embellir.

beauty, *n.* beauté *f.*

beauty mark, *n.* grain (*m.*) de beauté.

beauty parlor, *n.* salon (*m.*) de beauté.

beaver, *n.* castor *m.*

becalm, *vb.* calmer, apaiser; (naut.) abriter.

because, *conj.* parce que.

beckon, *vb.* faire signe (à).

become, *vb.* devenir.

becoming, *adj.* convenable; (dress) seyant.

bed, *n.* lit *m.*

bedbug, *n.* punaise *f.*

bedclothes, *n.* couvertures *f.pl.*

bedding, *n.* literie *f.*

bedfellow, *n.* camarade de lit *m.*

bedizen, *vb.* parer, attifer.

bedlam, *n.* chahut *m.*

bedraggled, *adj.* débraillé.

bedridden, *adj.* alité.

bedrock, *n.* roche solide *f.*

bedroom, *n.* chambre (*f.*) à coucher.

bedside, *n.* bord du lit *m.*

bedspread, *n.* dessus (*m.*) de lit.

bedstead, *n.* bois de lit *m.*

bedtime, *n.* heure (*f.*) de se coucher.

bee, *n.* abeille *f.*

beef, *n.* bœuf *m.*

beefsteak, *n.* bifteck *m.*

beefy, *adj.* musclé, costaud.

beehive, *n.* ruche *f.*

beeper, *n.* récepteur (*m.*) de poche

beer, *n.* bière *f.*

beeswax, *n.* cire jaune *f.*

beet, *n.* betterave *f.*

beetle, *n.* scarabée *m.*

befall, *vb.* arriver (à).

befit, *vb.* convenir (à).

befitting, *adj.* convenable.

before, 1. *adv.* (place) en avant; (time) avant. 2. *prep.* (place) devant; (time) avant. 3. *conj.* avant que.

beforehand, *adv.* d'avance.

befriend, *vb.* aider; traiter en ami.

befuddle, *vb.* embrouiller, déconcerter.

beg, *vb.* (of beggar) mendier; (ask) prier.

beget, *vb.* engendrer, produire.

beggar, *n.* mendiant *m.*

beggarly, *adj.* chétif, misérable.

begin, *vb.* commencer.

beginner, *n.* commençant *m.*

beginning, *n.* commencement *m.*

begrudge, *vb.* envier, donner à contrecoeur.

beguile, *vb.* tromper, séduire.

behalf, *n.* (on b. of) de la part de; (in b. of) en faveur de.

behave, *vb.* se conduire.

behavior, *n.* conduite *f.*

behead, *vb.* décapiter.

behind, 1. *adv. and prep.* derrière. 2. *n.* derrière *m.*

behold, 1. *vb.* voir. 2. *interj.* voici.

beige, *adj.* beige.

being, *n.* être *m.*

bejewel, *vb.* orner de bijoux.

belated, *adj.* attardé.

belch, *vb.* éructer, roter.

belfry, *n.* clocher *m.*, beffroi *m.*

Belgian, 1. *n.* Belge *m.f.* 2. *adj.* belge.

Belgium, *n.* Belgique *f.*

belie, *vb.* démentir.

belief, *n.* croyance *f.*; (confidence) confiance *f.*

believable, *adj.* croyable.

believe, *vb.* croire.

believer, *n.* croyant *m.*

belittle, *vb.* rabaisser.

bell, *n.* (house) sonnette *f.*; (church) cloche *f.*

bellboy, *n.* chasseur *m.*

bell buoy, *n.* bouée sonore *f.*

belligerence, *n.* belligérance *f.*

belligerent, *adj. and n.* belligérant *m.*

belligerently, *adv.* d'une manière belligérante.

bellow, *vb.* mugir.

bellows, *n.* soufflet *m.*

bell-tower, *n.* clocher *m.*

belly, *n.* ventre *m.*

belongings, *n.* effets *m.pl.*, affaires *f.pl.*

belong to, *vb.* appartenir à.

beloved, *adj. and n.* chéri *m.*

below, 1. *adv.* en bas. 2. *prep.* au-dessous de.

belt, *n.* ceinture *f.*

beltway, *n.* périphérique *m.*

bemused, *adj.* perplexe.

bemoan, *vb.* lamenter.

bench, *n.* banc *m.*

bend, *vb.* plier; (curve) courber, *tr.*

beneath, *see* below.

benediction, *n.* bénédiction *f.*

benefactor, *n.* bienfaiteur *m.*

benefactress, *n.* bienfaitrice *f.*

beneficent, *adj.* bienfaisant.

beneficial, *adj.* salutaire.

beneficiary, *n.* bénéficiaire *m.*

benefit, *n.* (favor) bienfait *m.*; (advantage) bénéfice *m.*

Benelux, *n.* Bénélux *m.*

benevolence, *n.* bienveillance *f.*

benevolent, *adj.* bienveillant.

benevolently, *adv.* bénévolement.

benign, *adj.* bénin *m.*, bénigne *f.*

benignity, *n.* bénignité *f.*

bent, *n.* penchant *m.*

benzene, *n.* benzène *m.*

benzine, *n.* benzine *f.*

bequeath, *vb.* léguer.

bequest, *n.* legs *m.*

berate, *vb.* gronder.

bereave, *vb.* priver (de).

bereavement, *n.* privation *f.*, perte *f.*, deuil *m.*

beriberi, *n.* béribéri *m.*

Bermuda, *n.* Bermudes *f.pl.*

berry, *n.* baie *f.*

berserk, *adj.* fou *m.*, folle *f.*

berth, *n.* couchette *f.*

beseech, *vb.* supplier.

beseechingly, *adv.* en suppliant.

beset, *vb.* attaquer, presser, assiéger.

beside, *prep.* à côté de.

besides, *adv.* en outre.

besiege, *vb.* assiéger.

besieged, *adj.* assiégé.

besieger, *n.* assiégeant *m.*

besmirch, *vb.* tacher, salir.

best, 1. *adj.* (le) meilleur. 2. *adv.* (le) mieux.

bestial, *adj.* bestial.

bestir, *vb.* remuer.

best man, *n.* garçon d'honneur (at weddings) *m.*

bestow, *vb.* accorder.

bestowal, *n.* dispensation *f.*

best-seller, *n.* best-seller *m.*, succès de librairie.

bet, 1. *n.* pari *m.* 2. *vb.* parier.

betake (oneself), *vb.* se rendre.

betray, *vb.* trahir.

betroth, *vb.* fiancer.

betrothal, *n.* fiançailles *f.pl.*

better, 1. *adj.* meilleur. **2.** *adv.* mieux.

between, *prep.* entre.

bevel, 1. *adj.* en biseau. **2.** *vb.* biaiser.

beverage, *n.* boisson *f.*

bevy, *n.* essaim *m.*

bewail, *vb.* lamenter, pleurer.

beware of, *vb.* prendre garde à.

bewilder, *vb.* égarer.

bewildered, *adj.* égaré, dérouté(e).

bewildering. *adj.* déconcertant.

bewilderment, *n.* égarement *m.*

bewitch, *vb.* ensorceler.

beyond, 1. *adv.* au delà. **2.** *prep.* au delà de.

biannual, *adj.* semestriel.

bias, *n.* (slant) biais *m.;* (prejudice) prévention *f.*

bib, *n.* bavette *f.*

Bible, *n.* Bible *f.*

biblical, *adj.* biblique.

bibliography, *n.* bibliographie *f.*

bicarbonate, *n.* bicarbonate *m.*

bicentennial, *n. and adj.* bicentenaire *m.*

biceps, *n.* biceps *m.*

bicker, *vb.* se quereller, se chamailler.

bicycle, 1 *n.* bicyclette *f.* **2.** *vb.* faire de la bicyclette.

bicyclist, *n.* cycliste *m.*

bid, 1. *n.* (auction) enchère *f.;* (bridge) appel *m.* **2.** *vb.* (order) ordonner; (invite) inviter; (auction) faire une offre.

bidder, *n.* enchérisseur *m.*

bide, *vb.* (live) demeurer; (wait) attendre.

biennial, *adj.* biennal.

bier, *n.* corbillard *m.,* civière *f.*

bifocal, 1. *adj.* bifocal. **2.** *n.* lunettes bifocales *f.pl.*

big, *adj.* grand.

bigamy, *n.* bigamie *f.*

big business, *n.* les grandes affaires *f.pl.*

bigot, *n.* bigot *m.*

bigotry, *n.* bigoterie *f.*

bike, *n.* vélo *m.*

bilateral, *adj.* bilatéral.

bile, *n.* bile *f.*

bilingual, *adj.* bilingue.

bilious, *adj.* bilieux.

bill, *n.* (restaurant) addition *f.;* (hotel, profession) note *f.;* (shop, public utility, etc.) facture *f.;* (money) billet *(m.)* de banque; (poster) affiche *f.;* (politics) projet *(m.)* de loi; **(b. of fare)** carte *(f.)* du jour; (bird) bec *m.*

billboard, *n.* panneau *(m.)* d'affichage.

billet, *n. (mil.)* billet de logement *m.*

billfold, *n.* portefeuille *m.*

billiard balls, *n.* billes *f.pl.*

billiards, *n.* billard *m.*

billion, *n.* (U.S.) milliard *m.,* (Britain) billion *m.*

bill of health, *n.* patente *(f.)* de santé.

bill of lading, *n.* connaissement *m.*

bill of sale, *n.* lettre de vente *f.,* acte *(m.)* de propriété.

billow, *n.* grande vague *f.,* lame *f.*

billy-goat, *n.* bouc *m.*

bimetallic, *adj.* bimétallique.

bimonthly, *adj. and adv.* bimensuel.

bin, *n.* coffre *m.*

bind, *vb.* lier; (books) relier.

bindery, *n.* atelier de reliure *m.*

binding, 1. *n.* (book) reliure *f.* **2.** *adj.* obligatoire.

binoculars, *n.* jumelles *f.pl.*

biochemistry, *n.* biochimie *f.*

biodegradable, *adj.* sujet à la putréfaction.

biofeedback, *n.* biofeedback *m.,* information *(f.)* reçue par un organisme pendant un processus biologique.

biographer, *n.* biographe *m.*

biographical, *adj.* biographique.

biography, *n.* biographie *f.*

biological, *adj.* biologique.

biologically, *adv.* biologiquement.

biology, *n.* biologie *f.*

biorhythm, *n.* biorythme *m.*

bipartisan, *adj.* représentant les deux partis.

biped, *n.* bipède *m.*

birch, *n.* bouleau *m.*

bird, *n.* oiseau *m.*

birdlike, *adj.* comme un oiseau.

bird of prey, *n.* oiseau de proie *m.*

bird's-eye view, *n.* vue *(f.)* à vol d'oiseau.

birth, *n.* naissance *f.*

birth certificate, *n.* acte *(m.)* de naissance.

birth control, *n.* contrôle *(m.)* des naissances.

birthday, *n.* anniversaire *(m.)* de naissance, fête *f.*

birthmark, *n.* tache *(f.)* de naissance.

birthplace, *n.* lieu *(m.)* de naissance.

birth rate, *n.* natalité *f.*

birthright, *n.* droit *(m.)* d'aînesse.

biscuit, *n.* (hard) biscuit *m.;* (soft) petit pain *(m.)* au lait.

bisect, *vb.* couper en deux.

bisexual, *adj.* bis(s)exuel.

bishop, *n.* évêque *m.*

bishopric, *n.* évêché *m.*

bismuth, *n.* bismuth *m.*

bison, *n.* bison *m.*

bit, *n.* (piece) morceau *m.;* **(a b. (of))** un peu (de); (harness) mors *m.;* (computer) unité d'information *f.*

bitch, *n.* chienne *f.;* (vulgar) garce *f.,* salope *f.*

bite, 1. *n.* morsure *f.* **2.** *vb.* mordre.

biting, *adj.* mordant.

bitter, *adj.* amer.

bitterly, *adv.* amèrement, avec amertume.

bitterness, *n.* amertume *f.*

bivouac, *n.* bivouac *m.*

biweekly, *adj. and adv.* tous les quinze jours.

blab, *vb.* jaser.

black, *adj.* noir.

Black, *n. and adj.* (for person) noir *m.;* noire *f.*

blackberry, n. mûre *(f.)* de ronce.

blackbird, *n.* merle *m.*

blackboard, *n.* tableau *(m.)* noir.

black currant, *n.* cassis *m.*

blacken, *vb.* noircir.

black eye, *n.* œil poché *m.*

blackguard, *n.* gredin *m.*, polisson *m.*, salaud *m.*

blackmail, 1. *n.* chantage *m.* **2.** *vb.* faire chanter.

black market, *n.* marché noir *m.*

blackout, *n.* panne *(f.)* d'-electricité; *(med.)* syncope *f.*

blacksmith, *n.* forgeron *m.*

bladder, *n.* vessie *f.*

blade, *n.* (sword, knife) lame *f.;* (grass) brin *m.*

blame, 1. *n.* blâme *m.* **2.** *vb.* blâmer.

blameless, *adj.* innocent, sans tache.

blanch, *vb.* blanchir, pâlir.

bland, *adj.* doux *m.*, douce *f.;* (insipid) fade.

blank, 1. *n.* (space) blanc *m.;* (void) vide *m.;* (printing) tiret *m.* **2.** *adj.* (page) blanc *m.*, blanche *f.;* (empty) vide.

blanket, *n.* couverture *f.*

blare, 1. *n.* son (de la trompette) *m.*, rugissement *m.* **2.** *vb.* retentir, *intr.*

blaspheme, *vb.* blasphémer.

blasphemer, *n.* blasphémateur *m.*

blasphemous, *adj.* blasphématoire.

blasphemy, *n.* blasphème *m.*

blast, *n.* (wind) rafale *f.;* (mine) explosion *f.*

blatant, *adj.* criard, bruyant.

blaze, 1. *n.* flambée *f.* **2.** *vb.* flamber.

blazer, *n.* blazer *m.*

blazing, *adj.* enflammé, flamboyant.

bleach, *vb.* décolorer, *tr.*

bleak, *adj.* morne.

bleakness, *n.* froidure *f.*

bleat, *vb.* bêler.

bleed, *vb.* saigner.

blemish, *n.* défaut *m.*

blend, 1. *n.* mélange *m.* **2.** *vb.* mêler, *tr.*

blended, *adj.* mélangé.

blender, *n.* mixeur *m.*, mixer *m.*

bless, *vb.* bénir.

blessed, *adj.* béni.

blessing, *n.* bénédiction *f.*

blight, 1. *vb.* flétrir, détruire, nieller, brouir. **2.** *n.* brouissure *f.*, flétrissure *f.*

blind, 1. *n.* store *m.* **2.** *adj.* aveugle; **(b. alley)** cul-de-sac *m.*

blindfold, *adj. and adv.* les yeux bandés.

blinding, *adj.* aveuglant.

blindly, *adv.* aveuglément.

blindness, *n.* cécité *f.*

blink, *vb.* clignoter.

bliss, *n.* béatitude *f.*

blissful, *adj.* bienheureux.

blissfully, *adv.* heureusement.

blister, *n.* ampoule *f.*

blithe, *adj.* gai, joyeux.

blizzard, *n.* tempête *(f.)* de neige.

bloat, *vb.* boursoufler.

bloated, *adj.* gonflé.

bloc, *n.* bloc *m.*

block, 1. *n.* bloc *m.;* (houses) pâté *m.* **2.** *vb.* bloquer.

blockade, *n.* blocus *m.*

blond, *adj. and n.* blond *m.*

blood, *n.* sang *m.*

blood-curdling, *adj.* à tourner le sang.

bloodhound, *n.* limier *m.*

bloodless, *adj.* exsangue, sans effusion de sang.

blood plasma, *n.* plasma *(m.)* du sang.

blood poisoning, *n.* empoisonnement *(m.)* du sang.

blood pressure, *n.* tension artérielle *f.*

bloodshed, *n.* effusion *(f.)* de sang.

bloodshot, *adj.* injecté de sang.

bloodthirsty, *adj.* sanguinaire.

bloody, *adj.* sanglant.

bloom, 1. *n.* fleur *f.* **2.** *vb.* fleurir.

blooming, 1. *n.* floraison *f.* **2.** *adj.* fleurissant.

blossom, *see* **bloom.**

blot, 1. *n.* tache *f.* **2.** *vb.* (spot) tacher; (dry ink) sécher l'encre.

blotch, *n.* tache *f.*

blotchy, *adj.* couvert de taches.

blotter, *n.* buvard *m.*

blouse, *n.* blouse *f.*

blow, 1. *n.* coup *m.* **2.** *vb.* souffler; **(b. out)** éteindre; **(b. over)** passer; **(b. up)** faire sauter, *tr.*

blowout, *n.* éclatement *(m.)* de pneu.

blowtorch, *n.* chalumeau *m.*

blubber, 1. *vb.* pleurer comme un veau. **2.** *n.* graisse de baleine *f.*

bludgeon, 1. *n.* matraque *f.* **2.** *vb.* donner des coups de matraque.

blue, *adj.* bleu; **(have the b.s)** avoir le cafard.

blue jeans, *n.* blue jeans *m.pl.*

blueprint, *n.* dessin négatif *m.*

bluff, *n.* bluff *m.*

bluffer, *n.* bluffeur *m.*

blunder, *n.* bévue *f.*

blunderer, *n.* maladroit *m.*

blunt, *adj.* (blade) émoussé; (person) brusque.

bluntly, *adv.* brusquement.

bluntness, *n.* brusquerie *f.*

blur, *vb.* (smear) barbouiller.

blurb, *n.* résumé *(m.)* publicitaire.

blurt, *vb.* **(b. out)** lâcher, dire.

blush, 1. *n.* rougeur *f.* **2.** *vb.* rougir.

bluster, *n.* fanfaronnade *f.*

boar, *n.* (wild) sanglier *m.*

board, *n.* (plank) planche *f.;* (daily meals) pension *f.;* (boat) bord *m.;* (politics) ministère *m.;* (administration) conseil *m.*

boarder, *n.* pensionnaire *m.f.*

boarding house, *n.* pension *f.*

boarding pass, *n.* carte *(f.)* d'embarquement.

boarding school, *n.* internat *m.*, pensionnat *m.*

boast (of), *vb.* se vanter (de).

boaster, *n.* vantard *m.*

boastful, *adj.* vantard.

boastfulness, *n.* vantardise *f.*

boat, *n.* bateau *m.*

boathouse, *n.* abri (*m.*) à bateaux.

boatswain, *n.* maître d'équipage *m.*

bob, *vb.* (hair) couper court.

bobbin, *n.* bobine *f.*

bode, *vb.* présager.

bodice, *n.* corsage *m.*

bodily, *adj.* corporel.

body, *n.* corps *m.*

bodyguard, *n.* garde (*f.*) du corps.

bog, 1. *n.* marécage *m.* **2.** *vb.* embourber.

bogus, *adj.* bidon.

Bohemia, *n.* (geographical) Bohême *f.*; (*fig.*) bohème *f.*

Bohemian, 1. *n.* (geographical) Bohémien *m.*; (*fig.*) bohème *m.f.* **2.** *adj.* (geographical) bohémien; (*fig.*) bohème.

boil, 1. *vb.* bouillir, *intr.*; faire bouillir, *tr.* **2.** *n.* (*med.*) furoncle *m.*, clou *m.*

boiler, *n.* chaudière *f.*

boisterous, *adj.* (person) bruyant.

boisterously, *adv.* bruyamment.

bold, *adj.* hardi.

boldface, *adj.* (type) caractères gras *m.pl.*

boldly, *adv.* hardiment, avec audace.

boldness, *n.* hardiesse *f.*

Bolivia, *n.* Bolivie *f.*

bologna, *n.* saucisson (*m.*) de Bologne.

bolster, *n.* traversin *m.*

bolster up, *vb.* soutenir.

bolt, 1. *n.* verrou *m.* **2.** *vb.* verrouiller.

bomb, *n.* bombe *f.*

bombard, *vb.* bombarder.

bombardier, *n.* bombardier *m.*

bombardment, *n.* bombardement *m.*

bombastic, *adj.* pompeux.

bomber, *n.* avion (*m.*) de bombardement; bombardier *m.*

bombproof, *adj.* à l'épreuve des bombes.

bombshell, *n.* bombe *f.*

bombsight, *n.* viseur (*m.*) de lancement.

bona fide, *adj.* véritable.

bonbon, *n.* bonbon *m.*

bond, *n.* lien *m.*; (law, finance) obligation *f.*

bondage, *n.* servitude *f.*

bonded, *adj.* entreposé.

bone, *n.* os *m.*

boneless, *adj.* sans os.

bonfire, *n.* feu (*m.*) de joie.

bonnet, *n.* chapeau *m.*

bonus, *n.* gratification *f.*

bony, *adj.* osseux.

boo, *vb.* huer.

book, 1. *n.* livre *m.* **2.** *vb.* (ticket) prendre, (space) réserver.

bookbindery, *n.* atelier (*m.*) de reliure.

bookcase, *n.* bibliothèque *f.*

bookkeeper, *n.* teneur (*m.*) de livres.

bookkeeping, *n.* comptabilité *f.*

booklet, *n.* opuscule *m.*, brochure *f.*

bookseller, *n.* libraire *m.*; (second-hand) bouquiniste *m.*

bookstore, bookshop, *n.* librairie *f.*

boom, 1. *n.* grondement *m.*; (in numbers) forte augmentation. **2.** *vb.* gronder; prospérer.

boon, *n.* bienfait *m.*, don *m.*

boor, *n.* rustre *m.*

boorish, *adj.* rustre.

boost, *vb.* (push) pousser; (praise) louer.

boot, 1. *n.* bottine *f.*, botte *f.* **2.** *vb.* initialiser.

bootblack, *n.* cireur *m.*

booth, *n.* (fair) baraque *f.*; (telephone) cabine *f.*

booty, *n.* butin *m.*

booze, *n.* boissons (*f.pl.*) alcooliques.

border, *n.* bord *m.*; (of country) frontière *f.*

borderline, *adj.* touchant (à), avoisinant.

bore, *vb.* (make a hole) forer; (annoy) ennuyer.

boredom, *n.* ennui *m.*

boric acid, *n.* acide borique *m.*

boring, *adj.* ennuyeux.

born, 1. *adj.* né. **2.** *vb.* (be b.) naître.

born-again, *adj.* réné.

borough, *n.* (administration) circonscription électorale *f.*; (large village) bourg *m.*

borrower, *n.* emprunteur *m.*

borrow from, *vb.* emprunter à.

Bosnia, *n.* Bosnie *f.*

bosom, *n.* sein *m.*

boss, 1. *n.* patron *m.* **2.** *vb.* diriger.

bossy, *adj.* comme un patron, impérieux.

botanical, *adj.* botanique.

botany, *n.* botanique *f.*

botch, 1. *n.* ravaudage *m.* **2.** *vb.* ravauder, faire une mauvaise besogne.

both, *adj. and pron.* tous (les) deux *m.*, toutes (les) deux *f.*

bother, 1. *n.* ennui *m.* **2.** *vb.* gêner.

bothersome, *adj.* gênant.

bottle, *n.* bouteille *f.*

bottleneck, *n.* (traffic) bouchon.

bottom, *n.* fond *m.*

bottomless, *adj.* sans fond.

bough, *n.* branche *f.*

bouillon, *n.* bouillon *m.*

boulder, *n.* galet *m.*

boulevard, *n.* boulevard *m.*

bounce, *vb.* (ball) rebondir.

bound, 1. *n.* (limit) borne *f.*; (jump) bond *m.* **2.** *vb.* (limit) borner; (jump) bondir.

boundary, *n.* frontière *f.*

bound for, *adj.* en route pour.

boundless, *adj.* sans bornes, illimité.

boundlessly, *adv.* sans bornes.

bounteous, *adj.* généreux, bienfaisant.

bounty, *n.* largesse *f.*; (premium) prime *f.*

bouquet, *n.* bouquet *m.*

bourgeois, *adj.* bourgeois.

bout, *n.* (fever) accès *m.*

bovine, *n.* bovine *f.*; *adj.* bovin.

bow, *n.* (weapon) arc *m.*; (violin) archet *m.*; (curtsy) révérence *f.*; (ship) avant *m.*

bow, *vb.* incliner *tr.*

bowels, *n.* entrailles *f.pl.*

bowl, 1. *n.* bol *m.* **2.** *vb.* jouer aux boules.

bowlegged, *adj.* à jambes arquées.

bowler, *n.* joueur *(m.)* de boule.

bowling, *n.* jeu *(m.)* de boules.

box, 1. *n.* boîte *f.*; (theater) loge *f.* **2.** *vb.* boxer.

boxcar, *n.* wagon *(m.)* de marchandises.

boxer, *n.* boxeur *m.*

boxing, *n.* boxe *f.*

box office, *n.* bureau *(m.)* de location.

boy, *n.* garçon *m.*

boycott, *vb.* boycotter.

boyfriend, *n.* (petit) ami *m.*

boyhood, *n.* première je-unesse *f.*

boyish, *adj.* enfantin, puéril.

boyishly, *adv.* comme un gamin.

bra, *n.* soutien-gorge *m.*

brace, 1. *vb.* fortifier. **2.** *n.* vilebrequin (tool) *m.*, paire *f.*, couple *m.*

bracelet, *n.* bracelet *m.*

bracket, *n.* (wall) console *f.*; (printing) crochet *m.*

brag, *vb.* se vanter.

braggart, *n.* fanfaron *m.*

braid, *n.* (hair) tresse *f.*; (sewing) galon *m.*

Braille, *n.* braille *m.*

brain, *n.* cerveau *m.*; **(b.s)** cervelle *f.*

brainwash, *vb.* faire un lavage de cerveau à.

brainy, *adj.* intelligent.

brake, *n.* frein *m.*

bramble, *n.* ronce *f.*

bran, *n.* son *m.*

branch, *n.* branche *f.*

brand, *n.* marque *f.*

brandish, *vb.* brandir.

brand-new, *adj.* tout neuf.

brandy, *n.* eau-de-vie *f.*

brash, *adj.* impertinent.

brass, *n.* cuivre *(m.)* jaune.

brassiere, *n.* soutien-gorge *m.*

brat, *n.* gosse *m.f.*

bravado, *n.* bravade *f.*

brave, *adj.* courageux.

bravery, *n.* courage *m.*

brawl, *n.* rixe *f.*

brawn, *n.* partie charnue *f.*, muscles *m.pl.*

bray, *vb.* braire.

brazen, *adj.* (person) ef-fronté.

Brazil, *n.* Brésil *m.*

breach, *n.* infraction *f.*; *(mil.)* brèche *f.*

bread, *n.* pain *m.*

breadcrumbs, *n.* chapelure *f.*

breadth, *n.* largeur *f.*

breadwinner, *n.* soutien *(m.)* de la famille.

break, 1. *n.* rupture *f.*; (pause) interruption *f.*; (rest) pause *f.* **2.** *vb.* rompre, briser, casser.

breakable, *adj.* cassable.

breakage, *n.* cassure *f.*, rup-ture *f.*

breakdown, *n.* panne *f.*; dé-pression *f.*; analyse *f.*

breakfast, *n.* (petit) déje-uner *m.*

breakwater, *n.* brise-lames *m.*, jetée *f.*

breast, *n.* poitrine *f.*, sein *m.*

breath, *n.* haleine *f.*; *(fig.,* wind) souffle *m.*

Breathalyzer, *n.* alcootest *m.*

breathe, *vb.* respirer.

breathless, *adj.* (out of breath) essoufflé.

breathlessly, *adv.* hors d'haleine.

breathtaking, *adj.* à vous couper le souffle.

bred, *adj.* élevé.

breeches, *n.* pantalon *m.sg.*

breed, *vb.* produire; (live-stock) élever.

breeder, *n.* (raiser) éleveur *m.*

breeding, *n.* (manners) édu-cation *f.*; (animals) éle-vage *m.*

breeze, *n.* brise *f.*

breezy, *adj.* (windy) ven-teux; (manner) dégagé.

Breton, 1. *n.* Breton *m.* **2.** *adj.* breton.

brevity, *n.* brièveté *f.*

brew, *vb.* (beer) brasser; (tea) faire infuser, *tr.*

brewery, *n.* brasserie *f.*

briar, *n.* ronce *f.*

bribe, *vb.* corrompre.

briber, *n.* corrupteur *m.*

bribery, *n.* corruption *f.*

brick, *n.* brique *f.*

bricklaying, *n.* maçonnerie *f.*

bricklike, *adj.* comme une brique.

bridal, *adj.* nuptial.

bride, *n.* mariée *f.*

bridegroom, *n.* marié *m.*

bridesmaid, *n.* demoiselle *(f.)* d'honneur.

bridge, *n.* pont *m.*; (boat) passerelle *f.*; (cards) bridge *m.*

bridged, *adj.* lié.

bridgehead, *n.* tête de pont *f.*

bridle, *n.* bride *f.*

brief, 1. *adj.* bref *m.*, brève *f.* **2.** *n.* dossier *m.* **3.** *vb.* donner des instructions à.

briefcase, *n.* serviette *f.*

briefly, *adv.* brièvement.

briefness, *n.* brièveté *f.*

brier, *n.* bruyère *f.*, ronces *f.pl.*

brig, *n.* brick *m.*

brigade, *n.* brigade *f.*

bright, *adj.* vif *m.*, vive *f.*; intelligent.

brighten, *vb.* faire briller, *tr.*

brightness, *n.* éclat *m.*

brilliance, *n.* éclat *m.*

brilliant, *adj.* brillant.

brim, *n.* bord *m.*

brine, *n.* saumure *f.*

bring, *vb.* (thing) apporter; (person) amener; **(b. about)** amener, causer; **(b. up)** élever.

brink, *n.* bord *m.*

briny, *adj.* salé.

brisk, *adj.* vif *m.*, vive *f.*

brisket, *n.* (meat) poitrine *f.*

briskly, *adv.* vivement.

briskness, *n.* vivacité *f.*

bristle, *n.* soie *f.*

bristly, *adj.* hérissé (de), poilu.

British, *adj.* britannique.

British Empire, *n.* Empire Britannique *m.*

British Isles, *n.* Îles Britanniques *f.pl.*

brittle, *adj.* fragile.

broad, *adj.* large.

broadcast, 1. *vb.* diffuser. **2.** *n.* émission *f.*

broadcaster, *n.* speaker *m.*

broadcloth, *n.* drap *(m.)* fin.

broaden, *vb.* élargir.

broadly, *adv.* largement.

broadminded, *adj.* large d'esprit.

broadside, *n.* côte *f.,* bordée *f.*

brocade, *n.* brocart *m.*

brocaded, *adj.* de brocart.

broccoli, *n.* brocoli *m.*

brochure, *n.* brochure *f.*

broil, *vb.* griller.

broiler, *n.* gril *m.*

broke, *adj.* fauché.

broken-hearted, *adj.* qui a le coeur brisé.

broker, *n.* courtier *m.;* **(stock-b.)** agent *(m.)* de change.

brokerage, *n.* courtage *m.*

bronchial, *adj.* bronchique.

bronchitis, *n.* bronchite *f.*

bronze, *n.* bronze *m.*

brooch, *n.* broche *f.*

brood, 1. *n.* couvée *f.* **2.** *vb.* couver.

brook, *n.* ruisseau *m.*

broom, *n.* balai *m.*

broomstick, *n.* manche *(m.)* à balai.

broth, *n.* bouillon *m.*

brothel, *n.* bordel *m.,* maison mal famée *f.*

brother, *n.* frère *m.*

brotherhood, *n.* fraternité *f.*

brother-in-law, *n.* beau-frère *m.*

brotherly, *adj.* fraternel.

brow, *n.* front *m.*

browbeat, *vb.* intimider.

brown, *adj.* brun.

browse, *vb.* (animals) brouter; (books) feuilleter (des livres).

bruise, 1. *n.* meurtrissure *f.* **2.** *vb.* meurtrir.

bruised, *adj.* couvert de bleus.

brunette, *adj. and n.* brune *f.*

brunt, *n.* choc *m.*

brush, 1. *n.* brosse *f.;* **(paint-b.)** pinceau *m.* **2.** *vb.* brosser.

brushwood, *n.* broussailles *f.pl.*

brusque, *adj.* brusque.

brusquely, *adv.* brusquement.

Brussels, *n.* Bruxelles, *f.*

brutal, *adj.* brutal.

brutality, *n.* brutalité *f.*

brutalize, *vb.* abrutir.

brute, *n.* brute *f.*

bubble, 1. *n.* bulle *f.* **2.** *vb.* bouillonner.

buck, *n.* daim *m.;* (male) mâle *m.;* (colloquial) dollar *m.*

bucket, *n.* seau *m.*

buckle, *n.* boucle *f.*

buckram, *n.* bougran *m.*

buckshot, *n.* chevrotine *f.*

buckwheat, *n.* sarrasin *m.,* blé noir *m.*

bud, 1. *n.* bourgeon *m.* **2.** *vb.* bourgeonner.

budding, *adj.* en herbe.

buddy, *n.* copain *m.,* pote *m.*

budge, *vb.* bouger.

budget, *n.* budget *m.*

buffalo, *n.* buffle *m.*

buffer, *n.* tampon *m.;* (computer) mémoire *(f.)* tampon.

buffet, *n.* (sideboard) buffet *m.*

buffoon, *n.* bouffon *m.*

bug, 1. *n.* insecte *m.;* (computer) erreur *f.* **2.** *v.* embêter; mettre des micros dans.

bugle, *n.* clairon *m.*

build, *vb.* bâtir.

builder, *n.* (buildings) entrepreneur *m.;* (ships) constructeur *m.*

building, *n.* bâtiment *m.*

bulb, *n.* (electricity) ampoule *f.;* (botany) bulbe *m.*

Bulgaria, *n.* Bulgarie *f.*

bulge, *n.* bosse *f.*

bulimia, *n.* boulimie *f.*

bulk, *n.* masse *f.*

bulkhead, *n.* cloison étanche *f.*

bulky, *adj.* volumineux.

bull, *n.* taureau *m.*

bulldog, *n.* bouledogue *m.*

bulldozer, *n.* machine à refouler *f.*

bullet, *n.* balle *f.*

bulletin, *n.* bulletin *m.*

bulletproof, *adj.* à l'épreuve des balles.

bullfight, *n.* corrida *f.*

bullfighting, *n.* tauromachie *f.*

bullfinch, *n.* bouvreuil *m.*

bullion, *n.* lingot *m.*

bully, 1. *n.* brute *f.,* tyran *m.* **2.** *vb.* rudoyer.

bulwark, *n.* rempart *m.*

bum, *n.* fainéant *m.*

bumblebee, *n.* bourdon *m.*

bump, 1. *n.* (blow) coup *m.;* (protuberance) bosse *f.* **2.** *vb.* cogner.

bumper, *n.* (auto) pare-chocs *m.*

bumpy, *adj.* cahoteux.

bun, *n.* brioche *f.*

bunch, *n.* (flowers) bouquet *m.;* (grapes) grappe *f.;* (keys) trousseau *m.*

bundle, *n.* paquet *m.*

bungalow, *n.* bungalow *m.*

bungle, *vb.* bousiller.

bunion, *n.* cor *m.*

bunk, *n.* couchette *f.;* (colloquial) foutaises *f.pl.*

bunny, *n.* lapin *m.*

bunting, *n.* drapeaux *m.pl.*

buoy, *n.* bouée *f.*

buoyant, *adj.* qui a du ressort.

burden, *n.* fardeau *m.*

burdensome, *adj.* onéreux.

bureau, *n.* (office) bureau *m.;* (chest of drawers) commode *f.*

bureaucracy, *n.* bureaucratie *f.*

bureaucrat, *n.* bureaucrate *m.f.*

burglar, *n.* cambrioleur *m.*

burglarize, *vb.* cambrioler.

burglary, *n.* vol *(m.)* avec effraction, cambriolage.

Burgundy, *n.* Bourgogne *f.*

burial, *n.* enterrement *m.*

burlap, *n.* gros canevas *m.*

burly, *adj.* corpulent.
Burma, *n.* Birmanie *f.*
burn, *vb.* brûler.
burner, *n.* bec *m.*
burning, *adj.* brûlant.
burnish, *vb.* brunir, polir.
burp, *vb.* roter.
burrow, *n.* terrier *m.*
burst, *vb.* éclater.
bury, *vb.* enterrer.
bus, *n.* autobus *m.*
bush, *n.* buisson *m.;* (land) brousse *f.*
bushel, *n.* boisseau *m.*
bushy, *adj.* buissonneux; (hair) touffu.
busily, *adv.* activement.
business, *n.* affaire *f.;* (*comm.*) affaires *f.pl.*
businesslike, *adj.* pratique.
businessman, *n.* homme (*m.*) d'affaires.
businesswoman, *n.* femme (*f.*) d'affaires.
bust, *n.* buste *m.*
bustle, *vb.* se remuer.

busy, *adj.* occupé.
busybody, *n.* officieux *m.*
but, *conj.* mais; (only) ne . . . que; (except) sauf.
butane, *n.* butane *m.*
butcher, *n.* boucher *m.*
butchery, *n.* tuerie *f.*, massacre *m.*
butler, *n.* maître (*m.*) d'hôtel.
butt, *n.* bout *m.;* (of jokes) plastron *m.;* (of cigarette) mégot *m.;* (colloquial) derrière *m.*
butter, *n.* beurre *m.*
buttercup, *n.* bouton (*m.*) d'or.
butterfly, *n.* papillon *m.*
buttermilk, *n.* babeurre *m.*
butterscotch, *n.* caramel (*m.*) au beurre.
buttock, *n.* fesse *f.*
button, *n.* bouton *m.*
buttonhole, *n.* boutonnière *f.*
buttress, *n.* contrefort *m.;* (flying b.) arc-boutant *m.*

buxom, *adj.* (of women) aux formes rebondies.
buy, *vb.* acheter.
buyer, *n.* acheteur *m.*
buzz, 1. *n.* bourdonnement *m.* 2. *vb.* bourdonner.
buzzard, *n.* buse *f.*
buzzer, *n.* trompe *f.*, sirène *f.*
by, *prep.* (through) par; (near) près de.
by-and-by, *adv.* bientôt.
bye(-bye), *interj.* au revoir, salut.
bygone, *adj.* passé, d'autrefois.
bylaw, *n.* règlement local *m.*
by-pass, 1. *n.* route (*f.*) d'évitement. 2. *vb.* faire un détour.
by-product, *n.* sous-produit *m.*
bystander, *n.* spectateur *m.*
byte, *n.* unité fondamentale de données *f.;* octet *m.*
byway, *n.* sentier détourné *m.*

C

cab *n.* (taxi) taxi *m.;* (horse) fiacre *m.*
cabaret, *n.* cabaret *m.*
cabbage, *n.* chou *m.*
cabin, *n.* (hut) cabane *f.;* (boat) cabine *f.*
cabinet, *n.* cabinet *m.*
cabinetmaker, *n.* ébéniste *m.*
cable, 1. *n.* câble *m.* 2. *vb.* câbler.
cable car, *n.* téléphérique *m.*
cablegram, *n.* câblogramme *m.*
caboose, *n.* fourgon *m.*
cachet, *n.* cachet *m.*
cackle, 1. *n.* caquet *m.* 2. *vb.* caqueter.
cacophony, *n.* cacophonie *f.*
cactus, *n.* cactus *m.*
cad, *n.* mufle *m.*
cadaver, *n.* cadavre *m.*
cadaverous, *adj.* cadavérique.
cadence, *n.* cadence *f.*
cadet, *n.* cadet *m.*
cadmium, *n.* cadmium *m.*
cadre, *n.* cadre *m.*

Caesarean (section), *n.* césarienne *f.*
café, *n.* café, (-restaurant) *m.*
cafeteria, *n.* restaurant *m.*
caffeine, *n.* caféine *f.*
cage, *n.* cage *f.*
caged, *adj.* mis en cage.
cagey, *adj.* méfiant.
caisson, *n.* caisson *m.*
cajole, *vb.* cajoler.
cake, *n.* gâteau *m.*
calamitous, *adj.* calamiteux, désastreux.
calamity, *n.* calamité *f.*
calcify, *vb.* calcifier.
calcium, *n.* calcium *m.*
calculable, *adj.* calculable.
calculate, *vb.* calculer.
calculating, *adj.* qui fait des calculs.
calculation, *n.* calcul *m.*
calculator, *n.* calculatrice *f.*
calculus, *n.* calcul *m.*
caldron, *n.* chaudron *m.*
calendar, *n.* calendrier *m.*
calender, *n.* calandre *f.*
calf, *n.* veau *m.*

calfskin, *adj.* en peau de veau.
caliber, *n.* calibre *m.*
calico, *n.* calicot *m.*
calisthenic, *adj.* callisthénique.
calisthenics, *n.* callisthénie *f.*
calk, *vb.* ferrer à glace.
call, 1. *n.* appel *m.;* (visit) visite *f.* 2. *vb.* appeler; (c. on) faire visite à.
calligraphy, *n.* calligraphie *f.*
calling, *n.* vocation *f.*, profession *f.*
calling card, *n.* carte de visite *f.*
callously, *adv.* d'une manière insensible.
callousness, *n.* insensibilité *f.*
callow, *adj.* blanc-bec.
callus, *n.* callosité *f.*
calm, 1. *adj.* calme. 2. *vb.* calmer.
calmly, *adv.* calmement.
calmness, *n.* calme *m.*, tranquillité *f.*
caloric, *adj.* calorique.
calorie, *n.* calorie *f.*

calorimeter, *n.* calorimètre *m.*

calumniate, *vb.* calomnier.

calumny, *n.* calomnie *f.*

Calvary, *n.* Calvaire *m.*

calve, *vb.* vêler.

calyx, *n.* calice *m.*

camaraderie, *n.* camaraderie *f.*

Cambodia, *n.* Cambodge *m.*

cambric, *n.* batiste *f.*

camcorder, *n.* camescope *m.*

camel, *n.* chameau *m.*

camellia, *n.* camélia *m.*

camel's hair, *n.* poil *(m.)* de chameau.

cameo, *n.* camée *m.*

camera, *n.* appareil photographique *m.*

Cameroons, *n.* la République fédérale du Cameroun.

camouflage, *vb.* camoufler.

camouflaged, *adj.* camouflé.

camouflaging, *adj.* camouflant.

camp, 1. *n.* camp *m.;* (holiday camp) camping *m.* **2.** *vb.* camper.

campaign, *n.* campagne *f.*

camper, *n.* qui fait du camping; (vehicle) camping-car *m.*

camphor, *n.* camphre *m.*

camphor ball, *n.* balle *(f.)* de camphre.

campsite, *n.* (terrain *m.* de) camping.

campus, *n.* terrains *(m.pl.)* de l'université.

can, 1. *n.* (food) boîte *f.;* (general) bidon *m.* **2.** *vb.* (be able) pouvoir; (put in a can) conserver.

Canada, *n.* Canada *m.*

Canadian, 1. *n.* Canadien *m.* **2.** *adj.* canadien.

canal, *n.* canal *m.*

canalize, *vb.* canaliser.

canapé, *n.* canapé *m.*

canard, *n.* canard *m.*

canary, *n.* serin *m.*

Canary Islands, *n.* Îles Canaries *f.pl.*

cancel, *vb.* annuler; (erase) biffer.

cancellation, *n.* annulation *f.*

cancer, *n.* cancer *m.*

candelabrum, *n.* candélabre *m.*

candid, *adj.* sincère.

candidacy, *n.* candidature *f.*

candidate, *n.* candidat *m.*

candidly, *adv.* franchement.

candidness, *n.* candeur *f.*

candied, *adj.* candi.

candle, *n.* bougie *f.;* (church) cierge *m.*

candler, *n.* fabricant *(m.)* de chandelles.

candlestick, *n.* chandelier *m.*

candor, *n.* sincérité *f.*

candy, *n.* bonbon *m.*

cane, *n.* canne *f.*

canine, *adj.* canin.

canister, *n.* boîte à thé *f.*

canker, *n.* chancre *m.*

cankerworm, *n.* ver rongeur *m.*

canned, *adj.* conservé en boîtes (de fer blanc).

canner, *n.* travailleur dans une conserverie *m.*

cannery, *n.* conserverie *f.*

cannibal, *adj. and n.* cannibale *m.f.*

canning, *n.* mise en conserve, en boîtes (de fer blanc) *f.*

cannon, *n.* canon *m.*

cannonade, *n.* canonnade *f.*

cannoneer, *n.* canonier *m.*

cannot, *vb.* ne peut pas.

canny, *adj.* avisé, rusé.

canoe, *n.* canot *m.*

canon, *n.* chanoine *m.;* (rule) canon *m.*

canonical, *adj.* canonique.

canonize, *vb.* canoniser.

can opener, *n.* ouvre-boîte *m.*

canopy, *n.* dais *m.*

cant, *n.* hypocrisie *f.*

can't, *vb.* ne peut pas.

cantaloupe, *n.* melon *m.,* cantaloup *m.*

cantankerous, *adj.* grincheux.

canteen, *n.* cantine *f.;* bidon *m.*

canter, 1. *n.* petit galop *f.* **2.** *vb.* aller au petit galop.

cantonment, *n.* cantonnement *m.*

canvas, *n.* toile *f.*

canvass, 1. *n.* sollicitation *f.* **2.** *vb.* solliciter; (discuss) débattre.

canyon, *n.* gorge *f.,* défilé *m.*

cap, *n.* bonnet *m.;* (peaked) casquette *f.*

capability, *n.* capacité *f.*

capable, *adj.* capable.

capably, *adv.* capablement.

capacious, *adj.* ample, spacieux.

capacity, *n.* capacité *f.*

caparison, 1. *n.* caparaçon *m.* **2.** *vb.* caparaçonner.

cape, *n.* (geography) cap *m.;* (cloak) cape *f.*

caper, 1. *n.* bond *m.;* (plant) câpre *f.* **2.** *vb.* bondir.

capillary, *adj.* capillaire.

capital, 1. *n.* (finance) capital *m.;* (city) capitale *f.;* (letter) majuscule *f.;* (architecture) chapiteau *m.* **2.** *adj.* capital.

capitalism, *n.* capitalisme *m.*

capitalist, *n.* capitaliste *m.f.*

capitalistic, *adj.* capitaliste.

capitalization, *n.* capitalisation *f.*

capitalize, *vb.* capitaliser.

capitulate, *vb.* capituler.

capon, *n.* chapon *m.*

caprice, *n.* caprice *m.*

capricious, *adj.* capricieux.

capriciously, *adv.* capricieusement.

capriciousness, *n.* caractère capricieux *m.,* humeur fantasque *f.*

capsize, *vb.* chavirer, *intr.;* faire chavirer, *tr.*

capsule, *n.* capsule *f.*

captain, *n.* capitaine *m.*

caption, *n.* en-tête *m.*

captious, *adj.* chicaneur.

captivate, *vb.* captiver.

captivating, *adj.* séduisant.

captive, *adj. and n.* captif *m.*

captivity, *n.* captivité *f.*

captor, *n.* capteur *m.*

capture, 1. *n.* capture *f.* **2.** *vb.* capturer.

car, *n.* (auto) voiture *f.;* (train) wagon *m.*

caracul, *n.* caracul *m.*

carafe, *n.* carafe *f.*

caramel, *n.* caramel *m.*

carat, *n.* carat *m.*

caravan, n. caravane f.
caraway, n. carvi m., cumin (m.) (des prés).
carbide, n. carbure m.
carbine, n. carabine f.
carbohydrate, n. carbohydrate m.
carbon, n. carbone m.
carbon dioxide, n. acide carbonique m.
carbon monoxide, n. oxyde de carbone m.
carbon paper, n. papier carbone m.
carbuncle, n. escarboucle f., (med.) charbon m.
carburetor, n. carburateur m.
carcass, n. carcasse f.
carcinogenic, adj. cancérogène.
card, n. carte f.
cardboard, n. carton m.
cardiac, adj. cardiaque.
cardigan, n. gilet de tricot m.
cardinal, n. cardinal m.
care, 1. n. (worry) souci m.; (attention) attention f.; (take c.!) faites attention!; (charge) soin m.; (take c. of) prendre soin de. 2. vb. (c. about) se soucier de; (c. for) aimer; (look after) soigner.
careen, vb. caréner.
career, n. carrière f.
carefree, adj. insouciant.
careful, adj. soigneux.
carefully, adv. soigneusement, attentivement.
carefulness, n. soin m., attention f.
careless, adj. insouciant.
carelessly, adv. nonchalamment, négligemment.
carelessness, n. insouciance f., négligence f.
caress, 1. n. caresse f. 2. vb. caresser.
caretaker, n. concierge m.f.
cargo, n. cargaison f.
Caribbean, n. the C. (sea) la mer des Caraïbes; the C. (islands) les Antilles.
caricature, n. caricature f.
caries, n. carie f.
carillon, n. carillon m.
carload, n. voiturée f.
carnage, n. carnage m.

carnal, adj. charnel.
carnation, n. œillet m.
carnival, n. carnaval m.
carnivorous, adj. carnivore.
carol, n. (Xmas c.) noël m.
carouse, vb. faire la fête.
carousel, n. carrousel m.
carpenter, n. charpentier m.
carpet, n. tapis m.
carpeting, n. pose de tapis f.
car pool, n. groupe (m.) de personnes qui voyagent régulièrement ensemble en auto.
carriage, n. (vehicle) voiture f.; (bearing) maintien m.; (transport) transport m.
carrier, n. porteur m., messager m.
carrier pigeon, n. pigeon voyageur m.
carrot, n. carotte f.
carry, vb. porter; (c. on) continuer; (c. out) exécuter; (c. through) mener à bonne fin.
cart, n. charrette f.
cartage, n. charriage m., transport m.
cartel, n. cartel m.
carter, n. charretier m.
cartilage, n. cartilage m.
carton, n. carton m.
cartoon, n. dessin satirique m., (cinema) dessin (m.) animé.
cartoonist, n. caricaturiste m.
cartridge, n. cartouche f.
carve, vb. (art) sculpter; (meat) découper.
carver, n. découpeur m., sculpteur m.
carving, n. découpage m., sculpture f.
cascade, n. cascade f.
case, n. (instance, state of things) cas m.; (law) cause f.; (packing) caisse f.; (holder) étui m.; (in any c.) en tout cas.
cash, 1. n. espèces f.pl.; (C.O.D.) livraison (f.) contre remboursement. 2. vb. (c. a check) toucher.
cashew, n. noix (f.) de cajou.
cashier, n. caissier m.
cashmere, n. cachemire m.
cash register, n. caisse f.

casing, n. revêtement m., enveloppe f.
casino, n. casino m.
cask, n. tonneau m.
casket, n. cassette f.
casserole, n. casserole f.
cassette, n. cassette f.
cast, 1. n. (throw) coup m.; (characteristic) trempe f.; (theater) distribution f.; (c. from mold) moulage m.; (hue) nuance f.; (med.) plâtre m. 2. vb. (throw) jeter; (metal) couler.
castaway, n. naufragé m.; rejeté m.
caste, n. caste f.
caster, n. fondeur m.
castigate, vb. châtier, punir.
cast iron, n. fonte f.
castle, n. château m.
castoff, adj. abandonné.
castrate, vb. châtrer.
casual, adj. (accidental) casuel; (person) insouciant.
casually, adv. fortuitement, en passant.
casualness, n. nonchalance f.
casualties, n. (mil.) pertes f.pl.
cat, n. chat m., chatte f.
cataclysm, n. cataclysme m.
catacomb, n. catacombe f.
catalogue, n. catalogue m.
catalyst, n. catalyseur m.
catapult, n. catapulte f.
cataract, n. cataracte f.
catarrh, n. catarrhe m.
catastrophe, n. catastrophe f.
catch, vb. attraper; (seize, understand) saisir; (c. up) se rattraper.
catcher, n. qui attrape.
catchword, n. mot d'ordre m.
catchy, adj. (musical air) facile à retenir; (question) insidieuse.
catechism, n. catéchisme m.
catechize, vb. catéchiser.
categorical, adj. catégorique.
category, n. catégorie f.
cater, vb. pourvoir à.
caterpillar, n. chenille f.
catgut, n. corde (f.) à boyau.
catharsis, n. catharsis f., (med.) purgation f.

cathartic, *adj.* cathartique, purgatif.

cathedral, *n.* cathédrale *f.*

cathode, *n.* cathode *f.*

Catholic, *adj.* catholique.

Catholic Church, *n.* Église catholique *f.*

Catholicism, *n.* catholicisme *m.*

cat nap, *n.* somme *m.*

catsup, *n.* sauce piquante *f.*

cattle, *n.* bétail *m.*, bestiaux *m.pl.*

cattleman, *n.* éleveur de bétail *m.*

catty, *adj.* méchant.

catwalk, *n.* coursive *f.*

caucus, *n.* comité *(m.)* local ou electoral.

cauliflower, *n.* chou-fleur *m.*

causation, *n.* causation *f.*

cause, *n.* cause *f.*

causeway, *n.* chaussée *f.*

caustic, *adj.* caustique.

cauterize, *vb.* cautériser.

cautery, *n.* cautère *f.*

caution, 1. *n.* prudence *f.* **2.** *vb.* avertir.

cautious, *adj.* prudent.

cavalcade, *n.* cavalcade *f.*

cavalier, *adj. and n.* cavalier *m.*

cavalry, *n.* cavalerie *f.*

cave, *n.* caverne *f.*

cave-in, *n.* effondrement *m.*

cavern, *n.* caverne *f.*

caviar, *n.* caviar *m.*

cavity, *n.* cavité *f.*

cavort, *vb.* cabrioler.

CD, *n.* compact disc *m.*

cease, *vb.* cesser (de).

ceaseless, *adj.* incessant, continuel.

cedar, *n.* cèdre *m.*

cede, *vb.* céder.

cedilla, *n.* cédille *f.*

ceiling, *n.* plafond *m.*

celebrant, *n.* célébrant *m.*

celebrate, *vb.* célébrer.

celebration, *n.* célébration *f.*

celebrity, *n.* célébrité *f.*

celerity, *n.* célérité *f.*, vitesse *f.*

celery, *n.* céleri *m.*

celestial, *adj.* céleste.

celibacy, *n.* célibat *m.*

celibate, *adj.* célibataire.

cell, *n.* cellule *f.*

cellar, *n.* cave *f.*

cellist, *n.* violoncelliste *m.f.*

cello, *n.* violoncelle *m.*

cellophane, *n.* cellophane *f.*

cellular, *adj.* cellulaire.

celluloid, *n.* celluloïd *m.*

cellulose, *n.* cellulose *f.*

Celtic, *adj.* celtique.

cement, 1. *n.* ciment *m.* **2.** *vb.* cimenter.

cemetery, *n.* cimetière *m.*

censor, 1. *n.* censeur *m.* **2.** *vb.* censurer.

censorious, *adj.* critique, hargneux.

censorship, *n.* censure *f.*

censure, *n.* censure *f.*

census, *n.* recensement *m.*

cent, *n.* cent *m.;* **(per c.)** pour cent.

centenary, centennial, *adj. and n.* centenaire *m.*

center, *n.* centre *m.*

centerfold, *n.* pages centrales *f.pl.*

centerpiece, *n.* pièce de milieu *f.*

centigrade, *adj.* centigrade.

centigrade thermometer, *n.* thermomètre centigrade *m.*

centipede, *n.* mille-pattes *m.*

central, *adj.* central.

Central America, *n.* Amérique *(f.)* Centrale.

central heating, *n.* chauffage *(m.)* central.

centralize, *vb.* centraliser.

century, *n.* siècle *m.*

century plant, *n.* agave *(m.)* d'Amérique.

ceramic, *adj.* céramique.

ceramics, *n.* céramique *f.*

cereal, *adj. and n.* céréale *f.*

cerebral, *adj.* cérébral.

ceremonial, *adj. and n.* cérémonial *m.*

ceremonious, *adj.* cérémonieux.

ceremony, *n.* cérémonie *f.*

certain, *adj.* certain.

certainly, *adv.* certainement.

certainty, *n.* certitude *f.*

certificate, *n.* certificat *m.;* **(birth c.)** acte *(m.)* de naissance.

certification, *n.* certification *f.*

certified, *adj.* certifié, diplômé, breveté.

certifier, *n.* (personne) qui certifie.

certify, *vb.* certifier.

certitude, *n.* certitude *f.*

cervical, *adj.* cervical.

cervix, *n.* col (de l'utérus) *m.*

cessation, *n.* cessation *f.*, suspension *f.*

cession, *n.* cession *f.*

cesspool, *n.* fosse *(f.)* d'aisances.

Chad, *n.* Tchad *m.*

chafe, *vb.* frictionner.

chaff, 1. *n.* menue paille *f.;* (colloquial) blague *f.* **2.** *vb.* blaguer.

chafing dish, *n.* réchaud *m.*

chagrin, *n.* chagrin *m.*

chain, *n.* chaîne *f.*

chain reaction, *n.* réaction caténaire *f.*

chain store, *n.* succursale *(f.)* de grand magasin.

chair, *n.* chaise *f.;* **(arm-c.)** fauteuil *m.*

chairman, *n.* président *m.*

chairmanship, *n.* présidence *f.*

chairperson, *n.* président *m.*, présidente *f.*

chairwoman, *n.* présidente *f.*

chalice, *n.* calice *m.*

chalk, *n.* craie *f.*

chalky, *adj.* de craie, calcaire.

challenge, 1. *n.* défi *m.* **2.** *vb.* défier; (dispute) contester.

challenger, *n.* qui fait un défi, prétendant *m.*

chamber, *n.* chambre *f.*

chamberlain, *n.* chambellan *m.*

chambermaid, *n.* femme de chambre *f.*

chamber music, *n.* musique de chambre *f.*

chameleon, *n.* caméléon *m.*

chamois, *n.* chamois *m.*

champ, *vb.* ronger, mâcher.

champagne, *n.* champagne *m.*

champion, *n.* champion *m.*

championship, *n.* championnat *m.*

chance, *n.* chance *f.;* **(by c.)** par hasard; **(take a c.)** prendre un risque.

chancel, *n.* sanctuaire *m.,* choeur *m.*

chancellery, *n.* chancellerie *f.*

chancellor, *n.* chancelier *m.*

chancy, *adj.* risqué.

chandelier, *n.* lustre *m.*

change, 1. *n.* changement *m.;* (money) monnaie *f.;* (exchange) change *m.* **2.** *vb.* changer.

changeability, *n.* variabilité *f.*

changeable, *adj.* changeant.

changer, *n.* changeur *m.*

channel, *n.* canal *m.;* **(the English C.)** la Manche *f.;* (television) chaîne *f.*

chant, 1. *n.* chant *m.* **2.** *vb.* chanter.

chaos, *n.* chaos *m.*

chaotic, *adj.* chaotique.

chap, *n.* (on skin) gerçure *f.;* (young man) gars *m.*

chapel, *n.* chapelle *f.*

chaperon, *n.* (person) duègne *f.,* chaperon *m.*

chaplain, *n.* aumônier *m.*

chapman, *n.* colporteur *m.*

chapped, *adj.* gercé.

chapter, *n.* chapitre *m.*

char, *vb.* carboniser.

character, *n.* caractère *m.;* (in fiction) personnage *m.;* (role) rôle *m.*

characteristic, 1. *n.* trait caractéristique *m.* **2.** *adj.* caractéristique.

characteristically, *adv.* d'une manière caractéristique.

characterization, *n.* action de caractériser *f.*

characterize, *vb.* caractériser.

charcoal, *n.* charbon *(m.)* de bois.

charge, 1. *n.* (guns, legal, office) charge *f.;* (price) prix *m.;* (care) soin *m.* **2.** *vb.* charger; **(c. with)** charger de; (price) demander.

charger, *n.* grand plat *m.;* cheval de bataille *m.*

chariot, *n.* char *m.,* chariot *m.*

charioteer, *n.* conducteur de chariot *m.*

charisma, *n.* charisme *m.*

charitable, *adj.* charitable.

charitableness, *n.* bienveillance *f.*

charitably, *adv.* charitablement.

charity, *n.* charité *f.*

charlatan, *n.* charlatan *m.*

charlatanism, *n.* charlatanisme *m.*

charm, 1. *n.* charme *m.* **2.** *vb.* charmer.

charmer, *n.* charmeur *m.,* enchanteur *m.*

charming, *adj.* charmant.

charred, *adj.* carbonisé.

chart, *n.* (map) carte *f.;* (graph) graphique *m.*

charter, 1. *n.* charte *f.* **2.** *vb.* (boat) affréter.

charter flight, *n.* vol frété *m.;* charter *m.*

charwoman, *n.* femme *(f.)* de journée; femme *(f.)* de ménage.

chase, 1. *n.* chasse *f.* **2.** *vb.* chasser.

chaser, *n.* chasseur *m.;* ciseleur *m.*

chasm, *n.* abîme *m.*

chassis, *n.* chassis *m.*

chaste, *adj.* chaste.

chasten, *vb.* châtier, corriger.

chasteness, *n.* pureté *f.*

chastise, *vb.* châtier.

chastisement, *n.* châtiment *m.*

chastity, *n.* chasteté *f.*

chat, 1. *n.* causette *f.* **2.** *vb.* causer.

chateau, *n.* château *m.*

chattel, *n.* bien *m.,* meuble *m.*

chatter, 1. *n.* bavardage *m.* **2.** *vb.* bavarder.

chatterbox, *n.* bavard *m.*

chatty, *adj.* bavard.

chauffeur, *n.* chauffeur *m.*

chauvinist, *adj.* (male) phallocrate; (nationalist) chauvin *m.*

cheap, *adj.* (inexpensive) bon marché; (mean) de peu de valeur.

cheapen, *vb.* déprécier.

cheaply, *adv.* à bon marché.

cheapness, *n.* bon marché *m.,* bas prix *m.;* basse qualité *f.*

cheat, *vb.* tromper; (at games) tricher.

cheater, *n.* tricheur *m.,* trompeur *m.*

check, 1. *n.* (restraint) frein *m.;* (verification) vérification *f.;* (stub) ticket *m.;* (bill) addition *f.;* (bank draft) chèque *m.* **2.** *vb.* (stop) arrêter; (restrain) modérer; (verify) vérifier; (luggage) enregistrer.

checker, *n.* enregistreur *m.,* contrôleur *m.*

checkbook, *n.* chéquier *m.,* carnet *(m.)* de chèques.

checkers, *n.* jeu de dames *m.*

checkmate, 1. *n.* échec et mat *m.* **2.** *vb.* mater.

checkroom, *n.* vestiaire *m.*

cheek, *n.* joue *f.*

cheer, 1. *n.* (applause) hourra *m.* **2.** *vb.* (acclaim) acclamer; **(c. up,** *tr.*) réjouir.

cheerful, *adj.* gai.

cheerfully, *adv.* gaiement, de bon cœur.

cheerfulness, *n.* gaieté *f.,* bonne humeur *f.*

cheerless, *adj.* triste, morne, sombre.

cheery, *adj.* gai, joyeux.

cheese, *n.* fromage *m.*

cheesecloth, *n.* gaze *f.*

cheesy, *adj.* fromageux.

cheetah, *n.* guépard *m.*

chef, *n.* chef *m.*

chemical, *adj.* chimique.

chemically, *adv.* chimiquement.

chemist, *n.* chimiste *m.f.*

chemistry, *n.* chimie *f.*

chemotherapy, *n.* chimiothérapie *f.*

chenille, *n.* chenille *f.*

cherish, *vb.* chérir.

cherry, *n.* cerise *f.*

cherub, *n.* chérubin *m.*

chess, *n.* échecs *m.pl.*

chessman, *n.* pièce *f.*

chest, *n.* (box) coffre *m.;* (body) poitrine *f.;* **(c. of drawers)** commode *f.*

chestnut, *n.* châtaigne *f.*

chevron, *n.* chevron *m.*

chew, vb. mâcher.

chewer, n. mâcheur m.

chic, adj. chic, élégant, smart.

chicanery, n. chicane f., chicanerie f.

chick, n. poussin m.

chicken, n. poulet m.

chicken-hearted, adj. peureux.

chicken-pox, n. varicelle f.

chickpea, n. pois (m.) chiche.

chicle, n. chiclé m.

chicory, n. chicorée f.

chide, vb. gronder, réprimander.

chief, 1. n. chef m. 2. adj. principal; (c. executive) directeur général.

chiefly, adv. surtout, principalement.

chieftain, n. chef de clan m.

chiffon, n. chiffon m.

chilblain, n. engelure f.

child, n. enfant m.f.

childbirth, n. enfantement m.; accouchement m.

childhood, n. enfance f.

childish, adj. enfantin.

childishness, n. puérilité f., enfantillage m.

childless, adj. sans enfant.

childlessness, n. l'état d'être sans enfants.

childlike, adj. comme un enfant, en enfant.

Chile, n. Chili m.

Chilean, 1. n. Chilien m. 2. adj. chilien.

chili, n. piment m.

chill, 1. n. froid m.; (shiver) frisson m. 2. vb. refroidir.

chilliness, n. froid m., frisson m.

chilly, adj. un peu froid.

chime, 1. n. carillon m. 2. vb. carillonner.

chimney, n. cheminée f.

chimney sweep, n. ramoneur m.

chimpanzee, n. chimpanzé m.

chin, n. menton m.

China, n. Chine f.

china, n. (ware) porcelaine f.

chinchilla, n. chinchilla m.

Chinese, 1. n. (person) Chinois m.; (language) chinois m. 2. adj. chinois.

chink, n. fente f., crevasse f.

chintz, n. perse f.

chip, 1. n.. éclat m.; (potato c.s) chips m.pl. 2. vb. ébrecher.

chipmunk, n. tamias m.

chiropractor, n. chiropracteur m.

chirp, vb. pépier, gazouiller.

chisel, 1. vb. ciseler. 2. n. ciseau m.

chitchat, n. bavardage m.

chivalrous, adj. chevaleresque.

chivalry, n. chevalerie f.

chive, n. ciboulette f.

chloride, n. chlorure m.

chlorine, n. chlore m.

chloroform, n. chloroforme m.

chlorophyll, n. chlorophylle m.

chockfull, adj. plein comme un œuf.

chocolate, n. chocolat m.

choice, n. choix m.

choir, n. chœur m.

choke, vb. étouffer.

choker, n. foulard m.

cholera, n. choléra m.

choleric, adj. cholérique.

cholesterol, n. cholestérol m.

choose, vb. choisir.

choosy, adj. exigeant.

chop, 1. n. (meat) côtelette f. 2. vb. couper.

chopper, n. couperet m.

choppy, adj. (sea) clapoteux.

chopstick, n. baguette f., bâtonnet m.

choral, adj. choral.

chord, n. (music) accord m.

chore, n. travail (m.) de ménage.

choreography, n. choréographie f.

chorister, n. choriste m., enfant de chœur m.

chortle, vb. glousser de joie.

chorus, n. chœur m.; (of song) refrain m.

chowder, n. (sorte de) bouillabaisse f.

Christ, n. le Christ m.

christen, vb. baptiser.

Christendom, n. chrétienté f.

christening, n. baptême m.

Christian, 1. n. Chrétian m. 2. adj. chrétien.

Christianity, n. christianisme m.

Christmas, n. Noël m.; (C. Day) jour (m.) de Noël; (C. Eve) veille (f.) de Noël; (C. tree) sapin (m.) de Noël.

chromatic, adj. chromatique.

chromium, n. chrome m.

chromosome, n. chromosome m.

chronic, adj. chronique.

chronically, adv. d'une manière chronique.

chronicle, n. chronique f.

chronological, adj. chronologique.

chronologically, adv. chronologiquement.

chronology, n. chronologie f.

chrysalis, n. chrysalide f.

chrysanthemum, n. chrysanthème m.

chubby, adj. joufflu.

chuck, n. petite tape f., gloussement (de volaille) m.

chuckle, vb. rire tout bas.

chug, 1. n. souffle m. (d'une machine à vapeur). 2. vb. souffler.

chum, n. camarade m., copain m.

chummy, adj. familier, intime.

chunk, n. gros morceau m.

chunky, adj. en gros morceaux.

church, n. église f.

churchman, n. homme (m.) d'église, ecclésiastique m.

churchyard, n. cimetière m.

churn, vb. baratter.

chute, n. glissière f.

chutney, n. chutney m.

cicada, n. cigale f.

cider, n. cidre m.

cigar, n. cigare m.

cigarette, n. cigarette f.

cilia, n. cils m.pl.

ciliary, adj. ciliaire.

cinch, n. (it's a c.) c'est facile.

cinchona, *n.* quinquina *m.*

cinder, *n.* cendre *f.*

Cinderella, *n.* Cendrillon *f.*

cinema, *n.* cinéma *m.*

cinematic, *adj.* cinématographique.

cinnamon, *n.* cannelle *f.*

cipher, *n.* chiffre *m.;* (nought) zéro *m.*

circle, 1. *n.* cercle *m.* **2.** *vb.* entourer (de).

circuit, *n.* circuit *m.*

circuitous, *adj.* détourné, sinueux.

circuitously, *adv.* d'une manière détournée, par des détours.

circular, *adj.* circulaire.

circularize, *vb.* envoyer des circulaires.

circulate, *vb.* circuler, *intr.;* faire circuler, *tr.*

circulation, *n.* circulation *f.;* (newspaper) tirage *m.*

circulator, *n.* circulateur *m.*

circulatory, *adj.* circulaire, circulatoire.

circumcise, *vb.* circoncire.

circumcision, *n.* circoncision *f.*

circumference, *n.* circonférence *f.*

circumflex, *n.* accent *(m.)* circonflexe.

circumlocution, *n.* circonlocution *f.*

circumscribe, *vb.* circonscrire.

circumspect, *adj.* circonspect.

circumstance, *n.* (condition) circonstance *f.;* (financial) moyens *m.pl.*

circumstantial, *adj.* circonstancié.

circumstantially, *adv.* en détail.

circumvent, *vb.* circonvenir.

circumvention, *n.* circonvention *f.*

circus, *n.* cirque *m.*

cirrhosis, *n.* cirrhose *f.*

cistern, *n.* citerne *f.*

citadel, *n.* citadelle *f.*

citation, *n.* citation *f.*

cite, *vb.* citer.

citizen, *n.* citoyen *m.*

citizenry, *n.* tous les citoyens *m.pl.*

citizenship, *n.* droit *(m.)* de cité.

citric acid, *n.* acide citrique *m.*

citrus fruit, *n.* agrume *m.*

city, *n.* ville *f.;* cité *f.*

city hall, *n.* hôtel *(m.)* de ville.

city planning, *n.* urbanisme.

civic, *adj.* civique.

civics, *n.* instruction *(f.)* civique.

civil, *adj.* civil; (polite) poli; (**c. servant**) fonctionnaire *m.*

civilian, *n.* civil *m.*

civility, *n.* civilité *f.*, politesse *f.*

civilization, *n.* civilisation *f.*

civilize, *vb.* civiliser.

civilized, *adj.* civilisé.

civil rights, *n.* droits *(m.pl.)* de l'homme.

civil servant, *n.* fonctionnaire *m.*

civil service, *n.* administration (civile) *f.*

civil war, *n.* guerre civile *f.*

clad, *adj.* habillé, vêtu.

claim, 1. *n.* (demand) demande *f.;* (right) droit *m.* **2.** *vb.* (demand) réclamer, prétendre; (insist) soutenir.

claimant, *n.* réclamateur *m.*, prétendant *m.*

clairvoyance, *n.* clairvoyance *f.*

clairvoyant, *n.* voyant *m.*

clam, *n.* palourde *f.*, mollusque *m.*

clamber, *vb.* grimper.

clammy, *adj.* visqueux, moite.

clamor, *n.* clameur *f.*

clamorous, *adj.* bruyant.

clamp, 1. *n.* (metal) crampon *m.;* (carpentry) serre-joint *m.* **2.** *vb.* cramponner, serrer.

clan, *n.* clan *m.*, clique *f.*, coterie *f.*

clandestine, *adj.* clandestin.

clandestinely, *adv.* clandestinement.

clang, 1. *n.* cliquetis *m.*, son métallique *m.* **2.** *vb.* résonner.

clangor, *n.* cliquetis *m.*

clannish, *adj.* de clan.

clap, *vb.* (applaud) applaudir.

clapboard, *n.* bardeau *m.*

clapper, *n.* claqueur *m.*, battant (of a bell) *m.*

claque, *n.* claque *f.*

claret, *n.* vin rouge *(m.)* de Bordeaux.

clarification, *n.* clarification *f.*

clarify, *vb.* (*lit.*) clarifier; (*fig.*) éclaircir.

clarinet, *n.* clarinette *f.*

clarinetist, *n.* clarinettiste *m.f.*

clarion, *n.* clairon *m.*

clarity, *n.* clarté *f.*

clash, 1. *vb.* choquer, *tr.;* s'entre-choquer, *intr.* **2.** *n.* choc *m.*

clasp, 1. *n.* agrafe *f.;* (embrace) étreinte *f.* **2.** *vb.* agrafer, étreindre.

class, *n.* classe *f.*

classic, classical, *adj.* classique.

classicism, *n.* classicisme *m.*

classifiable, *adj.* classifiable.

classification, *n.* classification *f.*

classified, *adj.* (information) secret.

classified ad, *n.* petite annonce *f.*

classify, *vb.* classifier, classer.

classmate, *n.* camarade *(m.)* de classe.

classroom, *n.* salle *(f.)* de classe.

clatter, *n.* bruit *m.*

clause, *n.* clause *f.*

claustrophobia, *n.* claustrophobie *f.*

claw, *n.* griffe *f.*

claw-hammer, *n.* marteau à dent *m.*

clay, *n.* argile *f.*, glaise *f.*

clean, 1. *adj.* propre. **2.** *vb.* nettoyer.

clean-cut, *adj.* net, fin.

cleaner, *n.* (**dry-c.**) teinturier *m.*

cleaning, *n.* nettoyage *m.*

cleanliness, cleanness, *n.* propreté *f.*

cleanse, *vb.* nettoyer, curer.

cleanser, *n.* chose qui nettoie *f.*, détersif *m.*; cureur *m.*

clear, 1. *adj.* clair. **2.** *vb.* **(c. up)** déblayer; (profit) gagner; (get over) franchir; (weather, *intr.*) s'éclaircir.

clearance sale, *n.* vente *f.*, liquidation *f.*

clear-cut, *adj.* nettement dessiné.

clearing, *n.* (open place) clairière *f.*, éclaircissement *m.*, *(comm.)* acquittement *m.*, (woods) éclaircie *f.*

clearing house, *n.* banque de virement *f.*, chambre de compensation *f.*

clearly, *adv.* clairement, nettement, évidemment.

clearness, *n.* clarté *f.*, netteté *f.*

cleat, *n.* fer *m.*, *(naut.)* taquet *m.*

cleavage, *n.* fendage *m.*, scission *f.*

cleave, *vb.* (split) fendre; (adhere) adhérer.

cleaver, *n.* fendeur (person) *m.*; fendoir *m.*, couperet (instrument) *m.*

cleft, *n.* fente *f.*

clemency, *n.* clémence *f.*

clench, *vb.* serrer.

clergy, *n.* clergé *m.*

clergyman, *n.* ecclésiastique *m.*

clerical, *adj.* (clergy) clérical; (business) de bureau.

clericalism, *n.* cléricalisme *m.*

clerk, *n.* (business) employé *m.*; (store) commis *m.*; (law, *eccles.*) clerc *m.*

clerkship, *n.* place de clerc *f.*, place de commis *f.*

clever, *adj.* habile.

cleverly, *adv.* habilement.

cleverness, *n.* adresse *f.*

clew, *n.* fil *m.*

cliché, *n.* cliché *m.*

click, 1. *n.* cliquetis *m.*, déclic *m.*; (computer)

clic *m.* **2.** *vb.* cliqueter; (computer) clicquer.

client, *n.* client *m.*

clientele, *n.* clientèle *f.*

cliff, *n.* falaise *f.*

climactic, *adj.* arrivé à son apogée.

climate, *n.* climat *m.*

climatic, *adj.* climatique.

climax, *n.* comble *m.*

climb, 1. *n.* montée *f.* **2.** *vb.* monter, grimper.

climber, *n.* grimpeur *m.*, ascensioniste *m.*

clinch, *vb.* river; (settle) conclure.

cling, *vb.* s'accrocher.

clinging, *adj.* qui se cramponne, qui s'accroche (à).

clinic, *n.* clinique *f.*

clinical, *adj.* clinique.

clinically, *adv.* d'une manière clinique.

clink, *vb.* tinter, cliqueter.

clip, 1. *vb.* couper. **2.** *n.* pince *f.*; (paper c.) trombone *m.*

clipper, *n.* rogneur *m.*, tondeuse (instrument) *f.*, *(naut.)* fin voilier *m.*

clipping, *n.* coupure *f.*

clique, *n.* clique *f.*

cloak, *n.* manteau *m.*; (c. room) vestiaire *m.*

clobber, *vb.* rosser.

clock, *n.* horloge *f.*; (two o'c.) deux heures.

clockwise, *adv.* dans le sens des aiguilles d'une montre.

clockwork, *n.* mouvement *(m.)* d'horlogerie.

clod, *n.* motte *(f.)* de terre; (person) lourdaud *m.*

clog, 1. *vb.* entraver. **2.** *n.* sabot *m.*

cloister, *n.* cloître *m.*

clone, *n.* reproduction exacte *f.*

close, 1. *adj.* (closed) fermé; (narrow) étroit; (near) proche; (secret) réservé. **2.** *vb.* fermer. **3.** *adv.* tout près. **4.** *prep.* (c. to) près de.

closely, *adv.* de près, étroitement.

closeness, *n.* proximité *f.*, lourdeur (of weather) *f.*, réserve *f.*

closet, *n.* (room) cabinet *m.*; (clothes) placard *m.*

close-up, *n.* gros plan *m.*

closure, *n.* fermeture *f.*

clot, *n.* (blood) caillot *m.*

cloth, *n.* étoffe *f.*

clothe, *vb.* vêtir (de); habiller.

clothes, *n.* habits *m.pl.*

clothes hanger, *n.* cintre *m.*

clothespin, *n.* pince *f.*

clothier, *n.* drapier *m.*, tailleur *m.*

clothing, *n.* vêtements *m.pl.*

cloud, *n.* nuage *m.*

cloudburst, *n.* trombe *f.*, rafale (f.) de pluie.

cloudiness, *n.* état nuageux *m.*, obscurité *f.*

cloudless, *adj.* sans nuage.

cloudy, *adj.* nuageux, couvert.

clout, 1. *n.* gifle *f.*, tape *f.*; (power) pouvoir *f.* **2.** *vb.* gifler, taper.

clove, *n.* clou *(m.)* de girofle; (c. of garlic) gousse *(f.)* d'ail.

clover, *n.* trèfle *m.*

clown, *n.* bouffon *m.*

clownish, *adj.* rustre, grossier, de paysan.

cloy, *vb.* rassasier.

cloying, *adj.* écœurant.

club, 1. *n.* (society) club *m.*, société *f.*, cercle *m.*; (stick) massue *f.*; (golf) crosse *f.*; (cards) trèfle *m.* **2.** *vb.* matraquer.

clubfoot, *n.* pied bot *m.*

clue, *n.* fil *m.*

clump, *n.* (trees) bosquet *m.*; massif *m.*

clumsiness, *n.* gaucherie *f.*, maladresse *f.*

clumsy, *adj.* gauche.

cluster, 1. *n.* (people) groupe *m.*; (fruit) grappe *f.*; (flowers, trees) bouquet *m.* **2.** *vb.* se grouper.

clutch, 1. *n.* (claw) griffe *f.*; (auto) embrayage *m.* **2.** *vb.* saisir.

clutter, 1. *vb.* encombrer. **2.** *n.* désordre *m.*

coach, 1. *n.* (carriage) carrosse *m.;* (train) wagon *m.;* (sports) entraîneur *m.* **2.** *vb.* (sports) entraîner; (school) donner des leçons particulières à.

coachman, *n.* cocher *m.*

coagulate, *vb.* se coaguler.

coagulation, *n.* coagulation *f.*

coal, *n.* charbon *(m.)* de terre, houille *f.*

coalesce, *vb.* se fondre, se fusionner, s'unir.

coalition, *n.* coalition *f.*

coal tar, *n.* goudron *(m.)* de houille.

coarse, *adj.* grossier.

coarsen, *vb.* rendre plus grossier.

coarseness, *n.* grossièreté *f.*

coast, 1. *n.* côte *f.* **2.** *vb.* (bicycle) descendre en roue libre.

coastal, *adj.* de la côte, littoral.

coaster, *n.* caboteur *m.,* dessous de carafe *m.*

coast guard, *n.* garde-côtes *m.*

coastline, *n.* littoral *m.*

coat, 1. *n.* (man) pardessus *m.;* (woman) manteau *m.;* (paint) couche *f.* **2.** *vb.* (c. with) revêtir de.

coating, *n.* couche *f.,* enduit *m.,* étoffe pour habits *f.*

coat of arms, *n.* écusson *m.*

coax, *vb.* cajoler.

cob, *n.* épi *m.*

cobalt, *n.* cobalt *m.*

cobbler, *n.* savetier *m.,* cordonnier *m.*

cobblestone, *n.* pavé *m.*

cobra, *n.* cobra *m.*

cobweb, *n.* toile *(f.)* d'araignée.

cocaine, *n.* cocaïne *f.*

cock, 1. *n.* (fowl) coq *m.;* (male) mâle *m.* **2.** *vb.* faire de l'œil.

cocker spaniel, *n.* épagneul cocker *m.*

cockeyed, *adj.* louche.

cockhorse, *n.* dada *m.*

cockpit, *n.* poste *(m.)* de pilotage.

cockroach, *n.* blatte *f.,* cafard *m.*

cocksure, *adj.* sûr et certain.

cocktail, *n.* cocktail *m.;* **(fruit c.)** macédoine *f.* (de fruits).

cocky, *adj.* suffisant.

cocoa, *n.* cacao *m.*

coconut, *n.* noix *(f.)* de coco.

cocoon, *n.* cocon *m.*

cod, *n.* morue *f.*

coddle, *vb.* dorloter.

code, *n.* code *m.*

codeine, *n.* codéine *f.*

codfish, *n.* morue *f.*

codify, *vb.* codifier.

cod-liver oil, *n.* huile *(f.)* de foie de morue.

coeducation, *n.* enseignement mixte *m.*

coequal, *adj.* égal.

coerce, *vb.* contraindre.

coercion, *n.* coercition *f.,* contrainte *f.*

coercive, *adj.* coercitif.

coexist, *vb.* coexister.

coffee, *n.* café *m.*

coffee break, *n.* pause-café *f.*

coffee pot, *n.* cafetière *f.*

coffee shop, *n.* cafétéria *f.*

coffee table, *n.* table *(f.)* basse.

coffer, *n.* coffre *m.*

coffin, *n.* cercueil *m.*

cog, *n.* dent *f.*

cogent, *adj.* puissant, fort.

cogitate, *vb.* méditer, penser.

cognac, *n.* cognac *m.*

cognizance, *n.* connaissance *f.*

cognizant, *adj.* instruit, (law) compétent.

cogwheel, *n.* roue *(f.)* d'engrenage.

cohabit, *vb.* vivre en concubinage.

coherent, *adj.* cohérent.

cohesion, *n.* cohésion *f.*

cohesive, *adj.* cohésif.

cohort, *n.* cohorte *f.*

coiffure, *n.* coiffure *f.*

coil, *n.* rouleau *m.*

coin, *n.* pièce *(f.)* de monnaie.

coinage, *n.* monnayage *m.,* monnaie *f.*

coincide, *vb.* coïncider.

coincidence, *n.* coïncidence *f.*

coincident, *adj.* coïncident.

coincidental, *adj.* coïncident, d'accord (avec).

coincidentally, *adv.* par coïncidence.

colander, *n.* passoire *f.*

cold, 1. *n.* (temperature) froid *m.;* (med.) rhume *m.* **2.** *adj.* froid; **(it is c.)** il fait froid; **(feel c.)** avoir froid; **(catch c.)** attraper un rhume.

cold-blooded, *adj.* de sang froid.

coldly, *adv.* froidement.

coldness, *n.* froideur *f.*

cold sore, *n.* bouton *(m.)* de fièvre.

colic, *n.* colique *f.*

collaborate, *vb.* collaborer.

collaboration, *n.* collaboration *f.*

collaborator, *n.* collaborateur *m.*

collapse, 1. *n.* effondrement *m.;* (med.) affaissement *m.* **2.** *vb.* s'effondrer; (med.) s'affaisser.

collapsible, *adj.* pliant.

collar, *n.* col *m.;* (dog) collier *m.*

collarbone, *n.* clavicule *f.*

collate, *vb.* collationner, comparer.

collateral, *adj. and n.* collatéral *m.*

collation, *n.* collation *f.,* comparaison *f.,* repas froid *m.*

colleague, *n.* collègue *m.f.*

collect, *vb.* rassembler.

collection, *n.* collection *f.;* (money) collecte *f.*

collective, *adj.* collectif.

collectively, *adv.* collectivement.

collector, *n.* (art) collectionneur *m.;* (tickets) contrôleur *m.*

college, *n.* collège *m.;* (higher education) université *f.*

collegiate, *adj.* de collège, collégial.

collide, *vb.* se heurter (contre).

collie, *n.* colley *m.*

colliery, *n.* houillère *f.*, mine *(f.)* de charbon.

collision, *n.* collision *f.*

colloquial, *adj.* familier.

colloquialism, *n.* expression de style familier *f.*

colloquially, *adv.* en style familier.

colloquy, *n.* colloque *m.*, entretien *m.*

collusion, *n.* collusion *f.*, connivence *f.*

colon, *n. (gramm.)* deux points *m.pl.*

colonel, *n.* colonel *m.*

colonial, *adj.* colonial.

colonist, *n.* colon *m.*

colonization, *n.* colonisation *f.*

colonize, *vb.* coloniser.

colony, *n.* colonie *f.*

color, 1. *n.* couleur *f.* **2.** *vb.* colorer, *tr.*

color-blind, *adj.* daltonien.

coloration, *n.* coloris *m.*

colored, *adj.* coloré, de couleur, colorié.

colorful, *adj.* coloré, pittoresque.

coloring, *n.* coloris *m.*, couleur *f.*; (skin) teint *m.*

colorless, *adj.* sans couleur, incolore, terne.

colossal, *adj.* colossal.

colt, *n.* poulain *m.*

colter, *n.* coutre *m.*

column, *n.* colonne *f.*

columnist, *n.* journaliste (qui a sa rubrique à lui) *m.*

coma, *n.* coma *m.*

comb, 1. *n.* peigne *m.* **2.** *vb.* peigner.

combat, 1. *n.* combat *m.* **2.** *vb.* combattre.

combatant, *adj. and n.* combattant *m.*

combative, *adj.* combatif.

combination, *n.* combinaison *f.*

combination lock, *n.* serrure *(f.)* à combinaisons.

combine, *vb.* combiner, *tr.*

combustible, *adj. and n.* combustible *m.*

combustion, *n.* combustion *f.*

come, *vb.* venir; **(c. about)** arriver; **(c. across)** rencontrer; **(c. away)** partir; **(c. back)** revenir; **(c. down)** descendre; **(c. in)** entrer; **(c. off)** se détacher; **(c. out)** sortir; **(c. up)** monter; **(c. upon)** tomber sur.

comedian, *n.* comédien *m.*

comedienne, *n.* comédienne *f.*

comedy, *n.* comédie *f.*

comely, *adj.* avenant.

comet, *n.* comète *f.*

comfort, 1. *n.* (mental) consolation *f.*; (material) confort *m.* **2.** *vb.* consoler.

comfortable, *adj.* commode.

comfortably, *adv.* confortablement, commodément.

comforter, *n.* consolateur *m.*; (quilt) édredon *m.*

comfortingly, *adv.* d'une manière réconfortante.

comfortless, *adj.* sans consolation, inconsolable, désolé.

comic, comical, *adj.* comique.

comic strip, *n.* bande *(f.)* dessinée.

coming, *n.* venue *f.*, arrivée *f.*, approche *f.*

comma, *n.* virgule *f.*

command, 1. *n.* commandement *m.* **2.** *vb.* commander (à).

commandeer, *vb.* réquisitionner.

commander, *n.* commandant *m.*

commander in chief, *n.* généralissime *m.*

commandment, *n.* commandement *m.*

commando, *n.* commando *m.*

commemorate, *vb.* commémorer.

commemoration, *n.* célébration *f.*, commémoration *f.*

commemorative, *adj.* commémoratif.

commence, *vb.* commencer.

commencement, *n.* (school) distribution *(f.)* des diplômes.

commend, *vb.* (entrust) recommander; (praise) louer.

commendable, *adj.* louable, recommandable.

commendably, *adv.* d'une manière louable.

commendation, *n.* louange *f.*

commensurate, *adj.* proportionné.

comment, 1. *n.* commentaire *m.* **2.** *vb.* commenter.

commentary, *n.* commentaire *m.*; reportage *m.*

commentator, *n.* commentateur *m.*

commerce, *n.* commerce *m.*

commercial, 1. *adj.* commercial. **2.** *n.* annonce *(f.)* publicitaire; spot *m.*

commercialism, *n.* commercialisme *m.*

commercialize, *vb.* commercialiser.

commercially, *adv.* commercialement.

commiserate, *vb.* plaindre, avoir pitié de.

commissary, *n.* (person) commissaire *m.*; (supply store) dépôt *(m.)* de vivres.

commission, *n.* (assignment) commande *f.*; (officer) brevet *m.*; (committee, percentage) commission *f.*

commissioner, *n.* commissaire *m.*

commit, *vb.* commettre; **(c. oneself)** s'engager.

commitment, *n.* engagement *m.*

committee, *n.* comité *m.*

commodious, *adj.* spacieux.

commodity, *n.* produit *m.*, commodité *f.*, denrée *f.*

common, *adj.* commun; (vulgar) vulgaire.

common law, *n.* droit coutumier *m.*

commonly, *adv.* communément, ordinairement.

Common Market, *n.* Marché *(m.)* commun.

commonness, *n.* vulgarité *f.*

commonplace, 1. *n.* lieucommun *m.* **2.** *adj.* banal.

common sense, *n.* bon sens *m.*

commonwealth, *n.* état *m.*

commotion, *n.* agitation *f.*

communal, *adj.* communal.

commune, *n.* commune *f.*

communicable, *adj.* communicable.

communicant, *n.* communiant *m.*

communicate, *vb.* communiquer.

communication, *n.* communication *f.*

communicative, *adj.* communicatif.

communion, *n.* communion *f.*

communiqué, *n.* communiqué *m.*

communism, *n.* communisme *m.*

communist, *adj. and n.* communiste *m.f.*

communistic, *adj.* communiste.

community, *n.* communauté *f.*

commutation, *n.* commutation *f.*

commutation ticket, *n.* carte (*f.*) d'abonnement.

commute, *vb.* changer; (law) commuer; faire la navette.

commuter, *n.* voyageur (*m.*) de banlieue.

compact, 1. *n.* (agreement) accord *m.;* (cosmetic) poudrier *m.* **2.** *adj.* compact.

compact disc, *n.* disque (*m.*) compact.

compact disc player, *n.* lecteur (*m.*) de disque compact.

compactness, *n.* compacité *f.*

companion, *n.* compagnon *m.*, compagne *f.*

companionable, *adj.* sociable.

companionship, *n.* camaraderie *f.*

company, *n.* compagnie *f.*

comparable with, *adj.* comparable à.

comparative, *adj. and n.* comparatif *m.*

comparatively, *adv.* comparativement, relativement.

compare, *vb.* comparer.

comparison, *n.* comparaison *f.*

compartment, *n.* compartiment *m.*

compass, *n.* (*naut.*) boussole *f.;* (*geom.*) compas *m.*

compassion, *n.* compassion *f.*

compassionate, *adj.* compatissant.

compassionately, *adv.* avec compassion.

compatible, *adj.* compatible.

compatriot, *n.* compatriote *m.f.*

compel, *vb.* forcer.

compelling, *adj.* irrésistible.

compendium, *n.* abrégé *m.*, résumé *m.*

compensate, *vb.* compenser.

compensation, *n.* compensation *f.*

compensatory, *adj.* compensateur.

compete, *vb.* rivaliser.

competence, *n.* compétence *f.*

competent, *adj.* capable.

competently, *adv.* convenablement, avec compétence.

competition, *n.* concurrence *f.*

competitive, *adj.* concurrentiel; de compétition.

competitor, *n.* concurrent *m.*

compile, *vb.* compiler.

complacency, *n.* contentement (*m.*) de soi-même.

complacent, *adj.* content de soi-même.

complacently, *adv.* avec un air (un ton) suffisant.

complain, *vb.* se plaindre.

complainer, *n.* plaignant *m.*, réclameur *m.*

complainingly, *adv.* d'une manière plaignante.

complaint, *n.* plainte *f.*

complement, *n.* complément *m.*

complementary, *adj.* complémentaire.

complete, *adj.* complet.

completely, *adv.* complètement, tout à fait.

completeness, *n.* état complet *m.*, perfection *f.*

completion, *n.* achèvement *m.*

complex, *adj. and n.* complexe *m.*

complexion, *n.* teint *m.*

complexity, *n.* complexité *f.*

compliance, *n.* acquiescement *m.*

compliant, *adj.* complaisant, accommodant.

complicate, *vb.* compliquer.

complicated, *adj.* compliqué.

complication, *n.* complication *f.*

complicity, *n.* complicité *f.*

compliment, *n.* compliment *m.*

complimentary, *adj.* flatteur, de félicitation; (ticket) de faveur.

comply with, *vb.* se conformer à.

component, *n.* composant *m.*, élément *m.*

comport, *vb.* s'accorder (avec), convenir (à).

compose, *vb.* composer; (**c. oneself**) se calmer.

composed, *adj.* composé, calme, tranquille.

composer, *n.* compositeur *m.*

composite, *adj.* composé.

composition, *n.* composition *f.*

compost, *n.* compost *m.*, terreau *m.*

composure, *n.* calme *m.*, tranquillité *f.*, sang-froid *m.*

compote, *n.* compote *f.*

compound, 1. *adj. and n.* composé *m.* **2.** *vb.* aggraver.

compound fracture, *n.* fracture (*f.*) compliquée.

compound interest, *n.* intérêt (*m.*) composé.

comprehend, *vb.* comprendre.

comprehensible, *adj.* compréhensible, intelligible.

comprehension, *n.* compréhension *f.*

comprehensive, *adj.* compréhensif.

compress, 1. *n.* compresse *f.* 2. *vb.* comprimer, *tr.*

compressed, *adj.* comprimé.

compression, *n.* compression *f.*

compressor, *n.* compresseur *m.*

comprise, *vb.* comprendre.

compromise, 1. *n.* compromis *m.* 2. *vb.* compromettre.

compromiser, *n.* comprometteur *m.*

compulsion, *n.* contrainte *f.*

compulsive, *adj.* coercitif, obligatoire; (psychological) compulsif; (liar, smoker) invétéré.

compulsory, *adj.* obligatoire.

compunction, *n.* componction *f.*, scrupule *f.*

computation, *n.* supputation *f.*

compute, *vb.* supputer.

computer, *n.* ordinateur *m.*

computerize, *vb.* informatiser.

computer programmer, *n.* programmeur *m.*

computer science, *n.* informatique *f.*

comrade, *n.* camarade *m.f.*

comradeship, *n.* camaraderie *f.*

con, *vb.* rouler, escroquer.

concave, *adj.* concave.

conceal, *vb.* cacher.

concealment, *n.* action (*f.*) de cacher.

concede, *vb.* concéder.

conceit, *n.* vanité *f.*

conceited, *adj.* vaniteux, suffisant.

conceivable, *adj.* concevable.

conceivably, *adv.* d'une manière concevable.

conceive, *vb.* concevoir.

concentrate, *vb.* concentrer, *tr.*

concentration, *n.* concentration *f.*

concentration camp, *n.* camp (*m.*) de concentration.

concept, *n.* concept *m.*

conception, *n.* conception *f.*

concern, 1. *n.* (what pertains to one) affaire *f.*; (comm.) entreprise *f.*; (solicitude) souci *m.* 2. *vb.* concerner; (c. oneself with) s'intéresser à; (be c.ed about) s'inquiéter de.

concerning, *prep.* concernant.

concert, *n.* concert *m.*

concerted, *adj.* concerté.

concerto, *n.* concerto *m.*

concession, *n.* concession *f.*

conciliate, *vb.* concilier.

conciliation, *n.* conciliation *f.*

conciliator, *n.* conciliateur *m.*

conciliatory, *adj.* conciliant, conciliatoire.

concise, *adj.* concis.

concisely, *adv.* avec concision, succinctement.

conciseness, *n.* concision *f.*

conclave, *n.* conclave *m.*

conclude, *vb.* conclure.

conclusion, *n.* conclusion *f.*

conclusive, *adj.* concluant.

conclusively, *adv.* d'une manière concluante.

concoct, *vb.* préparer.

concoction, *n.* mélange *m.*

concomitant, 1. *adj.* concomitant. 2. *n.* accessoire *m.*

concord, *n.* concorde *f.*

concordat, *n.* concordat *m.*

concourse, *n.* concours *m.*, affluence *f.*

concrete, 1. *n.* béton *m.* 2. *adj.* concret.

concretely, *adv.* d'une manière concrète.

concreteness, *n.* état concret *m.*

concubine, *n.* concubine *f.*

concur, *vb.* (events) concourir; (persons) être d'accord.

concurrence, *n.* assentiment *m.*, concours *m.*

concurrent, *adj.* concourant.

concussion, *n.* secousse *f.*, ébranlement *m.*

condemn, *vb.* condamner.

condemnable, *adj.* condamnable.

condemnation, *n.* condamnation *f.*

condensation, *n.* condensation *f.*

condense, *vb.* condenser, *tr.*

condenser, *n.* condenseur *m.*

condescend, *vb.* condescendre.

condescendingly, *adv.* avec condescendance.

condescension, *n.* condescendance *f.*

condiment, *n.* condiment *m.*, assaisonnement *m.*

condition, 1. *n.* condition *f.* 2. *vb.* conditionner.

conditional, *adj. and n.* conditionnel *m.*

conditionally, *adv.* conditionnellement.

conditioner, *n.* (hair) après-shampooing *m.*

condolence, *n.* condoléance *f.*

condole with, *vb.* faire ses condoléances à.

condom, *n.* préservatif *m.*

condominium, *n.* condominium *m.*

condone, *vb.* approuver (tacitement).

conducive, *adj.* favorable.

conduct, 1. *n.* conduite *f.* 2. *vb.* conduire.

conductivity, *n.* conductivité *f.*

conductor, *n.* conducteur *m.*; (bus) receveur *m.*; (rail) chef (*m.*) de train; (music) chef (*m.*) d'orchestre.

conduit, *n.* conduit *m.*, tuyau *m.*

cone, *n.* cône *m.*

confection, *n.* confection *f.*; (sweet) bonbon *m.*

confectioner, *n.* confiseur *m.*

confectionery, *n.* confiserie *f.*

confederacy, confederation, *n.* confédération *f.*

confederate, *adj. and n.* confédéré *m.*

confer, *vb.* conférer.

conference, *n.* (meeting) entretien *m.*; (congress) congrès *m.*

confess, *vb.* avouer; (eccles.) confesser, *tr.*

confession, *n.* confession *f.*

confessional, *n.* confessional *m.*

confessor, *n.* confesseur *m.*

confetti, *n.* confetti *m.*

confidant, *n.* confident *m.*

confidante, *n.* confidente *f.*

confide, *vb.* confier (à), *tr.*

confidence, *n.* (trust) confiance *f.*; (secret) confidence *f.*

confident, *adj.* confiant.

confidential, *adj.* confidentiel.

confidentially, *adv.* confidentiellement.

confidently, *adv.* avec confiance.

configure, *vb.* (computer) configurer.

confine, *vb.* (banish) confiner; (limit) limiter.

confinement, *n.* détention *f.*

confirm, *vb.* confirmer.

confirmation, *n.* confirmation *f.*

confirmed, *adj.* invétéré, incorrigible.

confiscate, *vb.* confisquer.

confiscation, *n.* confiscation *f.*

conflagration, *n.* conflagration *f.*, incendie *m.*

conflict, *n.* conflit *m.*

conflicting, *adj.* contradictoire.

conform, *vb.* conformer, *tr.*

conformation, *n.* conformation *f.*, conformité *f.*

conformer, *n.* conformiste *m.*

conformist, *n.* conformiste *m.*

conformity, *n.* conformité *f.*

confound, *vb.* confondre; **(c. him!)** que le diable l'emporte!

confront, *vb.* confronter.

confrontation, *n.* confrontation *f.*

confuse, *vb.* confondre.

confusing, *adj.* peu clair.

confusion, *n.* confusion *f.*

congeal, *vb.* congeler, *tr.*

congealment, *n.* congélation *f.*

congenial, *adj.* (person) sympathique; (thing) convenable.

congenital, *adj.* congénital.

congenitally, *adv.* d'une manière congénitale.

congested, *adj.* (area) surpeuplé; (road) bloqué; (medical) congestionné.

congestion, *n.* (*med.*) congestion *f.*; (traffic) encombrement *m.*

conglomerate, *adj.* conglomére.

conglomeration, *n.* conglomération *f.*

congratulate, *vb.* féliciter (de).

congratulation, *n.* félicitation *f.*

congratulatory, *adj.* de félicitation.

congregate, *vb.* rassembler, *tr.*

congregation, *n.* assemblée *f.*

congress, *n.* congrès *m.*

congressional, *adj.* congressionnel.

congressman, -woman, *n.* membre (*m.*) du congrès.

conic, *adj.* conique.

conjecture, *n.* conjecture *f.*

conjugal, *adj.* conjugal.

conjugate, *vb.* conjuguer.

conjugation, *n.* conjugaison *f.*

conjunction, *n.* conjonction *f.*

conjunctive, *adj.* conjonctif.

conjunctivitis, *n.* conjonctivite *f.*

conjure, *vb.* conjurer.

conk, *vb.* **(c. out)** (colloquial) tomber en panne.

con man, *n.* arnaqueur *m.*

connect, *vb.* joindre.

connection, *n.* connexion *f.*; (social) relations *f.pl.*; (train) correspondance *f.*

connivance, *n.* connivence *f.*

connive, *vb.* conniver (à).

connoisseur, *n.* connaisseur *m.*

connotation, *n.* connotation *f.*

connote, *vb.* signifier, vouloir dire.

connubial, *adj.* conjugal, du mariage.

conquer, *vb.* conquérir.

conquerable, *adj.* qui peut être vaincu, domptable.

conqueror, *n.* conquérant *m.*

conquest, *n.* conquête *f.*

conscience, *n.* conscience *f.*

conscientious, *adj.* consciencieux.

conscientiously, *adv.* consciencieusement.

conscious, *adj.* conscient.

consciously, *adv.* sciemment, en parfaite connaissance.

consciousness, *n.* conscience *f.*

conscript, *adj. and n.* conscrit *m.*

conscription, *n.* conscription *f.*

consecrate, *vb.* consacrer.

consecration, *n.* consécration *f.*

consecutive, *adj.* consécutif.

consecutively, *adv.* consécutivement, de suite.

consensus, *n.* consensus *m.*, assentiment général *m.*

consent, 1. *n.* consentement *m.* **2.** *vb.* consentir.

consequence, *n.* conséquence *f.*

consequent, *adj.* conséquent.

consequential, *adj.* conséquent, logique.

consequently, *adv.* par conséquent.

conservation, *n.* conservation *f.*; **(c. area)** zone (*f.*) classée.

conservationist, *n.* défenseur (*m.*) de l'environnement.

conservatism, *n.* conservatisme *m.*

conservative, *adj.* (politics) conservateur; (*comm.*) prudent.

conservatively, *adv.* d'une manière conservatrice.

conservatory, *n.* conservatoire *m.*

conserve, *vb.* conserver.

consider, *vb.* considérer.

considerable, *adj.* considérable.

considerably, *adv.* considérablement.

considerate, *adj.* prévenant, attentionné.

considerately, *adv.* avec égards, avec indulgence.

consideration, *n.* considération *f.*

considering, *prep.* vu que, attendu que.

consign, *vb.* consigner.

consignment, *n.* expédition *f.,* consignation *f.*

consistency, *n.* consistance *f.*

consistent, *adj.* consistant; **(c. with)** conforme à.

consist of, *vb.* consister en.

consolation, *n.* consolation *f.*

console, *vb.* consoler.

consolidate, *vb.* consolider.

consommé, *n.* consommé *m.*

consonant, *n.* consonne *f.*

consort, 1. *n.* compagnon *m.,* époux *m.* 2. *vb.* s'associer (à).

conspicuous, *adj.* en évidence.

conspicuously, *adv.* visiblement, éminemment.

conspicuousness, *n.* éclat *m.,* position éminente *f.*

conspiracy, *n.* conspiration *f.*

conspirator, *n.* conspirateur *m.*

conspire, *vb.* conspirer.

conspirer, *n.* conspirateur *m.*

constancy, *n.* constance *f.,* fermeté *f.*

constant, *adj.* constant.

constantly, *adv.* constamment.

constellation, *n.* constellation *f.*

consternation, *n.* consternation *f.*

constipate, *vb.* constiper.

constipation, *n.* constipation *f.*

constituency, *n.* circonscription électorale *f.*

constituent, *adj.* constituant.

constitute, *vb.* constituer.

constitution, *n.* constitution *f.*

constitutional, *adj.* constitutionnel.

constrain, *vb.* contraindre.

constrained, *adj.* contraint.

constraint, *n.* contrainte *f.,* gêne *f.*

constrict, *vb.* resserrer.

constriction, *n.* resserrement *f.*

construct, *vb.* construire.

construction, *n.* construction *f.*

constuction worker, *n.* ouvrier *(m.)* de bâtiment.

constructive, *adj.* constructif.

constructively, *adv.* constructivement, par induction.

constructor, *n.* constructeur *m.*

construe, *vb.* interpréter.

consul, *n.* consul *m.*

consular, *adj.* consulaire.

consulate, *n.* consulat *m.*

consult, *vb.* consulter.

consultant, *n.* conseiller *m.,* consultant *m.*

consultation, *n.* consultation *f.*

consume, *vb.* consumer.

consumer, *n.* consommateur *m.*

consumer goods, *n.* biens *(m.pl.)* de consommation.

consumerism, *n.* protection *(f.)* des consommateurs.

consummate, 1. *adj.* consommé. 2. *vb.* consommer.

consummation, *n.* consommation *f.*

consumption, *n.* consommation *f.; (med.)* phtisie *f.*

consumptive, *adj.* poitrinaire, tuberculeux.

contact, *n.* contact *m.*

contact lenses, *n.* lentilles *(f.pl.)* (de contact), verres *(m.pl.)* de contact.

contagion, *n.* contagion *f.*

contagious, *adj.* contagieux.

contain, *vb.* contenir.

container, *n.* récipient *m.*

contaminate, *vb.* contaminer.

contaminated, *adj.* contaminé.

contamination, *n.* contamination *f.*

contemplate, *vb.* contempler.

contemplation, *n.* contemplation *f.*

contemplative, *adj.* contemplatif.

contemporary, *adj.* contemporain.

contempt, *n.* mépris *m.*

contemptible, *adj.* méprisable.

contemptuous, *adj.* méprisant.

contemptuously, *adv.* avec mépris, dédaigneusement.

contend, *vb.* (struggle) lutter; (maintain) soutenir.

contender, *n.* compétiteur *m.*

content, *n.* (satisfaction) contentement *m.; (c.s)* contenu *m.*

contented with, *adj.* content de.

contention, *n.* contention *f.,* lutte *f.*

contentment, *n.* contentement *m.*

contents, *n.pl.* (of text) contenu *m.; (table of c.)* table *(f.)* des matières.

contest, 1. *n.* (struggle) lutte *f.;* (competition) concours *m.* 2. *vb.* contester.

contestable, *adj.* contestable.

contestant, *n.* concurrent *m.,* disputant *m.*

context, *n.* contexte *m.*

contiguous, *adj.* contigu *m.,* contiguë *f.*

continence, *n.* continence *f.,* retenue *f.*

continent, *adj. and n.* continent *m.*

continental, *adj.* continental.

contingency, *n.* contingence *f.; (c. plan)* plan *(m.)* d'urgence.

contingent, *adj.* contingent; **(be c. upon)** dépendre de.

continual, *adj.* continuel.

continuance, *n.* continuation *f.*

continuation, *n.* continuation *f.;* (of story) suite *f.;* (after interruption) reprise *f.*

continue, *vb.* continuer.

continuity, *n.* continuité *f.*

continuous, *adj.* continu.

continuously, *adv.* continûment, sans interruption.

contort, *vb.* tordre, défigurer.

contortion, *n.* torsion *f.;* contorsion *f.*

contortionist, *n.* contortionniste *m.f.*

contour, *n.* contour *m.*

contraband, *n.* contrebande *f.*

contraception, *n.* limitation des naissances *f.,* contraception *f.*

contraceptive, *n.* contraceptif *m.*

contract, 1. *n.* contrat *m.* **2.** *vb.* contracter, *tr.*

contracted, *adj.* contracté, resserré.

contraction, *n.* contraction *f.*

contractor, *n.* entrepreneur *m.*

contradict, *vb.* contredire.

contradictable, *adj.* qui peut être contredit.

contradiction, *n.* contradiction *f.,* démenti *m.*

contradictory, *adj.* contradictoire.

contraption, *n.* machin *m.*

contrary, *adj. and n.* contraire *m.;* **(on the c.)** au contraire.

contrast, 1. *n.* contraste *m.* **2.** *vb.* mettre en contraste, *tr.;* contraster, *intr.*

contravene, *vb.* contrevenir à.

contribute, *vb.* contribuer.

contribution, *n.* contribution *f.*

contributive, *adj.* contributif.

contributor, *n.* contribuant *m.*

contributory, *adj.* contribuant.

contrite, *adj.* contrit, pénitent.

contrition, *n.* contrition *f.*

contrivance, *n.* combinaison *f.,* invention *f.,* artifice *m.*

contrive, *vb.* inventer, imaginer, arranger.

control, 1. *n.* autorité *f.;* (machinery) commande *f.* **2.** *vb.* gouverner; (check) contrôler.

controllable, *adj.* vérifiable, gouvernable.

controller, *n.* contrôleur *m.*

control panel, *n.* tableau *(m.)* de commande.

control room, *n.* salle *(f.)* des commandes.

controversial, *adj.* de controverse, polémique.

controversy, *n.* controverse *f.*

contusion, *n.* contusion *f.*

conundrum, *n.* devinette *f.,* énigme *f.*

convalescence, *n.* convalescence *f.*

convalescent, *adj.* convalescent.

convector, *n.* radiateur *m.* (à convexion).

convene, *vb.* assembler, *tr.*

convenience, *n.* convenance *f.;* (comfort) commodité *f.*

convenient, *adj.* commode.

conveniently, *adv.* commodément.

convent, *n.* couvent *m.*

convention, *n.* convention *f.*

conventional, *adj.* conventionnel.

conventionally, *adv.* par convention.

converge, *vb.* converger.

convergence, *n.* convergence *f.*

convergent, *adj.* convergent.

conversant, *adj.* versé (dans), familier (avec).

conversation, *n.* conversation *f.*

conversational, *adj.* de conversation.

conversationalist, *n.* causeur *m.*

converse, 1. *vb.* converser. **2.** *adj and n.* inverse.

conversely, *adv.* réciproquement.

conversion, *n.* conversion *f.*

convert, *vb.* convertir, *tr.*

converter, *n.* convertisseur *m.*

convertible, *adj.* convertible (of things), convertissable (of persons), décapotable (of car).

convex, *adj.* convexe.

convey, *vb.* (transport) transporter; (transmit) transmettre.

conveyance, *n.* transport *m.*

conveyor, *n.* transporteur *m.,* conducteur (élec-

trique) *m.;* **(c. belt)** tapis *(m.)* roulant.

convict, 1. *n.* forçat *m.* **2.** *vb.* condamner.

conviction, *n.* (condemnation) condamnation *f.;* (persuasion) conviction *f.*

convince, *vb.* convaincre.

convincing, *adj.* convaincant.

convincingly, *adv.* d'une manière convaincante.

convivial, *adj.* jovial, joyeux.

convocation, *n.* convocation *f.*

convoke, *vb.* convoquer.

convoluted, *adj.* compliqué.

convoy, *n.* convoi *m.*

convulse, *vb.* convulser, bouleverser.

convulsion, *n.* convulsion *f.*

convulsive, *adj.* convulsif.

coo, *vb.* roucouler.

cook, 1. *n.* cuisinier *m.* **2.** *vb.* cuire, *intr.;* faire cuire, *tr.*

cookbook, *n.* livre *(m.)* de cuisine.

cookie, *n.* gâteau sec *m.*

cooking, *n.* cuisine *f.*

cool, 1. *adj.* frais *m.,* fraîche *f.* **2.** *vb.* rafraîchir.

cooler, *n.* rafraîchissoir *m.,* réfrigérant *m.,* (motor) radiateur *m.*

coolness, *n.* fraîcheur *f.*

coop, 1. *n.* cage *(f.)* à poules. **2.** *vb.* **(c. up)** enfermer.

cooperate, *vb.* coopérer.

cooperation, *n.* coopération *f.*

cooperative, 1. *n.* coopérative *f.* **2.** *adj.* coopératif.

cooperatively, *adj.* d'une manière coopérative.

co-opt, *vb.* coopter.

coordinate, *vb.* coordonner.

coordination, *n.* coordination *f.*

coordinator, *n.* coordinateur *m.*

co-ownership, *n.* copropriété *f.*

cop, 1. *n.* (slang) flic *m.* **2.** *vb.* (colloquial) attraper, pincer.

cope with, *vb.* tenir tête à.

copier, *n.* machine à copier *f.*

copious, *adj.* copieux.

copiously, *adv.* copieusement.

copiousness, *n.* abondance *f.*

copper, *n.* cuivre *m.*

copperplate, *n.* cuivre plané *m.;* taille-douce *f.*

copulate, *vb.* s'accoupler.

copy, 1. *n.* (duplicate) copie *f.;* (book) exemplaire *m.* **2.** *vb.* copier.

copyist, *n.* copiste *m.,* imitateur *m.*

copyright, *n.* droit (*m.*) d'auteur.

coquetry, *n.* coquetterie *f.*

coquette, *n.* coquette *f.*

coral, *n.* corail *m.; pl.* coraux.

cord, *n.* corde *f.*

cordial, *adj. and n.* cordial *m.*

cordiality, *n.* cordialité *f.*

cordially, *adv.* cordialement.

cordon, *n.* cordon *m.*

cordovan, *adj.* cordovan.

corduroy, *n.* velours côtelé *m.*

core, *n.* cœur *m.*

coriander, *n.* coriandre.

cork, *n.* (botany) liège *m.;* (stopper) bouchon *m.*

corkscrew, *n.* tire-bouchon *m.*

corn, *n.* maïs *m.;* (c. on the cob) épi (*m.*) de maïs.

cornea, *n.* cornée *f.*

corner, *n.* coin *m.*

cornerstone, *n.* pierre angulaire *f.*

cornet, *n.* cornet *m.*

cornetist, *n.* cornettiste *m.*

cornstarch, *n.* farine (*f.*) de maïs.

cornice, *n.* corniche *f.*

cornucopia, *n.* corne (*f.*) d'abondance.

corny, *adj.* rebattu.

corollary, *n.* corollaire *m.*

coronary, *adj.* coronaire.

coronation, *n.* couronnement *m.*

coroner, *n.* coroner *m.*

coronet, *n.* (petite) couronne *f.*

corporal, *n. (mil.)* caporal *m.*

corporate, *adj.* de corporation.

corporation, *n.* société *f.* (anonyme).

corps, *n.* corps *m.*

corpse, *n.* cadavre *m.*

corpulent, *adj.* corpulent, gros.

corpuscle, *n.* corpuscule *m.*

corral, *n.* corral *m.*

correct, 1. *adj.* correct. **2.** *vb.* corriger.

correction, *n.* correction *f.*

corrective, 1. *adj.* correctif. **2.** *n.* correctif *m.*

correctly, *adv.* correctement, justement.

correctness, *n.* correction *f.*

correlate, *vb.* être en corrélation, *intr.;* mettre en corrélation, *tr.*

correlation, *n.* corrélation *f.*

correspond, *vb.* correspondre.

correspondence, *n.* correspondance *f.*

correspondent, *n.* correspondant *m.*

corridor, *n.* couloir *m.*

corroborate, *vb.* corroborer.

corroboration, *n.* corroboration *f.,* confirmation *f.*

corroborative, *adj.* corroboratif.

corrode, *vb.* corroder.

corrosion, *n.* corrosion *f.*

corrosive, *adj.* corrosif.

corrugate, *vb.* rider, plisser.

corrugated, *adj.* ondulé.

corrupt, 1. *adj.* corrompu. **2.** *vb.* corrompre.

corruptible, *adj.* corruptible.

corruption, *n.* corruption *f.*

corruptive, *adj.* corruptif.

corsage, *n.* corsage *f.*

corset, *n.* corset *m.*

Corsica, *n.* Corse *f.*

cortege, *n.* cortège *m.*

cortisone, *n.* cortisone *f.*

corvette, *n.* corvette *f.*

cosmetic, *adj. and n.* cosmétique *m.*

cosmic, *adj.* cosmique.

cosmic rays, *n.* rayons cosmiques *m.pl.*

cosmonaut, *n.* cosmonaute *m.f.*

cosmopolitan, *adj. and n.* cosmopolite *m.f.*

cosmos, *n.* cosmos *m.*

Cossack, *n.* cosaque *m.*

cost, 1. *n.* coût *m.* **2.** *vb.* coûter.

costliness, *n.* haut prix *m.,* somptuosité *f.*

cost-effective, *adj.* rentable.

cost price, *n.* prix (*m.*) de revient.

co-star, *n.* partenaire *m.f.*

costly, *adj.* coûteux.

costume, *n.* costume *m.*

costume jewelry, *n.* bijoux (*m.pl.*) de fantaisie.

costumer, *n.* costumier *m.*

cot, *n.* (berth) couchette *f.;* (folding) lit-cage *m.*

coterie, *n.* coterie *f.,* clique *f.*

cotillion, *n.* cotillon *m*

cottage, *n.* chaumière *f.*

cottage industry, *n.* activité (*f.*) artisanale.

cotton, *n.* coton *m.*

cottonseed, *n.* graine (*f.*) de coton.

couch, *n.* divan *m.*

cougar, *n.* couguar *m.*

cough, 1. *n.* toux *f.* **2.** *vb.* tousser.

could, *vb.* pouvait, pourrait.

council, *n.* conseil *m.*

councilman, -woman, *n.* conseiller *m.,* conseillère *f.*

counsel, 1. *n.* conseil *m.* **2.** *vb.* conseiller.

counselor, *n.* conseiller *m.*

count, 1. *n.* (calculation) compte *m.;* (title) comte *m.* **2.** *vb.* compter; (c. on) compter sur.

countenance, *n.* expression *f.*

counter, 1. *n.* (shop) comptoir *m.* **2.** *adv.* (c. to) à l'encontre de.

counteract, *vb.* neutraliser.

counteraction, *n.* action contraire *f.*

counterattack, 1. *n.* contre-attaque *f.* **2.** *vb.* contreattaquer.

counterbalance, 1. *n.* contrepoids *m.* **2.** *vb.* contrebalancer.

counterclockwise, *adj. and adv.* dans le sens inverse des aiguilles d'une montre.

counterfeit, 1. *adj.* (money) faux *m.*, fausse *f.* **2.** *vb.* contrefaire.

countermand, *vb.* contremander.

counteroffensive, *n.* contre-offensive *f.*

counterpart, *n.* contre-partie *f.*, homologue *m.*

counterproductive, *adj.* qui produit l'effet contraire.

countersign, *vb.* contresigner.

countess, *n.* comtesse *f.*

countless, *adj.* innombrable.

country, 1. *n.* (nation) pays *m.*; (opposed to town) campagne *f.*; **(native c.)** patrie *f.*

countryman, *n.* (of same c.) compatriote *m.f.*; (rustic) campagnard *m.*

countryside, *n.* campagne *f.*

county, *n.* comté *m.*

coupé, *n.* coupé *m.*

couple, 1. *n.* couple *f.* **2.** *vb.* coupler.

coupon, *n.* coupon *m.*

courage, *n.* courage *m.*

courageous, *adj.* courageux.

courier, *n.* courrier *m.*

course, *n.* cours *m.*; **(of c.)** bien entendu; (route) route *f.*; (meal) service *m.*

court, 1. *n.* cour *f.*; (tennis) court. **2.** *vb.* faire la cour à.

courteous, *adj.* courtois.

courtesy, *n.* courtoisie *f.*

courthouse, *n.* palais (*m.*) de justice.

courtier, *n.* courtisan *m.*

courtly, *adj.* de cour, élégant, courtois.

courtmartial, *n.* conseil (*m.*) de guerre.

courtroom, *n.* salle (*f.*) d'audience.

courtship, *n.* cour *f.*

courtyard, *n.* cour *f.*

cousin, *n.* cousin *m.*, cousine *f.*

cove, *n.* anse *f.*, crique *f.*

covenant, *n.* pacte *m.*

cover, 1. *n.* (book, *comm.*, blanket) couverture *f.*; (pot) couvercle *m.*; (shelter) abri *m.*; (enve-lope) pli *m.*; (*mil.*) couvert *m.* **2.** *vb.* couvrir.

coverage, *n.* couverture *f.*

coveralls, *n.* bleus (*m.pl.*) de travail.

cover charge, *n.* couvert *m.*

covering, *n.* couverture *f.*, enveloppe *f.*

covert, *adj.* secret; voilé.

cover-up, *n.* tentative (*f.*) pour étouffer une affaire.

covet, *vb.* convoiter.

covetous, *adj.* avide, avaricieux.

cow, *n.* vache *f.*

coward, *adj. and n.* lâche *m.f.*

cowardice, *n.* lâcheté *f.*

cowardly, *adv.* lâche.

cowboy, *n.* cowboy *m.*

cower, *vb.* se blottir.

cow hand, *n.* vacher *m.*

cowhide, *n.* peau (*f.*) de vache.

cowshed, *n.* étable *f.*

coxswain, *n.* patron (*m.*) de chaloupe, barreur *m.*

coy, *adj.* faussement timide.

cozy, *adj.* confortable, douillet.

crab, 1. *n.* crabe *m.* **2.** *vb.* rouspéter.

crab apple, *n.* pomme sauvage *f.*

crack, 1. *n.* (fissure) fente *f.*; (noise) craquement *m.* **2.** *vb. tr.* (glass, china) fêler; (nuts) casser; (noise) faire craquer. **3.** *vb. intr.* (split) se fendiller; (noise) craquer.

cracked, *adj.* fendu, fêlé.

cracker, *n.* biscuit *m.*

cracking, *n.* craquement *m.*, claquement *m.*

crackle, 1. *n.* crépitement *m.* **2.** *vb.* crépiter.

crackup, *n.* crach *m.*

cradle, *n.* berceau *m.*

craft, *n.* (skill) habileté *f.*; (trade) métier *m.*; (boat) embarcation *f.*

craftsman, *n.* artisan *m.*

craftsmanship, *n.* habileté *f.*, technique *f.*, art *m.*

crafty, *adj.* rusé, astucieux.

crag, *n.* rocher à pic *m.*, rocher escarpé *m.*

cram, *vb.* remplir, farcir.

cramp, *n.* (*med.*) crampe *f.*; (mechanical) crampon *m.*

cranberry, *n.* canneberge *f.*, airelle *f.*

crane, *n.* grue *f.*

cranium, *n.* crâne *m.*

crank, *n.* manivelle *f.*

cranky, *adj.* d'humeur difficile.

cranny, *n.* crevasse *f.*, fente *f.*

craps, *n.* (slang) jeu de dés *m.*

crapshooter, *n.* (slang) joueur aux dés *m.*

crash, 1. *n.* (noise) fracas *m.*; (accident) accident *m.* **2.** *vb.* tomber avec fracas, *intr.*

crash landing, *n.* atterrissage (*m.*) forcé.

crass, *adj.* grossier.

crate, *n.* caisse *f.*

crater, *n.* cratère *m.*

crave, *vb.* désirer ardemment.

craven, *adj.* lâche, poltron.

craving, *n.* désir ardent *m.*, besoin impérieux *m.*

crawl, *vb.* (reptiles) ramper; (persons) se traîner.

crayfish, *n.* (freshwater) écrevisse *f.*; (saltwater) langouste *f.*

crayon, *n.* pastel *m.*, crayon *m.*

craze, *n.* engouement *m.*

crazed, *adj.* fou, dément.

crazy, *adj.* fou *m.*, folle *f.*

creak, *vb.* grincer.

creaky, *adj.* qui crie, qui grince.

cream, *n.* crème *f.*

cream cheese, *n.* fromage (*m.*) frais.

creamery, *n.* crêmerie *f.*

creamy, *adj.* crémeux, de crème.

crease, 1. *n.* pli *m.* **2.** *vb.* froisser, *tr.*

create, *vb.* créer.

creation, *n.* création *f.*

creative, *adj.* créateur *m.*, créatrice *f.*

creator, *n.* créateur *m.*, créatrice *f.*

creature, *n.* créature *f.*

credence, *n.* créance *f.,* croyance *f.*

credentials, *n.* lettres (*f.pl.*) de créance; (student, servant) certificat *m.*

credibility, *n.* crédibilité *f.*

credible, *adj.* croyable.

credit, *n.* crédit *m.;* (merit) honneur *m.*

creditable, *adj.* estimable.

creditably, *adv.* honorablement.

credit card, *n.* carte (*f.*) de crédit.

creditor, *n.* créancier *m.*

credo, *n.* credo *m.*

credulity, *n.* crédulité *f.*

credulous, *adj.* crédule.

creed, *n.* (belief) croyance *f.,* (theology) credo *m.*

creek, *n.* ruisseau *m.*

creep, *vb.* (reptiles, insects, plants) ramper; (persons) se glisser.

creepy, *adj.* qui fait frissonner.

cremate, *vb.* incinérer.

crematorium, *n.* four (*m.*) crématoire.

crematory, *n.* crématorium *m.*

Creole, *n.* créole *m.f.*

creosote, *n.* créosote *f.*

crepe, *n.* crêpe *m.*

crescent, *n.* croissant *m.*

crest, *n.* crête *f.*

crestfallen, *adj.* abattu, découragé.

Crete, *n.* Crète *f.*

cretin, *n.* crétin *m.*

cretonne, *n.* cretonne *f.*

crevice, *n.* crevasse *f.*

crew, *n.* (boat) équipage *m.;* (gang) équipe *f.*

crew cut, *n.* les cheveux (*m.pl.*) en brosse.

crib, *n.* (child's bed) lit (*m.*) d'enfant; (manger) mangeoire *f.*

cricket, *n.* (insect) grillon *m.;* (game) cricket *m.*

crier, *n.* crieur *m.,* huissier *m.*

crime, *n.* crime *m.*

criminal, *adj.* criminel.

criminologist, *n.* criminologue *m.f.*

criminology, *n.* criminologie *f.*

crimson, *adj. and n.* cramoisi *m.*

cringe, *vb.* faire des courbettes, se tapir, s'humilier.

crinkle, 1. *n.* pli *m.,* sinuosité *f.* **2.** *vb.* serpenter, former en zigzag.

cripple, 1. *n.* estropié *m.* **2.** *vb.* estropier.

crisis, *n.* crise *f.*

crisp, *adj.* (food) croquant; (manner) tranchant.

crispness, *n.* frisure *f.*

crisscross, 1. *adj. and adv.* entrecroisé. **2.** *vb.* (s')entrecroiser.

criterion, *n.* critérium *m.*

critic, *n.* critique *m.*

critical, *adj.* critique.

criticism, *n.* critique *f.*

criticize, *vb.* critiquer.

critique, *n.* critique *f.*

croak, *vb.* (frogs) coasser; (crows, persons) croasser.

Croatia, *n.* Croatie *f.*

crochet, 1. *vb.* broder au crochet. **2.** *n.* crochet *m.*

crock, *n.* pot (*m.*) de terre.

crockery, *n.* faïence *f.*

crocodile, *n.* crocodile *m.*

crocodile tears, *n.* larmes (*f.pl.*) de crocodile.

croissant, *n.* croissant *m.*

crone, *n.* vieille femme *f.*

crony, *n.* vieux camarade *m.,* compère *m.*

crook, *n.* escroc *m.;* (thief) voleur *m.*

crooked, *adj.* tortu.

croon, *vb.* chantonner, fredonner.

crop, 1. *n.* (farming) récolte *f.* **2.** *vb.* (c. up) surgir.

croquet, *n.* (jeu de) croquet *m.*

croquette, *n.* croquette *f.*

cross, 1. *n.* croix *f.* **2.** *adj.* maussade. **3.** *vb.* croiser, *tr.;* (c. oneself) se signer; (c. out) rayer; (go across) traverser.

crossbreed, *n.* race croisée *f.*

cross-examine, *vb.* contre-examiner.

cross-eyed, *adj.* louche.

cross-fertilization, *n.* croisement *m.*

crossfire, *n.* feux croisés *m.pl.*

cross-purpose, *n.* opposition *f.,* contradiction *f.,* malentendu *m.*

cross section, *n.* coupe (*f.*) en travers.

crossword puzzle, *n.* mots croisés *m.pl.*

crotch, *n.* (tree) fourche *f.;* (trousers) fourchet *m.*

crouch, *vb.* s'accroupir.

croup, *n.* croupe *f.;* (med.) croup *m.*

croupier, *n.* croupier *m.*

crouton, *n.* crouton *m.*

crow, 1. *n.* (bird) corneille *f.;* (cock-c.) chant (*m.*) du coq. **2.** *vb.* chanter.

crowd, 1. *n.* foule *f.* **2.** *vb.* serrer, *tr.;* (c. with) remplir de.

crowded, *adj.* (streets, etc.) encombré.

crown, 1. *n.* couronne *f.;* (of head) sommet *m.;* (of hat) calotte *f.* **2.** *vb.* couronner.

crown prince, *n.* prince héritier *m.*

crow's-foot, *n.* patte d'oie (near the eye) *f.;* (naut.) araignée *f.*

crucial, *adj.* crucial.

crucible, *n.* creuset *m.*

crucifix, *n.* crucifix *m.*

crucifixion, *n.* crucifixion *f.,* crucifiement *m.*

crucify, *vb.* crucifier.

crude, *adj.* (unpolished) grossier; (metals, etc.) brut.

crudeness, *n.* crudité *f.*

cruel, *adj.* cruel.

cruelty, *n.* cruauté *f.*

cruet, *n.* burette *f.*

cruise, *n.* croisière *f.*

cruiser, *n.* croiseur *m.*

crumb, *n.* (small piece) miette *f.;* (not crust) mie *f.*

crumble, *vb.* émietter, *tr.*

crumple, *vb.* chiffonner, *tr.*

crunch, 1. *vb.* croquer, broyer. **2.** *n.* grincement *m.*

crusade, *n.* croisade *f.*

crusader, *n.* croisé *m.*

crush, 1. *vb.* écraser. **2.** *n.* presse *f.,* foule *f.;* **(a c. on)** le béguin pour.

crust, *n.* croûte *f.*

crustacean, *adj.* crustacé.

crusty, *adj.* couvert d'une croûte; *(fig.)* bourru, maussade.

crutch, *n.* béquille *f.*

cry, 1. *n.* cri *m.* **2.** *vb.* (shout) crier; (weep) pleurer.

crybaby, *n.* pleurnicheur *m.*

crying, *adj.* criant.

cryosurgery, *n.* cryochirurgie *f.*

crypt, *n.* crypte *f.*

cryptic, *adj.* occulte, secret.

cryptography, *n.* cryptographie *f.*

crystal, *n.* cristal *m.*

crystalline, *adj.* cristallin.

crystallize, *vb.* cristalliser, *tr.*

cub, *n.* petit *m.* (d'un animal).

Cuba, *n.* Cuba *m.*

Cuban, 1. *n.* Cubain *m.* **2.** *adj.* cubain.

cubbyhole, *n.* retraite *f.,* cachette *f.,* placard *m.*

cube, *n.* cube *m.*

cubic, *adj.* cubique.

cubicle, *n.* compartiment *m.,* cabine *f.*

cubic measure, *n.* mesures *(f.pl.)* de volume.

cubism, *n.* cubisme *m.*

cuckold, 1. *n.* cocu *m.* **2.** *vb.* cocufier, faire cocu.

cuckoo, *n.* coucou *m.; (fig.)* niais *m.*

cucumber, *n.* concombre *m.*

cud, *n.* bol alimentaire *m.,* panse *f.,* chique (of tobacco) *f.*

cuddle, *vb.* serrer (dans ses bras), *tr.*

cudgel, 1. *n.* bâton *m.,* gourdin *m.,* trique *f.* **2.** *vb.* bâtonner.

cue, *n.* (theater) réplique *f.;* (hint) mot *m.*

cuff, *n.* poignet *m.*

cuff link, *n.* bouton (*m.*) de manchette.

cuisine, *n.* cuisine *f.*

cul-de-sac, *n.* cul de sac *m.,* impasse *f.*

culinary, *adj.* culinaire, de cuisine.

cull, *vb.* cueillir, recueillir.

culminate, *vb.* culminer.

culmination, *n.* point culminant *m.*

culpable, *adj.* coupable.

culprit, *n.* coupable *m.f.*

cult, *n.* culte *m.*

cultivate, *vb.* cultiver.

cultivated, *adj.* cultivé.

cultivation, *n.* culture *f.*

cultivator, *n.* cultivateur *m.*

cultural, *adj.* culturel.

culture, *n.* culture *f.*

cumbersome, *adj.* encombrant.

cumulative, *adj.* cumulatif.

cunning, 1. *n.* (guile) ruse *f.;* (skill) adresse *f.* **2.** *adj.* rusé; (attractive) charmant.

cup, *n.* tasse *f.*

cupboard, *n.* armoire *f.*

cupidity, *n.* cupidité *f.*

curable, *adj.* guérissable.

curator, *n.* conservateur *m.*

curb, 1. *n.* (horse) gourmette *f.;* (pavement) bord *m.* **2.** *vb.* (horse) gourmer; *(fig.)* brider.

curbstone, *n.* garde-pavé *m.*

curd, *n.* lait caillé *m.*

curdle, *vb.* cailler.

cure, 1. *n.* (healing) guérison *f.;* (remedy) remède *m.* **2.** *vb.* guérir.

curfew, *n.* couvre-feu *m.*

curio, *n.* curiosité *f.*

curiosity, *n.* curiosité *f.*

curious, *adj.* curieux.

curl, 1. *n.* boucle *f.* **2.** *vb.* friser.

curler, *n.* bigoudi *m.*

curly, *adj.* frisé.

currant, *n.* groseille *f.*

currency, *n.* monnaie *f.*

current, *adj. and n.* courant *m.*

current affairs, *n.* actualités *f.pl.*

currently, *adv.* actuellement.

curriculum, *n.* programme (*m.*) d'études., plan (*m.*) d'études.

curry, 1. *n.* (food) cari *m.* **2.** *vb.* **(c. favor with)** chercher à s'attirer les bonnes grâces de.

curse, 1. *n.* (malediction) malédiction *f.;* (oath) juron *m.;* (scourge) fléau *m.* **2.** *vb.* maudire; (swear) jurer.

cursed, *adj.* maudit.

cursor, *n.* curseur *m.*

cursory, *adj.* rapide, superficiel.

curt, *adj.* brusque.

curtail, *vb.* raccourcir.

curtain, *n.* rideau *m.*

curtsy, *n.* révérence *f.*

curvature, *n.* courbure *f.*

curve, 1. *n.* courbe *f.* **2.** *vb.* courber, *tr.*

cushion, *n.* coussin *m.*

cuspidor, *n.* crachoir *m.*

custard, *n.* crème *f.*

custodian, *n.* gardien *m.*

custody, *n.* (care) garde *f.;* (arrest) détention *f.*

custom, *n.* coutume *f.*

customary, *adj.* habituel.

customer, *n.* client *m.*

customize, *vb.* personnaliser.

customized, *adj.* fait sur demande.

custom-made, *adj.* fait sur mesure.

customs, *n.* douane *f.*

customs-officer, *n.* douanier *m.*

cut, 1. *n.* (wound) coupure *f.;* (clothes, hair) coupe *f.;* (reduction) réduction *f.* **2.** *vb.* couper.

cutaneous, *adj.* cutané.

cute, *adj.* gentil *m.,* gentille *f.*

cut glass, *n.* cristal *m.*

cuticle, *n.* cuticule *f.*

cutlery, *n.* coutellerie *f.*

cutlet, *n.* côtelette *f.*

cutout, *n.* découpage *m.,* coupe *f.*

cutter, *n.* coupeur *m.,* coupeuse *f.*

cutthroat, *n.* coupe-jarret *m.*

cutting, 1. *n.* incision *f.* **2.** *adj.* incisif, tranchant.

cyanide, *n.* cyanure *m.*

cybernetics, *n.* cybernétique *f.*

cyclamate, n. cyclamate m.
cycle, 1. n. cycle m. 2. vb. faire de la bicyclette.
cyclist, n. cycliste m.
cyclone, n. cyclone m.
cyclotron, n. cyclotron m.

cylinder, n. cylindre m.
cylindrical, adj. cylindrique.
cymbal, n. cymbale f.
cynic, n. cynique m.
cynical, adj. cynique.

cynicism, n. cynisme m.
cypress, n. cyprès m.
czar, n. tsar m.
Czechoslovakie, n. Tchécoslovaquie f.
cyst, n. kyste m.

D

dab, 1. n. coup léger m., tape f. 2. vb. toucher légèrement.
dabble, vb. humecter, faire l'amateur.
dad, n. papa m.
daddy, n. papa m.
daffodil, n. narcisse m.
daffy, adj. niais, sot.
dagger, n. poignard m.
dahlia, n. dahlia m.
daily, adj. quotidien.
daintiness, n. délicatesse f.
dainty, adj. délicat.
dairy, n. laiterie f.
dairyman, n. crémier m.
dais, n. estrade f.
daisy, n. marguerite f.
dale, n. vallon m., vallée f.
dam, n. digue f.
damage, 1. n. dommage m. 2. vb. endommager.
damaging, adj. nuisible.
damask, n. damas m.
damnation, n. damnation f.
damp, adj. humide.
dampen, vb. humecter.
dampness, n. humidité f., moiteur f.
damsel, n. demoiselle f., jeune fille f.
dance, 1. n. danse f. 2. vb. danser.
dancer, n. danseur m.
dandelion, n. pissenlit m.
dandruff, n. pellicules f.pl.
dandy, 1. n. dandy m. 2. adj. élégant.
Dane, n. Danois m.
danger, n. danger m.
dangerous, adj. dangereux.
dangle, vb. pendiller, intr.
Danish, 1. n. Danois m. 2. adj. danois.
dank, adj. humide et froid.
dapper, adj. pimpant, petit et vif.
dappled, adj. pommelé.

dare, vb. oser.
daredevil, n. casse-cou m.
daring, adj. audacieux.
dark, adj. sombre.
darken, vb. obscurcir, tr.
dark horse, n. tocard m.
darkness, n. obscurité f.
darkroom, n. chambre noire f.
darling, adj. and n. chéri m.
darn, 1. n. reprise f. 2. vb. repriser.
darning needle, n. aiguille à repriser f.
dart, 1. n. dard m.; (sewing) pince f. 2. vb. se précipiter.
dash, 1. n. (energy) fougue f.; (pen) trait m. 2. vb. (throw) lancer; (destroy) détruire; (rush) se précipiter.
dashboard, n. tableau (m.) de bord.
dashing, adj. fougueux, brillant, superbe.
data, n. données f.pl.
database, n. base (f.) de données.
data processing, n. élaboration f., traitement (m.) de données.
date, 1. n. date f.; (appointment) rendez-vous m.; (fruit) datte f. 2. vb. dater.
dated, adj. démodé.
date line, n. ligne (f.) de changement de date.
daub, 1. n. barbouillage m. 2. vb. barbouiller.
daughter, n. fille f.
daughter-in-law, n. belle-fille f.
daunt, vb. intimider.
dauntless, adj. intrépide, indomptable.
dauntlessly, adv. d'une manière intrépide.

davenport, n. divan m.
dawdle, vb. flâner, muser.
dawn, n. aube f.
day, n. jour m.; (span of day) journée f.
day care, n. garderie f.
daydream, n. rêverie f.
daylight, n. lumière (f.) du jour.
daylight-saving time, n. l'heure (f.) d'été.
daytime, n. jour m. journée f.
daze, vb. étourdir.
dazzle, vb. éblouir.
deacon, n. diacre m.
dead, adj. mort.
deaden, vb. amortir.
dead end, n. cul-de-sac m., impasse f.
dead letter, n. lettre morte f.
deadline, n. ligne (f.) de délimitation, date (f.) de limite.
deadlock, n. impasse f.
deadly, adj. mortel.
deadpan, adj. impassible.
deadwood, n. bois mort m.
deaf, adj. sourd.
deafen, vb. assourdir.
deaf-mute, adj. sourd-muet.
deafness, n. surdité f.
deal, 1. n. (business) affaire f.; (great d.) beaucoup; (cards) donne f. 2. vb. (d. with) traiter; (d. out) distribuer.
dealer, n. marchand m.
dealings, n. relations f.pl.
dean, n. doyen m.
dear, adj. and n. cher m.
dearly, adv. chèrement.
dearth, n. disette f.
death, n. mort f.
death certificate, n. acte (m.) de décès.
deathless, adj. impérissable.
deathly, adj. mortel.

death penalty, *n.* peine (*f.*) de mort.

debacle, *n.* débâcle *f.*

debase, *vb.* avilir.

debatable, *adj.* discutable.

debate, 1. *n.* débat *m.* **2.** *vb.* discuter.

debater, *n.* orateur parlementaire *m.*, argumentateur *m.*

debauch, 1. *n.* débauche *f.* **2.** *vb.* débaucher, corrompre.

debenture, *n.* obligation *f.*

debilitate, *vb.* débiliter, affaiblir.

debility, *n.* débilité *f.*

debit, *n.* débit *m.*

debonair, *adj.* courtois et jovial.

debris, *n.* débris *m.pl.*

debt, *n.* dette *f.*

debtor, *n.* débiteur *m.*

debunk, *vb.* dégonfler.

debut, *n.* début *m.*

debutante, *n.* débutante *f.*

decade, *n.* décennie *f.*

decadence, *n.* décadence *f.*

decadent, *adj.* décadent.

decaffeinated, *adj.* décaféiné.

decalcomania, *n.* décalcomanie *f.*

decanter, *n.* carafe *f.*

decapitate, *vb.* décapiter.

decay, 1. *n.* décadence *f.*; (state of ruin) délabrement *m.*; (teeth) carie *f.* **2.** *vb.* tomber en décadence.

deceased, *adj.* défunt.

deceit, *n.* tromperie *f.*

deceitful, *adj.* trompeur.

deceive, *vb.* tromper.

deceiver, *n.* imposteur.

December, *n.* décembre *m.*

decency, *n.* décence *f.*

decent, *adj.* décent.

decentralization, *n.* décentralisation *f.*

decentralize, *vb.* décentraliser.

deception, *n.* tromperie *f.*, duperie *f.*

deceptive, *adj.* décevant, trompeur.

decibel, *n.* décibel *m.*

decide, *vb.* décider.

decided, *adj.* décidé, prononcé.

decidedly, *adv.* décidément.

deciduous, *adj.* à feuillage caduc.

decimal, *adj.* décimal.

decimal point, *n.* virgule *f.*

decimate, *vb.* décimer.

decipher, *vb.* déchiffrer.

decision, *n.* décision *f.*

decisive, *adj.* décisif.

deck, *n.* (boat) pont *m.*; (cards) jeu *m.*

deck chair, *n.* chaise (*f.*) longue.

deck hand, *n.* matelot (*m.*) de pont.

declaim, *vb.* déclamer.

declamation, *n.* déclamation *f.*

declaration, *n.* déclaration *f.*

declarative, *adj.* explicatif, (law) déclaratif.

declare, *vb.* déclarer.

declension, *n.* déclinaison *f.*

decline, *vb.* décliner.

decode, *vb.* déchiffrer, décoder.

decoder, *n.* décodeur *m.*

décolleté, *adj.* décolleté.

decompose, *vb.* décomposer, *tr.*

decongestant, *adj.* décongestionnant.

decor, *n.* décor *m.*

decorate, *vb.* décorer.

decoration, *n.* décoration *f.*

decorative, *adj.* décoratif.

decorator, *n.* décorateur *m.*

decorous, *adj.* bienséant, convenable.

decorum, *n.* décorum *m.*

decoy, 1. *n.* leurre *m.* **2.** *vb.* leurrer.

decrease, 1. *n.* diminution *f.* **2.** *vb.* diminuer.

decree, *n.* décret *m.*

decrepit, *adj.* décrépit.

decry, *vb.* décrier, dénigrer.

dedicate, *vb.* dédier.

dedication, *n.* dédicace *f.*

deduce, *vb.* déduire.

deduct, *vb.* déduire.

deduction, *n.* déduction.

deductive, *adj.* déductif.

deed, *n.* action *f.*; (law) acte (*m.*) notarié.

deem, *vb.* juger.

deep, *adj.* profond.

deepen, *vb.* approfondir, *tr.*

deep freeze, *n.* surgélateur *m.*

deeply, *adv.* profondément.

deep-rooted, *adj.* enraciné.

deep-seated, *adj.* profond.

deer, *n.* cerf *m.*

deerskin, *n.* peau (*f.*) de daim.

deface, *vb.* défigurer.

defamation, *n.* diffamation *f.*

defame, *vb.* diffamer.

default, *n.* défaut *m.*

defeat, 1. *n.* défaite *f.* **2.** *vb.* vaincre.

defeatism, *n.* défaitisme *m.*

defect, 1. *n.* défaut *m.* **2.** *vb.* passer à l'ennemi.

defection, *n.* défection *f.*

defective, *adj.* défectueux.

defend, *vb.* défendre.

defendant, *n.* défendeur *m.*; (in court) accusé *m.*, prévenu *m.*

defender, *n.* défenseur *m.*

defense, *n.* défense *f.*

defenseless, *adj.* sans défense.

defensible, *adj.* défendable, soutenable.

defensive, *adj.* défensif.

defer, *vb.* (put off) différer; (show deference) déférer.

deference, *n.* déférence *f.*

deferential, *adj.* plein de déférence, respectueux.

defiance, *n.* défi *m.*

defiant, *adj.* de défi.

deficiency, *n.* insuffisance *f.*

deficient, *adj.* insuffisant.

deficit, *n.* déficit *m.*

defile, *vb.* souiller.

define, *vb.* définir.

definite, *adj.* défini.

definitely, *adv.* d'une manière déterminée.

definition, *n.* définition *f.*

definitive, *adj.* définitif.

deflate, *vb.* dégonfler.

deflation, *n.* dégonflement *m.*

deflect, *vb.* faire dévier, détourner.

deforestation, *n.* déforestation *f.*

deform, *vb.* déformer.

deformity, *n.* difformité *f.*

defraud, *vb.* frauder.

defray, *vb.* payer.

defrost, *vb.* déglacer.

defroster, *n.* déglaceur *m.*

deft, *adj.* adroit.

defunct, *adj.* défunt.

defy, *vb.* défier.

degenerate, *vb.* dégénérer.

degeneration, *n.* dégénérescence *f.*

degradation, *n.* dégradation *f.*

degrade, *vb.* dégrader.

degree, *n.* degré *m.;* (university) diplôme *m.*

dehydrate, *vb.* déshydrater.

de-ice, *vb.* dégivrer.

deify, *vb.* déifier.

deign, *vb.* daigner.

deity, *n.* divinité *f.*

dejected, *adj.* abattu.

dejection, *n.* abattement *m.*

delay, 1. *n.* retard *m.* **2.** *vb.* retarder, *tr.;* tarder, *intr.*

delectable, *adj.* délectable.

delegate, 1. *n.* délégué *m.* **2.** *vb.* déléguer.

delegation, *n.* délégation *f.*

delete, *vb.* rayer, biffer; (computer) effacer.

deletion, *n.* suppression *f.,* rature *f.*

deliberate, 1. *adj.* délibéré. **2.** *vb.* délibérer.

deliberately, *adv.* (carefully) de propos délibéré; (on purpose) exprès.

deliberation, *n.* délibération *f.*

deliberative, *adj.* délibératif.

delicacy, *n.* délicatesse *f.*

delicate, *adj.* délicat.

delicatessen, *n.* charcuterie *f.*

delicious, *adj.* délicieux.

delight, 1. *n.* délices *f.pl.* **2.** *vb.* enchanter.

delightful, *adj.* charmant.

delineate, *vb.* esquisser, dessiner.

delinquency, *n.* délit *m.*

delinquent, *adj. and n.* délinquant *m.*

delirious, *adj.* délirant.

delirium, *n.* délire *m.*

deliver, *vb.* délivrer; (speech) prononcer.

deliverance, *n.* délivrance *f.*

delivery, *n.* (child) accouchement *m.;* (speech) débit *m.;* (goods) livraison *f.;* (letters) distribu-

tion *f.;* **(general d.)** poste restante *f.*

delouse, *vb.* épouiller.

delta, *n.* delta *m.*

delude, *vb.* tromper.

deluge, *n.* déluge *m.*

delusion, *n.* illusion *f.*

deluxe, *adv.* de luxe.

delve, *vb.* creuser, pénétrer.

demagogue, *n.* démagogue *m.*

demand, 1. *n.* demande *f.* **2.** *vb.* demander; (as right) exiger.

demanding, *adj.* exigeant.

demarcation, *n.* démarcation *f.*

demean, *vb.* **(d. oneself)** s'avilir, s'abaisser.

demeanor, *n.* maintien *m.*

demented, *adj.* fou *m.,* folle *f.*

demerit, *n.* démérite *m.*

demigod, *n.* demi-dieu *n.*

demilitarize, *vb.* démilitariser.

demise, *n.* décès *m.,* mort *f.*

demo, *n.* démonstration *f.*

demobilization, *n.* démobilisation *f.*

demobilize, *vb.* démobiliser.

democracy, *n.* démocratie *f.*

democrat, *n.* démocrate *m.f.*

democratic, *adj.* démocratique.

demolish, *vb.* démolir.

demolition, *n.* démolition *f.*

demon, *n.* démon *m.*

demonstrable, *adj.* démonstrable.

demonstrate, *vb.* démontrer.

demonstration, *n.* démonstration *f.*

demonstrative, *adj.* démonstratif.

demonstrator, *n.* démonstrateur *m.*

demoralize, *vb.* démoraliser.

demote, *vb.* réduire à un grade inférieur.

demur, *vb.* hésiter, s'opposer à.

demure, *adj.* posé, d'une modestie affectée.

den, *n.* antre *m.,* repaire *m.*

denaturalize, *vb.* dénaturaliser.

denature, *vb.* dénaturer.

denial, *n.* dénégation *f.;* (refusal) refus *m.*

denim, *n.* treillis *m.*

Denmark, *n.* Danemark *m.*

denomination, *n.* dénomination *f.;* (religion) confession *f.*

denominator, *n.* dénominateur *m.*

denote, *vb.* dénoter.

denouement, *n.* dénouement *m.*

denounce, *vb.* dénoncer.

dense, *adj.* dense; (stupid) bête.

density, *n.* densité *f.*

dent, *n.* bosselure *f.*

dental, *adj.* dentaire; *(gramm.)* dental.

dentifrice, *n.* dentifrice *m.*

dentist, *n.* dentiste *m.*

dentistry, *n.* art *(m.)* du dentiste, dentisterie *f.*

denture, *n.* dentier *m.,* râtelier *m.*

denude, *vb.* dénuder.

denunciation, *n.* dénonciation *f.*

deny, *vb.* nier.

deodorant, *n.* désodorisant *m.*

deodorize, *vb.* désodoriser, désinfecter.

depart, *vb.* partir, s'en aller, quitter.

department, *n.* département *m.;* (government) ministère *m.;* **(d. store)** grand magasin *m.*

departmental, *adj.* départemental.

departure, *n.* départ *m.*

dependability, *n.* confiance *(f.)* que l'on inspire.

dependable, *adj.* digne de confiance.

dependence, *n.* dépendance *f.,* confiance *f.*

dependent, 1. *adj.* dépendant. **2.** *n.* personne *(f.)* à charge.

depend on, *vb.* dépendre de; (rely) compter sur.

depict, *vb.* peindre.

depiction, *n.* description *f.*

deplete, *vb.* épuiser.

deplorable, *adj.* déplorable.

deplore, *vb.* déplorer.

depopulate, *vb.* dépeupler.

deport, *vb.* déporter.

deportation, *n.* déportation *f.*

deportment, *n.* maintien *m.*

depose, *vb.* déposer.

deposit, 1. *n.* dépôt *m.* **2.** *vb.* déposer.

depositor, *n.* déposant *m.*

depository, *n.* dépôt *m.,* dépositaire *m.*

depot, *n.* dépôt *m.,* gare *f.*

deprave, *vb.* dépraver, corrompre.

depravity, *n.* dépravation *f.,* corruption *f.*

deprecate, *vb.* désapprouver, s'opposer à.

depreciate, *vb.* déprécier.

depreciation, *n.* dépréciation *f.*

depredation, *n.* déprédation *f.,* pillage *m.*

depress, *vb.* (lower) abaisser; *(fig.)* abattre.

depressed, *adj.* abattu, bas.

depression, *n.* dépression *f.;* (personal) abattement *m.; (comm.)* crise *f.*

deprivation, *n.* privation *f.*

deprive, *vb.* priver.

depth, *n.* profondeur *f.*

depth charge, *n.* grenade *(f.)* sous-marine.

deputy, *n.* délégué *m.;* (politics) député *m.*

derail, *vb.* dérailler.

derange, *vb.* déranger.

deranged, *adj.* dérangé, troublé.

derelict, 1. *n.* vaisseau abandonné *m.,* épave *f.* **2.** *adj.* abandonné, délaissé.

dereliction, *n.* abandon *m.*

deride, *vb.* tourner en dérision.

derision, *n.* dérision *f.*

derisive, *adj.* dérisoire.

derisory, *adj.* dérisoire.

derivation, *n.* dérivation *f.,* origine *f.*

derivative, *n.* dérivatif.

derive, *vb.* dériver.

dermatology, *n.* dermatologie *f.*

derogatory, *adj.* dérogatoire.

derrick, *n.* grue *f.*

descend, *vb.* descendre.

descendant, *n.* descendant *m.*

descent, *n.* descente *f.*

describe, *vb.* décrire.

description, *n.* description *f.*

descriptive, *adj.* descriptif.

desecrate, *vb.* profaner.

desensitize, *vb.* désensibiliser.

desert, 1. *n.* (place) désert *m.;* (merit) mérite *m.* **2.** *vb.* déserter.

deserter, *n.* déserteur *m.*

desertion, *n.* abandon *m.;* (military) désertion *f.*

deserve, *vb.* mériter.

deserving, *adj.* méritoire, de mérite.

design, 1. *n.* (project) dessein *m.;* (architecture) projet *m.* **2.** *vb.* dessiner; **(d. for)** destiner à.

designate, *vb.* désigner.

designation, *n.* désignation *f.*

designedly, *adv.* à dessein.

designer, *n.* dessinateur *m.*

designing, *adj.* intrigant, artificieux.

desirable, *adj.* désirable.

desire, 1. *n.* désir *m.* **2.** *vb.* désirer.

desirous, *adj.* désireux.

desist, *vb.* cesser.

desk, *n.* (office) bureau *m.;* (school) pupitre *m.*

desolate, *adj.* désolé.

desolation, *n.* désolation *f.*

despair, 1. *n.* désespoir *m.* **2.** *vb.* désespérer.

desperado, *n.* désespéré *m.,* cerveau brûlé *m.*

desperate, *adj.* désespéré.

desperation, *n.* désespoir *m.*

despicable, *adj.* méprisable.

despise, *vb.* mépriser.

despite, *prep.* en dépit de.

despondent, *adj.* découragé.

despot, *n.* despote *m.*

despotic, *adj.* despotique.

despotism, *n.* despotisme *m.*

dessert, *n.* dessert *m.*

destination, *n.* destination *f.*

destine, *vb.* destiner.

destiny, *n.* destin *m.*

destitute, *adj.* (deprived) dénué; (poor) indigent.

destitution, *n.* destitution *f.*

destroy, *vb.* détruire.

destroyer, *n.* destructeur *m.;* *(naval)* contre-torpilleur *m.*

destructible, *adj.* destructible.

destruction, *n.* destruction *f.*

destructive, *adj.* destructif.

desultory, *adj.* à bâtons rompus, décousu.

detach, *vb.* détacher.

detachment, *n.* détachement *m.*

detail, *n.* détail *m.*

detain, *vb.* retenir; (in prison) détenir.

detect, *vb.* découvrir.

detection, *n.* découverte *f.*

detective, *n.* agent *(m.)* de la police secrète; **(d. novel)** roman policier.

detente, *n.* détente *f.*

detention, *n.* détention *f.*

deter, *vb.* détourner, empêcher (de), dissuader (de).

detergent, *n.* détersif *m.*

deteriorate, *vb.* détériorer, tr.

deterioration, *n.* détérioration *f.*

determination, *n.* détermination *f.*

determine, *vb.* déterminer.

determined, *adj.* déterminé.

determinism, *n.* déterminisme *m.*

deterrence, *n.* préventif *m.*

deterrent, *n. and adj.* préventif *m.*

detest, *vb.* détester.

dethrone, *vb.* détrôner.

detonate, *vb.* détoner.

detour, *n.* détour *m.*

detract, *vb.* enlever, ôter (à), dénigrer, déroger (à).

detriment, *n.* détriment *m.,* préjudice *m.*

detrimental, *adj.* préjudiciable, nuisible (à).

devaluate, *vb.* dévaluer, déprécier.

devaluation, *n.* dévaluation *f.*

devastate, *vb.* dévaster.

devastating, *adj.* dévastateur, (news) accablant.

develop, *vb.* développer, tr.

developer, *n.* (photography) révélateur *m.*

developing nation, *n.* nation (*f.*) en voie de développement.

development, *n.* développement *m.*

deviant, 1. *adj.* anormal. **2.** *n.* déviant *m.*

deviate, *vb.* dévier, s'écarter (de).

deviation, *n.* déviation *f.*, écart *m.*

device, *n.* expédient *m.*

devil, *n.* diable *m.*

devilish, *adj.* diabolique.

devious, *adj.* détourné.

devise, *vb.* (plan) combiner; (plot) tramer.

devitalize, *vb.* dévitaliser.

devoid, *adj.* dépourvu.

devolution, *n.* décentralisation.

devote, *vb.* consacrer.

devoted, *adj.* dévoué.

devotee, *n.* dévot *m.*, dévote *f.*, adepte *m.f.*

devotion, *n.* (religious) dévotion *f.*; (to person or thing) dévouement *m.*

devour, *vb.* dévorer.

devout, *adj.* dévot.

dew, *n.* rosée *f.*

dewy, *adj.* de rosée.

dexterity, *n.* dextérité *f.*

dexterous, *adj.* adroit.

diabetes, *n.* diabète *m.*

diabolic, *adj.* diabolique.

diadem, *n.* diadème *m.*

diagnose, *vb.* diagnostiquer.

diagnosis, *n.* diagnose *f.*

diagnostic, *adj.* diagnostique.

diagonal, *adj.* diagonal.

diagonally, *adv.* diagonalement.

diagram, *n.* diagramme *m.*

dial, 1. *n.* cadran *m.* **2.** *vb.* (d. a number) composer.

dialect, *n.* dialecte *m.*

dialogue, *n.* dialogue *m.*

dial tone, *n.* tonalité *f.*

diameter, *n.* diamètre *m.*

diametrical, *adj.* diamétral.

diamond, *n.* diamant *m.*; (shape) losange *m.*; (cards) carreau *m.*

diaper, *n.* (babies) couche *f.*

diaphragm, *n.* diaphragme *m.*

diarrhea, *n.* diarrhée *f.*

diary, *n.* journal *m.*

diathermy, *n.* diathermie *f.*

diatribe, *n.* diatribe *f.*

dice, *n.* dés *m.pl.*

dicker, *vb.* marchander.

dictaphone, *n.* machine à dicter *f.*

dictate, *vb.* dicter.

dictation, *n.* dictée *f.*

dictator, *n.* dictateur *m.*

dictatorial, *adj.* dictatorial.

dictatorship, *n.* dictature *f.*

diction, *n.* diction *f.*

dictionary, *n.* dictionnaire *m.*

didactic, *adj.* didactique.

die, 1. *n.* dé *m.* **2.** *vb.* mourir.

die-hard, *n.* intransigeant *m.*, ultra *m.*

diesel, *n.* diesel *m.*

diet, *n.* régime *m.*

dietary, *adj.* diététique.

dietetics, *n.* diététique *f.*

dietitian, *n.* diététicien *m.*

differ, *vb.* différer.

difference, *n.* différence *f.*

different, *adj.* différent.

differential, *adj.* différentiel.

differentiate (between), *vb.* faire une différence (entre).

difficult, *adj.* difficile.

difficulty, *n.* difficulté *f.*

diffident, *adj.* hésitant, timide.

diffuse, *adj.* diffus.

diffusion, *n.* diffusion *f.*

dig, *vb.* bêcher; (hole) creuser.

digest, *vb.* digérer.

digestible, *adj.* digestible.

digestion, *n.* digestion *f.*

digestive, *adj. and n.* digestif *m.*

digit, *n.* chiffre *m.*

digital, *adj.* (in watches, etc.) digital, numérique.

digitalis, *n.* digitaline *f.*

dignified, *adj.* plein de dignité.

dignify, *vb.* honorer, élever.

dignitary, *n.* dignitaire *m.*

dignity, *n.* dignité *f.*

digress, *vb.* faire une digression.

digression, *n.* digression *f.*

dike, *n.* (ditch) fossé *m.*; (dam) digue *f.*

dilapidated, *adj.* délabré.

dilapidation, *n.* délabrement *m.*

dilate, *vb.* dilater, *tr.*

dilatory, *adj.* dilatoire, lent, négligent.

dilemma, *n.* dilemme *m.*

dilettante, *n.* dilettante *m.*, amateur *m.*

diligence, *n.* diligence *f.*

diligent, *adj.* diligent.

dill, *n.* aneth *m.*

dilute, *vb.* diluer.

dim, 1. *adj.* (light, sight) faible; (color) terne. **2.** *vb.* réduire, baisser.

dime, *n.* un dixième de dollar *m.*

dimension, *n.* dimension *f.*

diminish, *vb.* diminuer.

diminution, *n.* diminution *f.*

diminutive, 1. *adj.* tout petit. **2.** *n.* (*gramm.*) diminutif *m.*

dimness, *n.* (weakness) faiblesse *f.*; (darkness) obscurité *f.*

dimple, *n.* (face) fossette *f.*

din, *n.* tapage *m.*

dine, *vb.* dîner.

diner, dining-car, *n.* wagon-restaurant *m.*

dingy, *adj.* défraîchi.

dining room, *n.* salle (*f.*) à manger.

dinner, *n.* dîner *m.*; (d. jacket) smoking *m.*

dinosaur, *n.* dinosaurie *m.*

diocese, *n.* diocèse *m.*

dint, *n.* (by d. of) à force de.

dip, *vb.* plonger.

diphtheria, *n.* diphtérie *f.*

diphthong, *n.* diphtongue *f.*

diploma, *n.* diplôme *m.*

diplomacy, *n.* diplomatie *f.*

diplomat, *n.* diplomate *m.*

diplomatic, *adj.* diplomatique.

dipper, *n.* cuiller (*f.*) à pot.

dire, *adj.* affreux.

direct, 1. *vb.* (guide) diriger; (address) adresser; (film) réaliser; (play) mettre en scène. **2.** *adj.* direct.

direct current, *n.* courant continu *m.*

direction, *n.* direction *f.*; (orders) instructions *f.pl.*

directional, *adj.* de direction.

directive, 1. *n.* directif *m.* **2.** *adj.* dirigeant.

directly, *adv.* directement.

directness, *n.* rectitude *f.;* (frankness) franchise *f.*

director, *n.* directeur *m.,* (theater) metteur *(m.)* en scène, (cinema, TV) réalisateur *m.*

directorate, *n.* conseil *(m.)* d'administration.

directory, *n.* annuaire *m.*

dirge, *n.* chant funèbre *m.*

dirigible, *adj. and n.* dirigeable *m.*

dirt, *n.* saleté *f.*

dirty, 1. *adj.* sale. **2.** *vb.* salir.

disability, *n.* incapacité *f.*

disable, *vb.* mettre hors de combat, *tr.*

disabled, *adj.* invalide.

disabuse, *vb.* désabuser.

disadvantage, *n.* désavantage *m.*

disagree, *vb.* être en désaccord.

disagreeable, *adj.* désagréable.

disagreement, *n.* désaccord *m.*

disappear, *vb.* disparaître.

disappearance, *n.* disparition *f.*

disappoint, *vb.* désappointer.

disappointing, *adj.* décevant.

disappointment, *n.* déception *f.*

disapproval, *n.* désapprobation *f.*

disapprove, *vb.* désapprouver.

disarm, *vb.* désarmer.

disarmament, *n.* désarmement *m.*

disarray, *n.* désarroi *m.,* désordre *m.*

disassemble, *vb.* démonter, désassembler.

disaster, *n.* désastre *m.*

disastrous, *adj.* désastreux.

disavow, *vb.* désavouer.

disavowal, *n.* désaveu *m.*

disband, *vb.* congédier, *tr.;* se débander, *intr.*

disbar, *vb.* rayer du tableau des avocats.

disbelief, *n.* incrédulité *f.*

disbelieve, *vb.* ne pas croire, refuser de croire.

disburse, *vb.* débourser.

disc, *n.* disque *m.*

discard, *vb.* mettre de côté.

discern, *vb.* discerner.

discerning, *adj.* judicieux, éclairé.

discernment, *n.* discernement *m.*

discharge, 1. *n.* décharge *f.;* (mil.) congé *m.* **2.** *vb.* décharger; (mil.) congédier.

disciple, *n.* disciple *m.*

disciplinarian, *n.* disciplinaire *m.*

disciplinary, *adj.* disciplinaire.

discipline, *n.* discipline *f.*

disclaim, *vb.* désavouer, nier.

disclaimer, *n.* désaveu *m.*

disclose, *vb.* révéler.

disclosure, *n.* révélation *f.*

disco, *adj.* disco.

discolor, *vb.* décolorer.

discoloration, *n.* décoloration *f.*

discomfiture, *n.* défaite *f.,* déroute *f.*

discomfort, *n.* malaise *m.*

disconcert, *vb.* déconcerter.

disconnect, *vb.* désunir; (electric) débrancher.

disconnected, *adj.* (electricity) hors circuit.

disconsolate, *adj.* désolé.

discontent, *n.* mécontentement *m.*

discontented, *adj.* mécontent.

discontinue, *vb.* discontinuer.

discord, *n.* discorde *f.*

discordant, *adj.* discordant, en désaccord.

discotheque, *n.* discothèque *f.*

discount, 1. *n.* escompte *m.;* (reduction) remise *f.* **2.** *vb.* ne pas tenir compte de.

discourage, *vb.* décourager.

discouragement, *n.* découragement *m.*

discourse, *n.* discours *m.*

discourteous, *adj.* impoli.

discourtesy, *n.* impolitesse *f.*

discover, *vb.* découvrir.

discoverer, *n.* découvreur *m.*

discovery, *n.* découverte *f.*

discredit, 1. *n.* discrédit *m.* **2.** *vb.* discréditer.

discreditable, *adj.* déshonorant, peu honorable.

discreet, *adj.* discret.

discrepancy, *n.* contradiction *f.*

discretion, *n.* discrétion *f.*

discriminate, *vb.* distinguer.

discrimination, *n.* discernement *m.,* jugement *m.*

discursive, *adj.* discursif, sans suite.

discuss, *vb.* discuter.

discussion, *n.* discussion *f.*

disdain, *n.* dédain *m.*

disdainful, *adj.* dédaigneux.

disease, *n.* maladie *f.*

diseased, *adj.* malade.

disembark, *vb.* débarquer.

disembody, *vb.* dépouiller du corps.

disenchantment, *n.* désenchantement *m.*

disengage, *vb.* dégager.

disentangle, *vb.* démêler.

disfavor, *n.* défaveur *f.*

disfigure, *vb.* défigurer, enlaidir.

disfranchise, *vb.* priver du droit de vote.

disgorge, *vb.* dégorger.

disgrace, *n.* disgrâce *f.*

disgraceful, *adj.* honteux.

disgruntled, *adj.* mécontent, de mauvaise humeur.

disguise, 1. *n.* déguisement *m.* **2.** *vb.* dégoûter.

disgust, 1. *n.* dégout *m.* **2.** *vb.* dégouter.

disgusting, *adj.* dégoûtant.

dish, *n.* plat *m.;* (wash the d.s) laver la vaisselle.

dishcloth, *n.* torchon *m.*

dishearten, *vb.* décourager.

disheveled, *adj.* échevelé.

dishonest, *adj.* malhonnête.

dishonesty, *n.* malhonnêteté *f.*

dishonor, *n.* déshonneur *m.*

dishonorable, *adj.* (action) déshonorant.

dishwasher, *n.* lave-vaisselle *m.*

disillusion, *n.* désillusion *f.*

disinclined, *adj.* **(be d. to)** décourager.

disinfect, *vb.* désinfecter.

disinfectant, *n.* désinfectant *m.*

disinherit, *vb.* déshériter.

disintegrate, *vb.* désagréger.

disinterested, *adj.* désintéressé.

disjointed, *adj.* désarticulé, disloqué.

disk, *n.* disque *m.;* **(floppy d.)** disquette *f.;* **(d. drive)** lecteur *(m.)* de disquettes.

diskette, *n.* disquette *f.*

dislike, 1, *n.* aversion *f.* 2. *vb.* ne pas aimer.

dislocate, *vb.* disloquer.

dislodge, *vb.* déloger.

disloyal, *adj.* infidèle.

disloyalty, *n.* infidélité *f.,* perfidie *f.*

dismal, *adj.* sombre.

dismantle, *vb.* dépouiller (de).

dismay, *n.* consternation *f.*

dismember, *vb.* démembrer.

dismiss, *vb.* congédier.

dismissal, *n.* renvoi *m.*

dismount, *vb.* descendre.

disobedience, *n.* désobéissance *f.*

disobedient, *adj.* désobéissant.

disobey, *vb.* désobéir à.

disorder, *n.* désordre *m.*

disorderly, *adj.* désordonné.

disorganize, *vb.* désorganiser.

disorient, *vb.* désorienter.

disown, *vb.* désavouer.

disparage, *vb.* déprécier, dénigrer.

disparaging, *adj.* désobligeant.

disparate, *adj.* disparate.

disparity, *n.* inégalité *f.*

dispassionate, *adj.* calme.

dispatch, 1. *n.* (business) expédition *f.;* (speed) promptitude *f.;* (message) dépêche *f.* 2. *vb.* expédier.

dispatcher, *n.* expéditeur *m.*

dispel, *vb.* dissiper.

dispensable, *adj.* dont on peut se passer.

dispensary, *n.* dispensaire *m.*

dispensation, *n.* dispensation *f.*

dispense, *vb.* distribuer, dispenser.

dispersal, *n.* dispersion *f.*

disperse, *vb.* disperser.

dispirited, *adj.* découragé.

displace, *vb.* déplacer.

displaced person, *n.* réfugié *m.*

displacement, *n.* déplacement *m.*

display, 1. *n.* (show) exposition *f.;* (shop, ostentation) étalage *m.* 2. *vb.* étaler.

display window, *n.* vitrine *f.*

displease, *vb.* déplaire à.

disposable, *adj.* disponible, jetable.

disposal, *n.* disposition *f.*

dispose, *vb.* disposer.

disposition, *n.* disposition *f.;* (character) caractère *m.*

dispossess, *vb.* déposséder, exproprier.

disproportion, *n.* disproportion *f.*

disproportionate, *adj.* disproportionné.

disprove, *vb.* réfuter.

disputable, *adj.* contestable, disputable.

dispute, 1. *n.* (discussion) discussion *f.;* (quarrel) dispute *f.* 2. *vb.* (se) disputer.

disqualify, *vb.* (sports) disqualifier.

disregard, *vb.* ne tenir aucun compte de.

disrepair, *n.* délabrement *m.*

disreputable, *adj.* déshonorant, honteux.

disrespect, *n.* irrévérence *f.*

disrespectful, *adj.* irrespectueux.

disrobe, *vb.* déshabiller, dévêtir.

disrupt, *vb.* faire éclater, rompre.

dissatisfaction, *n.* mécontentement *m.*

dissatisfy, *vb.* mécontenter.

dissect, *vb.* disséquer.

dissemble, *vb.* dissimuler.

disseminate, *vb.* disséminer.

dissension, *n.* dissension *f.*

dissent, 1. *vb.* différer. 2. *n.* dissentiment *m.*

dissertation, *n.* dissertation *f.,* discours *m.*

disservice, *n.* mauvais service rendu *m.*

dissimilar, *adj.* dissemblable.

dissipate, *vb.* dissiper.

dissipated, *adj.* dissipé.

dissipation, *n.* dissipation *f.*

dissociate, *vb.* désassocier, dissocier.

dissolute, *adj.* dissolu.

dissolution, *n.* dissolution *f.*

dissolve, *vb.* dissoudre, *tr.*

dissonance, *n.* dissonance *f.,* désaccord *m.*

dissonant, *adj.* dissonant.

dissuade, *vb.* dissuader.

distance, *n.* distance *f.*

distant, *adj.* distant.

distaste, *n.* dégoût *m.*

distasteful, *adj.* désagréable.

distemper, 1. *n.* maladie *(f.)* des chiens. 2. *vb.* peindre en détrempe.

distend, *vb.* dilater, gonfler.

distended, *adj.* dilaté.

distill, *vb.* distiller.

distillation, *n.* distillation *f.*

distiller, *n.* distillateur *m.*

distillery, *n.* distillerie *f.*

distinct, *adj.* distinct.

distinction, *n.* distinction *f.*

distinctive, *adj.* distinctif.

distinctly, *adv.* distinctement, clairement.

distinguish, *vb.* distinguer.

distinguished, *adj.* distingué.

distort, *vb.* déformer.

distract, *vb.* (divert) distraire; (upset) affoler.

distracted, *adj.* affolé, bouleversé.

distraction, *n.* (diversion) distraction *f.;* (madness) folie *f.*

distraught, *adj.* affolé, éperdu, hors de soi.

distress, 1. *n.* détresse *f.* 2. *vb.* affliger.

distressing, *adj.* affligeant, pénible, désolant.

distribute, *vb.* distribuer.

distribution, *n.* distribution *f.*

distributor, *n.* distributeur *m.*

district, *n.* (region) contrée *f.;* (administration) district *m.;* (town) quartier *m.*

district attorney, *n.* procureur *(m.)* de la République.

distrust, 1. *n.* méfiance *f.* **2.** *vb.* se méfier de.

distrustful, *adj.* méfiant.

disturb, *vb.* déranger.

disturbance, *n.* dérangement *m.*

disunite, *vb.* désunir.

disuse, *n.* désuétude *f.*

ditch, *n.* fossé *m.*

ditto, *adv.* idem, de même.

diva, *n.* diva *f.*

divan, *n.* divan *m.*

dive, *vb.* plonger.

dive bomber, *n.* avion *(m.)* de bombardement qui fait des vols piqués.

diver, *n.* plongeur *m.*

diverge, *vb.* diverger.

divergence, *n.* divergence *f.*

divergent, *adj.* divergent.

diverse, *adj.* divers.

diversion, *n.* (amusement) divertissement *m.;* (turning aside) détournement *m.*

diversity, *n.* diversité *f.*

divert, *vb.* (turn aside) détourner; (amuse) divertir.

divest, *vb.* ôter, dépouiller, priver.

divide, *vb.* diviser.

divided, *adj.* divisé, séparé.

dividend, *n.* dividende *m.*

divine, *adj.* divin.

diving, *n.* plongée *f.;* **(d. board)** plongeoir *m.;* **(d. suit)** tenue *(f.)* de plongée.

divinity, *n.* divinité *f.*

divisible, *adj.* divisible.

division, *n.* division *f.*

divisive, *adj.* qui divise, qui sépare.

divorce, 1. *n.* divorce *m.* **2.** *vb.* divorcer.

divorcee, *n.* divorcé *m.,* divorcée *f.*

divulge, *vb.* divulguer.

dizziness, *n.* vertige *m.*

dizzy, *adj.* pris de vertige.

do, *vb.* faire; **(how d. you d.?)** comment allez-vous?

docile, *adj.* docile.

dock, *n.* bassin *m.*

docket, *n.* registre *m.,* bordereau *m.*

dockyard, *n.* chantier *(m.)* de construction de navires.

doctor, *n.* (academic) docteur *m.;* (med.) médecin *m.*

doctorate, *n.* doctorat *m.*

doctrinaire, *adj.* doctrinaire.

doctrine, *n.* doctrine *f.*

document, *n.* document *m.*

documentary, *adj.* documentaire.

documentation, *n.* documentation *f.*

dodge, *vb.* esquiver, éluder.

doe, *n.* daine *f.,* biche *f.*

doeskin, *n.* peau *(f.)* de daim.

dog, *n.* chien *m.*

dogfight, *n.* combat *(m.)* de chiens, mêlée générale *f.*

dogged, *adj.* obstiné, tenace.

doggerel, *n.* poésie burlesque *f.*

doghouse, *n.* chenil *m.*

dogma, *n.* dogme *m.*

dogmatic, *adj.* dogmatique.

dogmatism, *n.* dogmatisme *m.*

doily, *n.* petit napperon *m.*

do-it-yourself, *n.* bricolage *m.*

doldrum, *n.* (naut.) zone des calmes *f.;* cafard *m.*

dole, 1. *n.* pitance *f.;* aumône *f.* **2.** *vb.* distribuer parcimonieusement.

doleful, *adj.* lugubre.

doll, *n.* poupée *f.*

dollar, *n.* dollar *m.*

dolorous, *adj.* douloureux.

dolphin, *n.* dauphin *m.*

domain, *n.* domaine *m.*

dome, *n.* dôme *m.*

domestic, *adj.* domestique.

domesticate, *vb.* domestiquer, apprivoiser.

domicile, *n.* domicile *m.*

dominance, *n.* dominance *f.,* prédominance *f.*

dominant, *adj.* dominant.

dominate, *vb.* dominer.

domination, *n.* domination *f.*

domineer, *vb.* se montrer tyrannique.

domineering, *adj.* impérieux.

dominion, *n.* domination *f.;* (territory) possessions *f.pl.*

domino, *n.* domino *m.*

don, *vb.* endosser, revêtir.

donate, *vb.* donner.

donation, *n.* donation *f.*

done, *vb.* fait.

donkey, *n.* âne *m.*

don't, *vb.* ne faites pas!, ne fais pas!

doodle, *vb.* griffonner.

doom, *vb.* condamner.

doomsday, *n.* (jour du) jugement dernier *m.*

door, *n.* porte *f.;* **(d.-keeper)** concierge *m.f.*

doorbell, *n.* sonnette *f.*

doorman, *n.* portier *m.*

doorstep, *n.* seuil *m.,* pas *(m.)* de la porte.

doorway, *n.* (baie de) porte *f.,* encadrement *(m.)* de la porte.

dope, 1. *n.* stupéfiant *m.* **2.** *vb.* doper.

dormant, *adj.* endormi, assoupi.

dormer, *n.* lucarne *f.*

dormitory, *n.* maison *(f.)* d'étudiants.

dosage, *n.* dosage *m.*

dose, *n.* dose *f.*

dossier, *n.* dossier *m.*

dot, *n.* point *m.*

dotage, *n.* radotage *m.*

dote, *vb.* radoter; **(d. on)** aimer excessivement.

dot-matrix printer, *n.* imprimante *(f.)* matricielle.

double, 1. *adj. and n.* double *m.* **2.** *vb.* doubler.

double-bass, *n.* contre basse *f.*

double-breasted, *adj.* croisé.

double-cross, *vb.* duper, tromper.

double-dealing, *n.* duplicité *f.*

double room, *n.* chambre *(f.)* pour deux personnes.

double time, *n.* pas gymnastique *m.*

doubly, *adv.* doublement.

doubt, 1. *n.* doute *m.* 2. *vb.* douter (de).

doubtful, *adj.* douteux.

doubtless, *adv.* sans doute.

dough, *n.* pâte *f.;* (colloquial) fric *m.*

doughnut, *n.* pet (*m.*) de nonne, baignet *m.*

dour, *adj.* austère.

douse, *vb.* plonger, tremper.

dove, *n.* colombe *f.*

dowager, *n.* douairère *f.*

dowdy, *adj.* sans élégance, qui manque de chic.

dowel, 1. *n.* goujon *m.* 2. *vb.* goujonner.

down, 1. *n.* duvet *m.* 2. *adv.* en bas. 3. *prep.* (along) le long de.

downcast, *adj.* (look) baissé.

downfall, *n.* chute *f.*

downgrade, *vb.* déclasser.

downhearted, *adj.* découragé, déprimé.

downhill, 1. *n.* descente *f.* 2. *adj.* en pente, incliné.

downpour, *n.* averse *f.*

downright, *adv.* tout à fait.

downstairs, *adv.* en bas.

downtown, *adv.* en ville.

downtrodden, *adj.* opprimé, piétiné.

downward, *adj.* descendant.

downy, *adj.* duveteux.

dowry, *n.* dot *f.*

doze, *vb.* sommeiller.

dozen, *n.* douzaine *f.*

drab, *adj.* (color) gris; (dull) terne.

draft, 1. *n.* (drawing) dessin *m.;* (mil.) conscription *f.;* (air) courant (*m.*) d'air. 2. *vb.* (mil.) appeler sous le drapeau.

draftee, *n.* conscrit *m.*

draftsman, *n.* dessinateur *m.*

drafty, *adj.* plein de courants d'air.

drag, *vb.* traîner.

dragnet, *n.* drague *f.*, seine *f.*, chalut *m.*

dragon, *n.* dragon *m.*

dragon-fly, *n.* libellule *f.*

drain, *vb.* drainer, *tr.;* s'écouler, *intr.*

drainage, *n.* drainage *m.*

dram, *n.* drachme *f.*, goutte *f.*

drama, *n.* drame *m.*

dramatic, *adj.* dramatique.

dramatics, *n.* théâtre *m.*

dramatist, *n.* dramaturge *m.*

dramatize, *vb.* dramatiser.

dramaturgy, *n.* dramaturgie *f.*

drape, *vb.* draper.

drapery, *n.* draperie *f.*

drastic, *adj.* drastique.

draw, *vb.* (pull) tirer; (sketch) dessiner.

drawback, *n.* inconvénient *m.*

drawbridge, *m.* pont-levis *m.*

drawer, *n.* tiroir *m.*

drawing, *n.* dessin *m.*

drawl, 1. *n.* voix (*f.*) traînante. 2. *vb.* traîner la voix.

dray, *n.* camion *m.*

drayman, *n.* camionneur *m.*

dread, 1. *n.* crainte *f.* 2. *vb.* redouter.

dreadful, *adj.* affreux.

dreadfully, *adv.* terriblement, affreusement.

dream, *n.* rêve *m.*

dreamer, *n.* rêveur *m.*

dreamy, *adj.* rêveur *m.*, rêveuse *f.*

dreary, *adj.* morne.

dredge, *vb.* draguer.

dreg, *n.* lie *f.*

drench, *vb.* tremper.

dress, 1. *n.* robe *f.* 2. *vb.* habiller, *tr.;* s'habiller, *intr.*

dresser, *n.* commode *f.*

dressing, *n.* toilette *f.;* (surgical) pansement *m.*

dressing gown, *n.* robe (*f.*) de chambre, peignoir *m.*

dressmaker, *n.* couturière *f.*

dress rehearsal, *n.* répétition générale *f.*

dressy, *adj.* chic.

dribble, *vb.* baver.

drier, *n.* sécheur *m.*, dessécheur *m.*

drift, *vb.* (boat) dériver; (person) se laisser aller.

drifter, *n.* personne (*f.*) sans but.

driftwood, *n.* bois flottant *m.*

drill, 1. *n.* (tool) foret *m.;* (exercise) exercice *m.* 2. *vb.* (hole) forer; (exercise) exercer, *tr.;* faire l'exercice, *intr.*

drink, 1. *n.* boisson *f.* 2. *vb.* boire.

drinkable, *adj.* potable.

drip, 1. *vb.* dégoutter. 2. *n.* goutte *f.*

dripping, 1. *n.* dégouttement *m.* 2. *adj.* ruisselant.

drive, 1. *n.* promenade (*f.*) en voiture; (energy) énergie *f.* 2. *vb.* (auto, animals) conduire; (force) pousser.

drivel, *n.* bave *f.*

driver, *n.* (auto) chauffeur *m.*

driver's license, *n.* permis (*m.*) de conduire.

driveway, *n.* allée *f.*

driving, *n.* conduite *f.*

drizzle, 1. *n.* bruine *f.* 2. *vb.* bruiner.

dromedary, *n.* dromadaire *m.*

drone, 1. *n.* abeille mâle *f.;* bourdonnement *m.* 2. *vb.* bourdonner.

drool, *vb.* baver.

droop, *vb.* pencher.

drop, 1. *n.* goutte *f.;* (fall) chute *f.* 2. *vb.* tomber, *intr.;* laisser tomber, *tr.*

dropout, *n.* étudiant qui quitte l'école avant de recevoir son diplôme *m.*

dropper, *n.* compte-gouttes *m.*

dropsy, *n.* hydropisie *f.*

drought, *n.* sécheresse *f.*

drove, *n.* troupeau *m.*

drown, *vb.* noyer, *tr.*

drowse, *vb.* s'assoupir.

drowsiness, *n.* somnolence *f.*

drowsy, *adj.* somnolent.

drudge, *vb.* s'éreinter.

drudgery, *n.* corvée *f.*

drug, *n.* drogue *f.*

drug addict, *n.* toxicomane *m.f.*

druggist, *n.* pharmacien *m.*

drugstore, *n.* pharmacie *f.*

drum, *n.* tambour *m.;* (ear) tympan *m.*

drum major, *n.* tambour-major *m.*

drummer, *n.* tambour *m.*

drumstick, *n.* baguette (*f.*) de tambour.

drunk, *adj.* ivre.
drunkard, *n.* ivrogne *m.*
drunkenness, *n.* ivresse *f.;* (habitual) ivrognerie *f.*
dry, 1. *adj.* sec *m.,* sèche *f.* 2. *vb.* sécher.
dry-clean, *vb.* nettoyer à sec.
dry cleaner, *n.* teinturier *m.*
dry dock, 1. *n.* cale sèche *f.* 2. *vb.* mettre en cale sèche.
dry goods, *n.* articles *(m.pl.)* de nouveauté.
dryness, *n.* sécheresse *f.*
dual, *adj.* double.
dualism, *n.* dualisme *m.*
dubbed, *adj.* doublé.
dubious, *adj.* douteux.
duchess, *n.* duchesse *f.*
duchy, *n.* duché *m.*
duck, *n.* canard *m.*
duckling, *n.* caneton *m.*
duct, *n.* conduit *m.*
ductile, *adj.* ductile.
dud, 1. *adj.* incapable. 2. *n.* obus qui a raté *m.*
due, *adj.* dû *m.,* due *f.*
duel, *n.* duel *m.*
duelist, *n.* duelliste *m.*
duet, *n.* duo *m.*
duffel bag, *n.* sac *(m.)* pour les vêtements de rechange.
duffel coat, *n.* duffel-coat *m.*
dugout, *n.* abri-caverne *m.*
duke, *n.* duc *m.*
dukedom, *n.* duché *m.*
dulcet, *adj.* doux, suave.
dull, *adj.* (boring) ennuyeux; (blunt) émoussé.
dullard, *n.* lourdaud *m.*

dullness, *n.* (monotony) monotonie *f.*
duly, *adv.* dûment.
dumb, *adj.* muet *m.,* muette *f.;* (stupid) sot *m.,* sotte *f.*
dumbfound, *vb.* abasourdir, interdire.
dumbfounded, *adj.* sidéré.
dumbwaiter, *n.* monte-plats *m.*
dummy, *n.* (dressmaking) mannequin *m.;* (cards) mort *m.*
dump, 1. *n.* voirie *f.* 2. *vb.* déposer; (computer) vider, transférer.
dumpling, *n.* boulette (de pâte) *f.*
dumpy, *adj.* boulot.
dun, *vb.* importuner, talonner.
dunce, *n.* crétin *m.*
dunce cap, *n.* bonnet d'âne *m.*
dune, *n.* dune *f.*
dung, *n.* fiente *f.;* (agriculture) fumier *m.*
dungaree, *n.* salopette *f.,* bleus *m.pl.*
dungeon, *n.* cachot *m.*
dupe, 1. *n.* dupe *f.* 2. *vb.* duper.
duplex, *adj.* double.
duplicate, 1. *n.* double *m.* 2. *vb.* faire le double de.
duplication, *n.* duplication *f.*
duplicity, *n.* duplicité *f.*
durability, *n.* durabilité *f.*
durable, *adj.* durable.
duration, *n.* durée *f.*

duress, *n.* contrainte *f.,* coercition *f.*
during, *prep.* pendant.
dusk, *n.* crépuscule *m.*
dusky, *adj.* sombre.
dust, 1. *n.* poussière *f.* 2. *vb.* épousseter.
dustpan, *n.* ramasse-poussière *m.*
dust storm, *n.* tourbillon *(m.)* de poussière.
dusty, *adj.* poussiéreux.
Dutch, *adj. and n.* hollandais *m.*
Dutchman, *n.* Hollandais *m.*
dutiful, *adj.* respectueux, fidèle.
dutifully, *adv.* avec soumission.
duty, *n.* (moral, legal) devoir *m.;* (tax) droit *m.;* (be on d.) être de service.
duty-free, *adj.* exempt de droits, hors-taxe.
dwarf, *adj. and n.* nain *m.*
dwell, *vb.* demeurer.
dwindle, *vb.* diminuer.
dye, 1. *n.* teinture *f.* 2. *vb.* teindre.
dyer, *n.* teinturier *m.*
dyestuff, *n.* matière colorante *f.*
dynamic, *adj.* dynamique.
dynamics, *n.* dynamique *f.*
dynamite, *n.* dynamite *f.*
dynamo, *n.* dynamo *f.*
dynasty, *n.* dynastie *f.*
dysentery, *n.* dysenterie *f.*
dyslexia, *n.* dyslexie *f.*
dyspepsia, *n.* dyspepsie *f.*
dyspeptic, *adj.* dyspeptique.

E

each, 1. *adj.* chaque. 2. *pron.* chacun *m.,* chacune *f.;* (e. other) l'un l'autre.
eager, *adj.* ardent.
eagerly, *adv.* ardemment, avidement.
eagerness, *n.* empressement *m.*
eagle, *n.* (bird) aigle *m.;* *(mil.)* aigle *f.*
eaglet, *n.* aiglon *m.*
ear, *n.* oreille *f.*
earache, *n.* mal d'oreille *m.*

eardrum, *n.* tympan *m.*
earl, *n.* comte *m.*
early, 1. *adj.* (of morning) matinal; (first) premier. 2. *adv.* de bonne heure; tôt.
earmark, 1. *n.* marque distinctive *f.* 2. *vb.* marquer, assigner.
earn, *vb.* gagner.
earnest, *adj.* sérieux.
earnestly, *adv.* sérieusement, sincèrement.

earnestness, *n.* gravité *f.,* sérieux *m.*
earnings, *n.* salaire *m.*
earphone, *n.* casque (téléphonique) *m.*
earring, *n.* boucle *(f.)* d'oreille.
earshot, *n.* portée de voix *f.*
earth, *n.* terre *f.*
earthenware, *n.* poterie *f.,* argile cuite *f.,* faïence *f.*
earthly, *adj.* terrestre.

earthquake, *n.* tremblement (*m.*) de terre.

earthworm, *n.* ver de terre *m.*

earthy, *adj.* terreux.

ease, 1. *n.* aise *f.*; **(with e.)** avec facilité. **2.** *vb.* calmer, détendre.

easel, *n.* chevalet *m.*

easily, *adv.* facilement.

easiness, *n.* facilité *f.*

east, *n.* est *m.*; **(the E.)** l'Orient *m.*

Easter, *n.* Pâques *m.*

easterly, *adj.* d'est, vers l'est.

eastern, *adj.* de l'est, oriental.

eastward, *adv.* vers l'est.

easy, *adj.* facile; (of manners) aisé.

easy chair, *n.* fauteuil *m.*

easygoing, *adj.* insouciant, peu exigeant, accommodant.

eat, *vb.* manger.

eaves, *n.* avant-toit *m.*

eavesdrop, *vb.* écouter aux portes.

ebb, *n.* (water) reflux *m.*; (decline) déclin *m.*

ebony, *n.* ébène *m.*

ebullient, *adj.* bouillonnant.

eccentric, *adj.* excentrique.

eccentricity, *n.* excentricité *f.*

ecclesiastic, *adj. and n.* ecclésiastique *m.*

ecclesiastical, *adj.* ecclésiastique.

echelon, *n.* échelon *m.*

echo, *n.* écho *m.*

eclipse, *n.* éclipse *f.*

ecological, *adj.* écologique.

ecology, *n.* écologie *f.*

economic, *adj.* économique.

economical, *adj.* (person) économe.

economics, *n.* économie (*f.*) politique.

economist, *n.* économiste *m.f.*

economize, *vb.* économiser.

economy, *n.* économie *f.*

ecosystem, *n.* écosystème *m.*

ecru, *n.* écru *m.*

ecstasy, *n.* (religious) extase *f.*; (*fig.*) transport *m.*

ecumenical, *adj.* œcuménique.

eczema, *n.* eczéma *m.*

eddy, *n.* remous *m.*

edge, *n.* bord *m.*; (blade) fil *m.*

edging, *n.* pose *f.*, bordure *f.*

edgy, *adj.* d'un air agacé.

edible, *adj.* comestible.

edict, *n.* édit *m.*

edifice, *n.* édifice *m.*

edify, *vb.* édifier.

edit, *vb.* (text) corriger; (report) préparer; (film) monter.

edition, *n.* édition *f.*

editor, *n.* (text) correcteur *m.*, éditeur *m.*; (paper) rédacteur *m.*

editorial, *n.* éditorial *m.*

educate, *vb.* (upbringing) élever; (knowledge) instruire.

education, *n.* éducation *f.*; (schooling) instruction *f.*

educational, *adj.* pédagogique; scolaire.

educator, *n.* éducateur *m.*

eel, *n.* anguille *f.*

eerie, *adj.* inquiétant.

efface, *vb.* effacer.

effect, 1. *n.* effet *m.* **2.** *vb.* effectuer.

effective, *adj.* (having effect) efficace; (in effect) effectif.

effectively, *adv.* efficacement, effectivement.

effectiveness, *n.* efficacité *f.*

effectual, *adj.* efficace.

effeminate, *adj.* efféminé.

effervesce, *vb.* être en effervescence, pétiller d'animation.

effervescent, *adj.* gazeux.

effete, *adj.* epuisé, caduc.

efficacious, *adj.* efficace.

efficacy, *n.* efficacité *f.*

efficiency, *n.* (person) compétence *f.*; (machine) rendement *m.*

efficient, *adj.* (person) capable.

efficiently, *adv.* efficacement, avec compétence.

effigy, *n.* effigie *f.*

effort, *n.* effort *m.*

effortless, *adj.* sans effort.

effrontery, *n.* effronterie *f.*

effulgent, *adj.* resplendissant.

effusive, *adj.* démonstratif.

egalitarian, *adj.* égalitaire.

egg, *n.* œuf *m.*; **(boiled e.)** œuf à la coque; **(fried e.)** œuf sur le plat; **(poached e.)** œuf poché; **(scrambled e.)** œuf brouillé.

eggplant, *n.* aubergine *f.*

egg shell, *n.* coquille (*f.*) d'œuf.

ego, *n.* moi *m.*

egoism, *n.* égoïsme *m.*

egotism, *n.* égotisme *m.*

egotist, *n.* égotiste *m.*

Egypt, *n.* Égypte *m.*

Egyptian, 1. *n.* Égyptien *m.* **2.** *adj.* égyptien.

eiderdown, *n.* édredon *m.*

eight, *adj. and n.* huit *m.*

eighteen, *adj. and n.* dix-huit *m.*

eighteenth, *adj. and n.* dix-huitième *m.f.*

eighth, *adj. and n.* huitième *m.f.*

eightieth, *adj. and n.* quatrevingtième *m.f.*

eighty, *adj. and n.* quatre-vingts *m.*

Eire, *n.* République (*f.*) d'Irlande.

either, 1. *adj.* (each of two) chaque; (one or other) l'un ou l'autre. **2.** *pron.* chacun; l'un ou l'autre. **3.** *conj.* **(e. . . . or)** ou . . . ou . . .

ejaculate, *vb.* éjaculer, prononcer.

eject, *vb.* (throw) jeter.

ejection, *n.* jet *m.*, éjection *f.*, expulsion *f.*

eke, *vb.* suppléer à, subsister pauvrement.

elaborate, 1. *adj.* minutieux. **2.** *vb.* élaborer.

elapse, *vb.* (time) s'écouler.

elastic, *adj. and n.* élastique *m.*

elasticity, *n.* élasticité *f.*

elate, *vb.* exalter, transporter.

elated, *adj.* exalté.

elation, *n.* exaltation *f.*

elbow, *n.* coude *m.*

elbowroom, *n.* aisance (*f.*) des coudes.

elder, *adj. and n.* aîné *m.*

elderberry, *n.* baie de sureau *f.*

elderly, *adj.* d'un certain âge.

eldest, *adj.* aîné.

elect, 1. *vb.* élire. 2. *adj.* (the president e.) le président élu.

election, *n.* élection *f.*

electioneer, *vb.* faire une campagne électorale.

elective, *adj.* électif.

electorate, *n.* électorat *m.*, les votants *m.pl.*

electric, electrical, *adj.* électrique.

electric chair, *n.* fauteuil électrique *m.*

electric eel, *n.* anguille électrique *f.*

electrician, *n.* électricien *m.*

electricity, *n.* électricité *f.*

electrocardiogram, *n.* électrocardiogramme *m.*

electrocute, *vb.* électrocuter.

electrode, *n.* électrode *f.*

electrolysis, *n.* électrolyse *f.*

electron, *n.* électron *m.*

electronic, *adj.* électronique.

electronics, *n.* électronique *f.*

electroplate, 1. *vb.* plaquer. 2. *adj.* plaqué.

elegance, *n.* élégance *f.*

elegant, *adj.* élégant.

elegiac, *adj.* élégiaque.

elegy, *n.* élégie *f.*

element, *n.* élément *m.*

elemental, elementary, *adj.* élémentaire.

elephant, *n.* éléphant *m.*

elephantine, *adj.* éléphantin.

elevate, *vb.* élever.

elevation, *n.* élévation *f.*

elevator, *n.* ascenseur *m.*

eleven, *adj. and n.* onze *m.*

eleventh, *adj. and n.* onzième *m.f.*

elf, *n.* elfe *m.*, lutin *m.*

elfin, *adj.* d'elfe.

elicit, *vb.* tirer, faire jaillir.

eligibility, *n.* éligibilité *f.*

eligible, *adj.* éligible.

eliminate, *vb.* éliminer.

elimination, *n.* élimination *f.*

elixir, *n.* élixir *m.*

elk, *n.* élan *m.*

ellipse, *n.* ellipse *f.*

elm, *n.* orme *m.*

elocution, *n.* élocution *f.*

elongate, *vb.* allonger, étendre.

elope, *vb.* s'enfuir.

eloquence, *n.* éloquence *f.*

eloquent, *adj.* éloquent.

eloquently, *adv.* d'une manière éloquente.

else, 1. *adj.* autre; (someone e.) quelqu'un d'autre; (everyone e.) tous les autres. 2. *adv.* autrement.

elsewhere, *adv.* ailleurs.

elucidate, *vb.* élucider, éclaircir.

elude, *vb.* éluder.

elusive, *adj.* évasif, insaisissable.

emaciated, *adj.* émacié.

emanate, *vb.* émaner.

emancipate, *vb.* émanciper.

emancipation, *n.* émancipation *f.*

emancipator, *n.* émancipateur *m.*

emasculate, *vb.* émasculer.

embalm, *vb.* embaumer.

embankment, *n.* levée *f.*

embargo, *n.* embargo *m.*

embark, *vb.* embarquer, *tr.*

embarkation, *n.* embarquement *m.*

embarrass, *vb.* embarrasser.

embarrassing, *adj.* embarrassant.

embarrassment, *n.* embarras *m.*

embassy, *n.* ambassade *f.*

embed, *vb.* encastrer.

embellish, *vb.* embellir.

embellishment, *n.* embellissement *m.*

ember, *n.* braise *f.*, charbon ardent *m.*

embezzle, *vb.* détourner.

embitter, *vb.* aigrir, envenimer.

emblazon, *vb.* blasonner.

emblem, *n.* emblème *m.*

emblematic, *adj.* emblématique.

embody, *vb.* incarner, incorporer.

emboss, *vb.* graver en relief, travailler en bosse.

embrace, 1. *n.* étreinte *f.* 2. *vb.* embrasser.

embroider, *vb.* broder.

embroidery, *n.* broderie *f.*

embroil, *vb.* embrouiller.

embryo, *n.* embryon *m.*

embryology, *n.* embryologie *f.*

embryonic, *adj.* embryonnaire.

emerald, *n.* émeraude *f.*

emerge, *vb.* émerger.

emergency, *n.* circonstance (*f.*) critique; (e. exit) sortie (*f.*) de secours; (e. landing) atterrissage (*m.*) forcé.

emergent, *adj.* émergent.

emery, *n.* émeri *m.*

emetic, *n.* émétique *m.*

emigrant, *n.* émigrant *m.*

emigrate, *vb.* émigrer.

emigration, *n.* émigration *f.*

eminence, *n.* éminence *f.*

eminent, *adj.* éminent.

emissary, *n.* émissaire *m.*

emission control, *n.* appareil (*m.*) pour limiter l'émission de vapeurs nuisibles.

emit, *vb.* émettre.

emollient, *adj.* émollient.

emolument, *n.* traitement *m.*

emotion, *n.* émotion *f.*

emotional, *adj.* émotif; (excitable) émotionnable.

emperor, *n.* empereur *m.*

emphasis, *n.* (impressiveness) force *f.*; (stress) accent *m.*

emphasize, *vb.* mettre en relief, souligner.

emphatic, *adj.* (manner) énergique.

empire, *n.* empire *m.*

empirical, *adj.* empirique.

employ, *vb.* employer.

employee, *n.* employé *m.*

employer, *n.* patron *m.*

employment, *n.* emploi *m.*

employment agency, *n.* agence (*f.*) de placement.

empower, *vb.* autoriser.

empress, *n.* impératrice *f.*

emptiness, *n.* vide *m.*

empty, 1. *adj.* vide. 2. *vb.* vider.

emulate, *vb.* émuler.

emulsion, *n.* émulsion *f.*

enable, *vb.* mettre à même (de).

enact, vb. (law) décréter; (play) jouer.

enactment, n. promulgation f., acte législatif m.

enamel, n. émail m., pl. émaux.

enamored, adj. (be e. of) être épris de.

encamp, vb. camper, faire camper.

encampment, n. campement m.

encased, adj. (e. in) enfermé dans.

encephalitis, n. encéphalite f.

encephalon, n. encéphale m.

enchant, vb. enchanter.

enchanting, adj. ravissant.

enchantment, n. enchantement m.

encircle, vb. entourer.

enclose, vb. enclore; (in letter) joindre.

enclosure, n. enclos m.; (in letter) pièce (f.) jointe.

encompass, vb. entourer.

encounter, vb. rencontrer.

encourage, vb. encourager.

encouragement, n. encouragement m.

encroach, vb. empiéter.

encumber, vb. encombrer.

encyclical, n. encyclique f.

encyclopedia, n. encyclopédie f.

end, 1. n. fin f.; (extremity) bout m.; (aim) but m. 2. vb. finir.

endanger, vb. mettre en danger.

endear, vb. rendre cher.

endearing, adj. attachant.

endearment, n. charme m., attrait m.

endeavor, 1. n. effort m. 2. vb. s'efforcer.

endemic, adj. endémique.

ending, n. terminaison f.

endive, n. chicorée f., endive f.

endless, adj. sans fin.

endocrine gland, n. glande endocrine f.

endorse, vb. (sign) endosser; (support) appuyer.

endorsement, n. (signing) endossement m.; (approval) approbation f.

endow, vb. doter.

endowment, n. dotation f., fondation f.

endurance, n. résistance f.

endure, vb. supporter.

enduring, adj. durable.

enema, n. lavement m.

enemy, adj. and n. ennemi m.

energetic, adj. énergique.

energy, n. énergie f.

enervate, vb. énerver, affaiblir.

enervation, n. affaiblissement m.

enfold, vb. envelopper.

enforce, vb. imposer; (law) exécuter.

enforcement, n. exécution f.

enfranchise, vb. affranchir, accorder le droit de vote.

engage, vb. engager, tr.; (become e.d, to be married) se fiancer.

engaged, adj. occupé, pris; fiancé.

engagement, n. engagement m.; (marriage) fiançailles f.pl.

engaging, adj. attrayant, séduisant.

engender, vb. engendrer.

engine, n. machine f.; (train) locomotive f.; (motor) moteur m.

engineer, n. (profession) ingénieur m.; (engine operator) mécanicien m.; (mil.) soldat (m.) du génie.

engineering, n. génie m., ingénierie f.

England, n. Angleterre f.

English, adj. and n. anglais m.

Englishman, n. Anglais m.

Englishwoman, n. Anglaise f.

engrave, vb. graver.

engraver, n. graveur m.

engraving, n. gravure f.

engross, vb. (absorb) absorber.

engrossing, adj. absorbant.

engulf, vb. engouffrer.

enhance, vb. rehausser.

enigma, n. énigme f.

enigmatic, adj. énigmatique.

enjoin, vb. enjoindre.

enjoy, vb. jouir de; (e. oneself) s'amuser.

enjoyable, adj. agréable.

enjoyment, n. plaisir m.

enlace, vb. enlacer.

enlarge, vb. agrandir, tr.

enlargement, n. agrandissement m.

enlarger, n. agrandisseur m., amplificateur m.

enlighten, vb. éclairer.

enlightenment, n. éclaircissement m.; (the E.) le Siècle (m.) des Lumières.

enlist, vb. enrôler, tr.

enlisted man, n. gradé m.

enlistment, n. enrôlement m.

enliven, vb. animer.

enmesh, vb. engrener, embarrasser.

enmity, n. inimitié f.

ennoble, vb. anoblir.

ennui, n. ennui m.

enormity, n. énormité f.

enormous, adj. énorme.

enough, adj. and adv. assez (de).

enrage, vb. faire enrager.

enrapture, vb. ravir, enchanter.

enrich, vb. enrichir.

enroll, vb. enrôler, s'inscrire.

enrollment, n. inscription f.

ensemble, n. ensemble m.

enshrine, vb. enchâsser.

ensign, n. (navy) enseigne m.

enslave, vb. asservir.

ensnare, vb. prendre au piège.

ensue, vb. s'ensuivre.

entail, vb. (involve) entraîner; (law) substituer.

entangle, vb. empêtrer.

enter, vb. entrer (dans).

enterprise, n. entreprise f.

enterprising, adj. entreprenant.

entertain, vb. (amuse) amuser; (receive) recevoir.

entertainment, n. amusement m.

enthrall, vb. captiver, ensorceler.

enthusiasm, n. enthousiasme m.

enthusiast, *n.* enthousiaste *m.f.*

enthusiastic, *adj.* enthousiaste.

entice, *vb.* attirer.

entire, *adj.* entier.

entirely, *adv.* entièrement.

entirety, *n.* totalité *f.*

entitle, *vb.* donner droit à; (book) intituler.

entity, *n.* entité *f.*

entomb, *vb.* enterrer, ensevelir.

entrails, *n.* entrailles *f.pl.*

entrain, *vb.* embarquer en chemin de fer.

entrance, 1. *n.* entrée *f.* **2.** *vb.* enchanter.

entrant, *n.* débutant *m.,* inscrit *m.*

entrap, *vb.* attraper, prendre au piège.

entreat, *vb.* supplier.

entreaty, *n.* instance *f.*

entrench, *vb.* retrancher.

entrust to, *vb.* confier à.

entry, *n.* (entrance) entrée *f.;* (recording) inscription *f.*

enumerate, *vb.* énumérer.

enumeration, *n.* énumération *f.*

enunciate, *vb.* énoncer.

enunciation, *n.* énonciation *f.*

envelop, *vb.* envelopper.

envelope, *n.* enveloppe *f.*

enviable, *adj.* enviable.

envious, *adj.* envieux.

environment, *n.* milieu *m.;* (ecology) environnement *m.*

environmentalist, *n.* écologiste *m.f.;* environnementaliste *m.*

environmental protection, *n.* protection (*f.*) de l'environnement.

environs, *n.* environs *m.pl.,* alentours *m.pl.*

envisage, *vb.* envisager.

envoy, *n.* envoyé *m.*

envy, 1. *n.* envie *f.* **2.** *vb.* envier.

enzyme, *n.* enzyme *m.*

eon, *n.* éon *m.*

ephemeral, *adj.* éphémère.

epic, 1. *n.* épopée *f.* **2.** *adj.* épique.

epicure, *n.* gourmet *m.*

epidemic, *n.* épidémie *f.*

epidermis, *n.* épiderme *m.*

epigram, *n.* épigramme *f.*

epilepsy, *n.* épilepsie *f.*

epilogue, *n.* épilogue *m.*

episode, *n.* épisode *m.*

epistle, *n.* épître *f.*

epitaph, *n.* épitaphe *f.*

epithet, *n.* épithète *f.*

epitome, *n.* épitomé *m.,* résumé *m.*

epitomize, *vb.* résumer, abréger.

epoch, *n.* époque *f.*

equable, *adj.* uniforme, régulier.

equal, 1. *adj.* égal; **2.** *vb.* égaliser.

equality, *n.* égalité *f.*

equalize, *vb.* égaliser, *tr.*

equanimity, *n.* tranquillité (*f.*) d'esprit, équanimité *f.,* sérénité *f.*

equate, *vb.* égaler, mettre en équation.

equation, *n.* équation *f.*

equator, *n.* équateur *m.*

equatorial, *adj.* équatorial.

equestrian, *adj.* équestre.

equidistant, *adj.* équidistant.

equilateral, *adj.* équilatéral.

equilibrium, *n.* équilibre *m.*

equinox, *n.* équinoxe *m.*

equip, *vb.* équiper.

equipment, *n.* équipement *m.*

equitable, *adj.* équitable, juste.

equity, *n.* équité *f.,* action *f.*

equivalent, *adj. and n.* équivalent *m.*

equivocal, *adj.* équivoque.

equivocate, *vb.* équivoquer.

era, *n.* ère *f.*

eradicate, *vb.* déraciner.

eradicator, *n.* effaceur *m.,* grattoir *m.*

erase, *vb.* effacer.

eraser, *n.* gomme *f.*

erasure, *n.* rature *f.*

erect, *adj.* droit.

erection, *n.* érection *f.,* construction *f.*

erectness, *n.* attitude droite *f.*

ermine, *n.* hermine *f.*

erode, *vb.* éroder, ronger.

erosion, *n.* érosion *f.*

erosive, *adj.* érosif.

erotic, *adj.* érotique.

err, *vb.* errer.

errand, *n.* course *f.*

errant, *adj.* errant.

erratic, *adj.* irrégulier, excentrique.

erring, *adj.* égaré, dévoyé.

erroneous, *adj.* erroné.

error, *n.* erreur *f.*

erudite, *adj.* érudit.

erudition, *n.* érudition *f.*

erupt, *vb.* entrer en éruption.

eruption, *n.* éruption *f.*

escalate, *vb.* escalader.

escalator, *n.* escalier roulant *m.*

escapade, *n.* escapade *f.*

escape, 1. *n.* fuite *f.* **2.** *vb.* échapper.

escapism, *n.* évasion *f.,* échappement *m.*

eschew, *vb.* éviter, s'abstenir.

escort, 1. *n.* (mil.) escorte *f.;* (to a lady) cavalier *m.* **2.** *vb.* escorter.

esculent, *adj.* comestible.

escutcheon, *n.* écusson *m.*

Eskimo, 1. *n.* Esquimau *m.,* Esquimaude *f.* **2.** *adj.* esquimau *m.,* esquimaude *f.*

esoteric, *adj.* ésotérique.

especially, *adj.* surtout, particulièrement.

espionage, *n.* espionnage *m.*

espousal, *n.* adoption *f.,* adhésion (à) *f.*

espouse, *vb.* épouser, embrasser (une cause).

esquire, *n.* écuyer *m.;* titre honorifique d'un "gentleman" *m.*

essay, 1. *n.* essai *m.;* (school) composition *f.* **2.** *vb.* essayer.

essayist, *n.* essayiste *m.*

essence, *n.* essence *f.*

essential, *adj.* essentiel.

essentially, *adv.* essentiellement.

establish, *vb.* établir.

establishment, *n.* établissement *m.;* (the E.) l'ordre (*m.*) établi.

estate, *n.* (condition, class) état *m.;* (wealth) biens *m.pl.;* (land) propriété *f.*

esteem, 1. n. estime f. 2. vb. estimer.

estimable, adj. estimable.

estimate, 1. n.. estimation f.; (comm.) devis m. 2. vb. estimer.

estimation, n. (opinion) jugement m., estimation f.

estrange, vb. aliéner.

estuary, n. estuaire m.

etching, n. gravure (f.) à l'eau-forte.

eternal, adj. éternel.

eternity, n. éternité f.

ether, n. éther m.

ethereal, adj. éthéré.

ethical, adj. moral.

ethics, n. éthique f.

Ethiopia, n. Éthiopie f.

ethnic, adj. ethnique.

etiquette, n. étiquette f.

Etruscan, 1. n. Étrusque m.f. 2. adj. étrusque.

etymology, n. étymologie f.

eucalyptus, n. eucalyptus m.

eugenic, adj. eugénésique.

eugenics, n. eugénisme m., eugénique f.

eulogize, vb. faire l'éloge de.

eulogy, n. panégyrique m.

eunuch, n. eunuque m.

euphonious, adj. mélodieux, euphonique.

euphoria, n. euphorie f.

eurocheque, n. eurochèque m.

Europe, n. Europe f.

European, 1. n. Européen m. 2. adj. européen.

European Community, n. Communauté (f.) européenne.

euthanasia, n. euthanasie f.

evacuate, vb. évacuer.

evacuee, n. évacué m.

evade, vb. éluder.

evaluate, vb. évaluer.

evaluation, n. évaluation f.

evanescent, adj. évanescent, éphémère.

evangelist, n. évangéliste m.

evaporate, vb. évaporer, tr.

evaporation, n. évaporation f.

evasion, n. subterfuge f.

evasive, adj. évasif.

eve, n. veille f.

even, 1. adj. égal; (number) pair. 2. adv. même.

evening, n. soir m.; (span of e.) soirée f.

evenness, n. égalité f.

event, n. événement m.; (eventuality) cas m.

eventful, adj. mouvementé.

eventual, adj. (ultimate) définitif; (contingent) éventuel.

eventually, adv. en fin de compte, un jour ou l'autre.

ever, adv. (at all times) toujours; (at any time) jamais.

everglade, n. région marécageuse (de la Floride) f.

evergreen, adj. à feuilles persistantes, toujours vert.

everlasting, adj. éternel.

every, adj. (each) chaque; (all) tous les m.; toutes les f.

everybody, everyone, pron. tout le monde; chacun.

everyday, adj. de tous les jours.

everything, pron. tout.

everywhere, adv. partout.

evict, vb. évincer.

eviction, n. éviction f., expulsion f.

evidence, n. évidence f.; (proof) preuve f.

evident, adj. évident.

evidently, adv. évidemment.

evil, 1. n. mal m. 2. adj. mauvais.

evince, vb. démontrer.

eviscerate, vb. éviscérer.

evoke, vb. évoquer.

evolution, n. évolution f.

evolutionist, n. évolutionniste m.f.

evolve, vb. évoluer, développer.

ewe, n. agnelle f.

exacerbate, vb. exacerber.

exact, adj. exact.

exacting, adj. (person) exigeant.

exactly, adv. exactement.

exaggerate, vb. exagérer.

exaggerated, adj. exagéré.

exaggeration, n. exagération f.

exalt, vb. exalter; (raise) élever.

exaltation, n. exaltation f.

examination, n. examen m.

examine, vb. examiner.

example, n. exemple m.

exasperate, vb. exaspérer.

exasperation, n. exaspération f.

excavate, vb. creuser.

exceed, vb. excéder.

exceedingly, adv. extrêmement.

excel, vb. exceller, intr.

excellence, excellency, n. excellence f.

excellent, adj. excellent.

excelsior, n. copeaux (m.pl.) d'emballage.

except, 1. vb. excepter. 2. prep. excepté, sauf.

exception, n. exception f.

exceptional, adj. exceptionnel.

excerpt, n. extrait m.

excess, n. excès m.; (surplus) excédent m.

excessive, adj. excessif.

exchange, 1. n. échange m.; (money) change m. 2. vb. échanger.

exchangeable, adj. échangeable.

excise, n. contribution indirecte f., régie f.

excitable, adj. émotionnable, excitable.

excite, vb. exciter.

excitement, n. agitation f.

exciting, adj. passionnant.

exclaim, vb. s'écrier.

exclamation, n. exclamation f.

exclamation point or mark, n. point (m.) d'exclamation.

exclude, vb. exclure.

exclusion, n. exclusion f.

exclusive, adj. exclusif; (stylish) sélect.

excommunicate, vb. excommunier.

excommunication, n. excommunication f.

excoriate, vb. excorier, écorcher.

excrement, n. excrément m.

excruciating, *adj.* atroce, affreux.

exculpate, *vb.* disculper, exonérer.

excursion, *n.* excursion *f.*

excusable, *adj.* excusable.

excuse, 1. *n.* excuse *f.* **2.** *vb.* excuser.

execrable, *adj.* exécrable, abominable.

execute, *vb.* exécuter.

execution, *n.* exécution *f.*

executioner, *n.* bourreau *m.*

executive, *adj.* and *n.* exécutif *m.*, cadre *m.*

executive mansion, *n.* maison présidentielle *f.*

executor, *n.* exécuteur *m.*

exemplary, *adj.* exemplaire.

exemplify, *vb.* expliquer par des exemples.

exempt, 1. *adj.* exempt. **2.** *vb.* exempter.

exercise, 1. *n.* exercice *m.* **2.** *vb.* exercer.

exercise bike, *n.* vélo *(m.)* d'appartement.

exert, *vb.* employer; **(e. oneself)** s'efforcer de.

exertion, *n.* effort *m.*

exhale, *vb.* exhaler.

exhaust, 1. *n.* (machines) échappement *m.* **2.** *vb.* épuiser.

exhausted, *adj.* épuisé.

exhaustion, *n.* épuisement *m.*

exhaustive, *adj.* complet, approfondi.

exhibit, *vb.* (pictures, etc.) exposer; (show) montrer.

exhibition, *n.* exposition *f.*

exhibitionism, *n.* exhibitionnisme *m.*

exhilarate, *vb.* égayer.

exhort, *vb.* exhorter.

exhortation, *n.* exhortation *f.*

exhume, *vb.* exhumer.

exigency, *n.* exigence *f.*

exile, 1. *n.* exil *m.;* (person) exilé *m.* **2.** *vb.* exiler.

exist, *vb.* exister.

existence, *n.* existence *f.*

existent, *adj.* existant.

exit, 1. *n.* sortie *f.* **2.** *vb.* sortir.

exit ramp, *n.* bretelle *(f.)* d'accès.

exodus, *n.* exode *m.*

exonerate, *vb.* exonérer.

exorbitant, *adj.* exorbitant.

exorcise, *vb.* exorciser.

exotic, *adj.* exotique.

expand, *vb.* étendre, *tr.;* (dilate) dilater, *tr.*

expanse, *n.* étendue *f.*

expansion, *n.* expansion *f.*

expansive, *adj.* expansif.

expatiate, *vb.* discourir.

expatriate, *vb.* expatrier.

expect, *vb.* s'attendre à; (await) attendre.

expectancy, *n.* attente *f.*

expectant, *adj.* **(e. mother)** future maman *f.*

expectation, *n.* attente *f.;* (hope) espérance *f.*

expectorate, *vb.* expectorer.

expediency, *n.* convenance *f.*

expedient, *n.* expédient *m.*

expedite, *vb.* activer, accélérer.

expedition, *n.* expédition *f.*

expel, *vb.* expulser.

expend, *vb.* (money) dépenser; (use up) épuiser.

expenditure, *n.* dépense *f.*

expense, *n.* dépense *f.;* (expenses) frais *m.pl.*

expensive, *adj.* coûteux, cher.

expensively, *adv.* coûteusement.

experience, 1. *n.* expérience *f.* **2.** *vb.* éprouver.

experienced, *adj.* expérimenté.

experiment, *n.* expérience *f.*

experimental, *adj.* expérimental.

expert, *adj.* and *n.* expert *m.*

expiate, *vb.* expier.

expiration, *n.* expiration *f.*

expire, *vb.* expirer.

explain, *vb.* expliquer.

explanation, *n.* explication *f.*

explanatory, *adj.* explicatif.

expletive, *n.* explétif *m.*

explicit, *adj.* explicite.

explode, *vb.* (burst) éclater, *intr.*

exploit, 1. *n.* exploit *m.* **2.** *vb.* exploiter.

exploitation, *n.* exploitation *f.*

exploration, *n.* exploration *f.*

exploratory, *adj.* exploratif.

explore, *vb.* explorer.

explorer, *n.* explorateur *m.*

explosion, *n.* explosion *f.*

explosive, *adj.* and *n.* explosif *m.*

exponent, *n.* interprète *m.*

export, 1. *n.* (exportation) exportation *f.;* (exported object) article *(m.)* d'exportation. **2.** *vb.* exporter.

exportation, *n.* exportation *f.*

expose, *vb.* exposer.

exposé, *n.* exposé *m.*

exposition, *n.* exposition *f.*

expository, *adj.* expositoire.

expostulate, *vb.* faire des remontrances à.

exposure, *n.* exposition *f.*

expound, *vb.* exposer.

express, 1. *adj.* exprès. **2.** *vb.* exprimer.

expression, *n.* expression *f.*

expressive, *adj.* expressif.

expressly, *adv.* expressément.

expressman, *n.* agent *(m.)* de messageries.

expropriate, *vb.* exproprier.

expulsion, *n.* expulsion *f.*

expunge, *vb.* effacer, rayer.

expurgate, *vb.* expurger, épurer.

exquisite, *adj.* exquis.

extant, *adj.* existant.

extemporaneous, *adj.* improvisé, impromptu.

extend, *vb.* étendre; (prolong) prolonger.

extension, *n.* extension *f.*

extensive, *adj.* étendu.

extensively, *adv.* largement, considérablement.

extent, *n.* étendue *f.;* **(to some e.)** jusqu'à un certain point.

extenuate, *vb.* (tire out) exténuer; (diminish) atténuer.

extenuating circumstances, *n.* circonstances *(f.pl.)* atténuantes.

exterior, *adj.* and *n.* extérieur *m.*

exterminate, *vb.* exterminer.

extermination, *n.* extermination *f.*

external, *adj.* externe.
extinct, *adj.* éteint.
extinction, *n.* extinction *f.*
extinguish, *vb.* éteindre.
extol, *vb.* vanter.
extort, *vb.* extorquer.
extortion, *n.* extorsion *f.*
extortioner, *n.* extorqueur *m.*
extra, *adj.* (additional) supplémentaire; (spare) de réserve.
extra-, *prefix.* (outside of) en dehors de; (intensive) extra-.
extract, 1. *n.* extrait *m.* 2. *vb.* extraire.
extraction, *n.* extraction *f.*
extradite, *vb.* extrader.

extramarital, *adj.* extraconjugal.
extraneous, *adj.* étranger à.
extraordinary, *adj.* extraordinaire.
extravagance, *n.* extravagance *f.;* (money) prodigalité *f.*
extravagant, *adj.* extravagant; (money) prodigue.
extravaganza, *m.* œuvre fantaisiste *f.*
extreme, *adj. and n.* extrême *m.*
extremity, *n.* extrémité *f.*
extricate, *vb.* dégager, tirer.
extrovert, *n.* extroverti *m.*
exuberant, *adj.* exubérant.

exude, *vb.* exsuder.
exult, *vb.* exulter.
exultant, *adj.* exultant, joyeux.
eye, *n.* œil *m.*, *pl.* yeux.
eyeball, *n.* globe (*m.*) de l'œil.
eyebrow, *n.* sourcil *m.*
eyeglass, *n.* lorgnon *m.*
eyeglasses, *n.* lunettes *f.pl.*
eyelash, *n.* cil *m.*
eyelet, *n.* œillet *m.*
eyelid, *n.* paupière *f.*
eye shadow, *n.* fard (*m.*) à paupières.
eyesight, *n.* vue *f.*
eyewitness, *n.* témoin oculaire *m.*

F

fable *n.* fable *f.*
fabric, *n.* (structure) édifice *m.;* (cloth) tissu *m.*
fabricate, *vb.* fabriquer.
fabrication, *n.* fabrication *f.*
fabulous, *adj.* fabuleux.
façade, *n.* façade *f.*
face, 1. *n.* figure *f.* 2. *vb.* faire face à.
facet, *n.* facette *f.*
facetious, *adj.* facétieux.
face value, *n.* valeur nominale *f.*
facial, *adj.* facial.
facile, *adj.* facile.
facilitate, *vb.* faciliter.
facility, *n.* facilité *f.*
facing, *n.* revêtement *m.*, revers *m.*
facsimile, *n.* fac-similé *m.;* (document) télécopie *f.*, fax *m.;* (f. machine) télécopieur *m.*
fact, *n.* fait *m.;* (as a matter of f.) en effet.
faction, *n.* faction *f.*
factor, *n.* facteur *m.*
factory, *n.* fabrique *f.*, usine *f.*
factual, *adj.* effectif, positif.
faculty, *n.* faculté *f.*
fad, *n.* marotte *f.*
fade, *vb. intr.* se faner; (color) se décolorer; (f. away) s'évanouir.

fail, *vb.* manquer; (not succeed) échouer.
failing, 1. *n.* manquement *m.* 2. *adj.* faiblissant. 3. *prep.* au défaut de.
faille, *n.* faille *f.*
failure, *n.* (lack) défaut *m.;* (want of success) insuccès *m.*
faint, 1. *adj.* faible. 2. *vb.* s'évanouir.
faintly, *adv.* faiblement, timidement, légèrement.
fair, 1. *n.* foire *f.* 2. *adj.* (beautiful) beau *m.*, belle *f.;* (blond) blond; (honest) juste; (pretty good) passable.
fairly, *adv.* honnêtement, impartialement.
fairness, *n.* (honesty) honnêteté *f.*
fairy, *n.* fée *f.*
fairyland, *n.* pays (*m.*) des fées.
fairy tale, *n.* conte (*m.*) de fées.
faith, *n.* foi *f.*
faithful, *adj.* fidèle.
faithless, *adj.* infidèle.
fake, *vb.* truquer.
faker, *n.* truqueur *m.*
falcon, *n.* faucon *m.*
falconry, *n.* fauconnerie *f.*
fall, 1. *n.* chute *f.;* (autumn) automne *m.* 2. *vb.* tomber.

fallacious, *adj.* fallacieux.
fallacy, *n.* fausseté *f.*
fallen, *adj.* tombé, déchu.
fallible, *adj.* faillible.
fallout, *n.* pluie radioactive *f.*
fallow, *adj.* en jachère.
false, *adj.* faux *m.*, fausse *f.*
falsehood, *n.* mensonge *m.*
falseness, *n.* fausseté *f.*
falsetto, *n. and adj.* fausset *m.*
falsification, *n.* falsification *f.*
falsify, *vb.* falsifier.
falter, *vb.* hésiter.
fame, *n.* renommée *f.*
famed, *adj.* célèbre, renommé, fameux.
familiar, *adj.* familier.
familiarity, *n.* familiarité *f.*
familiarize, *vb.* familiariser.
family, *n.* famille *f.*
famine, *n.* (food) disette *f.;* (general) famine *f.*
famished, *adj.* affamé.
famous, *adj.* célèbre.
fan, *n.* éventail *m.;* (mechanical) ventilateur *m.;* (of person) admirateur *m.*
fanatic, *adj. and n.* fanatique *m.*
fanatical, *adj.* fanatique.
fanaticism, *n.* fanatisme *m.*
fan belt, *n.* courroie (*f.*) de ventilateur.

fanciful, *adj.* fantastique, fantaisiste.

fancy, 1. *n.* fantaisie *f.* **2.** *vb.* se figurer; avoir envie de.

fanfare, *n.* fanfare *f.*

fang, *n.* croc (of a dog) *m.*, crochet (of a snake) *m.*

fantastic, *adj.* fantastique.

fantasy, *n.* fantaisie *f.*

far, *adv.* loin; **(so f.)** jusqu'ici; **(as f. as)** autant que; **(much)** beaucoup; **(by f.)** de beaucoup.

faraway, *adj.* lointain.

farce, *n.* farce *f.*

farcical, *adj.* bouffon.

fare, 1. *n.* (price) prix *m.*; (food) chère *f.* **2.** *vb.* aller.

Far East, *n.* Extrême-Orient *m.*

farewell, *interj. and n.* adieu *m.*

far-fetched, *adj.* forcé.

far-flung, *adj.* très étendu, vaste.

farina, *n.* farine *f.*

farm, *n.* ferme *f.*

farmer, *n.* fermier *m.*

farmhouse, *n.* maison (*f.*) de ferme.

farming, *n.* culture *f.*

farmyard, *n.* cour de ferme *f.*

far-reaching, *adj.* de grande envergure.

far-sighted, *adj.* clairvoyant.

farther, 1. *adj.* plus éloigné. **2.** *adv.* plus loin.

farthest, *adj. and adv.* le plus lointain.

fascinate, *vb.* fasciner.

fascination, *n.* fascination *f.*

fascism, *n.* fascisme *m.*

fashion, *n.* mode *f.*; (manner) manière *f.*

fashionable, *adj.* à la mode.

fast, 1. *n.* jeûne *m.* **2.** *adj.* (speedy) rapide; (firm) ferme; (of clock) en avance. **3.** *vb.* jeûner. **4.** *adv.* (quickly) vite; (firmly) ferme.

fasten, *vb.* attacher, *tr.*

fastener, *n.* fermeture *f.*

fastening, *n.* attache *f.*

fastidious, *adj.* difficile.

fat, *adj.* gras *m.*, grasse *f.*

fatal, *adj.* fatal; (deadly) mortel.

fatality, *n.* fatalité *f.*

fatally, *adv.* fatalement, mortellement.

fate, *n.* destin *m.*

fateful, *adj.* fatal.

father, *n.* père *m.*

fatherhood, *n.* paternité *f.*

father-in-law, *n.* beau-père *m.*

fatherland, *n.* patrie *f.*

fatherless, *adj.* sans père.

fatherly, *adj.* paternel.

fathom, 1. *n.* (*naut.*) brasse *f.* **2.** *vb.* sonder.

fatigue, *n.* fatigue *f.*

fatten, *vb.* engraisser.

fatty, *adj.* graisseux.

fatuous, *adj.* sot.

faucet, *n.* robinet *m.*

fault, *n.* (mistake) faute *f.*; (defect) défaut *m.*

faultfinding, *n.* disposition (*f.*) à critiquer.

faultless, *adj.* sans défaut.

faultlessly, *adv.* d'une manière impeccable.

faulty, *adj.* défectueux.

fauna, *n.* faune *f.*

favor, 1. *n.* faveur *f.* **2.** *vb.* favoriser.

favorable, *adj.* favorable.

favored, *adj.* favorisé.

favorite, *adj. and n.* favori *m.*, favorite *f.*

favoritism, *n.* favoritisme *m.*

fawn, *n.* faon *m.*

fax, 1. *n.* (document) télécopie *f.*, fax *m.*; **(f. machine)** télécopieur *m.* **2.** *vb.* télécopier, faxer.

faze, *vb.* bouleverser.

fear, 1. *n.* crainte *f.* **2.** *vb.* craindre.

fearful, *adj.* (person) craintif; (thing) effrayant.

fearless, *adj.* intrépide.

fearlessness, *n.* intrépidité *f.*

fearsome, *adj.* redoutable.

feasible, *adj.* faisable.

feast, *n.* fête *f.*; (banquet) festin *m.*

feat, *n.* exploit *m.*

feather, *n.* plume *f.*

feathered, *adj.* emplumé.

featherweight, *n.* poids (*m.*) plume.

feathery, *adj.* plumeux.

feature, *n.* trait *m.*

February, *n.* février *m.*

fecund, *adj.* fécond.

federal, *adj.* fédéral.

federation, *n.* fédération *f.*

fedora, *n.* chapeau mou *m.*

fee, *n.* (for professional services) honoraires *m.pl.*; (school) frais *m.pl.*

feeble, *adj.* faible.

feeble-minded, *adj.* d'esprit faible.

feebleness, *n.* faiblesse *f.*

feed, 1. *n.* nourriture *f.* **2.** *vb.* nourrir, *tr.*

feedback, *n.* action (*f.*) de contrôle en retour.

feel, *vb.* sentir, *tr.*; (touch) tâter.

feeling, *n.* sentiment *m.*

feign, *vb.* feindre.

feint, *n.* feinte *f.*

felicitate, *vb.* féliciter.

felicitous, *adj.* heureux.

felicity, *n.* félicité *f.*

feline, *adj.* félin.

fell, *adj.* funeste.

fellow, *n.* (general) homme *m.*, garçon *m.*; (companion) compagnon *m.*

fellowship, *n.* camaraderie *f.*; (university) bourse (*f.*) universitaire.

fellow traveler, *n.* compagnon (*m.*) de route.

felon, *n.* criminel *m.*

felony, *n.* crime *m.*

felt, *n.* feutre *m.*

female, 1. *n.* (person) femme *f.*; (animals, plants) femelle *f.* **2.** *adj.* féminin, femelle.

feminine, *adj.* féminin.

femininity, *n.* féminité *f.*

fence, 1. *n.* clôture *f.* **2.** *vb.* (enclose) enclore; (sword, foil) faire de l'escrime.

fencer, *n.* escrimeur *m.*

fencing, *n.* escrime *f.*

fender, *n.* garde-boue *m.*; (fireplace) garde-feu *m.*

ferment, *vb.* fermenter.

fermentation, *n.* fermentation *f.*

fern, *n.* fougère *f.*

ferocious, *adj.* féroce.

ferociously, *adv.* d'une manière féroce.

ferocity, *n.* férocité *f.*

ferry, *n.* passage *(m.)* en bac; (**f. boat**) bac *m.*
fertile, *adj.* fertile.
fertility, *n.* fertilité *f.*
fertilization, *n.* fertilisation *f.*
fertilize, *vb.* fertiliser.
fervency, *n.* ardeur *f.*
fervent, *adj.* fervent.
fervently, *adv.* ardemment.
fervid, *adj.* fervent.
fervor, *n.* ferveur *f.*
fester, *vb.* suppurer.
festival, *n.* fête *f.*
festive, *adj.* de fête.
festivity, *n.* réjouissance *f.*
festoon, **1.** *n.* feston *m.* **2.** *vb.* festonner.
fetal, *adj.* foetal.
fetch, *vb.* (go and get) aller chercher; (bring) apporter.
fetching, *adj.* attrayant.
fete, *vb.* fêter.
fetid, *adj.* fétide.
fetish, *n.* fétiche *m.*
fetlock, *n.* fanon *m.*
fetter, **1.** *n.* lien *m.*, chaîne *f.* **2.** *vb.* enchaîner.
fetus, *n.* fœtus *m.*
feud, *n.* inimitié *f.*; (historical) fief *m.*
feudal, *adj.* féodal.
feudalism, *n.* régime féodal *m.*
fever, *n.* fièvre *f.*
feverish, *adj.* fiévreux.
feverishly, *adv.* fébrilement, fiévreusement.
few, **1.** *adj.* peu de; (**a f.**) quelques. **2.** *pron.* peu; (**a f.**) quelques-uns.
fiancé, *n.* fiancé *m.*
fiasco, *n.* fiasco *m.*
fiat, *n.* décret *m.*
fib, *n.* petit mensonge *m.*
fiber, *n.* fibre *f.*
fiberboard, *n.* fibre *(m.)* de bois.
fiberglass, *n.* fibre *(m.)* de verre.
fibrous, *adj.* fibreux.
fickle, *adj.* volage.
fickleness, *n.* inconstance *f.*
fiction, *n.* fiction *f.*; (literature) romans *m.pl.*
fictional, *adj.* de romans.

fictitious, *adj.* fictif, imaginaire.
fictitiously, *adv.* d'une manière factice.
fiddle, **1.** *n.* violon *m.* **2.** *vb.* jouer du violon.
fiddlesticks, *interj.* quelle blague!
fidelity, *n.* fidélité *f.*
fidget, *vb.* se remuer.
field, *n.* champ *m.*
fiend, *n.* démon *m.*
fiendish, *adj.* diabolique, infernal.
fierce, *adj.* féroce.
fiery, *adj.* ardent.
fiesta, *n.* fête *f.*
fife, *n.* fifre *m.*
fifteen, *adj. and n.* quinze *m.*
fifteenth, *adj. and n.* quinzième *m.f.*
fifth, *adj. and n.* cinquième *m.f.*
fifty, *adj. and n.* cinquante *m.*
fig, *n.* figue *f.*
fight, **1.** *n.* combat *m.*; (struggle) lutte *f.*; (quarrel) dispute *f.* **2.** *vb.* combattre; se disputer.
fighter, *n.* combattant *m.*
figment, *n.* invention *f.*
figurative, *adj.* figuré.
figuratively, *adv.* au figuré.
figure, **1.** *n.* figure *f.*; (of body) ligne *f.*; *(math.)* chiffre *m.* **2.** *vb.* figurer; calculer.
figured, *adj.* à dessin.
figurehead, *n.* homme de paille *m.*
figure of speech, *n.* façon *(f.)* de parler.
figurine, *n.* figurine *f.*
filament, *n.* filament *m.*
filch, *vb.* escamoter.
file, **1.** *n.* (tool) lime *f.*; (row) file *f.*; (papers) liasse *f.*; (for papers, etc.) classeur *m.*; (computer) fichier *m.*; (**f.s**) archives *f.pl.* **2.** *vb.* (tool) limer; (papers) classer; (**f. off**) défiler.
filial, *adj.* filial.
filigree, *n.* filigrane *m.*
filing cabinet, *n.* classeur *m.*
filings, *n.* limaille *f.*
fill, *vb.* remplir, *tr.*

fillet, *n.* (band) bandeau *m.*; (meat, fish) filet *m.*
filling, *n.* remplissage *m.*, (food) farce *f.*; (tooth) plombage *m.*
filling station, *n.* station-service *f.*
film, *n.* (cinema) film *m.*; (photo) pellicule *f.*
filmy, *adj.* couvert d'une pellicule.
filter, **1.** *n.* filtre *m.* **2.** *vb.* filtrer.
filth, *n.* ordure *f.*
filthy, *adj.* immonde; obscène.
fin, *n.* nageoire *f.*
final, *adj.* final.
finale, *n.* finale *m.*
finalist, *n.* finaliste *m.*
finality, *n.* finalité *f.*
finalize, *vb.* mettre au point.
finally, *adv.* finalement, enfin.
finance, **1.** *n.* finance *f.* **2.** *vb.* financer.
financial, *adj.* financier.
financier, *n.* financier *m.*
find, *vb.* trouver.
findings, *n.* conclusions *f.pl.*, verdict *m.*
fine, **1.** *n.* amende *f.* **2.** *adj.* (beautiful) beau *m.*, belle *f.*; (pure, thin) fin. **3.** *vb.* mettre à l'amende.
fine arts, *n.* beaux arts *m.pl.*
finery, *n.* parure *f.*
finesse, **1.** *n.* finesse *f.* **2.** *vb.* finasser.
finger, *n.* doigt *m.*
finger bowl, *n.* rince-bouche *m.*
fingernail, *n.* ongle *m.*
fingerprint, *n.* empreinte digitale *f.*
finicky, *adj.* affété.
finish, *vb.* finir.
finished, *adj.* fini, achevé.
finite, *adj.* fini.
Finland, *n.* Finlande *f.*
Finn, *n.* Finlandais, Finnois *m.*
Finnish, **1.** *n.* finnois *m.* **2.** *adj.* finlandais, finnois.
fir, *n.* sapin *m.*
fire, **1.** *n.* feu *m.*; (burning of house, etc.) incendie *m.* **2.** *vb.* (weapon) tirer.

fire alarm, *n.* avertisseur (*m.*) d'incendie.

firearm, *n.* arme (*f.*) à feu.

firecracker, *n.* pétard *m.*

firedamp, *n.* grisou *m.*

fire engine, *n.* pompe (*f.*) à incendie.

fire escape, *n.* échelle (*f.*) de sauvetage.

fire extinguisher, *n.* extincteur *m.*

firefly, *n.* luciole *f.*

fireman, *n.* pompier *m.*

fireplace, *n.* cheminée *f.*

fireproof, *adj.* à l'épreuve du feu.

fireside, *n.* coin du feu *m.*

firewood, *n.* bois (*m.*) de chauffage.

fireworks, *n.* feu (*m.*) d'artifice.

firing squad, *n.* peloton (*m.*) d'exécution.

firm, 1. *n.* maison (*f.*) de commerce. 2. *adj.* ferme.

firmness, *n.* fermeté *f.*

first, 1. *adj.* premier. 2. *adv.* d'abord.

first aid, *n.* premiers secours *m.pl.*

first-class, *adj.* de premier ordre.

firsthand, *adj.* de première main.

first-rate, *adj.* de premier ordre.

fiscal, *adj.* fiscal.

fish, 1. *n.* poisson *m.* 2. *vb.* pêcher.

fisherman, *n.* pêcheur *m.*

fishery, *n.* pêcherie *f.*

fishhook, *n.* hameçon *m.*

fishing, *n.* pêche *f.*

fishmonger, *n.* marchand (*m.*) de poisson.

fishwife, *n.* marchande (*f.*) de poisson.

fishy, *adj.* de poisson; (*slang*) louche.

fission, *n.* fission *f.*

fissure, *n.* fente *f.*

fist, *n.* poing *m.*

fistic, *adj.* au poing.

fit, 1. *n.* accès *m.* 2. *adj.* (suitable) convenable; (capable) capable; (*f.* for) propre à. 3. *vb.* (befit) convenir à;

(clothes) aller à; (adjust) ajuster, *tr.*

fitful, *adj.* agité, irrégulier.

fitness, *n.* à-propos *m.*; (person) aptitude *f.*; (medical) forme (*f.*) physique.

fitting, 1. *n.* ajustage *m.* 2. *adj.* convenable.

five, *adj. and n.* cinq *m.*

fix, 1. *n.* embarras *m.* 2. *vb.* fixer; (repair) réparer.

fixation, *n.* fixation *f.*

fixed, *adj.* fixe.

fixture, *n.* object (*m.*) d'attache.

fizzy, *adj.* pétillant, gazeux.

flabbergasted, *adj.* sidéré.

flabby, *adj.* flasque.

flaccid, *adj.* flasque.

flag, *n.* drapeau *m.*; (stone) dalle *f.*

flagellate, *vb.* flageller.

flagging, 1. *n.* relâchement *m.* 2. *adj.* qui s'affaiblit.

flagon, *n.* flacon *m.*

flagpole, *n.* mât de drapeau *m.*

flagrant, *adj.* flagrant.

flagrantly, *adv.* d'une manière flagrante.

flagship, *n.* vaisseau amiral *m.*

flagstone, *n.* dalle *f.*

flail, 1. *n.* fléau *m.* 2. *vb.* battre au fléau.

flair, *n.* flair *m.*

flake, 1. *n.* (snow) flocon *m.* 2. *vb.* s'écailler.

flamboyant, *adj.* flamboyant.

flame, 1. *n.* flamme *f.* 2. *vb.* flamboyer.

flame thrower, *n.* lanceur (*m.*) de flammes.

flaming, *adj.* flamboyant.

flamingo, *n.* flamant *m.*

flank, *n.* flanc *m.*

flannel, *n.* flanelle *f.*

flap, 1.*n.* (wing) coup *m.*; (pocket) patte *f.*; (table) battant *m.* 2. *vb.* battre.

flare, *n.* flamboyer.

flare-up, 1. *n.* emportement *m.* 2. *vb.* s'emporter.

flash, 1. *n.* éclair *m.* 2. *vb.* briller, clignoter.

flashback, *n.* retour (*m.*) en arrière.

flashcube, *n.* flash-cube *m.*

flashiness, *n.* faux brillant *m.*; éclat superficiel *m.*

flashlight, *n.* (lighthouse) feu (*m.*) à éclats; (pocket) lampe (*f.*) de poche.

flashy, *adj.* voyant.

flask, *n.* gourde *f.*

flat, 1. *n.* appartement *m.*; (tire) pneu (*m.*) crevé. 2. *adj.* plat *m.*, platte *f.*

flatcar, *n.* wagon en plateforme *m.*

flatness, *n.* (evenness) égalité *f.*; (dullness) platitude *f.*

flatten, *vb.* aplatir.

flatter, *vb.* flatter.

flatterer, *n.* flatteur *m.*

flattery, *n.* flatterie *f.*

flattop, *n.* porte-avion *m.*

flaunt, *vb.* parader, étaler.

flautist, *n.* flûtiste *m.f.*

flavor, *n.* (taste) saveur *f.*; (fragrance) arome *m.*

flavoring, *n.* assaisonnement *m.*

flavorless, *adj.* fade.

flaw, *n.* défaut *m.*

flawless, *adj.* sans défaut, parfait.

flawlessly, *adv.* d'une manière impeccable.

flax, *n.* lin *m.*

flay, *vb.* écorcher.

flea, *n.* puce *f.*

fleck, 1. *n.* tache *f.* 2. *vb.* tacheter.

fledgling, *n.* oisillon *m.*

flee, *vb.* s'enfuir.

fleece, 1. *n.* toison *f.* 2. *vb.* voler.

fleecy, *adj.* laineux, moutonneux.

fleet, *n.* flotte *f.*

fleeting, *adj.* fugitif.

Flemish, *adj.* flamand.

flesh, *n.* chair *f.*

fleshy, *adj.* charnu.

flex, *vb.* fléchir.

flexibility, *n.* flexibilité *f.*

flexible, *adj.* flexible.

flick, 1. *n.* petit coup *m.* 2. *vb.* donner un petit coup à.

flicker, 1. *n.* lueur (*f.*) vacillante. 2. *vb.* trembloter.

flier, *n.* aviateur *m.*

flight, n. (flying) vol m.; (fleeing) fuite f.

flight attendant, n. hôtesse (f.) de l'air.

flighty, adj. étourdi.

flimsy, adj. sans solidité.

flinch, vb. reculer, broncher.

fling, 1. vb. jeter. 2. n. (have a f.) faire la fête.

flint, n. (lighter) pierre (f.) à briquet; (mineral) silex m.

flip, vb. donner un petit coup à.

flippant, adj. léger.

flippantly, adv. légèrement.

flirt, vb. flirter.

flirtation, n. flirt m.

float, vb. flotter.

flock, 1. n. troupeau m. 2. vb. accourir.

flog, vb. fouetter.

flood, n. inondation f.

floodgate, n. écluse f.

floodlight, n. lumière (f.) à grand flots.

floor, n. plancher m.; (take the f.) prendre la parole; (story) étage m.

flooring, n. plancher m., parquet m.

floorwalker, n. inspecteur du magasin m.

flop, 1. vb. faire plouf, s'effondrer. 2. n. fiasco m.

floral, adj. floral.

florid, adj. fleuri, vermeil.

florist, n. fleuriste m.f.

flounce, 1. n. volant m. 2. vb. se démener.

flounder, n. flet m.

flour, n. farine f.

flourish, vb. prospérer.

flow, vb. couler.

flower, 1. n. fleur f. 2. vb. fleurir.

flowerpot, n. pot à fleurs m.

flowery, adj. fleuri.

flu, n. grippe f.

fluctuate, vb. osciller.

fluctuation, n. fluctuation f.

flue, n. tuyau (m.) de cheminée.

fluency, n. facilité f.

fluent, adj. (be a f. speaker of . . .) parler . . . couramment.

fluid, adj and n. fluide m.

fluidity, n. fluidité f.

flunk, vb. coller, recaler.

flunkey, n. laquais m.

fluorescent lamp, n. lampe fluorescente f.

fluoride, n. fluorure f.

fluoroscope, n. fluoroscope m.

flurry, 1. n. agitation f. 2. vb. agiter.

flush, n. (redness) rougeur f.; (plumbing) chasse f.

flustered, adj. énervé.

flute, n. flûte f.

flutter, 1. n. (bird) voltigement m.; (agitation) agitation f. 2. vb. s'agiter; (heart) palpiter.

flux, n. flux m.

fly, 1. n. mouche f.; (on pants) braguette f. 2. vb. voler.

foam, n. écume f.

focal, adj. focal.

focus, 1. n. foyer m.; (in f.) au point. 2. vb. (photo) mettre au point.

fodder, n. fourrage m.

foe, n. ennemi m.

fog, n. brouillard m.

foggy, adj. brumeux.

foil, n. (sheet) feuille f.; (set-off) repoussoir m.; (fencing) fleuret m.

foist, vb. fourrer.

fold, 1. n. pli m. 2. vb. plier.

folder, n. (booklet) prospectus m.

foliage, n. feuillage m.

folio, n. in-folio m.

folk, n. gens m.f.pl.

folklore, n. folk-lore m.

folksong, n. chanson (f.) folklorique.

follicle, n. follicule m.

follow, vb. suivre.

follower, n. disciple m.

folly, n. folie f.

foment, vb. fomenter.

fond, adj. tendre; (be f. of) aimer.

fondant, n. fondant m.

fondle, vb. caresser.

fondly, adv. tendrement.

fondness, n. tendresse f.

font, n. fonte f.

food, n. nourriture f.

foodstuff, n. comestible m.

fool, n. sot m., sotte f.; (jester) bouffon m.

foolhardiness, n. témérité f.

foolhardy, adj. téméraire.

foolish, adj. sot m., sotte f.

foolproof, adj. infaillible.

foolscap, n. papier écolier m.

foot, n. pied m.

footage, n. métrage m.

football, n. football m., ballon m.

foothill, n. colline basse f.

foothold, n. point d'appui m.

footing, n. pied m., point d'appui m.

footlights, n. rampe f.

footnote, n. note f.

footprint, n. empreinte de pas f.

footsore, adj. aux pieds endoloris.

footstep, n. pas m.

footstool, n. tabouret m.

footwork, n. jeu de pieds m.

fop, n. fat m.

for, 1. prep. pour. 2. conj. car.

forage, 1. n. fourrage m. 2. vb. fourrager.

foray, n. razzia f.

forbear, vb. (avoid) s'abstenir de; (be patient) montrer de la patience.

forbearance, n. patience f.

forbid, vb. défendre (à).

forbidding, adj. menaçant.

force, 1. n. force f. 2. vb. forcer.

forced, adj. forcé.

forceful, adj. énergique.

forcefulness, n. énergie f., vigueur f.

forceps, n. forceps m.

forcible, adj. forcé.

ford, 1. n. gué m. 2. vb. traverser à gué.

fore, 1. adj. antérieur, de devant. 2. n. avant m.

fore and aft, adv. de l'avant à l'arrière.

forearm, n. avant-bras m.

forebears, n. ancêtres m.pl.

forebode, vb. présager.

foreboding, 1. n. mauvais augure m., pressentiment m. 2. adj. qui présage le mal.

forecast, 1. *n.* prévision *f.* 2. *vb.* prévoir.

forecaster, *n.* pronostiqueur *m.*

forecastle, *n.* gaillard *m.*

foreclose, *vb.* exclure, forclore.

forefather, *n.* ancêtre *m.*

forefinger, *n.* index *m.*

forefront, *n.* premier rang *m.*

foregone, *adj.* décidé d'avance.

foreground, *n.* premier plan *m.*

forehead, *n.* front *m.*

foreign, *adj.* étranger.

foreign aid, *n.* aide (*f.*) aux pays étrangers.

foreigner, *n.* étranger *m.*

foreleg, *n.* jambe antérieure *f.*

foreman, *n.* contremaître *m.*

foremost, *adj.* premier.

forenoon, *n.* matinée *f.*

forensic, *adj.* judiciaire.

forerunner, *n.* avant-coureur *m.*

foresee, *vb.* prévoir.

foreseeable, *adj.* prévisible.

foreshadow, *vb.* présager.

foresight, *n.* prévoyance *f.*

forest, *n.* forêt *f.*

forestall, *vb.* anticiper, devancer.

forester, *n.* forestier *m.*

forestry, *n.* sylviculture *f.*

foretaste, *n.* avant-goût *m.*

foretell, *vb.* prédire.

forever, *adv.* pour toujours.

forevermore, *adv.* à jamais.

forewarn, *vb.* prévenir.

foreword, *n.* avant-propos *m.*

forfeit, *vb.* forfaire.

forfeiture, *n.* perte (*f.*) par confiscation, forfaiture *f.*

forgather, *vb.* se réunir.

forge, 1. *n.* forge *f.* 2. *vb.* forger; (signature, money) contrefaire.

forger, *n.* faussaire *m.*, falsificateur *m.*

forgery, *n.* faux *m.*

forget, *vb.* oublier.

forgetful, *adj.* oublieux.

forget-me-not, *n.* myosotis *m.*

forgive, *vb.* pardonner (à).

forgiveness, *n.* pardon *m.*

forgo, *vb.* renoncer à.

fork, *n.* fourchette *f.*; (tool, road) fourche *f.*

forlorn, *adj.* (hopeless) désespéré; (forsaken) abandonné.

form, 1. *n.* forme *f.*; (blank) formule *f.* 2. *vb.* former.

formal, *adj.* formel.

formaldehyde, *n.* formaldéhyde *f.*

formality, *n.* formalité *f.*

formally, *adv.* formellement.

format, 1. *n.* format *m.* 2. *vb.* formater.

formation, *n.* formation *f.*

formative, *adj.* formatif.

former, 1. *adj.* précédent; (with latter) premier. 2. *pron.* le premier.

formerly, *adv.* autrefois, jadis, auparavant.

formidable, *adj.* formidable.

formless, *adj.* informe.

formula, *n.* formule *f.*

formulate, *vb.* formuler.

formulation, *n.* formulation *f.*

forsake, *vb.* abandonner.

forsythia, *n.* forsythie *f.*

fort, *n.* fort *m.*

forte, *n.* fort *m.*

forth, *adv.* en avant; (and so f.) et ainsi de suite.

forthcoming, *adv.* à venir.

forthright, 1. *adj.* tout droit. 2. *adv.* carrément, nettement.

forthwith, *adv.* sur-le-champ, tout de suite.

fortieth, *adj. and n.* quarantième *m.f.*

fortification, *n.* fortification *f.*

fortify, *vb.* fortifier, renforcer.

fortissimo, *adv.* fortissimo.

fortitude, *n.* courage *m.*

fortnight, *n.* quinzaine *f.*

fortress, *n.* forteresse *f.*

fortuitous, *adj.* fortuit.

fortunate, *adj.* heureux.

fortune, *n.* fortune *f.*

fortuneteller, *n.* diseur (*m.*) de bonne aventure.

forty, *adj. and n.* quarante *m.*

forum, *n.* (Roman) forum *m.*

forward, 1. *adj.* en avant; (advanced) avancé; (bold) hardi. 2. *adv.* en avant. 3. *vb.* (letter) faire suivre.

forwardness, *n.* empressement *m.*, effronterie *f.*

fossil, *n.* fossile *m.*

fossilize, *vb.* fossiliser.

foster, *vb.* nourrir.

foster child, *n.* enfant (*m.*) adopté.

foul, *adj.* (dirty) sale; (disgusting) dégoûtant; (obscene) ordurier; (abominable) infâme.

found, *vb.* fonder.

foundation, *n.* fondation *f.*; (theory) fondement *m.*

founder, *n.* fondateur *m.*

foundling, *n.* enfant trouvé.

foundry, *n.* fonderie *f.*

fountain, *n.* fontaine *f.*

fountainhead, *n.* source *f.*

fountain pen, *n.* stylo(-graphe) *m.*

four, *adj. and n.* quatre *m.*

four-in-hand, *n.* attelage à quatre *m.*

fourscore, *adj.* quatre-vingts.

foursome, *n.* à quatre.

fourteen, *adj. and n.* quatorze *m.*

fourth, *adj. and n.* quatrième *m.f.*; (fraction) quart *m.*

fourth estate, *n.* quatrième état *m.*

fowl, *n.* volaille *f.*

fox, *n.* renard *m.*

foxglove, *n.* digitale *f.*

foxhole, *n.* renardière *f.*

fox terrier, *n.* fox-terrier *m.*

fox trot, *n.* fox-trot *m.*

foxy, *adj.* rusé.

foyer, *n.* foyer *m.*

fracas, *n.* fracas *m.*

fraction, *n.* fraction *f.*

fracture, *n.* fracture *f.*

fragile, *adj.* fragile.

fragment, *n.* fragment *m.*

fragmentary, *adj.* fragmentaire.

fragrance, *n.* parfum *m.*

fragrant, *adj.* parfumé.

frail, *adj.* frêle.

frailty, *n.* faiblesse *f.*

frame, *n.* (picture) cadre *m.*; (structure) structure *f.*

frame-up, 1. *n.* coup monté *m.* **2.** *vb.* monter un coup.

framework, *n.* charpente *f.*

France, *n.* France *f.*

franchise, *n.* droit (*m.*) électoral.

frank, *adj.* franc *m.*, franche *f.*

frankfurter, *n.* saucisse (*f.*) de Francfort.

frankincense, *n.* encens *m.*

frankly, *adv.* franchement.

frankness, *n.* franchise *f.*

frantic, *adj.* frénétique.

fraternal, *adj.* fraternel.

fraternally, *adv.* fraternellement.

fraternity, *n.* fraternité *f.*

fraternization, *n.* fraternisation *f.*

fraternize, *vb.* fraterniser.

fratricide, *n.* fratricide *m.*

fraud, *n.* fraude *f.*; (person) imposteur *m.*

fraudulent, *adj.* frauduleux.

fraudulently, *adv.* frauduleusement.

fraught, *adj.* chargé (de), plein, gros.

fray, 1. *n.* bagarre *f.* **2.** *vb.* érailler.

freak, *n.* (whim) caprice *m.*; (abnormality) phénomène *m.*

freckle, *n.* tache de rousseur *f.*

freckled, *adj.* taché de rousseur.

free, 1. *adj.* libre; (without cost) gratuit. **2.** *vb.* libérer, affranchir.

freedom, *n.* liberté *f.*

freelance, 1. *n.* journaliste ou politicien indépendant *m.* **2.** *vb.* faire du journalisme indépendant.

freestone, *n.* pêche (*f.*) dont la chair n'adhère pas au noyau.

free verse, *n.* vers libre *m.*

free will, *n.* libre arbitre *m.*

freeze, *vb.* geler; (food) surgeler.

freezer, *n.* glacière *f.*; congélateur *m.*

freezing point, *n.* point (*m.*) de congélation.

freight, *n.* fret *m.*

freightage, *n.* frètement *m.*

freighter, *n.* affréteur *m.*

French, *adj. and n.* français *m.*

French fries, *n.* frites *f.pl.*

French leave, *n.* filer à l'anglaise.

Frenchman, *n.* Français *m.*

French toast, *n.* tranche de pain frite *f.*

Frenchwoman, *n.* Française *f.*

frenzied, *adj.* affolé, frénétique.

frenzy, *n.* frénésie *f.*

frequency, *n.* fréquence *f.*

frequent, 1. *adj.* fréquent. **2.** *vb.* fréquenter.

frequently, *adv.* fréquemment.

fresco, *n.* fresque *f.*

fresh, *adj.* frais *m.*, fraîche *f.*; (new, recent) nouveau; nouvel *m.*, nouvelle *f.*; (impudent) culotté.

freshen, *vb.* rafraîchir.

freshman, *n.* étudiant (*m.*) de première année.

freshness, *n.* fraîcheur *f.*

fresh-water, *adj.* d'eau douce.

fret, *vb.* ronger, *tr.*

fretful, *adj.* chagrin.

fretfully, *adv.* avec irritation.

fretfulness, *n.* irritabilité *f.*

friar, *n.* moine *m.*, frère religieux *m.*

fricassee, *n.* fricassée *f.*

friction, *n.* friction *f.*

Friday, *n.* vendredi *m.*

fridge, *n.* frigo *m.*

friend, *n.* ami *m.*, amie *f.*

friendless, *adj.* sans amis.

friendliness, *n.* disposition (*f.*) amicale.

friendly, *adj.* amical.

friendship, *n.* amitié *f.*

fright, *n.* effroi *m.*

frighten, *vb.* effrayer.

frightening, *adj.* effrayant.

frightful, *adj.* affreux.

frigid, *adj.* glacial.

Frigid Zone, *n.* zone glaciale *f.*

frill, 1. *n.* volant *m.*; affectation *f.* **2.** *vb.* plisser.

frilly, *adj.* froncé, ruché.

fringe, *n.* frange *f.*

fringe benefits, *n.* avantages (*m.pl.*) sociaux.

frisk, *vb.* fouiller.

frisky, *adj.* folâtre.

frivolity, *n.* frivolité *f.*

frivolous, *adj.* frivole.

frivolousness, *n.* frivolité *f.*

frizzy, *adj.* crépu.

frock, *n.* robe *f.*; (monk's) froc *m.*

frog, *n.* grenouille *f.*

frolic, *vb.* folâtrer.

from, *prep.* de; (time) depuis.

front, *n.* front *m.*; (front part) devant *m.*; (in f. of) devant.

frontage, *n.* étendue de devant *f.*

frontal, *adj.* frontal, de face.

frontier, *n.* frontière *f.*

frost, *n.* gelée *f.*

frostbite, *n.* gelure *f.*

frosting, *n.* glaçage *m.*

frosty, *adj.* gelé, glacé.

froth, 1. *n.* écume *f.* **2.** *vb.* écumer.

frown, *vb.* froncer les sourcils.

frowzy, *adj.* mal tenu, peu soigné.

frozen, *adj.* gelé; (food) surgelé.

fructify, *vb.* fructifier.

frugal, *adj.* frugal.

frugality, *n.* frugalité *f.*

fruit, *n.* fruit *m.*

fruitful, *adj.* fructueux.

fruition, *n.* réalisation *f.*, fructification *f.*

fruitless, *adj.* infructueux.

frustrate, *vb.* faire échouer.

frustration, *n.* frustration *f.*

fry, *vb.* frire, *intr.*; faire frire, *tr.*

fryer, *n.* casserole *f.*

fuchsia, *n.* fuchsia *m.*

fudge, 1. *n.*. espèce de fondant américain. **2.** *interj.* bah!

fuel, *n.* combustible *m.*

fugitive, *adj.* fugitif.

fugue, *n.* fugue *f.*

fulcrum, *n.* pivot *m.*, point d'appui *m.*

fulfill, *vb.* accomplir.

fulfillment, *n.* accomplissement *m.*

full, *adj.* plein.

fullback, *n.* arrière *m.*

full dress, *adj.* en tenue de cérémonie.

fullness, *n.* plénitude *f.*

fully, *adv.* pleinement.

fulminate, *vb.* fulminer.

fulmination, *n.* fulmination *f.*

fumble, *vb.* tâtonner.

fume, *n.* fumée *f.*

fumigate, *vb.* désinfecter.

fumigator, *n.* fumigateur *m.*

fun, *n.* (amusement) amusement *m.;* **(have f.)** s'amuser; (joke) plaisanterie *f.;* **(make f. of)** se moquer de.

function, *n.* fonction *f.;* (social occasion) cérémonie *f.*

functional, *adj.* fonctionnel.

functionary, *n.* fonctionnaire *m.*

fund, *n.* fonds *m.*

fundamental, *adj.* fondamental.

fundamentalist, *n.* intégriste *m.*

fundamentalism, *n.* intégrisme *m.*

funeral, *n.* funérailles *f.pl.*

funereal, *adj.* funèbre, funéraire.

fungicide, *n.* fongicide *m.*

fungus, *n.* fongus *m.*

funk, *n.* **(be in a f.)** être déprimé.

funnel, *n.* entonnoir *m.;* (smoke-stack) cheminée *f.*

funny, *adj.* drôle.

fur, *n.* fourrure *f.*

furious, *adj.* furieux.

furlong, *n.* furlong *m.*

furlough, *n.* permission *f.*

furnace, *n.* fourneau *m.*

furnish, *vb.* fournir; (house) meubler.

furnishings, *n.* ameublement *m.*

furniture, *n.* meubles *m. pl.*

furor, *n.* fureur *f.*

furred, *adj.* fourré.

furrier, *n.* fourreur *m.*

furrow, *n.* sillon *m.*

furry, *adj.* qui ressemble à la fourrure.

further, 1. *adj.* ultérieur. **2.** *adv.* (distance) plus loin; (extent) davantage.

furtherance, *n.* avancement *m.*

furthermore, *adv.* en outre.

fury, *n.* furie *f.*

fuse, *vb.* fondre.

fuselage, *n.* fuselage *m.*

fusillade, *n.* fusillade *f.*

fusion, *n.* fusion *f.,* fusionnement *m.*

fuss, *n.* **(make a f.)** faire des histoires.

fussy, *adj.* difficile.

futile, *adj.* futile.

futility, *n.* futilité *f.*

future, 1. *n.* avenir *m.;* (gramm.) futur *m.* **2.** *adj.* futur.

futurity, *n.* avenir *m.*

futurology, *n.* futurologie *f.*

fuzz, *n.* duvet *m.,* flou *m.*

fuzzy, *adj.* flou, frisotté.

G

gab *vb.* jaser.

gabardine, *n.* gabardine *f.*

gable, *n.* pignon *m.*

gadabout, *n.* coureur *m.*

gadfly, *n.* taon *m.*

gadget, *n.* truc *m.*

Gaelic, *adj.* gaélique.

gaffe, *n.* gaffe *f.*

gag, 1. *vb.* bâillonner. **2.** *n.* blague *f.,* bobard *m.;* bâillon *m.*

gaiety, *n.* gaieté *f.*

gaily, *adv.* gaiement.

gain, 1. *n.* gain *m.* **2.** *vb.* gagner.

gainful, *adj.* profitable, rémunérateur.

gainfully, *adv.* profitablement.

gainsay, *vb.* contredire.

gait, *n.* allure *f.*

gal, *n.* (colloquial) femme *f.*

gala, *n.* fête de gala *f.*

galaxy, *n.* galaxie *f.,* assemblée brillante *f.*

gale, *n.* grand vent *m.*

gall, *n.* (bile) fiel *m.;* (sore) écorchure *f.*

gallant, *adj.* (brave) vaillant; (with ladies) galant.

gallantly, *adv.* galamment.

gallantry, *n.* vaillance *f.,* galanterie *f.*

gall bladder, *n.* vésicule biliaire *f.*

galleon, *n.* galion *m.*

gallery, *n.* galerie *f.*

galley, *n.* galère *f.,* (naut.) cuisine *f.,* (typographic) galée *f.*

galley proof, *n.* épreuve en première *f.*

Gallic, *adj.* gaulois, français.

gallivant, *vb.* courailler.

gallon, *n.* gallon *m.*

gallop, 1. *n.* galop *m.* **2.** *vb.* galoper.

gallows, *n.* potence *f.*

gallstone, *n.* calcul biliaire *m.*

galore, *adv.* à foison, à profusion.

galosh, *n.* galoche *f.,* caoutchouc *m.*

galvanize, *vb.* galvaniser.

Gambia, *n.* Gambie *f.*

gamble, 1. *n.* jeu *(m.)* de hasard. **2.** *vb.* jouer.

gambler, *n.* joueur *m.*

gambling, *n.* jeu *m.*

gambol, 1. *n.* gambade *f.* **2.** *vb.* gamboler.

game, *n.* jeu *m.;* (hunting) gibier *m.*

gamely, *adv.* courageusement, crânement.

gameness, *n.* courage *m.,* crânerie *f.*

gamin, *n.* gamin *m.*

gamut, *n.* gamme *f.*

gamy, *adj.* giboyeux.

gander, *n.* jars *m.*

gang, *n.* bande *f.;* (workers) équipe *f.*

gangling, *adj.* dégingandé.

gangplank, *n.* passerelle *f.*

gangrene, *n.* gangrène *f.*

gangrenous, *adj.* gangreneux.

gangster, *n.* gangster *m.*

gangway, *n.* passage *m.*

gap, *n.* (opening) ouverture *f.*; (empty space) vide *m.*

gape, *vb.* rester bouche bée.

garage, *n.* garage *m.*

garb, 1. *n.* vêtement *m.*, costume *m.* 2. *vb.* vêtir, habiller.

garbage, *n.* ordures *f.pl.*

garble, *vb.* tronquer, altérer.

garden, *n.* jardin *m.*

gardener, *n.* jardinier *m.*

gardenia, *n.* gardénia *m.*

gargle, 1. *n.* gargarisme *m.* 2. *vb.* se gargariser.

gargoyle, *n.* gargouille *f.*

garish, *adj.* voyant.

garland, *n.* guirlande *f.*

garlic, *n.* ail *m.*

garment, *n.* vêtement *m.*

garner, *vb.* mettre en grenier.

garnet, *n.* grenat *m.*

garnish, *vb.* garnir.

garnishee, *n.* tiers-saisi *m.*

garnishment, *n.* saisie-arrêt *f.*

garret, *n.* mansarde *f.*

garrison, *n.* garnison *f.*

garrote, 1. *n.* garrotte *f.* 2. *vb.* garrotter.

garrulous, *adj.* bavard, loquace.

garter, *n.* jarretière *f.*

gas, *n.* gaz *m.*; (auto) essence *f.* (g. station) station-service *f.*

gaseous, *adj.* gazeux.

gash, 1. *n.* coupure *f.*, entaille *f.* 2. *vb.* couper, entailler.

gasket, *n.* garcette *f.*

gasless, *adj.* sans gaz.

gas mask, *n.* masque à gaz *m.*

gasohol, *n.* essence *(f.)* fabriquée avec de l'alcool.

gasoline, *n.* essence *f.*

gasp, *vb.* (astonishment) sursauter; (lack of breath) haleter.

gassy, *adj.* gazeux; (talkative) bavard.

gastric, *adj.* gastrique.

gastric juice, *n.* suc gastrique *m.*

gastritis, *n.* gastrite *f.*

gastronomically, *adv.* d'une manière gastronomique.

gastronomy, *n.* gastronomie *f.*

gate, *n.* (city) porte *f.*; (with bars) barrière *f.*; (wrought-iron) grille *f.*

gateway, *n.* porte *f.*, entrée *f.*

gather, *vb.* rassembler, *tr.*; recueillir, *tr.*

gathering, *n.* rassemblement *m.*

gaudily, *adv.* de manière voyante.

gaudiness, *n.* éclat criard *m.*, ostentation *f.*

gaudy, *adj.* voyant.

gaunt, *adj.* décharné.

gauntlet, *n.* gantelet *m.*

gauze, *n.* gaze *f.*

gavel, *n.* marteau *m.*

gavotte, *n.* gavotte *f.*

gawky, *adj.* dégingandé.

gay, 1. *adj.* gai; (homosexual) homosexuel. 2. *n.* homosexuel *m.*

gaze, *vb.* regarder fixement.

gazelle, *n.* gazelle *f.*

gazette, *n.* gazette *f.*

gazetteer, *n.* gazetier *m.*, répertoire géographique *m.*

gear, *n.* (implements, device) appareil *m.*; (machines) engrenage *m.*; (in g.) engrené; (g. change) changement *(m.)* de vitesse.

gearing, *n.* engrenage *m.*

gearshift, *n.* changement *(m.)* de vitesse.

gel, *n.* gel *m.*

gelatin, *n.* gélatine *f.*

gelatinous, *adj.* gélatineux.

geld, *vb.* châtrer.

gelding, *n.* animal châtré *m.*

gem, *n.* pierre *(f.)* précieuse.

gender, *n.* genre *m.*

gene, *n.* gène *m.*

genealogical, *adj.* généalogique.

genealogy, *n.* généalogie *f.*

general, *adj. and n.* général *m.*

generality, *n.* généralité *f.*

generalization, *n.* généralisation *f.*

generalize, *vb.* généraliser.

generally, *adv.* généralement.

general practioner, *n.* généraliste *m.*

generalship, *n.* stratégie *f.*

generate, *vb.* engendrer, générer.

generation, *n.* génération *f.*

generator, *n.* (electricity) groupe *(m.)* électrogène.

generic, *adj.* générique.

generosity, *n.* générosité *f.*

generous, *adj.* généreux.

generously, *adv.* généreusement.

genetic, *adj.* génétique.

genetics, *n.* génétique *f.*

genial, *adj.* sympathique.

geniality, *n.* jovialité *f.*, bienveillance *f.*

genially, *adv.* affablement.

genital, *adj.* génital.

genitals, *n.* organes génitaux *m.pl.*

genitive, *n. and adj.* génitif *m.*

genius, *n.* génie *m.*

genocide, *n.* génocide *m.*

genre, *n.* genre *m.*

genteel, *adj.* de bon ton.

gentian, *n.* gentiane *f.*

gentile, *n.* gentil *m.*

gentility, *n.* prétention *(f.)* à la distinction.

gentle, *adj.* doux *m.*, douce *f.*

gentleman, *n.* monsieur *m.*, *pl.* messieurs; (character) galant homme *m.*

gentlemanly, *adj.* comme il faut, bien élevé.

gentlemen's agreement, *n.* convention verbale *f.*

gentleness, *n.* douceur *f.*

gently, *adv.* doucement.

gentry, *n.* petite noblesse *f.*

genuflect, *vb.* faire des génuflexions.

genuine, *adj.* véritable.

genuinely, *adv.* véritablement.

genuineness, *n.* authenticité *f.*

genus, *n.* genre *m.*

geographer, *n.* géographe *m.*

geographical, *adj.* géographique.

geography, *n.* géographie *f.*

geometric, *adj.* géométrique.

geometry, *n.* géométrie *f.*

geopolitics, *n.* géopolitique *f.*

geranium, *n.* géranium *m.*

geriatric, *adj.* gériatrique.

germ, *n.* germe *m.*

German, 1. *n.* (person) Allemand *m.*; (language) allemand *m.* **2.** *adj.* allemand.

germane, *adj.* approprié.

Germanic, *adj.* allemand, germanique.

German measles, *n.* rougeole bénigne *f.*

Germany, *n.* Allemagne *f.*

germicide, *n.* microbicide *m.*

germinal, *adj.* germinal.

germinate, *vb.* germer.

gestate, *vb.* enfanter.

gestation, *n.* gestation *f.*

gesticulate, *vb.* gesticuler.

gesticulation, *n.* gesticulation *f.*

gesture, *n.* geste *m.*

get, *vb.* (obtain) obtenir; (receive) recevoir; (take) prendre; (become) devenir; (arrive) arriver; (**g. in**) entrer; (**g. off**) descendre; (**g. on,** agree) s'entendre; (**g. on,** go up) monter; (**g. out**) sortir; (**g. up**) se lever.

getaway, *n.* fuite *f.*

geyser, *n.* geyser *m.*

Ghana, *n.* Ghana *m.*

ghastly, *adj.* horrible.

ghetto blaster, *n.* stéréo (*f.*) portable.

ghost, *n.* (specter) revenant *m.*; (**Holy G.**) Saint-Esprit *m.*

ghost writer, *n.* collaborateur anonyme *m.*, nègre *m.*

ghoul, *n.* goule *f.*, vampire *m.*

giant, *n.* géant *m.*

gibberish, *n.* baragouin *m.*

gibbon, *n.* gibbon *m.*

gibe, 1. *n.* raillerie *f.* **2.** *vb.* railler.

giblet, *n.* abatis (de volaille) *m.*

Gibraltar, *n.* Gibraltar.

giddy, *adj.* étourdi.

gift, *n.* don *m.*; (present) cadeau *m.*

gifted, *adj.* doué.

gigantic, *adj.* géant, gigantesque.

giggle, *vb.* rire nerveusement, glousser.

gigolo, *n.* gigolo *m.*

gild, *vb.* dorer.

gill, *n.* (of fish) ouïes *f.pl.*

gilt, 1. *n.* dorure *f.* **2.** *adj.* doré.

gilt-edged, *adj.* doré sur tranche.

gimcrack, 1. *n.* camelote *f.* **2.** *adj.* de camelote.

gimlet, *n.* vrille *f.*

gimmick, *n.* truc *m.*

gin, *n.* genièvre *m.*

ginger, *n.* gingembre *m.*

ginger ale, *n.* boisson (*f.*) gazeuse au gingembre.

gingerly, *adv.* avec précaution.

gingersnap, *n.* biscuit (*m.*) au gingembre.

gingham, *n.* guingan *m.*

giraffe, *n.* girafe *f.*

gird, *vb.* ceindre.

girder, *n.* support *m.*

girdle, *n.* gaine *f.*

girl, *n.* jeune fille *f.*

girlfriend, *n.* petite amie *f.*

girlish, *adj.* de jeune fille.

girth, *n.* sangle *f.*, circonférence *f.*, corpulence *f.*

gist, *n.* fond *m.*, essence *f.*

give, *vb.* donner; (**g. back**) rendre; (**g. in**) céder; (**g. out**) distribuer; (**g. up**) renoncer à.

give-and-take, *adv.* donnant donnant.

given, *adj.* donné.

given name, *n.*, prénom *m.*

giver, *n.* donneur *m.*

gizzard, *n.* gésier *m.*

glace, *adj.* glacé.

glacial, *adj.* glaciaire.

glacier, *n.* glacier *m.*

glad, *adj.* heureux.

gladden, *vb.* réjouir.

glade, *n.* clairière *f.*, éclaircie *f.*

gladiolus, *n.* glaïeul *m.*

gladly, *adv.* volontiers.

gladness, *n.* joie *f.*

Gladstone bag, *n.* sac américain *m.*

glamour, *n.* éclat *m.*

glance, 1. *n.* coup (*m.*) d'œil. **2.** *vb.* jeter un coup d'œil.

gland, *n.* glande *f.*

glandular, *adj.* glandulaire.

glare, 1. *n.* (light) clarté *f.*; (stare) regard (*m.*) enflammé. **2.** *vb.* (shine) briller; (look) jeter des regards enflammés.

glaring, *adj.* éclatant, flagrant, voyant, manifeste.

glass, *n.* verre *m.*

glass-blowing, *n.* soufflage *m.*

glasses, *n.* lunettes *f.pl.*

glassful, *n.* verre *m.*, verrée *f.*

glassware, *n.* verrerie *f.*

glassy, *adj.* vitreux.

glaucoma, *n.* glaucome *m.*

glaze, 1. *n.* lustre *m.* **2.** *vb.* vitrer.

glazier, *n.* vitrier *m.*

gleam, 1. *n.* lueur *f.* **2.** *vb.* luire.

glean, *vb.* glâner.

glee, *n.* allégresse *f.*

glee club, *n.* chœur d'hommes *m.*

gleeful, *adj.* joyeux, allègre.

glen, *n.* vallon *m.*, ravin *m.*

glib, *adj.* spécieux, facile.

glide, *vb.* glisser; (plane) planer.

glider, *n.* planeur *m.*

glimmer, 1. *n.* faible lueur *f.* **2.** jeter une faible lueur.

glimmering, *adj.* faible, vacillant.

glimpse, 1. *vb.* entrevoir. **2.** *n.* aperçu *m.*

glint, 1. *n.* éclair *m.*, reflet *m.* **2.** *vb.* entreluire, étinceler.

glisten, *vb.* briller.

glitter, *vb.* étinceler.

gloat, *vb.* se régaler de.

global, *adj.* global.

globe, *n.* globe *m.*

globetrotter, *n.* globe trotter *m.*

globular, *adj.* globulaire, globuleux.

globule, *n.* globule *m.*

glockenspiel, *n.* glockenspiel *m.*

gloom, *n.* (darkness) ténèbres *f.pl.*; (sadness) tristesse *f.*

gloomy, *adj.* sombre.

glorification, *n.* glorification *f.*

glorify, *vb.* glorifier.

glorious, *adj.* glorieux; (weather) radieux.

glory, *n.* gloire *f.*

gloss, *n.* **1.** lustre *m.*, vernis *m.*, glose *f.* **2.** *vb.* lustrer, glacer.

glossary, *n.* glossaire *m.*

glossy, *adj.* lustré, glacé.

glove, *n.* gant *m.*

glow, 1. *n.* (light) lumière *f.*; (heat) chaleur *f.* **2.** *vb.* briller.

glower, *vb.* **(g. at)** lancer des regards mauvais à.

glowing, *adj.* embrasé, rayonnant.

glowingly, *adv.* en termes chaleureux.

glowworm, *n.* ver luisant *m.*

glucose, *n.* glucose *f.*

glue, 1. *n.* colle (*f.*) forte. **2.** *vb.* coller.

glum, *adj.* maussade.

glumness, *n.* air maussade *m.*, tristesse *f.*

glut, 1. *n.* assouvissement *m.*, excès *m.*, pléthore *f.* **2.** *vb.* assouvir, rassasier, gorger.

glutinous, *adj.* glutineux.

glutton, *n.* gourmand *m.*

gluttonous, *adj.* gourmand, goulu.

glycerin, *n.* glycérine *f.*

gnarl, *n.* loupe *f.*, nœud *m.*

gnash, *vb.* grincer.

gnat, *n.* moucheron *m.*

gnaw, *vb.* ronger.

gnu, *n.* gnou *m.*

go, *vb.* aller; **(g. away)** s'en aller; **(g. back)** retourner; **(g. by)** passer; **(g. down)** descendre; **(g. in)** entrer; **(g. on)** continuer; **(g. out)** sortir; **(g. up)** monter; **(g. without)** se passer de.

goad, 1. *n.* aiguillon *m.* **2.** *vb.* aiguillonner, piquer.

goal, *n.* but *m.*

goat, *n.* chèvre *f.*

goatee, *n.* barbiche *f.*

goatherd, *n.* chevrier *m.*

goatskin, *n.* peau (*f.*) de chèvre.

gobble, *vb.* avaler goulûment, dévorer.

gobbler, *n.* avaleur *m.*; dindon *m.*

go-between, *n.* intermédiaire *m.*

goblet, *n.* gobelet *m.*

goblin, *n.* gobelin *m.*, lutin *m.*

God, *n.* Dieu *m.*

godchild, *n.* filleul *m.*

goddess, *n.* déesse *f.*

godfather, *n.* parrain *m.*

godless, *adj.* athée, impie, sans Dieu.

godlike, *adj.* comme un dieu, divin.

godly, *adj.* dévot, pieux, saint.

godmother, *n.* marraine *f.*

godsend, *n.* aubaine *f.*, bienfait du ciel *m.*

Godspeed, *interj.* bon voyage!

go-getter, *n.* homme (*m.*) d'affaires énergique, arriviste *m.*

goggles, *n.* lunettes (*f.pl.*) protectrices.

goiter, *n.* goitre *m.*

gold, *n.* or *m.*

gold brick, *n.* attrape-niais *m.*

golden, *adj.* d'or.

goldenrod, *n.* solidage *m.*

golden rule, *n.* règle (*f.*) par excellence.

gold-filled, *adj.* aurifié, en (or) doublé.

goldfinch, *n.* chardonneret *m.*

goldfish, *n.* poisson rouge *m.*

gold leaf, *n.* feuille d'or *f.*, or battu *m.*

gold-plated, *adj.* plaqué or.

goldsmith, *n.* orfèvre *m.*

gold standard, *n.* étalon or *m.*

golf, *n.* golf *m.*

gondola, *n.* gondole *f.*

gondolier, *n.* gondolier *m.*

gone, *adj.* disparu, parti.

gong, *n.* gong *m.*

gonorrhea, *n.* gonorrhée *f.*, blennorrhagie *f.*

good, 1. *adj.* bon *m.*, bonne *f.* **2.** *n.* bien *m.*; **(goods)** marchandises *f.pl.*

good-bye, *n. and interj.* adieu *m.*

Good Friday, *n.* Vendredi Saint *m.*

good-hearted, *adj.* qui a bon cœur, compatissant.

good-humored, *adj.* de bonne humeur, plein de bonhomie.

good-looking, *adj.* beau, joli.

good-natured, *adj.* au bon naturel, accommodant.

goodness, *n.* bonté *f.*

good will, *n.* bonne volonté *f.*

goody-goody, *n.* petit saint *m.*

goose, *n.* oie *f.*

gooseberry, *n.* groseille verte *f.*

gooseflesh, *n.* chair (*f.*) de poule.

gooseneck, *n.* col (*m.*) de cygne.

goose step, *n.* pas (*m.*) d'oie.

gore, 1. *n.* (dress) chanteau *m.*, soufflet *m.*; (blood) sang coagulé *m.* **2.** *vb.* corner.

gorge, *n.* gorge *f.*

gorgeous, *adj.* splendide.

gorilla, *n.* gorille *m.*

gory, *adj.* sanglant, ensanglanté.

gosh, *interj.* mince (alors).

gosling, *n.* oison *m.*

gospel, *n.* évangile *m.*

gossamer, *n.* filandre *f.*, gaze légère *f.*

gossip, 1. *n.* bavardage *m.* **2.** *vb.* bavarder.

Gothic, *adj.* gothique.

gouge, 1. *n.* gouge *f.* **2.** *vb.* gouger.

gourd, *n.* gourde *f.*, courge *f.*

gourmand, *n.* gourmand *m.*

gourmet, *n.* gourmet *m.*

govern, *vb.* gouverner.

governess, *n.* gouvernante *f.*

government, *n.* gouvernement *m.*

governmental, *adj.* gouvernemental.

governor, *n.* gouvernant *m.*

governorship, *n.* fonctions de gouverneur *f.pl.*, temps de gouvernement *m.*

gown, *n.* robe *f.*

grab, *vb.* saisir.

grace, *n.* grâce *f.*

graceful, *adj.* gracieux.

gracefully, *adv.* avec grâce.

graceless, *adj.* sans grâce, gauche.

gracious, *adj.* gracieux; (merciful) miséricordieux.

grackle, *n.* mainate *m.*

gradation, *n.* gradation *f.*

grade, 1. *n.* grade *m.;* (quality) qualité *f.* 2. *vb.* classer.

grade crossing, *n.* passage (*m.*) à niveau.

gradual, *adj.* graduel, progressif.

gradually, *adv.* graduellement.

graduate, *vb.* graduer; (school) obtenir son diplôme; prendre ses grades.

graduation, *n.* remise (*f.*) des diplômes.

graft, *n.* corruption *f.*

grail, *n.* graal *m.*

grain, *n.* grain *m.*

gram, *n.* gramme *m.*

grammar, *n.* grammaire *f.*

grammarian, *n.* grammairien *m.*

grammar school, *n.* école primaire *f.*

grammatical, *adj.* grammatical.

gramophone, *n.* phonographe.

granary, *n.* grenier *m.*

grand, *adj.* grandiose; (in titles) grand; (fine, *colloq.*) épatant.

grandchild, *n.* petit-fils *m.;* petite-fille *f.;* petits-enfants *m.pl.*

granddaughter, *n.* petite-fille *f.*

grandee, *n.* grand *m.*

grandeur, *n.* grandeur *f.*

grandfather, *n.* grand-père *m.*

grandiloquent, *adj.* grandiloquent.

grandiose, *adj.* grandiose.

grand jury, *n.* jury d'accusation *m.*

grandly, *adv.* grandement, magnifiquement.

grandmother, *n.* grand'mère *f.*

grand opera, *n.* grand opéra *m.*

grandson, *n.* petit-fils *m.*

grandstand, *n.* grande tribune *f.*

granger, *n.* régisseur *m.*

granite, *n.* granit *m.*

granny, *n.* bonne-maman *f.*

grant, 1. *n.* concession *f.;* (money) subvention *f.* 2. *vb.* accorder; (admit) admettre.

granular, *adj.* en grains, granulé.

granulate, *vb.* granuler, grener.

granulation, *n.* granulation *f.*

granule, *n.* granule *m.*

grape, *n.* raisin *m.*

grapefruit, *n.* pamplemousse *f.*

grapeshot, *n.* mitraille *f.*

grapevine, *n.* treille *f.*

graph, *n.* courbe *f.*

graphic, *adj.* graphique, pittoresque, explicite.

graphite, *n.* graphite *m.*

graphology, *n.* graphologie *f.*

grapple, 1. *n.* grappin *m.;* lutte *f.* 2. *vb.* accrocher; en venir aux prises.

grasp, 1. *n.* (hold) prise *f.* 2. *vb.* saisir.

grasping, *adj.* avide, cupide.

grass, *n.* herbe *f.*

grasshopper, *n.* sauterelle *f.*

grass-roots, *adj.* de la base, du people.

grassy, *adj.* herbeux, verdoyant.

grate, 1. *n.* grille *f.* 2. *vb.* (cheese, etc.) râper; (make noise) grincer.

grateful, *adj.* reconnaissant.

gratify, *vb.* contenter, satisfaire.

grating, 1. *n.* grille *f.* 2. *vb.* grinçant, discordant.

gratis, *adv.* gratis, gratuitement.

gratitude, *n.* gratitude *f.*

gratuitous, *adj.* gratuit.

gratuity, *n.* (tip) pourboire *m.*

grave, 1. *n.* tombe *f.* 2. *adj.* grave.

gravel, *n.* gravier *m.*

gravely, *adv.* gravement, sérieusement.

gravestone, *n.* pierre sépulcrale *f.,* tombe *f.*

graveyard, *n.* cimetière *m.*

gravitate, *vb.* graviter.

gravitation, *n.* gravitation *f.*

gravity, *n.* gravité *f.*

gravure, *n.* gravure *f.*

gravy, *n.* jus *m.*

gray, *adj.* gris.

grayish, *adj.* grisâtre.

gray matter, *n.* substance grise *f.,* cendrée *f.*

graze, *vb.* paître.

grazing, *n.* pâturage *m.*

grease, 1. *n.* graisse *f.* 2. *vb.* graisser.

great, *adj.* grand.

Great Dane, *n.* grand Danois *m.*

greatness, *n.* grandeur *f.*

Greece, *n.* Grèce *f.*

greediness, *n.* gourmandise *f.*

greedy, *adj.* gourmand.

Greek, 1. *n.* (person) Grec *m.,* Grecque *f.;* (language) grec *m.* 2. *adj.* grec *m.,* grecque *f.*

green, *adj.* vert.

greenery, *n.* verdure *f.*

greenhouse, *n.* serre *f.*

greet, *vb.* saluer.

greeting, *n.* salutation *f.;* (reception) accueil *m.*

gregarious, *adj.* grégaire.

grenade, *n.* grenade *f.*

grenadine, *n.* grenadine *f.*

greyhound, *n.* lévrier *m.*

grid, *n.* gril *m.*

griddle, *n.* gril *m.*

gridiron, *n.* gril *m.*

grief, *n.* chagrin *m.*

grievance, *n.* grief *m.*

grieve, *vb.* affliger, *tr.;* chagriner, *tr.*

grievous, *adj.* douloureux.

grill, 1. *n.* gril *m.* 2. *vb.* griller.

grillroom, *n.* grill-room *m.*

grim, *adj.* sinistre.

grimace, *n.* grimace *f.*

grime, *n.* saleté *f.,* noirceur *f.*

grimy, *adj.* sale, noirci, encrassé.

grin, *n.* large sourire *m.*

grind, *vb.* (crush) moudre; (sharpen) aiguiser.

grindstone, *n.* meule *f.*

gringo, *n.* Anglo-américain *m.*

grip, *n.* prise *f.*

gripe, *vb.* saisir, empoigner; grogner.

grisly, *adj.* hideux, horrible.

grist, *n.* blé à moudre *m.*, mouture *f.*

gristle, *n.* cartilage *m.*

grit, *n.* grès *m.*, sable *m.*; *(fig.)* cran *m.*, courage *m.*

grizzled, *adj.* grison, grisonnant.

groan, 1. *n.* gémissement *m.* 2. *vb.* gémir.

grocer, *n.* épicier *m.*

grocery, *n.* épicerie *f.*

grog, *n.* grog *m.*

groggy, *adj.* gris, titubant.

groin, *n.* aine *f.*

groom, 1.*n.* (horses) palefrenier *m.*; (bridegroom) nouveau marié *m.* 2. *vb.* (horses) panser.

groove, *n.* rainure *f.*

grope, *vb.* tâtonner.

grosgrain, *adj.* de grosgrain.

gross, *adj.* (bulky) gros *m.*, grosse *f.*; (coarse) grossier; *(comm.)* brut.

grossly, *adv.* grossièrement.

grossness, *n.* grossièreté *f.*, énormité *f.*

grotesque, *adj. and n.* grotesque *m.*

grotto, *n.* grotte *f.*

grouch, 1. *n.* maussaderie *f.*; grogneur *m.* 2. *vb.* grogner.

ground, *n.* (earth) terre *f.*; (territory) terrain *m.*; (reason) raison *f.*; (background) fond *m.*

ground hog, *n.* marmotte d'Amérique *f.*

groundless, *adj.* sans fondement.

ground swell, *n.* houle *f.*, lame de fond *f.*

groundwork, *n.* fondement *m.*, fond *m.*, base *f.*

group, 1. *n.* groupe *m.* 2. *vb.* grouper, *tr.*

groupie, *n.* groupie *f.*; membre *(m.)* d'un groupe de jeunes filles.

grouse, 1. *n.* tétras *m.* 2. *vb.* grogner.

grove, *n.* bocage *m.*, bosquet *m.*

grovel, *vb.* ramper, se vautrer.

grow, *vb.* croître; (persons) grandir; (become) devenir; (cultivate) cultiver.

growl, *vb.* grogner.

grown, *adj.* fait, grand.

grownup, *adj. and n.* grand *m.*, adulte *m.f.*

growth, *n.* croissance *f.*; (increase) accroissement *m.*

grub, 1. *n.* larve *f.*, ver blanc *m.*; (slang) nourriture *f.* 2. *vb.* défricher, fouiller.

grubby, *adj.* véreux, *(fig.)* sale.

grudge, *n.* rancune *f.*

gruel, *n.* gruau *m.*

gruesome, *adj.* lugubre, terrifiant.

gruff, *adj.* bourru.

grumble, *vb.* grommeler.

grumpy, *adj.* bourru, morose.

grunt, 1. *n.* grognement *m.* 2. *vb.* grogner.

guarantee, 1. *n.* garantie *f.* 2. *vb.* garantir.

guarantor, *n.* garant *m.*

guaranty, *n.* garantie *f.*

guard, 1. *n.* garde *f.* 2. *vb.* garder.

guarded, *adj.* prudent, circonspect, réservé.

guardhouse, *n.* corps de garde *m.*, poste *m.*

guardian, *n.* gardien *m.*; (law) tuteur *m.*

guardianship, *n.* tutelle *f.*

guardsman, *n.* garde *m.*

guava, *n.* goyave *f.*

gubernatorial, *adj.* du gouverneur, du gouvernement.

guerrilla, *n.* guérilla *f.*

guess, 1. *n.* conjecture *f.* 2. *vb.* deviner.

guesswork, *n.* conjecture *f.*

guest, *n.* invité *m.*

guffaw, 1. *n.* gros rire *m.* 2. *vb.* s'esclaffer.

guidance, *n.* direction *f.*

guide, 1. *n.* guide *m.* 2. *vb.* guider.

guidebook, *n.* guide *m.*

guided missile, *n.* missile *(m.)* téléguidé.

guidepost, *n.* poteau indicateur *m.*

guild, *n.* corporation *f.*, corps de métier *m.*

guile, *n.* astuce *f.*, artifice *m.*

guillotine, *n.* guillotine *f.*

guilt, *n.* culpabilité *f.*

guiltily, *adv.* criminellement.

guiltless, *adj.* innocent.

guilty, *adj.* coupable.

guimpe, *n.* guimpe *f.*

guinea fowl, *n.* pintade *f.*

guinea pig, *n.* cobaye *m.*

guise, *n.* guise *f.*, façon *f.*

guitar, *n.* guitare *f.*

gulch, *n.* ravin *m.*

gulf, *n.* (geog.) golfe *m.*; *(fig.)* gouffre *m.*

gull, *n.* mouette *f.*

gullet, *n.* gosier *m.*

gullible, *adj.* crédule, facile à duper.

gully, *n.* ravin *m.*

gulp, 1. *n.* goulée *f.*, gorgée *f.*, trait *m.* 2. *vb.* avaler, gober.

gum, *n.* gomme *f.*; (teeth) gencive *f.*

gumbo, *n.* gombo *m.*

gummy, *adj.* gommeux.

gumption, *n.* initiative *f.*, audace *f.*

gun, *n.* (cannon) canon *m.*; (rifle) fusil *m.*

gunboat, *n.* canonnière *f.*

gunman, *n.* partisan armé *m.*, voleur armé *m.*, bandit *m.*

gunner, *n.* artilleur *m.*

gunpowder, *n.* poudre *(f.)* à canon.

gunshot, *n.* portée *(f.)* de fusil.

gunwale, *n.* plat-bord *m.*

gurgle, *vb.* faire glouglou, gargouiller.

guru, *n.* gourou *m.*

gush, 1. *n.* jaillissement *m.* 2. *vb.* jaillir.

gusher, *n.* source jaillissante *f.*, personne exubérante *f.*

gusset, *n.* gousset *m.*, soufflet *m.*

gust, *n.* (wind) rafale *f.*

gustatory, *adj.* gustatif.

gusto, *n.* goût *m.*, délectation *f.*, verve *f.*

gusty, *adv.* venteux, orageux.

gut, 1. *n.* boyau *m.*, intestin *m.* **2.** *vb.* éventrer, vider.

gutter, *n.* (roof) gouttière *f.*; (street) ruisseau *m.*

guttural, *adj.* guttural.

guy, 1. *n.* type *m.*, individu *m.* **2.** *vb.* se moquer de.

guzzle, *vb.* ingurgiter, boire avidement.

gym, *n.* gymnase *m.*

gymnasium, *n.* gymnase *m.*

gymnast, *n.* gymnaste *m.*

gymnastic, *adj.* gymnastique.

gymnastics, *n.* gymnastique *f.*

gynecology, *n.* gynécologie *f.*

gypsum, *n.* gypse *m.*

gypsy, *n.* gitan *m.*

gyrate, *vb.* tournoyer.

gyroscope, *n.* gyroscope *m.*

H

habeas corpus *n.* habeas corpus *m.*

haberdasher, *n.* chemisier *m.*, mercier *m.*

haberdashery, *n.* chemiserie *f.*, mercerie *f.*

habiliment, *n.* habillement *m.*, apprêt *m.*

habit, *n.* habitude *f.*

habitable, *adj.* habitable.

habitat, *n.* habitat *m.*

habitation, *n.* habitation *f.*

habitual, *adj.* habituel.

habituate, *vb.* habituer, accoutumer.

habitué, *n.* habitué *m.*

hack, 1. *n.* (tool) pioche *f.*; (horse) cheval (*m.*) de louage; (vehicle) voiture (*f.*) de louage. **2.** *vb.* (h. up) hacher; (notch) entailler.

hackneyed, *adj.* banal, rebattu.

hacksaw, *n.* scie (*f.*) à métaux.

haddock, *n.* aigle fin *m.*

haft, *n.* manche *m.*, poignée *f.*

hag, *n.* vieille sorcière *f.*

haggard, *adj.* hagard.

haggle, *vb.* marchander.

hagridden, *adj.* tourmenté par le cauchemar.

Hague (The), *n.* La Haye *f.*

hail, 1. *n.* grêle *f.* **2.** *vb.* (weather) grêler; (salute) saluer; (come from) venir de. **3. interj.** salut.

Hail Mary, *n.* Ave Maria *m.*

hailstone, *n.* grêlon *m.*

hailstorm, *n.* tempête (*f.*) de grêle.

hair, *n.* cheveux *m.pl.*; (single, on head) cheveu *m.*; (on body, animals) poil *m.*

haircut, *n.* coupe (*f.*) de cheveux.

hairdo, *n.* coiffure *f.*

hairdresser, *n.* coiffeur *m.*

hairline, *n.* délié *m.*

hairpin, *n.* épingle (*f.*) à cheveux.

hair-raising, *adj.* horripilant, horrifique.

hair's-breadth, *n.* l'épaisseur d'un cheveu *f.*

hairspray, *n.* laque *f.*

hairy, *adj.* velu, poilu.

halcyon, 1. *n.* alcyon *m.* **2.** *adj.* calme.

hale, *adj.* sain.

half, 1. *n.* moitié *f.* **2.** *adj.* demi. **3.** *adv.* à moitié.

half-and-half, *n.* moitié de l'un, moitié de l'autre *f.*

halfback, *n.* demi-arrière *m.*

half-baked, *adj.* à moitié cuit, inexpérimenté, incomplet.

half-breed, *n.* métis *m.*

half brother, *n.* frère de père *m.*, frère de mère *m.*

half dollar, *n.* demi-dollar *m.*

half-hearted, *adj.* sans enthousiasme.

half-mast, *adv.* à mi-mât.

halfpenny, *n.* petit sou *m.*

halfway, *adv.* à mi-chemin.

half-wit, *n.* niais *m.*, sot *m.*

halibut, *n.* flétan *m.*

hall, *n.* (large room) salle *f.*; (entrance) vestibule *m.*

hallmark, *n.* contrôle *m.*

hallow, *vb.* sanctifier.

Halloween, *n.* la veille (*f.*) de la Toussaint.

hallucination, *n.* hallucination *f.*

hallway, *n.* corridor *m.*, vestibule *m.*

halo, *n.* auréole *f.*

halt, 1. *n.* halte *f.* **2.** *vb.* arrêter, *tr.*

halter, *n.* licou *m.*, longe *f.*, corde *f.*

halve, *vb.* diviser en deux, partager en deux.

halyard, *n.* drisse *f.*

ham, *n.* jambon *m.*

hamburger, *n.* hamburger *n.*

hamlet, *n.* hameau *m.*

hammer, 1. *n.* marteau *m.* **2.** *vb.* marteler.

hammock, *n.* hamac *m.*

hamper, 1. *n.* pannier *m.* **2.** *vb.* embarrasser, gêner.

hamstring, *vb.* couper le jarret à, couper les moyens à.

hand, *n.* main *f.*

handbag, *n.* sac (*m.*) à main.

handball, *n.* balle *f.*

handbook, *n.* manuel *m.*

handcuff, 1. *n.* menotte *f.* **2.** *vb.* mettre les menottes à.

handful, *n.* poignée *f.*

handicap, *n.* handicap *m.*, désavantage *m.*

handicraft, *n.* artisanat *m.*

handiwork, *n.* main-d'œuvre *f.*

handkerchief, *n.* mouchoir *m.*

handle, 1. *n.* manche *m.* **2.** *vb.* manier.

handlebar, *n.* guidon *m.*

handmade, *adj.* fait à la main, fabriqué à la main.

handmaid, *n.* servante *f.*

hand organ, *n.* orgue portatif *m.*, orgue de Barbarie *m.*

handout, *n.* aumône *f.*; compte rendu (*m.*) communiqué à la presse.

hand-pick, *vb.* trier à la main, éplucher à la main.

handsome, *adj.* beau *m.*, belle *f.*

hand-to-hand, *adj.* corps à corps.

handwriting, *n.* écriture *f.*

handy, *adj.* (person) adroit; (thing) commode; (at hand) sous la main.

handyman, *n.* homme (*m.*) à tout faire. bricoleur *m.*, factotum.

hang, *vb.* pendre.

hangar, *n.* hangar *m.*

hangdog, *adj.* avec une mine patibulaire, avec un air en dessous.

hanger-on, *n.* dépendant *m.*, parasite *m.*

hang glider, *n.* glisseur (*m.*) duquel l'usager pend.

hanging, 1. *n.* suspension *f.*, pendaison *f.* **2.** *adj.* suspendu, pendant.

hangman, *n.* bourreau *m.*

hangnail, *n.* envie *f.*

hangout, *n.* repaire *m.*, nid *m.*

hangover, *n.* gueule (*f.*) de bois.

hang-over, *n.* reste *m.*, reliquat *m.*

hangup, *n.* difficulté psychologique *f.*

hank, *n.* écheveau *m.*, torchette *f.*

hanker, *vb.* désirer vivement, convoiter.

haphazard, *adv.* au hasard.

happen, *vb.* (take place) arriver; (chance to be) se trouver.

happening, *n.* événement *m.*

happily, *adv.* heureusement.

happiness, *n.* bonheur *m.*

happy, *adj.* heureux.

happy-go-lucky, *adj.* sans souci, insouciant.

harakiri, *n.* hara-kiri *m.*

harangue, 1. *n.* harangue *f.* **2.** *vb.* haranguer.

harass, *vb.* harceler, tracasser.

harbinger, *n.* avant-coureur *m.*, précurseur *m.*

harbor, 1. *n.* (refuge) asile *m.*; (port) port *m.* **2.** *vb.* héberger.

hard, 1. *adj.* dur; (difficult) difficile. **2.** *adv.* fort.

hard-bitten, *adj.* tenace, dur à cuire.

hard-boiled, *adj.* dur, tenace, boucané.

hard coal, *n.* anthracite *m.*

hard disk, *n.* disque (*m.*) dur.

harden, *vb.* durcir.

hard-headed, *adj.* pratique, positif.

hard-hearted, *adj.* insensible, impitoyable, au cœur dur.

hardiness, *n.* robustesse *f.*, vigueur *f.*

hardly, *adv.* (in a hard manner) durement; (scarcely) à peine; (h. ever) presque jamais.

hardness, *n.* dureté *f.*; (difficulty) difficulté *f.*

hardship, *n.* privation *f.*

hardtack, *n.* galette *f.*, biscuit de mer *m.*

hardware, *n.* quincaillerie *f.*, matériel *m.*

hardwood, *n.* bois dur *m.*

hardy, *adj.* robuste.

hare, *n.* lièvre *m.*

harebrained, *adj.* écervelé, étourdi.

harelip, *n.* bec-de-lièvre *m.*

harem, *n.* harem *m.*

hark, 1. *vb.* prêter l'oreille à. **2.** *interj.* écoutez!

Harlequin, *n.* Arlequin *m.*

harlot, *n.* prostituée *f.*, fille de joie *f.*

harm, 1. *n.* mal *m.* **2.** *vb.* nuire à.

harmful, *adj.* nuisible.

harmless, *adj.* inoffensif.

harmonic, *adj.* harmonique.

harmonica, *n.* harmonica *m.*

harmonious, *adj.* harmonieux.

harmonize, *vb.* harmoniser.

harmony, *n.* harmonie *f.*

harness, 1. *n.* harnais *m.* **2.** *vb.* harnacher.

harp, *n.* harpe *f.*

harpoon, 1. *n.* harpon *m.* **2.** *vb.* harponner.

harpsichord, *n.* clavecin *m.*

harridan, *n.* vieille sorcière *f.*, vieille mégère *f.*

harrowing, *adj.* déchirant.

harry, *vb.* harceler.

harsh, *adj.* rude.

harshness, *n.* rudesse *f.*

harvest, 1. *n.* moisson *f.* **2.** *vb.* moissoner.

hash, 1. *n.* hachis *m.*, émincé *m.* **2.** *vb.* hacher (de la viande).

hashish, *n.* hachisch *m.*

hasn't, *vb.* n'a pas.

hassle, 1. *vb.* harceler. **2.** *n.* harcèlement *m.*

hassock, *n.* agenouilloir *m.*

haste, *n.* hâte *f.*

hasten, *vb.* hâter, *tr.*

hastily, *adv.* à la hâte.

hasty, *adj.* précipité.

hat, *n.* chapeau *m.*

hatch, *vb.* (hen) couver; (egg) éclore.

hatchback, *adj.* (auto) avec hayon arrière.

hatchery, *n.* établissement (*m.*) de pisciculture.

hatchet, *n.* hachette *f.*

hate, *vb.* haïr.

hateful, *adj.* odieux.

hatred, *n.* haine *f.*

haughtiness, *n.* arrogance *f.*, hauteur *f.*

haughty, *adj.* hautain.

haul, *vb.* traîner.

haunch, *n.* hanche *f.*, cuissot *m.*

haunt, *vb.* hanter.

have, *vb.* avoir; (h. to, necessity) devoir.

haven, *n.* havre *m.*; (refuge) asile *m.*

haven't, *vb.* n'ont pas.

havoc, *n.* ravage *m.*

hawk, 1. *n.* faucon *m.* **2.** *vb.* colporter.

hawker, *n.* colporteur *m.*, marchand ambulant *m.*

hawser, *n.* haussière *f.*, amarre *f.*

hawthorn, *n.* aubépine *f.*

hay, *n.* foin *m.*

hay fever, *n.* fièvre (*f.*) des foins.

hayfield, *n.* champs (*m.*) de foin.

hayloft, *n.* fenil *m.*, grenier *m.*

haystack, *n.* meule (*f.*) de foin.

hazard, 1. *n.* hasard *m.* **2.** *vb.* hasarder, risquer.

hazardous, *adj.* hasardeux.

haze, *n.* brume (*f.*) légère.

hazel, *n.* noisetier *m.*; couleur de noisette *f.*

hazy, *adj.* brumeux, nébuleux.

he, *pron.* il; (alone, stressed, with another subject) lui.

head, *n.* tête *f.*

headache, *n.* mal (*m.*) de tête.

headband, *n.* bandeau *m.*

headfirst, *adv.* la tête la première.

headgear, *n.* garniture (*f.*) de tête, coiffure *f.*

head-hunting, *n.* chasse (*f.*) aux têtes.

heading, *n.* rubrique *f.*

headlight, *n.* phare *m.*, projecteur *m.*

headline, *n.* titre *m.*

headlong, *adv.* la tête la première.

headman, *n.* chef *m.*

headmaster, *n.* directeur *m.*

head-on, *adj. and adv.* de front.

headquarters, *n.* (*mil.*) quartier (*m.*) général; (*comm.*) bureau (*m.*) principal.

headstone, *n.* pierre angulaire *f.*

headstrong, *adj.* volontaire, têtu, entêté.

headwaters, *n.* cours supérieur (d'une rivière) *m.*, eau d'amont *f.*

headway, *n.* progrès *m.*

headwork, *n.* travail de tête *m.*, travail intellectuel *m.*

heady, *adj.* impétueux, capiteux.

heal, *vb.* guérir.

health, *n.* santé *f.*

health foods, *n.* aliments (*m.pl.*) diététiques.

healthful, *adj.* salubre.

healthy, *adj.* sain.

heap, 1. *n.* tas *m.* **2.** *vb.* entasser.

hear, *vb.* entendre.

hearing, *n.* audition *f.*; ouïe *f.*

hearsay, *n.* ouï-dire *m.*

hearse, *n.* catafalque *m.*, corbillard *m.*

heart, *n.* cœur *m.*

heartache, *n.* chagrin *m.*

heart attack, *n.* crise (*f.*) cardiaque.

heartbreak, *n.* déchirement de cœur *m.*

heartbroken, *adj.* avec le cœur brisé, navré.

heartburn, *n.* brûlures (*f.pl.*) d'estomac. aigreur *f.*

heartfelt, *adj.* sincère, qui va au cœur.

hearth, *n.* foyer *m.*, âtre *m.*

heartless, *adj.* sans cœur, insensible, sans pitié.

heart-rending, *adj.* à fendre le cœur, navrant, déchirant.

heartsick, *adj.* écœuré.

heart-stricken, *adj.* frappé au cœur, navré.

heart-to-heart, *adj.* à cœur ouvert, intime.

hearty, *adj.* cordial.

heat, 1. *n.* chaleur *f.* **2.** *vb.* chauffer.

heated, *adj.* chaud, chauffé, animé.

heath, *n.* bruyère *f.*, lande *f.*

heathen, *adj. and n.* païen *m.*, païenne *f.*

heather, *n.* bruyère *f.*, brande *f.*

heatstroke, *n.* coup (*m.*) de chaleur.

heat wave, *n.* vague (*f.*) de chaleur, canicule *f.*

heave, *vb.* (lift) lever; (utter) pousser; (rise) se soulever, *intr.*

heaven, *n.* ciel *m.*, *pl.* cieux.

heavenly, *adj.* céleste.

heavy, *adj.* lourd.

heavyweight, *n.* poids lourd *m.*

Hebrew, 1. *n.* (language) hébreu *m.* **2.** *adj.* hébreu.

Hebrides, *n.* les Hébrides *f.pl.*

heckle, *vb.* poser des questions embarrassantes.

hectare, *n.* hectare *m.*

hectic, *adj.* (restless) agité.

hectograph, 1. *n.* hectographe *m.*, autocopiste *m.* **2.** *vb.* hectographier, autocopier.

hedge, *n.* haie *f.*

hedgehog, *n.* hérisson *m.*

hedgehop, *vb.* voler à ras de terre.

hedgerow, *n.* bordure de haies *f.*

hedonism, *n.* hédonisme *m.*

heed, 1. *n.* attention *f.* **2.** *vb.* faire attention à.

heedless, *adj.* étourdi, imprudent, insouciant.

heel, *n.* talon *m.*

hefty, *adj.* fort, solide, costaud.

hegemony, *n.* hégémonie *f.*

heifer, *n.* génisse *f.*

height, *n.* hauteur *f.*

heighten, *vb.* rehausser, augmenter.

heinous, *adj.* odieux, atroce, abominable.

heir, *n.* héritier *m.*

heir apparent, *n.* héritier présomptif *m.*

heirloom, *n.* meuble *m.* (or bijou *m.*) de famille.

heir presumptive, *n.* héritier présomptif *m.*

helicopter, *n.* hélicoptère *m.*

heliocentric, *adj.* héliocentrique.

heliograph, *n.* héliographe *m.*

heliotrope, *n.* héliotrope *m.*

heliport, *n.* héliport *m.*

helium, *n.* hélium *m.*

hell, *n.* enfer *m.*

Hellenism, *n.* hellénisme *m.*

hellish, *adj.* infernal, diabolique.

hello, *interj.* (telephone) allô.

helm, *n.* barre (*f.*) du gouvernail.

helmet, *n.* casque *m.*

helmsman, *n.* homme de barre *m.*, timonier *m.*

help, 1. *n.* aide *f.* **2.** *vb.* aider; (at table) servir. **3.** *interj.* au secours!

helper, *n.* aide *m.f.*

helpful, *adj.* (person) servi-able; (thing) utile.

helpfulness, *n.* serviabilité *f.,* utilité *f.*

helping, 1. *n.* portion *f.* **2.** *adj.* secourable.

helpless, *adj.* (forlorn) délaissé; (powerless) im-puissant.

helter-skelter, *adv.* pêle-mêle, en désordre.

hem, 1. *n.* ourlet *m.* **2.** *vb.* ourler.

hematite, *n.* hématite *f.*

hemisphere, *n.* hémisphère *m.*

hemlock, *n.* ciguë *f.*

hemoglobin, *n.* hémoglo-bine *f.*

hemophilia, *n.* hémophilie *f.*

hemorrhage, *n.* hémorragie *f.*

hemorrhoid, *n.* hémorroïde *f.*

hemp, *n.* chanvre *m.*

hemstitch, 1. *n.* ourlet *m.* **2.** *vb.* ourler.

hen, *n.* poule *f.*

hence, *adv.* (time, place) d'ici; (therefore) de là.

henceforth, *adv.* désormais.

henchman, *n.* homme de confiance *m.,* acolyte *m.,* satellite *m.*

henequen, *n.* henequen *m.*

henna, 1. *n.* henné *m.* **2.** *vb.* teindre au henné.

henpeck, *vb.* mener par le bout du nez.

hepatic, *adj.* hépatique.

hepatica, *n.* hépatique *f.*

hepatitis, *n.* hépatite *f.*

her, 1. *adj.* son *m.,* sa *f.,* ses *pl.* **2.** *pron.* (direct) la; (indirect) lui; (alone, stressed, with prep.) elle.

herald, *n.* héraut *m.*

heraldic, *adj.* héraldique.

heraldry, *n.* l'héraldique *f.*

herb, *n.* herbe *f.*

herbaceous, *adj.* herbacé.

herbarium, *n.* herbier *m.*

herculean, *adj.* herculéen.

herd, *n.* troupeau *m.*

here, *adv.* ici; (**h. is**) voici.

hereabout, *adv.* par ici, près d'ici.

hereafter, *adv.* dorénavant.

hereby, *adv.* par ceci, par ce moyen, par là.

hereditary, *adj.* héréditaire.

heredity, *n.* hérédité *f.*

herein, *adv.* ici; (**h. en-closed**) ci-enclus.

heresy, *n.* hérésie *f.*

heretic, *n.* hérétique *m.f.*

heretical, *adj.* hérétique.

hereto, *adv.* ci-joint.

heretofore, *adv.* jusqu'ici.

herewith, *adv.* avec ceci, ci-joint.

heritage, *n.* héritage *m.,* patrimoine *m.*

hermetic, *adj.* hermétique.

hermit, *n.* ermite *m.*

hermitage, *n.* ermitage *m.*

hernia, *n.* hernie *f.*

hero, *n.* héros *m.*

heroic, *adj.* héroïque.

heroically, *adv.* héroïque-ment.

heroin, *n.* héroïne *f.*

heroine, *n.* héroïne *f.*

heroism, *n.* héroïsme *m.*

heron, *n.* héron *m.*

herpes, *n.* herpès *m.*

herring, *n.* hareng *m.*

herringbone, *n.* arête (*f.*) de hareng.

hers, *pron.* le sien *m.,* la si-enne *f.*

herself, *pron.* elle-même; (reflexive) se.

hertz, *n.* hertz *m.*

hesitancy, *n.* hésitation *f.,* incertitude *f.*

hesitant, *adj.* hésitant, irré-solu.

hesitate, *vb.* hésiter.

hesitation, *n.* hésitation *f.*

heterodox, *adj.* hétérodoxe.

heterodoxy, *n.* hétérodoxie *f.*

heterogeneous, *adj.* hétérogène.

heterosexual, *adj.* hétéro-sexuel.

hew, *vb.* couper, tailler.

hexagon, *n.* hexagone *m.*

heyday, *n.* apogée *m.,* beaux jours *m.pl.*

hi, *interj.* salut!

hiatus, *n.* lacune *f.*

hibernate, *vb.* hiberner, hiverner.

hibernation, *n.* hibernation *f.*

hibiscus, *n.* hibiscus *m.*

hiccup, 1. *n.* hoquet *m.* **2.** *vb.* hoqueter.

hickory, *n.* noyer (blanc) d'Amérique *m.*

hide, 1. *vb.* cacher, *tr.* **2.** *n.* peau *f.*

hideous, *adj.* hideux.

hide-out, *n.* cachette *f.,* lieu (*m.*) de retraite.

hierarchical, *adj.* hiérar-chique.

hierarchy, *n.* hiérarchie *f.*

hieroglyphic, *adj.* hiéro-glyphique.

hi-fi, 1. *n.* hi-fi *f.* **2.** *adj.* hi-fi.

high, *adj.* haut.

highbrow, *n.* intellectuel *m.*

high fidelity, *n.* haute fidél-ité *f.*

high-handed, *adj.* arbi-traire, tyrannique.

high-hat, *vb.* traiter de haut en bas.

highland, *n.* haute terre *f.*

highlight, 1. *n.* clou *m.* **2.** *vb.* mettre en relief.

highly, *adv.* extrêmement.

high-minded, *adj.* à l'esprit élevé, généreux.

Highness, *n.* (title) Altesse *f.*

high school, *n.* lycée *m.*

high seas, *n.* haute mer *f.*

high-strung, *adj.* nerveux, impressionable.

high-tech, *n. and adj.* de pointe.

high tide, *n.* marée haute *f.*

highway, *n.* grande route *f.*

hijack, *vb.* détourner.

hijacker, *n.* pirate de l'air *m.*

hike, *n.* excursion (*f.*) à pied.

hilarious, *adj.* hilare.

hilariousness, *n.* hilarité *f.*

hilarity, *n.* hilarité *f.*

hill, *n.* colline *f.*

hilt, *n.* poignée *f.,* garde *f.*

him, *pron.* (direct) le; (indi-rect) lui; (alone, stressed, with prep.) lui.

himself, *pron.* lui-même; (reflexive) se.

hinder, *vb.* (impede) gêner; (prevent) empêcher.

hindmost, *adj.* dernier.

hindquarter, *n.* arrière-main *m.,* arrière-train *m.*

hindrance, *n.* empêchement *m.*, obstacle *m.*, entrave *f.*

hindsight, *n.* (with h.) avec du recul.

Hindu, 1. *n.* Hindou *m.* 2. *adj.* hindou.

hinge, *n.* gond *m.*

hint, 1. *n.* allusion *f.* 2. *vb.* insinuer.

hinterland, *n.* hinterland *m.*, arrière-pays *m.*

hip, *n.* hanche *f.*

hippie, *n.* hippie *m.f.*

hippodrome, *n.* hippodrome *m.*

hippopotamus, *n.* hippopotame *m.*

hire, *vb.* louer; (servant) engager.

hireling, *n.* mercenaire *m.*, stipendié *m.*

hirsute, *adj.* hirsute, velu.

his, 1. *adj.* son *m.*, sa *f.*, ses *pl.* 2. *pron.* le sien *m.*, la sienne *f.*

Hispanic, *adj.* hispanique.

hiss, *vb.* siffler.

historian, *n.* historien *m.*

historic, *adj.* historique.

historical, *adj.* historique.

history, *n.* histoire *f.*

histrionic, *adj.* histrionique, théâtral.

histrionics, *n.* parade d'émotions *f.*, démonstration peu sincère *f.*

hit, 1. *n.* coup *m.*; (success) succès *m.* 2. *vb.* frapper.

hitch, 1. *n.* (obstacle) anicroche *f.* 2. *vb.* (fasten) accrocher, *tr.*

hitchhike, *vb.* faire de l'auto-stop.

hither, 1. *adv.* ici. 2. *adj.* le plus rapproché.

hitherto, *adj.* jusqu'ici.

hive, *n.* ruche *f.*

hives, *n.* éruption *f.*, varicelle pustuleuse *f.*, urticaire *f.*

hoard, 1. *n.* amas *m.* 2. *vb.* amasser; (money) thésauriser.

hoarse, *adj.* enroué.

hoax, *n.* mystification *f.*

hobble, *vb.* boitiller, clopiner, entraver.

hobby, *n.* marotte *f.*

hobbyhorse, *n.* dada *m.*, cheval de bois *m.*

hobgoblin, *n.* lutin *m.*, esprit follet *m.*

hobnail, 1. *n.* caboche *f.*, clou (*n.*) à ferrer. 2. *vb.* ferrer.

hobnob, *vb.* boire avec, fréquenter.

hobo, *n.* vagabond *m.*, clochard *m.*, ouvrier ambulant *m.*

hock, 1. *n.* jarret *m.* 2. *vb.* mettre au clou.

hockey, *n.* hockey *m.*

hocuspocus, *n.* passe-passe *m.*

hod, *n.* auge *f.*

hodgepodge, *n.* mélange confus *m.*

hoe, 1. *n.* houe *f.* 2. *vb.* houer.

hog, *n.* porc *m.*

hogshead, *n.* tonneau *m.*, barrique *f.*

hog-tie, *vb.* lier les quatre pattes.

hoist, 1. *n.* treuil *m.*, grue *f.* 2. *vb.* hisser.

hold, 1. *n.* prise *f.*; (ship) cale *f.* 2. *vb.* tenir; (contain) contenir; (h. back) retenir; (h. up) arrêter, détenir, entraver.

holdup, *n.* arrêt *m.*, suspension *f.*; coup (*m.*) à main armée.

hole, *n.* trou *m.*

holiday, *n.* jour (*m.*) de fête; fête *f.*; (h.s) vacances *f.pl.*

holiness, *n.* sainteté *f.*

holistic, *adj.* holistique.

Holland, *n.* les Pays-Bas *m.pl.*, Hollande *f.*

hollow, *adj. and n.* creux *m.*

holly, *n.* houx *m.*

hollyhock, *n.* passe-rose *f.*, rose-trémière *f.*

holocaust, *n.* holocauste *m.*

hologram, *n.* hologramme *m.*

holography, *n.* holographie *f.*

holster, *n.* étui *m.*

holy, *adj.* saint.

Holy See, *n.* Saint-Siège *m.*

Holy Spirit, *n.* Saint-Esprit *m.*

Holy Week, *n.* semaine sainte *f.*

homage, *n.* hommage *m.*

home, *n.* maison *f.*; (hearth) foyer (*m.*) domestique; (at h.) à la maison, chez soi.

homeland, *n.* patrie *f.*

homeless, 1. *adj.* sans asile, sans abri. 2. *n.* sans abri *m.*

homelike, *adj.* qui ressemble au foyer domestique.

homely, *adj.* laid.

homemade, *adj.* fait à la maison.

home rule, *n.* autonomie *f.*

homesick, *adj.* (be h.) avoir le mal du pays.

homespun, *adj.* (étoffe) de fabrication domestique, fait à la maison, simple.

homestead, *n.* ferme *f.*, bien de famille *m.*

homeward, *adj.* de retour.

homework, *n.* travail fait à la maison *m.*, devoirs *m.pl.*

homicide, *n.* homicide *m.*

homily, *n.* homélie *f.*

homing pigeon, *n.* pigeon messager *m.*

hominy, *n.* bouillie (*f.*) de farine de maïs, semoule (*f.*) de maïs.

homogeneous, *adj.* homogène.

homonym, *n.* homonyme *m.*

homosexual, *n. and adj.* homosexuel *m.*, homosexuelle *f.*

Honduras, *n.* Honduras *m.*

hone, *vb.* aiguiser, affiler.

honest, *adj.* honnête.

honestly, *adv.* honnêtement, de bonne foi.

honesty, *n.* honnêteté *f.*

honey, *n.* miel *m.*

honeybee, *n.* abeille domestique *f.*

honeycomb, 1. *n.* rayon de miel *m.* 2. *vb.* cribler, affouiller.

honeydew melon, *n.* melon *m.*

honeymoon, *n.* lune (*f.*) de miel.

honeysuckle, *n.* chèvrefeuille *m.*

honor, 1. *n.* honneur *m.* **2.** *vb.* honorer.

honorable, *adj.* honorable.

honorary, *adj.* honoraire.

hood, *n.* capuchon *m.*; (vehicle) capote *f.*

hoodlum, *n.* voyou *m.*

hoodwink, *vb.* tromper, bander les yeux à.

hoof, *n.* sabot *m.*

hook, 1. *n.* croc *m.*; (fishing) hameçon *m.* **2.** *vb.* accrocher.

hooked, *adj.* crochu, recourbé; **(be h. on)** (drugs) se droguer à; (hobbies, etc.) être fana de.

hooked rug, *n.* tapis *(m.)* à points noués simples.

hooker, *n.* (colloquial) prostituée *f.*

hookworm, *n.* ankylostome *m.*

hoop, *n.* cercle *m.*

hoop skirt, *n.* jupe *(f.)* à paniers, vertugadin *m.*

hoot, 1. *n.* ululation *f.*, hululement *m.*, huée *f.* **2.** *vb.* hululer, huer.

hop, 1. *n.* (plant) houblon *m.* **2.** *vb.* sautiller.

hope, 1. *n.* espérance *f.*, espoir *m.* **2.** *vb.* espérer.

hopeful, *adj.* plein d'espoir.

hopeless, *adj.* désespéré.

hopelessness, *n.* désespoir *m.*, état désespéré *m.*

hopscotch, *n.* marelle *f.*

horde, *n.* horde *f.*

horizon, *n.* horizon *m.*

horizontal, *adj.* horizontal.

hormone, *n.* hormone *f.*

horn, *n.* corne *f.*; (music) cor *m.*; (auto) klaxon *m.*

hornet, *n.* frelon *m.*, guêpe-frelon *f.*

horny, *adj.* corné, calleux.

horoscope, *n.* horoscope *m.*

horrendous, *adj.* horrible, horripilant.

horrible, *adj.* horrible.

horrid, *adj.* affreux.

horrify, *vb.* horrifier.

horror, *n.* horreur *f.*

horror film, *n.* film *(m.)* d'horreur.

horse, *n.* cheval *m.*

horseback, *n.* **(on h.)** à cheval.

horsefly, *n.* taon *m.*

horsehair, *n.* crin *m.*

horseman, *n.* cavalier *m.*

horsemanship, *n.* équitation *f.*, manège *m.*

horseplay, *n.* jeu *(m.)* de mains, badinerie grossière *f.*

horsepower, *n.* puissance *(f.)* en chevaux.

horse-racing, *n.* courses *(f.pl.)* de chevaux.

horseradish, *n.* raifort *m.*

horseshoe, *n.* fer à cheval *m.*

horsewhip, 1. *n.* cravache *f.* **2.** *vb.* cravacher, sangler.

hortatory, *adj.* exhortatif.

horticulture, *n.* horticulture *f.*

hose, *n.* (pipe) tuyau *m.*; (stockings) bas *m.pl.*

hosiery, *n.* bonneterie *f.*

hospice, *n.* hospice *m.*

hospitable, *adj.* hospitalier.

hospital, *n.* hôpital *m.*

hospitality, *n.* hospitalité *f.*

hospitalization, *n.* hospitalisation *f.*

hospitalize, *vb.* hospitaliser.

host, *n.* hôte *m.*; (show) animateur *m.*; (religion) hostie *f.*

hostage, *n.* otage *m.*

hostel, *n.* hôtellerie *f.*, auberge *f.*

hostelry, *n.* hôtellerie *f.*, auberge *f.*

hostess, *n.* hôtesse *f.*

hostile, *adj.* hostile, agressif, contre.

hostility, *n.* hostilité *f.*

hot, *adj.* chaud.

hotbed, *n.* couche *f.*, foyer ardent *m.*

hot dog, *n.* saucisse chaude *f.*

hotel, *n.* hôtel *m.*

hot-headed, *adj.* impétueux, exalté, emporté.

hothouse, *n.* serre *f.*

hound, 1. *n.* chien *(m.)* de chasse. **2.** *vb.* poursuivre, pourchasser.

hour, *n.* heure *f.*

hourglass, *n.* sablier *m.*

hourly, *adv.* à chaque heure, à l'heure.

house, 1. *n.* maison *f.*; (legislature) chambre *f.* **2.** *vb.* loger; abriter.

housecoat, *n.* peignoir *m.*

housefly, *n.* mouche domestique *f.*

household, *n.* (house, family) ménage, *m.*, (family) famille *f.*; (servants) domestiques *m.pl.*

housekeeper, *n.* gouvernante *f.*

housekeeping, *n.* ménage *m.*, économie domestique *f.*

housemaid, *n.* fille *(f.)* de service, bonne *f.*, femme de chambre *f.*

housewarming (party), *n.* pendaison *(f.)* de la crémaillère.

housewife, *n.* ménagère *f.*, femme *(f.)* au foyer.

housework, *n.* ménage *m.*

housing, *n.* logement *m.*

hovel, *n.* taudis *m.*, bicoque *f.*

hover, *vb.* planer.

hovercraft, *n.* aéroglisseur *m.*

how, *adv.* comment; **(h. are you)** comment allez-vous?; **(h. much)** combien (de); (in exclamation) comme.

however, *adv.* (in whatever way) de quelque manière que; (with adj.) si . . . que; (nevertheless) cependant.

howitzer, *n.* obusier *m.*

howl, *vb.* hurler.

hub, *n.* moyeu *m.*, centre *m.*

hubbub, *n.* vacarme *m.*, tintamarre *m.*

huckleberry, *n.* airelle *f.*

huddle, 1. *n.* tas confus *m.*, fouillis *m.* **2.** *vb.* entasser.

hue, *n.* couleur *f.*

huff, 1. *n.* emportement *m.*, accès de colère *m.* **2.** *vb.* gonfler, enfler.

hug, 1. *n.* étreinte *f.* **2.** *vb.* serrer dans ses bras.

huge, *adj.* énorme.

hulk, *n.* carcasse *f.*, ponton *m.*

hull, *n.* coque *f.*, corps *m.*

hullabaloo, *n.* vacarme *m.*

hum, *vb.* (insect) bourdonner; (sing) fredonner.

human, humane, *adj.* humain.
human being, *n.* être *(m.)* humain.
humanism, *n.* humanisme *m.*
humanitarian, *adj.* humanitaire.
humanities, *n.* humanités *f.pl.*
humanity, *n.* humanité *f.*
humanly, *adv.* humainement.
humble, *adj.* humble.
humbug, *n.* blague *f.,* tromperie *f.,* fumisterie *f.*
humdrum, *adj.* monotone, assommant.
humid, *adj.* humide.
humidify, *vb.* humidifier.
humidor, *n.* boîte à cigares *f.*
humiliate, *adj.* humilier.
humiliation, *n.* humiliation *f.*
humility, *n.* humilité *f.*
humor, 1. *n.* (wit) humour *m.;* (medical, mood) humeur *f.* **2.** *vb.* se prêter aux caprices de.
humorous, *adj.* (witty) humoristique; (funny) drôle.
hump, *n.* bosse *f.*
humpback, *n.* bossu *m.*
humus, *n.* humus *m.,* terreau *m.*
hunch, 1. *n.* bosse *f.;* pressentiment *m.* **2.** *vb.* arrondir, voûter.
hunchback, *n.* bossu *m.*
hundred, *adj.* and *n.* cent *m.*
hundredth, *n.* and *adj.* centième *m.f.*
Hungarian, 1. *n.* (person) Hongrois *m.;* (language) hongrois *m.* **2.** *adj.* hongrois.
Hungary, *n.* Hongrie *f.*
hunger, *n.* faim *f.*
hunger strike, *n.* grève *(f.)* de la faim.
hungry, *adj.* affamé; (be h.) avoir faim.
hunk, *n.* gros morceau *m.*

hunt, *vb.* chasser.
hunter, *n.* chasseur *m.*
hunting, *n.* chasse *f.*
huntress, *n.* chasseuse *f.,* chasseresse *f.*
hurdle, *n.* claie *f.*
hurl, *vb.* lancer.
hurrah, hurray, *interj.* houra!
hurricane, *n.* ouragan *m.*
hurry, 1. *n.* hâte *f.;* (in a h.) à la hâte. **2.** *vb.* presser, *tr.;* se presser, *intr.*
hurt, *vb.* faire mal (à).
hurtful, *adj.* nuisible, pernicieux, préjudiciable.
hurtle, *vb.* se choquer, se heurter.
husband, *n.* mari *m.*
husbandry, *n.* agriculture *f.,* économie *f.*
hush, 1. *interj.* chut! paix! **2.** *vb.* taire, imposer silence à.
husk, 1. *n.* cosse *f.,* gousse *f.* **2.** *vb.* écosser, éplucher.
husky, 1. *adj.* (body) cossu; (voice) rauque, enroué. **2.** *n.* chien *(m.)* de traineau.
hustle, *vb.* bousculer, se presser.
hut, *n.* cabane *f.*
hutch, *n.* huche *f.,* clapier *m.*
hyacinth, *n.* jacinthe *f.*
hybrid, *adj.* hybride *m.*
hydrangea, *n.* hortensia *m.*
hydrant, *n.* prise d'eau *f.,* bouche d'incendie *f.*
hydraulic, *adj.* hydraulique.
hydrochloric acid, *n.* acide *(m.)* chlorhydrique.
hydroelectric, *adj.* hydroélectrique.
hydrofoil, *n.* hydroptère *m.*
hydrogen, *n.* hydrogène *m.*
hydrophobia, *n.* hydrophobie *f.*
hydroplane, *n.* hydroplane *m.*
hydrotherapy, *n.* hydrothérapie *f.*
hyena, *n.* hyène *f.*

hygiene, *n.* hygiène *f.*
hygienic, *adj.* hygiénique.
hymn, *n.* (song, anthem) hymne *m.;* (church) hymne *f.*
hymnal, *n.* hymnaire *m.,* recueil d'hymnes *m.*
hype, 1. *n.* tapage *(m.)* publicitaire. **2.** *vb.* faire du tapage autour de.
hyperacidity, *n.* hyperacidité *f.*
hyperbole, *n.* hyperbole *f.*
hypercritical, *adj.* hypercritique.
hypermarket, *n.* hypermarché *m.*
hypersensitive, *adj.* hypersensible.
hypertension, *n.* hypertension *f.*
hyphen, *n.* trait *(m.)* d'union.
hyphenate, *vb.* mettre un trait d'union à.
hypnosis, *n.* hypnose *f.*
hypnotic, *adj.* hypnotique.
hypnotism, *n.* hypnotisme *m.*
hypnotize, *vb.* hypnotiser.
hypochondria, *n.* hypocondrie *f.*
hypochondriac, *n.* and *adj.* hypocondriaque *m.*
hypocrisy, *n.* hypocrisie *f.*
hypocrite, *n.* hypocrite *m.f.*
hypocritical, *adj.* hypocrite.
hypodermic, *adj.* hypodermique.
hypotenuse, *n.* hypoténuse *f.*
hypothermia, *n.* hypothermie *f.*
hypothesis, *n.* hypothèse *f.*
hypothetical, *adj.* hypothétique.
hysterectomy, *n.* hystérectomie *f.*
hysteria, *n.* hystérie *f.*
hysterical, *adj.* hystérique.
hysterics, *n.pl.* crise *(f.)* de nerfs.

I

I *pron.* je; (alone, stressed, with another subject) moi.
iambic, *adj.* iambique.
Iberia, *n.* Ibérie *f.*
ice, *n.* glace *f.*
iceberg, *n.* iceberg *m.,* gros bloc de glace *m.*
ice-box, *n.* glacière *f.*

ice cream, *n.* glace *f.*
ice cube, *n.* glaçon *m.*
Iceland, *n.* Islande *f.*
ice skate, 1. *n.* patin à glace *m.* **2.** *vb.* patiner.
ichthyology, *n.* ichtyologie *f.*
icicle, *n.* glaçon *m.*
icing, *n.* glacé *m.*

icon, *n.* icône *f.*
icy, *adj.* glacial.
idea, *n.* idée *f.*
ideal, *adj.* and *n.* idéal *m.*
idealism, *n.* idéalisme *m.*
idealist, *n.* idéaliste *m.f.*
idealistic, *adj.* idéaliste.
idealize, *vb.* idéaliser.

ideally, *adv.* idéalement, en idée.

identical (with), *adj.* identique (à).

identifiable, *adj.* identifiable.

identification, *n.* identification *f.*

identify, *vb.* identifier.

identity, *n.* identité *f.*

ideology, *n.* idéologie *f.*

idiocy, *n.* idiotie *f.*, idiotisme *m.*

idiom, *n.* (language) idiome *m.*; (peculiar expression) idiotisme *m.*

idiot, *adj. and n.* idiot *m.*

idiotic, *adj.* idiot.

idle, *adj.* (unoccupied) désœuvré; (lazy) paresseux; (futile) vain.

idleness, *n.* oisiveté *f.*

idol, *n.* idole *f.*

idolatry, *n.* idolâtrie *f.*

idolize, *vb.* idolâtrer.

idyl, *n.* idylle *f.*

idyllic, *adj.* idyllique.

if, *conj.* si.

ignite, *vb.* allumer, mettre en feu.

ignition, *n.* ignition *f.*, allumage *m.*

ignoble, *adj.* ignoble; (low birth) plébéien.

ignominious, *adj.* ignominieux.

ignoramus, *n.* ignorant *m.*, ignare *m.*

ignorance, *n.* ignorance *f.*

ignorant, *adj.* ignorant; (be i. of) ignorer.

ignore, *vb.* feindre d'ignorer.

ill, 1. *n.* mal. 2. *adj.* (sick) malade; (bad) mauvais. 3. *adv.* mal.

illegal, *adj.* illégal.

illegible, *adj.* illisible.

illegibly, *adv.* illisiblement.

illegitimacy, *n.* illégitimité *f.*

illegitimate, *adj.* illégitime.

illicit, *adj.* illicite.

illiteracy, *n.* analphabétisme *m.*

illiterate, *adj.* illettré, analphabète.

illness, *n.* maladie *f.*

illogical, *adj.* illogique.

illuminate, *vb.* illuminer.

illumination, *n.* illumination *f.*, enluminure *f.*

illusion, *n.* illusion *f.*

illusive, *adj.* illusoire.

illustrate, *vb.* illustrer.

illustration, *n.* illustration *f.*; (example) exemple *m.*

illustrative, *adj.* explicatif, qui éclaircit.

illustrious, *adj.* illustre.

ill will, *adj.* mauvais vouloir *m.*, malveillance *f.*

image, *n.* image *f.*

imagery, *n.* images *f.pl.*, langage figuré *m.*

imaginable, *adj.* imaginable.

imaginary, *adj.* imaginaire.

imagination, *n.* imagination *f.*

imaginative, *adj.* imaginatif.

imagine, *vb.* imaginer, *tr.*

imam, *n.* imam *m.*

imbalance, *n.* déséquilibre *m.*

imbecile, *n.* imbécile *m.*

imbue, *vb.* imprégner.

imitate, *vb.* imiter.

imitation, *n.* imitation *f.*

imitative, *adj.* imitatif.

immaculate, *adj.* immaculé, sans tache.

immanent, *adj.* immanent.

immaterial, *adj.* immatériel, incorporel, sans conséquence.

immature, *adj.* pas mûr, prématuré.

immediate, *adj.* immédiat.

immediately, *adv.* immédiatement, tout de suite.

immense, *adj.* immense.

immerse, *vb.* immerger, plonger.

immigrant, *n.* immigrant *m.*, immigré *m.*

immigrate, *vb.* immigrer.

imminent, *adj.* imminent.

immobile, *adj.* fixe, immobile.

immobilize, *vb.* immobiliser.

immoderate, *adj.* immodéré, intempéré, outré.

immodest, *adj.* immodeste, impudique, présomptueux.

immoral, *adj.* immoral.

immorality, *n.* immoralité *f.*

immorally, *adv.* immoralement.

immortal, *adj. and n.* immortel *m.*

immortality, *n.* immortalité *f.*

immortalize, *vb.* immortaliser.

immovable, *adj.* fixe, immuable, inébranlable.

immune, *adj.* immunisé.

immunity, *n.* exemption *f.*, immunité *f.*

immunize, *vb.* immuniser.

immutable, *adj.* immuable, inaltérable.

impact, *n.* choc *m.*, impact *m.*

impair, *vb.* affaiblir, altérer, compromettre.

impale, *vb.* empaler.

impart, *vb.* donner, communiquer, transmettre.

impartial, *adj.* impartial.

impasse, *n.* impasse *f.*

impassioned, *adj.* passionné.

impassive, *adj.* impassible.

impatience, *n.* impatience *f.*

impatient, *adj.* impatient.

impeach, *vb.* attaquer, accuser, récuser.

impede, *vb.* entraver, empêcher.

impediment, *n.* entrave *f.*, obstacle *m.*, empêchement *m.*

impel, *vb.* pousser, forcer.

impending, *adj.* imminent.

impenetrable, *adj.* impénétrable.

impenitent, *adj.* impénitent.

imperative, 1. *n.* (gramm.) impératif *m.* 2. *adj.* (gramm.) impératif; urgent, impérieux.

imperceptible, *adj.* imperceptible.

imperfect, *adj. and n.* imparfait *m.*

imperfection, *n.* imperfection *f.*

imperial, *adj.* impérial.

imperialism, *n.* impérialisme *m.*

imperil, *vb.* mettre en péril, exposer au danger.

imperious, *adj.* impérieux, arrogant.

impersonal, *adj.* imperson-nel.

impersonate, *vb.* personni-fier, représenter.

impersonation, *n.* personni-fication *f.,* incarnation *f.*

impersonator, *n.* personni-ficateur *m.*

impertinence, *n.* imperti-nence *f.*

impervious, *adj.* impénétra-ble, imperméable.

impetuous, *adj.* impétueux.

impetus, *n.* élan *m.,* vitesse acquise *f.*

impinge, *vb.* se heurter à, empiéter sur.

implacable, *adj.* implacable.

implant, *vb.* inculquer, im-planter.

implement, *n.* outil *m.*

implicate, *vb.* impliquer, entremêler.

implication, *n.* implication *f.*

implicit, *adj.* implicite.

implied, *adj.* implicite, tacite.

implore, *vb.* implorer.

imply, *vb.* impliquer.

impolite, *adj.* impoli.

imponderable, *adj.* im-pondérable.

import, 1. *n.* article (*m.*) d'importation, importa-tion *f.* 2. *vb.* importer.

importance, *n.* importance *f.*

important, *adj.* important.

importation, *n.* importation *f.*

importune, *vb.* importuner.

impose (on), *vb.* imposer (à).

imposition, *n.* imposition *f.*

impossibility, *n.* impossibil-ité *f.*

impossible, *adj.* impossible.

impotence, *n.* impuissance *f.*

impotent, *adj.* impuissant.

impound, *vb.* confisquer.

impoverish, *vb.* appauvrir.

impractical, *adj.* pas pra-tique.

impregnable, *adj.* impren-able, inexpugnable.

impregnate, *vb.* imprégner, féconder.

impresario, *n.* imprésario *m.*

impress, *vb.* (imprint) im-primer; (affect) faire une impression à.

impression, *n.* impression *f.*

impressive, *adj.* impres-sionnant.

imprison, *vb.* emprisonner.

imprisonment, *n.* emprison-nement *m.*

improbable, *adj.* improba-ble.

impromptu, *adv., adj. and n.* impromptu *m.*

improper, *adj.* (inaccurate) impropre; (unbecoming) malséant.

improve, *vb.* améliorer, *tr.*

improvement, *n.* améliora-tion *f.*

improvise, *vb.* improviser.

impudent, *adj.* insolent, ef-fronté, impertinent.

impugn, *vb.* attaquer, con-tester, impugner.

impulse, *n.* impulsion *f.*

impulsion, *n.* impulsion *f.*

impulsive, *adj.* impulsif.

impunity, *n.* impunité *f.*

impure, *adj.* impur.

impurity, *n.* impureté *f.*

impute, *vb.* imputer.

in, *prep.* en; (with art. or adj.) dans; (town) à.

inability, *n.* incapacité *f.*

inaccurate, *adj.* inexact.

inadequate, *adj.* insuffisant.

inadvertent, *adj.* inattentif, négligent, involontaire.

inalienable, *adj.* inalién-able.

inane, *adj.* inepte, niais, bête.

inappropriate, *adj.* mal à propos.

inaugural, *adj.* inaugural.

inaugurate, *vb.* inaugurer.

inauguration, *n.* inaugura-tion *f.*

inborn, *adj.* inné.

inbred, *adj.* inné.

Inca, *n.* Inca *m.*

incandescence, *n.* incandes-cence *f.*

incandescent, *adj.* incan-descent.

incantation, *n.* incantation *f.,* conjuration *f.*

incapable, *adj.* incapable.

incapacitate, *vb.* rendre in-capable, priver de capac-ité légale.

incarcerate, *vb.* incarcérer, emprisonner.

incarnate, 1. *vb.* incarner. 2. *adj.* incarné, fait chair.

incarnation, *n.* incarnation *f.*

incendiary, 1. *n..* incendi-aire *m.* 2. *adj.* incendi-aire, séditieux.

incense, *n.* encens *m.*

incentive, *n.* stimulant *m.,* aiguillon *m.*

inception, *n.* commence-ment *m.,* début *m.*

incessant, *adj.* incessant, continuel.

incest, *n.* inceste *m.*

inch, *n.* pouce *m.*

incidence, *n.* incidence *f.*

incident, *n.* incident *m.*

incidental, *adj.* fortuit.

incidentally, *adv.* incidem-ment, en passant.

incinerator, *n.* incinérateur *m.*

incipient, *adj.* naissant, qui commence.

incision, *n.* incision *f.,* en-taille *f.*

incisive, *adj.* incisif, tran-chant.

incisor, *n.* incisive *f.*

incite, *vb.* inciter, instiguer.

inclination, *n.* inclinaison *f.,* penchant *m.*

incline, *vb.* incliner.

inclose, *see* enclose.

include, *vb.* comprendre.

inclusive, *adj.* inclusif.

incognito, *adj. and adv.* incognito.

income, *n.* revenu *m.*

incomparable, *adj.* incom-parable.

incompetent, *adj.* incompé-tent.

inconsiderate, *adj.* peu prévenant.

inconvenience, 1. *n.* incon-vénient *m.* 2. *vb.* incom-moder.

inconvenient, *adj.* incom-mode.

incorporate, *vb.* incorporer.

incorrigible, *adj.* incorrigi-ble.

increase, 1. *n.* augmentation *f.* 2. *vb.* augmenter.

incredible, *adj.* incroyable.

incredulity, *n.* incrédulité *f.*

incredulous, *adj.* incrédule.

increment, *n.* augmentation *f.,* accroissement *m.*

incriminate, *vb.* incriminer.

incrimination, *n.* incrimination *f.*

incrust, *vb.* incruster.

incubator, *n.* incubateur *m.*

inculcate, *vb.* inculquer.

incumbency, *n.* période *(f.)* d'exercice, charge *f.*

incumbent, 1. *n.* titulaire *m.,* bénéficiaire *m.* **2.** *adj.* couché, posé, appuyé.

incur, *vb.* encourir.

incurable, *adj.* incurable.

indebted, *adj.* endetté.

indecent, *adj.* indécent.

indecisive, *adj.* indécis.

indeed, *adv.* en effet.

indefatigable, *adj.* infatigable, inlassable.

indefinite, *adj.* indéfini.

indefinitely, *adv.* indéfiniment.

indelible, *adj.* indélébile, ineffaçable.

indemnify, *vb.* garantir, indemniser, dédommager.

indemnity, *n.* garantie *f.,* indemnité *f.,* dédommagement *m.*

indent, *vb.* denteler, découper, entailler.

indentation, *n.* découpage *m.,* renfoncement *m.,* endentement *m.*

independence, *n.* indépendance *f.*

independent, *adj.* indépendant.

in-depth, *adj.* profond.

index, *n.* index *m.*

India, *n.* Inde *f.*

Indian, 1. *n.* Indien *m.* **2.** *adj.* indien.

indicate, *vb.* indiquer.

indication, *n.* indication *f.*

indicative, *adj. and n.* indicatif *m.*

indicator, *n.* indicateur *m.*

indict, *vb.* accuser, inculper.

indictment, *n.* accusation *f.,* inculpation *f.,* réquisitoire *m.*

indifference, *n.* indifférence *f.*

indifferent, *adj.* indifférent.

indigenous, *adj.* indigène.

indigent, *adj.* indigent, pauvre.

indigestion, *n.* dyspepsie *f.,* indigestion *f.*

indignant, *adj.* indigné.

indignation, *n.* indignation *f.*

indignity, *n.* indignité *f.,* affront *m.*

indirect, *adj.* indirect.

indiscreet, *adj.* indiscret.

indiscretion, *n.* imprudence *f.*

indiscriminate, *adj.* aveugle, qui ne fait pas de distinction.

indispensable, *adj.* indispensable.

indisposed, *adj.* (unwilling) peu enclin, peu disposé; (ill) indisposé, souffrant.

individual, 1. *n.* individu *m.* **2.** *adj.* individuel.

individuality, *n.* individualité *f.*

individually, *adv.* individuellement.

indivisible, *adj.* indivisible.

indoctrinate, *vb.* endoctriner, instruire.

indolent, *adj.* indolent, paresseux.

Indonesia, *n.* Indonésie *f.*

indoor, *adj.* d'intérieur.

indoors, *adv.* à la maison.

indorse, *vb.* endosser, appuyer, sanctionner.

induce, *vb.* (persuade) persuader; (produce) produire.

induct, *vb.* installer, conduire.

induction, *n.* induction *f.;* installation *f.*

inductive, *adj.* inductif.

indulge, *vb.* contenter, favoriser.

indulgence, *n.* indulgence *f.*

indulgent, *adj.* indulgent.

industrial, *adj.* industriel.

industrialist, *n.* industriel *m.*

industrious, *adj.* travailleur.

industry, *n.* industrie *f.;* (diligence) assiduité *f.*

inebriated, *adj.* sou.

ineligible, *adj.* inéligible.

inept, *adj.* inepte, mal à propos.

inert, *adj.* inerte, apathique.

inertia, *n.* inertie *f.*

inevitable, *adj.* inévitable.

inexplicable, *adj.* inexplicable.

infallible, *adj.* infaillible.

infamous, *adj.* infâme.

infamy, *n.* infamie *f.*

infancy, *n.* (première) enfance *f.*

infant, *n.* enfant *m.f.*

infantile, *adj.* enfantin, infantile.

infantryman, *n.* soldat *(m.)* d'infanterie, fantassin *m.*

infatuated, *adj.* infauté, entiché.

infect, *vb.* infecter.

infection, *n.* infection *f.*

infectious, *adj.* infectieux, infect, contagieux.

infer, *vb.* déduire.

inference, *n.* inférence *f.*

inferior, *adj. and n.* inférieur *m.*

inferiority complex, *n.* complexe *(m.)* d'infériorité.

infernal, *adj.* infernal.

inferno, *n.* enfer *m.*

infest, *vb.* infester.

infidel, *n.* infidèle *m.,* incroyant *m.*

infidelity, *n.* infidélité *f.*

infighting, *n.* querelles *(f.pl.)* internes.

infiltrate, *vb.* infiltrer.

infinite, *adj. and n.* infini *m.*

infinitesimal, *adj.* infinitésimal.

infinitive, *n.* infinitif *m.*

infinity, *n.* infinité *f.*

infirm, *adj.* infirme, faible, maladif.

infirmary, *n.* infirmerie *f.*

infirmity, *n.* infirmité *f.*

inflame, *vb.* enflammer, *tr.*

inflammable, *adj.* inflammable.

inflammation, *n.* inflammation *f.*

inflammatory, *adj.* incendiaire, inflammatoire.

inflate, *vb.* gonfler.

inflation, *n.* (currency) inflation *f.*

inflection, *n.* inflection *f.*

inflict, vb. (penalty) infliger.
infliction, n. infliction f., châtiment m.
influence, n. influence f.
influential, adj. influent.
influenza, n. grippe f., influenza f.
inform, vb. (tell) informer.
informal, adj. (without formality) sans cérémonie.
informant, n. informateur m.
information, n. renseignements m.pl.
informative, adj. instructif.
informer, n. indicateur m.
infringe, vb. enfreindre, violer.
infuriate, vb. rendre furieux.
ingenious, adj. ingénieux.
ingenuity, n. ingéniosité f.
ingrained, adj. enraciné.
ingredient, n. ingrédient m.
inhabit, vb. habiter.
inhabitant, n. habitant m.
inhale, vb. inhaler, aspirer, humer.
inherent, adj. inhérent.
inherit, vb. hériter.
inheritance, n. héritage m.
inhibit, vb. empêcher; (psychology) inhiber.
inhibition, n. inhibition f., défense expresse f., prohibition f.
inhuman, adj. inhumain.
inimical, adj. ennemi, hostile, défavorable.
inimitable, adj. inimitable.
iniquity, n. iniquité f.
initial, 1. n. initiale f. **2.** adj. initial. **3.** vb. parafer.
initialize, vb. initialiser.
initiate, vb. (begin) commencer; (admit) initier.
initiation, n. commencement m., début m., initiation f.
initiative, n. initiative f.
inject, vb. injecter.
injection, n. injection f.
injunction, n. injonction f., ordre m.
injure, vb. (harm) nuire à; (wound) blesser; (damage) abîmer.
injurious, adj. (harmful) nuisible; (offensive) injurieux.

injury, n. (person) préjudice m.; (body) blessure f.; (thing) dommage m.
injustice, n. injustice f.
ink, n. encre f.
inland, adj. and n. intérieur m.
inlet, n. entrée f., admission f., débouché m.
inmate, n. habitant m., hôte m., pensionnaire m.
inn, n. auberge f.
innate, adj. inné.
inner, adj. intérieur.
inning, n. tour (m.) de batte.
innocence, n. innocence f.
innocent, adj. innocent.
innocuous, adj. inoffensif.
innovation, n. innovation f.
innuendo, n. insinuation f., allusion malveillante f.
innumerable, adj. innombrable.
inoculate, vb. inoculer.
inoculation, n. inoculation f., vaccination préventive f.
inoffensive, adj. inoffensif.
input, n. entrée (f.) (de données).
inquest, n. enquête f.
inquire (about), vb. se renseigner (sur).
inquiry, n. (investigation) recherche f.; (question) demande f.; (official) enquête f.
inquisition, n. Inquisition f.; enquête f., recherche f.
inquisitive, adj. curieux, questionneur, indiscret.
inroad, n. incursion f., invasion f., empiètement m.
insane, adj. fou m., folle f.
insanity, n. folie f., insanité f., démence f.
inscribe, vb. inscrire, graver.
inscription, n. inscription f.
insect, n. insecte m.
insecticide, n. insecticide m.
insecure, adj. peu sûr.
insensitive, adj. insensible.
inseparable, adj. inséparable.
insert, vb. insérer.
insertion, n. insertion f.
inside, 1. n. dedans m. **2.** adj. intérieur. **3.** prep. à

l'intérieur de. **4.** adv. (en) dedans.
insidious, adj. insidieux.
insight, n. perspicacité f., pénétration f.
insignia, n. insignes m.pl.
insignificance, n. insignifiance f.
insignificant, adj. insignifiant.
insinuate, vb. insinuer.
insinuation, n. insinuation f.
insipid, adj. insipide, fade.
insist, vb. insister.
insistence, n. insistance f.
insistent, adj. qui insiste, importun.
insolence, n. insolence f.
insolent, adj. insolent.
insomnia, n. insomnie f.
inspect, vb. examiner, inspecter.
inspection, n. inspection f.
inspector, n. inspecteur m.
inspiration, n. inspiration f.
inspire, vb. inspirer.
install, vb. installer.
installation, n. installation f., montage m.
installment, n. acompte m., versement partiel m., paiement à compte m.
instance, n. exemple m.
instant, n. instant m.
instantaneous, adj. instantané.
instantly, adv. à l'instant.
instead, adv. au lieu de cela.
instead of, prep. au lieu de.
instigate, vb. instiguer.
instill, vb. instiller, faire pénétrer, inculquer.
instinct, n. instinct m.
instinctive, adj. instinctif.
institute, vb. instituer.
institution, n. institution f.
instruct, vb. instruire.
instruction, n. instruction f.
instructive, adj. instructif.
instructor, n. (mil.) instructeur m.; (university) chargé (m.) de cours.
instrument, n. instrument m.
instrumental, adj. instrumental, contributif (à).
insufferable, adj. insupportable, intolérable.
insufficient, adj. insuffisant.

insular, *adj.* insulaire.

insulate, *vb.* isoler.

insulation, *n.* isolement *m.*, isolation *f.*

insulator, *n.* isolant *m.*, isolateur *m.*

insulin, *n.* insuline *f.*

insult, 1. *vb.* insulter. **2.** *n.* insulte *f.*

insuperable, *adj.* insurmontable.

insurance, *n.* assurance *f.*

insure, *vb.* assurer.

insurgent, *adj. and n.* insurgé *m.*

insurrection, *n.* insurrection *f.*, soulèvement *m.*

intact, *adj.* intact.

intake, *n.* admission(s) *f.pl.*; (technical) prise *f.*

intangible, *adj.* intangible, impalpable.

integral, *adj.* intégrant.

integrate, *vb.* intégrer, compléter, rendre entier.

integrity, *n.* intégrité *f.*

intellect, *n.* (mind) esprit *m.*; (faculty) intellect *m.*

intellectual, *adj. and n.* intellectuel *m.*

intelligence, *n.* intelligence *f.*; (information) renseignements *m.pl.*

intelligent, *adj.* intelligent.

intelligentsia, *n.* l'intelligence *f.*

intelligible, *adj.* intelligible.

intend, *vb.* avoir l'intention de; (destine for) destiner à.

intense, *adj.* intense.

intensify, *vb.* intensifier.

intensity, *n.* intensité *f.*

intensive, *adj.* intensif.

intent, *adj.* (**i. on**) (absorbed in) absorbé dans; (determined to) déterminé à.

intention, *n.* intention *f.*

intentional, *adj.* intentionnel, voulu, fait exprès.

inter, *vb.* enterrer.

interact, *vb.* communiquer, avoir une action réciproque.

intercede, *vb.* intervenir, intercéder.

intercept, *vb.* intercepter, capter.

interchange, *n.* échange *m.*

intercom, *n.* interphone *m.*

intercourse, *n.* commerce *m.*, relations *f.pl.*, rapports *m.pl.*

interdict, *vb.* interdire, prohiber.

interest, 1. *n.* intérêt *m.* **2.** *vb.* intéresser.

interesting, *adj.* intéressant.

interface, *n.* entreface *f.*

interfere, *vb.* (person) intervenir (dans); (**i. with**) (hinder) gêner.

interference, *n.* (person) intervention *f.*

interim, *adv.* entre temps, en attendant.

interior, *adj. and n.* intérieur *m.*

interject, *vb.* lancer, émettre.

interjection, *n.* interjection *f.*

interloper, *n.* intrus *m.*

interlude, *n.* intermède *m.*, interlude *m.*

intermarry, *vb.* se marier.

intermediary, *n.* intermédiaire *m.f.*

intermediate, *adj. and n.* intermédiaire *m.f.*

interment, *n.* enterrement *m.*

intermission, *n.* interruption *f.*, relâche *f.*; (theater) entr'acte *m.*

intermittent, *adj.* intermittent.

intern, 1. *n.* interne *m.* **2.** *vb.* interner.

internal, *adj.* interne.

Internal Revenue Service, *n.* fisc *m.*

international, *adj.* international.

internationalism, *n.* internationalisme *m.*

interne, *n.* interne *m.*

interplay, *n.* effect (*m.*) réciproque, interaction *f.*

interpolate, *vb.* interpoler.

interpose, *vb.* interposer, *tr.*

interpret, *vb.* interpréter.

interpretation, *n.* interprétation *f.*

interpreter, *n.* interprète *m.f.*

interrogate, *vb.* interroger, questionner.

interrogation, *n.* interrogation *f.*

interrogative, 1. *adj.* interrogateur. **2.** *n.* interrogatif *m.*

interrupt, *vb.* interrompre.

interruption, *n.* interruption *f.*

intersect, *vb.* entrecouper, intersecter, entrecroiser.

intersection, *n.* intersection *f.*

intersperse, *vb.* entremêler, parsemer, intercaler.

intertwine, *vb.* (s') entrelacer.

interval, *n.* intervalle *m.*

intervene, *vb.* intervenir.

intervention, *n.* intervention *f.*

interview, *n.* entrevue *f.*; (press) interview *m.f.*

intestine, *n.* intestin *m.*

intimacy, *n.* intimité *f.*

intimate, *adj.* intime.

intimidate, *vb.* intimider.

intimidation, *n.* intimidation *f.*

into, *prep.* en; (with art. or adj.) dans.

intonation, *n.* intonation *f.*

intone, *vb.* entonner, psalmodier.

intoxicate, *vb.* enivrer.

intoxication, *n.* intoxication *f.*, ivresse *f.*

intractable, *adj.* très difficile.

intransigent, *adj.* intransigeant.

intravenous, *adj.* intraveineux.

intrepid, *adj.* intrépide, brave, courageux.

intricacy, *n.* complexité *f.*, nature compliquée *f.*

intricate, *adj.* compliqué.

intrigue, *n.* intrigue *f.*

intrinsic, *adj.* intrinsèque.

introduce, *vb .* (bring in) introduire; (present) présenter.

introduction, *n.* introduction *f.*; (presenting) présentation *f.*

introductory, *adj.* introductoire, d'introduction.

introspection, *n.* introspection *f.*, recueillement *m.*

introvert, *n.* introverti *m.*

intrude on, *vb.* importuner.

intruder, *n.* intrus *m.*

intuition, *n.* intuition *f.*

intuitive, *adj.* intuitif.

inundate, *vb.* inonder.

invade, *vb.* envahir.

invader, *n.* envahisseur *m.*, transgresseur *m.*

invalid, *adj. and n.* infirme *m.f.*

invaluable, *adj.* inestimable.

invariable, *adj.* invariable.

invasion, *n.* invasion *f.*

invective, *n.* invective *f.*

inveigle, *vb.* attirer, séduire, leurrer.

invent, *vb.* inventer.

invention, *n.* invention *f.*

inventive, *adj.* inventif, trouveur.

inventor, *n.* inventeur *m.*

inventory, *n.* inventaire *m.*

inverse, *adj.* inverse.

invertebrate, 1. *n.* invertébré *m.* 2. *adj.* invertébré.

invest, *vb.* investir; (money) placer.

investigate, *vb.* faire des recherches (sur).

investigation, *n.* investigation *f.*

investment, *n.* placement *m.*

inveterate, *adj.* invétéré, enraciné.

invidious, *adj.* odieux, haïssable, ingrat.

invigorate, *vb.* fortifier, vivifier.

invincible, *adj.* invincible.

invisible, *adj.* invisible.

invitation, *n.* invitation *f.*

invite, *vb.* inviter.

invocation, *n.* invocation *f.*

invoice, *n.* facture *f.*

invoke, *vb.* invoquer.

involuntary, *adj.* involontaire.

involve, *vb.* (implicate) impliquer; (entail) entraîner.

invulnerable, *adj.* invulnérable.

inward, *adj.* intérieur.

iodine, *n.* iode *m.*

Iran, *n.* Iran *m.*

Iraq, *n.* Irak *m.*, Iraq *m.*

irate, *adj.* en colère, courroucé, furieux.

Ireland, *n.* Irlande *f.*

iridium, *n.* iridium *m.*

iris, *n.* iris *m.*

Irish, *adj.* irlandais.

Irishman, *n.* Irlandais *m.*

irk, *vb.* ennuyer.

iron, *n.* fer *m.*

ironworks, *n.* fonderie de fonte *f.*, usine métallurgique *f.*

irony, *n.* ironie *f.*

irrational, *adj.* irrationnel, déraisonnable, absurde.

irrefutable, *adj.* irréfutable, irrécusable.

irregular, *adj.* irrégulier.

irregularity, *n.* irrégularité *f.*

irrelevant, *adj.* non pertinent, hors de propos.

irresistible, *adj.* irrésistible.

irresponsible, *adj.* irresponsable.

irreverent, *adj.* irrévérent, irrévérencieux.

irrevocable, *adj.* irrévocable.

irrigate, *vb.* irriguer, arroser.

irrigation, *n.* irrigation *f.*

irritability, *n.* irritabilité *f.*

irritable, *adj.* irritable, irascible.

irritant, *n.* irritant *m.*

irritate, *vb.* irriter.

irritation, *n.* irritation *f.*

Islam, *n.* Islam *m.*

Islamic, *adj.* islamique.

island, *n.* île *f.*

isolate, *vb.* isoler.

isolation, *n.* isolement *m.*

isolationist, *n.* isolationniste *m.*

isosceles, *adj.* isoscèle.

Israel, *n.* Israël *m.*

Israeli, 1. *n.* Israëlien *m.* 2. *adj.* israëlien.

issuance, *n.* délivrance *f.*

issue, 1. *n.* (way out, end) issue *f.*; (result) résultat *m.*; (question) question *f.*; (publication) numéro *m.*; (money, bonds) émission *f.* 2. *vb.* (come out) sortir; (publish) publier; (money) émettre.

isthmus, *n.* isthme *m.*

it, *pron.* (subject) il *m.*; elle *f.*; (object) le *m.*, la *f.*; (of it) en; (in it, to it) y.

Italian, 1. *n.* (person) Italien *m.*; (language) italien *m.* 2. *adj.* italien.

italics, *n.* italique *m.*

Italy, *n.* Italie *f.*

itch, 1. *n.* démangeaison *f.* 2. *vb.* démanger.

item, *n.* (article) article *m.*; (detail) détail *m.*

itemize, *vb.* détailler.

itinerant, *adj.* ambulant.

itinerary, *n.* itinéraire *m.*

its, 1. *adj.* son *m.*, sa *f.*, ses *pl.* 2. *pron.* le sien *m.*, la sienne *f.*

itself, *pron.* lui-même *m.*, elle-même *f.*; (reflexive) se.

ivory, *n.* ivoire *m.*

ivy, *n.* lierre *m.*

J

jab *n.* coup *m.*, coup sec *m.* 2. *vb.* piquer, donner un coup sec.

jackal, *n.* chacal *m.*

jackass, *n.* âne *m.*; idiot *m.*

jacket, *n.* (man) veston *m.*; (woman) jaquette *f.*

jackknife, *n.* couteau *(m.)* de poche.

jack-of-all-trades, *n.* maître

Jacques *m.*, factotum *m.*, homme *(m.)* à tous les métiers.

jade, *n.* (horse) rosse *f.*, haridelle *f.*; (woman) drôlesse *f.*, coureuse *f.*; (mineral) jade *m.*

jaded, *adj.* surmené, éreinté, blasé, fatigué.

jagged, *adj.* déchiqueté, entaillé, dentelé.

jaguar, *n.* jaguar *m.*

jail, *n.* prison *f.*

jailer, *n.* gardien *m.*, geôlier *m.*

jam, 1. *n.* foule *f.*, presse *f.*; (traffic) embouteillage *m.*; (food) confiture *f.* 2. *vb.* serrer, presser.

Jamaica, n. Jamaïque f.

jamb, n. jambage m., montant m., chambranle m.

jangle, 1. n. cliquetis m. **2.** vb. cliqueter.

janitor, n. concierge m.

January, n. janvier m.

Japan, n. Japon m.

Japanese, 1. n. (person) Japonais m.; (language) japonais m. **2.** adj. japonais.

jar, 1. n. (container) pot m.; (sound) son (m.) discordant; (shock) secousse f. **2.** vb. secouer, heurter.

jargon, n. jargon m.

jasmine, n. jasmin m.

jaundice, n. jaunisse f.

jaunt, n. petite excursion f., balade f.

javelin, n. javelot m., javeline f.

jaw, n. mâchoire f.

jay, n. geai m.

jaywalk, vb. se promener d'une façon distraite ou imprudente.

jazz, n. jazz m.

jealous, adj. jaloux.

jealousy, n. jalousie f.

jeans, n. jeans m.pl.

jeer, 1. n. raillerie f.; moquerie f., huée f. **2.** vb. se moquer de, huer.

jelly, n. gelée f.

jellyfish, n. méduse f.

jeopardize, vb. exposer au danger, mettre en danger, hasarder.

jeopardy, n. danger m., péril m.

jerk, n. saccade f.; (person) pauvre type m.

jerkin, n. justaucorps m., pourpoint m.

jerky, adj. saccadé, coupé.

jersey, n. jersey m., tricot (m.) de laine.

Jerusalem, n. Jérusalem m.

jest, 1. n. plaisanterie f., raillerie f., badinage m. **2.** vb. plaisanter, railler, badiner.

jester, n. railleur m., farceur m., bouffon m.

Jesuit, n. jésuite m.

Jesus, n. Jésus m.

jet, n. (mineral) jais m.; (water, gas) jet m.; (**j. plane**) avion (m.) à réaction.

jet lag, n. (réaction au) décalage (m.) horaire.

jetsam, n. épaves f.pl.

jettison, vb. se délester.

jetty, n. jetée f., môle m.

Jew, n. Juif m., Juive f.

jewel, n. bijou m.

jeweler, n. bijoutier m., jouaillier m.

jewelry, n. bijouterie f.

Jewish, adj. juif m., juive f.

jib, n. foc m.

jibe, vb. être en accord, s'accorder.

jiffy, n. instant m., clin d'œil m.

jig, 1. n. gigue f.; calibre m., gabarit m. **2.** vb. danser la gigue, sautiller.

jilt, vb. délaisser, plaquer, planter.

jingle, 1. n. tintement m., cliquetis m. **2.** vb. tinter, cliqueter.

jinx, n. porte-malheur m.

jittery, adj. très nerveux.

job, n. (work) travail m.; (employment) emploi m.

jobber, n. intermédiaire m., marchandeur m., soustraitant m.

jockey, n. jockey m.

jocular, adj. facétieux, jovial, rieur.

jocund, adj. enjoué.

jodhpurs, n. pantalon (m.) d'équitation.

jog, 1. n. coup m., secousse f., cahot m. **2.** vb. pousser, secouer, cahoter; faire du jogging.

jogging, n. jogging m.

joggle, 1. n. petite secousse f. **2.** vb. secouer légèrement.

join, vb. (things) joindre; (group, etc.) se joindre à.

joiner, n. menuisier m.

joint, 1. n.. joint m.; (anatomy) articulation f. **2.** adj. (in common) commun; (in partnership) co-.

jointly, adv. ensemble, conjointement.

joist, n. solive f., poutre f.

joke, 1. n. plaisanterie f. **2.** vb. plaisanter.

joker, n. farceur m., blagueur m.; joker m.

jolly, adj. joyeux.

jolt, 1. n. cahot m., choc m., secousse f. **2.** vb. cahoter, secouer, ballotter.

jonquil, n. jonquille f.

Jordan, n. Jordanie f.

jostle, vb. coudoyer tr.

jot, vb. (**j. down**) noter.

jounce, 1. n. cahot m., secousse f. **2.** vb. cahoter.

journal, n. journal m.

journalism, n. journalisme m.

journalist, n. journaliste m.f.

journey, 1. n. voyage m. **2.** vb. voyager.

journeyman, n. compagnon m.

jovial, adj. jovial, gai.

jowl, n. mâchoire f.

joy, n. joie f.

joyful, adj. joyeux.

joyous, adj. joyeux.

joystick, n. manette f.

jubilant, adj. réjoui, jubilant, exultant.

jubilee, n. jubilé m.

Judaism, n. judaïsme m.

judge, 1. n. juge m. **2.** vb. juger.

judgment, n. jugement m.

judicial, adj. judiciaire.

judiciary, adj. judiciaire.

judicious, adj. judicieux, sensé.

jug, n. cruche f.

juggle, vb. jongler.

jugular, adj. jugulaire.

juice, n. jus m.

juicy, adj. juteux.

July, n. juillet m.

jumble, 1. n. brouillamini m., fouillis m., fatras m. **2.** vb. brouiller, mêler confusément.

jump, 1. n. saut m. **2.** vb. sauter.

jumper cables, n. câbles (m.pl.) de démarrage.

jumpy, adj. nerveux.

junction, n. jonction f.; (rail) embranchement m.

juncture, *n.* jointure *f.,* jonction *f.,* conjoncture *f.*

June, *n.* juin *m.*

jungle, *n.* jungle *f.,* brousse *f.*

junior, *adj. and n.* (age) cadet *m.;* (rank) subalterne *m.*

juniper, *n.* genévrier *m.,* genièvre *m.*

junk, *n.* (waste) rebut *m.*

junket, *n.* jonchée *f.;* festin *m.;* partie de plaisir *f.*

jurisdiction, *n.* juridiction *f.*

jurisprudence, *n.* jurisprudence *f.*

jurist, *n.* juriste *m.,* légiste *m.*

juror, *m.* juré *m.,* membre du jury *m.*

jury, *n.* jury *m.*

just, 1. *adj.* juste. **2.** *adv.*

(exactly) juste; (barely) à peine; **(have j.)** venir de.

justice, *n.* justice *f.*

justifiable, *adj.* justifiable, justifié.

justification, *n.* justification *f.*

justify, *vb.* justifier.

jut, *vb.* être en saillie.

jute, *n.* jute *m.*

juvenile, *adj.* juvénile.

K

kale *n.* chou *m.*

kaleidoscope, *n.* kaléidoscope *m.*

kangaroo, *n.* kangourou *m.*

karakul, *n.* karakul *m.,* caracul *m.*

karat, *n.* carat *m.*

karate, *n.* karaté *m.*

keel, *n.* quille *f.*

keen, *adj.* (edge) aiguisé; (pain, point) aigu; (look, mind) pénétrant; **(k. on)** enthousiaste de.

keep, *vb.* tenir; (reserve, protect, retain) garder; (remain) rester; (continue) continuer à.

keeper, *n.* gardien *m.*

keepsake, *n.* souvenir *m.*

keg, *n.* caque *f.,* barillet *m.,* tonnelet *m.*

kennel, *n.* chenil *m.*

Kenya, *n.* Kenya *m.*

kerchief, *n.* fichu *m.,* mouchoir *m.*

kernel, *n.* (grain) grain *m.;* (nut) amande *f.; (fig.)* noyau *m.*

kerosene, *n.* pétrole *m.*

ketchup, *n.* sauce *(f.)* piquante à base de tomates.

kettle, *n.* bouilloire *f.*

kettledrum, *n.* timbale *f.*

key, *n.* clef, clé *f.;* (piano, typewriter) touche *f.*

keyboard, *n.* clavier *m.*

keyhole, *n.* entrée *(f.)* de clef.

khaki, *n.* kaki *m.*

kick, 1. *n.* coup *(m.)* de pied; (gun) recul *m.* **2.** *vb.* donner un coup de pied à.

kid, *n.* (animal, skin) chevreau *m.;* (child) gosse *m.f.*

kidnap, *vb.* enlever de vive force.

kidnapper, *n.* auteur *(m.)* de l'enlèvement, ravisseur *m.*

kidney, *n.* rein *m.;* (food) rognon *m.*

kidney bean, *n.* haricot nain *m.*

kill, *vb.* tuer.

killer, *n.* tueur *m.,* meurtrier *m.*

killing, *n.* meurtre *m.*

kiln, *n.* four (céramique) *m.,* séchoir *m.*

kilobyte, *n.* kilo-octet *m.*

kilocycle, *n.* kilocycle *m.*

kilogram, *n.* kilogramme *m.*

kilohertz, *n.* kilohertz *m.*

kilowatt, *n.* kilowatt *m.*

kilt, *n.* kilt *m.*

kimono, *n.* kimono *m.*

kin, *n.* (relation) parent *m.*

kind, 1. *n.* genre *m.* **2.** *adj.* aimable.

kindergarten, *n.* jardin *(m.)* d'enfants, école maternelle *f.*

kindle, *vb.* allumer, *tr.*

kindling, *n.* allumage *m.,* bois d'allumage *m.*

kindly, *adv.* avec bonté.

kindness, *n.* bonté *f.*

kindred, 1. *n.* parenté *f.,* affinité *f.* **2.** *adj.* analogue.

kinetic, *adj.* cinétique.

king, *n.* roi *m.*

kingdom, *n.* royaume *m.*

kink, 1. *n.* nœud *m.,* tortillement *m.* **2.** *vb.* se nouer.

kinky, *adj.* excentrique.

kiosk, *n.* kiosque *m.*

kipper, *n.* kipper *m.,* hareng *(m.)* légèrement salé et fumé.

kiss, 1. *n.* baiser *m.* **2.** *vb.* embrasser.

kitchen, *n.* cuisine *f.*

kite, *n.* cerf-volant *m.*

kitten, *n.* petit chat *m.*

kitty, *n.* (money) cagnotte *f.*

kleptomania, *n.* kleptomanie *f.*

kleptomaniac, *n.* kleptomane *m.*

knack, *n.* tour de main *m.,* talent *m.,* truc *m.*

knapsack, *n.* havresac *m.*

knead, *vb.* pétrir, malaxer.

knee, *n.* genou *m.*

kneecap, *n.* genouillère *f.*

kneel, *vb.* s'agenouiller.

knell, *n.* glas *m.*

knickers, *n.* pantalon *m.;* (underwear) culotte *f.*

knife, *n.* couteau *m.*

knight, *n.* chevalier *m.*

knit, *vb.* (with needles) tricoter.

knob, *n.* bouton *m.*

knock, 1. *n.* coup *m.* **2.** *vb.* frapper.

knot, *n.* nœud *m.*

knotty, *adj.* plein de nœuds.

know, *vb.* savoir; (be acquainted with) connaître.

knowledge, *n.* connaissance *f.;* (learning) savoir *m.*

knuckle, *n.* articulation *(f.)* du doigt, jointure *(f.)* du doigt.

Kodak, *n.* kodak *m.*

Koran, *n.* Coran *m.*

Korea, *n.* Corée *f.*

Kosher, *adj.* kascher.

L

lab n. labo m.

label, n. étiquette f.

labor, 1. n. travail m.; (workers) ouvriers m.pl. 2. vb. peiner.

laboratory, n. laboratoire m.

laborer, n. travailleur m.

laborious, adj. laborieux.

labor union, n. syndicat m.

laburnum, n. cytise m.

labyrinth, n. labyrinthe m.

lace, n. dentelle f.; (string) lacet m.

lacerate, vb. lacérer, déchirer.

laceration, n. lacération f.

lack, 1. n. manque m. 2. vb. manquer de.

lackadaisical, adj. affecté.

laconic, adj. laconique.

lacquer, n. vernis-laque m.

lactic, adj. lactique.

lactose, n. lactose f.

lacy, adj. de dentelle.

ladder, n. échelle f.

ladle, n. cuiller (f.) à pot.

lady, n. dame f.

ladybug, n. coccinelle f.

lag behind, vb. rester en arrière.

lagoon, n. lagune f.

laid-back, adj. décontracté.

lair, n. tanière f., repaire m.

laissez faire, n. laisser-faire m.

laity, n. les laïques m.pl.

lake, n. lac m.

lamb, n. agneau m.

lame, adj. boiteux.

lament, vb. se lamenter (sur); (mourn) pleurer.

lamentable, adj. lamentable, déplorable.

lamentation, n. lamentation f.

laminate, vb. laminer, écacher.

lamp, n. lampe f.

lampoon, 1. n. pasquinade f., satire f. 2. vb. lancer des satires.

lance, n. lance f.

land, 1. n. terre f. 2. vb. (boat) débarquer; (plane) atterrir.

landholder, n. propriétaire foncier m.

landing, n. débarquement m., mise à terre f.

landlord, n. propriétaire m.f.

landmark, n. borne f.

landscape, n. paysage m.

landslide, n. éboulement m.

landward, adv. vers la terre.

lane, n. (country) sentier m., (town) ruelle f., (highway) file f.

language, n. langue f.; (form of expression) langage m.

languid, adj. languissant.

languish, vb. languir.

languor, n. langueur f.

lanky, adj. grand et maigre.

lanolin, n. lanoline f.

lantern, n. lanterne f.

lap, n. (of body) genoux m.pl.; (of track) tour (m.) (de piste).

lapel, n. revers m.

lapin, n. lapin m.

lapse, 1. n. (of time) laps m.; (error) faute f. 2. vb. passer.

laptop computer, n. portable m.

larceny, n. larcin m., vol m.

lard, n. saindoux m.

large, adj. grand.

largely, adv. en grande partie.

largo, n. largo m.

lariat, n. lasso m.

lark, n. alouette f.

larkspur, n. pied d'alouette m., delphinium m.

larva, n. larve f.

laryngitis, n. laryngite f.

larynx, n. larynx m.

lascivious, adj. lascif.

laser, n. laser m.

lash, 1. n. (whip) lanière f.; (blow) coup (m.) de fouet. 2. vb. fouetter.

lass, n. jeune fille f.

lassitude, n. lassitude f.

lasso, n. lasso m.

last, 1. adj. dernier; (at l.) enfin. 2. vb. durer.

lasting, adj. durable.

latch, n. loquet m.

late, adj. and adv. (on in day, etc.) tard; (after due time) en retard; (dead) feu; (recent) dernier.

latecomer, n. retardataire m.

lately, adv. dernièrement.

latent, adj. latent, caché.

lateral, adj. latéral.

lath, n. latte f.

lathe, n. tour m.

lather, n. (soap) mousse f.; (horse) écume f.

Latin, 1. n. (person) Latin m.; (language) latin m. 2. adj. latin.

Latin America, n. Amérique (f.) latine.

latitude, n. latitude f.

latrine, n. latrine f.

latter, adj. and pron. dernier.

lattice, n. treillis m.

laud, vb. louer.

laudable, adj. louable.

laudanum, n. laudanum m.

laudatory, adj. élogieux.

laugh, n. rire m.

laugh (at), vb. rire (de).

laughable, adj. risible.

laughter, n. rire m.

launch, 1. n. (boat) chaloupe f. 2. vb. lancer, tr.

launder, n. blanchir.

launderette, n. buanderie f., laverie (f.) (automatique).

laundry, n. (works) blanchisserie f.; (washing) lessive f.

laundryman, n. blanchisseur m.

laureate, adj. and n. lauréat m.f.

laurel, n. laurier m.

lava, n. lave f.

lavaliere, n. lavallière f.

lavatory, n. lavabo m.; cabinet (m.) de toilette.

lavender, n. lavande f.

lavish, 1. adj. (person) prodigue; (thing) somptueux. 2. vb. prodiguer.

law, n. loi f.; (jurisprudence) droit m.

law court, n. tribunal m.

lawful, adj. légal.

lawless, *adj.* sans loi.
lawn, *n.* pelouse *f.*
lawsuit, *n.* procès *m.*
lawyer, *n.* (counselor) avocat *m.; * (attorney) avoué *m.;* (jurist) jurisconsulte *m.*
lax, *adj.* lâche, mou, relâché.
laxative, *n.* laxatif *m.*
laxity, *n.* relâchement *m.*
lay, 1. *vb.* poser; (l. off) licencier. 2. *adj.* laïque.
layer, *n.* couche *f.*
layman, *n.* laïque *m.*
lazy, *adj.* paresseux.
lead, 1. *n.* plomb *m.; * (pencil) mine *f.* 2. *vb.* mener, conduire.
leaden, *adj.* de plomb.
leader, *n.* chef *m.*
leading, *adj.* principal.
lead pencil, *n.* crayon *(m.)* à la mine de plomb.
leaf, *n.* feuille *f.*
leaflet, *n.* feuillet *m.*
leafy, *adj.* feuillu.
league, *n.* (compact) ligue *f.;* (measure) lieue *f.*
League of Nations, *n.* La Société *(f.)* des Nations.
leak, 1. *n.* (liquid) fuite *f.;* (boat) voie *(f.)* d'eau. 2. *vb.* fuir; faire eau.
leakage, *n.* fuite d'eau *f.*
leaky, *adj.* qui coule, qui fait eau.
lean, 1. *adj.* maigre. 2. *vb. intr.* (l. against) s'appuyer sur; (stoop) se pencher. 3. *vb., tr.,* appuyer.
leap, *vb.* sauter.
leap year, *n.* année bissextile *f.*
learn, *vb.* apprendre.
learned, *adj.* savant, docte.
learning, *n.* science *f.,* instruction *f.,* érudition *f.*
lease, *n.* bail *m.*
leash, *n.* laisse *f.,* attache *f.*
least, 1. *n.* moins *m.* 2. *adj.* (le) moindre. 3. *adv.* (le) moins.
leather, *n.* cuir *m.*
leathery, *adj.* coriace.
leave, 1. *n.* permission *f.* 2. *vb.* laisser; (go away from) quitter.

leaven, 1. *n.* levain *m.* 2. *vb.* faire lever, modifier.
Lebanon, *n.* Liban *m.*
lecherous, *adj.* lascif, libertin.
lecture, *n.* conférence *f.*
lecturer, *n.* conférencier *m.*
ledge, *n.* bord *m.; * (of rocks) chaîne *f.*
ledger, *n.* grand livre *m.*
lee, *n.* côté *(m.)* sous le vent.
leech, *n.* sangsue *f.*
leek, *n.* poireau *m.*
leer, 1. *n.* œillade *f.,* regard de côté *m.* 2. *vb.* lorgner.
leeward, *adj. and adv.* sous le vent.
left, *adj. and n.* gauche *f.;* (on, to the l.) à gauche.
leftist, *n.* gaucher *m.;* (politics) gauchiste *m.*
left wing, *n.* l'aile gauche *f.;* (politics) la gauche.
leg, *n.* (man, horse) jambe *f.;* (most animals) patte *f.*
legacy, *n.* legs *m.*
legal, *adj.* légal.
legalize, *vb.* rendre légal.
legation, *n.* légation *f.*
legend, *n.* légende *f.*
legendary, *adj.* légendaire.
legible, *adj.* lisible.
legion, *n.* légion *f.*
legislate, *vb.* faire les lois.
legislation, *n.* législation *f.*
legislator, *n.* législateur *m.*
legislature, *n.* législature *f.*
legitimate, *adj.* légitime.
legume, *n.* légume *m.*
leisure, *n.* loisir *m.*
leisurely, *adv.* à loisir.
lemon, *n.* citron *m.*
lemonade, *n.* citron *(m.)* pressé.
lend, *vb.* prêter.
length, *n.* (dimension) longueur *f.;* (time) durée *f.*
lengthen, *vb.* allonger, *tr.*
lengthwise, *adv.* en long.
lengthy, *adj.* assez long.
lenient, *adj.* indulgent.
lens, *n.* lentille *f.;* (camera) objectif *m.*
Lent, *n.* carême *m.*
Lenten, *adj.* de carême.
lentil, *n.* lentille *f.*
lento, *adv.* lento.
leopard, *n.* léopard *m.*

leotard, *n.* maillot *(m.)* (de danseur, etc.).
leper, *n.* lépreux *m.*
leprosy, *n.* lèpre *f.*
lesbian, 1. *adj.* lesbien. 2. *n.* lesbienne *f.;* tribade *f.*
lesion, *n.* lésion *f.*
less, 1. *adj.* (smaller) moindre; (not so much) moins de. 2. *adv.* (l. than) moins (de).
lessen, *vb.* diminuer.
lesser, *adj.* moindre.
lesson, *n.* leçon *f.*
lest, *conj.* de peur que . . . (ne).
let, *vb.* laisser; (lease) louer.
letdown, *n.* déception *f.*
lethal, *adj.* mortel.
lethargic, *adj.* léthargique.
lethargy, *n.* léthargie *f.*
letter, *n.* lettre *f.*
letterhead, *n.* en-tête de lettre *m.*
lettuce, *n.* laitue *f.*
leukemia, *n.* leucémie *f.*
levee, *n.* lever *m.*
level, 1. *adj.* (flat) égal; (l. with) au niveau de. 2. *n.* niveau *m.*
lever, *n.* levier *m.*
levity, *n.* légèreté *f.*
levy, 1. *n.* levée *f.* 2. *vb.* lever.
lewd, *adj.* impudique.
lexicon, *n.* lexique *m.*
liability, *n.* responsabilité *f.*
liable, *adj.* (responsible for) responsable de; (subject to) sujet à.
liar, *n.* menteur *m.*
libation, *n.* libation *f.*
libel, *n.* diffamation *f.*
libelous, *adj.* diffamatoire.
liberal, *adj.* libéral; (generous) généreux.
liberalism, *n.* libéralisme *m.*
liberality, *n.* libéralité *f.*
liberate, *vb.* libérer.
liberation, *n.* libération *f.*
libertine, 1. *n.* libre-penseur *m.* 2. *adj.* libertin.
liberty, *n.* liberté *f.*
libidinous, *adj.* libidineux.
libido, *n.* libido *m.*
librarian, *n.* bibliothécaire *m.f.*
library, *n.* bibliothèque *f.*
libretto, *n.* livret *m.*

Libya, *n.* Libye *f.*

license, 1. *n.* permis *m.;* (tradesmen) patente *f.;* (abuse of freedom) licence *f.*

licentious, *adj.* licencieux.

lick, *vb.* lécher.

licorice, *n.* réglisse *f.*

lid, *n.* couvercle *m.*

lie, 1. *n.* mensonge *m.* **2.** *vb.* (fib) mentir; (recline) être couché; (**l. down**) se coucher; (be situated) se trouver.

lien, *n.* privilège *m.*

lieutenant, *n.* lieutenant *m.*

life, *n.* vie *f.*

lifeboat, *n.* bateau *(m.)* de sauvetage.

life buoy, *n.* bouée *(f.)* de sauvetage.

lifeguard, *n.* maître-nageur *m.*

life insurance, *n.* assurance-vie *f.*

lifeless, *adj.* sans vie.

life preserver, *n.* appareil *(m.)* de sauvetage.

life sentence, *n.* condamnation *(f.)* à perpétuité.

life style, *n.* manière de vivre *f.*

life-support system, *n.* respirateur *(m.)* artificiel.

lifetime, *n.* vie *f.*, vivant *m.*

lift, *vb.* lever.

ligament, *n.* ligament *m.*

ligature, *n.* ligature *f.*

light, 1. *n.* lumière *f.* **2.** *adj.* (not heavy) léger; (not dark) clair. **3.** *vb.* allumer, *tr.*

lighten, *vb.* (relieve) alléger, *tr.;* (brighten) éclairer, *tr.*

lighter, *n.* (cigarette) briquet *m.*

lighthouse, *n.* phare *m.*

lighting, *n.* éclairage *n.*

lightly, *adv.* légèrement.

lightness, *n.* légèreté *f.*

lightning, *n.* (flash of) éclair *m.*

lightweight, 1. *adj.* léger. **2.** *n.* (boxing) poids *(m.)* léger.

lignite, *n.* lignite *m.*

likable, *adj.* agréable.

like, 1. *adj.* pareil. **2.** *vb.* aimer; plaire à. **3.** *prep.* comme.

likelihood, *n.* probabilité *f.*

likely, *adj.* probable.

liken, *vb.* comparer.

likeness, *n.* ressemblance *f.*

likewise, *adv.* de même.

lilac, *n.* lilas *m.*

lilt, 1. *n.* forte cadence *f.* **2.** *vb.* chanter gaiement.

lily, *n.* lis *m.;* (**l. of the valley**) muguet *m.*

limb, *n.* membre *m.;* (tree) grosse branche *f.*

limber, 1. *adj.* souple, flexible. **2.** *vb.* assouplir.

limbo, *n.* limbes *m.pl.*

lime, *n.* (mineral) chaux *f.;* (tree) tilleul *m.;* (fruit) lime *f.*, citron *(m.)* vert.

limelight, *n.* lumière oxhydrique *f.*

limestone, *n.* pierre à chaux *f.*, calcaire *m.*

limewater, *n.* eau de chaux *f.*

limit, 1. *n.* limite *f.* **2.** *vb.* limiter.

limitation, *n.* limitation *f.*

limitless, *adj.* sans limite, sans bornes.

limousine, *n.* limousine *f.*

limp, 1. *adj.* flasque. **2.** *vb.* boiter.

limpid, *adj.* limpide.

linden, *n.* tilleul *n.*

line, *n.* ligne *f.*

lineage, *n.* lignée *f.*, race *f.*

lineal, *adj.* linéaire.

linen, *n.* (cloth) toile *f.;* (sheets, etc.) linge *m.*

linger, *vb.* s'attarder.

lingerie, *n.* lingerie *f.*

linguist, *n.* linguiste *m.f.*

linguistic, *adj.* linguistique.

linguistics, *n.* linguistique *f.*

liniment, *n.* liniment *m.*

lining, *n.* (clothes) doublure *f.*

link, 1. *n.* (chain) chaînon *m.; (fig.)* lien *m.* **2.** *vb.* (re)lier.

linoleum, *n.* linoléum *m.*

linseed, *n.* graine *(f.)* de lin.

lint, *n.* charpie *f.*

lion, *n.* lion *m.*

lip, *n.* lèvre *f.*

lipstick, *n.* rouge *(m.)* à lèvres.

liquefy, *vb.* liquéfier.

liqueur, *n.* liqueur *f.*

liquid, *adj. and n.* liquide *m.*

liquidate, *vb.* liquider.

liquidation, *n.* liquidation *f.*, acquittement *m.*

liquor, *n.* boisson *(f.)* alcoolique.

lisp, *vb.* zézayer.

list, 1. *n.* liste *f.* **2.** *vb.* enregistrer.

listen (to), *vb.* écouter.

listless, *adj.* inattentif.

litany, *n.* litanie *f.*

literacy, *n.* degré *(m.)* d'aptitude à lire et à écrire.

literal, *adj.* littéral.

literary, *adj.* littéraire.

literate, *adj.* lettré.

literature, *n.* littérature *f.*

lithe, *adj.* flexible, pliant.

lithograph, *vb.* lithographier.

lithography, *n.* lithographie *f.*

litigant, *n.* plaideur *m.*

litigation, *n.* litige *m.*

litmus, *n.* tournesol *m.*

litter, *n.* (vehicle, animals' bedding) litière *f.;* (disorder) fouillis *m.;* (animals' young) portée *f.*

little, 1. *n. and adv.* peu *m.* **2.** *adj.* (small) petit; (not much) peu (de).

liturgical, *adj.* liturgique.

liturgy, *n.* liturgie *f.*

live, *vb.* vivre.

livelihood, *n.* vie *f.*, subsistance *f.*, gagne-pain *m.*

lively, *adj.* vif *m.*, vive *f.*

liven, *vb.* animer, activer.

liver, *n.* foie *m.*

livery, *n.* livrée *f.*

livestock, *n.* bétail *m.*

livid, *adj.* livide, blême.

lizard, *n.* lézard *m.*

llama, *n.* lama *m.*

lo, *interj.* voilà.

load, 1. *n.* (cargo) charge *f.;* (burden) fardeau *m.* **2.** *vb.* charger.

loaf, 1. *n.* pain *m.* **2.** *vb.* flâner.

loafer, *n.* fainéant *m.*

loam, *n.* terre grasse *f.*

loan, 1. *n.* (thing) prêt *m.;* (borrowing) emprunt *m.* **2.** *vb.* prêter.

loath, *adj.* fâché, peiné.

loathe, *vb.* détester.

loathing, *n.* dégoût *m.*

loathsome, *adj.* dégoûtant.

lobby, 1. *n.* (hall) vestibule *m.;* (politics) groupe *(m.)* de pression. **2.** *vb.* faire pression sur.

lobe, *n.* lobe *m.*

lobster, *n.* homard *m.*

local, *adj.* local.

locale, *n.* localité *f.,* scène *f.*

locality, *n.* localité *f.*

localize, *vb.* localiser.

locate, *vb.* localiser.

location, *n.* placement *m.*

lock, 1. *n.* (door) serrure *f.;* (hair) mèche *f.* **2.** *vb.* fermer à clef.

locker, *n.* armoire *f.;* (baggage) consigne automatique *f.*

locket, *n.* médaillon *m.*

lockjaw, *n.* tétanos *m.*

locksmith, *n.* serrurier *m.*

locomotion, *n.* locomotion *f.*

locomotive, *n.* locomotive *f.*

locust, *n.* sauterelle *f.*

locution, *n.* locution *f.*

lode, *n.* filon *m.*

lodge, *vb.* loger.

lodger, *n.* locataire *m.*

lodging, *n.* logement *m.*

loft, *n.* grenier *m.*

lofty, *adj.* élevé; (proud) hautain.

log, *n.* (wood) bûche *f.;* (boat) loch *m.*

logarithm, *n.* logarithme *m.*

loge, *n.* loge *f.*

logic, *n.* logique *f.*

logical, *adj.* logique.

logo, *n.* emblème *m.*

loins, *n.* reins *m.pl.*

loiter, *vb.* flâner.

lollipop, *n.* sucre d'orge *m.,* sucette *f.*

London, *n.* Londres *m.*

lone, lonely, lonesome, *adj.* solitaire.

loneliness, *n.* solitude *f.*

long, 1. *adj.* long *m.,* longue *f.* **2.** *adv.* longtemps.

longevity, *n.* longévité *f.*

long for, *vb.* désirer ardemment.

longing, *n.* désir ardent *m.*

longitude, *n.* longitude *f.*

longitudinal, *adj.* longitudinal.

look, 1. *n.* regard *m.;* aspect *m.* **2.** *vb.* (**l. at**) regarder; (**l. for**) chercher; (**l. after**) soigner; (seem) paraître.

looking glass, *n.* miroir *m.*

loom, 1. *n.* métier *m.* **2.** *vb.* se dessiner.

loop, *n.* boucle *f.*

loophole, *n.* meurtrière *f.,* échappatoire *f.*

loose, *adj.* (not tight) lâche; (detached) détaché; (morals) relâché.

loosen, *vb.* desserrer.

loot, 1. *n.* butin *m.* **2.** *vb.* piller.

lop, *vb.* élaguer, ébrancher.

loquacious, *adj.* loquace.

lord, *n.* seigneur *m.;* (title) lord *m.*

lordship, *n.* seigneurie *f.*

lorgnette, *n.* lorgnette *f.*

lose, *vb.* perdre.

loss, *n.* perte *f.*

lot, *n.* (fortune) sort *m.;* (land) terrain *m.;* (much) beaucoup.

lotion, *n.* lotion *f.*

lottery, *n.* loterie *f.*

lotus, *n.* lotus *m.,* lotos *m.*

loud, 1. *adj.* fort; (noisy) bruyant. **2.** *adv.* haut.

loudspeaker, *n.* haut-parleur *m.*

lounge, 1. *n.* sofa *m.;* hall *m.* **2.** *vb.* flâner.

louse, *n.* pou *m.*

lout, *n.* rustre *m.*

louver, *n.* auvent *m.*

lovable, *adj.* aimable.

love, 1. *n.* amour *m.* **2.** *vb.* aimer.

love affair, *n.* liaison *(f.)* amoureuse.

lovely, *adj.* beau *m.,* belle *f.*

lover, *n.* amoureux *m.*

low, *adj.* bas *m.,* basse *f.*

lowboy, *n.* commode basse *f.*

lowbrow, *adj.* peu intellectual.

lower, *vb.* baisser.

lowly, *adj.* humble.

loyal, *adj.* loyal.

loyalist, *n.* loyaliste *m.f.*

loyalty, *n.* loyauté *f.*

lozenge, *n.* pastille *f.*

lubricant, *n.* lubrifiant *m.*

lubricate, *vb.* lubrifier.

lucid, *adj.* lucide.

luck, *n.* chance *f.*

lucky, *adj.* (person) heureux.

lucrative, *adj.* lucratif.

ludicrous, *adj.* risible.

lug, *vb.* traîner, tirer.

luggage, *n.* bagages *m.pl.*

lukewarm, *adj.* tiède.

lull, *n.* moment *(m.)* de calme.

lullaby, *n.* berceuse *f.*

lumbago, *n.* lumbago *m.*

lumber, *n.* bois *(m.)* de charpente.

luminous, *adj.* lumineux.

lump, 1. *n.* (gros) morceau *m.* **2.** *vb.* (**l. together**) mettre en tas.

lumpy, *adj.* grumeleux.

lunacy, *n.* folie *f.*

lunar, *adj.* lunaire.

lunatic, *n.* aliéné *m.*

lunch, 1. *n.* déjeuner *m.* **2.** *vb.* déjeuner.

luncheon, *n.* déjeuner *m.*

lung, *n.* poumon *m.*

lunge, 1. *n.* botte *f.* **2.** *vb.* se fendre.

lurch, 1. *n.* embardée *f.* **2.** *vb.* faire une embardée.

lure, *vb.* (animal) leurrer; (attract) attirer.

lurid, *adj.* blafard, sombre.

lurk, *vb.* se cacher, rôder.

luscious, *adj.* délicieux.

lush, *adj.* luxuriant.

lust, *n.* luxure *f.*

luster, *n.* lustre *m.*

lustful, *adj.* lascif, sensuel.

lustrous, *adj.* brillant, lustré.

lusty, *adj.* vigoureux.

lute, *n.* luth *m.*

Lutheran, *n.* Luthérien *m.*

Luxemburg, *n.* Luxembourg *m.*

luxuriant, *adj.* exubérant.

luxurious, *adj.* (thing) luxueux.

luxury, *n.* luxe *m.*

lying, *n.* mensonge *m.*

lymph, *n.* lymphe *f.*

lynch, *vb.* lyncher.

lyre, *n.* lyre *f.*

lyric, *adj.* lyrique.

lyricism, *n.* lyrisme *m.*

lyrics, *n.* (of song) paroles *f.pl.*

M

macaroni *n.* macaroni *m.*

machine, *n.* machine *f.*

machine gun, *n.* mitrailleuse *f.*

machinery, *n.* machines *f.pl.; (fig.)* mécanisme *m.*

machinist, *n.* machiniste *m.*

machismo, *n.* phallocratie *f.*

macho, 1. *adj.* phallocrate, macho. 2. *n.* homme phallocrate *m.*

mackerel, *n.* maquereau *m.*

mackinaw, *n.* mackinaw *m.*

macrobiotic, *adj.* macrobiotique.

mad, *adj.* fou *m.*, folle *f.*

madness, *n.* folie *f.*

Madagascar, *n.* Madagascar *m.*

madam, *n.* madame *f.*

madcap, *n. and adj.* écervelé.

madden, *vb.* exaspérer.

made, *adj.* fait, fabriqué.

mafia, *n.* mafia *f.*

magazine, *n.* revue *f.*

maggot, *n.* ver *m.*

magic, 1. *n.* magie *f.* 2. *adj.* magique.

magician, *n.* magicien *m.*

magistrate, *n.* magistrat *m.*

magnanimous, *adj.* magnanime.

magnate, *n.* magnat *m.*

magnesium, *n.* magnésium *m.*

magnet, *n.* aimant *m.*

magnetic, *adj.* magnétique.

magnificence, *n.* magnificence *f.*

magnificent, *adj.* magnifique.

magnify, *vb.* grossir.

magnitude, *n.* grandeur *f.*

mahogany, *n.* acajou *m.*

maid, *n.* (servant) bonne *f.;* (old m.) vieille fille *f.*

maiden, *adj.* de jeune fille.

mail, 1. *n.* courrier *m.* 2. *vb.* envoyer par la poste.

mailbox, *n.* boîte *(f.)* aux lettres.

mail carrier, mailman, *n.* facteur *m.*

maim, *vb.* estropier, mutiler.

main, *adj.* principal.

mainframe, *n.* unité centrale (d'un informateur) *f.*

mainland, *n.* terre *(f.)* ferme.

mainly, *adv.* surtout.

mainspring, *n.* grand ressort *m.;* mobile essentiel *m.*

maintain, *vb.* maintenir; (support) soutenir.

maintenance, *n.* entretien *m.*

maize, *n.* maïs *m.*

majestic, *adj.* majestueux.

majesty, *n.* majesté *f.*

major, 1. *n.* (mil.) commandant *m.;* (school) sujet *(m.)* principal. 2. *adj.* majeur.

majority, *n.* majorité *f.*

major scale, mode, or key, *n.* ton majeur *m.*, mode majeur *m.*

make, 1. *n.* fabrication *f.* 2. *vb.* faire.

make-believe, 1. *n.* trompe l'œil *m.* 2. *vb.* feindre.

maker, *n.* fabricant *m.*

makeshift, 1. *n.* expédient *m.* 2. *adj.* provisoire.

make-up, *n.* (face) maquillage *m.*

maladjusted, *adj.* mal adapté, mal ajusté.

maladjustment, *n.* mauvaise adaptation *f.*

malady, *n.* maladie *f.*

malaria, *n.* malaria *f.*

male, *adj. and n.* mâle *m.*

malevolent, *adj.* malveillant.

malice, *n.* méchanceté *f.*

malicious, *adj.* méchant.

malign, *vb.* calomnier.

malignant, *adj.* malin *m.*, maligne *f.*

mall, *n.* centre *(m.)* commercial.

malleable, *adj.* malléable.

malnutrition, *n.* mauvaise hygiène *(f.)* alimentaire.

malpractice, *n.* faute *(f.)* professionnelle.

malt, *n.* malt *m.*

Malta, *n.* Malte *f.*

mammal, *n.* mammifère *m.*

man, *n.* homme *m.*

manage, 1. *vb. tr.* (administer) gérer; (conduct) diriger; (person, animal) dompter. 2. *vb. intr.* se tirer d'affaire; (m. to) réussir à.

management, *n.* direction *f.*, gestion *f.*

manager, *n.* directeur *m.;* (household) ménager *m.;* gérant *m.*

mandate, *n.* (politics) mandat *m.*

mandatory, *adj.* obligatoire.

mandolin, *n.* mandoline *f.*

mane, *n.* crinière *f.*

maneuver, *n.* manœuvre *f.*

manganese, *n.* manganèse *m.*

manger, *n.* mangeoire *f.*

mangle, *vb.* mutiler.

manhood, *n.* virilité *f.*

mania, *n.* (craze) manie *f.;* (madness) folie *f.*

maniac, *adj. and n.* fou *m.*, folle *f.*

manic-depressive, *n. and adj.* maniaco-dépressif *m.*

manicure, *n.* (person) manucure *m.f.;* (care of hands) soin *(m.)* des mains.

manifest, 1. *adj.* manifeste. 2. *vb.* manifester.

manifesto, *n.* manifeste *m.*

manifold, *adj.* (varied) divers; (numerous) nombreux.

manipulate, *vb.* manipuler.

mankind, *n.* genre *(m.)* humain.

manly, *adj.* viril.

man-made, *adj.* artificiel.

manner, *n.* manière *f.;* (customs) mœurs *f.pl.*

mannerism, *n.* maniérisme *m.*, affectation *f.*

manor, *n.* manoir *m.*

manpower, *n.* main-d'œuvre *f.*

mansion, *n.* (country) château *m.;* (town) hôtel *m.*

manslaughter, *n.* homicide involontaire *m.*

mantel, *n.* (framework) manteau *m.;* (shelf) tablette *f.*

mantle, *n.* manteau *m.*

manual, *adj. and n.* manuel *m.*

manufacture, 1. *n.* manufacture *f.;* (product) produit *(m.)* manufacturé. **2.** *vb.* fabriquer.

manufacturer, *n.* fabricant *m.*

manure, *n.* fumier *m.*

manuscript, *adj. and n.* manuscrit *m.*

many, 1. *adj.* beaucoup de, un grand nombre de; (**too m.**) trop de; (**so m.**) tant de; (**how m.**) combien de. **2.** *pron.* beaucoup.

map, *n.* carte *(f.)* géographique.

maple, *n.* érable *m.*

mar, *vb.* gâter.

marble, *n.* marbre *m.*

march, 1. *n.* marche *f.* **2.** *vb.* marcher.

March, *n.* mars *m.*

mare, *n.* jument *f.*

margarine, *n.* margarine *f.*

margin, *n.* marge *f.*

marijuana, *n.* marijuana *f.;* marie-jeanne *f.*

marinate, *vb.* faire mariner.

marine, 1. *n.* (ships) marine *f.;* (soldier) fusilier *(m.)* marin. **2.** *adj.* marin; (insurance) maritime.

mariner, *n.* marin *m.*

marionette, *n.* marionnette *f.*

marital, *adj.* conjugal.

maritime, *adj.* maritime.

marjoram, *n.* marjolaine *f.*

mark, 1. *n.* marque *f.;* (target) but *m.;* (school) point *m.* **2.** *vb.* marquer.

market, 1. *n.* marché *m.* **2.** *vb.* commercialiser.

marketing, *n.* marketing *m.*

market place, *n.* place *(f.)* du marché.

market research, *n.* étude *(f.)* de marché.

marmalade, *n.* confiture *f.*

maroon, 1. *adj. and n.* rouge *(m.)* foncé. **2.** *vb.* abandonner (dans une île déserte).

marquee, *n.* (tente) marquise *f.*

marquis, *n.* marquis *m.*

marriage, *n.* mariage *m.*

married, *adj.* marié.

marrow, *n.* moelle *f.*

marry, *vb.* épouser; se marier (avec).

marsh, *n.* marais *m.*

marshal, *n.* maréchal *m.*

marshmallow, *n.* guimauve (plant) *f.*

martial, *adj.* martial.

martinet, *n.* officier *(m.)* strict sur la discipline.

martyr, *n.* martyr *m.*

martyrdom, *n.* martyre *m.*

marvel, 1. *n.* merveille *f.* **2.** *vb.* (**m. at**) s'étonner de.

marvelous, *adj.* merveilleux.

Marxist, *n. and adj.* marxiste *m.f.*

mascara, *n.* mascara *m.*

mascot, *n.* mascotte *f.*

masculine, *adj.* masculin.

mash, *n.* (food) purée *f.*

mask, 1. *n.* masque *m.* **2.** *vb.* masquer.

masochist, *n.* masochiste *m.f.*

mason, *n.* maçon *m.*

masquerade, *n.* mascarade *f.,* bal masqué *m.*

mass, *n.* masse *f.*

Mass, *n.* messe *f.*

massacre, 1. *n.* massacre *m.* **2.** *vb.* massacrer.

massage, *n.* massage *m.*

masseur, *n.* masseur *m.*

massive, *adj.* massif.

mass media, *n.* mass-media *m.pl.*

mass meeting, *n.* réunion *f.*

mass production, *n.* fabrication *(f.)* en série.

mast, *n.* mât *m.*

master, 1. *n.* maître *m.* **2.** *vb.* maîtriser.

masterpiece, *n.* chef-d'œuvre *m.*

mastery, *n.* maîtrise *f.*

masticate, *vb.* mâcher.

mat, *n.* (door) paillasson *m.*

match, 1. *n.* (for fire) allumette *f.;* (equal) égal *m.;* (marriage) mariage *m.;* (person to marry)

parti *m.;* (sport) partie *f.* **2.** *vb.* assortir, *tr.*

match box, *n.* boîte *(f.)* d'allumettes.

mate, 1. *n..* (fellow-worker) camarade *m.f.;* (of pair) compagnon *m.;* compagne *f.;* (boat) officier *m.* **2.** *vb.* s'accoupler.

material, 1. *n.* matière *f.;* (cloth) étoffe *f.* **2.** *adj.* matériel.

materialism, *n.* matérialisme *m.*

materialize, *vb.* matérialiser, *tr.;* se réaliser, *intr.*

maternal, *adj.* maternel.

maternity, *n.* maternité *f.*

math, *n.* maths *f.pl.*

mathematical, *adj.* mathématique.

mathematics, *n.* mathématiques *f.pl.*

matinee, *n.* matinée *f.*

mating, *n.* accouplement *m.*

mating season, *n.* saison *(f.)* des amours.

matriarch, *n.* femme *(f.)* qui porte les chausses.

matrimony, *n.* mariage *m.*

matrix, *n.* matrice *f.*

matron, *n.* (institution) intendante *f.*

matter, 1. *n.* (substance) matière *f.;* (subject) sujet *m.;* (question, business) affaire *f.;* (**what is the m.?**) qu'est-ce qu'il y a? **2.** *vb.* importer.

mattress, *n.* matelas *m.*

mature, 1. *adj.* mûr. **2.** *vb.* mûrir.

maturity, *n.* maturité *f.;* (comm.) échéance *f.*

maudlin, *adj.* larmoyant.

mausoleum, *n.* mausolée *m.*

maxim, *n.* maxime *f.*

maximum, *n.* maximum *m.*

may, *vb.* pouvoir.

May, *n.* mai *m.*

maybe, *adv.* peut-être.

mayhem, *n.* mutilation *f.*

mayonnaise, *n.* mayonnaise *f.*

mayor, *n.* maire *m.*

maze, *n.* labyrinthe *m.*

me, *pron.* (unstressed direct and indirect) me; (alone, stressed, with *prep.*) moi.

meadow, *n.* (small) pré *m.;* (large) prairie *f.*

meager, *adj.* maigre.

meal, *n.* (repast) repas *m.;* (grain) farine *f.*

mean, **1.** *n.* *(math.)* moyenne *f.;* **(m.s,** financial) moyens *m.pl.;* (m.s, way to do) moyen *m.* **2.** *adj.* humble; (stingy) avare; (contemptible) méprisable. **3.** *vb.* (signify) vouloir dire; (purpose) se proposer (de); (destine) destiner (à).

meaning, *n.* sens *m.*

meaningful, *adj.* significatif.

meanness, *n.* méchanceté *f.*

meantime, meanwhile, *adv.* sur ces entrefaites.

measles, *n.* rougeole *f.*

measure, **1.** *n.* mesure *f.* **2.** *vb.* mesurer.

measurement, *n.* mesurage *m.*

meat, *n.* viande *f.*

mechanic, *n.* mécanicien *m.;* (auto) garagiste *m.*

mechanical, **1.** *adj.* mécanique. **2.** *(fig.)* machinal.

mechanism, *n.* mécanisme *m.*

mechanize, *vb.* mécaniser.

medal, *n.* médaille *f.*

meddle, *vb.* se mêler (de).

media, *n.* media *m.pl.*

median, *n.* médian.

mediate, *vb.* agir en médiateur.

medical, *adj.* médical.

medicate, *vb.* médicamenter.

medication, *n.* médicament *m.*

medicine, *n.* médecine *f.*

medieval, *adj.* médiéval.

mediocre, *adj.* médiocre.

mediocrity, *n.* médiocrité *f.*

meditate, *vb.* méditer.

meditation, *n.* méditation *f.*

Mediterranean, **1.** *adj.* méditerranéen. **2.** *n.* (M. Sea) Méditerranée *f.*

medium, **1.** *n.* milieu *m.;* (agent) intermédiaire *m.;*

(psychic person) médium *m.* **2.** *adj.* moyen.

medley, *n.* mélange *m.*

meek, *adj.* doux *m.,* douce *f.*

meekness, *n.* douceur *f.*

meet, *vb.* rencontrer, *tr.;* (become acquainted with) faire la connaissance de; (expenses) faire face à.

meeting, *n.* réunion *f.*

megabyte, *n.* méga-octet *m.*

megahertz, *n.* mégahertz *m.*

megaphone, *n.* mégaphone *m.*

melancholic, *adj.* mélancolique.

melancholy, *n.* mélancolie *f.*

mellow, *adj.* moelleux.

melodious, *adj.* mélodieux.

melodrama, *n.* mélodrame *m.*

melody, *n.* mélodie *f.*

melon, *n.* melon *m.*

melt, *vb.* fondre.

meltdown, *n.* fusion *f.*

member, *n.* membre *m.*

membership, *n.* adhésion *f.*

membrane, *n.* membrane *f.*

memento, *n.* mémento *m.*

memo, *n.* note *f.*

memoir, *n.* mémoire *m.*

memorable, *adj.* mémorable.

memorandum, *n.* mémorandum *m.*

memorial, **1.** *n.* souvenir *m.,* monument *m.* **2.** *adj.* commémoratif.

memorize, *vb.* apprendre par cœur.

memory, *n.* mémoire *f.*

menace, **1.** *n.* menace *f.* **2.** *vb.* menacer.

menagerie, *n.* ménagerie *f.*

mend, *vb.* (clothes) raccommoder; (correct) corriger.

mendacious, *adj.* menteur.

mendicant, *n. and adj.* mendiant *m.*

menial, *adj.* servile.

meningitis, *n.* méningite *f.*

menstruation, *n.* menstruation *f.*

menswear, *n.* habillements masculins *m.pl.*

mental, *adj.* mental.

mentality, *n.* mentalité *f.*

menthol, *n.* menthol *m.*

mention, **1.** *n.* mention *f.* **2.** *vb.* mentionner; (don't m. it) il n'y a pas de quoi.

menu, *n.* menu *m.*

mercantile, *adj.* mercantile.

mercenary, *adj. and n.* mercenaire *m.*

merchandise, *n.* marchandise(s) *f.(pl.).*

merchant, **1.** *n.* négociant *m.* **2.** *adj.* marchand.

merchant marine, *n.* marine marchande *f.*

merciful, *adj.* miséricordieux.

merciless, *adj.* impitoyable.

mercury, *n.* mercure *m.*

mercy, *n.* miséricorde *f.;* (at the m. of) à la merci de.

mere, *adj.* simple.

merely, *adv.* simplement.

merge, *vb.* fusionner.

merger, *n.* fusion *f.*

merit, **1.** *n.* mérite *m.* **2.** *vb.* mériter.

meritorious, *adj.* (person) méritant; (deed) méritoire.

mermaid, *n.* sirène *f.*

merriment, *n.* gaieté *f.*

merry, *adj.* gai.

merry-go-round, *n.* carrousel *m.*

mesh, *n.* maille *f.*

mesmerize, *n.* magnétiser.

mess, **1.** *n.* (muddle) fouillis *m.;* gâchis *m.;* *(mil.)* popote *f.* **2.** *vb.* gâcher.

message, *n.* message *m.*

messenger, *n.* messager *m.,* coursier *m.*

messy, *adj.* (dirty) malpropre.

metabolism, *n.* métabolisme *m.*

metal, *n.* métal *m.*

metallic, *adj.* métallique.

metamorphosis, *n.* métamorphose *f.*

metaphor, *n.* métaphore *f.*

metaphysics, *n.* métaphysique *f.*

meteor, *n.* météore *m.*

meteorology, *n.* météorologie *f.*

meter, **1.** *n.* (measure) mètre *m.;* (device) compteur *m.*

method, *n.* méthode *f.*

meticulous, *adj.* méticuleux.

metric, *n.* métrique.

metropolis, *n.* métropole *f.*

metropolitan, *adj.* métropolitain.

mettle, *n.* ardeur *f.*

Mexican, 1. *n.* Mexicain *m.* 2. *adj.* mexicain.

Mexico, *n.* Mexique *m.*

mezzanine, *n.* mezzanine *f.*

microbe, *n.* microbe *m.*

microchip, *n.* microplaquette *f.*, puce *f.*

microcomputer, *n.* micro-ordinateur *m.*

microcosm, *n.* microcosme *m.*

microfiche, *n.* microfiche *f.*

microfilm, *n.* microfilm *m.*

microform, *n.* microforme *f.*

microphone, *n.* microphone *m.*

microscope, *n.* microscope *m.*

microscopic, *adj.* microscopique.

microwave, *n.* micro-onde *f.*; (m. oven) four *(m.)* à micro-ondes.

mid, *adj.* mi-.

middle, 1. *n.* milieu *m.* 2. *adj.* du milieu.

middle-aged, *adj.* d'un certain âge.

Middle Ages, *n.* moyen âge *m.*

middle class, *n.* classe moyenne *f.*, bourgeoisie *f.*

Middle East, *n.* Moyen Orient *m.*

midget, *n.* nain *m.*

midnight, *n.* minuit *m.*

midriff, *n.* diaphragme *m.*

midwife, *n.* sage-femme *f.*

mien, *n.* mine *f.*, air *m.*

might, *n.* puissance *f.*

mighty, *adj.* puissant.

migraine, *n.* migraine *f.*

migrate, *vb.* émigrer.

migration, *n.* migration *f.*

mike, *n.* (colloquial) micro *m.*

mild, *adj.* doux *m.*, douce *f.*

mildew, *n.* rouille *f.*

mile, *n.* mille *m.*

mileage, *n.* kilométrage *m.*

milestone, *n.* borne routière *f.*

militarism, *n.* militarisme *m.*

military, *adj.* militaire.

militia, *n.* milice *f.*

milk, *n.* lait *m.*

milkman, *n.* laitier *m.*

milky, *adj.* laiteux.

mill, 1. *n.* (grinding) moulin *m.*; (spinning) filature *f.*; (factory) usine *f.* 2. *vb.* (grind) moudre; (crowd) fourmiller.

millennium, *n.* millénaire *m.*

miller, *n.* meunier *m.*

millimeter, *n.* millimètre *m.*

milliner, *n.* modiste *f.*

millinery, *n.* modes *f.pl.*

million, *n.* million *m.*

millionaire, *adj. and n.* millionnaire *m.f.*

mimic, 1. *n.* mime *m.* 2. *adj.* mimique. 3. *vb.* imiter.

mince, *vb.* (chop) hacher.

mind, 1. *n.* esprit *m.*; (opinion) avis *m.*; (desire) envie *f.* 2. *vb.* (heed) faire attention à; (listen to) écouter; (apply oneself to) s'occuper de; (take care) prendre garde; (look after) garder; (never m.) n'importe.

mindful, *adj.* attentif.

mine, 1. *n.* mine *f.* 2. *pron.* le mien *m.*, la mienne *f.*, les miens *m.pl.*, les miennes *f.pl.*

mine field, *n.* champ *(m.)* de mines.

miner, *n.* mineur *m.*

mineral, *adj. and n.* minéral *m.*

mine sweeper, *n.* dragueur *(m.)* de mines.

mingle, *vb.* mêler, *tr.*

miniature, *n.* miniature *f.*

miniaturize, *vb.* miniaturiser.

minimize, *vb.* réduire au minimum.

minimum, *n.* minimum *m.*

minimum wage, *n.* salaire minimum *m.*

mining, *n.* exploitation minière *f.*, pose de mines *f.*

minister, *n.* ministre *m.*

ministry, *n.* ministère *m.*

mink, *n.* vison *m.*

minnow, *n.* vairon *m.*

minor, *adj. and n.* mineur *m.*

minority, *n.* minorité *f.*

minstrel, *n.* ménestrel *m.*

mint, *n.* (plant) menthe *f.*; (place) Hôtel *(m.)* de la Monnaie.

minus, *prep.* moins.

minute, 1. *n.* minute *f.*; (of meeting) procès-verbal *m.* 2. *adj.* (very small) minuscule; (detailed) minutieux.

miracle, *n.* miracle *m.*

miraculous, *adj.* miraculeux.

mirage, *n.* mirage *m.*

mire, *n.* boue *f.*, bourbier *m.*

mirror, *n.* miroir *m.*

mirth, *n.* gaieté *f.*

misadventure, *n.* mésaventure *f.*, contretemps *m.*

misappropriate, *vb.* détourner, dépréder.

misbehave, *vb.* se conduire mal.

miscellaneous, *adj.* divers.

mischief, *n.* (harm) mal *m.*; (mischievousness) malice *f.*

mischievous, *adj.* espiègle; (wicked) méchant.

misconstrue, *vb.* mal interpréter, tourner en mal.

misdemeanor, *n.* délit *m.*

miser, *n.* avare *m.f.*

miserable, *adj.* (unhappy) malheureux; (wretched) misérable.

miserly, *adj.* avare.

misery, *n.* (affliction) souffrance(s) *f.(pl.)*; (poverty) misère *f.*

misfit, *n.* vêtement manqué *m.*; inadapté *m.*, inapte *m.*

misfortune, *n.* malheur *m.*

misgiving, *n.* doute *m.*

mishap, *n.* mésaventure *f.*

mislead, *vb.* tromper, égarer.

misplace, *vb.* mal placer.

misprint, *n.* faute *(f.)* d'impression.

mispronounce, *vb.* mal prononcer, estropier.

miss, *vb.* manquer; (I m. you) vous me manquez.

miss, *n.* mademoiselle *f.*

missile, *n.* projectile *m.*

missing, *adj.* (thing) qui manque; (person) disparu.

mission, *n.* mission *f.*

missionary, *adj. and n.* missionnaire *m.f.*

misspell, *vb.* mal orthographier.

mist, *n.* brume *f.*

mistake, 1. *n.* erreur *f.* **2.** *vb.* (misunderstand) comprendre mal; (make a mistake) se tromper (de).

mister, *n.* monsieur *m.*

mistletoe, *n.* gui *m.*

mistreat, *vb.* maltraiter.

mistress, *n.* maîtresse *f.*

mistrust, 1. *n.* méfiance *f.* **2.** *vb.* se méfier de.

misty, *adj.* brumeux.

misunderstand, *vb.* mal comprendre.

misuse, *vb.* (misapply) faire mauvais usage (de); (maltreat) maltraiter.

mite, *n.* denier *m.,* obole *f.*

mitigate, *vb.* atténuer.

mitten, *n.* moufle *f.*

mix, *vb.* mêler, *tr.*

mixture, *n.* mélange *m.*

mix-up, *n.* embrouillement *m.*

moan, 1. *n.* gémissement *m.* **2.** *vb.* gémir.

moat, *n.* fossé *m.*

mob, 1. *n.* foule *f.*; (pejorative) populace *f.* **2.** *vb.* assaillir.

mobile, *adj.* mobile.

mobile phone, *n.* téléphone *(m.)* portatif.

mobilization, *n.* mobilisation *f.*

mobilize, *vb.* mobiliser.

mock, *vb.* **(m. at)** se moquer de; (imitate) singer.

mockery, *n.* moquerie *f.*

mod, *adj.* à la mode.

mode, *n.* mode *m.*

model, *n.* modèle *m.*

modem, *n.* modem *m.*

moderate, 1. *adj.* modéré. **2.** *vb.* modérer.

moderation, *n.* modération *f.*

modern, *adj.* moderne.

modernize, *vb.* moderniser.

modest, *adj.* modeste.

modesty, *n.* modestie *f.*

modify, *vb.* modifier.

modish, *adj.* à la mode.

modulate, *vb.* moduler.

module, *n.* module *m.*

moist, *adj.* moite.

moisten, *vb.* humecter.

moisture, *n.* humidité *f.*

molar, *n. and adj.* molaire *f.*

molasses, *n.* mélasse *f.*

mold, 1. *n.* (casting) moule *m.*; (mildew) moisissure *f.* **2.** *vb.* (shape) mouler; (get moldy) moisir.

moldy, *adj.* moisi.

mole, *n.* (animal) taupe *f.*; (spot) grain *(m.)* de beauté.

molecule, *n.* molécule *f.*

molest, *vb.* molester.

mollify, *vb.* adoucir, apaiser.

molten, *adj.* fondu, coulé.

moment, *n.* moment *m.*

momentary, *adj.* momentané.

momentous, *adj.* important.

mommy, *n.* maman *f.*

Monaco, *n.* Monaco *f.*

monarch, *n.* monarque *m.*

monarchy, *n.* monarchie *f.*

monastery, *n.* monastère *m.*

Monday, *n.* lundi *m.*

monetary, *adj.* monétaire.

money, *n.* argent *m.*; (comm.) monnaie *f.*

money order, *n.* mandat *m.*

mongrel, *n.* métis *m.*

monitor, *n.* moniteur *m.*

monk, *n.* moine *m.*

monkey, *n.* singe *m.*

monologue, *n.* monologue *m.*

monoplane, *n.* monoplan *m.*

monopolize, *vb.* monopoliser.

monopoly, *n.* monopole *m.*

monosyllable, *n.* monosyllabe *m.*

monotone, *n.* monotone *m.*

monotonous, *adj.* monotone.

monotony, *n.* monotonie *f.*

monsoon, *n.* mousson *f.*

monster, *n.* monstre *m.*

monstrosity, *n.* monstruosité *f.*

monstrous, *adj.* monstrueux.

month, *n.* mois *m.*

monthly, *adj.* mensuel.

monument, *n.* monument *m.*

monumental, *adj.* monumental.

mood, *n.* humeur *f.*; (gramm.) mode *m.*

moody, *adj.* de mauvaise humeur.

moon, *n.* lune *f.*

moonlight, 1. *n.* clair *(m.)* de lune. **2.** *vb.* travailler au noir.

moor, *n.* lande *f.*

mooring, *n.* amarrage *m.*

moot, *adj.* discutable.

mop, *n.* balai *(m.)* à laver.

mope, *vb.* bouder.

moped, *n.* cyclomoteur *m.*

moral, 1. *n.* morale *f.*; **(m.s)** moralité *f.* **2.** *adj.* moral.

morale, *n.* moral *m.*

moralist, *n.* moraliste *m.f.*

morality, *n.* moralité *f.*; (ethics) morale *f.*

morally, *adv.* moralement.

morbid, *adj.* morbide.

more, z1. *pron.* en . . . davantage. **2.** *adj. and adv.* plus; **(m. than)** plus de; (no m.) ne . . . plus.

moreover, *adv.* de plus.

mores, *n.* mœurs *f.pl.*

morgue, *n.* morgue *f.*

morning, *n.* matin *m.*; (length of m.) matinée *f.*; **(good m.)** bonjour.

Morocco, *n.* Maroc *m.*

moron, *n.* idiot *m.*

morose, *adj.* morose.

morphine, *n.* morphine *f.*

Morse code, *n.* l'alphabet Morse *m.*

morsel, *n.* morceau *m.*

mortal, *adj. and n.* mortel *m.*

mortality, *n.* mortalité *f.*

mortar, *n.* mortier *m.*

mortgage, 1. *n.* hypothèque *f.* **2.** *vb.* hypothéquer.

mortician, *n.* entrepreneur *(m.)* de pompes funèbres.

mortify, *vb.* mortifier.

mortuary, *adj.* mortuaire.

mosaic, 1. *n.* mosaïque *f.* **2.** *adj.* en mosaïque.

Moscow, *n.* Moscou *m.*

Moslem, *adj. and n.* musulman *m.*

mosque, *n.* mosquée *f.*

mosquito, *n.* moustique *m.*

moss, *n.* mousse *f.*

most, 1. *n.* le plus. **2.** *adj.* le plus (de); la plupart (de).

3. *adv.* (with adj. and vb.) le plus; (intensive) très.

mostly, *adv.* pour la plupart; (time) la plupart du temps.

moth, *n.* papillon *(m.)* de nuit; (clothes) mite *f.*

mother, *n.* mère *f.*

mother-in-law, *n.* belle-mère *f.*

mother-of-pearl, *n.* nacre *f.*

mother tongue, *n.* langue *(f.)* maternelle.

motif, *n.* motif *m.*

motion, *n.* mouvement *m.;* (gesture) signe *m.;* (proposal) motion *f.*

motionless, *adj.* immobile.

motion-picture, *n.* film *m.*

motivate, *vb.* motiver.

motive, *n.* motif *m.*

motley, 1. *adj.* bigarré. **2.** *n.* livrée de bouffon *m.*

motor, *n.* moteur *m.*

motorboat, *n.* canot *(m.)* automobile.

motorcycle, *n.* motocyclette *f.*

motorist, *n.* automobiliste *m.*

motto, *n.* devise *f.*

mound, *n.* tertre *m.*

mount, 1. *n.* (hill) mont *m.;* (horse, structure) monture *f.* **2.** *vb.* monter.

mountain, *n.* montagne *f.*

mountain bike, *n.* vélo *(m.)* tout terrain, VTT *m.*

mountaineer, *n.* montagnard *m.*, alpiniste *m.*

mountainous, *adj.* montagneux.

mountebank, *n.* saltimbanque *m.*, charlatan *m.*

mourn, *vb.* pleurer.

mournful, *adj.* triste.

mourning, *n.* deuil *m.*

mouse, *n.* souris *f.*

mouth, *n.* bouche *f.*

mouthful, *n.* bouchée *f.*

mouthpiece, *n.* embouchure *f.*, embout *m.*

movable, *adj.* mobile.

move, *vb.* mouvoir, *tr.;* remuer; (stir) bouger; (af-fect with emotion) émouvoir; (change residence) déménager; (propose) proposer.

movement, *n.* mouvement *m.*

movie, *n.* film *m.*

movie camera, *n.* caméra *f.*

moving, 1. *n.* déménagement *m.* **2.** *adj.* touchant.

mow, *vb.* faucher; (lawn) tondre.

Mr., *n.* M. *m. (abbr.* for Monsieur).

Mrs., *n.* Mme. *f. (abbr.* for Madame).

much, *adj., pron. and adv.* beaucoup (de); **(too m.)** trop (de); **(so m.)** tant (de); **(how m.)** combien (de).

mucilage, *n.* mucilage *m.*

muck, *n.* fumier *m.*

mucous, *adj.* muqueux.

mud, *n.* boue *f.*

muddy, *adj.* boueux.

muff, *n.* manchon *m.*

muffin, *n.* petit pain *m.*

muffle, *vb.* emmitoufler.

mug, 1. *n.* gobelet *m.*, pot *m.*, chope *f.* **2.** *vb.* attaquer.

muggy, *adj.* lourd, moite.

mulatto, *n.* mulâtre *m.*

mule, *n.* mulet *m.*

mullah, *n.* mollah *m.*

multicolored, *adj.* multicolore.

multifarious, *adj.* divers.

multinational, *adj.* multinational.

multiple, *adj.* multiple.

multiplication, *n.* multiplication *f.*

multiplicity, *n.* multiplicité *f.*

multiply, *vb.* multiplier, *tr.*

multitude, *n.* multitude *f.*

mumble, *vb.* marmonner.

mummy, *n.* (embalmed) momie *f.;* maman *f.*

mumps, *n.* oreillons *m.pl.*

munch, *vb.* mâcher.

mundane, *adj.* banal.

municipal, *adj.* municipal.

munificent, *adj.* munificent.

munition, *n.* munition(s) *f.(pl.).*

mural, *n.* (painting) peinture *(f.)* murale.

murder, *n.* meurtre *m.*

murderer, *n.* meurtrier *m.*

murmur, 1. *n.* murmure *m.* **2.** *vb.* murmurer.

muscle, *n.* muscle *m.*

muscular, *adj.* musculaire; (strong) musculeux.

muse, 1. *n.* muse *f.* **2.** *vb.* méditer.

museum, *n.* musée *m.*

mushroom, *n.* champignon *m.*

music, *n.* musique *f.*

musical, *adj.* musical; (person) musicien.

musical comedy, *n.* comédie musicale *f.*

musician, *n.* musicien *m.*

Muslim, *adj. and n.* musulman *m.*

muslin, *n.* mousseline *f.*

mussel, *n.* moule *f.*

must, *vb.* devoir; falloir (used impersonally, il faut que).

mustache, *n.* moustache *f.*

mustard, *n.* moutarde *f.*

muster, *vb.* rassembler, *tr.*

musty, *adj.* moisi, suranné.

mutation, *n.* mutation *f.*

mute, *adj.* muet.

mutilate, *vb.* mutiler.

mutiny, *n.* mutinerie *f.*

mutter, *vb.* grommeler.

mutton, *n.* mouton *m.*

mutual, *adj.* mutuel.

muzzle, *n.* muselière *f.*

my, *adj.* mon *m.*, ma *f.*, mes *pl.*

myopia, *n.* myopie *f.*

myriad, *n.* myriade *f.*

myself, *pron.* moi-même; (reflexive) me.

mysterious, *adj.* mystérieux.

mystery, *n.* mystère *m.*

mystic, *adj.* mystique.

mystify, *vb.* mystifier.

myth, *n.* mythe *m.*

mythical, *adj.* mythique.

mythology, *n.* mythologie *f.*

N

nab *vb.* attraper, saisir.

nag, *vb.* gronder.

nail, 1. *n.* (person, animal) ongle *m.;* (metal) clou *m.;* (n. polish) vernis (*m.*) à ongles. **2.** *vb.* clouer.

naïve, *adj.* naïf *m.,* naïve *f.*

naked, *adj.* nu.

name, 1. *n.* nom *m.* **2.** *vb.* nommer.

namely, *adv.* à savoir.

namesake, *n.* homonyme *m.*

nanny, *n.* nounou *f.*

nap, *n.* petit somme *m.*

nape, *n.* nuque *f.*

napkin, *n.* serviette *f.*

narcissus, *n.* narcisse *m.*

narcotic, *adj. and n.* narcotique *m.*

narrate, *vb.* raconter.

narrative, *n.* récit *m.*

narrow, *adj.* étroit.

narrow-minded, *adj.* à l'esprit étroit.

nasal, *adj.* nasal.

nasty, *adj.* méchant.

natal, *adj.* natal.

nation, *n.* nation *f.*

national, *adj.* national.

nationalism, *n.* nationalisme *m.*

nationality, *n.* nationalité *f.*

nationalization, *n.* nationalisation *f.*

nationalize, *vb.* nationaliser.

nationwide, 1. *adj.* à l'échelle du pays entier. **2.** *adv.* à travers tout le pays.

native, 1. *n.*. autochtone *m.f.,* (non-European) indigène *m.f.* **2.** *adj.* natif; (place) natal; (language) maternel.

nativity, *n.* naissance *f.*

NATO, *n.* OTAN *f.*

natural, *adj.* naturel.

naturalist, *n.* naturaliste *m.f.*

naturalize, *vb.* naturaliser.

naturalness, *n.* naturel *m.*

nature, *n.* nature *f.*

naughty, *adj.* méchant.

nausea, *n.* nausée *f.*

nauseous, *adj.* nauséeux.

nautical, *adj.* marin.

naval, *adj.* naval.

nave, *n.* nef *f.*

navigable, *adj.* navigable.

navigate, *vb.* naviguer.

navigation, *n.* navigation *f.*

navigator, *n.* navigateur *m.*

navy, *n.* marine *f.*

navy yard, *n.* arsenal maritime *m.*

Nazi, *n.* Nazi *m.*

near, 1. *adj.* proche. **2.** *adv.* près. **3.** *prep.* près de.

nearly, *adv.* de près; (almost) presque.

near-sighted, *adj.* myope.

neat, *adj.* soigné, net.

neatness, *n.* propreté *f.*

nebula, *n.* nébuleuse *f.*

nebulous, *adj.* nébuleux.

necessary, *adj.* nécessaire.

necessity, *n.* nécessité *f.*

neck, 1. *n.*cou *m.* **2.** *vb.* se peloter.

necklace, *n.* collier *m.*

necktie, *n.* cravate *f.*

nectar, *n.* nectar *m.*

need, 1. *n.* besoin *m.* **2.** *vb.* avoir besoin de.

needful, *adj.* nécessaire.

needle, *n.* aiguille *f.*

needle point, *n.* pointe d'aiguille *f.*

needless, *adj.* inutile.

needy, *adj.* nécessiteux.

nefarious, *adj.* infâme.

negative, *adj.* négatif.

neglect, 1. *n.* négligence *f.* **2.** *vb.* négliger (de).

negligee, *n.* négligée *f.*

negligent, *adj.* négligent.

negligible, *adj.* négligeable.

negotiate, *vb.* négocier.

negotiation, *n.* négociation *f.*

Negro, *adj. and n.* nègre *m.*

neighbor, *n.* voisin *m.;* (fellow man) prochain *m.*

neighborhood, *n.* voisinage *m.*

neighborly, *adj.* amical.

neither, 1. *adj. and pron.* ni l'un ni l'autre. **2.** *adv.* non plus. **3.** *conj.* (n. ... nor) ni ... ni.

neon, *n.* néon *m.*

neophyte, *n.* néophyte *m.*

nephew, *n.* neveu *m.*

nepotism, *n.* népotisme *m.*

nerve, *n.* nerf *m.*

nerve-racking, *adj.* angoissant.

nervous, *adj.* nerveux.

nervous system, *n.* système nerveux *m.*

nest, *n.* nid *m.*

nestle, *vb.* se nicher.

net, 1. *n.* filet *m.* **2.** *adj.* net *m.,* nette *f.*

Netherlands, the, *n.* les Pays-Bas *m.pl.,* Hollande *f.*

network, *n.* réseau *m.*

neuralgia, *n.* névralgie *f.*

neurology, *n.* neurologie *f.*

neurotic, *adj. and n.* névrosé *m.*

neutral, *adj. and n.* neutre *m.*

neutron, *n.* neutron *m.*

neutron bomb, *n.* bombe (*f.*) à neutrons.

never, *adv.* jamais.

nevertheless, *adv.* néanmoins.

new, *adj.* nouveau *m.,* nouvelle *f.;* (not used) neuf *m.,* neuve *f.*

newborn, *adj.* nouveau né.

newlyweds, *n.* jeunes mariés *m.pl.*

news, *n.* (piece of news) nouvelle *f.*

newsboy, *n.* vendeur (*m.*) de journaux.

newscast, *n.* journal parlé *m.,* informations *f.pl.*

newscaster, *n.* présentateur *m.*

newspaper, *n.* journal *m.*

newsreel, *n.* film (*m.*) d'actualité.

newsstand, *n.* kiosque (*m.*) à journaux.

New Testament, *n.* le Nouveau Testament *m.*

new year, *n.* nouvel an *m.*

New Zealand, *n.* Nouvelle-Zélande *f.*

next, 1. *adj.* prochain. **2.** *adv.* ensuite. **3.** *prep.* auprès de.

nibble, *vb.* grignoter.

nice, *adj.* (person) gentil; (thing) joli.

niche, *n.* niche *f.*, *(fig.)*
place *f.*, situation *f.*

nick, *n.* entaille *f.*

nickel, *n.* nickel *m.*

nickname, *n.* surnom *m.*

nicotine, *n.* nicotine *f.*

niece, *n.* nièce *f.*

Nigeria, *n.* Nigéria *m.f.*

niggardly, *adj.* chiche.

night, *n.* nuit *f.;* (evening)
soir *m.*

nightclub, *n.* boîte *(f.)* de
nuit, établissement *(m.)*
de nuit.

nightgown, *n.* chemise *(f.)*
de nuit.

nightingale, *n.* rossignol *m.*

nightly, *adv.* tous les soirs;
toutes les nuits.

nightmare, *n.* cauchemar *m.*

night-school, *n.* cours *(m.)*
du soir.

nimble, *adj.* agile.

nine, *adj. and n.* neuf *m.*

nineteen, *adj. and n.* dix-
neuf *m.*

ninety, *adj. and n.* quatre-
vingt-dix *m.*

ninth, *adj. and n.* neuvième
m.f.

nip, **1.** *n..* pincement *m.*,
pinçade *f.* **2.** *vb.* pincer.

nipple, *n.* mamelon *m.*

nitrogen, *n.* nitrogène *m.*

no, **1.** *adj.* pas de. **2.** *interj.*,
adv. non.

nobility, *n.* noblesse *f.*

noble, *adj.* noble.

nobleman, *n.* gentilhomme
m.

nobly, *adv.* noblement.

nobody, *pron.* personne.

nocturnal, *adj.* nocturne.

nod, **1.** *n.* signe *(m.)* de la
tête. **2.** *vb.* incliner la tête.

node, *n.* nœud *m.*

no-frills, *adj.* simple.

noise, *n.* bruit *m.*

noiseless, *adj.* silencieux.

noisome, *adj.* puant, fétide.

noisy, *adj.* bruyant.

nomad, *n.* nomade *m.f.*

nominal, *adj.* nominal.

nominate, *vb.* (appoint) nommer; (propose) désigner.

nomination, *n.* (appointment) nomination *f.;*
(proposal) désignation *f.*

nominee, *n.* personne nom-
mée *f.*, candidat choisi *m.*

nonaligned, *adj.* (in politics) non-aligné.

nonchalant, *adj.* nonchalant.

noncombatant, *adj. and n.*
non-combattant *m.*

noncommissioned, *adj.* sans
brevet.

noncommittal, *adj.* qui
n'engage à rien.

nondescript, *adj.* indéfinissable.

none, *pron.* aucun.

nonentity, *n.* nullité *f.*

nonplussed, *adj.* perplexe.

non-proliferation, *n.* non-
prolifération *f.*

nonresident, *n. and adj.*
non-résident *m.*

nonsense, *n.* absurdité *f.*

non-smoker, *n.* non-fumeur
m.

nonstop, *adj.* sans arrêt.

noodles, *n.* nouilles *f.pl.*

nook, *n.* coin *m.*, recoin *m.*

noon, *n.* midi *m.*

noose, *n.* nœud coulant *m.*

nor, *conj.* ni; (and not) et ne
. . . pas.

norm, *n.* norme *f.*

normal, *adj.* normal.

normally, *adv.* normalement.

Normandy, *n.* Normandie *f.*

north, *n.* nord *m.*

North America, *n.*
Amérique *(f.)* du Nord.

northeast, *n.* nord-est *m.*

northern, *adj.* du nord.

North Pole, *n.* pôle nord *m.*

northwest, *n.* nord-ouest *m.*

Norway, *n.* Norvège *f.*

Norwegian, **1.** *n.* (person)
Norvégien *m.;* (lan-
guage) norvégien *m.* **2.**
adj. norvégien.

nose, *n.* nez *m.*

nosebleed, *n.* saignement
(m.) du nez.

nose dive, *n.* vol piqué *m.*

nostalgia, *n.* nostalgie *f.*

nostril, *n.* narine *f.;* (animals) naseau *m.*

nostrum, *n.* panacée *f.*,
remède *(m.)* de charla-
tan.

nosy, *adj.* curieux.

not, *adv.* (ne) pas.

notable, *adj. and n.* notable
m.

notary, *n.* notaire *m.*

notation, *n.* notation *f.*

note, **1.** *n.* note *f.;* (letter, finance) billet *m.;* (distinc-
tion) marque *f.* **2.** *vb.*
noter.

notebook, *n.* (small) carnet
m.; (large) cahier *m.*

noted, *adj.* célèbre.

notepaper, *n.* papier *(m.)* à
notes.

noteworthy, *adj.* remarquable, mémorable.

nothing, *pron.* rien.

notice, **1.** *n.* (announcement) avis *m.;* (atten-
tion) attention *f.;* (fore-
warning) préavis *m.* **2.**
vb. remarquer.

noticeable, *adj.* remarquable; apparent.

notification, *n.* notification *f.*

notify, *vb.* avertir.

notion, *n.* idée *f.*

notoriety, *n.* notoriété *f.*

notorious, *adj.* notoire.

notwithstanding, **1.** *adv.* tout
de même. **2.** *prep.* malgré.

noun, *n.* substantif *m.*

nourish, *vb.* nourrir.

nourishment, *n.* nourriture *f.*

novel, **1.** *n.* roman *m.* **2.** *adj.*
nouveau, original.

novelist, *n.* romancier *m.*

novelty, *n.* nouveauté *f.*

November, *n.* novembre *m.*

novice, *n.* novice *m.f.*

now, *adv.* maintenant; (**n.**
and then) de temps en
temps.

nowadays, *adv.* de nos jours.

nowhere, *adv.* nulle part.

nozzle, *n.* ajutage *m.*, jet *m.*

nuance, *n.* nuance *f.*

nuclear, *adj.* nucléaire.

nuclear physics, *n.*
physique nucléaire *f.*

nuclear warhead, *n.* cône
(m.) de charge nucléaire.

nuclear waste, *n.* déchets
nucléaires *m.pl.*

nucleus, *n.* noyau *m.*

nude, *adj. and n.* nu *m.*

nugget, *n.* pépite *f.*

nuisance, *n.* (thing) ennui
m.; (person) peste *f.*

nuke, 1. *n.* arme nucléaire *f.* **2.** *vb.* détruire avec des armes nucléaires.

nullify, *vb.* annuler, nullifier.

numb, 1. *adj.* engourdi. **2.** *vb.* engourdir.

number, 1. *n.* nombre *m.;* (in a series, street, etc.) numéro *m.* **2.** *vb.* compter, numéroter.

numeral, *n.* chiffre *m.*

numerical, *adj.* numérique.

numerous, *adj.* nombreux.

nun, *n.* religieuse *f.,* nonne *f.*

nuncio, *n.* nonce *m.*

nuptial, *adj.* nuptial.

nurse, 1. *n.* (hospital) infirmière *f.;* (wet-n.) nourrice *f.* **2.** *vb.* soigner; (suckle) allaiter.

nursery, *n.* (children) chambre (*f.*) des enfants; (plants) pépinière *f.*

nurture, 1. *n.* nourriture *f.* **2.** *vb.* nourrir, entretenir.

nut, 1. *n.* noix *f.;* (metal) écrou *m.* **2.** *adj.* (n.s) (colloquial) dingue.

nutcracker, *n.* casse-noix *m.*

nutmeg, *n.* muscade *f.*

nutrition, *n.* nutrition *f.*

nutritious, *adj.* nutritif.

nutshell, *n.* coquille (*f.*) de noix; (in a n.) en deux mots.

nylon, *n.* nylon *m.*

nymph, *n.* nymphe *f.*

O

oak *n.* chêne *m.*

oar, *n.* rame *f.*

oasis, *n.* oasis *f.*

oath, *n.* serment *m.;* (curse) juron *m.*

oatmeal, *n.* farine (*f.*) d'avoine.

oats, *n.* avoine *f.*

obdurate, *adj.* obstiné, têtu.

obedience, *n.* obéissance *f.*

obedient, *adj.* obéissant.

obeisance, *n.* salut *m.*

obelisk, *n.* obélisque *m.*

obese, *adj.* obèse.

obey, *vb.* obéir à.

obituary, *n.* nécrologe *m.*

object, 1. *n.* objet *m.* **2.** *vb.* objecter.

objection, *n.* objection *f.*

objectionable, *adj.* répréhensible.

objective, *adj. and n.* objectif *m.*

obligation, *n.* obligation *f.*

obligatory, *adj.* obligatoire.

oblige, *vb.* obliger.

oblivion, *n.* oubli *m.*

obnoxious, *adj.* odieux.

oboe, *n.* hautbois *m.*

obscene, *adj.* obscène.

obscure, *adj.* obscur.

obsequious, *adj.* obséquieux.

observance, *n.* observance *f.*

observation, *n.* observation *f.*

observe, *vb.* observer.

observer, *n.* observateur *m.*

obsess, *vb.* obséder.

obsession, *n.* obsession *f.*

obsolescence, *n.* vieillissement *m.*

obsolete, *adj.* désuet.

obstacle, *n.* obstacle *m.*

obstetrician, *n.* médecin-accoucheur *m.*

obstinate, *adj.* obstiné.

obstreperous, *adj.* tapageur.

obstruct, *vb.* obstruer.

obstruction, *n.* obstruction *f.*

obtain, *vb.* obtenir.

obtrude, *vb.* mettre en avant.

obtuse, *adj.* obtus.

obviate, *vb.* prévenir, éviter.

obvious, *adj.* évident.

occasion, *n.* occasion *f.*

occasional, *adj.* (not regular) de temps en temps.

occult, *adj.* occulte.

occupant, *n.* occupant *m.*

occupation, *n.* occupation *f.;* (vocation) métier *m.*

occupy, *vb.* occuper.

occur, *vb.* (happen) avoir lieu; (come to the mind) se présenter à l'esprit.

occurrence, *n.* occurrence *f.*

ocean, *n.* océan *m.*

o'clock, *see* clock.

octagon, *n.* octogone *m.*

octave, *n.* octave *f.*

October, *n.* octobre *m.*

octopus, *n.* poulpe *m.*

ocular, *adj.* oculaire.

oculist, *n.* oculiste *m.f.*

odd, *adj.* (not even) impair; (unmatched) dépareillé; (strange) bizarre.

oddity, *n.* singularité *f.*

odds, *n.* inégalité *f.,* (betting) cote *f.*

odious, *adj.* odieux.

odor, *n.* odeur *f.*

of, *prep.* de.

off, 1. *adv.* (away) à ... de distance; (cancelled) rompu. **2.** *prep.* de.

offend, *vb.* offenser; (o. against the law) enfreindre la loi.

offender, *n.* offenseur *m.;* (law) délinquant *m.*

offense, *n.* offense *f.;* (transgression) délit *m.*

offensive, 1. *n.* offensive *f.* **2.** *adj.* (mil., etc.) offensif; (word, etc.) offensant.

offer, 1. *n.* offre *f.* **2.** *vb.* offrir.

offering, *n.* offre *f.,* offrande *f.*

offhand, 1. *adj.* spontané. **2.** *adv.* sans préparation.

office, *n.* (service) office *m.;* (function) fonctions *f.pl.;* (room) bureau *m.*

officer, *n.* (mil.) officier *m.;* (public) fonctionnaire *m.*

official, *adj.* officiel.

officiate, *vb.* officier.

officious, *adj.* officieux.

off-line, *adj. and adv.* (computer) (en mode) autonome.

off-peak, *adj.* aux heures creuses.

offshore, 1. *adv.* vers le large. **2.** *adj.* du côté de la terre.

offspring, *n.* descendant *m.*

often, *adv.* souvent.

oil, *n.* huile *f.*

oilcloth, *n.* toile cirée *f.*

oily, *adj.* huileux.

ointment, *n.* onguent *m.*

okay, *interj.* très bien, d'accord.

old, *adj.* vieux (vieil) *m.,* vieille *f.;* **(how o. are you?)** quel âge avez-vous?

old-fashioned, *adj.* démodé.

Old Testament, *n.* l'Ancien Testament *m.*

olfactory, *adj.* olfactif.

oligarchy, *n.* oligarchie *f.*

olive, *n.* (tree) olivier *m.;* (fruit) olive *f.*

ombudsman, *n.* (in France) médiateur *m.;* (in Quebec) protecteur *(m.)* du citoyen.

omelet, *n.* omelette *f.*

omen, *n.* présage *m.*

ominous, *adj.* de mauvais augure.

omission, *n.* omission *f.*

omit, *vb.* omettre.

omnibus, *n.* omnibus *m.*

omnipotent, *adj.* omnipotent, tout-puissant.

on, *prep.* sur.

once, *adv.* une fois; (formerly) autrefois; **(at o.,** without delay) tout de suite; **(at o., at the same time)** à la fois.

one, **1.** *adj.* un; (only) seul. **2.** *n.* un *m.* **3.** *pron.* un; (indefinite subject) on, (indefinite object) vous; **(the o.)** celui; **(this o.)** celui-ci; **(that o.)** celui-là; **(which o.)** lequel.

oneself, *pron.* soi-même; (reflexive) se.

one-sided, *adj.* unilatéral.

one-way, *adj.* (street, traffic) à sens unique; non connecté.

onion, *n.* oignon *m.*

onionskin, *n.* pelure *(f.)* d'oignon, (paper) papier pelure *m.*

on-line, *adj. and adv.* en ligne; connecté.

only, **1.** *adj.* seul. **2.** *adv.* seulement.

onslaught, *n.* assaut *m.*

onward, *adj. and adv.* en avant.

opal, *n.* opale *f.*

opaque, *adj.* opaque.

OPEC, *n.* OPEP *f.*

open, **1.** *adj.* ouvert; **(o.-minded)** à l'esprit ouvert. **2.** *vb.* ouvrir.

opening, *n.* ouverture *f.*

opera, *n.* opéra *m.*

opera glasses, *n.* jumelles *f.pl.*

operate, *vb.* opérer; (put into operation) actionner.

operatic, *adj.* d'opéra.

operation, *n.* opération *f.;* (functioning) fonctionnement *m.*

operator, *n.* opérateur *m.;* (switchboard) standardiste *m.f.*

operetta, *n.* opérette *f.*

opinion, *n.* opinion *f.*

opponent, *n.* adversaire *m.f.*

opportunism, *n.* opportunisme *m.*

opportunity, *n.* occasion *f.*

oppose, *vb.* (put in opposition) opposer; (resist) s'opposer à.

opposite, **1.** *adj.* opposé. **2.** *adv.* vis-à-vis. **3.** *prep.* en face de.

opposition, *n.* opposition *f.*

oppress, *vb.* opprimer.

oppression, *n.* oppression *f.*

oppressive, *adj.* oppressif; (heat, etc.) accablant.

opt, *vb.* **(o. for)** opter pour; **(o. out of)** refuser de participer à.

optic, *adj.* optique.

optician, *n.* opticien *m.*

optimism, *n.* optimisme *m.*

optimistic, *adj.* optimiste.

option, *n.* option *f.*

optional, *adj.* facultatif.

optometry, *n.* optométrie *f.*

opulent, *adj.* opulent, riche.

or, *conj.* ou; (with negative) ni.

oracle, *n.* oracle *m.*

oral, *adj.* oral.

orange, *n.* orange *f.*

orangeade, *n.* orangeade *f.*

oration, *n.* discours *m.*

orator, *n.* orateur *m.*

oratory, *n.* art *(m.)* oratoire.

orbit, *n.* orbite *f.*

orchard, *n.* verger *m.*

orchestra, *n.* orchestre *m.*

orchid, *n.* orchidée *f.*

ordain, *vb.* ordonner.

ordeal, *n.* épreuve *f.*

order, **1.** *n.* ordre *m.;* (comm.) commande *f.* **2.** *vb.* ordonner; (comm.) commander.

orderly, *adj.* ordonné.

ordinance, *n.* ordonnance *f.*

ordinary, *adj. and n.* ordinaire *m.*

ordination, *n.* ordination *f.*

ore, *n.* minerai *m.*

organ, *n.* (music) orgue *m.;* (body) organe *m.*

organdy, *n.* organdi *m.*

organic, *adj.* organique.

organism, *n.* organisme *m.*

organist, *n.* organiste *m.f.*

organization, *n.* organisation *f.;* (group) organisme *m.*

organize, *vb.* organiser.

orgasm, *n.* orgasme *m.*

orgy, *n.* orgie *f.*

orient, *vb.* orienter.

Orient, *n.* Orient *m.*

Oriental, **1.** *n.* Oriental *m.* **2.** *adj.* oriental.

orientation, *n.* orientation *f.*

orifice, *n.* orifice *m.*

origin, *n.* origine *f.*

original, *adj.* (new, unique) original; (from the origin) originel.

originality, *n.* originalité *f.*

originate from, *vb.* provenir de.

ornament, *n.* ornement *m.*

ornamental, *adj.* ornemental.

ornate, *adj.* orné.

ornithology, *n.* ornithologie *f.*

orphan, *n.* orphelin *m.*

orphanage, *n.* orphelinat *m.*

orthodox, *adj.* orthodoxe.

orthopedics, *n.* orthopédie *f.*

osmosis, *n.* osmose *f.*

ostensible, *adj.* prétendu.

ostentation, *n.* ostentation *f.*

ostentatious, *adj.* plein d'ostentation, ostentatoire.

osteopath, *n.* ostéopathe *m.f.*

ostracize, *vb.* ostraciser.

ostrich, *n.* autruche *f.*

other, *adj. and pron.* autre.

otherwise, *adv.* autrement.

ought, *vb.* devoir.

ounce, *n.* once *f.*

our, *adj.* notre *sg.,* nos *pl.*

ours, *pron.* le nôtre.

ourself, *pron.* nous-même; (reflexive) nous.

oust, *vb.* évincer.

ouster, *n.* éviction *f.*

out, *adv.* dehors.

outbreak, *n.* (beginning) commencement *m.;* (insurrection) révolte *f.,* éruption *f.*

outburst, *n.* éruption *f.*

outcast, *n.* paria *m.*

outcome, *n.* résultat *m.*

outdated, *adj.* suranné.

outdoors, *adv.* dehors.

outer, *adj.* extérieur.

outfit, *n.* équipement *m.;* (clothes) tenue *f.*

outgrow, *vb.* devenir trop grand pour.

outgrowth, *n.* conséquence *f.*

outing, *n.* promenade *f.*

outlandish, *adj.* bizarre.

outlaw, 1. *vb.* proscrire. **2.** *n.* hors-la-loi *m.*

outlet, *n.* issue *f.;* prise (*f.*) de courant.

outline, 1. *n.* contour *m.;* (general idea) aperçu *m.* **2.** *vb.* (drawing) tracer; (plan) exposer à grands traits.

out of, *prep.* hors de; (because of) par; (without) sans.

out-of-date, *adj.* suranné.

output, *n.* rendement *m.*

outrage, *n.* outrage *m.*

outrageous, *adj.* outrageant.

outrank, *vb.* occuper un rang supérieur.

outright, *adv.* complètement.

outrun, *vb.* dépasser.

outset, *n.* début *m.*

outside, 1. *adv.* dehors. **2.** *prep.* en dehors de.

outsider, *n.* étranger *m.*

outskirts, *n.* limites *f.pl.*

outstanding, *adj.* exceptionnel; non réglé.

outward, *adj.* extérieur.

oval, *adj.* and *n.* ovale *m.*

ovary, *n.* ovaire *m.*

ovation, *n.* ovation *f.*

oven, *n.* four *m.*

over, 1. *prep.* (on) sur; (above) au-dessus de; (beyond) au delà de; (more than) plus de. **2.** *adv.* (all o.) partout; (more) davantage; (finished) fini; (with adj.) trop.

overbearing, *adj.* arrogant.

overcast, *adj.* (weather) couvert.

overcoat, *n.* pardessus *m.*

overcome, *vb.* vaincre; (be o. by) succomber à.

overdose, *n.* dose (*f.*) excessive, overdose *f.*

overdue, *adj.* arriéré, échu.

overflow, *vb.* déborder.

overhaul, *vb.* examiner en détail, remettre au point.

overhead, 1. *adj.* (comm.) général. **2.** *adv.* en haut.

overkill, *n.* exagération rhétorique *f.*

overlook, *vb.* (look onto) avoir vue sur; (neglect) négliger.

overnight, *adv.* pendant la nuit.

overpower, *vb.* (subdue) subjuguer; (crush) accabler.

overrule, *vb.* décider contre.

overrun, *vb.* envahir.

overseas, *adv.* outre-mer, à l'étranger.

oversee, *vb.* surveiller.

oversight, *n.* inadvertance *f.*

overstuffed, *adj.* rembourré.

overt, *adj.* manifeste.

overtake, *vb.* rattraper; (accident, etc.) arriver à.

overthrow, *vb.* renverser.

overtime, *n.* heures (*f.pl.*) supplémentaires.

overture, *n.* ouverture *f.*

overturn, *vb.* renverser, *tr.*

overview, *n.* vue d'ensemble *f.*

overweight, *n.* excédent *m.*

overwhelm, *vb.* accabler (de).

overwork, *vb.* surmener, *tr.*

owe, *vb.* devoir.

owing, 1. *prep.* à cause de, en raison de. **2.** *adj.* dû.

owl, *n.* hibou *m.*

own, 1. *adj.* propre. **2.** *vb.* posséder; (admit) avouer; (acknowledge) reconnaître.

owner, *n.* propriétaire *m.f.*

ox, *n.* bœuf *m.*

oxygen, *n.* oxygène *m.*

oxygen mask, *n.* masque (*m.*) d'oxygène.

oyster, *n.* huître *f.*

ozone, *n.* ozone *m.;* (o. hole) trou (*m.*) d'ozone; (o. layer) couche (*f.*) d'ozone.

P

pace, 1. *n.* (step) pas *m.;* (gait) allure *f.* **2.** *vb.* arpenter.

pacemaker, *n.* stimulateur (*m.*) cardiaque.

pacific, *adj.* pacifique.

Pacific Ocean, *n.* océan Pacifique *m.*

pacifism, *n.* pacifisme *m.*

pacify, *vb.* pacifier.

pack, 1. *n.* paquet *m.;* (animals) meute *f.;* (persons) bande *f.* **2.** *vb.* emballer; (crowd) entasser.

package, *n.* paquet *m.*

packet, *n.* paquet *m.*

packing, *n.* emballage *m.*

pact, *n.* pacte *m.,* contrat *m.*

pad, 1. *n.* (stuffing) bourrelet *m.;* (cotton, ink) tampon *m.;* (paper) bloc *m.* **2.** *vb.* (clothes) ouater; (stuff) bourrer.

padding, *n.* remplissage *m.,* rembourrage *m.*

paddle, *n.* pagaie *f.*

paddock, *n.* enclos *m.*

padlock, *n.* cadenas *m.*

pagan, *adj.* and *n.* païen *m.*

page, *n.* (book) page *f.;* (attendant) page *m.*

pageant, *n.* spectacle *m.*

pager, *n.* récepteur (*m.*) d'appels.

pagoda, *n.* pagode *f.*

pail, *n.* seau *m.*

pain, 1. *n.* douleur *f.;* (trouble) peine *f.* **2.** *vb.* (hurt) faire mal (à); (distress) faire de la peine (à).

painful, *adj.* douloureux.

painstaking, *adj.* soigneux.

paint, 1. *n.* peinture *f.* **2.** *vb.* peindre.

painter, *n.* peintre *m.*

painting, *n.* peinture *f.*

pair, *n.* paire *f.*

pajamas, *n.* pyjama *m.*

Pakistan, *n.* Pakistan *m.*

pal, *n.* copain *m.*

palace, *n.* palais *m.*

palatable, *adj.* d'un goût agréable, agréable au palais.

palate, *n.* palais *m.*

palatial, *adj.* qui ressemble à un palais, magnifique.

pale, *adj.* pâle.

paleness, *n.* pâleur *f.*

Palestine, *n.* Palestine *f.*

palette, *n.* palette *f.*

pall, 1. *n.* drap funéraire *m.* **2.** *vb.* s'affadir.

pallbearer, *n.* porteur (d'un cordon du poêle) *m.*

pallid, *adj.* pâle, blême.

palm, *n.* (tree) palmier *m.;* (branch) palme *f.;* (hand) paume *f.*

palpable, *adj.* manifeste.

palpitate, *vb.* palpiter.

paltry, *adj.* mesquin.

pamper, *vb.* choyer.

pamphlet, *n.* brochure *f.*

pan, *n.* (cooking) casserole *f.*

panacea, *n.* panacée *f.*

Pan-American, *adj.* panaméricain.

pancake, *n.* crêpe *f.*

pancreas, *n.* pancréas *m.*

pandemonium, *n.* tumulte *m.,* chaos *m.*

pander to, *vb.* flatter bassement.

pane, *n.* (window) vitre *f.*

panel, *n.* panneau *m.*

pang, *n.* angoisse *f.*

panic, *n.* panique *f.*

panorama, *n.* panorama *m.*

pant, *vb.* haleter.

pantomime, *n.* pantomime *m.*

pantry, *n.* office *f.*

pants, *n.* pantalon *m.*

panty hose, *n.* collant *m.*

papal, *adj.* papal.

paper, *n.* papier *m.*

paperback, *n.* livre *(m.)* de poche.

par, *n.* pair *m.,* égalité *f.*

parable, *n.* parabole *f.*

parachute, *n.* parachute *m.*

parade, *n.* parade *f.*

paradise, *n.* paradis *m.*

paradox, *n.* paradoxe *m.*

paraffin, *n.* paraffine *f.*

paragon, *n.* modèle *m.*

paragraph, *n.* alinéa *m.,* paragraphe *m.*

parakeet, *n.* perruche *f.*

parallel, 1. *n.* (line) parallèle *f.;* (geography, comparison) parallèle *m.* **2.** *adj.* parallèle.

paralyze, *vb.* paralyser.

paramedic, *n.* assistant médical *m.*

parameter, *n.* paramètre *m.*

paramount, *adj.* souverain.

paranoia, *n.* paranoïa *f.*

paranoid, *adj.* paranoïaque.

paraphrase, *vb.* paraphraser.

parasite, *n.* parasite *m.*

parcel, *n.* paquet *m.;* **(p. post)** colis postal *m.*

parch, *vb.* dessécher, *tr.*

parchment, *n.* parchemin *m.*

pardon, 1. *n.* pardon *m.* **2.** *vb.* pardonner.

pare, *vb.* (fruit) peler.

parent, *n.* père *m.;* mère *f.;* **(parents)** parents *m.pl.*

parentage, *n.* naissance *f.*

parenthesis, *n.* parenthèse *f.*

parish, *n.* paroisse *f.*

Parisian, 1. *n.* Parisien *m.* **2.** *adj.* parisien.

parity, *n.* parité *f.,* égalité *f.*

park, 1. *n.* parc *m.* **2.** *vb.* stationner.

parking lot, *n.* parking *m.*

parking meter, *n.* parcmètre *m.*

parley, *n.* conférence *f.,* pourparler *m.*

parliament, *n.* parlement *m.*

parliamentary, *adj.* parlementaire.

parlor, *n.* petit salon *m.*

parochial, *adj.* paroissial; (limited in outlook) de clocher.

parody, *n.* parodie *f.*

parole, 1. *n.* parole *f.* **2.** *vb.* libérer conditionnellement.

paroxysm, *n.* paroxysme *m.*

parrot, *n.* perroquet *m.*

parsley, *n.* persil *m.*

parsimonious, *adj.* parcimonieux.

parson, *n.* pasteur *m.*

part, 1. *n.* (of a whole) partie *f.;* (share) part *f.* **2.** *vb.* (divide) diviser; (share) partager; (of people) se séparer.

partake of, *vb.* participer à.

partial, *adj.* partiel; (favoring) partial.

participant, *adj. and n.* participant *m.*

participate, *vb.* participer.

participation, *n.* participation *f.*

participle, *n.* participe *m.*

particle, *n.* particule *f.*

particular, 1. *n.* détail *m.* **2.** *adj.* particulier; (person) exigeant.

parting, *n.* séparation *f.;* (hair) raie *f.*

partisan, *n.* partisan *m.*

partition, *n.* partage *m.;* (wall) cloison *f.*

partly, *adv.* en partie.

partner, *n.* associé *m.*

part of speech, *n.* partie *(f.)* du discours.

partridge, *n.* perdrix *f.*

part-time, *adj. and adv.* à temps partiel.

party, *n.* (faction) parti *m.;* (social) réception *f.;* (group of people) groupe *m.;* (law) partie *f.*

pass, 1. *n.* (mountain) col *m.;* (permission) laissez-passer *m.* **2.** *vb.* passer.

passable, *adj.* traversable, passable, assez bon.

passage, *n.* passage *m.*

passenger, *n.* (land) voyageur *m.;* (sea, air) passager *m.*

passer-by, *n.* passant *m.*

passion, *n.* passion *f.*

passionate, *adj.* passionné.

passive, *adj. and n.* passif *m.*

Passover, *n.* Pâque *f.*

passport, *n.* passeport *m.*

password, *n.* mot *(m.)* de passe.

past, 1. *adj. and n.* passé *m.* **2.** *prep.* (beyond) au delà de; (more than) plus de; **(half p. four)** quatre heures et demie.

paste, 1. *n.* pâte *f.;* (glue) colle *f.* **2.** *vb.* coller.

pasteurize, *vb.* pasteuriser.

pastime, *n.* passe-temps *m.*

pastor, *n.* pasteur *m.*

pastry, *n.* pâtisserie *f.*

pasture, *n.* pâturage *m.*

pasty, *adj.* empâté, pâteux.

pat, *vb.* taper.

patch, *n.* pièce *f.* **2.** *vb.* rapiécer.

patchwork, *n.* patchwork *m.*

patent, *n.* brevet *(m.)* d'invention.

patent leather, *n.* cuir *(m.)* verni.

paternal, *adj.* paternel.

paternity, *n.* paternité *f.*

path, *n.* sentier *m.*

pathetic, *adj.* pathétique.

pathology, *n.* pathologie *f.*

pathos, *n.* pathétique *m.*

patience, *n.* patience *f.*

patient, 1. *n.* malade *m.f.* **2.** *adj.* patient.

patio, *n.* patio *m.*

patriarch, *n.* patriarche *m.*

patriot, *n.* patriote *m.f.*

patriotic, *adj.* patriotique.

patriotism, *n.* patriotisme *m.*

patrol, *n.* patrouille *f.*

patrolman, *n.* agent (de police) *m.,* patrouilleur *m.*

patron, *n.* protecteur *m.; (comm.)* client *m.*

patronize, *vb.* subventionner; traiter avec condescendance.

pattern, *n.* modèle *m.;* (design) dessin *m.;* schéma *m.*

pauper, *n.* indigent *m.,* pauvre *m.,* mendiant *m.*

pause, *n.* pause *f.*

pave, *vb.* paver.

pavement, *n.* pavé *m.;* (sidewalk) trottoir *m.*

pavestone, *n.* pavé *m.*

pavilion, *n.* pavillon *m.*

paw, *n.* patte *f.*

pawn, 1. *n.* pion *m.* **2.** *vb.* mettre en gage, engager.

pay, 1. *n.* salaire *m.* **2.** *vb.* payer.

payment, *n.* paiement *m.*

pay phone, *n.* cabine *(f.)* téléphonique.

pea, *n.* pois *m.*

peace, *n.* paix *f.*

peaceable, peaceful, *adj.* paisible.

peach, *n.* pêche *f.*

peacock, *n.* paon *m.*

peak, *n.* sommet *m.*

peal, 1. *n.* retentissement *m.* **2.** *vb.* sonner, retentir.

peanut, *n.* arachide *f.*

pear, *n.* poire *f.*

pearl, *n.* perle *f.*

peasant, *n.* paysan *m.*

pebble, *n.* caillou *m.*

peck, *vb.* becqueter.

peculiar, *adj.* particulier; (unusual) singulier.

pecuniary, *adj.* pécuniaire.

pedagogue, *n.* pédagogue *m.*

pedagogy, *n.* pédagogie *f.*

pedal, *n.* pédale *f.*

pedant, *n.* pédant *m.*

peddle, *vb.* colporter.

peddler, *n.* colporteur *m.,* camelot *m.*

pedestal, *n.* piédestal *m.*

pedestrian, *n.* piéton *m.*

pediatrician, *n.* pédiatre *m.*

pedigree, *n.* généalogie *f.*

pee, *vb.* (colloquial) faire pipi.

peek, 1. *n.* coup d'œil furtif *m.* **2.** *vb.* regarder à la dérobée.

peel, 1. *n.* pelure *f.* **2.** *vb.* peler.

peep, *vb.* regarder furtivement.

peer, 1. *n.* pair *m.* **2.** *vb.* scruter.

peevish, *adj.* irritable.

peg, *n.* cheville *f.*

pejorative, *adj.* péjoratif.

pelican, *n.* pélican *m.*

pelt, 1. *n.* peau *f.,* fourrure *f.* **2.** *vb.* lancer, jeter.

pelvis, *n.* bassin *m.*

pen, *n.* plume *f.;* (ballpoint) stylo *(m.)* à bille.

penalty, *n.* peine *f.*

penance, *n.* pénitence *f.*

penchant, *n.* penchant *m.*

pencil, *n.* crayon *m.*

pendant, *n.* pendentif *m.*

pending, *prep.* pendant.

penetrate, *vb.* pénétrer.

penetration, *n.* pénétration *f.*

penicillin, *n.* pénicilline *f.*

peninsula, *n.* péninsule *f.*

penis, *n.* pénis *m.*

penitent, 1. *adj.* pénitent, contrit. **2.** *n.* pénitent *m.*

penknife, *n.* canif *m.*

penniless, *adj.* sans le sou.

penny, *n.* sou *m.*

pension, *n.* pension *f.*

pensive, *adj.* pensif.

Pentecost, *n.* Pentecôte *f.*

pent-up, *adj.* refoulé.

penury, *n.* pénurie *f.*

people, 1. *n.* gens *m.f.pl.;* (of a country) peuple *m.* **2.** *vb.* peupler.

pep, *n.* énergie *f.*

pepper, *n.* poivre *m.*

per, *prep.* par; **(p. hour)** par heure; **(p. year)** par an.

perambulator, *n.* voiture *(f.)* d'enfant.

perceive, *vb.* apercevoir, *tr.*

percent, pour cent.

percentage, *n.* pourcentage *m.*

perceptible, *adj.* perceptible.

perception, *n.* perception *f.*

perch, 1. *n.* (for birds) perchoir *m.;* (fish) perche *f.* **2.** *vb.* se percher.

perdition, *n.* perte *f.*

peremptory, *adj.* péremptoire.

perennial, *adj.* perpétuel; (plant) vivace.

perfect, *adj.* parfait.

perfection, *n.* perfection *f.*

perforation, *n.* perforation *f.*

perform, *vb.* accomplir; (theater) jouer.

performance, *n.* (task) accomplissement *m.;* (theater) représentation *f.*

perfume, *n.* parfum *m.*

perfunctory, *adj.* fait pour la forme, superficiel.

perhaps, *adv.* peut-être.

peril, *n.* péril *m.*

perilous, *adj.* périlleux.

perimeter, *n.* périmètre *m.*

period, *n.* période *f.;* (full stop) point *m.*

periodic, *adj.* périodique.

periodical, *n.* périodique *m.*

peripheral, *adj.* périphérique.

periphery, *n.* périphérie *f.*

perish, *vb.* périr.

perishable, *adj.* périssable.

perjury, *n.* parjure *m.*

permanent, *adj.* permanent.

permeate, *vb.* filtrer.

permissible, *adj.* admissible.

permission, *n.* permission *f.*

permit, 1. *n.* permis *m.* **2.** *vb.* permettre.

pernicious, *adj.* pernicieux.

peroxide, *n.* eau *(f.)* oxygénée.

perpendicular, *adj.* perpendiculaire, vertical.

perpetrate, *vb.* perpétrer.

perpetual, *adj.* perpétuel.

perplex, *vb.* mettre dans la perplexité.

perplexity, *n.* perplexité *f.,* embarras *m.*

persecute, *vb.* persécuter.

persecution, *n.* persécution *f.*

perseverance, *n.* persévérance *f.*

persevere, *vb.* persévérer.

Persian, *adj.* persan; **(P. Gulf)** golfe *(m.)* persique.

persist, *vb.* persister.

persistent, *adj.* persistant.

person, *n.* personne *f.*

personage, *n.* personnage *m.*

personal, *adj.* personnel.

personal computer, *n.* ordinateur *(m.)* personnel.

personality, *n.* personnalité *f.*

personally, *adv.* personnellement.

personnel, *n.* personnel *m.*

perspective, *n.* perspective *f.*

perspiration, *n.* transpiration *f.*

perspire, *vb.* transpirer.

persuade, *vb.* persuader.

persuasive, *adj.* persuasif.

pertain, *vb.* appartenir.

pertinent, *adj.* pertinent.

perturb, *vb.* troubler.

Peru, *n.* Pérou *m.*

peruse, *vb.* lire attentivement.

pervade, *vb.* pénétrer.

perverse, *adj.* entêté (dans l'erreur).

perversion, *n.* perversion *f.*

pessimism, *n.* pessimisme *m.*

pester, *vb.* importuner.

pestilence, *n.* pestilence *f.*

pet, *n.* (animal) animal *(m.)* familier.

petal, *n.* pétale *m.*

petition, *n.* pétition *f.*

petrified, *adj.* mort de peur.

petroleum, *n.* pétrole *m.*

petticoat, *n.* jupon *m.*

petty, *adj.* insignifiant.

petulant, *adj.* boudeur.

pew, *n.* banc *(m.)* (d'église).

phantom, *n.* fantôme *m.*

pharmacist, *n.* pharmacien *m.*

pharmacy, *n.* pharmacie *f.*

phase, *n.* phase *f.*

phenomenal, *adj.* phénoménal.

phenomenon, *n.* phénomène *m.*

philanthropy, *n.* philanthropie *f.*

Philippines, *n.* Philippines *f.pl.*

philosopher, *n.* philosophe *m.*

philosophical, *adj.* philosophique.

philosophy, *n.* philosophie *f.*

phobia, *n.* phobie *f.*

phone, 1. *n.* téléphone *m.* **2.** *vb.* téléphoner.

phone booth, *n.* cabine *(f.)* téléphonique.

phonetics, *n.* phonétique *f.*

phonograph, *n.* phonographe *m.*

photocopier, *n.* photocopieur *m.*

photocopy, 1. *n.* photocopie *f.* **2.** *vb.* photocopier.

photograph, photography, *n.* photographie *f.*

photographer, *n.* photographe *m.*

phrase, *n.* expression *f.;* *(gramm.)* bout *(m.)* de phrase.

physical, *adj.* physique.

physical therapy, *n.* kinésithérapie *f.*

physician, *n.* médecin *m.*

physics, *n.* physique *f.*

physiology, *n.* physiologie *f.*

pianist, *n.* pianiste *m.f.*

piano, *n.* piano *m.*

pick, 1. *vb.* (choose) choisir; (gather) cueillir. **2.** *n.* pioche *f.*

pickles, *n.* conserves *(f.pl.)* au vinaigre.

picnic, *n.* pique-nique *m.*

picture, *n.* tableau *m.;* (motion picture) film *m.*

picturesque, *adj.* pittoresque.

pie, *n.* tarte *f.*

piece, *n.* morceau *m.*

pier, *n.* jetée *f.;* quai *m.*

pierce, *vb.* percer.

piety, *n.* piété *f.*

pig, *n.* cochon *m.*

pigeon, *n.* pigeon *m.*

pigeonhole, *n.* (for papers, etc.) case *f.*

pigment, *n.* pigment *m.*

pigtail, *n.* natte *f.*

pile, 1. *n.* (construction) pieu *m.;* (heap) tas *m.* **2.** *vb.* entasser.

pilgrim, *n.* pèlerin *m.*

pilgrimage, *n.* pèlerinage *m.*

pill, *n.* pilule *f.*

pillage, 1. *n.* pillage *m.* **2.** *vb.* piller.

pillar, *n.* pilier *m.*

pillow, *n.* oreiller *m.*

pillowcase, *n.* taie *(f.)* d'oreiller.

pilot, *n.* pilote *m.*

pimp, *n.* maquereau *m.,* souteneur *m.*

pimple, *n.* bouton *m.*

pin, 1. *n.* épingle *f.* **2.** *vb.* épingler.

pinball, *n.* flipper *m.*

pinch, *vb.* pincer.

pine, 1. *n.* pin *m.* **2.** *vb.* languir.

pineapple, *n.* ananas *m.*

pink, *adj.* and *n.* rose *m.*

pinnacle, *n.* pinacle *m.*

pint, *n.* pinte *f.*

pioneer, *n.* pionnier *m.*

pious, *adj.* pieux.

pipe, *n.* tuyau *m.;* (smoking) pipe *f.*

pipeline, *n.* pipeline *m.*

piper, *n.* (bagpipe) joueur *(m.)* de cornemuse.

piquant, *adj.* piquant.

pirate, *n.* pirate *m.*

pistol, *n.* pistolet *m.*

piston, *n.* piston *m.*

pit, *n.* fosse *f.*

pitch, 1. *n.* (substance) poix *f.;* (throw) jet *m.;* (height) hauteur *f.;* (music) ton *m.* **2.** *vb.* (throw) lancer.

pitcher, *n.* (vessel) cruche *f.;* (baseball) lanceur *m.*

pitfall, *n.* trappe *f.*

pitiful, *adj.* pitoyable.

pitiless, *adj.* impitoyable.

pity, 1. *n.* pitié *f.;* **(what a p.!)** quel dommage! **2.** *vb.* plaindre.

pivot, *n.* pivot *m.,* axe *m.*

pizza, *n.* pizza *f.*

placate, *vb.* calmer.

place, 1. *n.* endroit *m.;* (locality) lieu *m.;* (position occupied) place *f.* **2.** *vb.* mettre.

placid, *adj.* placide.

plagiarize, *vb.* plagier.

plague, *n.* (disease) peste *f.;* *(fig.)* fléau *m.*

plaid, *n.* (blanket) plaid *m.;* (textile) tartan *m.*

plain, 1. *n.* plaine *f.* **2.** *adj.* (clear) clair; (simple) simple; (of person) quelconque.

plaintiff, *n.* demandeur *m.,* plaignant *m.*

plan, 1. *n.* plan *m.* **2.** *vb.* prévoir, projeter.

plane, *n.* (surface) plan *m.;* (tool) rabot *m.;* (tree) platane *m.;* (airplane) avion *m.*

planet, *n.* planète *f.*

plank, *n.* planche *f.*

planning, *n.* planification *f.;* **(family p.)** planning *(m.)* familial.

plant, 1. *n.* plante *f.* **2.** *vb.* planter.

plantation, *n.* plantation *f.*

planter, *n.* planteur *m.*

plasma, *n.* plasma *m.*

plaster, *n.* plâtre *m.*

plastic, *adj.* plastique.

plate, *n.* plaque *f.;* (for eating) assiette *f.*

plateau, *n.* plateau *m.*

platform, *n.* plate-forme *f.;* (railroad) quai *m.*

platinum, *n.* platine *m.*

platonic, *adj.* platonique.

platoon, *n.* (military) section *f.*

platter, *n.* plat *m.*

plausible, *adj.* plausible.

play, 1. *n.* jeu *m.;* (drama) pièce *(f.)* de théâtre. **2.** *vb.* jouer; (game) jouer à; (instrument) jouer de.

player, *n.* jouer *m.;* (theater) acteur *m.*

playful, *adj.* enjoué.

playground, *n.* (children) terrain *(m.)* de jeu.

playmate, *n.* camarade *(m.f.)* de jeu.

playwright, *n.* dramaturge *m.*

plea, *n.* défense *f.;* (excuse) excuse *f.*

plead, *vb.* plaider; (allege) alléguer.

pleasant, *adj.* agréable.

please, *vb.* plaire à; (satisfy) contenter; **(if you p.)** s'il vous plaît.

pleasure, *n.* plaisir *m.*

pleat, *n.* pli *m.*

pledge, *n.* gage *m.;* (promise) engagement *m.*

plentiful, *adj.* abondant.

plenty, *n.* abondance *f.*

pliable, *adj.* pliable.

pliers, *n.* pinces *f.pl.*

plight, *n.* état *m.*

plot, 1. *n.* (literature) intrigue *f.;* (conspiracy) complot *m.* **2.** *vb.* comploter.

plow, 1. *n.* charrue *f.* **2.** *vb.* labourer.

pluck, *n.* courage *m.*

plug, *n.* tampon *m.;* (electric) prise *(f.)* de courant.

plum, *n.* prune *f.*

plumber, *n.* plombier *m.*

plume, *n.* panache *m.*

plump, *adj.* grassouillet.

plunder, *vb.* piller.

plunge, 1. *n.* plongeon *m.* **2.** *vb.* plonger.

pluperfect, *n.* plus-que-parfait *m.*

plural, *adj. and n.* pluriel *m.*

plus, *n.* plus *m.*

pneumonia, *n.* pneumonie *f.*

poach, *vb.* (of eggs) pocher.

poacher, *n.* braconnier *m.*

pocket, *n.* poche *f.*

pocketbook, *n.* sac *(m.)* à main.

podiatrist, *n.* podologue *m.f.*

poem, *n.* poésie *f.;* (long) poème *f.*

poet, *n.* poète *m.*

poetic, *adj.* poétique.

poetry, *n.* poésie *f.*

poignant, *adj.* poignant.

point, 1. *n.* point *m.;* (sharp end) pointe *f.* **2.** *vb.* (gun, etc.) pointer; (indicate) désigner.

pointed, *adj.* pointu; (ironical) mordant.

poise, *n.* équilibre *m.*

poison, 1. *n.* poison *m.* **2.** *vb.* empoisonner.

poisonous, *adj.* empoisonné; (plant) vénéneux; (animal) venimeux.

Poland, *n.* Pologne *f.*

polar, *adj.* polaire.

polar bear, *n.* ours *(m.)* blanc.

Pole, *n.* Polonais *m.*

pole, *n.* (geography) pôle *m.;* (wood) perche *f.*

polemic, *n.* polémique *f.*

police, *n.* police *f.*

policeman, *n.* agent *(m.)* de police.

policy, *n.* politique *f.;* (insurance) police *f.*

polio, *n.* polio *f.*

Polish, *adj. and n.* polonais *m.*

polish, *vb.* polir; (shoes) cirer.

polite, *adj.* poli.

politic, political, *adj.* politique.

politician, *n.* politicien *m.*

politics, *n.* politique *f.*

poll, *n.* (voting) scrutin *m.;* (opinion) sondage *m.*

pollen, *n.* pollen *m.*

pollute, *vb.* polluer.

polygamy, *n.* polygamie *f.*

pomegranate, *n.* grenade *f.*

pomp, *n.* pompe *f.*

pompous, *adj.* pompeux.

pond, n. étang m.
ponder, vb. réfléchir.
ponderous, adj. pesant.
pony, n. poney m.
poodle, n. caniche m.
pool, n. mare f.; (swimming) piscine f.
poor, adj. pauvre.
pop, n. petit bruit (m.) sec.
pope, n. pape m.
popular, adj. populaire.
popularity, n. popularité f.
population, n. population f.
porcelain, n. porcelaine f.
porch, n. véranda f.
porcupine, n. porc-épic m.
pore, 1. n. pore m. 2. vb. (p. over) s'absorber dans.
pork, n. porc m.
pornography, n. pornographie f.
porous, adj. poreux.
porpoise, n. marsouin m.
port, n. (harbor) port m.; (naut.) bâbord m.; (wine) porto m.
portable, adj. portatif.
portal, n. portail m.
portfolio, n. portefeuille m.
portion, n. portion f.
portrait, n. portrait m.
portray, vb. (paint) peindre; (describe) dépeindre.
Portugal, n. Portugal m.
Portuguese, 1. n. (person) Portugais m.; (language) portugais m. 2. adj. portugais.
pose, 1. n. pose f. 2. vb. poser.
position, n. position f.
positive, 1. n. positif m. 2. adj. positif.
possess, vb. posséder.
possession, n. possession f.
possibility, n. possibilité f.
possible, adj. possible.
possibly, adv. il est possible que . . .; (perhaps) peut-être.
post, 1. n. (mail) poste f.; (wood) poteau m.; (place) poste m. 2. vb. (mail) mettre à la poste; (placard) afficher.
postage, n. affranchissement m.
postal, adj. postal.

post card, n. carte (f.) postale.
poster, n. affiche f.
posterior, adj. postérieur.
posterity, n. postérité f.
post office, n. bureau (m.) de poste.
postman, n. facteur m.
postmark, n. cachet (m.) de la poste.
postpone, vb. remettre.
postscript, n. post-scriptum m.
posture, n. posture f.
postwar, adj. d'après-guerre.
pot, n. pot m.; (saucepan) marmite f.; (marijuana) herbe f., kif m.
potato, n. pomme (f.) de terre; (French-fried p.s) frites f.pl.
potent, adj. puissant.
potential, adj. and n. potentiel m.
pottery, n. poterie f.
pouch, n. sac m.
poultry, n. volaille f.
pound, n. livre f.
pour, vb. verser; (rain) tomber à verse.
pout, vb. bouder.
poverty, n. pauvreté f.
powder, n. poudre f.
power, n. pouvoir m.; (nation, mathematics) puissance f.
powerful, adj. puissant.
powerless, adj. impuissant.
practical, adj. pratique.
practically, adv. pratiquement.
practice, 1. n. (exercise) exercice m.; (habit) habitude f.; (not theory) pratique f. 2. vb. pratiquer; (piano, etc.) s'exercer (à).
practiced, adj. expérimenté.
pragmatic, adj. pragmatique.
prairie, n. savane f.
praise, 1. n. éloge m. 2. vb. louer.
prank, n. fredaine f.
pray, vb. prier.
prayer, n. prière f.
preach, vb. prêcher.
preacher, n. prédicateur m.
precarious, adj. précaire.

precaution, n. précaution f.
precede, vb. précéder.
precedent, n. précédent m.
precept, n. précepte m.
precinct, n. circonscription f.
precious, adj. précieux.
precipice, n. précipice m.
precipitate, vb. précipiter.
precise, adj. précis.
precision, n. précision f.
preclude, vb. empêcher.
precocious, adj. précoce.
precondition, n. condition (f.) requise.
predecessor, n. prédécesseur m.
predestination, n. prédestination f.
predicament, n. situation (f.) difficile.
predict, vb. prédire.
predispose, vb. prédisposer.
predominant, adj. prédominant.
preempt, vb. (acquire) acquérir d'avance; (forestall) prévenir.
prefabricate, vb. préfabriquer.
preface, n. préface f.
prefer, vb. préférer.
preferable, adj. préférable.
preference, n. préférence f.
prefix, n. préfixe m.
pregnant, adj. enceinte.
prejudice, n. préjugé m.
preliminary, adj. préliminaire.
prelude, n. prélude m.
premarital, adj. avant le mariage.
premature, adj. prématuré.
premeditate, vb. préméditer.
premier, n. premier ministre m.
première, n. première f.
premise, n. (place) lieux m.pl.; (logic) prémisse f.
premium, n. prix m.
preoccupation, n. préoccupation f.
preparation, n. préparation f.; préparatifs m.pl.
preparatory, adj. préparatoire.
prepare, vb. préparer, tr.
preponderant, adj. prépondérant.

preposition, n. préposition f.

preposterous, adj. absurde.

prerequisite, n. nécessité (f.) préalable.

prerogative, n. prérogative f.

prescribe, vb. prescrire.

prescription, n. prescription f.; (medical) ordonnance f.

presence, n. présence f.

present, 1. adj. présent. 2. n. présent m.; (gift) cadeau m. 3. vb. présenter.

presentable, adj. présentable.

presentation, n. présentation f.

presently, adv. tout à l'heure.

preservative, n. préservateur m., conservateur m.

preserve, 1. n. (jam) confiture f. 2. vb. (protect) préserver; (keep) conserver.

preside, vb. présider.

president, n. président m.

press, 1. n. presse f. 2. vb. presser; (iron) repasser.

press conference, n. conférence (f.) de presse.

pressure, n. pression f.

prestige, n. prestige m.

presume, vb. présumer.

presumptuous, adj. présomptueux.

pretend, vb. (claim, aspire) prétendre; (feign) simuler.

pretense, n. faux semblant m.

pretentious, adj. prétentieux.

pretext, n. prétexte m.

pretty, adj. joli.

prevail, vb. prévaloir; (p. upon) décider.

prevalent, adj. répandu.

prevent, vb. (impede) empêcher; (forestall) prévenir.

prevention, n. empêchement m.

preventive, adj. préventif.

preview, n. avant-première f.

previous, adj. antérieur.

prewar, adj. d'avant-guerre.

prey, n. proie f.

price, n. prix m.

priceless, adj. inestimable.

prick, 1. n. piqûre f. 2. vb. piquer.

pride, n. orgueil m.

priest, n. prêtre m.

prim, adj. guindé.

primarily, adv. principalement.

primary, adj. premier; (school, geology) primaire.

prime, 1. n. comble m. 2. adj. premier, de première qualité. 3. vb. amorcer.

prince, n. prince m.

princess, n. princesse f.

principal, adj. principal.

principle, n. principe m.

print, 1. n. (mark) empreinte f.; (book) impression f.; (photo) épreuve f. 2. vb. imprimer.

printout, n. feuille (f.) imprimée produite par un ordinateur.

prior, 1. adj. antérieur. 2. adv. (p. to doing) avant de faire.

priority, n. priorité f.

prism, n. prisme m.

prison, n. prison f.

prisoner, n. prisonnier m.

privacy, n. intimité f., solitude f., vie (f.) privée.

private, adj. particulier; (not public) privé.

privation, n. privation f.

privilege, n. privilège m.

prize, n. prix m.

probability, n. probabilité f.

probable, adj. probable.

probation, n. (on p.) en liberté (f.) surveillée.

probe, vb. sonder.

problem, n. problème m.

procedure, n. procédé m.

proceed, vb. procéder; (advance) avancer.

process, n. (method) procédé m., processus m.; (progress) développement m.

procession, n. cortège m.; (religious) procession f.

proclaim, vb. proclamer.

proclamation, n. proclamation f.

procrastinate, vb. différer.

procure, vb. procurer.

prodigal, adj. and n. prodigue m.

prodigy, n. prodige m.

produce, vb. produire.

product, n. produit m.

production, n. production f.

production line, n. chaîne (f.) (de fabrication).

productive, adj. productif.

profane, adj. profane.

profess, vb. professer.

profession, n. profession f.

professional, adj. professionnel.

professor, n. professeur m.

proficient, adj. capable.

profile, n. profil m.

profit, 1. n. profit m. 2. vb. profiter.

profitable, adj. profitable.

profound, adj. profond.

profuse, adj. (of thing) profus; (of person) prodigue.

program, 1. n. programme m. 2z. vb. programmer.

programming, n. programmation f.

progress, n. progrès m.; (motion forward) marche f.

progressive, adj. progressif.

prohibit, vb. défendre.

prohibition, n. défense f.

prohibitive, adj. prohibitif.

project, 1. n. projet m. 2. vb. projeter; (jut out) faire saillie.

projection, n. projection f.; (jutting out) saillie f.

projector, n. projecteur m.

proletariat, n. prolétariat m.

proliferation, n. prolifération f.

prologue, n. prologue m.

prolong, vb. prolonger.

prominent, adj. saillant.

promiscuous, adj. (indiscriminate) sans distinction.

promise, 1. n. promesse f. 2. vb. promettre.

promote, vb. (raise) promouvoir; (encourage) encourager.

promotion, n. promotion f.

prompt, 1. adj. prompt. 2. n. (computer) message (m.) (de guidage). 3. vb.

provoquer, (theater) souffler.
pronoun, *n.* pronom *m.*
pronounce, *vb.* prononcer.
pronunciation, *n.* prononciation *f.*
proof, *n.* (evidence) preuve *f.;* (test) épreuve *f.*
prop, *n.* appui *m.*
propaganda, *n.* progagande *f.*
propagate, *vb.* propager, *tr.*
propel, *vb.* propulser.
propeller, *n.* hélice *f.*
proper, *adj.* propre; (respectable, fitting) convenable.
property, *n.* propriété *f.*
prophecy, *n.* prophétie *f.*
prophesy, *vb.* prophétiser.
prophet, *n.* prophète *m.*
prophetic, *adj.* prophétique.
proportion, *n.* proportion *f.*
proportionate, *adj.* proportionné.
proposal, *n.* proposition *f.;* demande (*f.*) en mariage.
propose, *vb.* proposer, *tr.*
proposition, *n.* (proposal, grammar) proposition *f.;* (undertaking) affaire *f.*
proprietor, *n.* propriétaire *m.f.*
prosaic, *adj.* prosaïque.
proscribe, *vb.* proscrire.
prose, *n.* prose *f.*
prosecute, *vb.* poursuivre.
prosecution, *n.* poursuites (*f.pl.*) judiciaires.
prosecuting attorney, *n.* procureur *m.*
prospect, *n.* perspective *f.*
prospective, *adj.* en perspective.
prosper, *vb.* prospérer.
prosperity, *n.* prospérité *f.*
prosperous, *adj.* prospère.
prostate, *n.* prostate *f.*
prostitute, 1. *n.* prostituée *f.* 2. *vb.* prostituer.
prostrate, *adj.* prosterné.
protagonist, *n.* protagoniste *m.*
protect, *vb.* protéger.
protection, *n.* protection *f.*
protective, *adj.* protecteur.
protector, *n.* protecteur *m.*
protégé, *n.* protégé *m.*

protein, *n.* protéine *f.*
protest, 1. *n.* protestation *f.;* (comm.) protêt *m.* 2. *vb.* protester.
Protestant, 1. *n.* Protestant *m.* 2. *adj.* protestant.
protocol, *n.* protocole *m.*
protrude, *vb.* saillir.
proud, *adj.* fier.
prove, *vb.* prouver; (test) éprouver.
proverb, *n.* proverbe *m.*
provide (with), *vb.* pourvoir (de), *tr.*
providence, *n.* (foresight) prévoyance *f.;* (divine) providence *f.*
provincze, *n.* province *f.*
provincial, *adj. and n.* provincial *m.*
provision, *n.* (stock) provision *f.*
provocation, *n.* provocation *f.*
provoke, *vb.* provoquer; (irritate) irriter.
prowess, *n.* prouesse *f.*
prowl, *vb.* rôder.
proximity, *n.* proximité *f.*
prude, *n.* prude *f.*
prudence, *n.* prudence *f.*
prudent, *adj.* prudent.
prune, *n.* pruneau *m.*
Prussia, *n.* Prusse *f.*
Prussian, 1. *n.* Prussien *m.* 2. *adj.* prussien.
pry, *vb.* fureter.
psalm, *n.* psaume *m.*
psychedelic, *adj.* psychédélique.
psychiatry, *n.* psychiatrie *f.*
psychoanalysis, *n.* psychanalyse *f.*
psychological, *adj.* psychologique.
psychology, *n.* psychologie *f.*
psychothérapie, *n.* psychothérapie *f.*
ptomaine, *n.* ptomaïne *f.*
public, 1. *n.* public *m.* 2. *adj.* public *m.,* publique *f.*
publication, *n.* publication *f.*
publicity, *n.* publicité *f.*
public transport, *n.* transports (*m.pl.*) en commun.
publish, *vb.* publier.
publisher, *n.* éditeur *m.*
pudding, *n.* pouding *m.*

puddle, *n.* flaque *f.*
puff, *n.* (smoke etc.) bouffée *f.*
pugnacious, *adj.* batailleur, combattif.
pull, *vb.* tirer.
pulley, *n.* poulie *f.*
pulp, *n.* pulpe *f.*
pulpit, *n.* chaire *f.*
pulsar, *n.* pulsar *m.*
pulsate, *vb.* battre.
pulse, *n.* pouls *m.*
pump, 1. *n.* pompe *f.* 2. *vb.* pomper.
pumpkin, *n.* potiron *m.;* citrouille *f.*
pun, *n.* calembour *m.*
punch, 1. *n.* (tool) poinçon *m.;* (blow) coup (*m.*) de poing; (beverage) punch *m.* 2. *vb.* (pierce) percer; (pummel) gourmer.
punctual, *adj.* ponctuel.
punctuate, *vb.* ponctuer.
puncture, *n.* piqûre *f.*
punish, *vb.* punir.
punishment, *n.* punition *f.*
pupil, *n.* (school) élève *m.f.;* (eye) pupille *f.*
puppet, *n.* marionnette *f.*
puppy, *n.* petit chien *m.*
purchase, 1. *n.* achat *m.* 2. *vb.* acheter.
pure, *adj.* pur.
puree, *n.* purée *f.*
purge, *vb.* purger.
purify, *vb.* purifier.
puritan, *n.* puritain *m.*
purity, *n.* pureté *f.*
purple, *adj.* violet.
purpose, *n.* but *m.;* (to the p.) à propos.
purposely, *adv.* exprès.
purse, *n.* bourse *f.*
pursue, *vb.* poursuivre.
pursuit, *n.* poursuite *f.;* (occupation) occupation *f.;* (p. plane) avion (*m.*) de chasse.
push, 1. *n.* poussée *f.* 2. *vb.* pousser.
pussy(cat), *n.* minet *m.*
put, *vb.* mettre.
puzzle, 1. *n.* problème *m.* 2. *vb.* embarrasser.
pyramid, *n.* pyramide *f.*
Pyrenees, *n.* Pyrénées *f.pl.*
python, *n.* python *m.*

Q

quadrangle *n.* cour *f.*

quadraphonic, *adj.* quadriphonique.

quail, *n.* caille *f.*

quaint, *adj.* (strange) étrange.

quake, *vb.* trembler.

qualification, *n.* (reservation) réserve *f.;* (aptitude) compétence *f.;* (description) qualification *f.*

qualify, *vb.* qualifier; (modify) modifier.

quality, *n.* qualité *f.*

qualm, *n.* scrupule *m.*

quandary, *n.* dilemme *m.*

quantity, *n.* quantité *f.*

quarantine, *n.* quarantaine *f.*

quarrel, 1. *n.* querelle *f.* **2.** *vb.* se quereller.

quarry, *n.* carrière *f.*

quart, *n.* (approximately) litre *m.*

quarter, *n.* quart *m.;* (district, moon, beef) quartier *m.*

quarterly, *adj.* trimestriel.

quartet, *n.* quatuor *m.*

quartz, *n.* quartz *m.*

quasar, *n.* quasar *m.*

quaver, *vb.* chevroter.

queen, *n.* reine *f.*

queer, *adj.* bizarre.

quell, *vb.* réprimer.

quench, *vb.* éteindre.

querulous, *adj.* récriminateur.

query, *n.* question *f.*

quest, *n.* recherche *f.*

question, 1. *n.* question *f.* **2.** *vb.* interroger; (raise questions) mettre en doute.

questionable, *adj.* douteux.

question mark, *n.* point *(m.)* d'interrogation.

questionnaire, *n.* questionnaire *m.*

quibble, *vb.* ergoter.

quick, 1. *adj.* rapide; (lively) vif. **2.** *adv.* vite.

quicken, *vb.* accélérer.

quiet, 1. *n.* tranquillité *f.* **2.** *adj.* tranquille.

quilt, *n.* courtepointe *f.*

quinine, *n.* quinine *f.*

quip, *n.* mot *(m.)* piquant.

quit, *vb.* quitter.

quite, *adv.* tout à fait.

quiver, *vb.* trembloter.

quiz, 1. *n.* petit examen *m.* **2.** *vb.* examiner.

quorum, *n.* quorum *m.*

quota, *n.* (share) quote-part *f.;* (immigration, etc.) contingent *m.*

quotation, *n.* citation *f.;* *(comm.)* cote *f.*

quote, *vb.* citer.

quotient, *n.* quotient *m.*

R

rabbi *n.* rabbin *m.*

rabbit, *n.* lapin *m.*

rabble, *n.* tourbe *f.*

rabid, *adj.* enragé.

rabies, *n.* rage *f.*

race, 1. *n.* (people) race *f.;* (contest) course *f.* **2.** *vb.* lutter à la course (avec).

race-track, *n.* piste *f.*

racial, *adj.* racial.

racism, *n.* racisme *m.*

rack, *n.* râtelier *m.;* (torture) chevalet *(m.)* de torture.

racket, *n.* (tennis) raquette *f.;* (noise) tintamarre *m.*

radar, *n.* radar *m.*

radiance, *n.* éclat *m.*

radiant, *adj.* radieux.

radiate, *vb.* irradier.

radiation, *n.* rayonnement *m.*

radiator, *n.* radiateur *m.*

radical, *adj. and n.* radical *m.*

radio, *n.* télégraphie *(f.)* sans fil *(commonly* T.S.F.), radio *f.*

radioactive, *adj.* radio-actif.

radish, *n.* radis *m.*

radium, *n.* radium *m.*

radius, *n.* rayon *m.*

raft, *n.* radeau *m.*

rafter, *n.* chevron *m.*

rag, *n.* chiffon *m.*

rage, *n.* rage *f.*

ragged, *adj.* en haillons.

ragweed, *n.* ambrosie *f.*

raid, 1. *n.* (police) descente *f.;* (mil.) raid *m.* **2.** *vb.* faire un raid sur.

rail, *n.* (bar) barre *f.;* (railroad) rail *m.*

railroad, *n.* chemin *(m.)* de fer.

railway station, *n.* gare *f.*

rain, 1. *n.* pluie *f.* **2.** *vb.* pleuvoir.

rainbow, *n.* arc-en-ciel *m.*

raincoat, *n.* imperméable *m.*

rainfall, *n.* chute *(f.)* de pluie.

rain forest, *n.* forêt *(f.)* tropicale humide.

rainy, *adj.* pluvieux.

raise, *vb.* (bring up, erect, promote) élever; (lift) lever; (plants) cultiver.

raisin, *n.* raisin *(m.)* sec.

rake, 1. *n.* râteau *m.* **2.** *vb.* râteler.

rally, *n.* (mil.) ralliement *m.;* (meeting) rassemblement *m.*

ram, *n.* bélier *m.*

ramble, *vb.* rôder; (speech) divaguer.

ramp, *n.* rampe *f.*

rampart, *n.* rempart *m.*

rancid, *adj.* rance.

random, *n.* hasard *m.*

range, 1. *n.* (scope) étendue *f.;* (mountains) chaîne *f.;* (distance) portée *f.;* (stove) fourneau *m.* **2.** *vb.* s'étendre.

rank, 1. *n.* rang *m.* **2.** *vb.* zranger, *tr.*

ransack, *vb.* (search) fouiller; (pillage) saccager.

ransom, *n.* rançon *f.*

rant, *vb.* fulminer.

rap, 1. *n.* coup *m.;* (r. music) rap *m.* or *f.* **2.** *vb.* frapper.

rape, *n.* viol *m.*

rapid, *adj. and n.* rapide *m.*

rapture, *n.* ravissement *m.*

rare, *adj.* rare; (meat) saignant.

rascal, *n.* coquin *m.*

rash, 1. *n.* éruption *f.* **2.** *adj.* téméraire.

raspberry, *n.* framboise *f.*

rat, *n.* rat *m.*

rate, 1. *n.* taux *m.;* (speed) vitesse *f.;* **(at any r.)** en tout cas; **(first-r.)** de premier ordre. **2.** *vb.* estimer.

rather, *adv.* plutôt.

ratify, *vb.* ratifier.

rating, *n.* classement *m.;* **(TV r.s)** Audimat *m.*

ration, *n.* ration *f.*

rational, *adj.* raisonnable; (mathematics, philosophy) rationnel.

rat race, *n.* foire *(f.)* empoigne.

rattle, *n.* (toy) hochet *m.;* (noise) fracas *m.*

raucous, *adj.* rauque.

rave, *vb.* délirer; **(r. about)** s'extasier sur.

raven, *n.* corbeau *m.*

ravenous, *adj.* vorace.

raw, *adj.* cru.

ray, *n.* rayon *m.*

rayon, *n.* rayonne *f.*

razor, *n.* rasoir *m.*

reach, 1. *n.* portée *f.* **2.** *vb.* atteindre; (extend) étendre, *tr.;* (arrive) arriver à.

react, *vb.* réagir.

reaction, *n.* réaction *f.*

reactionary, *adj.* réactionnaire.

read, *vb.* lire.

reader, *n.* (person) lecteur *m.;* (book) livre *(m.)* de lecture.

readily, *adv.* promptement.

ready, *adj.* prêt.

real, *adj.* réel.

realist, *n.* réaliste *m.f.*

reality, *n.* réalité *f.*

realization, *n.* réalisation *f.*

realize, *vb.* (notice) s'apercevoir de; (make real) réaliser, *tr.*

really, *adv.* vraiment.

realm, *n.* royaume *m.*

Realtor, *n.* agent *(m.)* immobilier.

reap, *vb.* moissonner.

rear, 1. *n.* (hind part) queue *f.;* *(mil.)* arrière-garde *f.* **2.** *adj.* situé à l'arrière. **3.** *vb.* élever.

rear-view mirror, *n.* rétroviseur *m.*

reason, 1. *n.* raison *f.* **2.** *vb.* raisonner.

reasonable, *adj.* raisonnable.

reassure, *vb.* rassurer.

rebate, *n.* rabais *m.*

rebel, 1. *adj. and n.* rebelle *m.f.* **2.** *vb.* se rebeller.

rebellion, *n.* rébellion *f.*

rebellious, *adj.* rebelle.

rebirth, *n.* renaissance *f.*

rebound, *n.* rebond *m.*

rebuff, *vb.* repousser.

rebuke, 1. *n.* réprimande *f.* **2.** *vb.* réprimander.

rebuttal, *n.* réfutation *f.*

recall, *vb.* (call back) rappeler; (remember) se rappeler.

recap, *vb.* récapituler.

recede, *vb.* s'éloigner.

receipt, *n.* (for payment) quittance *f.*

receive, *vb.* recevoir.

receiver, *n.* (phone) récepteur *m.*

recent, *adj.* récent.

receptacle, *n.* réceptacle *m.;* récipient *m.*

reception, *n.* réception *f.;* (welcoming) accueil *m.*

receptive, *adj.* réceptif.

recess, *n.* recoin *m.;* (parliament) vacances *f.pl.;* (school) récréation *f.*

recession, *n.* récession *f.*

recipe, *n.* recette *f.*

reciprocal, *adj.* réciproque.

reciprocate, *vb.* payer de retour.

recite, *vb.* réciter.

reckless, *adj.* téméraire.

reckon, *vb.* compter.

reclaim, *v.* (person) corriger; (land) défricher.

recline, *vb.* reposer, *tr.*

recognition, *n.* reconnaissance *f.*

recognize, *vb.* reconnaître.

recoil, *vb.* reculer.

recollect, *vb.* se rappeler.

recommend, *vb.* recommander.

recommendation, *n.* recommandation *f.*

recompense, *n.* récompense *f.*

reconcile, *vb.* réconcilier.

record, 1. *n.* (register) registre *m.;* (mention) mention *f.;* (known facts of person) antécédents *m.pl.;* (sports) record *m.;* (phonograph) disque *m.* **2.** *vb.* enregistrer.

record player, *n.* tourne-disques *m.*

recount, *vb.* raconter.

recoup, *vb.* récupérer.

recover, *vb.* recouvrer; (from illness) se rétablir.

recovery, *n.* recouvrement *m.;* (health) rétablissement *m.*

recreation, *n.* récréation *f.*

recruit, 1. *n.* recrue *f.* **2.** *vb.* recruter.

rectangle, *n.* rectangle *m.*

rectify, *vb.* rectifier.

recuperate, *vb.* se rétablir, *intr.*

recur, *vb.* revenir.

recycle, *vb.* recycler.

recycling, *n.* recyclage *m.*

red, *adj. and n.* rouge *m.*

red tape, *n.* paperasse *f.*

redeem, *vb.* racheter.

redemption, *n.* rachat *m.;* (theology) rédemption *f.*

redo, *vb.* refaire.

redress, 1. *n.* justice *f.;* réparation *f.* **2.** *vb.* redresser, réparer; faire justice à.

reduce, *vb.* réduire.

reduction, *n.* réduction *f.;* (on price) remise *f.*

redundant, *adj.* superflu.

reed, *n.* roseau *m.;* (music) anche *f.*

reef, *n.* récif *m.*

reel, *n.* bobine *f.*

refer, *vb.* référer.

referee, *n.* arbitre *m.*

reference, *n.* référence *f.*

referendum, *n.* référendum *m.*

refill, *vb.* remplir (à nouveau).

refine, *vb.* raffiner.

refinement, *n.* raffinement *m.*

reflect, *vb.* réfléchir.
reflection, *n.* réflexion *f.*
reflex, *adj. and n.* réflexe *m.*
reform, 1. *n.* réforme *f.* **2.** *vb.* réformer, *tr.*
reformation, *n.* réforme *f.*
refractory, *adj.* réfractaire.
refrain from, *vb.* se retenir de.
refresh, *vb.* rafraîchir.
refreshment, *n.* rafraîchissement *m.*
refrigerator, *n.* frigidaire *m.*
refuge, *n.* refuge *m.*
refugee, *n.* réfugié *m.*
refund, 1. *n.* remboursement *m.* **2.** *vb.* rembourser.
refurbish, *vb.* remettre à neuf.
refusal, *n.* refus *m.*
refuse, 1. *n.* rebut *m.* **2.** *vb.* refuser.
refute, *vb.* réfuter.
regain, *vb.* regagner.
regal, *adj.* royal.
regard, 1. *n.* égard *m.; (r.s, compliments)* amitiés *f.pl.* **2.** *vb.* regarder.
regardless of, *adj.* sans tenir compte de.
regent, *adj. and n.* régent *m.*
regime, *n.* régime *m.*
regiment, *n.* régiment *m.*
region, *n.* région *f.*
register, 1. *n.* registre *m.* **2.** *vb.* enregistrer; *(letter)* recommander.
registration, *n.* enregistrement *m.*
regret, 1. *n.* regret *m.* **2.** *vb.* regretter.
regroup, *vb.* (se) regrouper.
regular, *adj.* régulier.
regularity, *n.* régularité *f.*
regulate, *vb.* régler.
regulation, *n.* règlement *m.*
regulator, *n.* régulateur *m.*
rehabilitate, *vb.* réhabiliter.
rehearse, *vb.* répéter.
reign, 1. *n.* règne *m.* **2.** *vb.* régner.
reimburse, *vb.* rembourser.
rein, *n.* rêne *f.*
reindeer, *n.* renne *m.*
reinforce, *vb.* renforcer.
reinforcement, *n.* renfort *m.*
reinstate, *vb.* rétablir, réintégrer.

reject, *vb.* rejeter.
rejoice, *vb.* réjouir, *tr.*
rejoin, *vb.* (join again) rejoindre; (reply) répliquer.
relapse, 1. *n.* rechute *f.* **2.** *vb.* rechuter.
relate, *vb.* raconter; (have reference to) se rapporter (à); **(r. to)** entrer en rapport avec.
relation, *n.* relation *f.; (relative)* parent *m.*
relationship, *n.* rapport *m.,* relations *f.pl.*
relative, 1. *n.* parent *m.* **2.** *adj.* relatif.
relax, *vb.* relâcher.
relay, 1. *n.* relais *m.* **2.** *vb.* relayer.
release, 1. *n.* délivrance *f.* **2.** *vb.* libérer.
relent, *vb.* se laisser attendrir.
relevant, *adj.* pertinent.
reliability, *n.* sûreté *f.*
reliable, *adj.* digne de confiance.
reliant, *adj.* confiant.
relic, *n.* relique *f.*
relief, *n.* (ease) soulagement *m.;* (help) secours *m.;* (projection) relief *m.*
relieve, *vb.* (ease) soulager; (help) secourir.
religion, *n.* religion *f.*
religious, *adj.* religieux.
relinquish, *vb.* abandonner.
relish, 1. *n.* goût *m.* **2.** *vb.* goûter.
relocate, *vb.* s'installer ailleurs.
reluctant, *adj.* peu disposé (à).
rely upon, *vb.* compter sur.
remain, *vb.* rester.
remainder, *n.* reste *m.*
remark, 1. *n.* remarque *f.* **2.** *vb.* remarquer.
remarkable, *adj.* remarquable.
remedy, 1. *n.* remède *m.* **2.** *vb.* remédier à.
remember, *vb.* se souvenir de.
remembrance, *n.* souvenir *m.*
remind of, *vb.* rappeler à (person recalling).

reminisce, *vb.* raconter ses souvenirs.
remiss, *adj.* negligent.
remission, *n.* rémission *f.*
remit, *vb.* remettre.
remnant, *n.* reste *m.,* vestige *m.,* (of cloth) coupon *m.*
remorse, *n.* remords *m.*
remote, *adj.* éloigné; (vague) vague.
removable, *adj.* transportable.
removal, *n.* enlèvement *m.*
remove, *vb.* enlever.
rend, *vb.* déchirer.
render, *vb.* rendre.
rendezvous, *n.* rendez-vous *m.*
renew, *vb.* renouveler.
renewal, *n.* renouvellement *m.*
renounce, *vb.* (give up) renoncer à; (repudiate) répudier.
renovate, *vb.* renouveler.
renown, *n.* renommée *f.*
rent, 1. *n.* loyer *m.* **2.** *vb.* louer.
repair, 1. *n.* réparation *f.* **2.** *vb.* réparer.
repay, *vb.* (give back) rendre; (refund) rembourser.
repeat, *vb.* répéter.
repel, *vb.* repousser.
repent, *vb.* se repentir (de).
repentance, *n.* repentir *m.*
repertoire, repertory, *n.* répertoire *m.*
repetition, *n.* répétition *f.*
replace, *vb.* (place again) replacer; (take place of) remplacer.
replay, *n.* répétition *f.*
replenish, *vb.* réapprovisionner.
reply, 1. *n.* réponse *f.* **2.** *vb.* répondre.
report, 1. *n.* rapport *m.;* (rumor) bruit *m.* **2.** *vb.* rapporter; (inform against) dénoncer.
report card, *n.* bulletin *(m.)* scolaire.
repose, *n.* repos *m.*
represent, *vb.* représenter.
representation, *n.* représentation *f.*

representative, 1. *n.* représentant *m.;* (politics) député *m.* **2.** *adj.* représentatif.
repress, *vb.* réprimer.
reprimand, *n.* réprimande *f.*
reprisals, *n.* représailles *f.pl.*
reproach, 1. *n.* reproche *f.* **2.** *vb.* faire des reproches à.
reproduce, *vb.* reproduire, *tr.*
reproduction, *n.* reproduction *f.*
reproof, *n.* réprimande *f.*
reprove, *vb.* réprimander.
reptile, *n.* reptile *m.*
republic, *n.* république *f.*
republican, *adj. and n.* républicain *m.*
repudiate, *vb.* répudier.
repugnant, *adj.* répugnant.
repulse, *vb.* repousser.
repulsive, *adj.* répulsif.
reputation, *n.* réputation *f.*
repute, 1. *n.* renom *m.* **2.** *vb.* réputer.
request, 1. *n.* requête *f.* **2.** *vb.* demander.
require, *vb.* exiger.
requirement, *n.* exigence *f.*
requisite, *adj.* nécessaire.
requisition, *n.* réquisition *f.*
rescind, *vb.* annuler.
rescue, 1. *n.* délivrance *f.* **2.** *vb.* délivrer.
research, *n.* recherche *f.*
resemble, *vb.* ressembler à.
resent, *vb.* être froissé de.
reservation, *n.* réserve *f.*
reserve, 1. *n.* réserve *f.* **2.** *vb.* réserver.
reservoir, *n.* réservoir *m.*
reside, *vb.* résider.
residence, *n.* résidence *f.*
resident, 1. *n.* habitant *m.* **2.** *adj.* résidant.
resign, *vb.* résigner; (from post) se démettre (de), démissionner.
resignation, *n.* résignation *f.;* (from post) démission *f.*
resist, *vb.* résister (à).
resistance, *n.* résistance *f.*
resolute, *adj.* résolu.
resolution, *n.* résolution *f.*
resolve, *vb.* résoudre.
resonant, *adj.* résonnant.

resort, 1. *n.* (resource) ressource *f.;* (recourse) recours *m.;* (place) lieu *(m.)* de séjour. **2.** *vb.* avoir recours.
resound, *vb.* résonner.
resource, *n.* ressource *f.*
respect, 1. *n.* respect *m.;* (reference) rapport *m.* **2.** *vb.* respecter.
respectable, *adj.* respectable.
respectful, *adj.* respectueux.
respective, *adj.* respectif.
respiration, *n.* respiration *f.*
respite, *n.* répit *m.*
respond, *vb.* répondre.
response, *n.* réponse *f.*
responsibility, *n.* responsabilité *f.*
responsible, *adj.* responsable.
rest, 1. *n.* (repose) repos *m.;* (remainder) reste *m.;* (the r., the others) les autres *m.f.pl.* **2.** *vb.* se reposer.
restaurant, *n.* restaurant *m.*
restful, *adj.* qui repose.
restive, *adj.* agité.
restless, *adj.* (anxious) inquiet.
restoration, *n.* restauration *f.*
restore, *vb.* remettre; (repair) restaurer.
restrain, *vb.* contenir.
restraint, *n.* contrainte *f.*
restrict, *vb.* restreindre.
result, 1. *n.* résultat *m.* **2.** *vb.* résulter.
resume, *vb.* reprendre.
résumé, *n.* résumé *m.*
resurrect, *vb.* ressusciter.
retail, *n.* détail *m.*
retain, *vb.* retenir.
retaliate, *vb.* user de représailles.
retard, *vb.* retarder.
retarded, *adj.* arriéré.
reticent, *adj.* réservé.
retina, *n.* rétine *f.*
retire, *vb.* se retirer.
retort, *n.* riposte *f.*
retract, *vb.* (se) rétracter.
retreat, 1. *n.* retraite *f.* **2.** *vb.* se retirer.
retribution, *n.* châtiment *m.*
retrieve, *vb.* recouvrer.

retrospect, *n.* renvoi *m.*, (in r.) coup d'œil *(m.)* rétrospectif.
return, 1. *n.* retour *m.;* (returns, *comm.)* recettes *f.pl.* **2.** *vb.* (give back) rendre; (go back) retourner; (come back) revenir.
reunion, *n.* réunion *f.*
reunite, *vb.* réunir.
reveal, *vb.* révéler.
revel, *vb.* s'ébattre.
revelation, *n.* révélation *f.*
revelry, *n.* bacchanale *f.*
revenge, 1. *n.* vengeance *f.* **2.** *vb.* (r. oneself) se venger.
revenue, *n.* revenu *m.*
reverberate, *vb.* réverbérer, réfléchir, répercuter.
revere, *vb.* révérer.
reverence, *n.* révérence *f.*
reverend, *adj.* révérend.
reverent, *adj.* respectueux.
reverie, *n.* rêverie *f.*
reverse, 1. *n.* (opposite) contraire *m.;* (defeat, medal) revers *m.;* (gear) marche *(f.)* arrière. **2.** *vb.* renverser.
revert, *vb.* revenir.
review, *n.* revue *f.*
revise, *vb.* réviser.
revision, *n.* révision *f.*
revival, *n.* renaissance *f.;* (religious) réveil *m.*, renouveau *m.*
revive, *vb.* revivre, *intr.;* faire revivre, *tr.*
revoke, *vb.* révoquer.
revolt, 1. *n.* révolte *f.* **2.** *vb.* se révolter.
revolution, *n.* révolution *f.*
revolutionary, *adj.* révolutionnaire.
revolve, *vb.* tourner, *intr.*
revolver, *n.* revolver *m.*
reward, 1. *n.* récompense *f.* **2.** *vb.* récompenser.
rewind, *vb.* rembobiner.
rheumatism, *n.* rhumatisme *m.*
Rhine, *n.* Rhin *m.*
Rhone, *n.* Rhône *m.*
rhinoceros, *n.* rhinocéros *m.*
rhubarb, *n.* rhubarbe *f.*
rhyme, 1. *n.* rime *f.* **2.** *vb.* rimer.
rhythm, *n.* rythme *m.*

rhythmical, *adj.* rythmique.

rib, *n.* côte *f.*

ribbon, *n.* ruban *m.*

rice, *n.* riz *m.*

rich, *adj.* riche.

rid, *vb.* débarrasser.

riddle, *n.* énigme *f.*

ride, 1. *n.* promenade *f.* **2.** *vb.* (horse) aller à cheval; (vehicle) aller en voiture.

rider, *n.* (on horse) cavalier *m.*

ridge, *n.* crête *f.*

ridicule, 1. *n.* ridicule *m.* **2.** *vb.* se moquer de.

ridiculous, *adj.* ridicule.

rifle, *n.* fusil *m.*

rift, *n.* désaccord *m.*

rig, 1. *n.* (vessel) gréement *m.;* (outfit) tenue *f.* **2.** *vb.* gréer.

right, 1. *n.* droit *m.;* (not left) droite *f.* **2.** *adj.* (straight, not left) droit; (correct, proper) juste; **(be r.,** of person) avoir raison; **(all r.)** c'est bien. **3.** *adv.* (straight) droit; (not left) à droite; (justly) bien.

righteous, *adj.* vertueux.

righteousness, *n.* justice *f.*

right of way, *n.* droit de passage *m.,* (automobiles) priorité (*f.*) de passage.

right wing, *n.* la droite.

rigid, *adj.* rigide.

rigor, *n.* rigueur *f.*

rigorous, *adj.* rigoureux.

rim, *n.* bord *m.;* (wheel) jante *f.*

ring, 1. *n.* anneau *m.;* (ornament) bague *f.;* (circle) cercle *m.;* (arena) arène *f.;* (sound) son *m.;* (phone) coup (*m.*) de téléphone. **2.** *vb.* sonner.

rinse, *vb.* rincer.

riot, *n.* émeute *f.*

rip, 1. *n.* fente *f.* **2.** *vb.* fendre, *tr.*

ripe, *adj.* mûr.

ripen, *vb.* mûrir.

ripoff, 1. *n.* vol *m.* **2.** *vb.* voler.

ripple, 1. *n.* (on water) ride *f.* **2.** *vb.* rider, *tr.*

rise, 1. *n.* (ground) montée *f.;* (increase) augmenta-tion *f.;* (rank) avancement *m.* **2.** *vb.* se lever.

risk, 1. *n.* risque *m.* **2.** *vb.* risquer.

rite, *n.* rite *m.*

ritual, *adj.* rituel.

rival, 1. *adj.* and *n.* rival *m.* **2.** *vb.* rivaliser avec.

rivalry, *n.* rivalité *f.*

river, *n.* fleuve *m.*

river bank, *n.* rive *f.,* berge *f.*

rivet, *n.* rivet *m.*

Riviera, *n.* Côte (*f.*) d'Azur.

road, *n.* route *f.*

roam, *vb.* errer (par).

roar, *vb.* (person) hurler; (lion) rugir; (bull, sea) mugir; (thunder, cannon) gronder; (laughter) éclater de.

roast, 1. *n.* rôti *m.* **2.** *vb.* rôtir.

rob, *vb.* voler.

robber, *n.* voleur *m.*

robbery, *n.* vol *m.*

robe, *n.* robe *f.*

robin, *n.* rouge-gorge *m.*

robot, *n.* automate *m.,* robot *m.*

robust, *adj.* robuste.

rock, 1. *n.* rocher *m.* **2.** *vb.* balancer; (child) bercer. **3.** *adj.* (music) rock.

rocket, *n.* fusée *f.*

rocking chair, *n.* fauteuil (*m.*) à bascule.

rocky, *adj.* rocheux.

rod, *n.* verge *f.*

rodent, *adj.* and *n.* rongeur *m.*

roe, *n.* (animal) chevreuil *m.;* (of fish) œufs (*m.pl.*) de poisson.

rogue, *n.* coquin *m.*

roguish, *adj.* coquin.

role, *n.* rôle *m.*

roll, 1. *n.* rouleau *m.;* (bread) petit pain *m.;* (list) liste *f.;* **(r.-call)** appel *m.;* (boat) roulis *m.* **2.** *vb.* rouler.

roller, *n.* rouleau *m.*

roller skate, *n.* patin (*m.*) à roulette.

Roman, 1. *n.* Romain *m.* **2.** *adj.* romain.

romance, *n.* roman (*m.*) de chevalerie.

Romania, *n.* Roumanie *f.*

Romanian, 1. *n.* (person) Roumain *m.;* (language) roumain *m.* **2.** *adj.* roumain.

romantic, *adj.* romanesque; (poetry, music) roman-tique.

romp, 1. *n.* tapage *m.* **2.** *vb.* batifoler.

roof, *n.* toit *m.*

room, *n.* (space) place *f.;* (private use) chambre *f.;* (public use) salle *f.*

roommate, *n.* camarade (*m.f.*) de chambre.

rooster, *n.* coq *m.*

root, 1. *n.* racine *f.;* (source) source *f.* **2.** *vb.* enraciner, *tr.*

rope, *n.* corde *f.*

rosary, *n.* rosaire *m.*

rose, *n.* rose *f.*

rosemary, *n.* romarin *m.*

rosin, *n.* colophane *f.*

rosy, *adj.* de rose.

rot, 1. *n.* pourriture *f.* **2.** *vb.* pourrir.

rotary, *adj.* rotatoire.

rotate, *vb.* tourner.

rotation, *n.* rotation *f.*

rotten, *adj.* pourri.

rouge, *n.* rouge *m.*

rough, *adj.* rude; (sea weather) gros *m.,* grosse *f.*

round, 1. *adj.* rond. **2.** *n.* rond *m.;* (circuit) tournée *f.*

round trip, *n.* voyage (*m.*) aller et retour.

rouse, *vb.* (wake) réveiller; (stir up) secouer.

rout, *n.* (mil.) déroute *f.*

route, *n.* route *f.*

routine, *n.* routine *f.*

rove, *vb.* errer (par).

rover, *n.* rôdeur *m.*

row, 1. *n.* rang *m.;* dispute *f.* **2.** *vb.* ramer.

rowboat, *n.* barque *f.*

rowdy, *adj.* tapageur.

rowing, *n.* aviron *m.*

royal, *adj.* royal.

royalty, *n.* royauté *f.;* (of author) droits (*m.pl.*) d'auteur.

rub, *vb.* frotter.

rubber, *n.* caoutchouc *m.*

rubbish, *n.* rebuts *m.pl.*; (nonsense) bêtises *f.pl.*
ruby, *n.* rubis *m.*
rudder, *n.* gouvernail *m.*
ruddy, *adj.* rouge.
rude, *adj.* (rough) rude; (impolite) impoli.
rudiment, *n.* rudiment *m.*
rue, *vb.* regretter.
ruffian, *n.* bandit *m.*
ruffle, *n.* (frill) fraise *f.*
rug, *n.* tapis *m.*
rugged, *adj.* (rough) rude; (uneven) raboteux.
ruin, 1. *n.* ruine *f.* 2. *vb.* ruiner.
ruinous, *adj.* ruineux.
rule, 1. *n.* règle *f.*; (authority) autorité *f.* 2. *vb.* gouverner; (decide) décider.

ruler, *n.* souverain *m.*; (for lines) règle *f.*
rum, *n.* rhum *m.*
rumba, *n.* rumba *f.*
rumble, *vb.* gronder.
rumor, *n.* rumeur *f.*
run, *vb. intr.* courir; (of engine) marcher; (of colors) déteindre; (of liquids) couler; (**r. away**) s'enfuir.
run-down, *adj.* épuisé.
rung, *n.* échelon *m.*
runner, *n.* (person) coureur *m.*; (table) chemin (*m.*) de table.
running, *n.* course *f.*, gestion *f.*, direction *f.*
rupture, *n.* rupture *f.*
rural, *adj.* rural.

rush, 1. *n.* (haste) hâte *f.*; (onrush) ruée *f.*; (air, water) coup *m.*; (plant) jonc *m.* 2. *vb.* se précipiter, *intr.*
Russia, *n.* Russie *f.*
Russian, 1. *n.* (person) Russe *m.f.*; (language) russe *m.* 2. *adj.* russe.
rust, 1. *n.* rouille *f.* 2. *vb.* rouiller, *tr.*
rustic, *adj.* rustique.
rustle, *n.* (leaves) bruissement *m.*; (skirt) froufrou *m.*
rusty, *adj.* rouillé.
rut, *n.* ornière *f.*
ruthless, *adj.* impitoyable.
rye, *n.* seigle *m.*; (whiskey) whisky *m.*

S

Sabbath *n.* sabbat *m.*
saber, *n.* sabre *m.*
sable, *n.* zibeline *f.*
sabotage, 1. *n.* sabotage *m.* 2. *vb.* saboter.
saboteur, *n.* saboteur *m.*
saccharin, *n.* saccharine *f.*
sachet, *n.* sachet *m.*
sack, 1. *n.* sac *m.* 2. *vb.* saccager.
sacrament, *n.* sacrement *m.*
sacred, *adj.* sacré.
sacrifice, 1. *n.* sacrifice *m.* 2. *vb.* sacrifier.
sacrilege, *n.* sacrilège *m.*
sad, *adj.* triste.
sadden, *vb.* attrister, *tr.*
saddle, *n.* selle *f.*
sadism, *n.* sadisme *m.*
sadistic, *adj.* sadique.
sadness, *n.* tristesse *f.*
safe, 1. *n.* coffre-fort *m.* 2. *adj.* sûr; (s. *and* sound) sain et sauf; (s. from) à l'abri de.
safeguard, *vb.* sauvegarder.
safe sex, *n.* rapports (*m.pl.*) sexuels sans risques.
safety, *n.* sûreté *f.*, sécurité *f.*
safety pin, *n.* épingle (*f.*) anglaise.
sag, *vb.* s'affaisser.
sage, *n.* (person) sage *m.*; (plant) sauge *f.*

sail, 1. *n.* voile *f.* 2. *vb.* naviguer; (depart) partir.
sailboat, *n.* canot (*m.*) à voiles.
sailor, *n.* marin *m.*
saint, *adj. and n.* saint *m.*
sake, *n.* (for the s. of) pour l'amour de.
salad, *n.* salade *f.*
salami, *n.* salami *m.*
salary, *n.* appointements *m.pl.*
sale, *n.* vente *f.*
salesman, *n.* vendeur *m.*
sales tax, *n.* impôt (*m.*) sur les ventes.
saliva, *n.* salive *f.*
salmon, *n.* saumon *m.*
salt, 1. *n.* sel *m.* 2. *vb.* saler.
salute, 1. *n.* salut *m.* 2. *vb.* saluer.
salvage, *n.* sauvetage *m.*
salvation, *n.* salut *m.*
salve, *n.* onguent *m.*
same, 1. *adj. and pron.* même. 2. *adv.* de même.
sample, *n.* échantillon *m.*
sanatorium, *n.* sanatorium *m.*
sanctify, *vb.* sanctifier.
sanction, *n.* sanction *f.*
sanctity, *n.* sainteté *f.*
sanctuary, *n.* sanctuaire *m.*
sand, *n.* sable *m.*

sandal, *n.* sandale *f.*
sandwich, *n.* sandwich *m.*
sandy, *adj.* sablonneux.
sane, *adj.* sain d'esprit.
sanitary, *adj.* sanitaire.
sanitary napkin, *n.* serviette (*f.*) hygiénique.
sanitation, *n.* hygiène *f.*
sanity, *n.* santé (*f.*) d'esprit.
Santa Claus, *n.* Père Noël *m.*
sap, *n.* sève *f.*
sapphire, *n.* saphir *m.*
sarcasm, *n.* sarcasme *m.*
sardine, *n.* sardine *f.*
Sardinia, *n.* Sardaigne *f.*
sash, *n.* ceinture *f.*
satellite, *n.* satellite *m.*
satellite dish, *n.* antenne (*f.*) parabolique.
satellite television, *n.* télévision (*f.*) par cable.
satin, *n.* satin *m.*
satire, *n.* satire *f.*
satisfaction, *n.* satisfaction *f.*
satisfactory, *adj.* satisfaisant.
satisfy, *vb.* satisfaire.
saturate, *vb.* saturer.
Saturday, *n.* samedi *m.*
sauce, *n.* sauce *f.*
saucer, *n.* soucoupe *f.*
saucy, *adj.* impertinent.
Saudi Arabia, *n.* Arabie (*f.*) Saoudite.
sausage, *n.* saucisse *f.*

savage, *adj. and n.* sauvage *m.f.*

save, *vb.* sauver; (put aside) mettre de côté; (economize) épargner.

saving, *n.* épargne *f.*

savings bank, *n.* caisse (*f.*) d'épargne.

savior, *n.* sauveur *m.*

savor, *n.* saveur *f.*

savory, *adj.* savoureux.

saw, 1. *n.* scie *f.* **2.** *vb.* scier.

say, *vb.* dire.

scab, *n.* croûte *f.*, gale *f.*

scaffold, *n.* échafaud *m.*

scald, *vb.* échauder.

scale, 1. *n.* (fish) écaille *f.*; (balance) balance *f.*; (series, graded system, map) échelle *f.*; (music) gamme *f.* **2.** *vb.* escalader.

scallop, *n.* coquille (*f.*) Saint-Jacques; (sewing) feston *m.*

scalp, 1. *n.* cuir (*m.*) chevelu. **2.** *vb.* scalper.

scan, 1. *vb.* (examine) scruter; (verse) scander. **2.** *n.* échographie *f.*

scandal, *n.* scandale *m.*

scandalous, *adj.* scandaleux.

Scandinavia, *n.* Scandinavie *f.*

Scandinavian, 1. *n.* Scandinave *m.f.* **2.** *adj.* scandinave.

scant(y), *adj.* limité, faible.

scar, *n.* cicatrice *f.*

scarce, *adj.* rare.

scare, *vb.* effrayer.

scarf, *n.* écharpe *f.*

scarlet, *adj. and n.* écarlate *f.*; (s. fever) scarlatine *f.*

scary, *adj.* effrayant.

scathing, *adj.* cinglant.

scatter, *vb.* éparpiller.

scavenger, *n.* boueur *m.*

scenario, *n.* scénario *m.*

scene, *n.* scène *f.*

scenery, *n.* (theater) décors *m.pl.*; (landscape) paysage *m.*

scent, 1. *n.* parfum *m.*, odeur *f.* **2.** *vb.* flairer, sentir.

schedule, *n.* horaire *m.*

scheme, *n.* plan *m.*

schizophrenic, *adj. and n.* schizophrène *m.f.*

scholar, *n.* savant *m.*

scholarship, *n.* (school) bourse *f.*

school, *n.* école *f.*

sciatica, *n.* sciatique *f.*

science, *n.* science *f.*

science fiction, *n.* science-fiction *f.*

scientist, *n.* scientifique *m.f.*

scissors, *n.* ciseaux *m.pl.*

scoff at, *vb.* se moquer de.

scold, *vb.* gronder.

scoop out, *vb.* évider.

scope, *n.* (extent) portée *f.*; (outlet) carrière *f.*

scorch, *vb.* roussir.

score, *n.* (games) points *m.pl.*; (twenty) vingtaine *f.*; (music) partition *f.*

scorn, 1. *n.* mépris *m.* **2.** *vb.* mépriser.

scornful, *adj.* dédaigneux.

Scotch, Scottish, *adj.* écossais.

Scotchman, Scotsman, *n.* Écossais *m.*

Scotch tape, *n.* ruban adhésif *m.*

Scotland, *n.* Écosse *f.*

scour, *vb.* nettoyer.

scourge, *n.* fléau *m.*

scout, *n.* éclaireur *m.*; (boy s.) boy-scout *m.*

scowl, *vb.* se renfrogner.

scramble, *vb.* avancer péniblement.

scrap, 1. *n.* petit morceau *m.* **2.** *vb.* mettre au rebut.

scrape, scratch, 1. *n.* égratignure *f.* **2.** *vb.* gratter.

scream, 1. *n.* cri *m.* **2.** *vb.* crier.

screen, *n.* écran *m.*; (folding s.) paravent *m.*

screen play, *n.* scénario *m.*

screw, 1. *n.* vis *f.* **2.** *vb.* visser, *tr.*

screwdriver, *n.* tournevis *m.*

scribble, *vb.* griffonner.

script, *n.* écriture *f.*, scénario *m.*

scroll, *n.* rouleau *m.*

scrub, *vb.* frotter.

scruple, *n.* scrupule *m.*

scrupulous, *adj.* scrupuleux.

scrutinize, *vb.* scruter.

scuba-diving, *n.* plongée (*f.*) sous-marine.

sculptor, *n.* sculpteur *m.*

sculpture, *n.* sculpture *f.*

scythe, *n.* faux *f.*

sea, *n.* mer *f.*

seabed, *n.* lit (*m.*) de la mer.

seacoast, *n.* littoral *m.*

seagull, *n.* mouette *f.*

seal, 1. *n.* (animal) phoque *m.*; (stamp) sceau *m.* **2.** *vb.* sceller.

seam, *n.* couture *f.*

seaport, *n.* port (*m.*) de mer.

search, 1. *n.* recherche *f.* **2.** *vb.* chercher.

seasickness, *n.* mal (*m.*) de mer.

season, 1. *n.* saison *f.* **2.** *vb.* assaisonner.

seat, 1. *n.* siège *m.* **2.** *vb.* asseoir.

seat-belt, *n.* ceinture (*f.*) de sécurité.

seclude, *vb.* isoler.

second, 1. *n.* seconde *f.* **2.** *adj.* second, deuxième.

secondary, *adj.* secondaire.

secret, *adj. and n.* secret *m.*

secretary, *n.* secrétaire *m.f.*

sect, *n.* secte *f.*

section, *n.* section *f.*

sectional, *adj.* régional.

secular, *adj.* (church) séculier; (education) laïque; (time) séculaire.

secure, 1. *adj.* sûr. **2.** *vb.* (make s.) mettre en sûreté; (make fast) fixer; (obtain) obtenir.

security, *n.* sûreté *f.*; (comm., law) caution *f.*; (finance, pl.) valeurs *f.pl.*

sedative, *adj. and n.* sédatif *m.*

sediment, *n.* sédiment *m.*

seduce, *vb.* séduire.

see, *vb.* voir.

seed, *n.* semence *f.*; (vegetables, etc.) graine *f.*

seek, *vb.* chercher.

seem, *vb.* sembler.

seep, *vb.* suinter.

segment, *n.* segment *m.*

segregate, *vb.* séparer.

seize, *vb.* saisir.

seizure, *n.* crise *f.*, attaque *f.*

seldom, *adv.* rarement.

select, *vb.* choisir.
selection, *n.* sélection *f.*
self, *n.* moi *m.*, personne *f.*
self-centered, *adj.* égocentrique.
selfish, *adj.* égoïste.
selfishness, *n.* égoïsme *m.*
self-righteous, *adj.* suffisant.
self-service, *adj. and n.* libre-service *m.*
sell, *vb.* vendre, *tr.*
semantics, *n.* sémantique *f.*
semester, *n.* semestre *m.*
semicircle, *n.* demi-cercle *m.*
semicolon, *n.* point-virgule *m.*
seminary, *n.* séminaire *m.*
Semite, *n.* Sémite *m.f.*
senate, *n.* sénat *m.*
senator, *n.* sénateur *m.*
send, *vb.* envoyer; (**s. back**) renvoyer.
senile, *adj.* sénile.
senior, *adj. and n.* (age) aîné *m.*; (rank) supérieur *m.*
senior citizen, *n.* personne (*f.*) du troisième âge.
seniority, *n.* ancienneté *f.*
sensation, *n.* sensation *f.*
sensational, *adj.* sensationnel.
sense, *n.* sens *m.*
sensible, *adj.* (wise) sensé; (appreciable) sensible.
sensitive, *adj.* sensible.
sensual, *adj.* sensuel.
sensuous, *adj.* sensuel.
sentence, *n.* (*gramm.*) phrase *f.*; (law) sentence *f.*
sentiment, *n.* sentiment *m.*
sentimental, *adj.* sentimental.
separate, 1. *adj.* séparé. 2. *vb.* séparer, *tr.*
separation, *n.* séparation *f.*
September, *n.* septembre *m.*
sequence, *n.* suite *f.*
serene, *adj.* serein.
serenade, *n.* sérénade *f.*
serene, *adj.* serein.
sergeant, *n.* sergent *m.*
serial, *n.* roman-feuilleton *m.*
series, *n.* série *f.*
serious, *adj.* sérieux.
sermon, *n.* sermon *m.*
serpent, *n.* serpent *m.*
serum, *n.* sérum *m.*

servant, *n.* (domestic) domestique *m.f.*; (public) employé *m.*
serve, *vb.* servir.
service, *n.* service *m.*; (church) office *m.*
service station, *n.* station-service *f.*
servitude, *n.* servitude *f.*
session, *n.* session *f.*
set, 1. *n.* ensemble *m.* 2. *adj.* fixe; (decided) résolu. 3. *vb. tr.* (put) mettre; (regulate) régler; (jewels) monter; (fix) fixer. 4. *vb. intr.* (sun, etc.) se coucher; (**s. about**) se mettre à.
settle, *vb.* (establish) établir, *tr.*; (fix) fixer; (decide) décider; (arrange) arranger; (pay) payer; (**s. down to,** *intr.*) se mettre à.
settlement, *n.* (colony) colonie *f.*; (accounts) règlement *m.*
settler, *n.* colon *m.*
seven, *adj. and n.* sept *m.*
seventeen, *adj. and n.* dix-sept *m.*
seventh, *adj. and n.* septième *m.f.*
seventy, *adj. and n.* soixante-dix *m.*
sever, *vb.* séparer, couper.
several, *adj. and pron.* plusieurs.
severe, *adj.* sévère.
severity, *n.* sévérité *f.*
sew, *vb.* coudre.
sewer, *n.* égout *m.*
sex, *n.* sexe *m.*
sexism, *n.* sexisme *m.*
sexist, *adj.* sexiste.
sexual, *adj.* sexuel.
shabby, *adj.* (clothes) usé; (person) mesquin.
shack, *n.* cabane *f.*
shade, 1. *n.* ombre *f.*; (colors) nuance *f.*; (window) store *m.* 2. *vb.* ombrager.
shadow, *n.* ombre *f.*
shady, *adj.* ombragé; (not honest) louche.
shaft, *n.* (mine) puits *m.*
shaggy, *adj.* poilu, hirsute.
shake, *vb. tr.* secouer; trembler; (**s. hands**) serrer la main à.

shallow, *adj.* peu profond.
shame, *n.* honte *f.*
shameful, *adj.* honteux.
shampoo, *n.* shampooing *m.*
shape, 1. *n.* forme *f.* 2. *vb.* former.
share, 1. *n.* part *f.*; (finance) action *f.* 2. *vb.* partager.
shareholder, *n.* actionnaire *m.*
shark, *n.* requin *m.*
sharp, *adj.* (cutting) tranchant; (clever) fin; (piercing) perçant; (music) dièse.
sharpen, *vb.* aiguiser.
shatter, *vb.* briser.
shave, *vb.* raser, *tr.*
shaving brush, *n.* blaireau *m.*
shaving cream, *n.* crème (*f.*) à raser.
shawl, *n.* châle *m.*
she, *pron.* elle.
sheaf, *n.* (grain) gerbe *f.*
shear, *vb.* tondre.
shears, *n.* cisailles *f.pl.*
sheath, *n.* étui *m.*
shed, 1. *n.* hangar *m.* 2. *vb.* verser.
sheen, *n.* lustre *m.*
sheep, *n.* mouton *m.*
sheet, *n.* (bed) drap *m.*; (paper, metal) feuille *f.*
shelf, *n.* rayon *m.*
shell, *n.* coquille *f.*; (of building) carcasse *f.*; (explosive) obus *m.*
shellac, *n.* laque *f.*
shellfish, *n.* coquillages *m.pl.*
shelter, 1. *n.* abri *m.* 2. *vb.* abriter.
shepherd, *n.* berger *m.*
sherbet, *n.* sorbet *m.*
sherry, *n.* xérès *m.*
shield, *n.* bouclier *m.*
shift, 1. *n.* (change) changement *m.*; (workers) équipe *f.*; (expedient) expédient *m.*; (shirt) chemise *f.* 2. *vb.* changer; (**s. gears**) changer de vitesse.
shin, *n.* tibia *m.*
shine, *vb.* briller, *intr.*; (shoes) cirer.
shiny, *adj.* luisant.
ship, *n.* navire *m.*; vaisseau *m.*

shipment, *n.* envoi *m.*

shirk, *vb.* esquiver.

shirt, *n.* chemise *f.*

shiver, 1. *n.* frisson *m.* 2. *vb.* frissonner.

shock, 1. *n.* choc *m.* 2. *vb.* choquer.

shock absorber, *n.* amortisseur *m.*

shoe, *n.* soulier *m.*, chaussure *f.*

shoelace, *n.* lacet *m.*

shoemaker, *n.* cordonnier *m.*

shoot, *vb.* tirer; (person) fusiller; (hit) atteindre; (rush) se précipiter.

shop, 1. *n.* boutique *f.*; (factory) atelier *m.* 2. *vb.* faire des emplettes.

shopping, *n.* achats *m.pl.*

shop window, *n.* vitrine *f.*

shore, *n.* rivage *m.*

short, *adj.* court.

shortage, *n.* manque *m.*, insuffisance *f.*

short-circuit, *n.* court-circuit *m.*

shorten, *vb.* raccourcir.

shorthand, *n.* sténographie *f.*

short story, *n.* nouvelle *f.*

shot, *n.* coup *m.*

should, *vb.* devoir (in conditional).

shoulder, *n.* épaule *f.*

shoulder blade, *n.* omoplate *f.*

shout, 1. *n.* cri *m.* 2. *vb.* crier.

shove, *vb.* pousser.

shovel, *n.* pelle *f.*

show, 1. *n.* (exhibition) exposition *f.*; (spectacle, performance) spectacle *m.*; (semblance) semblant *m.*; (display) parade *f.* 2. *vb.* montrer, *tr.*

shower, *n.* (rain) averse *f.*; (washing) douche *f.*

shrapnel, *n.* éclats (*m.pl.*) d'obus.

shrewd, *adj.* sagace.

shriek, 1. *n.* cri (*m.*) perçant. 2. *vb.* hurler.

shrill, *adj.* aigu.

shrimp, *n.* crevette *f.*

shrine, *n.* châsse *f.*

shrink, *vb.* rétrécir, *tr.*

shroud, *n.* linceul *m.*

shrub, *n.* arbrisseau *m.*

shudder, 1. *n.* frisson *m.* 2. *vb.* frissonner.

shun, *vb.* fuir.

shut, *vb.* fermer.

shuttle, 1. *n.* navette *f.* 2. *vb.* faire la navette.

shutter, *n.* volet *m.*

shy, *adj.* timide.

sick, *adj.* malade.

sickness, *n.* maladie *f.*

side, *n.* côté *m.*

sidewalk, *n.* trottoir *m.*

siege, *n.* siège *m.*

sieve, *n.* tamis *m.*

sift, *vb.* cribler.

sigh, 1. *n.* soupir *m.* 2. *vb.* soupirer.

sight, *n.* vue *f.*; (spectacle) spectacle *m.*

sightseeing, *n.* tourisme *m.*

sign, 1. *n.* signe *m.*; (placard) enseigne *f.* 2. *vb.* signer.

signal, *n.* signal *m.*

signature, *n.* signature *f.*

significance, *n.* (meaning) signification *f.*; (importance) importance *f.*

significant, *adj.* significatif.

signify, *vb.* signifier.

sign language, *n.* langage (*m.*) des sourds-muets.

silence, *n.* silence *m.*

silent, *adj.* silencieux.

silicon, *n.* silicium *m.*; (s. chip) microplaquette *f.*

silk, *n.* soie *f.*

silken, *adj.* de soie.

silly, *adj.* sot *m.*, sotte *f.*

silver, 1. *n.* argent *m.* 2. *adj.* d'argent.

silverware, *n.* argenterie *f.*

similar, *adj.* semblable.

simple, *adj.* simple.

simplicity, *n.* simplicité *f.*

simplify, *vb.* simplifier.

simply, *adv.* simplement.

simultaneous, *adj.* simultané.

sin, 1. *n.* péché *m.* 2. *vb.* pécher.

since, 1. *adv.*, *prep.* depuis. 2. *conj.* (time) depuis que; (cause) puisque.

sincere, *adj.* sincère.

sincerity, *n.* sincérité *f.*

sinful, *adj.* (person) pécheur *m.*, pécheresse *f.*; (act) coupable.

sing, *vb.* chanter.

singer, *n.* chanteur *m.*

single, *adj.* (only one) seul; (particular) particulier; (not married) célibataire.

singular, *adj.* and *n.* singulier *m.*

sinister, *adj.* sinistre.

sink, 1. *n.* (kitchen) évier *m.*, (bathroom) lavabo *m.* 2. *vb.* enfoncer, *tr.*; (vessel) couler à fond; (diminish, weaken) baisser.

sinner, *n.* pécheur *m.*, pécheresse *f.*

sinus, *n.* sinus *m.*

sip, *vb.* siroter.

sir, *n.* monsieur *m.*; (title) Sir *m.*

sirloin, *n.* aloyau *m.*

sister, *n.* sœur *f.*

sister-in-law, *n.* belle-sœur *f.*

sit, *vb.* (s. down) s'asseoir; (be seated) être assis.

sitcom, *n.* comédie (*f.*) de situation.

site, *n.* emplacement *m.*

sit-in, *n.* occupation (*f.*) (de locaux).

situate, *vb.* situer.

situation, *n.* situation *f.*

six, *adj.* and *n.* six *m.*

sixteen, *adj.* and *n.* seize *m.*

sixteenth, *adj.* and *n.* seizième *m.f.*

sixth, *adj.* and *n.* sixième *m.f.*

sixty, *adj.* and *n.* soixante *m.*

size, *n.* grandeur *f.*; (person) taille *f.*; (shoes, gloves) pointure *f.*; (book, packaged merchandise) format *m.*

skate, 1. *n.* patin *m.* 2. *vb.* patiner.

skateboard, *n.* planche (*f.*) à roulettes.

skeleton, *n.* squelette *m.*

skeptic, *n.* sceptique *m.f.*

skeptical, *adj.* sceptique.

sketch, 1. *n.* croquis *m.* 2. *vb.* esquisser.

ski, 1. *n.* ski *m.* 2. *vb.* faire du ski.

skill, *n.* adresse *f.*

skillful, *adj.* adroit.

skim, *vb.* (milk) écrémer; (book) feuilleter; (surface) effleurer.

skin, 1. *n.* peau *f.* 2. *vb.* écorcher.

skinny, *adj.* maigre.

skip, *vb.* sauter.

skirt, *n.* jupe *f.*

skull, *n.* crâne *m.*

sky, *n.* ciel *m.*

skyscraper, *n.* gratte-ciel *m.*

slab, *n.* dalle *f.*

slack, *adj.* lâche.

slacken, *vb.* (slow up) ralentir; (loosen) relâcher.

slacks, *n.* pantalon *m.*

slander, 1. *n.* calomnie *f.* 2. *vb.* calomnier.

slang, *n.* argot *m.*

slant, 1. *n.* (slope) pente *f.;* (bias) biais *m.* 2. *vb.* incliner.

slap, 1. *n.* claque *f.* 2. *vb.* gifler.

slash, *n.* taillade *f.*

slate, *n.* ardoise *f.*

slaughter, 1. *n.* (people) massacre *m.;* (animals) abattage *m.* 2. *vb.* massacrer; abattre.

slaughterhouse, *n.* abattoir *m.*

slave, *n.* esclave *m.f.*

slavery, *n.* esclavage *m.*

slay, *vb.* tuer.

sled, *n.* traîneau *m.*

sleep, 1. *n.* sommeil *m.;* (go to s.) s'endormir. 2. *vb.* dormir.

sleeping bag, *n.* sac de couchage *m.*

sleeping pill, *n.* somnifère *m.*

sleepy, *adj.* somnolent; (be s.) avoir sommeil.

sleet, 1. *n.* grésil *m.* 2. *vb.* grésiller.

sleeve, *n.* manche *f.*

sleigh, *n.* traîneau *m.*

slender, *adj.* mince; svelte.

slice, *n.* tranche *f.*

slide, 1. *n.* (sliding) glissade *f.;* (microscope) lamelle *f.;* (lantern) plaque *(f.)* de projection. 2. *vb.* glisser.

slight, *adj.* léger; mince.

slim, *adj.* mince.

sling, 1. *n.* fronde *f.;* (medical) écharpe *f.* 2. *vb.*

(throw) lancer; (hang) suspendre.

slip, 1. *n.* (sliding) glissade *f.;* (tongue, pen) lapsus *m.;* (mistake) faux pas *m.;* (paper) fiche *f.;* (garment) sous-jupe *f.* 2. *vb.* glisser; (err) faire une faute.

slipper, *n.* pantoufle *f.*

slippery, *adj.* glissant.

slit, 1. *n.* fente *f.* 2. *vb.* fendre.

slogan, *n.* mot *(m.)* d'ordre; (politics) cri *(m.)* de guerre.

slope, 1. *n.* pente *f.* 2. *vb.* incliner.

sloppy, *adj.* mal soigné.

slot, *n.* fente *f.*

slow, *adj.* lent; (clock) en retard.

slowness, *n.* lenteur *f.*

sluggish, *adj.* paresseux.

slum, *n.* quartier *(m.)* pauvre.

slumber, *vb.* sommeiller.

sly, *adj.* (crafty) rusé; (secretive) sournois.

smack, 1. *n.* (a bit) soupçon *m.;* (noise) claquement *m.* 2. *vb.* gifler.

small, *adj.* petit.

smallpox, *n.* petite vérole *f.*

smart, 1. *adj.* (clever) habile; (stylish) élégant. 2. *vb.* cuire.

smash, 1. *vb.* briser, *tr.* 2. *n.* coup *m.;* (fig.) collision *f.*

smear, 1. *n.* tache *f.* 2. *vb.* salir.

smell, 1. *n.* odeur *f.* 2. *vb.* sentir.

smelt, 1. *n.* éperlan *m.* 2. *vb.* fondre.

smile, *n., vb.* sourire *m.*

smite, *vb.* frapper.

smog, *n.* brouillard *(m.)* mélangé de fumée.

smoke, 1. *n.* fumée *f.* 2. *vb.* fumer.

smolder, *vb.* couver.

smooth, 1. *adj.* lisse. 2. *vb.* lisser.

smother, *vb.* étouffer.

smug, *adj.* suffisant.

smuggle, *vb.* faire passer en contrebande.

snack, *n.* casse-croûte *m.*

snag, *n.* obstacle *(m.)* caché.

snail, *n.* escargot *m.*

snake, *n.* serpent *m.*

snap, 1. *n.* (bite) coup *(m.)* de dents; (sound) coup *(m.)* sec. 2. *vb.tr.* (with teeth) happer; (sound) faire claquer.

snapshot, *n.* instantané *m.*

snare, *n.* piège *m.*

snarl, *vb.* grogner.

snatch, *vb.* saisir.

sneak, *vb.* se glisser furtivement.

sneakers, *n.* tennis *m.pl.,* basket *m.pl.*

sneer, *vb.* ricaner.

sneeze, 1. *n.* éternuement *m.* 2. *vb.* éternuer.

sniff, *vb.* renifler.

snob, *n.* snob *m.*

snore, *vb.* ronfler.

snorkel, *n.* tuba *m.*

snow, 1. *n.* neige *f.* 2. *vb.* neiger.

snug, *adj.* confortable.

snuggle, *vb.* se pelotonner.

so, *adv.* si; tellement; (thus) ainsi; (s. that) de sorte que.

soak, *vb.* tremper.

soap, *n.* savon *m.*

soar, *vb.* prendre son essor.

sob, 1. *n.* sanglot *m.* 2. *vb.* sangloter.

sober, *adj.* (sedate) sérieux; (not drunk) qui n'est pas ivre.

soccer, *n.* football *m.*

sociable, *adj.* sociable.

social, *adj.* social.

socialism, *n.* socialisme *m.*

socialist, *adj. and n.* socialiste *m.f.*

social worker, *n.* assistant *(m.f.)* social.

society, *n.* société *f.*

sociology, *n.* sociologie *f.*

sock, *n.* chaussette *f.*

socket, *n.* douille *f.*

sod, *n.* motte *f.*

soda, *n.* soude *f.;* (s. water) eau *(f.)* de Seltz.

sofa, *n.* canapé *m.*

soft, *adj.* doux *m.,* douce *f.;* (yielding) mou *m.,* molle *f.*

soften, *vb.* amollir, *tr.*

software, *n.* logiciel *m.*

soil, 1. *n.* terroir *m.* 2. *vb.* souiller.

sojourn, 1. *n.* séjour *m.* 2. *vb.* séjourner.

solace, *n.* consolation *f.*

solar, *adj.* solaire.

soldier, *n.* soldat *m.*

sole, *n.* (shoe) semelle *f.;* (fish) sole *f.*

solemn, *adj.* solennel.

solemnity, *n.* solennité *f.*

solicit, *vb.* solliciter.

solicitous, *adj.* empressé.

solid, *adj. and n.* solide *m.*

solidity, *n.* solidité *f.*

solidarity, *n.* solidarité *f.*

solitary, *adj.* solitaire.

solitude, *n.* solitude *f.*

solo, *n.* solo *m.*

solution, *n.* solution *f.*

solve, *vb.* résoudre.

solvent, *adj. (comm.)* solvable.

somber, *adj.* sombre.

some, 1. *adj.* quelque; (partitive) de. 2. *pron.* certains; (with verb) en.

somebody, someone, *pron.* quelqu'un.

something, *pron.* quelque chose *m.*

sometime, *adv.* (past) autrefois; (future) quelque jour.

sometimes, *adv.* quelquefois.

somewhat, *adv.* quelque peu.

somewhere, *adv.* quelque part.

son, *n.* fils *m.*

song, *n.* chanson *f.;* chant *m.*

son-in-law, *n.* gendre *m.*

soon, *adv.* bientôt, tôt.

soot, *n.* suie *f.*

soothe, *vb.* calmer.

sophisticated, *adj.* blasé.

soprano, *n.* soprano *m.*

sordid, *adj.* sordide.

sore, *adj.* (aching) douloureux; (have a s. throat, etc.) avoir mal à. . . .

sorrow, *n.* tristesse *f.,* douleur *f.,* chagrin *m.*

sorrowful, *adj.* (person) affligé.

sorry, 1. *adj.* désolé, triste; (be s.) regretter. 2. *interj.* pardon!

sort, 1. *n.* sorte *f.* 2. *vb.* trier.

soul, *n.* âme *f.*

sound, 1. *n.* son *m.* 2. *adj.* (healthy) sain, solide. 3. *vb.* sonner.

soundproof, *adj.* insonorisé.

soup, *n.* potage *m.,* soupe, *f.*

sour, *adj.* aigre.

source, *n.* source *f.*

south, *n.* sud *m.*

South America, *n.* Amérique *(f.)* du Sud.

southeast, *n.* sud-est *m.*

southern, *adj.* du sud.

South Pole, *n.* pôle sud *m.*

southwest, *n.* sud-ouest *m.*

souvenir, *n.* souvenir *m.*

Soviet, *adj.* soviétique; (S. Union) Union *(f.)* soviétique.

sow, *vb.* semer.

spa, *n.* station *(f.)* thermale.

space, *n.* espace *m.*

space shuttle, *n.* navette spatiale *f.*

spacious, *adj.* spacieux.

spade, *n.* bêche *f.;* (cards) pique *m.*

Spain, *n.* Espagne *f.*

span, *n.* (hand) empan *m.;* (bridge) travée *f.*

Spaniard, *n.* Espagnol *m.*

Spanish, *adj. and n.* espagnol *m.*

spank, *vb.* fesser.

spanking, *n.* fessée *f.*

spare, 1. *adj.* (in reserve) de réserve. 2. *vb.* épargner.

spark, *n.* étincelle *f.*

sparkle, *vb.* étinceler.

sparrow, *n.* moineau *m.*

spasm, *n.* spasme *m.*

speak, *vb.* parler.

speaker, *n.* (public) orateur *m.*

spec, *n.* (on s.) à tout hasard.

special, *adj.* spécial.

specialist, *n.* spécialiste *m.f.*

specially, *adv.* spécialement.

specialty, *n.* spécialité *f.*

species, *n.* espèce *f.*

specific, *adj.* spécifique.

specify, *vb.* spécifier.

specimen, *n.* spécimen *m.*

spectacle, *n.* spectacle *m.*

spectacular, *adj.* spectaculaire.

spectator, *n.* spectateur *m.*

speculate, *vb.* spéculer.

speculation, *n.* spéculation *f.*

speech, *n.* (address) discours *m.;* (utterance) parole *f.*

speed, *n.* vitesse *f.*

speedometer, *n.* compteur *(m.)* (de vitesse).

speedy, *adj.* rapide.

spell, 1. *n.* (incantation) charme *m.;* (period) période *f.* 2. *vb.* épeler.

spelling, *n.* orthographe *f.*

spend, *vb.* (money) dépenser; (time) passer.

sphere, *n.* sphère *f.*

spice, *n.* épice *f.*

spider, *n.* araignée *f.*

spike, *n.* pointe *f.*

spill, *vb.* répandre, *tr.*

spin, *vb.* (thread) filer; (twirl) tourner.

spinach, *n.* épinards *m.pl.*

spine, *n.* épine *f.;* (backbone) épine *(f.)* dorsale.

spiral, 1. *n.* spirale *f.* 2. *adj.* spiral.

spirit, *n.* esprit *m.*

spiritual, *adj.* spirituel.

spiritualism, *n.* spiritisme *m.;* spiritualisme *m.*

spit, 1. *n.* (saliva) crachat *m.;* (for roast) broche *f.* 2. *vb.* cracher.

spite, *n.* dépit *m.;* (in s. of) malgré.

spiteful, *adj.* méchant.

splash, *vb.* éclabousser.

splendid, *adj.* splendide.

splendor, *n.* splendeur *f.*

splinter, *n.* éclat *m.*

split, *vb.* fendre.

spoil, 1. *n.* butin *m.* 2. *vb.* gâter.

sponge, *n.* éponge *f.*

sponsor, *n.* (law) garant *m.*

spontaneity, *n.* spontanéité *f.*

spontaneous, *adj.* spontané.

spool, *n.* bobine *f.*

spoon, *n.* cuiller *f.*

spoonful, *n.* cuillerée *f.*

sporadic, *adj.* sporadique.

sport, *n.* sport *m.;* (fun) jeu *m.*

spot, 1. *n.* (stain) tache *f.;* (place) endroit *m.* 2. *vb.* tacher; (recognize) reconnaître.

spotless, *adj.* immaculé.

spouse, n. époux m., épouse f.

spout, 1. n. (teapot, etc.) bec m. 2. vb. jaillir.

sprain, n. entorse f.

sprawl, vb. s'étaler.

spray, n. (sea) embrun m.

spread, 1. n. étendue f. 2. vb. étendre, tr.

spreadsheet, n. tableur m.

spree, n. (go on a s.) faire la noce.

sprightly, adj. éveillé.

spring, 1. n. (season) printemps m.; (source) source f.; (leap) saut m.; (device) ressort m. 2. vb. (leap) sauter; (water) jaillir.

sprinkle, vb. asperger.

spry, adj. alerte.

spur, 1. n. éperon m. 2. vb. éperonner.

spurious, adj. faux m., fausse f.

spurn, vb. repousser.

spurt, 1. n. jet m. 2. vb. jaillir.

spy, 1. n. espion m. 2. espionner, apercevoir.

squad, n. escouade f.

squadron, n. escadron m.

squalid, adj. misérable.

squall, n. rafale f.

squander, vb. gaspiller.

square, 1. n. (geom.) carré m.; (in town) place f. 2. adj. carré.

squash, n. (vegetable) courge f.; (game) squash m. 2. vb. écraser.

squat, vb. s'accroupir.

squeak, 1. vb. crier, grincer. 2. n. grincement m.

squeeze, vb. serrer; (lemon) presser.

squid, n. calamar m.

squirrel, n. écureuil m.

squirt, vb. seringuer.

stab, vb. poignarder.

stability, n. stabilité f.

stabilize, vb. stabiliser.

stable, 1. n. écurie f. 2. adj. stable.

stack, n. (hay) meule f.; (pile) pile f.; (chimney) souche f.

staff, n. (stick) bâton m.; (mil.) état-major m.; (personnel) personnel m.

stage, n. (theater) scène f.; (in development) période f.; (stopping-place) étape f.

stagflation, n. stagflation f.

stagger, vb. (totter) chanceler.

stagnant, adj. stagnant.

stain, 1. n. tache f. 2. vb. (spot) tacher; (color) teinter.

staircase, stairway, n. escalier m.

stairs, n. escalier m.

stake, 1. n. (post) pieu m.; (at s.) en jeu. 2. vb. (gaming) mettre au jeu.

stale, adj. (bread) rassis; (food) pas frais.

stalk, 1. n. tige f. 2. vb. traquer.

stall, 1. n. (stable, church) stalle f. 2. vb. temporiser.

stamina, n. vigueur f.

stammer, vb. bégayer.

stamp, 1. n. timbre(-poste) m. 2. vb. (letter) timbrer; (with foot) frapper du pied.

stampede, n. sauve-qui-peut n.; débandade f.

stand, 1. n. (position) position f.; (resistance) résistance f.; (stall) étalage m.; (vehicles) station f. 2. vb. tr. (put) poser; (endure) supporter. 3. vb. intr. (upright) se tenir debout; (be situated, be located) se trouver; (stop) s'arrêter.

standard, n. (flag) étendard m.; (measure, etc.) étalon m.; (living, etc.) niveau m.

stanza, n. strophe f.

staple, 1. n. agrafe f. 2. vb. agrafer.

stapler, n. agrafeuse f.

star, n. étoile f.; (movie) vedette f.

starch, n. amidon m.

stare, vb. regarder fixement.

stark, adj. pur, austère.

start, 1. n. (beginning) commencement m.; (surprise, etc.) tressaillement

m. 2. vb. commencer, tressaillir.

startle, vb. effrayer.

starvation, n. faim f.

starve, vb. intr. mourir de faim.

state, 1. n. état m. 2. vb. déclarer.

statement, n. déclaration f.

statesman, n. homme (m.) d'état.

static, adj. statique.

station, n. (railroad) gare f.; (bus, subway) station f.

stationary, adj. stationnaire.

stationery, n. papeterie f.

statistics, n. statistique f.

statue, n. statue f.

stature, n. stature f.

statute, n. statut m.

stay, vb. rester.

steady, adj. ferme; (constant) soutenu.

steak, n. bifteck m.

steal, vb. voler.

steam, n. vapeur f.

steamboat, n. bateau (m.) à vapeur.

steamship, n. vapeur m.

steel, n. acier m.

steep, adj. raide.

steeple, n. clocher m.

steer, 1. n. jeune bœuf m. 2. vb. gouverner.

stem, n. (plant) tige f.

stenographer, n. sténographe m.f.

stenography, n. sténographie f.

step, 1. n. pas m.; (of staircase) marche f. 2. vb. faire un pas.

stereo, n. stéréo f.; chaîne (f.) stéréo.

stepbrother, n. demi-frère m.

stepdaughter, n. belle-fille f.

stepfather, n. beau-père m.

stepmother, n. belle-mère f.

stepsister, n. belle-sœur f.

stereophonic, adj. stéréophonique.

stereotype, n. stéréotype m.

sterile, adj. stérile.

stern, adj. sévère.

stethoscope, n. stéthoscope m.

stew, n. ragoût m.

steward, *n.* (airline) steward *m.*

stewardess, *n.* (airline) hôtesse *(f.)* de l'air.

stick, 1. *n.* bâton *m.* **2.** *vb.* (paste) coller, *tr.;* (remain) rester.

sticker, *n.* autocollant *m.*

sticky, *adj.* gluant.

stiff, *adj.* raide.

stiffness, *n.* raideur *f.*

stifle, *vb.* étouffer.

still, 1. *adj.* tranquille. **2.** *adv.* encore. **3.** *conj.* cependant.

stillness, *n.* tranquillité *f.*

stimulant, *n.* stimulant *m.*

stimulate, *vb.* stimuler.

stimulus, *n.* stimulant *m.*

sting, 1. *n.* piqûre *f.* **2.** *vb.* (prick) piquer; (smart) cuire.

stingy, *adj.* mesquin.

stink, 1. *vb.* puer. **2.** *n.* puanteur *f.*

stir, 1. *vb.* remuer; (person, *intr.)* bouger. **2.** *n.* mouvement *m.*

stitch, 1. *n.* (sewing) point *m.;* (knitting) maille *f.* **2.** *vb.* coudre.

stock, *n.* (goods on hand) marchandises *f.pl.;* (finance) valeurs *f.pl.,* action *f.*

stockbroker, *n.* agent de change *m.*

stock exchange, *n.* Bourse *f.*

stocking, *n.* bas *m.*

stole, *n.* étole *f.*

stomach, *n.* estomac *m.;* (s. ache) mal *(m.)* à l'estomac.

stone, *n.* pierre *f.*

stool, *n.* escabeau *m.*

stoop, *vb.* se pencher.

stop, 1. *n.* arrêt *m.* **2.** *vb.* arrêter, *tr.;* (prevent) empêcher (de); (cease) cesser.

storage, *n.* emmagasinage *m.*

store, 1. *n.* (shop) magasin *m.;* (supply) provision *f.* **2.** *vb.* emmagasiner.

storm, 1. *n.* orage *m.* **2.** *vb.* prendre d'assaut.

stormy, *adj.* orageux.

story, *n.* histoire *f.;* (floor) étage *m.*

stout, *adj.* gros *m.,* grosse *f.*

stove, *n.* fourneau *m.*

straight, *adj. and adv.* droit.

straighten, *vb.* redresser.

strain, 1. *n.* effort *m.* **2.** *vb.* (stretch) tendre; (filter) passer.

strait, *n.* (geography) détroit *m.*

strand, *n.* (beach) plage *f.;* (hair) mèche *f.;* (thread) fil *m.*

strange, *adj.* étrange; (foreign) étranger.

stranger, *n.* étranger *m.*

strangle, *vb.* étrangler.

strap, *n.* courroie *f.*

strategic, *adj.* stratégique.

strategy, *n.* stratégie *f.*

straw, *n.* paille *f.*

strawberry, *n.* fraise *f.*

stray, *adj.* égaré.

streak, 1. *n.* raie *f.* **2.** *vb.* rayer.

stream, *n.* courant *m.;* (small river) ruisseau *m.*

streamline, *vb.* caréner, simplifier, moderniser.

street, *n.* rue *f.*

strength, *n.* force *f.*

strengthen, *vb.* fortifier.

strenuous, *adj.* énergique.

streptococcus, *n.* streptocoque *m.*

stress, 1. *n.* force *f.;* tension *f.; (gramm.)* accent *m.* **2.** *vb.* accentuer.

stretch, *vb.* étendre, *tr.*

stretcher, *n.* brancard *m.*

strict, *adj.* strict.

stride, *n.* enjambée *f.*

strife, *n.* lutte *f.*

strike, 1. *n.* grève *f.* **2.** *vb.* frapper; (match, *tr.)* allumer; (clock) sonner; (workers) se mettre en grève.

string, *n.* ficelle *f.;* (music) corde *f.*

string bean, *n.* haricot vert *m.*

strip, 1. *n.* bande *f.* **2.** *vb.* dépouiller.

stripe, *n.* bande *f.; (mil.)* galon *m.*

strive, *vb.* s'efforcer (de).

stroke, 1. *n.* coup *m.,* caresse *f.* **2.** *vb.* caresser.

stroll, *n.* tour *m.*

stroller, *n.* poussette *f.*

strong, *adj.* fort.

structure, *n.* structure *f.*

struggle, 1. *n.* lutte *f.* **2.** *vb.* lutter.

stub, *n.* souche *f.*

stubborn, *adj.* opiniâtre, obstiné, têtu.

student, *n.* étudiant *m.*

studio, *n.* atelier *m.*

studious, *adj.* studieux.

study, 1. *n.* étude *f.;* (room) cabinet *(m.)* de travail. **2.** *vb.* étudier.

stuff, 1. *n.* (materials) matériaux *m.pl.;* (textile) étoffe *f.* **2.** *vb.* bourrer; (cooking) farcir.

stuffing, *n.* bourre *f.;* (cooking) farce *f.*

stumble, *vb.* trébucher.

stump, *n.* (tree) souche *f.*

stun, *vb.* étourdir.

stunt, *n.* tour *(m.)* de force.

stupid, *adj.* stupide.

stupidity, *n.* stupidité *f.*

sturdy, *adj.* vigoureux.

stutter, *vb.* bégayer.

style, *n.* style *m.*

stylish, *adj.* élégant.

subconscious, *adj.* subconscient.

subdue, *vb.* subjuguer.

subject, 1. *n.* sujet *m.* **2.** *adj.* (people, country) assujetti; (liable) sujet. **3.** *vb.* assujettir.

sublet, *vb.* sous-louer.

sublimate, *vb.* sublimer.

sublime, *adj.* sublime.

submarine, *n.* sous-marin *m.*

submerge, *vb.* submerger.

submission, *n.* soumission *f.*

submit, *vb.* soumettre, *tr.*

subnormal, *adj.* sous-normal.

subordinate, *adj. and n.* subordonné *m.*

subpoena, *n.* citation *f.*

subscribe, *vb.* (consent, support) souscrire; (to paper, etc.) s'abonner.

subscription, *n.* souscription *f.;* (to paper, etc.) abonnement *m.*

subsequent, *adj.* subséquent, ultérieur.

subsidy, *n.* subvention *f.*

substance, *n.* substance *f.*

substantial, *adj.* substantiel; (well-to-do) aisé.

substitute, 1. *n.* remplaçant *m.*, remplacement *m.* **2.** *vb.* substituer.

substitution, *n.* substitution *f.*

subterfuge, *n.* subterfuge *m.*, faux-fuyant *m.*

subterranean, *adj.* souterrain.

subtitle, *n.* sous-titre *m.*

subtle, *adj.* subtil.

subtract, *vb.* soustraire.

suburb, *n.* faubourg *m.*, banlieue *f.*

subversive, *adj.* subversif.

subway, *n.* métro(politain) *m.*

succeed, *vb.* (come after) succéder à; (be successful) réussir (à).

success, *n.* succès *m.*

successful, *adj.* heureux.

succession, *n.* succession *f.*

successive, *adj.* successif.

successor, *n.* successeur *m.*

succumb, *vb.* succomber.

such, *adj.* tel; (intensive, **s. a** + *adj.*) un . . . aussi + *adj.*

suck, *vb.* sucer.

suction, *n.* succion *f.*

sudden, *adj.* soudain.

sue, *vb.* poursuivre.

suffer, *vb.* souffrir.

suffice, *vb.* suffire.

sufficient, *adj.* suffisant.

suffocate, *vb.* suffoquer.

sugar, *n.* sucre *m.*

suggest, *vb.* suggérer.

suggestion, *n.* suggestion *f.*

suicide, 1. *n.* suicide *m.* **2.** *vb.* (**commit s.**) se suicider, *intr.*

suit, 1. *n.* (law) procès *m.*; (clothes) (man's) complet *m.*, (woman's) tailleur *m.*; (cards) couleur *f.* **2.** *vb.* convenir (à).

suitable, *adj.* convenable.

suitcase, *n.* valise *f.*

sulk, *vb.* bouder.

sulphur, *n.* soufre *m.*

sum, *n.* somme *f.*

summary, 1. *n.* résumé *m.*, abrégé *m.* **2.** *adj.* sommaire, immédiat.

summer, *n.* été *m.*

summit, *n.* sommet *m.*

summon, *vb.* (convoke) convoquer; (bid to come) appeler.

sun, *n.* soleil *m.*

sunburn, *n.* hâle *m.*, coup (*m.*) de soleil.

Sunday, *n.* dimanche *m.*

sunglasses, *n.* lunettes (*f.pl.*) de soleil.

sunny, *adj.* ensoleillé.

sunshine, *n.* soleil *m.*

suntan, *n.* bronzage *m.*

superb, *adj.* superbe.

superficial, *adj.* superficiel.

superfluous, *adj.* superflu.

superimpose, *vb.* superposer.

superintendent, *n.* surveillant *m.*

superior, *adj. and n.* supérieur *m.*

superiority, *n.* supériorité *f.*

superlative, *n.* superlatif *m.*

supermarket, *n.* supermarché *m.*

supernatural, *adj. and n.* surnaturel *m.*

superpower, *n.* superpuissance *f.*

supersede, *vb.* remplacer.

superstar, *n.* superstar *m.*

superstition, *n.* superstition *f.*

superstitious, *adj.* superstitieux.

superstore, *n.* hypermarché *m.*

supervise, *vb.* surveiller.

supper, *n.* souper *m.*

supplement, *n.* supplément *m.*

supply, 1. *n.* approvisionnement *m.*; provision *f.* **2.** *vb.* fournir (de).

support, 1. *n.* appui *m.*, soutien *m.* **2.** *vb.* soutenir; (bear) supporter; (back up) appuyer.

suppose, *vb.* supposer.

suppress, *vb.* supprimer.

suppression, *n.* suppression *f.*

supreme, *adj.* suprême.

surcharge, *n.* prix (*m.*) supplémentaire; (tax) surtaxe *f.*

sure, *adj.* sûr.

surf, *n.* ressac *m.*

surface, *n.* surface *f.*

surfboard, *n.* planche (*f.*) de surf.

surfing, *n.* surf *m.*

surge, *n.* houle *f.*

surgeon, *n.* chirurgien *m.*

surgery, *n.* chirurgie *f.*

surpass, *vb.* surpasser.

surplus, *n.* surplus *m.*

surprise, 1. *n.* surprise *f.* **2.** *vb.* surprendre.

surrender, *vb.* rendre, *tr.*

surround, *vb.* entourer.

survey, 1. *vb.* contempler; (investigate) examiner. **2.** *n.* enquête *f.*

survival, *n.* survivance *f.*, survie *f.*

survive, *vb.* survivre.

susceptible, *adj.* susceptible (de).

suspect, 1. *vb.* soupçonner. **2.** *adj. and n.,* suspect *m.*

suspend, *vb.* suspendre.

suspense, *n.* incertitude *f.*; (**in s.**) en suspens; (film, book) suspense *m.*

suspension, *n.* suspension *f.*

suspicion, *n.* soupçon *m.*

suspicious, *adj.* soupçonneux; (questionable) suspect.

sustain, *vb.* soutenir.

swallow, 1. *n.* (bird) hirondelle *f.* **2.** *vb.* avaler.

swamp, *n.* marais *m.*

swan, *n.* cygne *m.*

swap, *vb.* échanger.

swarm, *n.* essaim *m.*

sway, 1. *n.* (rule) domination *f.*; (motion) oscillation *f.* **2.** *vb.* (rule) gouverner; (motion) se balancer.

swear, *vb.* jurer.

sweat, 1. *n.* sueur *f.* **2.** *vb.* suer.

sweater, *n.* pull-over *m.*

Swede, *n.* Suédois *m.*

Sweden, *n.* Suède *f.*

Swedish, *adj. and n.* suédois *m.*

sweep, 1. n. (bend) courbe f.; (movement) mouvement (m.) circulaire. **2.** vb. balayer.

sweepstakes, n. poule f.

sweet, adj. doux m., douce f.; sucré.

sweetheart, n. chéri m., chérie f.

sweetness, n. douceur f.

swell, vb. gonfler, tr.; enfler, tr.

swift, adj. rapide.

swim, vb. nager.

swimsuit, n. maillot de bain m.

swindle, vb. escroquer.

swine, n. cochon m.

swing, vb. balancer, tr.

Swiss, 1. n. Suisse m. **2.** adj. suisse, helvétique.

switch, n. (elect.) interrupteur m.

switchboard, n. standard m.

Switzerland, n. Suisse f.

sword, n. épée f.

syllable, n. syllabe f.

symbol, n. symbole m.

symbolic, adj. symbolique.

symmetry, n. symétrie f.

sympathetic, adj. compatissant.

sympathy, n. compassion f.

symphony, n. symphonie f.

symptom, n. symptôme m.

synagogue, n. synagogue f.

synchronize, vb. synchroniser, tr.

syndicate, n. syndicat m.

syndrome, n. syndrome m.

synonym, n. synonyme m.

synthetic, adj. synthétique.

syphilis, n. syphilis f.

Syria, n. Syrie f.

syringe, n. seringue f.

syrup, n. sirop m.

system, n. système m.

systems analyst, n. analyste-programmeur m.

systematic, adj. systématique.

T

tabernacle n. tabernacle m.

table, n. table f.

tablecloth, n. nappe f.

tablespoon, n. cuiller (f.) à soupe.

tablet, n. tablette f.

tabloid, n. (t. press) la presse (f.) populaire.

tack, 1. n. (nail) broquette f. **2.** vb. clouer.

tackle, 1. n. matériel m. **2.** vb. s'attaquer à.

tact, n. tact m.

tag, n. étiquette f.

tail, n. queue f.

tailor, n. tailleur m.

take, vb. prendre; (lead) conduire; (carry) porter; **(t. off)** (plane) décoller.

tale, n. conte m.

talent, n. talent m.

talk, 1. n. conversation f. **2.** vb. parler.

talkative, adj. bavard.

tall, adj. grand.

tame, adj. (animal) apprivoisé.

tamper, vb. toucher à.

tampon, n. tampon hygiénique m.

tan, 1. n. (leather) tan m.; (skin) hâle m.; (color) tanné m. **2.** vb. tanner.

tangible, adj. tangible.

tangle, n. embrouillement m.

tank, n. réservoir m.; (mil.) char (m.) d'assaut.

tap, 1. n. (water) robinet m.; (knock) petit coup m. **2.** vb. frapper légèrement.

tape, n. ruban m.

tape recorder, n. magnétophone m.

tapestry, n. tapisserie f.

tar, n. goudron m.

target, n. cible f.

tariff, n. tarif m.

tarnish, vb. ternir, tr.

tarragon, n. estragon m.

tart, 1. n. tarte f. **2.** adj. âpre.

task, n. tâche f.

taste, 1. n. goût m. **2.** vb. goûter.

tasty, adj. savoureux.

taut, adj. raide.

tavern, n. taverne f.

tax, 1. n. impôt m. **2.** vb. imposer.

taxi, n. taxi m.

taxi driver, n. chauffeur (m.) de taxi.

taxpayer, n. contribuable m.

tea, n. thé m.

teach, vb. enseigner; (to do) apprendre à.

teacher, n. instituteur m.; (school) professeur m.

team, n. (animals) attelage m.; (people) équipe f.

teapot, n. théière f.

tear, 1. n. larme f.; (rip) déchirure f. **2.** vb. déchirer.

tease, vb. taquiner.

teaspoon, n. cuiller (f.) à thé.

technical, adj. technique.

technician, n. technicien m.

technique, n. technique f.

technological, adj. technologique.

tedious, adj. ennuyeux.

teenager, n. adolescent m.

telegram, n. télégramme m.

telegraph, n. télégraphe m.

telephone, 1. n. téléphone m. **2.** vb. téléphoner.

telephone booth, n. cabine (f.) téléphonique.

telephone directory, n. annuaire m. (du téléphone).

telescope, n. télescope m.

televise, vb. téléviser.

television, n. télévision f.

tell, vb. dire; (story, etc.) raconter.

teller, n. (bank) caissier m., guichetier m.

temper, n. (humor) humeur f.; (lose one's t.) s'emporter; (anger) colère f.; (metals) trempe f.

temperament, n. tempérament m.

temperamental, adj. instable.

temperance, n. tempérance f.

temperate, adj. (habit) sobre; (climate) tempéré.

temperature, n. température f.

tempest, n. tempête f.

template, *n.* patron *m.*

temple, *n.* temple *m.;* (forehead) tempe *f.*

temporary, *adj.* temporaire, provisoire.

tempt, *vb.* tenter.

temptation, *n.* tentation *f.*

ten, *adj. and n.* dix *m.*

tenant, *n.* locataire *m.f.*

tend, *vb.* tendre, *intr.;* (care for) soigner.

tendency, *n.* tendance *f.*

tender, *adj.* tendre.

tenderness, *n.* tendresse *f.*

tendon, *n.* tendon *m.*

tenement, *n.* taudis *m.*

tennis, *n.* tennis *m.*

tenor, *n.* (music) ténor *m.*

tense, *adj.* tendu.

tension, *n.* tension *f.*

tent, *n.* tente *f.*

tentative, *adj.* tentatif, expérimental.

tenth, *adj. and n.* dixième *m.f.*

term, *n.* terme *m.;* (school) trimestre *m.;* (conditions) conditions *f.pl.;* (political) mandat *m.*

terminal, 1. *n.* (electricity) borne *f.;* (computer) terminal *m.;* (airport) aérogare *f.* 2. *adj.* incurable, terminal.

terrace, *n.* terrasse *f.*

terrible, *adj.* terrible.

terrific, *adj.* fantastique.

terrify, *vb.* terrifier.

territory, *n.* territoire *m.*

terror, *n.* terreur *f.*

test, 1. *n.* épreuve *f.* 2. *vb.* mettre à l'épreuve.

testament, *n.* testament *m.*

testify, *vb.* témoigner (de); (declare) affirmer.

testimony, *n.* témoignage *m.*

text, *n.* texte *m.*

textile, *adj.* textile.

texture, *n.* texture *f.*

Thai, 1. *n.* Thaïlandais *m.* 2. *adj.* thaïlandais.

than, *conj.* que; (with numerals) de.

thank, *vb.* remercier; (t. you) merci.

thankful, *adj.* reconnaissant.

that *sg.,* those *pl.* 1. *adj.* ce, cet *m.,* cette *f.,* ces

pl.; (opposed to *this)* ce . . .-là, *etc.* 2. *demonstrative pron.* celui-là *m.,* celle-là *f.,* ceux-là *m.pl.,* celles-là *f.pl.;* (object not named) cela, *abbr.* ça; (what is t.?) qu'est-ce que c'est que ça? 3. *relative pron.* qui (subject); que (object). 4. *conj.* que; (purpose) pour que.

the, *art.* le *m.,* la *f.,* les *pl.*

theater, *n.* théâtre *m.*

theft, *n.* vol *m.*

their, *adj.* leur *sg.,* leurs *pl.*

theirs, *pron.* le leur *m.,* la leur *f.,* les leurs *pl.*

them, *pron.* eux *m.,* elles *f.;* (unstressed, with verb) les (direct); leur (indirect).

theme, *n.* thème *m.*

themselves, *pron.* eux-mêmes *m.,* elles-mêmes *f.;* (reflexive) se.

then, *adv.* alors; (after that) ensuite.

thence, *adv.* (place) de là; (reason) pour cette raison.

theology, *n.* théologie *f.*

theoretical, *adj.* théorique.

theory, *n.* théorie *f.*

therapy, *n.* thérapie *f.*

there, *adv.* là; (with verb) y.

therefore, *adv.* donc.

thermometer, *n.* thermomètre *m.*

thermonuclear, *adj.* thermonucléaire.

thermostat, *n.* thermostat *m.*

these, *see* this.

they, *pron.* ils *m.,* elles *f.*

thick, *adj.* épais.

thicken, *vb.* épaissir, *tr.*

thickness, *n.* épaisseur *f.*

thief, *n.* voleur *m.*

thigh, *n.* cuisse *f.*

thimble, *n.* dé *m.*

thin, *adj.* mince.

thing, *n.* chose *f.*

think (of), *vb.* penser (à).

thinker, *n.* penseur *m.*

third, 1. *n.* tiers *m.* 2. *adj.* troisième.

Third World, *n.* Tiers Monde *m.*

thirst, *n.* soif *f.*

thirsty, *adj.* (be t.) avoir soif.

thirteen, *adj. and n.* treize *m.*

thirty, *adj. and n.* trente *m.*

this, *sg.* these *pl.* 1. *adj.* ce, cet *m.,* cette *f.,* ces *pl.;* (opposed to *that)* ce . . .-ci, *etc.* 2. *demonstrative pron.* celui-ci *m.,* celle-ci *f.,* ceux-ci *m.pl.,* celles-ci *f.pl.;* (object not named) ceci.

thorough, *adj.* complet.

those, *see* that.

though, *conj.* quoique.

thought, *n.* pensée *f.*

thoughtful, *adj.* pensif.

thoughtless, *adj.* étourdi.

thousand, *adj. and n.* mille *m.*

thread, *n.* fil *m.*

threat, *n.* menace *f.*

threaten, *vb.* menacer.

three, *adj. and n.* trois *m.*

thrift, *n.* économie *f.*

thrill, 1. *n.* tressaillement *m.* 2. *vb.* tressaillir, *intr.;* faire frémir, *tr.*

thriller, *n.* livre *(m.)*/film *(m.)* à suspense.

thrive, *vb.* prospérer.

throat, *n.* gorge *f.*

throne, *n.* trône *m.*

through, *prep. and adv.* à travers; (be t.) avoir fini.

throughout, *adv.* partout.

throw, *vb.* jeter.

thrust, *vb.* pousser.

thumb, *n.* pouce *m.*

thumbtack, *n.* punaise *f.*

thunder, 1. *n.* tonnerre *m.* 2. *vb.* tonner.

Thursday, *n.* jeudi *m.*

thus, *adv.* ainsi.

thwart, *vb.* contrarier.

thyme, *n.* thym *m.*

thyroid, *n.* thyroïde *f.*

ticket, *n.* billet *m.*

tickle, *vb.* chatouiller.

ticklish, *adj.* chatouilleux.

tide, *n.* marée *f.*

tidy, *adj.* ordonné, en ordre.

tie, 1. *n.* lien *m.;* (neck-t.) cravate *f.* 2. *vb.* attacher; (bind) lier; (knot) nouer.

tier, *n.* gradin *m.*

tiger, *n.* tigre *m.*

tight, *adj.* serré; (drunk) gris.

tighten, *vb.* serrer.

tile, *n.* (roof) tuile *f.*

till, 1. *prep.* jusqu'a. 2. *conj.* jusqu'à ce que.

tilt, *vb.* pencher.

timber, *n.* (building) bois *(m.)* de construction.

time, 1. *n.* temps *m.;* (occasion) fois *f.;* (clock) heure *f.;* (what t. is it?) quelle heure est-il?; (have a good t.) s'amuser bien. 2. *vb.* (race) chronométrer; (program) minuter.

timeless, *adj.* éternel.

timetable, *n.* horaire *m.*

timid, *adj.* timide.

timidity, *n.* timidité *f.*

tin, *n.* étain *m.*

tin foil, *n.* papier *(m.)* d'aluminium.

tint, *n.* teinte *f.*

tiny, *adj.* tout petit.

tip, 1. *n.* (money) pourboire *m.;* (end) bout *m.* 2. *vb.* (money) donner un pourboire à; (t. over) renverser.

tire, 1. *n.* (car, etc.) pneu *m.* 2. *vb.* fatiguer.

tired, *adj.* fatigué.

tissue, *n.* tissu *m.;* mouchoir *m.z*

title, *n.* titre *m.*

to, *prep.* à; (in order t.) pour.

toast, *n.* pain *(m.)* grillé.

tobacco, *n.* tabac *m.*

today, *adv.* aujourd'hui.

toe, *n.* orteil *m.*

together, *adv.* ensemble.

toil, *vb.* travailler dur.

toilet, *n.* toilettes *f.pl.;* (t. paper) papier *(m.)* hygiénique.z

token, *n.* témoignage *m.;* (coin) jeton *m.*

tolerance, *n.* tolérance *f.*

tolerant, *adj.* tolérant.

tolerate, *vb.* tolérer.

toll, *n.* péage *m.*

tomato, *n.* tomate *f.*

tomb, *n.* tombeau *m.*

tomorrow, *adv.* demain.

ton, *n.* tonne *f.*

tone, *n.* ton *m.*

tongue, *n.* langue *f.*

tonic, *adj. and n.* tonique *m.*

tonight, *adv.* cette nuit; (evening) ce soir.

tonsil, *n.* amygdale *f.*

tonsillitis, *n.* amygdalite *f.*

too, *adv.* trop; (also) aussi.

tool, *n.* outil *m.*

tooth, *n.* dent *f.*

toothache, *n.* mal *(m.)* de dents.

toothbrush, *n.* brosse *(f.)* à dents.

toothpaste, *n.* dentifrice *m.*

top, *n.* (mountain, etc.) sommet *m.;* (table) dessus *m.*

topcoat, *n.* pardessus *m.*

topic, *n.* sujet *m.*

torch, *n.* torche *f.*

torment, 1. *n.* tourment *m.* 2. *vb.* tourmenter.

tornado, *n.* tornade *f.*

torrent, *n.* torrent *m.*

torture, 1. *n.* torture *f.* 2. *vb.* torturer.

toss, *vb.* (throw) jeter; s'agiter.

total, *adj. and n.* total *m.*

totalitarian, *adj.* totalitaire.

touch, 1. *n.* (touching) attouchement *m.;* (sense) toucher *m.;* (small amount) pointe *f.;* (contact) contact *m.* 2. *vb.* toucher.

touching, *adj.* touchant.

tough, *adj.* dur.

tour, 1. *n.* tour *m.* 2. *vb.* visiter.

tourist, *n.* touriste *m.f.*

tournament, *n.* tournoi *m.*

tow, *vb.* remorquer.

toward, *prep.* (place, time) vers; (feelings, etc.) envers.

towel, *n.* serviette *f.*

tower, *n.* tour *f.*

town, *n.* ville *f.*

toy, *n.* jouet *m.*

trace, *n.* trace *f.*

track, *n.* piste *f.;* (railroad) voie *f.*

tract, *n.* (space) étendue *f.*

tractor, *n.* tracteur *m.*

trade, 1. *n.* commerce *m.;* (job) métier *m.* 2. *vb.* commercer, échanger.

trader, *n.* commerçant *m.*

trade union, *n.* syndicat *m.*

tradition, *n.* tradition *f.*

traditional, *adj.* traditionnel.

traffic, *n.* circulation *f.*

tragedy, *n.* tragédie *f.*

tragic, *adj.* tragique.

trail, *n.* trace *f.*

train, 1. *n.* train *m.;* (dress) traîne *f.;* (retinue) suite *f.* 2. *vb.* (sports) entraîner, *tr.;* (mil.) exercer, *tr.*

trait, *n.* trait *m.*

traitor, *n.* traître *m.*

tramp, *n.* (steps) bruit *(m.)* de pas; (person) chemineau *m.*

tranquil, *adj.* tranquille.

tranquillity, *n.* tranquillité *f.*

transaction, *n.* opération *f.*

transcript, *n.* transcription *f.*

transfer, 1. *n.* transport *m.;* (ticket) billet *(m.)* de correspondance. 2. *vb.* transférer, *tr.*

transform, *vb.* transformer.

transfusion, *n.* transfusion *f.*

transistor, *n.* transistor *m.*

transition, *n.* transition *f.*

translate, *vb.* traduire.

translation, *n.* traduction *f.*

transmit, *vb.* transmettre.

transparent, *adj.* transparent.

transplant, 1. *vb.* transplanter. 2. *n.* transplantation *f.*

transport, transportation, 1. *n.* transport *m.* 2. *vb.* transporter.

transsexual, *adj.* transsexuel.

transvestite, *adj.* travesti.

trap, 1. *n.* piège *m.* 2. *vb.* prendre au piège.

trash, *n.* (rubbish) rebut *m.*

trauma, *n.* traumatisme *m.*

travel, 1. *n.* voyage *m.* 2. *vb.* voyager.

traveler, *n.* voyageur *m.*

traveler's check, *n.* chèque *(m.)* de voyage.

tray, *n.* plateau *m.*

treacherous, *adj.* traître.

tread, *vb.* marcher.

treason, *n.* trahison *f.*

treasure, 1. *n.* trésor *m.* 2. *vb.* tenir beaucoup à.

treasurer, *n.* trésorier *m.*

treasury, *n.* trésor *m.*

treat, *vb.* traiter.

treatment, *n.* traitement *m.*

treaty, *n.* traité *m.*

tree, *n.* arbre *m.*

trek, *n.* voyage *(m.)* difficile.
tremble, *vb.* trembler.
tremendous, *adj.* terrible.
trench, *n.* tranchée *f.*
trend, *n.* tendance *f.,* mode *f.*
trespass, *vb.* empiéter.
triage, *n.* présélection *f.*
trial, *n.* (law) procès *m.;* (test) épreuve *f.*
triangle, *n.* triangle *m.*
tribe, *n.* tribu *f.*
tribulation, *n.* tribulation *f.*
tributary, 1. *n.* (river) affluent *m.* **2.** *adj.* tributaire.
tribute, *n.* tribut *m.*
trick, 1. *n.* ruse *f.* **2.** *vb.* duper.
trickle, *vb.* dégouliner.
tricky, *adj.* astucieux.
trifle, *n.* bagatelle *f.*
trigger, 1. *n.* détente *f.* **2.** *vb.* déclencher.
trim, 1. *adj.* soigné, svelte. **2.** *vb.* (put in order) arranger; (adorn) garnir; (cut) tailler.
Trinity, *n.* Trinité *f.*
trinket, *n.* breloque *f.*
trip, 1. *n.* voyage *m.* **2.** *vb.* trébucher.
triple, *adj. and n.* triple *m.*
trite, *adj.* rebattu.
triumph, *n.* triomphe *m.*
triumphant, *adj.* triomphant.
trivial, *adj.* trivial.
trolley-car, *n.* tramway *m.*
troop, *n.* troupe *f.*
trophy, *n.* trophée *m.*
tropic, *n.* tropique *m.*
trot, 1. *n.* trot *m.* **2.** *vb. intr.* trotter.
trouble, 1. *n.* (misfortune) malheur *m.;* (difficulty) difficulté *f.;* (inconvenience, med.) dérangement *m.* **2.** *vb.* (worry) inquiéter, *tr.;* (inconvenience) déranger; (afflict) affliger.
troublesome, *adj.* gênant.

trough, *n.* auge *f.*
trousers, *n.* pantalon *m.*
trousseau, *n.* trousseau *m.*
trout, *n.* truite *f.*
truce, *n.* trêve *f.*
truck, *n.* camion *m.*
true, *adj.* vrai.
truly, *adv.* vraiment.
trumpet, *n.* trompette *f.*
trunk, *n.* (clothes) malle *f.;* (body, tree) tronc *m.*
trust, 1. *n.* confiance *f.;* (business) trust *m.* **2.** *vb.* se confier à; (entrust) confier.
trustworthy, *adj.* digne de confiance.
truth, *n.* vérité *f.*
truthful, *adj.* sincère.
try, *vb.* essayer; (law) mettre en jugement.
tryst, *n.* rendez-vous *m.*
T-shirt, *n.* maillot *m.,* tee-shirt *m.*
tub, *n.* baignoire *f.*
tube, *n.* tube *m.*
tuberculosis, *n.* tuberculose *f.*
tuck, 1. *n.* (fold) pli *m.* **2.** *vb.* ranger, rentrer.
Tuesday, *n.* mardi *m.*
tug, 1. *n.* (boat) remorqueur *m.* **2.** *vb.* (pull) tirer; (boat) remorquer.
tuition, *n.* (frais de l')enseignement *m.*
tulip, *n.* tulipe *f.*
tumble, *vb.* (fall) tomber.
tummy, *n.* ventre *m.*
tumor, *n.* tumeur *f.*
tumult, *n.* tumulte *m.*
tuna, *n.* thon *m.*
tune, 1. *n.* air *m.;* (concord, harmony) accord *m.* **2.** *vb.* accorder.
Tunisia, *n.* Tunisie *f.*
tunnel, *n.* tunnel *m.*
turban, *n.* turban *m.*
turf, *n.* gazon *m.*
Turk, *n.* Turc *m.,* Turque *f.*

turkey, *n.* dindon *m.*
Turkey, *n.* Turquie *f.*
Turkish, 1. *n.* (language) turc *m.* **2.** *adj.* turc *m.,* turque *f.*
turmoil, *n.* tumulte *m.*
turn, 1. *n.* tour *m.;* (road) détour *m.* **2.** *vb.* tourner, virer.
turning point, *n.* tournant *m.*
turnip, *n.* navet *m.*
turnover, *n.* (money) chiffre *(m.)* d'affaires.
turnpike, *n.* autoroute *(f.)* à péage.
turret, *n.* tourelle *f.*
turtle, *n.* tortue *f.*
tutor, 1. *n.* précepteur *m.* **2.** *vb.* donner des leçons particulières à.
TV, *n.* télé *f.*
twelfth, *adj. and n.* douzième *m.f.*
twelve, *adj. and n.* douze *m.*
twentieth, *adj. and n.* vingtième *m.f.*
twenty, *adj. and n.* vingt *m.*
twice, *adv.* deux fois.
twig, *n.* brindille *f.*
twilight, *n.* crépuscule *m.*
twin, *adj. and n.* jumeau *m.,* jumelle *f.*
twine, *n.* ficelle *f.*
twinkle, *vb.* scintiller.
twirl, *vb.* (faire) tournoyer.
twist, *vb.* tordre.
two, *adj. and n.* deux *m.*
tycoon, *n.* magnat *m.*
type, 1. *n.* type *m.;* (printing) caractère *m.* **2.** *vb.* taper à la machine.
typewriter, *n.* machine *(f.)* à écrire.
typhoid fever, *n.* fièvre *(f.)* typhoïde.
typical, *adj.* typique.
typist, *n.* dactylo(graphe) *m.f.*
tyranny, *n.* tyrannie *f.*
tyrant, *n.* tyran *m.*

U

ubiquitous *adj.* omniprésent.

udder, *n.* mamelle *f.*

Uganda, *n.* Ouganda *m.*

ugliness, *n.* laideur *f.*

ugly, *adj.* laid.

ulcer, *n.* ulcère *m.*

ulterior, *adj.* ultérieur.

ultimate, *adj.* dernier.

ultrasound, *n.* ultrason *m.*

umbrella, *n.* parapluie *m.*

umpire, *n.* arbitre *m.f.*

unable, *adj.* incapable; (u. to) dans l'impossibilité de.

unanimous, *adj.* unanime.

uncalled for, *adj.* déplacé.

uncanny, *adj.* bizarre.

uncertain, *adj.* incertain.

uncle, *n.* oncle *m.*

unconscious, 1. *n.* inconscient *m.* 2. *adj.* (aware) inconscient; (faint) sans connaissance; (u. of) sans conscience de.

uncouth, *adj.* grossier.

uncover, *vb.* découvrir.

under, 1. *prep.* sous. 2. *adv.* au-dessous.

underdeveloped, *adj.* sous-développé.

underestimate, *vb.* sous-estimer.

undergo, *vb.* subir.

underground, *adj.* souterrain, clandestin.

underline, *vb.* souligner.

underneath, *adv.* en dessous.

underpants, *n.pl.* caleçon *m.*, slip *m.*

underprivileged, *adj.* défavorisé.

undershirt, *n.* gilet *(m.)* de dessous.

understand, *vb.* comprendre.

understatement, *n.* litote *f.*

undertake, *vb.* entreprendre.

undertaker, *n.* entrepreneur *(m.)* de pompes funèbres.

underwear, *n.*, sous-vêtements *m.pl.*

underworld, *n.* (crime) milieu *m.*, pègre *f.*

undo, *vb.* défaire.

undress, *vb.* déshabiller, *tr.*

uneasy, *adj.* gêné.

uneven, *adj.* inégal.

unexpected, *adj.* inattendu.

unfair, *adj.* injuste.

unfit, *adj.* peu propre (à).

unfold, *vb.* déplier.

unforgettable, *adj.* inoubliable.

unfortunate, *adj.* malheureux.

unhappy, *adj.* malheureux.

uniform, *adj. and n.* uniforme *n.*

unify, *vb.* unifier.

union, *n.* union *f.*

unique, *adj.* unique.

unisex, *adj.* unisexuel.

unison, *n.* (in u.) à l'unisson.

unit, *n.* unité *f.*

unite, *vb.* unir, *tr.*

United Kingdom, *n.* Royaume *(m.)* Uni.

United Nations, *n.* Nations *(f.pl.)* Unies.

United States, *n.* États-Unis *m.pl.*

unity, *n.* unité *f.*

universal, *adj.* universel.

universe, *n.* univers *m.*

university, *n.* université *f.*

unless, *conj.* à moins que . . . ne.

unlike, *adj.* dissemblable.

unload, *vb.* décharger.

unlock, *vb.* ouvrir.

untie, *vb.* dénouer.

until, *conj.* jusqu'à ce que.

unusual, *adj.* insolite.

up, *prep.* vers le haut de.

upbringing, *n.* éducation *f.*

update, *vb.* mettre à jour.

uphold, *vb.* soutenir.

upholster, *vb.* tapisser.

upon, *prep.* sur.

upper, *adj.* supérieur.

upright, *adj.* droit.

uprising, *n.* soulèvement *m.*

uproar, *n.* vacarme *m.*

upset, *vb.* renverser.

upstairs, *adv.* en haut.

uptight, *adj.* tendu, crispé.

upward, 1. *adj.* dirigé en haut. 2. *adv.* en montant.

uranium, *n.* uranium *m.*

urban, *adj.* urbain.

urge, *vb.* (beg) prier.

urgency, *n.* urgence *f.*

urgent, *adj.* urgent.

us, *pron.* nous.

use, 1. *n.* usage *m.* 2. *vb.* employer, se servir de.

useful, *adj.* utile.

useless, *adj.* inutile.

usher, *n.* huissier *m.*

usual, *adj.* usuel.

utensil, *n.* ustensile *m.*

uterus, *n.* utérus *m.*

utilize, *vb.* utiliser, se servir de.

utmost, 1. *n.* le plus; (all one can) tout son possible. 2. *adj.* (greatest) le plus grand.

utter, 1. *adj.* absolu. 2. *vb.* prononcer; (cry) pousser.

utterance, *n.* émission *f.*

V

vacancy *n.* vide *m.*, vacance *f.*

vacant, *adj.* vide.

vacate, *vb.* quitter, évacuer.

vacation, *n.* vacances *f.pl.*

vaccinate, *vb.* vacciner.

vaccine, *n.* vaccin *m.*

vacuum, *n.* vide *m.*; (v. cleaner) aspirateur *m.*

vagina, *n.* vagin *m.*

vagrant, *adj.* vagabond.

vague, *adj.* vague.

vain, *adj.* vain.

valiant, *adj.* vaillant.

valid, *adj.* valide.

valise, *n.* valise *f.*

valley, *n.* vallée *f.*

valor, *n.* valeur *f.*

valuable, *adj.* de valeur.

value, 1. *n.* valeur *f.* 2. *vb.* évaluer.

value-added tax, *n.* taxe à la valeur ajoutée *f.*
valve, *n.* soupape *f.*
van, *n.* camionnette *f.*
vandal, *n.* vandale *m.f.*
vanguard, *n.* avant-garde *f.*
vanilla, *n.* vanille *f.*
vanish, *vb.* s'évanouir.
vanity, *n.* vanité *f.*
vanquish, *vb.* vaincre.
vapor, *n.* vapeur *f.*
variable, *adj.* variable.
variation, *n.* variation *f.*
varied, *adj.* varié.
variety, *n.* variété *f.*
various, *adj.* divers.
varnish, *n.* vernis *m.*
vary, *vb.* varier.
vase, *n.* vase *m.*
vasectomy, *n.* vasectomie *f.*
vassal, *n.* vassal *m.*
vast, *adj.* vaste.
vat, *n.* cuve *f.*
vault, *n.* voûte *f.*
veal, *n.* veau *m.*
vegetable, *n.* légume *m.*
vegetarian, *n.* végétarien *m.*
vehement, *adj.* véhément.
vehicle, *n.* véhicule *m.*
veil, *n.* voile *m.*
vein, *n.* veine *f.*
velocity, *n.* vitesse *f.*
velvet, *n.* velours *m.*
vending machine, *n.* distributeur *(m.)* automatique
venereal, *adj.* vénérien.
vengeance, *n.* vengeance *f.*
vent, *n.* ouverture *f.*
ventilate, *vb.* ventiler.
venture, 1. *n.* aventure *f.* **2.** *vb.* hasarder, *tr.*
verb, *n.* verbe *m.*
verbose, *adj.* verbeux.
verdict, *n.* verdict *m.*
verge, *n.* bord *m.*
verify, *vb.* vérifier.
vermouth, *n.* vermouth *m.*
versatile, *adj.* versatile.
verse, *n.* vers *m.pl.;* (line of poetry) vers *m.*

version, *n.* version *f.*
vertical, *adj.* vertical.
vertigo, vertige *m.*
very, *adv.* très.
vessel, *n.* vaisseau *m.*
vest, *n.* gilet *m.*
veteran, *n.* vétéran *m.*
veterinarian, *n.* vétérinaire *m.f.*
veto, *n.* véto *m.*
vex, *vb.* vexer.
viaduct, *n.* viaduc *m.*
vibrate, *vb.* vibrer.
vibration, *n.* vibration *f.*
vice, *n.* vice *m.*
vicinity, *n.* voisinage *m.*
vicious, *adj.* méchant.
victim, *n.* victime *f.*
victor, *n.* vainqueur *m.*
victorious, *adj.* victorieux.
victory, *n.* victoire *f.*
videocassette recorder, *n.* magnétoscope *m.*
videodisc, *n.* vidéodisque *m.*
videotape, *n.* bande vidéo *f.*
Vietnam, *n.* Viêt-nam *m.*
view, *n.* vue *f.*
vigil, *n.* veille *f.*
vigilant, *adj.* vigilant.
vigor, *n.* vigueur *f.*
vile, *adj.* vil, abominable.
village, *n.* village *m.*
villain, *n.* scélérat *m.*
vindicate, *vb.* défendre.
vindictive, *adj.* vindicatif.
vine, *n.* vigne *f.*
vinegar, *n.* vinaigre *m.*
vineyard, *n.* vigne *f.,* vignoble *m.*
vintage, *n.* (grapes gathered) vendange *f.;* (year of wine) année *f.,* millésime, *m.*
viola, *n.* alto *m.*
violate, *vb.* violer.
violation, *n.* violation *f.*
violence, *n.* violence *f.*
violent, *adj.* violent.
violet, 1. *n.* violette *f.* **2.** *adj.* violet.

violin, *n.* violon *m.*
virgin, *n.* vierge *f.*
virile, *adj.* viril.
virtual, *adj.* vrai.
virtual reality, *n.* réalité *(f.)* virtuelle.
virtue, *n.* vertu *f.*
virtuous, *adj.* vertueux.
virus, *n.* virus *m.*
visa, *n.* visa *m.*
visible, *adj.* visible.
vision, *n.* vision *f.*
visit, 1. *n.* visite *f.* **2.** *vb.* visiter.
visitor, *n.* visiteur *m.*
visual, *adj.* visuel.
vital, *adj.* vital.
vitality, *n.* vitalité *f.*
vitamin, *n.* vitamine *f.*
vivacious, *adj.* vif *m.,* vive *f.*
vivid, *adj.* vif *m.,* vive *f.*
vocabulary, *n.* vocabulaire *m.*
vocal, *adj.* vocal.
vocation, *n.* vocation *f.*
vodka, *n.* vodka *f.*
vogue, *n.* vogue *f.*
voice, *n.* voix *f.*
void, *adj.* (law) nul.
volcano, *n.* volcan *m.*
volley, *n.* (gun fire) salve *f.*
volleyball, *n.* volley(-ball) *m.*
volt, *n.* volt *m.*
voltage, *n.* tension *f.,* voltage *m.*
volume, *n.* volume *m.*
voluntary, *adj.* volontaire.
volunteer, 1. *n.* volontaire *m.* **2.** *vb.* s'engager.
vomit, *vb.* vomir.
vote, 1. *n.* vote *m.* **2.** *vb.* voter.
voter, *n.* votant *m.*
vouch for, *vb.* répondre de.
vow, *n.* vœu *m.*
vowel, *n.* voyelle *f.*
voyage, *n.* voyage *m.*
vulgar, *adj.* vulgaire.
vulnerable, *adj.* vulnérable.
vulture, *n.* vautour *m.*

W

wade *vb.* traverser à gué.
wafer, *n.* gaufrette *f.*
waffle, *n.* gaufre (américaine) *f.*
wag, *vb.* agiter.
wage, *vb.* (war) faire la guerre.
wages, *n.* salaire *m.*
wagon, *n.* chariot *m.*
wail, *vb.* gémir.
waist, *n.* taille *f.*
wait (for), *vb.* attendre.
waiter, *n.* garçon *m.,* serveur *m.*
waitress, *n.* serveuse *f.*
wake (up), *vb.* réveiller, *tr.;* s'éveiller, *intr.*
Wales, *n.* pays *(m.)* de Galles.
walk, 1. *n.* promenade *f.* **2.** *vb.* marcher; **(take a w.)** se promener.
Walkman, *n.* baladeur *m.,* walkman *m.*
wall, *n.* mur *m.*
wallcovering, *n.* tenture *f.*
wallet, *n.* portefeuille *m.*
wallpaper, *n.* papier peint *m.;* papier à tapisser *m.*
walnut, *n.* noix *f.*
walrus, *n.* morse *m.*
waltz, *n.* valse *f.*
wander, *vb.* errer.
want, 1. *n.* besoin *m.* **2.** *vb.* vouloir.
war, *n.* guerre *f.*
ward, *n.* (hospital) salle *f.;* (charge) pupille *m.f.*
ware, *n.* marchandises *f.pl.*
warehouse, *n.* entrepôt *m.*
warhead, *n.* ogive *f.*
warlike, *adj.* guerrier.
warm, 1. *adj.* chaud; **(be w.)** avoir chaud. **2.** *vb.* chauffer.
warmth, *n.* chaleur *f.*
warn, *vb.* avertir.
warning, *n.* avertissement *m.*
warp, *vb.* détourner.
warrant, 1. *n.* mandat *m.* **2.** *vb.* garantir.
warranty, *n.* garantie *f.*
warrior, *n.* guerrier *m.*
warship, *n.* navire *(m.)* de guerre.

wash, *vb.* laver, *tr.*
washing machine, *n.* laveuse mécanique *f.*
washroom, *n.* salle *(f.)* de bain.
wasp, *n.* guêpe *f.*
waste, 1. *n.* (money) gaspillage *m.;* (time) perte *f.;* (rubbish) déchets *m.pl.* **2.** *vb.* gaspiller, perdre.
wastepaper basket, *n.* corbeille *(f.)* à papier.
watch, 1. *n.* (timepiece) montre *f.;* (guard) garde *f.* **2.** *vb.* veiller.
watchful, *adj.* vigilant.
watchmaker, *n.* horloger *m.*
watchman, *n.* gardien *m.*
water, *n.* eau *f.*
waterbed, *n.* aqualit *m.*
water color, *n.* aquarelle *f.*
watercress, *n.* cresson *m.*
waterfall, *n.* chute *(f.)* d'eau.
waterproof, *adj.* imperméable.
wave, 1. *n.* (sea) vague *f.;* (sound) onde *f.;* **(permanent w.)** ondulation *(f.)* permanente. **2.** *vb.* agiter; (hair) onduler; saluer.
waver, *vb.* vaciller.
wax, *n.* cire *f.*
way, *n.* (road) chemin *m.;* (distance) distance *f.;* (direction) côté *m.;* (manner) manière *f.*
we, *pron.* nous.
weak, *adj.* faible.
weaken, *vb.* affaiblir.
weakness, *n.* faiblesse *f.*
wealth, *n.* richesse *f.*
wealthy, *adj.* riche.
weapon, *n.* arme *f.*
wear, *vb.* porter; **(w. down)** user; **(w. out)** épuiser.
weary, *adj.* las.
weasel, *n.* belette *f.*
weather, *n.* temps *m.*
weave, *vb.* tisser.
weaver, *n.* tisserand *m.*
web, *n.* (fabric) tissu *m.;* (spider) toile *f.*
wedding, *n.* noces *f.pl.*
wedge, *n.* coin *m.*
Wednesday, *n.* mercredi *m.*

weed, *n.* mauvaise herbe *f.*
week, *n.* semaine *f.*
weekday, *n.* jour *(m.)* de semaine.
weekend, *n.* week-end *m.,* fin de semaine *f.*
weekly, *adj.* hebdomadaire.
weep, *vb.* pleurer.
weigh, *vb.* peser.
weight, *n.* poids *m.*
weird, *adj.* mystérieux.
welcome, *adj.* bienvenu.
welfare, *n.* bien-être *m.*
welfare work, *n.* travail *(m.)* social.
well, 1. *n.* (water) puits *m.* **2.** *adv.* bien.
well-known, *adj.* bien connu.
well-meaning, *adj.* bien intentionné.
well-off, *adj.* aisé.
Welsh, *adj.* gallois.
west, *n.* ouest *m.*
western, *adj.* de l'ouest.
westward, *adv.* vers l'ouest.
wet, 1. *adj.* mouillé; (weather) pluvieux. **2.** *vb.* mouiller.
whale, *n.* baleine *f.*
wharf, *n.* quai *m.*
what, 1. *adj.* quel. **2.** *pron. (relative,* that which) ce qui (subject), ce que (object); *interr.* qu'est-ce qui; quoi. **3.** *interj.* quoi!
whatever, 1. *adj.* quelque ... qui (subject), ... que (object). **2.** *pron.* quoi qui (subject), ... que (object).
wheat, *n.* blé *m.*
wheel, *n.* roue *f.*
wheel chair, *n.* fauteuil *(m.)* roulant.
when, *conj.* quand.
whenever, *conj.* toutes les fois que.
where, *conj.* où.
wherever, *conj.* partout où.
whether, *conj.* soit que; (if) si.
which, 1. *adj.* quel. **2.** *pron. (relative)* qui; lequel; *interr.* lequel.
whichever, *pron.* n'importe lequel.

while, *conj.* pendant que; (whereas) tandis que.

whim, *n.* caprice *m.*, lubie *f.*

whip, *n.* fouet *m.*

whirl, *vb.* faire tourner, *tr.;* tourner sur soi, *intr.*

whirlpool, *n.* tourbillon *m.*

whirlwind, *n.* tornade *f.*

whisker, *n.* (man) favori *m.;* (animals) moustache *f.*

whiskey, *n.* whiskey *m.*

whisper, *vb.* chuchoter.

whistle, 1. *n.* sifflet *m.* 2. *vb.* siffler.

white, *adj.* blanc *m.*, blanche *f.*

who, *pron.* qui.

whoever, *pron.* qui que.

whole, *adj.* entier.

wholesale, *adj. and adv.* en gros.

wholesome, *adj.* sain.

wholly, *adv.* entièrement.

whom, *pron. (relative)* que; lequel; *interr.* qui.

whooping cough, *n.* coqueluche *f.*

whose, *pron. (relative)* dont; *interr.* de qui.

why, *adv.* pourquoi.

wicked, *adj.* méchant.

wickedness, *n.* méchanceté *f.*

wide, *adj.* large.

widen, *vb.* élargir, *tr.*

widespread, *adj.* répandu.

widow, *n.* veuve *f.*

widower, *n.* veuf *m.*

width, *n.* largeur *f.*

wield, *vb.* manier.

wife, *n.* femme *f.*

wig, *n.* perruque *f.*

wild, *adj.* sauvage.

wilderness, *n.* désert *m.*

wildlife, *n.* faune *f.*

will, 1. *n.* volonté *f.;* (last w.) testament *m.* 2. *vb.* vouloir; (bequeath) léguer.

willful, *adj.* obstiné.

willing, *adj.* bien disposé.

willpower, *n.* volonté *f.*

wilt, *vb.* flétrir.

win, *vb.* gagner.

wind, *n.* vent *m.*

window, *n.* fenêtre *f.*

windshield, *n.* pare-brise *m.*

windsurfing, *n.* planche (*f.*) à voile.

windy, *adj.* venteux.

wine, *n.* vin *m.*

wing, *n.* aile *f.*

wink, 1. *n.* clin (*m.*) d'œil. 2. *vb.* clignoter.

winner, *n.* gagnant *m.*

winter, *n.* hiver *m.*

wipe, *vb.* essuyer.

wire, *n.* fil (*m.*) de fer.

wireless, *n.* télégraphie (*f.*) sans fil (*abbr.* T.S.F.).

wisdom, *n.* sagesse *f.*

wise, *adj.* sage.

wish, 1. *n.* désir, souhait *m.* 2. *vb.* désirer, souhaiter.

wit, *n.* esprit *m.*

witch, *n.* sorcière *f.*

with, *prep.* avec.

withdraw, *vb.* retirer, *tr.*

wither, *vb.* flétrir.

withhold, *vb.* refuser.

within, *adv.* dedans.

without, *prep.* sans.

witness, *n.* témoin *m.*

witty, *adj.* spirituel.

wizard, *n.* sorcier *m.*

woe, *n.* malheur *m.*

wolf, *n.* loup *m.*

woman, *n.* femme *f.*

womb, *n.* matrice *f.*

wonder, *vb.* (ask oneself) se demander; (be surprised) être étonné.

wonderful, *adj.* merveilleux.

woo, *vb.* faire la cour à.

wood, *n.* bois *m.*

wooden, *adj.* de bois.

wool, *n.* laine *f.*

woolen, *adj.* de laine.

word, *n.* mot *m.*

word processing, *n.* traitement (*m.*) de texte.

word processor, *n.* machine (*f.*) de traitement de texte.

work, 1. *n.* travail *m.* 2. *vb.* travailler.

workaholic, *n.* bourreau (*m.*) de travail.

worker, *n.* travailleur *m.*

working class, *n.* classe (*f.*) ouvrière.

workman, *n.* ouvrier *m.*

world, *n.* monde *m.*

worldly, *adj.* mondain.

worldwide, *adj.* mondial.

worm, *n.* ver *m.*

worn, *adj.* usé.

worry, 1. *n.* souci *m.* 2. *vb.* tracasser, préoccuper, *tr.*

worse, 1. *adj.* pire. 2. *adv.* pis.

worship, 1. *n.* culte *m.* 2. *vb.* adorer.

worst, 1. *adj.* (le) pire. 2. *adv.* (le) pis.

worth, *n.* valeur *f.;* (be w. while to) valoir la peine de.

worthless, *adj.* indigne; (without value) sans valeur.

worthy, *adj.* digne.

would, *vb.* vouloir.

wound, 1. *n.* blessure *f.* 2. *vb.* blesser.

wrap, *vb.* envelopper, emballer.

wrapping, *n.* couverture *f.*, emballage *m.*

wrath, *n.* courroux *m.*

wreath, *n.* couronne *f.*

wreck, *n.* (ship) naufrage *m.;* (remains) débris *m .pl.*

wrench, *vb.* tordre.

wrestle, *vb.* lutter.

wretched, *adj.* misérable.

wring, *vb.* tordre.

wrinkle, 1. *n.* ride *f.* 2. *vb.* rider *tr.*

wrist, *n.* poignet *m.*

wristwatch, *n.* montre-bracelet *f.*

write, *vb.* écrire.

writer, *n.* écrivain *m.*

writhe, *vb.* se tordre.

writing, *n.* écriture *f.*

wrong, 1. *n.* tort *m.* 2. *adj.* faux *m.*, fausse *f.;* (be w.) avoir tort.

X, Y, Z

xerox *vb.* photocopier.
x-rays, *n.* rayons X *m.pl.*
xylophone, *n.* xylophone *m.*
yacht, *n.* yacht *m.*
yam, *n.* igname *f.*
yard, *n.* (house, etc.) cour *f.;* (lumber, etc.) chantier *m.;* (measure) yard *m.*
yarn, *n.* fil *m.*
yawn, 1. *n.* bâillement *m.* **2.** *vb.* bâiller.
year, *n.* an *m.;* (duration) année *f.*
yearly, *adj.* annuel.
yearn for, *vb.* soupirer après.
yeast, *n.* levure *f.*
yell, *vb.* hurler.
yellow, *adj. and n.* jaune *m.*
yes, *adv.* oui; (after negative question) si.
yesterday, *adv.* hier.
yet, 1. *adv.* encore. **2.** *conj.* néanmoins.
Yiddish, *n.* yiddish *m.*

yield, *vb.* (resign, submit) céder; (produce) produire.
yoga, *n.* yoga *m.*
yogurt, *n.* yaourt *m.*
yoke, *n.* joug *m.*
yolk, *n.* jaune *m.*
you, *pron.* vous; (familiar, *sg.*) tu (subject), toi (object), te (object, unstressed, with verb).
young, *adj.* jeune.
your, *adj.* votre *sg.*, vos *pl.;* (familiar form) ton *m.sg.*, ta *f.sg.*, tes *pl.*
yours, *pron.* le vôtre; *m.*, la vôtre *f.*, les vôtres *pl.*, (familiar form) le tien *m.*, la tienne *f.*, les tiens *m.pl.*, les tiennes *f.pl.*
yourself, *pron.* vous-même; (familiar form) toi-même; (reflexive) vous, te.
youth, *n.* jeunesse *f.*

youthful, *adj.* (young) jeune; (of youth) de jeunesse.
Yugoslavia, *n.* Yougoslavie *f.*
yuppie, *n.* yuppie *m.*
zap, *vb.* (kill) descendre; (computer) effacer; (TV) zapper.
zeal, *n.* zèle *m.*
zealous, *adj.* zélé.
zebra, *n.* zèbre *m.*
zenith, *n.* zénith *m.*
zero, *n.* zéro *m.*
zest, *n.* entrain *m.;* (taste) saveur *f.*
zip code, *n.* code postal **m.**
zipper, *n.* fermeture *f.* éclair.
zone, *n.* zone *f.*
zoo, *n.* jardin (*m.*) zoologique.
zoology, *n.* zoologie *f.*
zoom, 1. *vb.* passer en trombe. **2.** *n.* zoom *m.*
zucchini, *n.* courgette *f.*

Numerals

Cardinal

1 un, une	21 vingt et un	75 soixante-quinze
2 deux	22 vingt-deux	76 soixante-seize
3 trois	23 vingt-trois	77 soixante-dix-sept
4 quatre	24 vingt-quatre	78 soixante-dix-huit
5 cinq	25 vingt-cinq	79 soixante-dix-neuf
6 six	26 vingt-six	80 quatre-vingts
7 sept	27 vingt-sept	81 quatre-vingt-un
8 huit	28 vingt-huit	82 quatre-vingt-deux
9 neuf	29 vingt-neuf	90 quatre-vingt-dix
10 dix	30 trente	91 quatre-vingt-onze
11 onze	31 trente et un	92 quatre-vingt-douze
12 douze	32 trente-deux	100 cent
13 treize	40 quarante	101 cent un
14 quatorze	50 cinquante	102 cent deux
15 quinze	60 soixante	200 deux cents
16 seize	70 soixante-dix	300 trois cents
17 dix-sept	71 soixante et onze	301 trois cent un
18 dix-huit	72 soixante-douze	1,000 mille
19 dix-neuf	73 soixante-treize	5,000 cinq mille
20 vingt	74 soixante-quatorze	1,000,000 un million

Ordinal

1st	premier, première	19th	dix-neuvième
2nd	deuxième, second	20th	vingtième
3rd	troisième	21st	vingt-et-unième
4th	quatrième	22nd	vingt-deuxième
5th	cinquième	30th	trentième
6th	sixième	40th	quarantième
7th	septième	50th	cinquantième
8th	huitième	60th	soixantième
9th	neuvième	70th	soixante-dixième
10th	dixième	80th	quatre-vingtième
11th	onzième	90th	quatre-vingt-dixième
12th	douzième	100th	centième
13th	treizième	101st	cent-unième
14th	quatorzième	102nd	cent-deuxième
15th	quinzième	103rd	cent-troisième
16th	seizième	300th	trois-centième
17th	dix-septième	1,000th	millième
18th	dix-huitième	1,000,000th	millionième

Days of the Week

Sunday	dimanche
Monday	lundi
Tuesday	mardi
Wednesday	mercredi
Thursday	jeudi
Friday	vendredi
Saturday	samedi

Months

January	janvier
February	février
March	mars
April	avril
May	mai
June	juin
July	juillet
August	août
September	septembre
October	octobre
November	novembre
December	décembre

Weights and Measures

The French use the *Metric System* of weights and measures, a decimal system in which multiples are shown by the prefixes **déci-** (one-tenth); **centi-** (one hundredth); **milli-** (one thousandth); **hecto-** (hundred); and **kilo-** (thousand).

1 centimètre	=	.3937 inch
1 mètre	=	39.37 inches
1 kilomètre	=	.621 mile
1 centigramme	=	.1543 grain
1 gramme	=	15.432 grains
100 grammes	=	3.527 ounces
1 kilogramme	=	2.2046 pounds
1 tonne	=	2.204 pounds
1 centilitre	=	.338 ounce
1 litre	=	1.0567 quart (liquid); .908 quart (dry)
1 kilolitre	=	264.18 gallons

Useful Words and Phrases

Good day.	Bonjour.
Good afternoon.	Bonjour.
Good evening.	Bonsoir.
Good night.	Bonne nuit.
Good-bye.	Au revoir.
How are you?	Comment allez-vous?
Fine, thank you.	Très bien, merci.
Glad to meet you.	Enchanté de faire votre connaissance.
Thank you very much.	Merci beaucoup.
You're welcome.	Pas de quoi.
Please.	S'il vous plaît.
Good luck.	Bonne chance.
To your health.	A votre santé.
I am lost.	Je me suis égaré(e).
Please help me.	Aidez-moi, s'il vous plaît.
Do you understand?	Comprenez-vous?
I don't understand.	Je ne comprends pas.
Speak slowly, please.	Parlez lentement, s'il vous plaît.
Please repeat.	Répétez, s'il vous plaît.
I don't speak French.	Je ne parle pas français.
Do you speak English?	Parlez-vous anglais?
Does anyone here speak English?	Y a-t-il quelqu'un qui parle anglais?
How do you say . . . in French?	Comment dit-on . . . en français?
What do you call this?	Comment appelle-t-on ceci?
What is your name?	Comment vous appelez-vous?
My name is . . .	Je m'appelle . . .
I am an American.	Je suis américain.
May I introduce . . .	Permettez-moi de vous présenter . . .
How is the weather?	Quel temps fait-il?
What time is it?	Quelle heure est-il?
What is it?	Qu'est-ce que c'est?
I would like . . .	Je voudrais . . .
Please give me . . .	S'il vous plaît, donnez-moi . . .
Please bring me . . .	S'il vous plaît, apportez-moi . . .
How much does this cost?	Combien est ceci?
It is too expensive.	C'est trop cher.
May I see something cheaper?	Pourrais-je voir quelque chose à meilleur marché?
May I see something better?	Pourrais-je voir quelque chose de meilleur?
It is not exactly what I want.	Ce n'est pas exactement ce que je cherche.

I want to buy . . .	Je voudrais acheter . . .
Do you accept traveler's checks?	Acceptez-vous les chèques de voyage?
I want to eat.	Je voudrais manger.
Can you recommend a restaurant?	Pouvez-vous recommander un restaurant?
I am hungry.	J'ai faim.
I am thirsty.	J'ai soif.
May I see the menu?	Pourrais-je voir le menu?
Check, please.	L'addition, s'il vous plaît.
Is service included in the bill?	Le service est-il compris?
Where can I get a taxi?	Où pourrais-je trouver un taxi?
What is the fare to . . .	Quel est le tarif jusqu 'à . . . ?
Please take me to this address.	Veuillez me conduire à cette adresse.
I have a reservation.	J'ai une réservation.
Where is the nearest drugstore?	Où est la pharmacie la plus proche?
Is there a hotel here?	Y a-t-il un hôtel ici?
Where is . . . ?	Où est . . . ?
Where is the men's (women's) room?	Où est la toilette pour messieurs (dames)?
What is the way to . . . ?	Quelle est la route de . . . ?
Take me to . . .	Conduisez-moi à . . .
I need . . .	J'ai besoin de . . .
I am ill.	Je suis malade.
Please call a doctor.	Appelez un docteur, s'il vous plaît.
Is there any mail for me?	Y a-t-il du courrier pour moi?
Please call the police.	Appelez la police, s'il vous plaît.
I want to send a telegram.	Je voudrais envoyer un télégramme.
Where can I change money?	Où puis-je changer de l'argent?
Where is the nearest bank?	Où est la banque la plus proche?
Will you accept checks?	Acceptez-vous des chèques?
What is the postage?	Quel est l'affranchissement?
Where can I mail this letter?	Où est-ce que je peux mettre cette lettre à la poste?
Please help me with my baggage	S'il vous plaît, aidez-moi avec mes bagages.
Right away.	Tout de suite.
Help!	Au secours!
Who is it?	Qui est-ce que c'est?
Come in.	Entrez.
Stop.	Arrêtez.
Hurry.	Dépêchez-vous.
Go on.	Continuez.
Right.	A droite.
Left.	A gauche.
Straight ahead.	Tout droit.
Hello! *(on telephone)*	Allô!
As soon as possible.	Aussitôt que possible.
Pardon me.	Pardon *or* Pardonnez-moi *or* Je m'excuse.
Look out!	Attention! *or* Faites attention!
Just a minute!	Un instant!

Signs

Caution	Attention	**Go Slow**	Ralentir
Danger	Danger	**No smoking**	Défense de fumer
Exit	Sortie	**No admittance**	Défense d'entrer
Entrance	Entrée	**Women**	Dames
Stop	Halte, Arrêtez	**Men**	Hommes
Closed	Fermé	**Lavatory**	Lavabos, toilettes
Open	Ouvert		

Food and Menu Terms

Les Entrées *f.pl.*   Appetizers

artichaut *m.*	artichoke
assiette *f.* **de charcuterie**	cold cuts
assiette *f.* **de crudités**	raw vegetables
céleri *m.* **rémoulade** *f.*	shredded celery root in mayonnaise sauce
champignons *m.pl.* **à la grecque**	mushrooms in oil, lemon juice and herbs
coeur *m.* **de palmier**	hearts of palm
coquilles *f.pl.* **St. Jacques**	bay scallops in cream sauce
escargots *m.pl.*	snails (usually in garlic butter)
moules *f.pl.* **(rémoulade)**	mussels (in mayonnaise)
pâté *m.* **de foie**	liver pâté
pâté de campagne	pork pâté
pâté impérial	spring roll
salade *f.* **verte**	green salad
salade niçoise	salad usually including tuna, tomatoes, green beans, anchovies and olives
sardines *f.pl.* **à l'huile**	sardines in oil
saucisse *f.*	small fresh sausage
saucisson *m.*	large sausage, like salami
saucisson à l'ail	garlic sausage
saumon *m.* **fumé**	smoked salmon
terrine *f.*	cold pâté baked in earthenware casserole
thon *m.* **mayonnaise**	tuna salad with mayonnaise

Potages *m.pl.* and Soupes *f.pl.*   Soups

bisque *f.*	shellfish soup
bouillabaisse *f.*	Provençal fish soup
bouillon *m.*	clear broth
consommé *m.* **(de volaille)**	clear (chicken) soup

petite marmite *f.*	meat and vegetable broth cooked in earthenware casserole
pistou *m.*	rich vegetable, bean and pasta soup flavored with basil, garlic and olive oil
potage *m.* aux légumes	vegetable soup
potage crème Saint-Germain	cream of pea soup
soupe *f.* à l'oignon	onion soup
vichyssoise *f.*	cold, creamy leek and potato soup

Les Plats *m.pl*   Main Courses

Viandes *f.pl.*	Meats
agneau *m.*	lamb
carré *m.* d'agneau	rack of lamb
côte *f.* d'agneau	lamb chop
gigot *m.* d'agneau	leg of lamb
bifteck *m.*	steak
blanquette *f.*	traditional stew of veal, chicken, lamb or seafood in cream sauce
boeuf *m.* bourguignon	stew of beef chunks and vegetables in Burgundy wine sauce
boudin *m.*	meat sausage
boudin blanc	white sausage of veal, chicken or pork
boudin noir	pork blood sausage
brochette *f.*	cubes of meat or fish and vegetables cooked on skewer
chateaubriand *m.*	thick beef fillet, traditionally served with sautéed potatoes and sauce
côtelette *f.*	thin chop or cutlet
entrecôte *m. or f.*	beef rib steak
escalope *f.*	thin slice of meat or fish
filet mignon *m.*	filet mignon
jambon *m.*	ham
jarret *m.* (de veau, de porc, de boeuf)	knuckles (veal, pork, beef)
lapin *m.*	rabbit
pavé *m.*	thick slice of boned beef or calf's liver
porc *m.*	pork
carré de porc	pork loin
steak *m.* frites	steak with French fries
steak *m.* tartare	raw chopped steak
tournedos *m.*	center part of beef fillet
tripes *f.pl.* à la mode de Caen	beef entrails, carrots, leeks, and onions, cooked in water, cider and Calvados
veau *m.*	veal
côte de veau	veal chop
Volailles *f.pl.*	Poultry
caille *f.*	quail
canard *m.*	duck
canard à la presse	roast duck with sauce of natural juices, red wine and cognac
canard sauvage	wild duck, usually mallard
caneton *m.*	young male duck
coq *m.* (au vin)	mature male chicken (cooked in wine sauce)

coq jaune	chicken cooked in the local wine with butter, cream and tarragon
coq *m.* de bruyère	wood grouse
coquelet *m.* (sauté)	sautéed baby rooster
foie *m.*	liver
fricassé *m.*	stewed or sautéed mixture of fish or meat
perdrix *f.*	partridge
poulet *m.* rôti	roast chicken
poulet à la Kiev	chicken Kiev
poulet impérial	Vietnamese chicken
poulet basquaise	chicken Basque-style with tomatoes and sweet peppers
poulet fermier	free-range chicken

Fruits *m.pl.* de Mer and Poissons *m.pl.*   Fish

bar *m.*	bass
colin *m.*	hake
coquillage *m.*	shellfish
crevettes *f.pl.*	shrimp
escargots *m.pl.*	snails
grenouilles *f.pl.*	frogs' legs
homard *m.*	lobster
huîtres *f.pl.*	oysters
langouste *f.*	crayfish
langoustines *f.pl.*	prawns
moules *f.pl.*	mussels
saumon *m.*	salmon
sôle *f.*	sole
thon *m.*	tuna
truite *f.*	trout
turbot *m.*	turbot

Légumes *m.pl.*   Vegetables

asperges *f.pl.*	asparagus
avocat *m.*	avocado
brocoli *m.*	broccoli
carotte *f.*	carrot
champignons *m.pl.*	mushrooms
chou-fleur *m.*	cauliflower
choux *m.*	cabbage
concombre *m.*	cucumber
courgette *f.*	zucchini
endive *f.*	chicory, endive
fenouil *m.*	fennel
flageolet *m.*	small kidney-shaped bean
haricots *m.pl.*	beans
haricots rouges	kidney beans
haricots verts	string beans
laitue *f.*	lettuce

maïs *m.*	corn
navet *m.*	turnip
petits pois *m.pl.*	green peas
poireaux *m.pl.*	leeks
poivron (doux) *m.*	(sweet bell) pepper

Oeufs *m.pl.*   Eggs

oeuf *m.* à la coque	soft-boiled egg
oeuf brouillé	scrambled egg
oeuf dur	hard-boiled egg
oeuf poché	poached egg
oeuf sur le plat	fried egg

Desserts *m.pl.*   Desserts

crème *f.* caramel	caramel custard
flan *m.*	custard
gâteau *m.*	cake
glace *f.*	ice cream
marron *m.* glacé	glazed chestnut
mousse *f.* au chocolat	chocolate mousse
oeufs *m.pl.* à la neige	poached meringues in custard sauce
pêche *f.* melba	poached peach with vanilla ice cream and raspberry sauce
petit-four *m.*	tiny cake
poire *f.* belle Hélène	pear with ice cream, cookie and hot chocolate sauce
profiteroles *f.pl.*	ice cream–filled cream puffs topped with hot chocolate sauce
sorbet *m.*	sorbet
tarte *f.* aux fruits	fruit pie

Fruits *m.pl.*   Fruits

abricot *m.*	apricot
banane *f.*	banana
cantaloup *m.*	cantaloupe
cerise *f.*	cherry
citron *m.*	lemon
figue *f.*	fig
fraise *f.*	strawberry
framboise *f.*	raspberry
melon *m.*	melon
myrtille *f.*	bilberry
pamplemousse *f.*	grapefruit
pêche *f.*	peach
pomme *f.*	apple
pruneau *m.*	prune

Boissons *f.pl.*   Drinks, Beverages

sans alcool	(nonalcoholic)
café *m.*	coffee
eau *f.* minérale	mineral water
jus *m.*	juice
jus d'orange	orange juice
jus de tomate	tomato juice
jus de raisin	grape juice
lait *m.*	milk
thé *m.*	tea
avec alcool	(alcoholic)
champagne *m.*	champagne
cognac *m.*	cognac
vin *m.*	wine
vin rouge	red wine
vin blanc	white wine
vin rosé	rosé wine

Spanish speakers aren't just from Spain. They're from all over Latin America, and each country shapes and adds to the language. Become a *global* speaker of Spanish—look for:

RANDOM HOUSE LATIN-AMERICAN SPANISH DICTIONARY
SPANISH-ENGLISH/ENGLISH-SPANISH

Featuring more than 50,000 entries and 100,000 definitions, including vocabulary and usages unique to Mexico, Cuba, Venezuela, Chile, and other Latin-American countries.

RANDOM HOUSE
LATIN-AMERICAN
SPANISH DICTIONARY
by David L. Gold

Published by Ballantine Books.
Available in bookstores everywhere.